Professional
Visual Studio® 2008

(Continued)

Professional
Visual Studio® 2008

Professional
Visual Studio® 2008

By
Nick Randolph
David Gardner

WILEY

Wiley Publishing, Inc.

Professional Visual Studio® 2008

Published by
Wiley Publishing, Inc.
10475 Crosspoint Boulevard
Indianapolis, IN 46256
www.wiley.com

Copyright © 2008 by Wiley Publishing, Inc., Indianapolis, Indiana

ISBN: 978-0-470-229880

Manufactured in the United States of America

10 9 8 7 6 5 4 3 2 1

Library of Congress Cataloging-in-Publication Data is available from the publisher.

About the Authors

Nick Randolph is currently the Chief Development Officer for N Squared Solutions, having recently left his role as lead developer at Intilecta Corporation where he was integrally involved in designing and building that firm's application framework.

After graduating with a combined Engineering (Information Technology)/Commerce degree, Nick went on to be nominated as a Microsoft MVP in recognition of his work with the Perth .NET user group and his focus on mobile devices. He is still an active contributor in the device application development space via his blog at `http://community.softteq.com/blogs/nick/` and via the Professional Visual Studio web site, `http://www.professionalvisualstudio.com/`.

Over the past two years, Nick has been invited to present at a variety of events including Tech Ed Australia, MEDC, and Code Camp. He has also authored articles for MSDN Magazine (ANZ edition) and a book entitled *Professional Visual Studio 2005*, and has helped judge the 2004, 2005, and 2007 world finals for the Imagine Cup.

David Gardner is a seasoned .NET developer and the Chief Software Architect at Intilecta Corporation. David has an ongoing passion to produce well-designed, high-quality software products that engage and delight users. For the past decade and a bit, David has worked as a solutions architect, consultant, and developer, and has provided expertise to organizations in Australia, New Zealand, and Malaysia.

David is a regular speaker at the Perth .NET user group, and has presented at events including the .NET Framework Launch, TechEd Malaysia, and the Microsoft Executive Summit. He holds a Bachelor of Science (Computer Science) and is a Microsoft Certified Systems Engineer.

David regularly blogs about Visual Studio and .NET at `http://www.professionalvisualstudio.com/`, and maintains a personal web site at `http://peaksite.com/`.

Guest Authors

Miguel Madero

Miguel Madero is a Senior Developer with Readify Consulting in Australia. Miguel has architected different frameworks and solutions for disconnected mobile applications, ASP.NET, and Distributed Systems, worked with Software Factories, and trained other developers in the latest Microsoft technologies. Miguel was also the founder of DotNetLaguna, the .NET User Group in Torreón, Coahuila, México. In his spare time Miguel enjoys being with his beautiful fiancée, Carina, practicing rollerblading, and trying to surf at Sydney's beaches. You can find Miguel's blog at `http://www.miguelmadero.com/`.

Miguel wrote Chapters 54 through 58 of this book, covering Visual Studio Team Suite and Team Foundation Server.

Keyvan Nayyeri

Keyvan Nayyeri is a software architect and developer with a Bachelor of Science degree in Applied Mathematics. Keyvan's main focus is Microsoft development and related technologies. He has published articles on many well-known .NET online communities and is an active team leader and developer for several .NET open-source projects.

Keyvan is the author of *Professional Visual Studio Extensibility* and co-authored *Professional Community Server*, also published by Wrox Press. You can find his thoughts on .NET, Community Server and Technology at http://www.nayyeri.net/.

Keyvan was a guest author on this book, writing Chapters 51 through 53 on Visual Studio Automation.

Joel Pobar

Joel Pobar is a habituated software tinkerer originally from sunny Brisbane, Australia. Joel was a Program Manager on the .NET Common Language Runtime team, sharing his time between late-bound dynamic CLR features (Reflection, Code Generation), compiler teams, and the Shared Source CLI program (Rotor). These days, Joel is on sabbatical, exploring the machine learning and natural language processing worlds while consulting part-time for Microsoft Consulting Services. You can find Joel's recent writings at http://callvirt.net/blog/.

Joel lent his expertise to this book by authoring Chapter 15 on the Languages Ecosystem.

Credits

Acquisitions Editor
Katie Mohr

Development Editor
William Bridges

Technical Editors
Todd Meister
Keyvan Nayyeri
Doug Holland

Production Editor
William A. Barton

Copy Editors
Kim Cofer
S.D. Kleinman

Editorial Manager
Mary Beth Wakefield

Production Manager
Tim Tate

Vice President and Executive Group Publisher
Richard Swadley

Vice President and Executive Publisher
Joseph B. Wikert

Project Coordinator, Cover
Lynsey Osborne

Proofreaders
David Fine, Corina Copp,
Word One

Indexer
Robert Swanson

Acknowledgments

I was expecting that writing the second edition of this book would be relatively straightforward — a little tweak here and a bit extra there — but no, the reality was that it was again one of the most time-demanding exercises I've undertaken in recent years. I must thank my partner, Cynthia, who consistently encouraged me to "get it done," so that we can once again have a life.

I would especially like to thank everyone at Wrox who has helped me re-learn the art of technical writing — in particular, Bill Bridges, whose attention to detail has resulted in consistency throughout the book despite there being five authors contributing to the process, and Katie Mohr (whose ability to get us back on track was a life-saver), who made the whole process possible.

I have to pass on a big thank you to my co-author, David Gardner, who agreed to work with me on the second edition of this book. I doubt that I really gave an accurate representation of exactly how much work would be involved, and I really appreciated having someone of such high caliber to bounce ideas off of and share the workload. As we approached the mid-point of this book, I really appreciated a number of guest authors stepping in to help ensure we were able to meet the deadline. So a big thanks to Keyvan Nayyeri, Miguel Madero, and Joel Pobar for their respective contributions.

Lastly, I would like to thank all of my fellow Australian MVP developers and the Microsoft staff (Dave Glover and Andrew Coates particularly), who were always able to answer any questions along the way.

— *Nick Randolph*

This book represents one of the most rewarding and challenging activities I've ever undertaken. Writing while maintaining a full-time job is certainly not for the fainthearted. However, in the process I have amassed a wealth of knowledge that I never would have found the time to learn otherwise.

The process of writing a book is very different from writing code, and I am especially thankful to the team at Wrox for helping guide me to the finish line. Without Katie Mohr and Bill Bridges working as hard as they did to cajole the next chapter out of us, we never would have gotten this finished. Katie put her trust in me as a first-time author, and fully supported our decisions regarding the content and structure of the book. Bill improved the clarity and quality of my writing and corrected my repeated grammatical transgressions and Aussie colloquialisms. It was a pleasure to be in such experienced hands, and I thank them both for their patience and professionalism.

A huge thank you goes to my co-author Nick Randolph, who invited me to join him in writing this book, and managed to get us organized early on when I had very little idea what I was doing. I enjoyed collaborating on such a big project and the ongoing conversations about the latest cool feature that we'd just discovered.

Much appreciation and thanks go to our guest authors, Keyvan Nayyeri, Miguel Madero, and Joel Pobar, whose excellent contributions to this book have improved it significantly. Also thanks to my fellow

Acknowledgments

coffee drinkers and .NET developers, Mitch Wheat, Michael Minutillo, and Ola Karlsson, for their feedback and suggestions on how to improve various chapters.

Most of all I would like to thank my beautiful and supportive wife, Julie. She certainly didn't know what she was getting herself into when I agreed to write this book, but had she known I've no doubt that she would still have been just as encouraging and supportive. Julie did more than her fair share for our family when I needed to drop almost everything else, and I am truly grateful for her love and friendship.

Finally, thanks to my daughters Jasmin and Emily, who gave up countless cuddles and tickles so that Daddy could find the time to write this book. I promise I'll do my best to catch up on the tickles that I owe you, and pay them back with interest.

— *David Gardner*

Contents

Contents

Contents

Contents

Contents

Contents

Contents

Contents

Contents

Contents

Contents

Contents

Contents

Contents

Contents

Contents

Introduction

Visual Studio 2008 is an enormous product no matter which way you look at it. Incorporating the latest advances in Microsoft's premier programming languages, Visual Basic and C#, along with a host of improvements and new features in the user interface, it can be intimidating to both newcomers and experienced .NET developers.

Professional Visual Studio 2008 looks at every major aspect of this developer tool, showing you how to harness each feature and offering advice about how best to utilize the various components effectively. It shows you the building blocks that make up Visual Studio 2008, breaking the user interface down into manageable chunks for you to understand.

It then expands on each of these components with additional details about exactly how it works both in isolation and in conjunction with other parts of Visual Studio to make your development efforts even more efficient.

Who This Book Is For

Professional Visual Studio 2008 is for all developers new to Visual Studio as well as those programmers who have some experience but want to learn about features they may have previously overlooked.

If you are familiar with the way previous versions of Visual Studio worked, you may want to skip Part I, which deals with the basic constructs that make up the user interface, and move on to the remainder of the book where the new features found in Visual Studio 2008 are discussed in detail.

If you're just starting out, you'll greatly benefit from the first part, where basic concepts are explained and you're introduced to the user interface and how to customize it to suit your own style.

This book does assume that you are familiar with the traditional programming model, and it uses both the C# and Visual Basic languages to illustrate features within Visual Studio 2008. In addition, it is assumed that you can understand the code listings without an explanation of basic programming concepts in either language. If you're new to programming and want to learn Visual Basic, please take a look at *Beginning Visual Basic 2008* by Thearon Willis and Bryan Newsome. Similarly, if you are after a great book on C#, track down *Beginning Visual C# 2008*, written collaboratively by a host of authors.

What This Book Covers

Microsoft Visual Studio 2008 is arguably the most advanced integrated development environment (IDE) available for programmers today. It is based on a long history of programming languages and interfaces and has been influenced by many different iterations of the theme of development environments.

The next few pages introduce you to Microsoft Visual Studio 2008, how it came about, and what it can do for you as a developer. If you're already familiar with what Visual Studio is and how it came to be, you may want to skip ahead to the next chapter and dive into the various aspects of the integrated development environment itself.

A Brief History of Visual Studio

Microsoft has worked long and hard on its development tools. Actually, its first software product was a version of BASIC in 1975. Back then, programming languages were mainly interpretive languages in which the computer would process the code to be performed line by line. In the past three decades, programming has seen many advances, one of the biggest by far being development environments aimed at helping developers be efficient at producing applications in their chosen language and platform.

In the 32-bit computing era, Microsoft started releasing comprehensive development tools, commonly called IDEs (short for integrated development environments), which contained not just a compiler but also a host of other features to supplement it, including a context-sensitive editor and rudimentary IntelliSense features that helped programmers determine what they could and couldn't do in a given situation. Along with these features came intuitive visual user interface designers with drag-and-drop functionality and associated tool windows that gave developers access to a variety of properties for the various components on a given window or user control.

Initially, these IDEs were different for each language, with Visual Basic being the most advanced in terms of the graphical designer and ease of use, and Visual C++ having the most power and flexibility. Under the banner of Visual Studio 6, the latest versions of these languages were released in one large development suite along with other "Visual" tools such as FoxPro and InterDev. However, it was obvious that each language still had a distinct environment in which to work, and as a result, development solutions had to be in a specific language.

One Comprehensive Environment

When Microsoft first released Visual Studio .NET in 2002, it inherited many features and attributes of the various, disparate development tools the company had previously offered. Visual Basic 6, Visual InterDev, Visual C++, and other tools such as FoxPro all contributed to a development effort that the Microsoft development team mostly created on its own. The team had some input from external groups, but Visual Studio .NET 2002 and .NET 1.0 were primarily founded on Microsoft's own principles and goals.

Visual Studio .NET 2003 was the next version released, and it provided mostly small enhancements and big fixes. Two years later, Visual Studio 2005 and the .NET Framework 2.0 were released. This was a major new edition with new foundation framework classes that went far beyond anything Microsoft had released previously. However, the most significant part of this release was realized in the IDE where the various components fit together in a cohesive way to provide you with an efficient tool set where everything was easily accessible.

The latest release, Visual Studio 2008 and .NET Framework 3.5, builds on this strong foundation. LINQ promises to revolutionize the way you access data, and features that were previously separate downloads, such as ASP.NET AJAX and Visual Studio Tools for Office, are now included by default.

The Visual Studio 2008 development environment (see Figure I-1) takes the evolution of Microsoft IDEs even further along the road to a comprehensive set of tools that can be used regardless of your purpose as a developer. A quick glance at Figure I-1 shows the cohesive way in which the various components fit together to provide you with an efficient tool set with everything easily accessible.

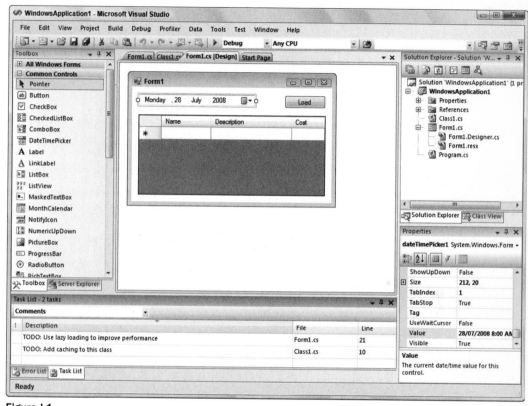

Figure I-1

Visual Studio 2008 comes in several versions: Express, Standard, Professional, and Team System (to be accurate, there are four distinct flavors of Team System for different roles, but their core Visual Studio functionality remains the same). The majority of this book deals with the Professional Edition of Visual Studio 2008, but some parts utilize features found only in Team System. If you haven't used Team System before, read through Chapters 54 to 58 for an overview of the features it offers over and above the Professional Edition.

How This Book Is Structured

This book's first section is dedicated to familiarizing you with the core aspects of Visual Studio 2008. Everything you need is contained in the first five chapters, from the IDE structure and layout to the various options and settings you can change to make the user interface synchronize with your own way of doing things.

From there, the remainder of the book is broken into 11 parts:

❑ **Getting Started:** In this part, you learn how to take control of your projects, how to organize them in ways that work with your own style, and how to edit application configuration and XML resource files.

❑ **Languages:** The .NET languages continue to evolve to support new features that are added to the framework. In the latest version of the framework, enhancements were added to support the introduction of LINQ, namely implicit typing, object initialization, and lambda expressions. Add these to features introduced in earlier versions, such as generics and partial types, and you've got an extremely expressive and powerful framework for building applications. This part covers all these features and more.

❑ **Coding:** Though the many graphical components of Visual Studio that make a programmer's job easier are discussed in many places throughout this book, you often need help when you're in the process of actually writing code. This part deals with features that support the coding of applications such as IntelliSense, code refactoring, and creating and running unit tests.

❑ **Data:** A large proportion of applications use some form of data storage. Visual Studio 2008 and the .NET Framework include strong support for working with databases and other data sources. This part examines how to use DataSets, the Visual Database Tools, LINQ, and Synchronization Services to build applications that work with data.

❑ **Security:** Application security is a consideration that is often put off until the end of a development project or, in all too many cases, ignored completely. Rather than follow the trend and leave this topic to the end of the book, it is placed in a more appropriate place.

❑ **Platforms:** For support building everything from Office add-ins to mobile applications, Visual Studio enables you to develop applications for a wide range of platforms. This part covers the application platforms that have always been supported, including ASP.NET, Office, and Mobile, as well as the application types that were introduced with .NET 3.0 (WPF, WCF, and WF). At the end of this part, you'll find a chapter on building the next-generation web with Silverlight 2 and ASP.NET MVC.

❑ **Configuration and Internationalization:** The built-in support for configuration files allows you to adjust the way an application functions on the fly without having to rebuild it. Furthermore, resource files can be used to both access static data and easily localize an application into foreign languages and cultures. This part of the book shows how to use .NET configuration and resource files.

❑ **Debugging:** Application debugging is one of the more challenging tasks developers have to tackle, but correct use of the Visual Studio 2008 debugging features will help you analyze the state of the application and determine the cause of any bugs. This part examines the rich debugging support provided by the IDE.

❑ **Build and Deployment:** In addition to discussing how to build your solutions effectively and getting applications into the hands of your end users, this part also deals with the process of upgrading your projects from previous versions.

❑ **Automation:** If the functionality found in the previous part isn't enough to help you in your coding efforts, Microsoft has provided many other features related to the concept of automating your programming work. This part starts by looking at the automation model, and then discusses add-ins and macros.

❑ **Visual Studio Team System:** Visual Studio Team System gives organizations a single tool that can be used to support the entire software lifecycle. The final part of the book examines the additional features only available in the Team System versions of Visual Studio 2008. In addition, you'll also learn how the Team Foundation Server provides an essential tool for managing software projects.

Though this breakdown of the Visual Studio feature set provides the most logical and easily understood set of topics, you may need to look for specific functions that will aid you in a particular activity. To address this need, references to appropriate chapters are provided whenever a feature is covered in more detail elsewhere in the book.

What You Need to Use This Book

To use this book effectively, you'll need only one additional item — Microsoft Visual Studio 2008 Professional Edition. With this software installed and the information found in this book, you'll be able to get a handle on how to use Visual Studio 2008 effectively in a very short period of time.

Some chapters discuss additional products and tools that work in conjunction with Visual Studio. The following are all available to download either on a trial basis, or for free:

❑ **Sandcastle:** Using Sandcastle, you can generate comprehensive documentation for every member and class within your solutions from the XML comments in your code. XML comments and Sandcastle are discussed in Chapter 9.

❑ **F#:** A multi-paradigm functional language, F# was incubated out of Microsoft Research in Cambridge, England. Chapter 15 covers the F# programming language.

❑ **Code Snippet Editor:** This is a third-party tool developed for creating code snippets in Visual Basic. The Snippet Editor tool is discussed in Chapter 17.

❑ **SQL Server 2005:** The installation of Visual Studio 2008 includes an install of SQL Server 2005 Express, enabling you to build applications that use database files. However, for more comprehensive enterprise solutions, you can use SQL Server 2005 instead. Database connectivity is covered in Chapter 22.

❑ **Silverlight 2:** Silverlight 2 is a cross-platform, cross-browser runtime that includes a lightweight version of the .NET Framework and delivers advanced functionality such as vector graphics, animation, and streaming media. Silverlight 2 is discussed in Chapter 37.

- **ASP.NET MVC:** The ASP.NET MVC framework provides a way to cleanly separate your application into model, view, and controller parts, thus enabling better testability and giving you more control over the behavior and output produced by your web application. Chapter 37 explains how to build applications with the ASP.NET MVC framework.

- **Web Deployment Projects:** Using a Web Deployment Project, you can effectively customize your application so that it can be deployed with a minimal set of files. Web Deployment Projects are covered in Chapter 50.

- **Visual Studio 2008 Team System:** A more powerful version of Visual Studio, Team System introduces tools for other parts of the development process such as testing and design. Team System is discussed in Chapters 54–58.

Conventions

To help you get the most from the text and keep track of what's happening, we've used a number of conventions throughout the book.

Tips, hints, tricks, and asides to the current discussion are offset and placed in italics like this.

As for styles in the text:

- We *highlight* new terms and important words when we introduce them.

- We show keyboard strokes like this: Ctrl+A.

- URLs and code that are referenced within the text use this format: `persistence.properties`.

- We present code in two different ways:

```
Normal code examples are listed like this.
In code examples we highlight important code with a gray background.
```

Source Code

As you work through the examples in this book, you may choose either to type in all the code manually or to use the source code files that accompany the book. All of the source code used in this book is available for download at `www.wrox.com`. Once at the site, simply locate the book's title (either by using the Search box or by using one of the title lists) and click the Download Code link on the book's detail page to obtain all the source code for the book.

Because many books have similar titles, you may find it easiest to search by ISBN; this book's ISBN is 978-0-470-22988-0.

Once you download the code, just decompress it with your favorite compression tool. Alternatively, you can go to the main Wrox code download page at `www.wrox.com/dynamic/books/download.aspx` to see the code available for this book and all other Wrox books.

Errata

We make every effort to ensure that there are no errors in the text or in the code. However, no one is perfect, and mistakes do occur. If you find an error in one of our books, such as a spelling mistake or faulty piece of code, we would be very grateful for your feedback. By sending in errata you may save another reader hours of frustration, and at the same time you will be helping us provide even higher quality information.

To find the errata page for this book, go to www.wrox.com and locate the title using the Search box or one of the title lists. Then, on the book details page, click the Book Errata link. On this page you can view all errata that have been submitted for this book and posted by Wrox editors. A complete book list, including links to each book's errata, is also available at www.wrox.com/misc-pages/booklist.shtml.

If you don't spot "your" error on the Book Errata page, go to www.wrox.com/contact/techsupport.shtml and complete the form there to send us the error you have found. We'll check the information and, if appropriate, post a message to the book's errata page and fix the problem in subsequent editions of the book.

p2p.wrox.com

For author and peer discussion, join the P2P forums at http://p2p.wrox.com. The forums are a web-based system for you to post messages relating to Wrox books and related technologies, and to interact with other readers and technology users. The forums offer a subscription feature to e-mail you topics of interest of your choosing when new posts are made to the forums. Wrox authors, editors, other industry experts, and your fellow readers are present on these forums.

At http://p2p.wrox.com you will find a number of different forums that will help you not only as you read this book, but also as you develop your own applications. To join the forums, just follow these steps:

1. Go to http://p2p.wrox.com and click the Register link.

2. Read the terms of use and click Agree.

3. Complete the required information to join as well as any optional information you wish to provide and click Submit.

4. You will receive an e-mail with information describing how to verify your account and complete the joining process.

> *You can read messages in the forums without joining P2P, but in order to post your own messages, you must join.*

Once you join, you can post new messages and respond to messages other users post. You can read messages at any time on the Web. If you would like new messages from a particular forum e-mailed to you, click the Subscribe to this Forum icon by the forum name in the forum listing.

For more information about how to use the Wrox P2P, be sure to read the P2P FAQs for answers to questions about how the forum software works as well as many common questions specific to P2P and Wrox books. To read the FAQs, click the FAQ link on any P2P page.

Part I

Integrated Development Environment

1

A Quick Tour

Ever since we have been developing software, there has been a need for tools to help us write, compile, and debug our applications. Microsoft Visual Studio 2008 is the next iteration in the continual evolution of a best-of-breed integrated development environment (IDE). If this is your first time using Visual Studio, then you will find this chapter a useful starting point. Even if you have worked with a previous version of Visual Studio, you may want to quickly skim it.

This chapter introduces the Visual Studio 2008 user experience and will show you how to work with the various menus, toolbars, and windows. It serves as a quick tour of the IDE, and as such it won't go into detail about what settings can be changed or how to go about customizing the layout, as these topics will be explored in the following chapters.

Let's Get Started

Each time you launch Visual Studio you will notice the Microsoft Visual Studio 2008 splash screen appear. Like a lot of splash screens, it provides information about the version of the product and to whom it has been licensed, as shown in Figure 1-1.

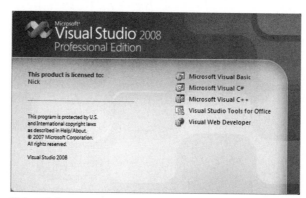

Figure 1-1

More importantly, the Visual Studio splash screen includes a list of the main components that have been installed. If you install third-party add-ins, you may see those products appear in this list.

The first time you run Visual Studio 2008, you will see the splash screen only for a short period before you are prompted to select the default environment settings. It may seem unusual to ask those who haven't used a product before how they imagine themselves using it. As Microsoft has consolidated a number of languages and technologies into a single IDE, that IDE must account for the subtle (and sometimes not so subtle) differences in the way developers work.

If you take a moment to review the various options in this list, as shown in Figure 1-2, you'll find that the environment settings that will be affected include the position and visibility of various windows, menus, and toolbars, and even keyboard shortcuts. For example, if you select the General Development Settings option as your default preference, this screen describes the changes that will be applied.

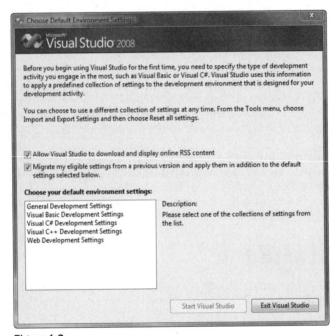

Figure 1-2

A tip for Visual Basic .NET developers coming from previous versions of Visual Studio is that they should NOT use the Visual Basic Development Settings option. This option has been configured for VB6 developers and will only infuriate Visual Basic .NET developers, as they will be used to different shortcut key mappings. We recommend that you use the general development settings, as these will use the standard keyboard mappings without being geared toward another development language.

The Visual Studio IDE

Depending on which set of environment settings you select, when you click the Start Visual Studio button you will most likely see a dialog indicating that Visual Studio is configuring the development environment. When this process is complete, Visual Studio 2008 will open, ready for you to start work, as shown in Figure 1-3.

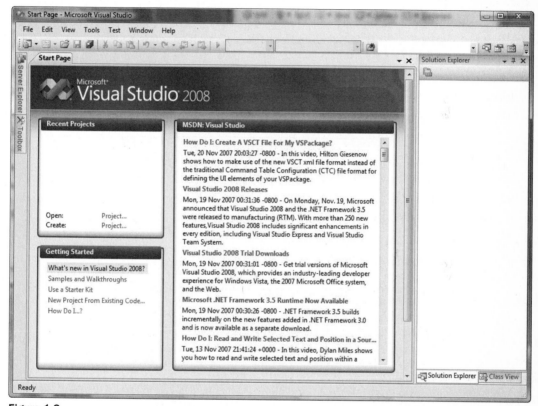

Figure 1-3

Regardless of the environment settings you selected, you will see the Start Page in the center of the screen. However, the contents of the Start Page and the surrounding toolbars and tool windows can vary. At this stage it is important to remember that your selection only determined the default settings, and that over time you can configure Visual Studio to suit your working style.

The contents shown in the right-hand portion of the Start Page are actually just the contents of an RSS feed. You can change this to be your favorite blog, or even a news feed (so you can catch up on the latest news while your solution is loading), by changing the news channel property on the Environment ➪ Startup node in the Options dialog, accessible via the Options item on the Tools menu.

Before we launch into building our first application, it's important that we take a step back and look at the components that make up the Visual Studio 2008 IDE. Menus and toolbars are positioned along the top of the environment (as in most Windows applications), and a selection of sub-windows, or panes, appears on the left and right of the main window area. In the center is the main editor space: Whenever you open a code file, an XML document, a form, or some other file, it will appear in this space for editing. With each file you open, a new tab is created so that you can toggle among opened files.

On either side of the editor space is a set of tool windows: These areas provide additional contextual information and functionality. In the case of the general developer settings, the default layout includes the Solution Explorer and Class View on the right, and the Server Explorer and Toolbox on the left. The tool windows on the left are in their collapsed, or *unpinned*, state. If you click on a tool window's title, it will expand; it will collapse again when it no longer has focus or you move the cursor to another area of the screen. When a tool window is expanded you will see a series of three icons at the top right of the window, similar to those shown in the left image of Figure 1-4.

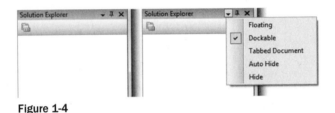

Figure 1-4

If you want the tool window to remain in its expanded, or *pinned*, state, you can click the middle icon, which looks like a pin. The pin will rotate 90 degrees to indicate that the window is now pinned. Clicking the third icon, the X, will close the window. If later you want to reopen this or another tool window, you can select it from the View menu.

Some tool windows are not accessible via the View menu, for example those having to do with debugging, such as threads and watch windows. In most cases these windows are available via an alternative menu item: in the case of the debugging windows it is the Debug menu.

The right image in Figure 1-4 shows the context menu that appears when the first icon, the down arrow, is clicked. Each item in this list represents a different way of arranging the tool window. In the left image of Figure 1-5 the Solution Explorer is set as dockable, whereas in the right image the floating item has been selected. The latter option is particularly useful if you have multiple screens, as you can move the various tool windows onto the additional screen, allowing the editor space to use the maximum screen real estate. Selecting the Tabbed Document option will make the tool window into an additional tab in the editor space. In Chapter 4 you will learn how to effectively manage the workspace by docking and pinning tool windows.

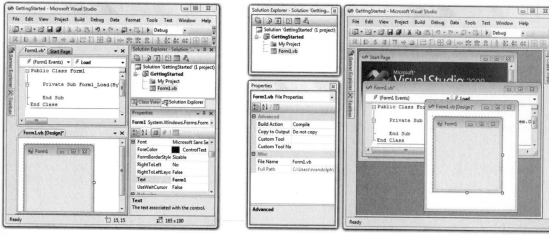

Figure 1-5

The other thing to note about the left image of Figure 1-5 is that the editor space has been divided into two horizontal regions. If you right-click an existing tab in the editor space, you can elect to move it to a new horizontal or vertical tab group. This can be particularly useful if you are working on multiple forms, or if you want to view the layout of a form while writing code in the code-behind file.

In the right image of Figure 1-5 the editor space is no longer rendered as a series of tabs. Instead, it is a series of child windows, in classic multiple-document-interface style. Unfortunately, this view is particularly limiting, because the child windows must remain within the bounds of the parent window, making it unusable across multiple monitors. To toggle between tabbed and multiple document window layouts, simply select the Environment ⇨ General node from the Options dialog.

Develop, Build, and Debug Your First Application

Now that you have seen an overview of the Visual Studio 2008 IDE, let's walk through creating a simple application that demonstrates working with some of these components. This is, of course, the mandatory "Hello World" sample that every developer needs to know, and it can be done in either Visual Basic .NET or C#, depending on what you feel more comfortable with.

1. Start by selecting File ⇨ New ⇨ Project. This will open the New Project dialog, as shown in Figure 1-6. A couple of new features are worth a mention here. Based on numerous feedback requests, this dialog is now resizable. More importantly, there is an additional drop-down box in the top right-hand corner, which is used to select the version of the .NET Framework that the application will target. The ability to use a single tool to create applications that target different framework versions means that developers can use fewer products and can take advantage of all the new features, even if they are maintaining an older product.

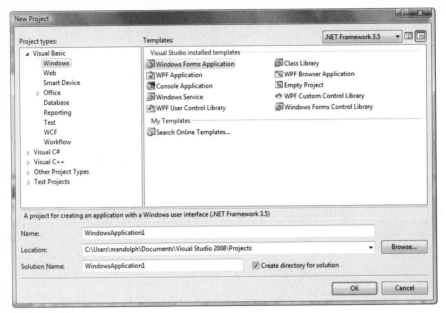

Figure 1-6

Select the Windows Forms Application from the Templates area (this item exists under the root Visual Basic and Visual C# nodes, or under the sub-node Windows) and set the Name to "GettingStarted," before selecting OK. This should create a new windows application project, which includes a single startup form and is contained within a "GettingStarted" solution, as shown in the Solution Explorer window of Figure 1-7. This startup form has automatically opened in the visual designer, giving you a graphical representation of what the form will look like when you run the application. You will notice that there is now an additional command bar visible and that the Properties tool window is in the right tool windows area.

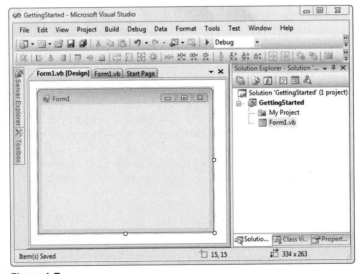

Figure 1-7

2. Click on the Toolbox tool window, which will cause the window to expand, followed by the pin icon, which will pin the tool window open. To add controls to the form, select the appropriate items from the Toolbox and drag them onto the form. In Figure 1-8, you can see how the Toolbar tool window appears after being pinned and the result of clicking and dragging a button onto the form visual designer.

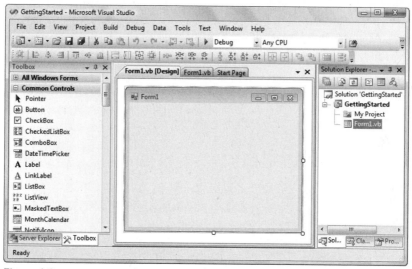

Figure 1-8

3. Add a button and textbox to the form so that the layout looks similar to the one shown in Figure 1-9. Select the textbox and select the Properties tool window (you can press F4 to automatically open the Properties tool window). Use the scrollbar to locate the (Name) property and set it to txtToSay. Repeat for the button control, naming it btnSayHello and setting the Text property to "Say Hello!"

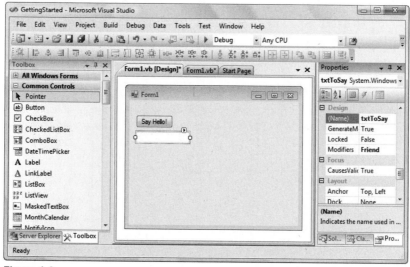

Figure 1-9

4.   When a form is opened in the editor space, an additional command bar is added to the top of Visual Studio 2008. If you select both controls on the form, you will see that certain icons on this command bar are enabled. Selecting the Make Same Width icon will align the edges of the two controls, as illustrated in Figure 1-10.

You will also notice that after you add controls to the form the tab will be updated with an asterisk (*) after the text to indicate that there are unsaved changes to that particular item. If you attempt to close this item while changes are pending, you will be asked if you want to save the changes. When you build the application, any unsaved files will automatically be saved as part of the build process.

One thing to be aware of is that some files, such as the solution file, are modified when you make changes within Visual Studio 2008 without your being given any indication that they have changed. If you try to exit the application or close the solution, you will still be prompted to save these changes.

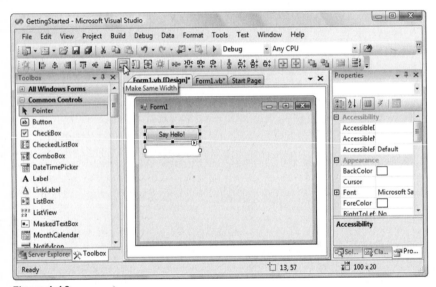

Figure 1-10

5.   Deselect all controls and then double-click the button. This will not only open the code editor with the code-behind file for this form; it will also create and wire up an event handler for the Click Event on the button. Figure 1-11 shows the code window after we have added a single line to echo the message to the user.

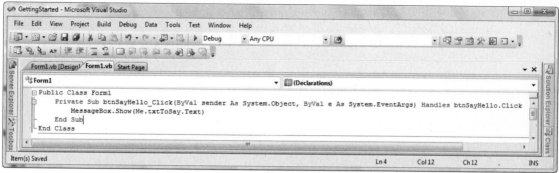

Figure 1-11

6. The last step in the process is to build and execute the application. Before doing so, place the cursor somewhere on the line containing `Messagebox.Show` and press F9. This will set a breakpoint — when you run the application by pressing F5 and then click the Say Hello! button, the execution will halt at this line. Figure 1-12 illustrates this breakpoint being reached. The data tip, which appears when the mouse hovers over the line, shows the contents of the `txtToSay.ext` property.

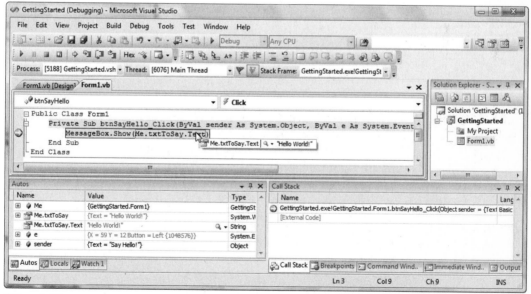

Figure 1-12

The layout of Visual Studio in Figure 1-12 is significantly different from the previous screenshots, as there are a number of new tool windows visible in the lower half of the screen and new command bars at the top. When you stop the application you will notice that Visual Studio returns to the previous layout. Visual Studio 2008 maintains two separate layouts: design time and runtime. Menus, toolbars, and various windows have default layouts for when you are editing a project, whereas a different setup is defined for when a project is being executed and debugged. You can modify each of these layouts to suit your own style and Visual Studio 2008 will remember them.

It's always a good idea to export your layout and settings (see Chapter 3) once you have them set up just the way you like them. That way you can take them to another PC or restore them if your PC gets rebuilt.

Summary

You've now seen how the various components of Visual Studio 2008 work together to build an application. As a review of the default layout for Visual Basic programs, the following list outlines the typical process of creating a solution:

1. Use the File menu to create a solution.

2. Use the Solution Explorer to locate the form that needs editing and click the View Designer button to show it in the main workspace area.

3. Drag the necessary components onto the form from the Toolbox.

4. Select the form and each component in turn, and edit the properties in the Properties window.

5. Use the Solution Explorer to locate the form and click the View Code button to access the code behind the form's graphical interface.

6. Use the main workspace area to write code and design the graphical interface, switching between the two via the tabs at the top of the area.

7. Use the toolbars to start the program.

8. If errors occur, review them in the Error List and Output windows.

9. Save the project using either toolbar or menu commands, and exit Visual Studio 2008.

While many of these actions can be performed in other ways (for instance, right-click the design surface of a form and you'll find the View Code command), this simplified process shows how the different sections of the IDE work in conjunction with each other to create a comprehensive application design environment.

In subsequent chapters, you'll learn how to customize the IDE to more closely fit your own working style, and how Visual Studio 2008 takes a lot of the guesswork out of the application development process. You will also see a number of best practices for working with Visual Studio 2008 that you can reuse as a developer.

2

The Solution Explorer, Toolbox, and Properties

In Chapter 1 you briefly saw and interacted with a number of the components that make up the Visual Studio 2008 IDE. Now you will get an opportunity to work with three of the most commonly used tool windows — the Solution Explorer, the Toolbox, and Properties.

Throughout this and other chapters you will see references to keyboard shortcuts, such as Ctrl+S. In these cases we assume the use of the general development settings, as shown in Chapter 1. Other profiles may have different key combinations.

The Solution Explorer

Whenever you create or open an application, or for that matter just a single file, Visual Studio 2008 uses the concept of a solution to tie everything together. Typically, a solution is made up of one or more projects, each of which in turn can have multiple items associated with it. In the past these items were typically just files, but increasingly projects are made up of items that may consist of multiple files, or in some cases no files at all. Chapter 6 will go into more detail about projects, the structure of solutions, and how items are related.

The Solution Explorer tool window (Ctrl+Alt+L) provides a convenient visual representation of the solution, projects, and items, as shown in Figure 2-1. In this figure you can see that there are three projects presented in a tree: a Visual Basic .NET Windows application, a WCF service library, and a C# class library.

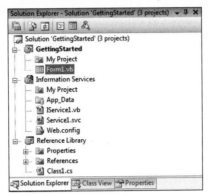

Figure 2-1

Each project has an icon associated with it that typically indicates the type of project and the language it is written in. There are some exceptions to this rule, such as setup projects that don't have a language.

One node is particularly noticeable, as the font is boldfaced. This indicates that this project is the startup project — in other words, the project that is launched when you select Debug ⇨ Start Debugging or press F5. To change the startup project, right-click the project you want to nominate and select "Set as Startup Project." It is also possible to nominate multiple projects as startup projects via the Solution Properties dialog, which you can reach by selecting Properties from the right-click menu of the solution node.

With certain environment settings (see "Let's Get Started" in Chapter 1), the solution node is not visible when only a single project exists. The problem with this is that it becomes difficult to access the Solution Properties window. To get the solution node to appear you can either add another project to the solution or check the "Always show solution" item from the Projects and Solutions node in the Options dialog, accessible via Tools ⇨ Options.

The toolbar across the top of the Solution Explorer enables you to customize the way the contents of the window appear to you, as well as giving you shortcuts to the different views for individual items. For example, the first button accesses the Properties window for the currently selected node, with the exception of the solution node, which opens the Solution Properties dialog. The second button, "Show All Files," expands the solution listing to display the additional files and folders, shown in Figure 2-2. You can see that even a simple item, such as a form, can be made up of multiple files. In this case Form1 has Form1.vb, which is where your code goes, Form1.designer.vb, which is where the generated code goes, and Form1.resx, an XML document where all the resources used by this form are captured.

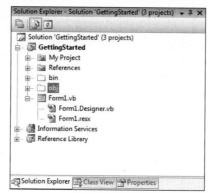

Figure 2-2

In this expanded view you can see all the files and folders contained under the project structure. Unfortunately, if the file system changes, the Solution Explorer will not automatically update to reflect these changes. The third button, "Refresh," can be used to make sure you are seeing the correct list of files and folders.

The Solution Explorer toolbar is contextually aware, with different buttons displayed depending on what type of node is selected. This is shown in Figure 2-2, where a folder not contained in the project (as indicated by the faded icon color) is selected and the remaining buttons from Figure 2-1 are not visible. In short, these buttons when visible can be used to view code (in this case the Form1.vb file), open the designer, which displays a visual representation of the Form1.designer.vb file, and lastly see the Class Diagram.

If you don't already have a class diagram in your project, clicking the "View Class Diagram" button will insert one and automatically add all the classes. For a project with a lot of classes this can be quite time-consuming and will result in a large and unwieldy class diagram. It is generally a better idea to manually add one or more class diagrams, which gives you total control.

Common Tasks

In addition to providing a convenient way to manage projects and items, the Solution Explorer has a dynamic context menu that gives you quick access to some of the most common tasks, such as building the solution or individual projects, accessing the build configuration manager, and opening files. Figure 2-3 shows how the context menu varies depending on which item is selected in the Solution Explorer.

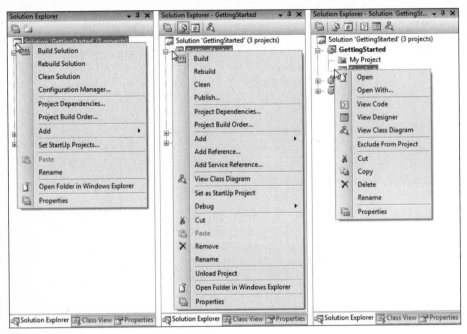

Figure 2-3

The first items in the left-hand and center menus relate to building either the entire solution or the selected project. In most cases selecting "Build" will be the most efficient option, as it will only build projects that have changed. However, in some cases you may need to force a rebuild, which will build all dependent projects regardless of their states. If you just want to remove all the additional files that are created during the build process, you can invoke "Clean." This option can be useful if you want to package your solution in order to e-mail it to someone — you wouldn't want to include all the temporary or output files that are created by the build.

For most items in the Solution Explorer, the first section of the context menu is similar to the right-hand menu in Figure 2-3: there is a default "Open," and "Open With . . .", item that allows you to determine how the item will be opened. This is of particular use when you are working with XML resource files. Visual Studio 2008 will open this file type using the built-in resource editor, but this prevents you from making certain changes and doesn't support all data types you might want to include (Chapter 40 goes into how you can use your own data types in resource files.) Using the "Open With . . ." menu item, you can instead use the Visual Studio 2008 XML editor.

A notable addition to the context menu is the "Open Folder in Windows Explorer" item. This enables you to open Windows Explorer quickly to the location of the selected item, saving you the hassle of having to navigate to where your solution is located and then find the appropriate sub-folder.

Adding Projects and Items

The most common activities carried out in the Solution Explorer are the addition, removal, and renaming of projects and items. In order to add a new project to an existing solution, you select Add ⇨ New Project from the context menu off the solution node. This will invoke the dialog in Figure 2-4, which has undergone a few minor changes since previous versions of Visual Studio. Frequently requested features, such as the ability to resize the dialog, have now been implemented, making it much easier to locate the project type you want to add.

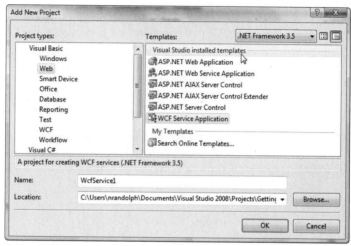

Figure 2-4

In the Project types hierarchy on the left of the Add New Project dialog, the types are primarily arranged by language, and then by technology. The types include Office project types, enabling you to build both application- and document-level add-ins for most of the Office products. While the Office add-ins still make use of Visual Studio Tools for Office (VSTO), this is now built into Visual Studio 2008 instead of being an additional installer. You will see in Chapter 33 how you can use these project types to build add-ins for the core Office applications.

The other thing you will notice in this dialog is the ability to select different Framework versions. This is a significant improvement for most development teams. If you have existing projects that you don't want to have to migrate forward to the new version of the .NET Framework, you can still immediately take advantage of the new features, such as improved IntelliSense. The alternative would have been to have both Visual Studio 2008 and a previous version installed in order to build projects for earlier Framework versions.

In fact, this is still the case if you have any applications that require version 1.0 or 1.1 of the .NET Framework. However, in this case you can still get away without having to install Visual Studio 2005.

One warning about this feature is that when you open your existing solutions or projects in Visual Studio 2008, they will still go through the upgrade wizard (see Chapter 44 for more information) but will essentially make only minor changes to the solution and project files. Unfortunately, these minor changes, which involve the inclusion of additional properties, will break your existing build process if you are using a previous version of MSBuild. For this reason, you will still need to migrate your entire development team across to using Visual Studio 2008 and the new version of MSBuild.

One of the worst and most poorly understood features that was added to Visual Studio 2005 was the concept of a Web Site project. This is distinct from a Web Application project, which can be added via the aforementioned Add New Project dialog (this is covered in detail in Chapter 31). To add a Web Site project you need to select Add ⇨ Web Site . . . from the context menu off the solution node. This will display a dialog similar to the one shown in Figure 2-5, where you can select the type of web project to be created. In most cases, this simply determines the type of default item that is to be created in the project.

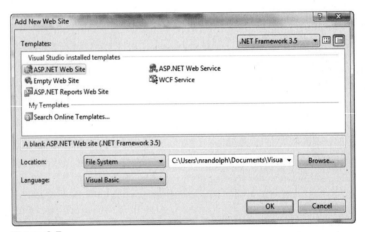

Figure 2-5

It is important to note that the types of web project listed in Figure 2-5 are the same as the types listed under the Web node in the Add New Project dialog. However, understand that they will not generate the same results, as there are significant differences between Web Site projects (created via the Add New Web Site dialog) and Web Application projects (created via the Add New Project dialog).

Once you have a project or two, you will need to start adding items. This is done via the "Add" context menu item off the project node in the Solution Explorer. The first sub-menu, "New Item . . .", will launch the Add New Item dialog, as seen in Figure 2-6.

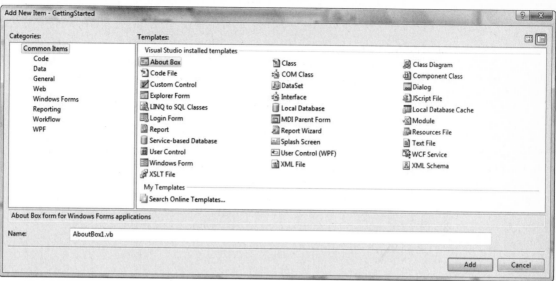

Figure 2-6

Returning to the Add context menu, you will notice that there are a number of predefined shortcuts such as Windows Form, User Control, and Class. These do little more than bypass the stage of locating the appropriate template within the Add New Item dialog. This dialog is still displayed, since you need to assign a name to the item being created.

It is important to make the distinction that you are adding items rather than files to the project. While a lot of the templates contain only a single file, some, like the Windows Form, will add multiple files to your project.

Adding References

Each new software development technology that is released promises better reuse, but few are able to actually deliver on this promise. One way that Visual Studio 2008 supports reusable components is via the references for a project. If you expand out any project you will observe that there are a number of .NET Framework libraries, such as System and System.Core, that need to be referenced by a project in order to be built. Essentially, a reference enables the compiler to resolve type, property, field, and method names back to the assembly where they are defined. If you want to reuse a class from a third-party library, or even your own .NET assembly, you need to add a reference to it via the "Add Reference . . ." context menu item on the project nodes of the Solution Explorer.

When you launch the Add Reference dialog, shown in Figure 2-7, Visual Studio 2008 will interrogate the local computer, the global assembly cache, and your solution in order to present a list of known libraries that can be referenced. This includes both .NET and COM references that are separated into different lists, as well as project and recently used references. If the component you need to reference isn't present in the appropriate list, you can choose the Browse tab, which enables you to locate the file containing the component directly in the file system.

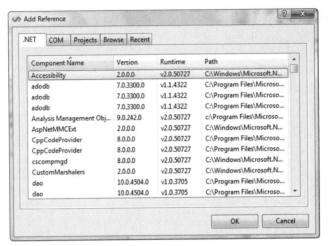

Figure 2-7

As in other project-based development environments going back as far as the first versions of Visual Basic, you can add references to projects contained in your solution, rather than adding the compiled binary components. The advantage to this model is that it's easier to debug into the referenced component, but for large solutions this may become unwieldy.

> *Where you have a solution with a large number of projects (large can be relevant to your computer but typically anything over 20), you should consider having multiple solutions that reference subsets of the projects. This will continue to give you a nice debugging experience throughout the entire application while improving Visual Studio performance during both loading and building of the solution.*

Adding Service References

The other type of reference that the Solution Explorer caters to is service references. In previous versions these were limited to web references, but with the advent of the Windows Communication Foundation (WCF) there is now a more generic "Add Service Reference . . ." menu item. This invokes the Add Service Reference dialog, which you can see in Figure 2-8. In this example the drop-down feature of the "Discover" button has been used to look for Services in Solution.

Unfortunately, this dialog is another case of Microsoft not understanding the usage pattern properly. While the dialog itself is resizable, the status response message area is not. Luckily, if any errors are thrown while Visual Studio 2008 attempts to access the service information, it will provide a hyperlink that will open the Add Service Reference Error dialog. This will generally give you enough information to resolve the problem.

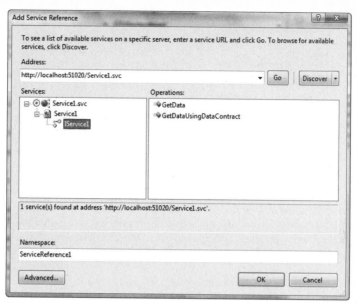

Figure 2-8

In the lower left-hand corner of Figure 2-8 is an "Advanced . . ." button. The Service Reference Settings dialog that this launches enables you to customize which types are defined as part of the service reference. By default, all local system types are assumed to match those being published by the service. If this is not the case, you may want to adjust the values in the Data Type area of this dialog. There is also an "Add Web Reference" button in the lower left-hand corner of the Service Reference Settings dialog, which enables you to add more traditional .NET Webservice references. This might be important if you have some limitations or are trying to support intersystem operability.

The Toolbox

One of the major advantages over many other IDEs that Microsoft has offered developers is true drag-and-drop placement of elements during the design of both web and Windows (and now WPF) forms. These elements are all available in what is known as the Toolbox (Ctrl+Alt+X), a tool window accessible via the View menu, as shown in Figure 2-9.

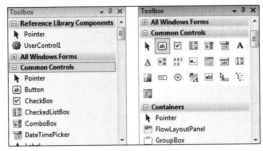

Figure 2-9

The Toolbox window contains all of the available components for the currently-active document being shown in the main workspace. These can be visual components, such as buttons and textboxes; invisible, service-oriented objects, such as timers and system event logs; or even designer elements, such as class and interface objects used in the Class Designer view.

Visual Studio 2008 presents the available components in groups rather than as one big mess of components. This default grouping enables you to more easily locate the controls you need — for example, data-related components are in their own Data group.

By default, groups are presented in list view (see the left side of Figure 2-9). Each component is represented by its own icon and the name of the component. This differs from the old way of displaying the available objects, in which the Toolbox was simply a stacked list of icons that left you guessing as to what some of the more obscure components were, as shown with the Common Controls group on the right side of Figure 2-9. You can change the view of each control group individually — right-click anywhere within the group area and deselect the "List View" option in the context menu.

Regardless of how the components are presented, the way they are used in a program is usually the same: click and drag the desired component onto the design surface of the active document, or double-click the component's entry for Visual Studio to automatically add an instance. Visual components, such as buttons and textboxes, will appear in the design area where they can be repositioned, resized, and otherwise adjusted via the property grid. Nonvisual components, such as the Timer control, will appear as icons, with associated labels, in a nonvisual area below the design area, as shown in Figure 2-10.

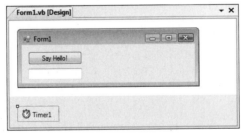

Figure 2-10

At the top left-hand side of Figure 2-9 is a group called Reference Library Components with a single component, UserControl1. "Reference Library" is actually the name of a class library that is defined in the same solution, and it contains the UserControl1 control. When you start to build your own components or controls, instead of your having to manually create a new tab and go through the process of adding each item, Visual Studio 2008 automatically interrogates all the projects in your solution. If any components (classes that inherit from *System.ComponentModel.Component*) or controls (classes that inherit from *System.Windows.Forms.Control*) are identified, a new tab will be created for that project and the appropriate items will be added with a default icon and class name (in this case UserControl1), as you can see on the left in Figure 2-9. For components, this is the same icon that will appear in the nonvisual part of the design area when you use the component.

> *Visual Studio 2008 interrogates all projects in your solution, both at startup and after build activities. This can take a significant amount of time if you have a large number of projects. If this is the case, you should consider disabling this feature by setting the* `AutoToolboxPopulate` *property to* `false` *under the Windows Forms Designer node of the Options dialog (Tools ⇨ Options).*

To customize how your items appear in the Toolbox, you need to add a 16×16 pixel bitmap to the same project as your component or control. Next, select the newly inserted bitmap in the Solution Explorer and navigate to the Properties window. Make sure the `Build` property is set to `Embedded Resource`. All you now need to do is attribute your control with the `ToolboxBitmap` attribute.

```
<ToolboxBitmap(GetType(UserControl1), "MyControlIcon.bmp")> _
Public Class UserControl1
```

This attribute uses the type reference for UserControl1 to locate the appropriate assembly from which to extract the `MyControlIcon.bmp` embedded resource. There are other overloads of this attribute that can use a file path as the only argument. In this case you don't need even to add the bitmap to your project.

> *Unfortunately, it appears that you can't customize the way the automatically generated items appear in the Toolbox. However, if you manually add an item to the Toolbox and select your components, you will see your custom icon. Alternatively, if you have a component and you drag it onto a form, you will see your icon appear in the nonvisual space on the designer.*

Arranging Components

Alphabetical order is a good default because it enables you to locate items that are unfamiliar. However, if you're only using a handful of components and are frustrated by having to continuously scroll up and down, you can create your own groups of controls and move existing object types around.

Repositioning an individual component is easy. Locate it in the Toolbox and click and drag it to the new location. When you're happy with where it is, release the mouse button and the component will move to the new spot in the list. You can move it to a different group in the same way — just keep dragging the component up or down the Toolbox until you've located the right group. These actions work in both List and Icon views.

If you want to copy the component from one group to another, rather than move it, hold down the Ctrl key as you drag, and the process will duplicate the control so that it appears in both groups.

Sometimes it's nice to have your own group to host the controls and components you use the most. To create a new group in the Toolbox, right-click anywhere in the Toolbox area and select the "Add Tab" command. A new blank tab will be added to the bottom of the Toolbox with a prompt for you to name it. Once you have named the tab, you can then add components to it by following the steps described in this section.

When you first start Visual Studio 2008, the items within each group are arranged alphabetically. However, after moving items around, you may find that they're in a bewildering state and decide that you simply need to start again. All you have to do is right-click anywhere within the group and choose the "Sort Items Alphabetically" command.

By default, controls are added to the Toolbox according to their base names. This means you end up with some names that are hard to understand, particularly if you add COM controls to your Toolbox. Visual Studio 2008 enables you to modify a component's name to something more understandable.

To change the name of a component, right-click the component's entry in the Toolbox and select the "Rename Item" command. An edit field will appear inline in place of the original caption, enabling you to name it however you like, even with special characters.

If you've become even more confused, with components in unusual groups, and you have lost sight of where everything is, you can choose "Reset Toolbox" from the same right-click context menu. This will restore all of the groups in the Toolbox to their original states, with components sorted alphabetically and in the groups in which they started.

> *Remember: Selecting "Reset Toolbox" will delete any of your own custom-made groups of commands, so be very sure you want to perform this function!*

Adding Components

Sometimes you'll find that a particular component you need is not present in the lists displayed in the Toolbox. Most of the main .NET components are already present, but some are not. For example, the WebClient class component is not displayed in the Toolbox by default. Managed applications can also use COM components in their design. Once added to the Toolbox, COM objects can be used in much the same way as regular .NET components, and if coded correctly you can program against them in precisely the same way, using the Properties window and referring to their methods, properties, and events in code.

To add a component to your Toolbox layout, right-click anywhere within the group of components you wish to add it to and select "Choose Items". After a moment (this process can take a few seconds on a slower machine, as the machine needs to interrogate the .NET cache to determine all the possible components you can choose from), you will be presented with a list of .NET Framework components, as Figure 2-11 shows.

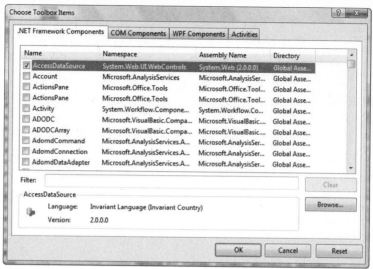

Figure 2-11

Scroll through the list to locate the item you wish to add to the Toolbox and check the corresponding checkbox. You can add multiple items at the same time by selecting each of them before clicking the OK button to apply your changes. At this time you can also remove items from the Toolbox by deselecting them from the list. Note that this will remove the items from any groups to which they belong, not just from the group you are currently editing.

If you're finding it hard to locate the item you need, you can use the Filter box, which will filter the list based on name, namespace, and assembly name. On rare occasions the item may not be listed at all. This can happen with nonstandard components, such as ones that you build yourself or that are not registered in the Global Assembly Cache. You can still add them by using the "Browse" button to locate the physical file on the computer. Once you've selected and deselected the items you need, click the "OK" button to save them to the Toolbox layout.

COM components, WPF components, and (workflow) activities can be added in the same manner. Simply switch over to the relevant tab in the dialog window to view the list of available, properly registered COM components to add. Again, you can use the "Browse" button to locate controls that may not appear in the list.

Properties

One of the most frequently used tool windows built into Visual Studio 2008 is the Properties window (F4), as shown in Figure 2-12. The Properties window is made up of a property grid and is contextually aware, displaying only relevant properties of the currently selected item, whether that item is a node in the Solution Explorer or an element in the form design area. Each line represents a property with its name and corresponding value in two columns.

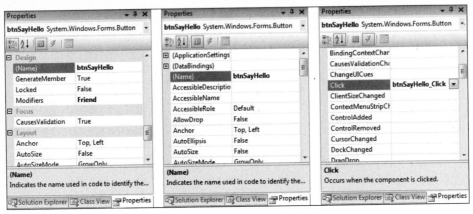

Figure 2-12

The property grid used in the Properties window is the same grid that can be found in the Toolbox and can be reused by your application. It is capable of grouping properties, or sorting them alphabetically — you can toggle this layout using the first two buttons at the top of the Properties window. There are built-in editors for a range of system types, such as colors, fonts, anchors, and docking, which are invoked when you click into the value column of the property to be changed. When a property is selected, as shown in the center of Figure 2-12, the property name is highlighted and a description is presented in the lower region of the property grid.

In addition to displaying properties for a selected item, the Properties window also provides a design experience for wiring up event handlers. The right side of Figure 2-12 illustrates the event view that is accessible via the fourth button, the lightning bolt, across the top of the Properties window. In this case you can see that there is an event handler for the click event. To wire up another event you can either select from a list of existing methods via a drop-down list in the value column, or you can double-click the value column. This will create a new event-handler method and wire it up to the event. If you use the first method you will notice that only methods that match the event signature are listed.

In the Properties window, read-only properties are indicated in gray and you will not be able to modify their values. The value SayHello for the Text property on the left side of Figure 2-12 is boldfaced, which indicates that this is not the default value for this property. If you inspect the code that is generated, you will notice that a line exists for each property that is boldfaced in the property grid — adding a line of code for every single property on a control would significantly increase the time to render the form. For example:

```
Me.btnSayHello.Location = New System.Drawing.Point(12, 12)
Me.btnSayHello.Name = "btnSayHello"
Me.btnSayHello.Size = New System.Drawing.Size(100, 23)
Me.btnSayHello.TabIndex = 0
Me.btnSayHello.Text = "Say Hello!"
Me.btnSayHello.UseVisualStyleBackColor = True
```

Certain components, such as the DataGridView, expose a number of commands, or shortcuts, that can be executed via the Properties window. On the left side of Figure 2-13 you can see that there are two commands for the DataGridView: "Edit Columns . . ." and "Add Column . . .". When you click either of these command links, you will be presented with a dialog for performing that action.

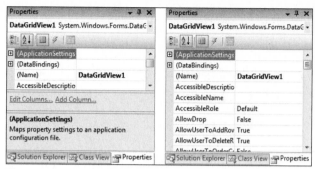

Figure 2-13

As you can see on the left of Figure 2-13, if the Properties window only has a small amount of screen real estate, it can be difficult to scroll through the list of properties. If you right-click in the property grid you can uncheck the "Command" and "Description" checkboxes to hide these sections of the Properties window, as shown on the right side of Figure 2-13.

Extending the Properties Window

You have just seen how Visual Studio 2008 highlights properties that have changed by boldfacing the value. The question that you need to ask is, How does Visual Studio 2008 know what the default value is? The answer is that when the Properties window interrogates an object to determine what properties to display in the property grid, it looks for a number of design attributes. These attributes can be used to control which properties are displayed, the editor that is used to edit the value, and what the default value is. To show how you can use these attributes on your own components, start with adding a simple field-backed property to your component:

```
Public Property Description() As String
    Get
        Return mDescription
    End Get
    Set(ByVal value As String)
        mDescription = value
    End Set
End Property
```

The Browsable Attribute

By default, all public properties will be displayed in the property grid. However, you can explicitly control this behavior by adding the Browsable attribute. If you set it to false the property will not appear in the property grid.

```
<System.ComponentModel.Browsable(False)> _
Public Property Description() As String
```

DisplayName Attribute

The `DisplayName` attribute is somewhat self-explanatory, as it enables you to modify the display name of the property. In our case, we can change the name of the property as it appears in the property grid from `Description` to `VS2008 Description`.

```
<System.ComponentModel.DisplayName("VS2008 Description")> _
Public Property Description() As String
```

Description

In addition to defining the friendly or display name for the property, it is also worth providing a description, which will appear in the bottom area of the Properties window when the property is selected. This will ensure that users of your component understand what the property does.

```
<System.ComponentModel.Description("My first custom property")> _
Public Property Description() As String
```

Category

By default any property you expose will be placed in the Misc group when the Properties window is in grouped view. Using the `Category` attribute you can place your property in any of the existing groups, such as Appearance or Data, or a new group if you specify a group name that doesn't exist.

```
<System.ComponentModel. Category("Appearance")> _
Public Property Description() As String
```

DefaultValue

Earlier you saw how Visual Studio 2008 highlights properties that have changed from their initial or default values. The `DefaultValue` attribute is what Visual Studio 2008 looks for to determine the default value for the property.

```
Private Const cDefaultDescription As String = "<enter description>"
<System.ComponentModel.DefaultValue(GetType(String), cDefaultDescription)> _
Public Property Description() As String
```

In this case, if the value of the `Description` property is set to `"<enter description>"`, Visual Studio 2008 will remove the line of code that sets this property. If you modify a property and want to return to the default value, you can right-click the property in the Properties window and select "Reset" from the context menu.

It is important to note that the `DefaultValue` attribute does not set the initial value of your property. In this case, the `Description` property will start with a value of `nothing` (null for C#) but the following line will appear in the designer-generated code, because `nothing` is not the default value.

```
Me.MyFirstControl1.Description = ""
```

It is recommended that if you specify the DefaultValue attribute you also set the initial value of your property to the same value.

```
Private mDescription As String = cDefaultDescription
```

AmbientValue

One of the features we all take for granted but that few truly understand is the concept of ambient properties. Typical examples are background and foreground colors and fonts: unless you explicitly set these via the Properties window they are inherited — not from their base classes, but from their parent control. A broader definition of an ambient property is a property that gets its value from another source.

Like the DefaultValue attribute, the AmbientValue attribute is used to indicate to Visual Studio 2008 when it should not add code to the designer file. Unfortunately, with ambient properties you can't hard-code a value for the designer to compare the current value to, as it is contingent on the property's source value. Because of this, when you define the AmbientValue attribute this tells the designer to look for a function called ShouldSerialize*PropertyName*. In our case it would be ShouldSerializeDescription, and this method is called to determine whether the current value of the property should be persisted to the designer code file.

```
Private mDescription As String = cDefaultDescription
<System.ComponentModel.AmbientValue(GetType(String), cDefaultDescription)> _
Public Property Description() As String
    Get
        If Me.mDescription = cDefaultDescription _
                            AndAlso Me.Parent IsNot Nothing Then
            Return Parent.Text
        End If
        Return mDescription
    End Get
    Set(ByVal value As String)
        mDescription = value
    End Set
End Property
Private Function ShouldSerializeDescription() As Boolean
    If Me.Parent IsNot Nothing Then
        Return Not Me.Description = Me.Parent.Text
    Else
        Return Not Me.Description = cDefaultDescription
    End If
End function
```

When you create a control with this property, the initial value would be set to the value of the cDefaultDescription constant, but in the designer you would see a value corresponding to the Parent.Text value. There would also be no line explicitly setting this property in the designer code file, as reflected in the Properties window by the value being non-boldfaced. If you change the value of this property to anything other than the cDefaultDescription constant, you will see that it becomes bold and a line is added to the designer code file. If you reset this property, the underlying value will be set back to the value defined by AmbientValue, but all you will see is that it has returned to displaying the Parent.Text value.

Summary

In this chapter you have seen three of the most common tool windows in action. Knowing how to manipulate these windows can save you considerable time during development. However, the true power of Visual Studio 2008 is exposed when you start to incorporate the designer experience into your own components. This can be useful even if your components aren't going to be used outside your organization. Making effective use of the designer can improve not only the efficiency with which your controls are used, but also the performance of the application you are building.

3

Options and Customizations

Now that you're familiar with the general layout of Visual Studio 2008, it's time to learn how you can customize the IDE to suit your working style. In this chapter you will learn how to manipulate tool windows, optimize the code window for maximum viewing space, and change fonts and colors to reduce developer fatigue.

As Visual Studio has grown, so too has the number of settings that you can adjust in order to optimize your development experience. Unfortunately, unless you've periodically spent time sifting through the Options dialog (Tools ⇨ Options), it's likely that you've overlooked one or two settings that might be important. Through the course of this chapter you will see a number of recommendations of settings you might want to investigate further.

> *A number of Visual Studio add-ins will add their own nodes to the Options dialog as this provides a one-stop shop for configuring settings within Visual Studio. Note also that some developer setting profiles, as selected in Chapter 1, will show only a cut-down list of options. In this case, checking the Advanced checkbox will show the complete list of available options.*

Window Layout

If you are unfamiliar with Visual Studio, the behavior of the numerous tool windows may strike you as erratic, because they seem to appear in random locations and then come and go when you move from writing code (design time) to running code (runtime) and back again. Visual Studio 2008 will remember the locations of tool windows in each of these modes separately. This way you can optimize the way you write and debug code.

As you open different items from the Solution Explorer, you'll see that the number of Toolbars across the top of the screen varies depending on the type of file being opened. Each Toolbar has a built-in association to specific file extensions so that Visual Studio knows to display the Toolbar when a file with one of those extensions is opened. If you close a Toolbar when a file is open that has a matching file extension, Visual Studio will remember this when future files with the same extension are opened.

You can reset the association between Toolbars and the file extensions via the Customize dialog (Tools ⇨ Customize). Select the appropriate Toolbar and click the "Reset" button.

Viewing Windows and Toolbars

Once a tool window or Toolbar has been closed it can be difficult to locate it again. Luckily most of the most frequently used tool windows are accessible via the View menu. Other tool windows, mainly related to debugging, are located under the Debug menu.

All the Toolbars available in Visual Studio 2008 are listed under the View ⇨ Toolbars menu item. Each Toolbar that is currently visible is marked with a tick against the appropriate menu item. You can also access the list of Toolbars by right-clicking in any empty space in the Toolbar area at the top of the Visual Studio window.

Once a Toolbar is visible you can customize which buttons are displayed, either via View ⇨ Toolbars ⇨ Customize or under the Tools menu. Alternatively, as shown in Figure 3-1, if you select the down arrow at the end of a Toolbar you will see a list of all Toolbars that are on the same line in the Toolbar area. Selecting a Toolbar presents a list of all the buttons available on that Toolbar, from which you can check the buttons you want to appear on the Toolbar.

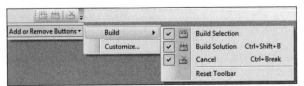

Figure 3-1

Navigating Open Items

After opening multiple items you'll notice that you run out of room across the top of the editor space and that you can no longer see the tabs for all the items you have open. Of course you can go back to the Solution Explorer window and select a specific item. If the item is already open it will be displayed without reverting to its saved state. However, it is still inconvenient to have to find the item in the Solution Explorer.

Luckily, Visual Studio 2008 has a number of shortcuts to the list of open items. As with most document-based applications, Visual Studio has a Windows menu. When you open an item its title is added to the bottom section of this menu. To display an open item just select the item from the Windows menu, or click the generic Windows item, which will display a modal dialog from which you can select the item you want.

Another alternative is to use the drop-down menu at the end of the tab area of the editor space. Figure 3-2 shows the drop-down list of open items from which you can select the item you want to access.

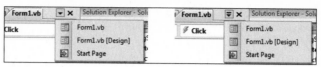

Figure 3-2

Figure 3-2 (right) is the same as Figure 3-2 (left) except for the drop-down icon. This menu also displays a down arrow, but this one has a line across the top. This line indicates that there are more tabs than can fit across the top of the editor space.

Another way to navigate through the open items is to press Ctrl+Tab, which will display a temporary window, as shown in Figure 3-3. It is a temporary window because when you release the Ctrl key it will disappear. However, while the window is open you can use the arrow keys or press Tab to move among the open windows.

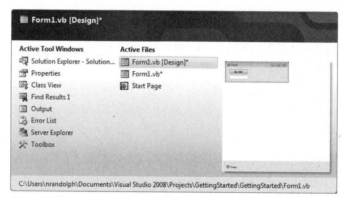

Figure 3-3

The Ctrl+Tab window is broken into three sections, which include the active tool windows, active files (this should actually be active items because it contains some items that don't correspond to a single file), and a preview of the currently selected item. As the number of either active files or active tool windows increases, the windows will expand vertically until there are 15 items, at which point an additional column will be formed.

> *If you get to the point where you are seeing multiple columns of active files, you might consider closing some or all of the unused files. The more files Visual Studio 2008 has open, the more memory it uses and the more slowly it performs.*

Docking

Each tool window has a default position, which it will resume when it is opened from the View menu. For example, View ⇨ Toolbox will open the Toolbox docked to the left edge of Visual Studio. Once a tool window is opened and is docked against an edge, it has two states, pinned and unpinned. As you saw in Chapter 1, you can toggle between these states by clicking on the vertical pin to unpin the tool window or on the horizontal pin to pin the tool window.

*You will notice that as you unpin a tool window it will slide back against the edge of the IDE,
leaving visible a tag displaying the title of the tool window. This animation can be annoying and
time-consuming when you have tool windows unpinned. On the Environment node of the Options
dialog you can control whether Visual Studio should "Animate environment tools." If you uncheck the
box, the tool windows will simply appear in their expanded state when you click the minimized tab.
Alternatively, you can adjust the speed at which the animation occurs.*

For most people the default location will suffice, but occasionally you'll want to adjust where the tool
windows appear. Visual Studio 2008 has one of the most advanced systems for controlling the layout of
tool windows. In Chapter 1 you saw how you could use the drop-down, next to the "Pin" and "Close"
buttons at the top of the tool window, to make the tool window floating, dockable, or even part of the
main editor space (using the Tabbed Document option).

When a tool window is dockable, you have a lot of control over where it is positioned. In Figure 3-4 you
can see the top of the Properties window, which has been dragged away from its default position at the
right of the IDE. To begin dragging you need to make sure the tool window is pinned and then click on
either the title area at the top of the tool window or the tab at the bottom of the tool window and drag
the mouse in the direction you want the window to move. If you click in the title area you'll see that all
tool windows in that section of the IDE will also be moved. Clicking the tab will result in only the
corresponding tool window moving.

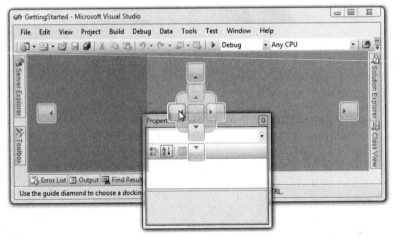

Figure 3-4

As you drag the tool window around Visual Studio 2008, you'll see that translucent icons appear at
different locations around the IDE. These icons are a useful guide to help you position the tool window
exactly where you want. In Figure 3-5, the Properties window has been dragged over the left icon of
the center image. The blue shading indicates where the Properties will be located when you release the
"Mouse" button. (In the case shown in the figure, the effect will be the same regardless of whether
we use the left icon of the center image or the icon on the far left of the IDE.) In Figure 3-5, similarly, the
Server Explorer tool window has been pinned against the left side. Now when the Properties window is
positioned over the left icon of the center image, the blue shading again appears on the inside of the
existing tool window. This indicates that both the Server Explorer and Properties tool windows will be
pinned and visible if this layout is chosen.

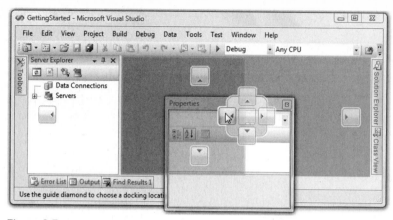

Figure 3-5

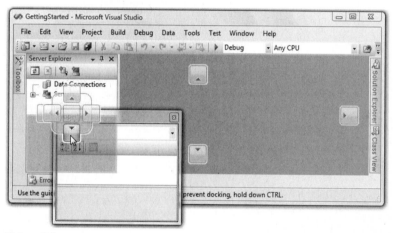

Figure 3-6

Alternatively, if the Properties tool window is dragged over the left icon of Figure 3-6, the center image will move over the existing tool window. This indicates that the Properties tool window will be positioned within the existing tool window area. As you drag the window over the different quadrants, you will see that the blue shading again indicates where the tool window will be positioned when the mouse is released. In Figure 3-6 it indicates that the Properties tool window will appear below the existing tool windows.

It should be noted that if you have a large screen, or multiple screens, it is worth spending time laying out the tool windows you use frequently. With multiple screens, using floating tool windows means that you can position them away from the main editor space, maximizing your screen real estate. If you have a small screen you may find that you continually have to adjust which tool windows are visible, so becoming familiar with the docking and layout options is essential.

The Editor Space

Like most IDEs, Visual Studio 2008 has been built up around the central code-editing window. Over time it has evolved and is now much more than a simple text editor. While most developers will spend considerable time writing code in the editor space, there are an increasing number of designers for performing tasks such as building forms, adjusting project settings, and editing resources. Regardless of whether you are writing code or doing form design, you are going to spend a lot of your time within Visual Studio 2008 in the editor space. Because of this it is important for you to know how to tweak the layout so you can work more efficiently.

Fonts and Colors

Some of the first things that presenters change in Visual Studio are the fonts and colors used in the editor space, in order to make the code more readable. However, it shouldn't just be presenters who adjust these settings. Selecting fonts and colors that are easy for you to read and that aren't harsh on the eyes will make you more productive and enable you to code for longer without feeling fatigued. Figure 3-7 shows the Fonts and Colors node of the Options dialog, where you can make adjustments to the font, size, color, and styling of different display items. One thing to note about this node in the Options dialog is that it is very slow to load, so try to avoid accidentally clicking it.

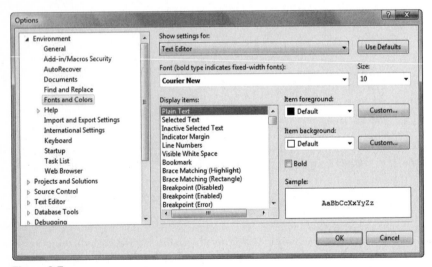

Figure 3-7

In order to adjust the appearance of a particular text item within Visual Studio 2008, you first need to select the area of the IDE that it applies to. In Figure 3-7 the Text Editor has been selected, and has been used to determine which items should appear in the "Display items" list. Once you have found the relevant item in this list, you can make adjustments to the font and colors.

Some items in this list, such as Plain Text, are reused by a number of areas within Visual Studio 2008, which can result in some unpredictable changes when you tweak fonts and colors.

When choosing a font, remember that proportional fonts are usually not as effective for writing code as non-proportional fonts (also known as fixed-width fonts). As indicated in Figure 3-7, fixed-width fonts are distinguished in the list from the variable-width types so they are easy to locate. One of the problems with Courier New is that it is less readable on the screen than other fixed-width fonts. A viable alternative as a readable screen font is Consolas (you may need to download and install the Consolas Font Pack from www.microsoft.com).

Visual Guides

When you are editing a file, Visual Studio 2008 will automatically color-code the code based on the type of file. For example, in Figure 3-8, which shows a VB.NET code file, it has highlighted keywords in blue, variable names and class references are in black, and string literals are in red. You will also note that there is a line running up the left side of the code. This is used to indicate where the code blocks are. You can click on the minus sign to condense the btnSayHello_Click method or the entire Form1 code block.

Various points about visual guides are illustrated in Figures 3-8 to 3-10. Those readers familiar with VB.NET will realize that Figure 3-8 is missing the end of the line where the method is set to handle the Click event of the btnSayHello button. This is because the rest of the line is being obscured by the edge of the code window. To see what is at the end of the line, the developer has to either scroll the window to the right or use the keyboard to navigate the cursor to the end of the line. In Figure 3-9 word wrap has been enabled via the Options dialog (see the Text Editor ⇨ All Languages ⇨ General node).

```
Public Class Form1
    Private Sub btnSayHello_Click(ByVal sender As System.Object, ByVal e As System.EventArgs)
        MessageBox.Show(Me.txtToSay.Text)
    End Sub
End Class
```

Figure 3-8

```
Public Class Form1
    Private Sub btnSayHello_Click(ByVal sender As System.Object, ByVal e As System.EventArgs)
Handles btnSayHello.Click
        MessageBox.Show(Me.txtToSay.Text)
    End Sub
End Class
```

Figure 3-9

```
1 Public·Class·Form1
2     ····Private·Sub·btnSayHello_Click(ByVal·sender·As·System.Object,·ByVal·e·As·System.EventArgs)·↵
  Handles·btnSayHello.Click
3 ········MessageBox.Show(Me.txtToSay.Text)
4     ····End·Sub
5 End·Class
6 □
```

Figure 3-10

Unfortunately, enabling word wrapping can make it hard to work out which lines have been wrapped. Luckily Visual Studio 2008 has an option (immediately below the checkbox to enable word wrapping in the Options dialog) that can display visual glyphs at the end of each line that with have been wrapped to the next line, as you can see in Figure 3-10. In this figure you can also see two other visual guides. On the left, outside the code block markers, are line numbers. These can be enabled via the "Line numbers" checkbox below both the Word Wrap and Visual Glyphs checkboxes. The other guide is the dots that represent space in the code. Unlike the other visual guides, this one can be enabled via the Edit ➪ Advanced ➪ View White Space menu item when the code editor space has focus.

Full-Screen Mode

If you have a number of tool windows and multiple Toolbars visible, you will have noticed that you quickly run out of space for actually writing code. For this reason, Visual Studio 2008 has a full-screen mode that you can access via the View ➪ Full Screen menu item. Alternatively, you can press Shift+Alt+Enter to toggle in and out of full-screen mode. Figure 3-11 shows the top of Visual Studio 2008 in full-screen mode. As you can see, no Toolbars or tool windows are visible and the window is completely maximized, even to the exclusion of the normal Minimize, Restore, and Close buttons.

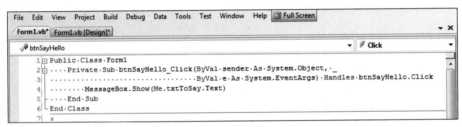

Figure 3-11

If you are using multiple screens, full-screen mode can be particularly useful. Undock the tool windows and place them on the second monitor. When the editor window is in full-screen mode you still have access to the tool windows, without having to toggle back and forth.

Tracking Changes

To enhance the experience of editing, Visual Studio 2008 uses line-level tracking to indicate which lines of code you have modified during an editing session. When you open a file to begin editing there will be no line coloring. However, when you begin to edit you will notice that a yellow mark appears next to the lines that have been modified. In Figure 3-12 you can see that the MsgBox line has been modified since this file was last saved.

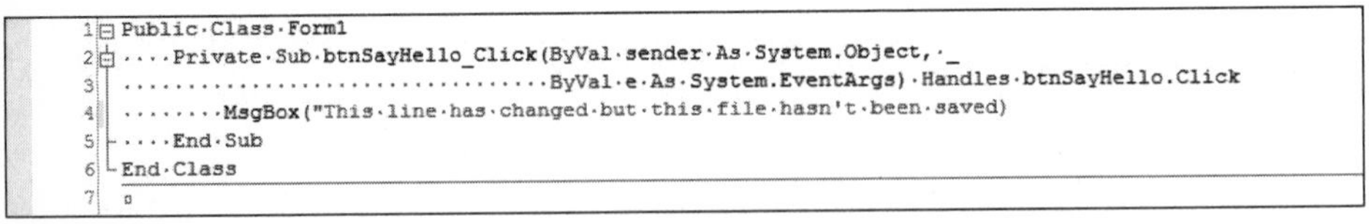

```
1 ⊟ Public·Class·Form1
2 ⊟ ····Private·Sub·btnSayHello_Click(ByVal·sender·As·System.Object,·_
3 ································ByVal·e·As·System.EventArgs)·Handles·btnSayHello.Click
4 ········MsgBox("This·line·has·changed·but·this·file·hasn't·been·saved)
5 ┕····End·Sub
6 ┕End·Class
7    ▫
```

Figure 3-12

When the file is saved the modified lines will change to having a green mark next to them. In Figure 3-13 the first MsgBox line has changed since the file was opened, but those changes have been saved to disk. However, the second MsgBox line has not yet been saved.

```
1  Public·Class·Form1
2      ····Private·Sub·btnSayHello_Click(ByVal·sender·As·System.Object,·_
3      ································ByVal·e·As·System.EventArgs)·Handles·btnSayHello.Click
4      ········MsgBox("This·line·has·changed·and·the·file·has·been·saved,")
5      ········MsgBox("but·this·line·has·changed·since·then!")
6      ····End·Sub
7  End·Class
8
```

Figure 3-13

If you don't find tracking changes to be useful, you can disable this feature by unchecking the Text Editor ⇨ General ⇨ Track Change item in the Options dialog.

Other Options

Many options that we haven't yet touched on can be used to tweak the way Visual Studio operates. Through the remainder of this chapter you will see some of the more useful options that can help you be more productive.

Keyboard Shortcuts

Visual Studio 2008 ships with many ways to perform the same action. Menus, Toolbars, and various tool windows provide direct access to many commands, but despite the huge number available, many more are not accessible through the graphical interface. Instead, these commands are accessed (along with most of those in the menus and Toolbars) via keyboard shortcuts.

These shortcuts range from the familiar Ctrl+Shift+S to save all changes, to the obscure Ctrl+Alt+E to display the Exceptions dialog window. As you might have guessed, you can set your own keyboard shortcuts and even change the existing ones. Even better, you can filter the shortcuts to operate only in certain contexts, meaning you can use the same shortcut differently depending on what you're doing.

Figure 3-14 shows the Keyboard node in the Environment section of the Options dialog with the default keyboard mapping scheme selected. If you want to change to use a different keyboard mapping scheme, simply select it from the drop-down and hit the Reset button.

The keyboard mapping schemes are stored as .VSK files at C:\Program Files\Microsoft Visual Studio 9.0\Common7\IDE. *This is the keyboard mapping file format used in versions of Visual Studio prior to Visual Studio 2005. To import keyboard mappings from Visual Studio 2005, use the import settings feature (see the end of this chapter); for earlier versions copy the appropriate .VSK file into the aforementioned folder, and you will be able to select it from the mapping scheme drop-down the next time you open the Options dialog.*

The listbox in the middle of Figure 3-14 lists every command that is available in Visual Studio 2008. Unfortunately, this list is quite extensive and the Options dialog is not resizable, which makes navigating this list difficult. To make it easier to search for commands, you can filter the command list using the "Show commands containing" textbox. In Figure 3-14 the word *build* has been used to filter the list down to all the commands starting with or containing that word. From this list the `Build.BuildSolution` command has been selected. As there is already a keyboard shortcut assigned to this command, the "Shortcuts for selected command" drop-down and "Remove" button have been enabled. It is possible to have multiple shortcuts for the same command, so the drop-down enables you to remove individual assigned shortcuts.

Having multiple shortcuts is useful if you want to keep a default shortcut — so that other developers feel at home using your setup — but also add your own personal one.

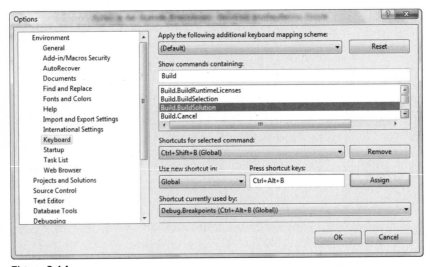

Figure 3-14

The remainder of this dialog enables you to assign a new shortcut to the command you have selected. Simply move to the "Press shortcut keys" textbox and, as the label suggests, press the appropriate keys. In Figure 3-14 the keyboard chord Ctrl+Alt+B has been entered, but this shortcut is already being used by another command, as shown at the bottom of the dialog window. If you click the "Assign" button, this keyboard shortcut will be remapped to the `Build.BuildSolution` command.

To restrict a shortcut's use to only one contextual area of Visual Studio 2008, select the context from the "Use new shortcut in" drop-down list. The Global option indicates that the shortcut should be applied across the entire environment, but we want this new shortcut to work only in the editor window, so the Text Editor item has been selected in Figure 3-14.

Chapter 53 deals with macros that you can create and maintain to make your coding experience easier. These macros can also be assigned to keyboard shortcuts.

Projects and Solutions

Several options relate to projects and solutions. The first of these is perhaps the most helpful — the default locations of your projects. By default, Visual Studio 2008 uses the standard Documents and Settings path common to many applications (see Figure 3-15), but this might not be where you'll want to keep your development work.

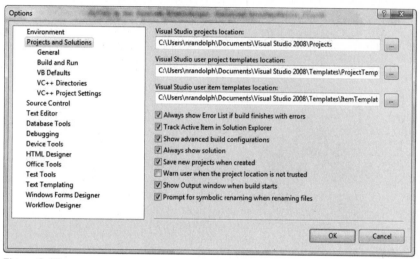

Figure 3-15

You can also change the location of template files at this point. If your organization uses a common network location for corporate project templates, you can change the default location in Visual Studio 2008 to point to this remote address rather than map the network drive.

There are a number of other options that you can adjust to change how projects and solutions are managed in Visual Studio 2008. One of particular interest is Track Active Item in Solution Explorer. With this option enabled, the layout of the Solution Explorer changes as you switch among items to ensure the current item is in focus. This includes expanding (but not collapsing again) projects and folders, which can be frustrating on a large solution as you are continually having to collapse projects so that you can navigate.

Another option that relates to solutions, but doesn't appear in Figure 3-15, is to list miscellaneous files in the Solution Explorer. Say you are working on a solution and you have to inspect an XML document that isn't contained in the solution. Visual Studio 2008 will happily open the file, but you will have to reopen it every time you open the solution. Alternatively, if you enable Environment ⇨ Documents ⇨ Show Miscellaneous Files in Solution Explorer via the Options dialog, the file will be temporarily added to the solution. The miscellaneous files folder to which this file is added is shown in Figure 3-16.

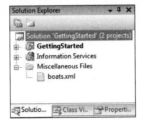

Figure 3-16

Visual Studio 2008 will automatically manage the list of miscellaneous files, keeping only the most recent ones, based on the number of files defined in the Options dialog. You can get Visual Studio to track up to 256 files in this list, and files will be evicted based on when they were last accessed.

Build and Run

The Projects and Solutions ➪ Build and Run node, shown in Figure 3-17, can be used to tailor the build behavior of Visual Studio 2008. The first option to notice is "Before building." With the default option of "Save all changes," Visual Studio will apply any changes made to the solution prior to compilation. In the event of a crash during the build process or while you're debugging the compiled code, you can be assured that your code is safe. You may want to change this option to "Prompt to save all changes" if you don't want changes to be saved prematurely, though this is not recommended. This setting will inform you of unsaved modifications made in your solution, enabling you to double-check those changes prior to compilation.

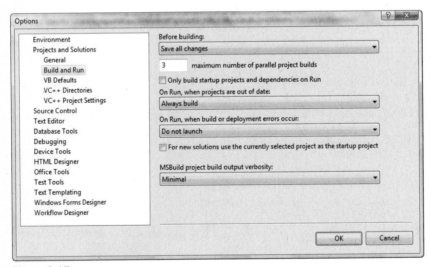

Figure 3-17

In order to reduce the amount of time it takes to build your solution, you may want to increase the maximum number of parallel builds that are performed. Visual Studio 2008 can build in parallel only those projects that are not dependent, but if you have a large number of independent projects this might yield a noticeable benefit. Be aware that on a single-core or single-processor machine this may actually increase the time taken to build your solution.

Figure 3-17 shows that projects will "Always build" when they are out of date, and that if there are build errors the solution will not launch. Both these options can increase your productivity, but be warned that they eliminate dialogs letting you know what's going on.

> *The last option worth noting in Figure 3-17 is "MSBuild project build output verbosity." In most cases the Visual Studio 2008 build output is sufficient for debugging build errors. However, in some cases, particularly when building ASP.NET projects, you will need to increase verbosity in order to diagnose the build error.*

VB.NET Options

VB.NET programmers have four compiler options that can be configured at a project or a file level. You can also set the defaults on the Projects and Solutions ⇨ VB Defaults node of the Options dialog. Previous versions of Visual Basic had an Option Explicit, which forced variables to be defined prior to their use in code. When it was introduced, many experts recommended that it be turned on permanently because it did away with many runtime problems in Visual Basic applications that were caused by improper use of variables.

Option Strict takes enforcing good programming practices one step further by forcing developers to explicitly convert variables to their correct types, rather than let the compiler try to guess the proper conversion method. Again, this results in fewer runtime issues and better performance.

> *We advise strongly that you use Option Strict to ensure that your code is not implicitly converting variables inadvertently. If you are not using Option Strict, with all the new language features, you may not be making the most effective use of the language.*

Importing and Exporting Settings

Once you have the IDE in exactly the configuration you want, you may want to back up the settings for future use. You can do this by exporting the IDE settings to a file that can then be used to restore the settings or even transfer them to a series of Visual Studio 2008 installations, so that they all share the same IDE setup.

> *The Environment ⇨ Import and Export Settings node in the Options dialog enables you to specify a team settings file. This can be located on a network share, and Visual Studio 2008 will automatically apply new settings if the file changes.*

To export the current configuration, select Tools ⇨ Import and Export Settings to start the Import and Export Settings Wizard, shown in Figure 3-18. The first step in the wizard is to select the Export option and which settings are to be backed up during the export procedure.

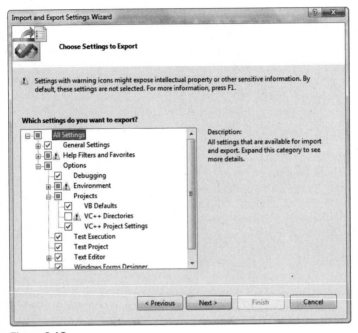

Figure 3-18

As shown in Figure 3-18, a variety of grouped options can be exported. The screenshot shows the Options section expanded, revealing that the Debugging and Projects settings will be backed up along with the Text Editor and Windows Forms Designer configurations. As the small exclamation icons indicate, some settings are not included in the export by default, because they contain information that may infringe on your privacy. You will need to select these sections manually if you wish them to be included in the backup. Once you have selected the settings you want to export, you can progress through the rest of the wizard, which might take a few minutes depending on the number of settings being exported.

Importing a settings file is just as easy. The same wizard is used, but you select the Import option on the first screen. Rather than simply overwriting the current configuration, the wizard enables you to back up the current setup first (see Figure 3-19).

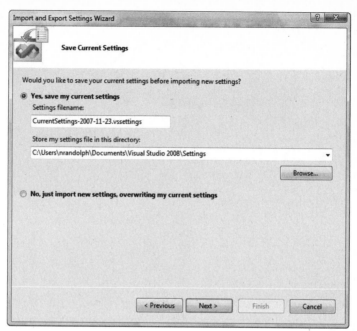

Figure 3-19

You can then select from a list of preset configuration files — the same set of files from which you can choose when you first start Visual Studio 2008 — or browse to a settings file that you created previously. Once the settings file has been chosen, you can then choose to import only certain sections of the configuration, or import the whole lot.

The wizard excludes some sections by default, such as External Tools or Command Aliases, so that you don't inadvertently overwrite customized settings. Make sure you select these sections if you want to do a full restore.

> *If you just want to restore the configuration of Visual Studio 2008 to one of the default presets, you can choose the Reset All Settings option in the opening screen of the wizard, rather than go through the import process.*

Summary

This chapter covered only a core selection of the useful options available to you as you start to shape the Visual Studio interface to suit your own programming style; many other options are available. These numerous options enable you to adjust the way you edit your code, add controls to your forms, and even select the methods to use when debugging code. The settings within the Visual Studio 2008 Options page also enable you to control how and where applications are created, and even to customize the keyboard shortcuts you use. Throughout the remainder of this book, you'll see the Options dialog revisited according to specific functionality such as macros, debugging, and compiling.

4

Workspace Control

So far you have seen how to get started with Visual Studio 2008 and how to customize the IDE to suit the way that you work. In this chapter, you will learn to take advantage of some of the built-in commands, shortcuts, and supporting tool windows that will help you to write code and design forms.

Command Window

As you become more familiar with Visual Studio 2008, you will spend less time looking for functionality and more time using keyboard shortcuts to navigate and perform actions within the IDE. One of the tool windows that's often overlooked is the Command Window, accessible via View ➪ Other Windows ➪ Command Window (Ctrl+Alt+A). From this window you can execute any existing Visual Studio command or macro, as well as any additional macros you may have recorded or written. Figure 4-1 illustrates the use of IntelliSense to show the list of commands that can be executed from the Command Window. This list will include all macros defined within the current solution.

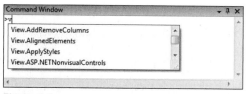

Figure 4-1

A full list of the Visual Studio commands is available via the Environment ➪ Keyboard node of the Options dialog (Tools ➪ Options). The commands all have a similar syntax based on the area of the IDE that they are derived from. For example, you can open the debugging output window (Debug ➪ Windows ➪ Output) by typing Debug.Output into the command window.

The commands fall into three rough groups. Many commands are shortcuts to either tool windows (which are made visible if they aren't already open) or dialogs. For example, `File.NewFile` will open the new file dialog. Other commands query information about the current solution or the debugger. Using `Debug.ListThreads` will list the current threads, in contrast to `Debug.Threads`, which will open the Threads tool window. The third type includes those commands that perform an action without displaying a dialog. This would include most macros and a number of commands that accept arguments (a full list of these, including the arguments they accept, is available within the MSDN documentation). There is some overlap between these groups: for example, the `Edit.Find` command can be executed with or without arguments. If this command is executed without arguments, the Find and Replace dialog will be displayed. Alternatively, the following command will find all instances of the string `MyVariable` in the current document (`/d`) and place a marker in the code window border against the relevant lines (`/m`):

```
>Edit.Find MyVariable /m /d
```

Although there is IntelliSense within the command window, you may find typing a frequently used command somewhat painful. Visual Studio 2008 has the ability to assign an alias to a particular command. For example, the `alias` command can be used to assign an alias, `e?`, to the find command used previously:

```
>alias e? Edit.Find MyVariable /m /d
```

With this alias defined you can easily perform this command from anywhere within the IDE: press Ctrl+Alt+A to give the Command Window focus, then type `e?` to perform the find-and-mark command.

A number of default aliases belong to the environment settings you will have imported when you began working with Visual Studio 2008. You can list these using the `alias` command with no arguments. Alternatively, if you wish to find out what command a specific alias references, you can execute the command with the name of the alias. For example, querying the previously defined alias, `e?`, would look like the following:

```
>alias e?
alias e? Edit.Find SumVals /m /doc
```

Two additional switches can be used with the `alias` command. The `/delete` switch, along with an alias name, will remove a previously defined alias. If you want to remove all aliases you may have defined and revert any changes to a predefined alias, you can use the `/reset` switch.

Immediate Window

Quite often when you are writing code or debugging your application, you will want to evaluate a simple expression either to test a bit of functionality or to remind yourself of how something works. This is where the Immediate window comes in handy. This window enables you to run expressions as you type them. Figure 4-2 shows a number of statements — from basic assignment and print operations to more advanced object creation and manipulation.

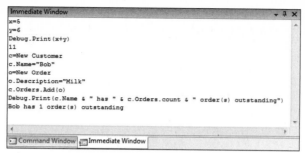

Figure 4-2

Although you can't do explicit variable declaration (for example, `Dim x as Integer`), it is done implicitly via the assignment operator. The example shown in Figure 4-2 shows a new customer being created, assigned to a variable `c`, and then used in a series of operations.

The Immediate window supports a limited form of IntelliSense, and you can use the arrow keys to track back through the history of previous commands executed. Variable values can be displayed by means of the `Debug.Print` statement. Alternatively, you can use the `?` alias.

In earlier versions of Visual Studio, your application had to be in Break mode (i.e., at a breakpoint or pausing execution) for the expressions to be evaluated. Although this is no longer a requirement, your solution cannot have any compile errors. When you execute a command in the Immediate window without being in Break mode, Visual Studio will build the solution and then execute the command. If the command execute code has an active breakpoint, the command will break there. This can be useful if you are working on a particular method that you want to test without running the entire application.

You can access the Immediate window via the keyboard chord Ctrl+Alt+I, but if you are working between the Command and Immediate windows you may want to use the predefined aliases `cmd` and `immed`, respectively.

> Note that in order to execute commands in the Immediate window you need to add > as a prefix (e.g., >cmd to go to the Command window); otherwise Visual Studio tries to evaluate the command.

> Also, you should be aware that the language used in the Immediate window is that of the active project. The examples shown in Figure 4-2 will work only if a Visual Basic project is currently active.

Class View

Although the Solution Explorer is probably the most useful tool window for navigating your solution, it can sometimes be difficult to locate particular classes and methods. The Class View tool window provides you with an alternative view of your solution that lists namespaces, classes, and methods so that you can easily navigate to them. Figure 4-3 shows a simple Windows application that contains a single form, Form1, which is selected in the class hierarchy. Note that there are two SampleWindowsApplication nodes. The first is the name of the project (not the assembly as you might expect), while the second is the namespace that Form1 belongs to. If you were to expand the References node, you would see a list of assemblies that this project references. Drilling further into each of these would yield a list of namespaces, followed by the classes contained in the assembly.

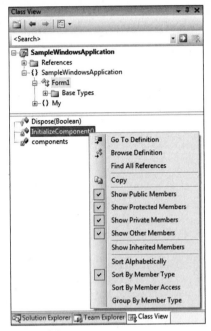

Figure 4-3

In the lower portion of Figure 4-3 you can see the list of members that are available for the class Form1. Using the right-click shortcut menu, you can either filter this list based on accessibility, sort and group the list, or use it to navigate to the selected member. For example, clicking Go To Definition on InitializeComponent() would take you to the Form1.Designer.vb file, which would normally be hidden in the Solution Explorer.

The Class View is useful for navigating to generated members, which are usually in a file hidden in the default Solution Explorer view. It can also be a useful way to navigate to classes that have been added to an existing file — this would result in multiple classes in the same file, which is not a recommended practice. As the file does not have a name that matches the class name, it becomes hard to navigate to that class using the Solution Explorer; hence the Class View is a good alternative.

Object Browser

Another way of viewing the classes that make up your application is via the Object Browser. Unlike most other tool windows, which appear docked to a side of Visual Studio 2008 by default, the Object Browser appears in the editor space. As you can see in Figure 4-4, at the top of the Object Browser window is a drop-down box that defines the object browsing scope. This includes a set of predefined values, such as All Components, .NET Framework 3.5, and My Solution, as well as a Custom Component Set. Here, My Solution is selected and a search string of `sample` has been entered. The contents of the main window are then all the namespaces, classes, and members that match this search string.

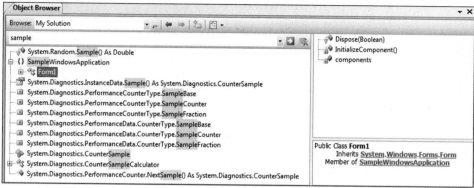

Figure 4-4

In the top right-hand portion of Figure 4-4 you can see the list of members for the selected class, Form1, and in the lower window the full class definition, which includes its base class and namespace information. One of the options in the Browse drop-down of Figure 4-4 is a Custom Component Set. To define what assemblies are included in this set you can either click the ellipsis next to the drop-down or select Edit Custom Component Set from the drop-down itself. This will present you with an edit dialog similar to the one shown in Figure 4-5.

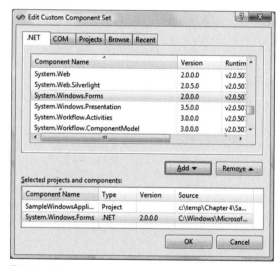

Figure 4-5

Selecting items in the top section and clicking "Add" will insert that assembly into the component set. Similarly, selecting an item in the lower section and clicking "Remove" will delete that assembly from the component set. Once you have finished customizing the component set, it will be saved between Visual Studio sessions.

Object Test Bench

Implementing classes can be quite a tedious process that usually involves several iterations of the design, write, and execute cycles. This is particularly true when the classes are part of a large system that can take considerable time to initiate in order to test the class being created. Visual Studio 2008 has what is known as the *object test bench*, which can be used to instantiate entities and invoke methods without your having to load the entire application. The object test bench is itself another tool window that appears empty by default and acts as a sandbox in which you can create and work with objects.

Invoking Static Methods

For this example we have a class, Order, which has a static method, CalculateItemTotal.

```
Public Class Order
    Public Shared Function CalculateItemTotal(ByVal itemCost As Double, _
                                              ByVal quantity As Integer _
                                              ) As Double
        Return itemCost * quantity
    End Function
End Class
```

Starting from either the Class View window or the class diagram, you can invoke static methods. Right-clicking the class will bring up the context menu from which you can select the appropriate method from the Invoke Static Method sub-menu.

> *If the Invoke Static Method menu item doesn't exist, it may be that the project you are working on is not set as the startup project. In order for the object test bench to work with your class, you need to set the project it belongs to as the startup project by right-clicking the project and selecting "Set as Startup Project."*

This will bring up the Invoke Method dialog shown in Figure 4-6, which prompts you to provide parameters for the method.

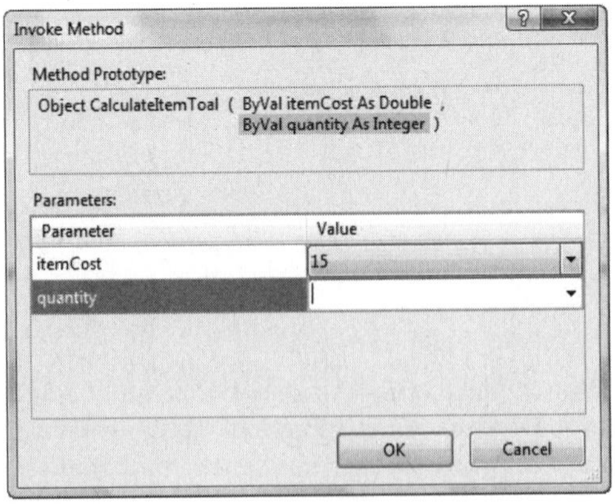

Figure 4-6

Specify values for each of the parameters and click "OK" to invoke the method. This causes Visual Studio to enter Debugging mode in order to execute the method. This means that any breakpoints in the code will be hit. If there is a return value, a Method Call Result dialog will appear, as shown in Figure 4-7.

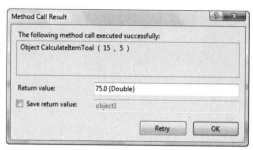

Figure 4-7

Checking the "Save return value" checkbox will enable you to retain this return value in the object test bench. You need to associate a title with the return value so that it is easily identifiable, as shown in Figure 4-8.

Figure 4-8

Once an object or value is residing in the object test bench, it can be consumed as arguments for future method invocations. Unfortunately, if Visual Studio has to rebuild your solution, the current state of the object test bench will be immediately discarded.

In some instances the "Save return value" checkbox in Figure 4-7 may be disabled, as Visual Studio 2008 has decided that it is unable to preserve the output from invoking your static method. You can usually resolve this problem by rebuilding your solution or saving an instance of an object to the test bench, covered in the next section.

Instantiating Objects

You can use a similar technique to create an instance of a class from either the Class View or the class diagram. Right-click the class and select Create Instance from the context menu. You will be prompted for a name for the instance, as shown in Figure 4-9. The name you give the instance has no relationship to any property that may be called Name in your class. All it does is provide a user-friendly name for referring to the instance when working with it.

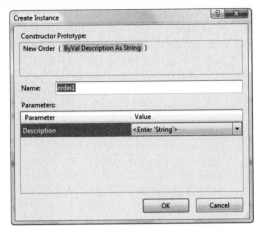

Figure 4-9

After you enter a description, for example `Milk`, clicking "OK" will create an instance of the `Order` class and place it in the object test bench. Figure 4-10 shows the newly created instance `order1` alongside a previously created `customer1` object. The friendly name that you gave the instance appears above the object type so that you can clearly distinguish it from any other objects of the same type that may have been created.

Figure 4-10

Accessing Fields and Properties

Within the object test bench you can access fields and properties using the same technique available to you during application debugging. You can hover the mouse over an object to access the properties of that object. When the mouse hovers over the object, a datatip appears that can be used to drill down to obtain the current values of both fields and properties, as shown in Figure 4-11. The datatip also enables you to modify the public properties of the object to adjust its state.

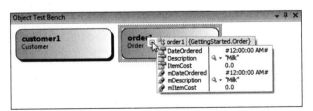

Figure 4-11

Invoking Instance Methods

The final step in working with items in the object test bench is to invoke instance, or nonstatic, methods. You can do this by right-clicking the object on the test bench and selecting Invoke Method. In Figure 4-12, the AddOrder method has been invoked on the customer1 object of the test bench. The parameter for this method needs to be an Order. In the Value column of the Parameters list you can select any object that appears on the object test bench. Because an Order is required, the order1 object seems a good candidate.

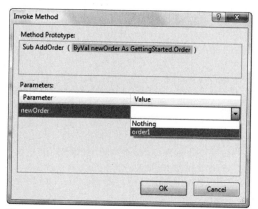

Figure 4-12

Invoking this method will return the number of orders that have been added to the customer, which you can then save to the object test bench for future use. Once you have populated the object test bench with instances of your classes, you can manipulate them using either the user interface previously described or the Immediate window. In fact, as you invoke methods or create instances of objects you will see the methods being invoked appear in the Immediate window. Unfortunately, the reverse is not applicable: if you create a new instance of an object in the Immediate window, it doesn't appear in the object test bench. The flow-on effect of this is that you can't automate the creation of an object, which can lead to a lot of frustration as you have to recreate your test scenario each time you compile a project.

Code View

As a developer you're likely to spend a considerable portion of your time writing code, which means that knowing how to tweak the layout of your code and being able to navigate it effectively are particularly important.

Forward/Backward

As you move within and between items, Visual Studio 2008 tracks where you have been, in much the same way that a web browser tracks the sites you have visited. Using the Navigate Forward and Navigate Backward items from the View menu, you can easily go back and forth between files that you are working on. The keyboard shortcut to navigate backward is Ctrl+–. To navigate forward again it is Ctrl+Shift+–.

Regions

Effective class design usually results in classes that serve a single purpose and are not overly complex or lengthy. However, there will be times when you have to implement so many interfaces that your code file will become unwieldy. In this case you have a number of options, such as partitioning the code into multiple files or using regions to condense the code, thereby making it easier to navigate.

The introduction of partial classes means that at design time you can place code into different physical files representing a single logical class. The advantage of using separate files is that you can effectively group all methods that are related, for example, methods that implement an interface. The problem with this strategy is that navigating the code then requires continual switching between code files.

An alternative is to use named code regions to condense sections of code that are not currently in use. In Figure 4-13 you can see that two regions are defined, My Region and IComparable. Clicking the minus sign next to #Region will condense the region into a single line and clicking the plus sign will expand it again.

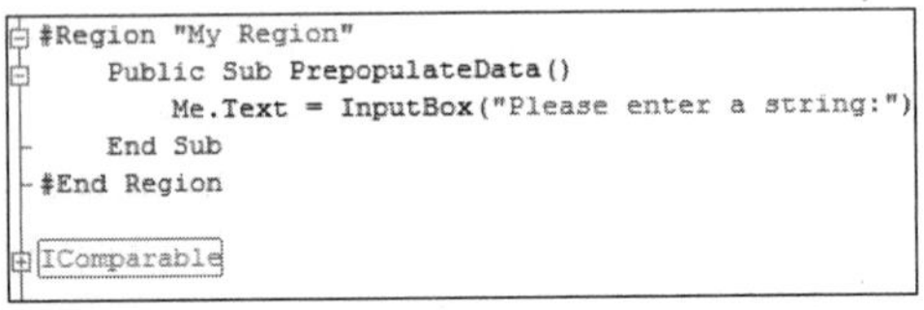

```
#Region "My Region"
    Public Sub PrepopulateData()
        Me.Text = InputBox("Please enter a string:")
    End Sub
#End Region

IComparable
```

Figure 4-13

The other way to expand and condense regions is via the keyboard shortcut Ctrl+M, Ctrl+M. This shortcut will toggle between the two layouts.

Outlining

In addition to regions that you have defined, Visual Studio 2008 has the ability to auto-outline your code, making it easy to collapse methods, comments, and class definitions. Figure 4-14 shows three condensable regions wrapping the class, constructor, and associated comments, respectively. Automatic outlines can be condensed and expanded in the same way as regions you define manually.

```
Public Class Order
     ''' <summary>
     ''' Creates a new ORder of items with the description provided
     ''' </summary>
     ''' <param name="Description">The item being ordered</param>
     ''' <remarks></remarks>
     Public Sub New(ByVal Description As String)
          Me.mDescription = Description
     End Sub
End Class
```

Figure 4-14

One trick for C# developers is that Ctrl+] enables you to easily navigate from the beginning of a region, or outline, to the end and back again.

Code Formatting

By default, Visual Studio 2008 will assist you in writing readable code by automatically indenting and aligning. However, it is also configurable so that you can control how your code is arranged. Common to all languages is the ability to control what happens when you create a new line. In Figure 4-15 you can see that there is a Tabs node under the Text Editor ⇨ All Languages node of the Options dialog. Setting values here defines the default value for all languages, which you can then overwrite for an individual language using the Basic ⇨ Tabs node (for VB.NET), C# ⇨ Tabs, or other language nodes.

By default, the indenting behavior for both C# and VB.NET is smart indenting, which will, among other things, automatically add indentation as you open and close enclosures. Smart indenting is not available for all languages, in which case block indenting will be used.

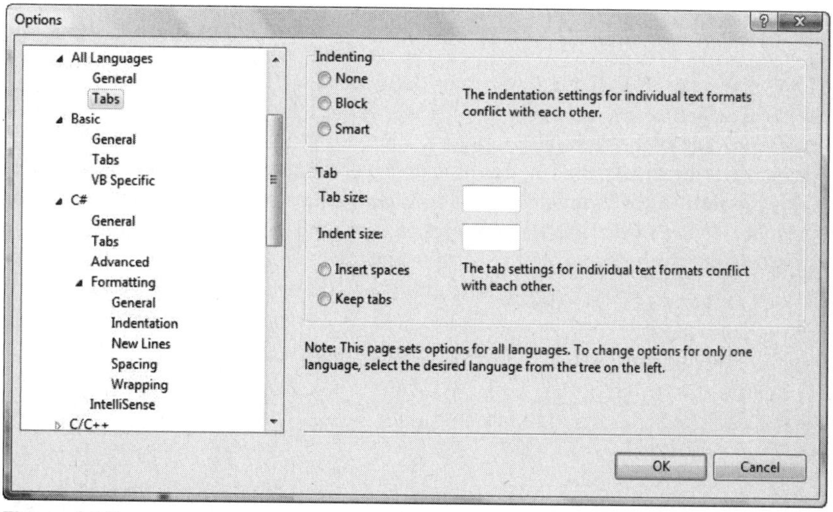

Figure 4-15

If you are working on a small screen, you might want to reduce the tab and indent sizes to optimize screen usage. Keeping the tab and indent sizes the same will ensure that you can easily indent your code with a single tab keypress.

What is interesting about this dialog is the degree of control C# users have over the layout of their code. Under the VB Specific node is a single checkbox entitled "Pretty listing (reformatting) of code", which if enabled will keep your code looking uniform without your having to worry about aligning methods, closures, class definitions, or namespaces. C# users, on the other hand, can control nearly every aspect of how the code editor reformats code, as you can see from the additional nodes for C# in Figure 4-15.

Document Outline Tool Window

Editing HTML files, using either the visual designer or code view, is never as easy as it could be, particularly when you have a large number of nested elements. When Visual Studio .NET first arrived on the scene, a feature known as *document outlining* came to at least partially save the day. In fact, this feature was so successful for working with HTML files that it was repurposed for working with non-web forms and controls. This section introduces you to the Document Outline window and demonstrates how effective it can be at manipulating HTML documents, and forms and controls.

HTML Outlining

The primary purpose of the Document Outline window was to present a navigable view of HTML pages so that you could easily locate the different HTML elements and the containers they were in. Because it was difficult to get HTML layouts correct, especially with the many .NET components that could be included on an ASP.NET page, the Document Outline view provided a handy way to find the correct position for a specific component.

Figure 4-16 shows a typical HTML page with standard tags used in most web pages. DIV, TABLE, and other tags are used to define layout, while a FORM tag, along with its subordinate components for a login form, are also displayed. Without the Document Outline window, the only way to determine the hierarchical position of a particular component is to select it and examine the bottom of the workspace area. Beside the "Design" and "Source" buttons is an area populated with the current hierarchy for the selected component. In the example shown in Figure 4-16, you can see that the selected item is a FORM tag. In the current case, this helps locate the component, as that class value is unique; but a more logical property would be the ID or Name property so that you could be sure you had the correct HTML element.

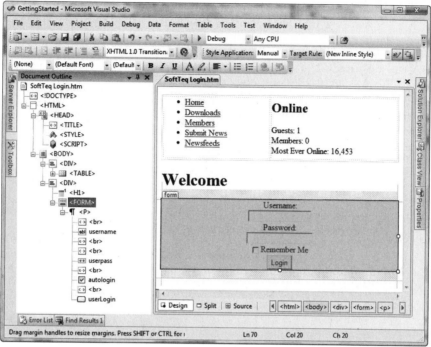

Figure 4-16

The Document Outline pane (View ⇨ Other Windows ⇨ Document Outline), on the left of Figure 4-16, presents that same information about the HTML page but does so exhaustively and with a much more intuitive interface. Visual Studio analyzes the content of the currently active file and populates it with a tree view containing every element and its containers. In this case the Name or ID value of each element is used to identify the component, while unnamed components are simply listed with their HTML tags. The password field selected in Figure 4-16 can be seen in the tree with its name, userpass, and an icon indicating that not only is it a form text entry field, but also that it is a password field — a lot more information!

As you select each entry in the Document Outline window, the Design view is updated to select the component and its children. In Figure 4-16, the FORM tag containing the login form's contents is selected, and it and all its contained HTML tags are highlighted in the Design view, giving you instant feedback as to what is included in that FORM area.

Control Outline

The Document Outline window has been available in Visual Studio since the first .NET version for HTML files but has been of little use for other file views. When Visual Studio 2003 was released, an add-in called the *Control view* was developed that allowed a similar kind of access to Windows forms.

The tool was so popular that Microsoft incorporated its functionality into the Document Outline tool window, so now you can browse Windows forms in the same way.

Figure 4-17 shows a typical complex form, with many panels to provide structure and controls to provide the visual elements. Each component is represented in the Document Outline by its name and component type. As each item is selected in the Document Outline window, the corresponding visual element is selected and displayed in the Design view.

This means that when the item is in a menu (as is the case in Figure 4-17) Visual Studio will automatically open the menu and select the menu item ready for editing. As you can imagine, this is an incredibly useful way of navigating your form layouts, and it can often provide a shortcut for locating wayward items.

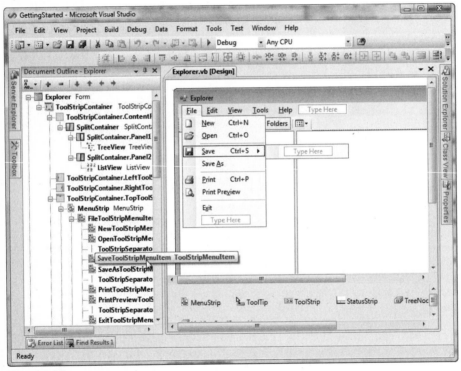

Figure 4-17

The Document Outline window has more functionality when used in Control Outline mode than just a simple navigation tool. Right-clicking an entry gives you a small context menu of actions that can be performed against the selected item. The most obvious is to access the Properties window.

One tedious chore is renaming components after you've added them to the form. You can select each one in turn and set its Name property in the Properties window, but using the Document Outline window you can simply choose the Rename option in the context menu and Visual Studio will automatically rename the component in the design code, thus updating the Name property for you without your needing to scroll through the Properties list.

Complex form design can sometimes produce unexpected results. This often happens when a component is placed in an incorrect or inappropriate container control. In such a case you'll need to move the component to the correct container. Of course, you have to locate the issue before you even know that there is a problem.

The Document Outline window can help with both of these activities. First, using the hierarchical view, you can easily locate each component and check its parent container elements. The example shown in Figure 4-17 indicates that the TreeView control is in Panel1, which in turn is in SplitContainer, which is itself contained in a ContentPanel object. In this way you can easily determine when a control is incorrectly placed on the form's design layout.

When you need to move a component it can be quite tricky to get the layout right. In the Document Outline window it's easy. Simply drag and drop the control to the correct position in the hierarchy. For example, dragging the TreeView control to Panel2 results in its sharing the Panel2 area with the ListView control.

You also have the option to cut, copy, and paste individual elements or whole sets of containers and their contents by using the right-click context menu. The copy-and-paste function is particularly useful, as you can duplicate whole chunks of your form design in other locations on the form without having to use trial and error to select the correct elements in the Design view, or resort to duplicating them in the code-behind in the Designer.vb file.

When you cut an item, remember to paste it immediately into the destination location.

Summary

In this chapter you have seen that there are a number of tool windows that can help you not only write code but also prototype and try it out. Making effective use of these windows will dramatically reduce the number of times you have to run your application in order to test the code you are writing. This, in turn, will improve your overall productivity and eliminate idle time spent waiting for your application to run.

5

Find and Replace, and Help

In the current wave of development technology, find-and-replace functionality is expected as a fundamental part of the tool set, and Visual Studio 2008 delivers on that expectation. However, unlike other development environments that enable you to perform only simple searches against the active code module, Visual Studio includes the capability to perform rapid find-and-replace actions on the active code module or project, or right across the solution. It then goes an extra step by giving you the capability to search external files and even whole folder hierarchies for different kinds of search terms and to perform replacement actions on the results automatically. In the first part of this chapter you will see how to invoke and control this powerful tool.

Visual Studio 2008 is an immensely complex development environment that encompasses multiple languages based on an extensive framework of libraries and components. You will find it almost impossible to know everything about the IDE, let alone each of the languages or even the full extent of the .NET Framework. As both the .NET Framework and Visual Studio evolve it becomes increasingly difficult to stay abreast of all the changes; moreover it is likely that you need to know only a subset of this knowledge. Of course you'll periodically need to obtain more information on a specific topic. To help you in these situations, Visual Studio 2008 comes with comprehensive documentation in the form of the MSDN Library, Visual Studio 2008 Edition. The second part of this chapter walks through the methods of researching documentation associated with developing projects in Visual Studio 2008.

Introducing Find and Replace

The find-and-replace functionality in Visual Studio 2008 is split into two broad tiers with a shared dialog and similar features: *Quick Find*, and the associated *Quick Replace*, are for searches that you need to perform quickly on the document or project currently open in the IDE. The two tools have limited options to filter and extend the search, but as you'll see in a moment, even those options provide a powerful search engine that goes beyond what you'll find in most applications.

The second, extended tier consists of the *Find in Files* and *Replace in Files* commands. These functions enable you to broaden the search beyond the current solution to whole folders and folder structures, and even to perform mass replacements on any matches for the given criteria and filters. Additional options are available to you when using these commands, and search results can be placed in one of two tool windows so you can easily navigate them.

In addition to these two groups of find-and-replace tools, Visual Studio also offers two other ways to navigate code:

- ❑ **Find Symbols:** You can use Find Symbols to locate the symbols of various objects and members within your code, rather than strings of text.

- ❑ **Bookmarks:** You can bookmark any location throughout your code and then easily go back to it, either with the Bookmarks window or by using the Bookmark menu and Toolbar commands.

Quick Find

Quick Find is the term that Visual Studio 2008 uses to refer to the most basic search functionality. By default it enables you to search for a simple word or phrase within the current document, but even Quick Find has additional options that can extend the search beyond the active module, or even incorporate wildcards and regular expressions in the search criteria.

To start a Find action, press the standard keyboard shortcut Ctrl+F or select Edit ⇨ Find and Replace ⇨ Quick Find. Visual Studio will display the basic Find and Replace dialog, with the default Quick Find action selected (see Figure 5-1).

Figure 5-1

Type the search criteria into the Find What textbox, or select from previous searches by clicking the drop-down arrow and scrolling through the list of criteria that have been used. By default the scope of the search is restricted to the current document or window you're editing, unless you have a number of lines selected, in which case the default scope is the selection. The "Look in" drop-down list gives you additional options based on the context of the search itself, including Selection, Current Block, Current Document, Current Window, Current Project, and All Open Documents.

Find-and-replace actions will always wrap around the selected scope looking for the search terms, stopping only when the find process has reached the starting point again. As Visual Studio finds each result, it will highlight the match and scroll the code window so you can view it. If the match is already visible in the code window, Visual Studio will not scroll the code. Instead, it will just highlight the new match. However, if it does need to scroll the window, it will attempt to position the listing so the match is in the middle of the code editor window.

If the next match happens to be in a document other than the active one, Visual Studio will open that document in a new tab in the workspace.

In the Standard Toolbar there is a Quick Find drop-down area, as shown in Figure 5-2. This drop-down actually has multiple purposes. The keyboard shortcut Ctrl+D will place focus on the drop-down. You can then enter a search phrase and press Enter to find the next match in the currently open file. If you prefix what you type with >, Visual Studio 2008 will attempt to execute the command as if it had been entered into the Command window (see Chapter 4 for more information).

Figure 5-2

Pressing Ctrl+/ will not only put focus into the Quick Find drop-down but will also add the > prefix.

Performing a Quick Replace is similar to performing a Quick Find. You can switch between Quick Find and Quick Replace by clicking their respective buttons at the top of the dialog window. If you want to go directly to Quick Replace, you can do so with the keyboard shortcut Ctrl+H or the menu command Edit ⇨ Find and Replace ⇨ Quick Replace. The Quick Replace options (see Figure 5-3) are the same as those for Quick Find, but with an additional field where you can specify what text should be used in the replacement.

Figure 5-3

The "Replace with" field works in the same way as "Find what" — you can either type a new replacement string or, with the drop-down list provided, choose any you've previously entered.

A simple way to delete recurring values is to use the replace functionality with nothing specified in the "Replace with" text area. This will enable you to find all occurrences of the search text and decide if it should be deleted.

Quick Find and Replace Dialog Options

Sometimes you will want to filter the search results in different ways, and that's where the find options come into play. First, to display the options section (available in all find-and-replace actions), click the expand icon next to Find options. The dialog will expand to show a set of checkbox options and drop-down lists from which you can choose, as shown in Figure 5-4.

Figure 5-4

These options enable you to refine the search to be case-sensitive ("Match case") or an exact match ("Match whole word"). You can also change the direction of the search ("Search up"), search within collapsed regions ("Search hidden text"), and use more advanced search symbols such as wildcards or regular expressions.

Wildcards

Wildcards are simple text symbols that represent one or more characters, and are familiar to many users of Windows applications. Figure 5-5 illustrates the Expression Builder when the wildcard option is specified under the "Use" drop-down. While additional characters can be used in a wildcard search, the most common characters are ? for a single character, and * for multiple characters that are unknown or variable in the search.

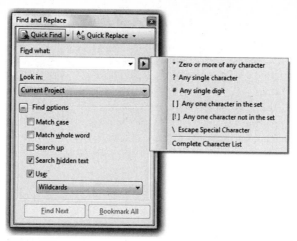

Figure 5-5

Regular Expressions

Regular expressions take searching to a whole new level, with the capability to do complex text matching based on the full RegEx engine built into Visual Studio 2008. Although this book doesn't go into great detail on the advanced matching capabilities of regular expressions, it's worth mentioning the additional help provided by the Find and Replace dialog if you choose to use them in your search terms.

Figure 5-6 again shows the Expression Builder, this time for building a regular expression as specified in the "Use" drop-down. From here you can easily build your regular expressions with a menu showing the most commonly used regular expression phrases and symbols, along with English descriptions of each.

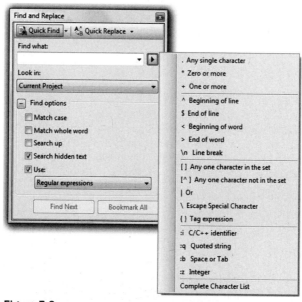

Figure 5-6

Find in Files

The really powerful part of the search engine built into Visual Studio is found in the Find in Files command. Rather than restrict yourself to a single document or project, Find in Files gives you the ability to search entire folders (along with all their sub-folders), looking for files that contain the search criteria.

The Find in Files dialog, shown in Figure 5-7, can be invoked via the menu command Edit ➪ Find and Replace ➪ Find in Files. Alternatively, if you have the Quick Find dialog open, you can switch over to Find in Files mode by clicking the small drop-down arrow next to Quick Find and choosing Find in Files. You can also use the keyboard shortcut Ctrl+Shift+F to launch this dialog.

Figure 5-7

Most of the Quick Find options are still available to you, including wildcard and regular expressions searching, but instead of choosing a scope from the project or solution, you use the "Look in" field to specify where the search is to be performed. Either type the location you wish to search or click the ellipsis to display the Choose Search Folders dialog, shown in Figure 5-8.

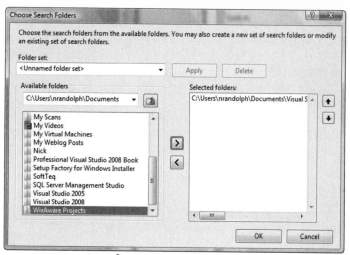

Figure 5-8

You can navigate through the entire file system, including networked drives, and add the folders you want to the search scope. This enables you to add disparate folder hierarchies to the one single search. Start by using the "Available folders" list on the left to select the folder(s) that you would like to search. Add them to the "Selected folders" list by clicking the right arrow. Within this list you can adjust the search order using the up and down arrows. Once you have added folders to the search, you can simply click "OK" to return a semicolon-delimited list of folders. If you want to save this set of folders for future use you can enter a name into the "Folder set" drop-down and click "Apply."

The process of saving search folders is less than intuitive, but if you think of the "Apply" button as more of a Save button then you can make sense of this dialog.

Find Dialog Options

Because the search is being performed on files that are not normally open within the IDE, the two Find options normally used for open files — namely, "Search up" and "Search hidden text" — are not present. However, in their place is a filter that can be used to search only on specific file types.

The Look at These File Types drop-down list contains several extension sets, each associated with a particular language, making it easy to search for code in Visual Basic, C#, J#, and other languages. You can type in your own extensions too, so if you're working in a non-Microsoft language, or just want to use the Find in Files feature for non-development purposes, you can still limit the search results to those that correspond to the file types you want.

In addition to the Find options, there are also configuration settings for how the results will be displayed. For searching you can choose one of two results windows, which enables you to perform a subsequent search without losing your initial action. The results can be quite lengthy if you show the full output of the search, but if you're interested only in finding out which files contain the information you're looking for, check the Display Filenames Only option and the results window will be populated with only one line per file.

Results Window

When you perform a Find in Files action, results are displayed in one of two Find Results windows. These appear as open tool windows docked to the bottom of the IDE workspace. For each line that contained the search criteria, the results window displays a full line of information, containing the filename and path, the line number that contained the match, and the actual line of text itself, so you can instantly see the context (see Figure 5-9).

```
Find Results 1                                                                      ▼ ▫ X
🖩 | 📇📑 | ⯗ | 🔍
\GettingStarted\Form1.vb(2):      Private Sub btnSayHello_Click(ByVal sender As System.Object, _
\GettingStarted\Form1.vb(3):                    ByVal e As System.EventArgs) Handles btnSayHello.Click
\GettingStarted\Form1.Designer.vb(1):<Global.Microsoft.VisualBasic.CompilerServices.DesignerGenerated()> _
\GettingStarted\Form1.Designer.vb(3):      Inherits System.Windows.Forms.Form
\GettingStarted\Form1.Designer.vb(5):      'Form overrides dispose to clean up the component list.
\GettingStarted\Form1.Designer.vb(6):      <System.Diagnostics.DebuggerNonUserCode()> _
\GettingStarted\Form1.Designer.vb(10):               components.Dispose()
\GettingStarted\Form1.Designer.vb(12):          MyBase.Dispose(disposing)
```

Figure 5-9

Along the top of each results window is a small Toolbar, as shown in Figure 5-10 (left), for navigation within the results themselves. These commands are also accessible through a context menu, as shown in Figure 5-10 (right).

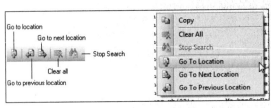

Figure 5-10

Right-click the particular match you want to look at and choose the Go To Location command. Alternatively, double-click a specific match.

Replace in Files

Although it's useful to search a large number of files and find a number of matches to your search criteria, even better is the Replace in Files action. Accessed via the keyboard shortcut Ctrl+Shift+H or the drop-down arrow next to Quick Replace, Replace in Files performs in much the same way as Find in Files, with all the same options.

The main difference is that you can enable an additional Results option when you're replacing files. When you're performing a mass replacement action like this, it can be handy to have a final confirmation before committing changes. To have this sanity check available to you, enable the "Keep modified files open after Replace All" checkbox (shown at the bottom of Figure 5-11).

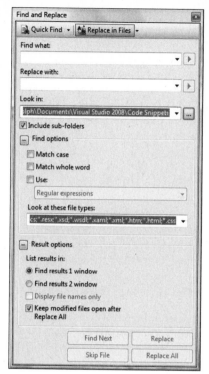

Figure 5-11

Note that this feature works only when you're using "Replace All"; if you just click "Replace," Visual Studio will open the file containing the next match and leave the file open in the IDE anyway.

> *Important: If you leave this option unchecked and perform a mass replacement on a large number of files, they* will *be changed permanently without your having any recourse to an undo action. Be* very *sure that you know what you're doing.*

Whether you have this option checked or not, after performing a "Replace All" action, Visual Studio will report back to you how many changes were made. If you don't want to see this dialog box, you have an option to hide the dialog with future searches.

Incremental Search

If you're looking for something in the current code window and don't want to bring up a dialog, the Incremental Search function might be what you need. Invoked by either the Edit ⇨ Advanced ⇨ Incremental Search menu command or the keyboard shortcut Ctrl+I, Incremental Search locates the next match based on what you type.

Immediately after invoking Incremental Search, simply begin typing the text you need to find. The mouse pointer will change to a set of binoculars and a down arrow. As you type each character, the editor will move to the next match. For example, typing *f* would find the first word containing an *f* — such as *offer*. Typing an *o* would then move the cursor to the first word containing *fo* — such as *form*; and so on.

Using this feature is an incredibly efficient way of navigating through long code blocks when you want to quickly locate the next place you need to work.

Find Symbol

In addition to these already comprehensive find-and-replace tools, there is an additional search feature in Visual Studio 2008. You can now search for symbols that are objects, classes, and procedural names. The Find Symbol dialog is invoked by the keyboard shortcut Alt+F12 or the menu command Edit ⇨ Find and Replace ⇨ Find Symbol. Alternatively, you can switch the normal Find and Replace dialog over to Find Symbol by clicking the drop-down arrow next to Quick Find or Find in Files.

The Find Symbol dialog (see Figure 5-12) has slightly different options from the dialogs for the other Find actions. Rather than having its scope based on a current document or solution like Quick Find, or on the file system like Find in Files, Find Symbol can search through your whole solution, a full component list, or even the entire .NET Framework. In addition, you can include any references added to the solution as part of the scope. To create your own set of components in which to search, click the ellipsis next to the "Look in" field and browse through and select the .NET and COM components registered in the system, or browse to files or projects.

The Find options are also simplified. You can search only for whole words, substrings (the default option), or prefixes.

After you click "Find All," the search results are compiled and presented in a special tool window entitled Find Symbol Results. By default this window shares space with the Find Results windows at the bottom of the IDE, and displays each result with any references to the particular object or component. This is extremely handy when you're trying to determine where and how a particular object is used or referenced from within your project.

Figure 5-12

Find and Replace Options

Believe it or not, you can further customize the find-and-replace functionality with its own set of options in the main Options dialog. Found in the Environment group, the Find and Replace options enable you to reset informational and warning message settings as well as to indicate whether the "Find what" field should be automatically filled with the current selection in the editor window. There is also an option to hide the Find dialog after performing a Quick Find or Quick Replace, which can be handy if you typically look only for the first match.

Once you have performed the first Quick Find search you no longer need the dialog to be visible. You can simply press F3 to repeat the same search.

Accessing Help

The easiest way to get help for Visual Studio 2008 is to use the same method you would use for almost every Windows application ever created — press the F1 key, the universal shortcut key for help. If you do so, the first thing you'll notice is that help is contextual. For instance, if the cursor is currently positioned on or inside a class definition in a Visual Basic project, the help window will open immediately with a mini-tutorial about what the Class statement is and how it works, as shown in Figure 5-13.

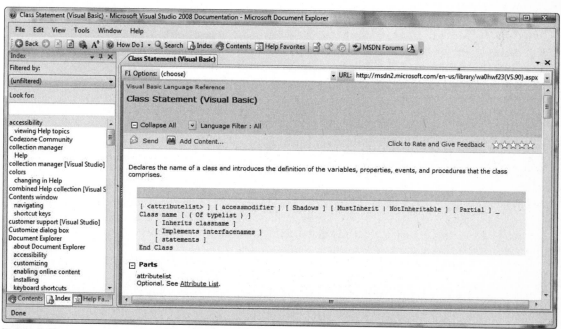

Figure 5-13

This is incredibly useful because more often than not, simply by choosing the right-click context menu and pressing F1, you can go directly to a help topic that deals with the problem you're currently researching.

However, in some situations you will want to go directly to the table of contents, or the search page within the help system. Visual Studio 2008 enables you to do this through its main Help menu (see Figure 5-14).

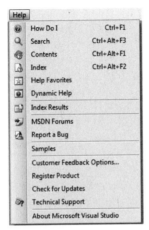

Figure 5-14

In addition to the several help links there are also shortcuts to MSDN forums and for reporting a bug.

Document Explorer

The help commands shown in Figure 5-14, with the exception of Dynamic Help, will open the main help documentation for Visual Studio 2008. Microsoft has introduced a completely new help system, using an interface known as the *Document Explorer*. Based on a combination of HTML Help, modern web browsers, and the Visual Studio 2008 IDE, the Document Explorer is a feature-rich application in its own right.

Despite the revolutionary changes made to the documentation system, the Document Explorer still presents a familiar interface. It's constructed according to regular Windows application standards: customizable menus, a Toolbar at the top of the interface, a tabbed tool window docked by default to the left side of the main window, and a primary workspace that displays the documents you're working in, as well as the Search pane.

The phrase "tool window" was not used by accident in the previous paragraph. The pane on the left side of Figure 5-15 works in exactly the same way as the tool windows of Visual Studio 2008 itself. In fact, it's actually three tool windows: Contents, Index, and Help Favorites. Each window can be repositioned independently — to float over the main interface or be docked to any side of the Document Explorer user interface. The tool windows can be made to share the same space, as they do by default, or be docked above, below, or alongside each other, as the example in Figure 5-15 illustrates.

Figure 5-15

You can use the Help system much as you would previous versions of Help. Using the Contents tool window, you can browse through the hierarchy of topics until you locate the information you're seeking. Alternatively, the Index window gives you direct access to the full index generated by the currently compiled local documentation. Finally, just as in previous versions, a particular topic contains multiple hyperlinks to other related parts of the documentation.

In addition to these traditional means of navigation, the Document Explorer also has a bar at the top of most topics that provides other commands. Figure 5-13 illustrates this with the Class statement topic: directly underneath the heading are two direct hotlinks to sections of the current topic, and two functions that collapse the information or filter it based on a particular language, respectively.

Figure 5-16 shows the latter feature, Language Filter, in action. When the mouse pointer is placed over the Language Filter label, a drop-down list of the main Microsoft languages appears. If you know that the information you want to view is not related to specific languages, you can switch them off by unchecking their respective boxes.

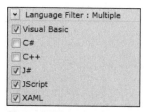

Figure 5-16

Dynamic Help

The only help-related command in the Help menu that does not display the Document Explorer interface is Dynamic Help. Using this command will display the Dynamic Help tool window, shown in Figure 5-17. By default, this window shares space with the Properties tool window, but it can be repositioned just like any other part of the Visual Studio IDE.

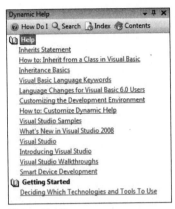

Figure 5-17

The Dynamic Help window contents are constantly updated based on the context in which you are working. This feature works regardless of what mode you're working under, so contextually it updates when you're working in Design or Class Diagram modes, changing as you select or add controls or classes.

Using the Dynamic Help tool window has always been very CPU-intensive. With Visual Studio 2008 the performance of this window has noticeably improved, but it can still adversely affect machines that only barely meet the system requirements for Visual Studio 2008.

The Search Window

While these small features of the Help system are appreciated, the real advance made in the Help engine is the Search window. Figure 5-18 shows the Search window in its default state, with the local help documentation selected and abstracts for each topic result displayed. Enter the search terms in the top text field and click "Search." If you wish you can filter the results before or after you perform the search, or change the way the results will be sorted.

The search engine starts searching all four main categories of documentation: the local Help, MSDN Online, the community of developer web sites approved through Codezone, and the Question database. As it receives information from each group, the corresponding tab is populated with the number of results and the headings of the first three topics. In addition, the main area of the Search window is populated with the topics that met the criteria, with a heading and brief abstract showing you the first chunk of documentation that will be found in each topic.

As well as these two items, depending on the category you're viewing you may find a footer line containing extra information. Figure 5-18 shows the footer information for local documentation searches — language information and documentation source — but MSDN Online and Codezone Community categories will display a rating value, while the Questions results will feature author and date information as well as the rating and source values.

To view a topic that met the search terms, locate it in the results list and click the heading, which is a hyperlink (or double-click anywhere in the abstract area). This will open a new tab if the Search tab is the only one open, or reuse the most recently accessed tab if other documents are already being viewed. To force the Document Explorer to open the topic in a new tab, right-click it and select Open in New Window.

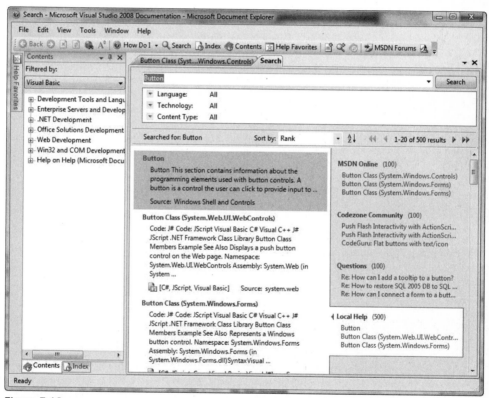

Figure 5-18

Some of the online search categories will have star ratings. This can be useful when you're trying to find an authority on a particular subject.

Keeping Favorites

There will be times when you find topics that you want to keep for later review. The Document Explorer includes a Help Favorites tool window (shown in Figure 5-19) that enables you to do just that.

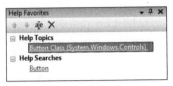

Figure 5-19

To add topics to the Help Favorites window, right-click the result in the search results window and select the Add to Help Favorites command from the context menu. This menu is also available when you're viewing the actual topic, or you can access the command from the Toolbar. You can also save common searches, as evidenced by the appropriately named Help Searches list. To add a search, click the Save Search button on the Toolbar.

From the Help Favorites list, you can rename both topics and searches by right-clicking an entry and choosing Rename or clicking the Rename command on the Help Favorites Toolbar. This can be useful for excessively long headings or some of those esoterically named topics sometimes found in MSDN documentation.

Customizing Help

Just as with earlier versions of Visual Studio, you can customize the way the Help system works through a number of options. Rather than go through each one here, this section provides a summary of the options you may want to take a closer look at.

By default the Help system will look online for results and the contents of topics you're trying to look up. Only if it cannot find the results in the online system (or cannot contact the online documentation) will the Document Explorer try the local, offline version. The advantage of this is that you'll always have the most up-to-date information — a godsend for programmers who work with modern tools and find themselves frustrated with outdated documentation. However, if you have a slow or intermittent Internet connection, you may want to change this option to use the local version of the documentation first, or even not to search the online documentation at all. Both of these options are available from the Online group in the Options window (see Figure 5-20). You can also filter the Codezone Community groups down to only the sites you prefer.

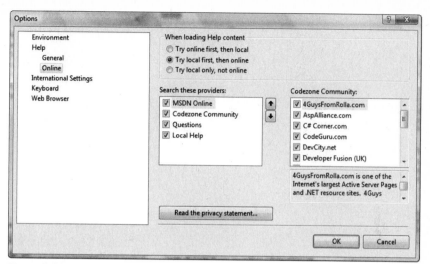

Figure 5-20

The other main options group you may want to take a look at is the Keyboard group. This should be immediately familiar to you because it is a direct clone of the Keyboard group of options in Visual Studio 2008. It enables you to set keyboard shortcuts for any command that can be performed in the Document Explorer, which can be useful for actions you want to perform often that may be difficult to access.

Summary

As you've seen in this chapter, Visual Studio 2008 comes with an excellent set of search-and-replacement functionalities that makes your job a lot easier, even if you need to search entire computer file systems for regular expressions. The additional features, such as Find Symbol and Incremental Search, also add to your tool set, simplifying the location of code and objects as well.

The Help Document Explorer is a powerful interface to the documentation that comes with Visual Studio 2008. While it has some new features, the general presentation should be immediately familiar, so you can very easily get accustomed to researching your topics of interest. The ability to switch easily between online and local documentation ensures that you can balance the speed of offline searches with the relevance of information found on the Web. And the abstract paragraphs that are shown in all search results, regardless of their locations, help reduce the number of times you might click a false positive.

Part II
Getting Started

6

Solutions, Projects, and Items

Other than the simplest, such as Hello World, most applications require more than one source file. This raises a number of questions, such as how the files will be named, where they will be located, and whether they can be reused. Within Visual Studio 2008, the concept of a *solution*, containing a series of *projects*, made up of a series of *items*, is used to enable developers to track, manage, and work with their source files. The IDE has a number of built-in features meant to simplify this process, while still enabling developers to get the most out of their applications. This chapter examines the structure of solutions and projects, looking at available project types and how they can be configured.

Solution Structure

Whenever you're working within Visual Studio, you will have a solution open. When you're editing an ad hoc file, this will be a temporary solution that you can elect to discard when you have completed your work. However, the solution enables you to manage the files that you're currently working with, so in most cases saving the solution means that you can return to what you were doing at a later date without having to locate and reopen the files on which you were working.

> Solutions should be thought of as containers of related projects. The projects within a solution do not need to be of the same language or project type. For example, a single solution could contain an ASP.NET web application written in Visual Basic, a C# control library, and an IronRuby WPF application. The solution enables you to open all these projects together in the IDE and manage the build and deployment configuration for them as a whole.

The most common way to structure applications written within Visual Studio is to have a single solution containing a number of projects. Each project can then be made up of a series of both code files and folders. The main window in which you work with solutions and projects is the Solution Explorer, shown in Figure 6-1.

Figure 6-1

Within a project, folders are used to organize the source code, and have no application meaning associated with them (with the exception of web applications, which have folders whose names have specific meanings in this context). Some developers use folder names that correspond to the namespace to which a class belongs. For example, if class Person is found within a folder called DataClasses in a project called FirstProject, the fully qualified name of the class could be FirstProject.DataClasses.Person.

Solution folders are a useful means of organizing the projects in a large solution. They are visible only in the Solution Explorer — a physical folder is not created on the file system. Actions such as building or unloading can be performed easily on all projects in a solution folder. They can also be collapsed or hidden so that you can work more easily in the Solution Explorer. Hidden projects are still built when you build the solution. Because solution folders do not map to a physical folder, you can add, rename, or delete them at any time without causing invalid file references or source control issues.

> *Miscellaneous Files is a special solution folder that can be used to keep track of other files that have been opened in Visual Studio but are not part of any projects in the solution. The Miscellaneous Files solution folder is not visible by default. The settings to enable it can be found under Tools ⇨ Options ⇨ Environment ⇨ Documents.*

There is a common misconception that projects necessarily correspond to .NET assemblies. While this is mostly true, it is possible for multiple DLL files to represent a single .NET assembly. However, such an arrangement is not supported by Visual Studio 2008, so this book assumes that a project will correspond to an assembly.

In Visual Studio 2008, although the format for the solution file has not changed significantly, solution files are not backward-compatible with Visual Studio 2005. However, project files are fully forward- and backward-compatible between Visual Studio 2005 and Visual Studio 2008.

In addition to tracking which files are contained within an application, solution and project files can record other information, such as how a particular file should be compiled, its project settings and resources, and much more. Visual Studio 2008 includes a non-modal dialog for editing project properties, while solution properties still open in a separate window. As you might expect, the project properties are those pertaining only to the project in question, such as assembly information and references, whereas solution properties determine the overall build configurations for the application.

Solution File Format

Visual Studio 2008 actually creates two files for a solution, with extensions .suo and .sln (solution file). The first of these is a rather uninteresting binary file, and hence difficult to edit. It contains user-specific information — for example, which files were open when the solution was last closed, and the location of breakpoints. This file is marked as hidden, so it won't appear in the solution folder if you are using Windows Explorer unless you have enabled the option to show hidden files.

Occasionally the .suo file will become corrupted and cause unexpected behavior when you are building and editing applications. If Visual Studio becomes unstable for a particular solution, you should delete the .suo file. It will be recreated by Visual Studio the next time the solution is opened.

The .sln solution file contains information about the solution, such as the list of projects, the build configurations, and other settings that are not project-specific. Unlike many files used by Visual Studio 2008, the solution file is not an XML document. Instead, it stores information in blocks, as shown in the following example solution file:

```
Microsoft Visual Studio Solution File, Format Version 10.00
# Visual Studio 2008
Project("{F184B08F-C81C-45F6-A57F-5ABD9991F28F}") = "FirstProject",
    "FirstProject\FirstProject.vbproj", "{D4FAF2DD-A26C-444A-9FEE-2788B5F5FDD2}"
EndProject
Global
    GlobalSection(SolutionConfigurationPlatforms) = preSolution
        Debug|Any CPU = Debug|Any CPU
    EndGlobalSection
    GlobalSection(ProjectConfigurationPlatforms) = postSolution
        {D4FAF2DD-A26C-444A-9FEE-2788B5F5FDD2}.Debug|Any CPU.ActiveCfg = Debug|Any CPU
        {D4FAF2DD-A26C-444A-9FEE-2788B5F5FDD2}.Debug|Any CPU.Build.0 = Debug|Any CPU
    EndGlobalSection
    GlobalSection(SolutionProperties) = preSolution
        HideSolutionNode = FALSE
    EndGlobalSection
EndGlobal
```

In this example the solution consists of a single project, FirstProject, and a Global section outlining settings that apply to the solution. For instance, the solution itself will be visible in the Solution Explorer because the HideSolutionNode setting is FALSE. If you were to change this value to TRUE, the solution name would not be displayed in Visual Studio.

Solution Properties

You can open the Solution Properties dialog by right-clicking the Solution node in the Solution Explorer and selecting Properties. This dialog contains two nodes, Common Properties and Configuration Properties, as shown in Figure 6-2.

If your dialog is missing the Configuration Properties node, you need to check the Show Advanced Build Configurations property in the Projects and Solutions node of the Options window, accessible from the Tools menu. Unfortunately, this property is not checked for some of the setting profiles — for example, the Visual Basic Developer profile. Checking this option not only displays this node, but also displays the configuration selection drop-down in the Project Settings window, discussed later in this chapter.

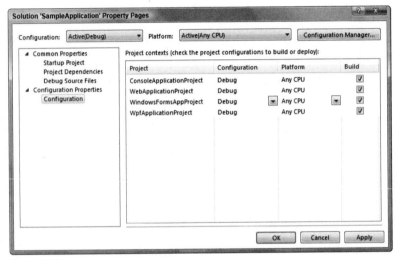

Figure 6-2

The following sections describe the Common Properties and Configuration Properties nodes in more detail.

Common Properties

You have three options when defining the startup project for an application, and they're somewhat self-explanatory. Selecting Current Selection will start the project that has current focus in the Solution Explorer. Single Startup will ensure that the same project starts up each time. (This is the default selection, as most applications have only a single startup project.) The last option, Multiple Startup Projects, allows multiple projects to be started in a particular order. This can be useful if you have a client/server application specified in a single solution and you want them both to be running. When you are running multiple projects, it is also relevant to control the order in which they start up. Use the up and down arrows next to the project list to control the order in which projects are started.

The Project Dependencies section is used to indicate other projects on which a specific project is dependent. For the most part, Visual Studio will manage this for you as you add and remove project references for a given project. However, sometimes you may want to create dependencies between projects to ensure that they are built in the correct order. Visual Studio uses its list of dependencies to determine the order in which projects should be built. This window prevents you from inadvertently adding circular references and from removing necessary project dependencies.

In the Debug Source Files section, you can provide a list of directories through which Visual Studio can search for source files when debugging. This is the default list that is searched before the Find Source dialog is displayed. You can also list source files that Visual Studio should not try to locate. If you click Cancel when prompted to locate a source file, the file will be added to this list.

Configuration Properties

Both projects and solutions have build configurations associated with them that determine which items are built and how. It can be somewhat confusing because there is actually no correlation between a project configuration, which determines how things are built, and a solution configuration, which determines which projects are built, other than that they might have the same name. A new solution will define both Debug and Release (solution) configurations, which correspond to building all projects within the solution in Debug or Release (project) configurations.

For example, a new solution configuration called Test can be created, which consists of two projects: MyClassLibrary and MyClassLibraryTest. When you build your application in Test configuration, you want MyClassLibary to be built in Release mode so you're testing as close to what you would release as possible. However, in order to be able to step through your test code, you want to build the test project in Debug mode.

When you build in Release mode, you don't want the Test solution to be built or deployed with your application. In this case you can specify in the Test solution configuration that you want the MyClassLibrary project to be built in Release mode, and that the MyClassLibraryTest project should not be built.

You can switch between configurations easily via the Configuration drop-down on the standard toolbar. However, it is not as easy to switch between platforms, as the Platform drop-down is not on any of the toolbars. To make it available, select View ➪ Toolbars ➪ Customize. From the Build category on the Commands, the Solution Platforms item can be dragged onto a toolbar.

You will notice that when the Configuration Properties node is selected from the Solution Properties dialog, as shown in Figure 6-2, the Configuration and Platform drop-down boxes are enabled. The Configuration drop-down contains each of the available solution configurations (Debug and Release by default), Active, and All. Similarly, the Platform drop-down contains each of the available platforms (any CPU by default), Active, and All. Whenever these drop-downs appear and are enabled, you can specify the settings on that page on a per-configuration and/or per-platform basis. You can also use the Configuration Manager button to add additional solution configurations and/or platforms.

When you are adding additional solution configurations, there is an option (checked by default) to create corresponding project configurations for existing projects (projects will be set to build with this configuration by default for this new solution configuration), and an option to base the new configuration on an existing one. If the Create Project Configurations option is checked and the new configuration is based on an existing one, the new project configurations will be the same as those specified for the existing configuration.

The options available for creating new platform configurations are limited by the types of CPUs available: Itanium, x86, and x64. Again, the new platform configuration can be based on existing configurations, and the option to create project platform configurations is also available.

The other thing you can specify in the solution configuration file is the type of CPU for which you are building. This is particularly relevant if you want to deploy to 64-bit architecture machines.

All these solution settings can be reached directly from the right-click context menu from the Solution node in the Solution Explorer window. While the Set Startup Projects menu item opens the Solution Configuration window, the Configuration Manager and Project Dependencies items open the Configuration Manager and Project Dependencies windows, respectively. Interestingly, an additional option in the right-click context menu, the Build Order, doesn't appear in the solution configuration. When selected, this opens the Project Dependencies window, which lists the build order in a separate tab, as shown in Figure 6-3. This tab reveals the order in which projects will be built, according to the dependencies. This can be useful if you are maintaining references to project output DLLs rather than project references, and you can use it to double-check that projects are being built in the correct order.

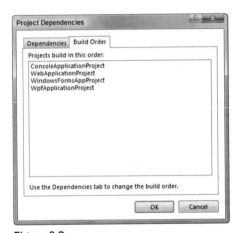

Figure 6-3

Project Types

Within Visual Studio, the most common projects for Visual Basic and C# have been broadly classified into six categories. With the exception of Web Site Projects, which are discussed separately later in this chapter, each project contains a project file (.vbproj or .csproj) that conforms to the MSBuild schema. Selecting a project template will create a new project of a specific project type and populate it with initial classes and settings. Following are the six most common project types:

❑ **Windows:** The Windows project category is the broadest and includes most of the common project types that run on end-user operating systems. This includes the Windows Forms executable projects, Console application projects, and Windows Presentation Foundation (WPF) applications. These project types create an executable (.exe) assembly that is executed directly by an end user. The Windows category also includes several types of library assemblies that can easily be referenced by other projects. These include both class libraries and control libraries for

Windows Forms and WPF applications. A class library reuses the familiar .dll extension. The Windows Service project type can also be found in this category.

❑ **Office:** As its name suggests, the Office category creates managed code add-ins for Microsoft office products such as Outlook, Word, and Excel. These project types use Visual Studio Tools for Office (VSTO), and are capable of creating add-ins for most products in both the Office 2003 and Office 2007 product suites.

❑ **Smart Device:** Similar to Windows, the Smart Device category provides project types for applications and libraries that run on the Windows Mobile or Windows CE platforms.

❑ **WCF:** This category contains a number of project types for creating applications that provide Windows Communication Foundation (WCF) services.

❑ **Web:** The Web category includes the project types that run under ASP.NET. This includes ASP.NET web applications, XML web services, and control libraries for use in web applications and rich, AJAX-enabled web applications.

❑ **Workflow:** This contains a number of project types for sequential and state machine workflow libraries and applications.

The New Project dialog box in Visual Studio 2008, shown in Figure 6-4, enables you to browse and create any of these project types. The target .NET Framework version is listed in a drop-down selector in the top right-hand corner of this dialog box. If a project type is not supported by the selected .NET Framework version, such as a WPF application under .NET Framework 2.0, then that project type will not be displayed.

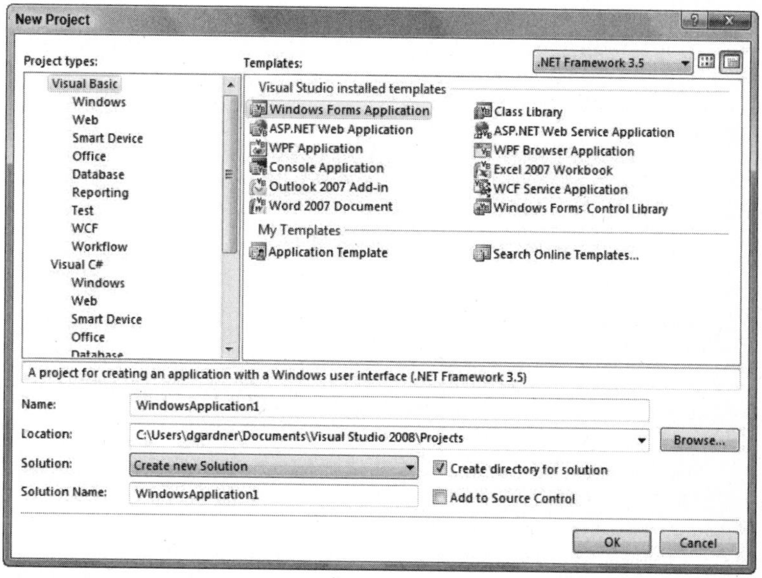

Figure 6-4

Project Files Format

The project files (.csproj or .vbproj) are text files in an XML document format that conforms to the MSBuild schema. The XML schema files for the latest version of MSBuild are installed with the .NET Framework, by default in C:\WINDOWS\Microsoft.NET\Framework\v3.5\MSBuild\Microsoft .Build.Core.xsd).

> *To view the project file in XML format, right-click the project and select Unload. Then right-click the project again and select Edit* [project name]. *This will display the project file in the XML editor, complete with IntelliSense.*

The project file stores the build and configuration settings that have been specified for the project, and details about all the files that are included in the project. In some cases, a user-specific project file is also created (.csproj.user or .vbproj.user), which stores user preferences such as startup and debugging options. The .user file is also an XML file that conforms to the MSBuild schema.

Project Properties

You can reach the project properties by either right-clicking the Project node in the Solution Explorer and then selecting Properties, or double-clicking My Project (Properties in C#) just under the Project node. In contrast to solution properties, the project properties do not display in a modal dialog. Instead, they appear as additional tabs alongside your code files. This was done in part to make it easier to navigate between code files and project properties, but it also enables you to open project properties of multiple projects at the same time. Figure 6-5 illustrates the project settings for a Visual Basic Windows Forms project. This section walks you through the vertical tabs on the project editor for both Visual Basic and C# projects.

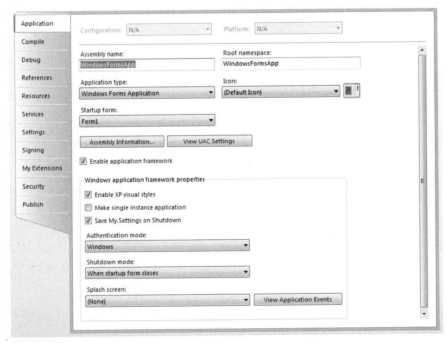

Figure 6-5

The project properties editor contains a series of vertical tabs that group the properties. As changes are made to properties in the tabs, stars are added to the corresponding vertical tabs. This functionality is limited, however, as it does not indicate which fields within a tab have been modified.

Application

The Application tab, visible in Figure 6-5, enables the developer to set the information about the assembly that will be created when the project is compiled. Included are attributes such as the output type (i.e., Windows or Console Application, Class Library, Windows Service, or a Web Control Library), application icon, and startup object. C# applications can also select the target .NET Framework version on the Application tab.

Assembly Information

Attributes that previously had to be configured by hand in the `AssemblyInfo` file contained in the project can also be set via the "Assembly Information" button. This information is important, as it shows up when an application is installed and when the properties of a file are viewed in Windows Explorer. Figure 6-6 (left) shows the assembly information for a sample application and Figure 6-6 (right) shows the properties of the compiled executable.

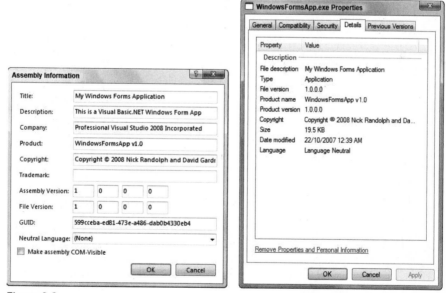

Figure 6-6

Each of the properties set in the Assembly Information dialog is represented by an attribute that is applied to the assembly. This means that you can query the assembly in code to retrieve this information. In Visual Basic, the My namespace (covered in Chapter 12) can be used to retrieve this information.

User Account Control Settings

Visual Studio 2008 provides support for developing applications that work with User Account Control (UAC) under Windows Vista. This involves generating an assembly manifest file, which is an XML file that notifies the operating system if an application requires administrative privileges at startup. In Visual Basic applications, the "View UAC Settings" button on the Application tab can be used to generate and add an assembly manifest file for UAC to your application. The following listing shows the default manifest file that is generated by Visual Studio.

```
<?xml version="1.0" encoding="utf-8"?>
<asmv1:assembly manifestVersion="1.0" xmlns="urn:schemas-
    microsoft-com:asm.v1" xmlns:asmv1="urn:schemas-
    microsoft-com:asm.v1" xmlns:asmv2="urn:schemas-
    microsoft-com:asm.v2"
    xmlns:xsi="http://www.w3.org/2001/XMLSchema-instance">
  <assemblyIdentity version="1.0.0.0" name="MyApplication.app"/>
  <trustInfo xmlns="urn:schemas-microsoft-com:asm.v2">
    <security>
      <requestedPrivileges xmlns="urn:schemas-microsoft-com:asm.v3">
        <!-- UAC Manifest Options
            If you want to change the Windows User Account Control level replace the
            requestedExecutionLevel node with one of the following.

            <requestedExecutionLevel  level="asInvoker" />
            <requestedExecutionLevel  level="requireAdministrator" />
            <requestedExecutionLevel  level="highestAvailable" />

            If you want to utilize File and Registry Virtualization for backward
            compatibility then delete the requestedExecutionLevel node.
        -->
        <requestedExecutionLevel level="asInvoker" />
      </requestedPrivileges>
    </security>
  </trustInfo>
</asmv1:assembly>
```

If the UAC-requested execution level is changed from the default asInvoker to requireAdministrator, Windows Vista will present a UAC prompt when the application is launched. Visual Studio 2008 will also prompt to restart in Administrator mode if an application requiring admin rights is started in Debug mode. Figure 6-7 shows the prompt that is raised, enabling us to restart Visual Studio in Administrator mode.

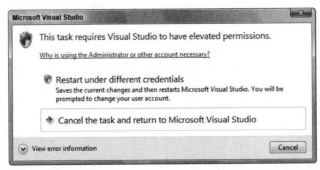

Figure 6-7

If you agree to the restart, Visual Studio will not only restart with administrative privileges, it will also reopen your solution including all the files you had opened. It will even remember the last cursor position.

Application Framework (Visual Basic only)

Additional application settings are available for Visual Basic projects because they can use the Application Framework that is exclusive to Visual Basic. This extends the standard event model to provide a series of application events and settings that control the behavior of the application. You can enable the Application Framework by checking the Enable Application Framework checkbox. The following three checkboxes control the behavior of the Application Framework:

❑ **Enable XP visual styles:** XP visual styles are a feature that significantly improves the look and feel of Windows XP, as it provides a much smoother interface through the use of rounded buttons and controls that dynamically change color as the mouse passes over them. Visual Basic applications enable XP styles by default and can be disabled from the Project Settings dialog, or controlled from within code.

❑ **Make single instance application:** Most applications support multiple instances running concurrently. However, an application opened more than two or three times may be run only once, with successive executions simply invoking the original application. Such an application could be a document editor, for which successive executions simply open different documents. You can easily add this functionality by marking the application as a single instance.

❑ **Save My.Settings on Shutdown:** This option will ensure that any changes made to user-scoped settings will be preserved, saving the settings provided prior to the application's shutting down.

This section also enables you to select an authentication mode for the application. By default this is set to Windows, which uses the currently logged-on user. Selecting Application-defined enables you to use a custom authentication module.

You can also identify a form to be used as a splash screen when the application is first launched, and specify the shutdown behavior of the application.

The Visual Basic Application Framework is discussed further in Chapter 11.

Compile (Visual Basic only)

The Compile section of the project settings, shown in Figure 6-8, enables the developer to control how and where the project is built. For example, the output path can be modified so that it points to an alternative location. This might be important if the output is to be used elsewhere in the build process.

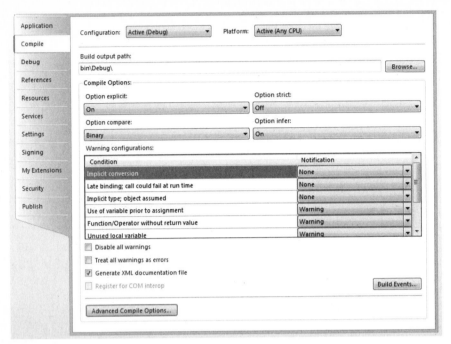

Figure 6-8

Within the Advanced Compile Options, various attributes can be adjusted, including the compilation constants. The DEBUG and TRACE constants can be enabled here. Alternatively, you can easily define your own constant, which can then be queried. For example, the DEBUG constant can be queried as follows:

```
#If DEBUG Then
    MsgBox("Constant Defined")
#End If
```

Some Visual Basic-specific properties can also be configured in the Compile pane. "Option explicit" determines whether variables that are used in code have to be explicitly defined. "Option strict" forces the type of variables to be defined, rather than be late-bound. "Option compare" determines whether strings are compared by means of binary or text comparison operators. "Option infer" specifies whether local type inference in variable declarations is allowed or the type must explicitly stated.

All four of these compiler options can be controlled at either the project or file level. File-level compiler options will override project-level options.

The Compile pane also defines a number of different compiler options that can be adjusted to improve the reliability of your code. For example, unused variables may warrant only a warning, whereas a path that doesn't return a value is more serious and should generate a build error. It is possible to either disable all these warnings or treat all of them as errors.

Visual Basic developers also have the capability to generate XML documentation. Of course, as the documentation takes time to generate, it is recommended that you disable this option for debug builds.

This will speed up the debugging cycle; however, when this option is turned off warnings will not be given for missing XML documentation.

The last element of the Compile pane is the "Build Events" button. Click this button to view commands that can be executed prior to and after the build. Because not all builds are successful, the execution of the post-build event can depend on a successful build. Build Events is listed as a separate vertical tab for C# projects.

Build (C# only)

The Build tab, shown is Figure 6-9, is the C# equivalent of the Visual Basic Compile tab. It enables the developer to specify the project's build configuration settings. For example, you can enable the use of the C# unsafe keyword or enable optimizations during compilation to make the output file smaller, faster, and more efficient. These optimizations typically increase the build time, and because of this are not recommended for the Debug build.

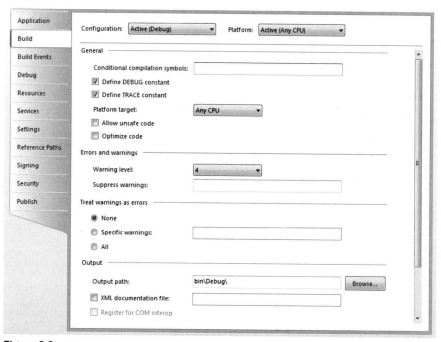

Figure 6-9

The Configuration drop-down selector at the top of the tab page allows different build settings for the Debug and Release build configurations.

Debug

The Debug tab, shown in Figure 6-10, determines how the application will be executed when run from within Visual Studio 2008.

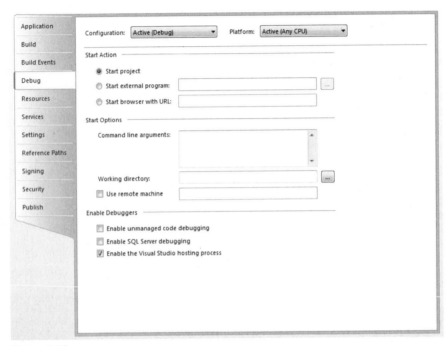

Figure 6-10

Start Action

When a project is set to start up, this set of radio buttons controls what actually happens when the application is run. Initially, these buttons are set to start the project, meaning that the startup object specified on the Application tab will be called. The other options are to either run an executable or launch a specific web site.

Startup Options

The options that you can specify when running an application are additional command-line arguments (generally used in conjunction with an executable start action) and the initial working directory. You can also specify to start the application on a remote computer. Of course, this is possible only when debugging is enabled on a remote machine.

Enable Debuggers

Debugging can be extended to include unmanaged code and the SQL Server. The Visual Studio hosting process can also be enabled here. This process has a number of benefits associated with the performance and functionality of the debugger. The benefits fall into three categories. First, the hosting process acts as a background host for the application you are debugging. In order for a managed application to be debugged, various administrative tasks must be performed, such as creating an AppDomain and associating the debugger, which take time. With the hosting process enabled, these tasks are handled in the background, resulting in a much quicker load time during debugging.

Second, in Visual Studio 2008 it is quite easy to create, debug, and deploy applications that run under partial trust. The hosting process is an important tool in this process because it gives you the ability to run and debug an application in partial trust. Without this process, the application would run in full trust mode, preventing you from debugging the application in partial trust mode.

The last benefit that the hosting process provides is design-time evaluation of expressions. This is, in effect, an optical illusion, as the hosting process is actually running in the background. However, using the Immediate window as you're writing your code means that you can easily evaluate expressions, call methods, and even hit breakpoints without running up the entire application.

References (Visual Basic only)

The References tab enables the developer to reference classes in other .NET assemblies, projects, and native DLLs. Once the project or DLL has been added to the references list, a class can be accessed by its full name, including namespace, or the namespace can be imported into a code file so the class can be referenced by just the class name. Figure 6-11 shows the References tab for a project that has a reference to a number of framework assemblies.

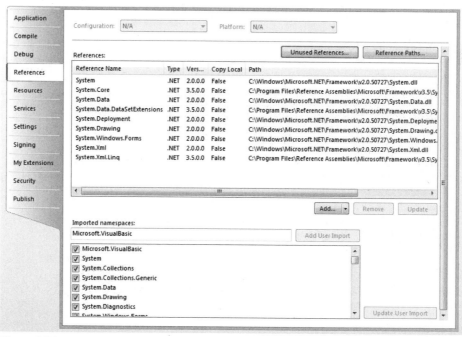

Figure 6-11

One of the added features of this tab for Visual Basic developers is the "Unused References" button, which performs a search to determine which references can be removed. It is also possible to add a reference path, which will include all assemblies in that location.

Once an assembly has been added to the reference list, any public class contained within that assembly can be referenced within the project. Where a class is embedded in a namespace (which might be a nested hierarchy), referencing a class requires the full class name. Both Visual Basic and C# provide a mechanism for importing namespaces so that classes can be referenced directly. The References section allows namespaces to be globally imported for all classes in the project, without their being explicitly imported within the class file.

References to external assemblies can either be file references or project references. File references are direct references to an individual assembly. You create them using the Browse tab of the Add Reference dialog box. Project references are references to a project within the solution. All assemblies outputted by that project are dynamically added as references. You create them using the Project tab of the Add Reference dialog box.

> *It is recommended that you never add a file reference to a project that exists in the same solution. If a project requires a reference to another project in that solution, a project reference should always be used.*

The advantage of a project reference is that it creates a dependency among the projects in the build system. The dependent project will be built if it has changed since the last time the referencing project was built. A file reference doesn't create a build dependency, so it's possible to build the referencing project without building the dependent project. However, this can result in problems with the referencing project expecting a different version from what is included in the output.

Resources

Project resources can be added and removed via the Resources tab, shown in Figure 6-12. In the example shown, three icons have been added to this application. Resources can be images, text, icons, files, or any other serializable class.

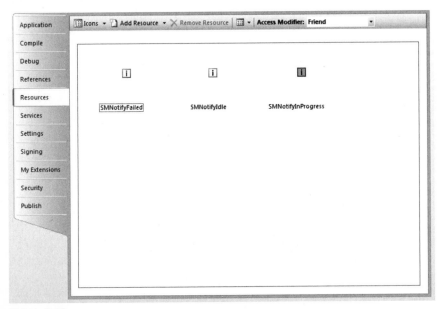

Figure 6-12

This interface makes working with resource files at design time very easy. Chapter 38 examines in more detail how resource files can be used to store application constants and internationalize your application.

Services

Client application services are a new feature in Visual Studio 2008 that allows Windows-based applications to use the authentication, roles, and profile services from Microsoft ASP.NET 2.0. The client services enable multiple web- and Windows-based applications to centralize user profiles and user-administration functionality.

Figure 6-13 shows the Services tab, which is used to configure client application services for Windows applications. When the services are being enabled, the URL of the ASP.NET service host must be specified for each service. This will be stored in the app.config file. The following client services are supported:

❏ **Authentication:** This enables the user's identity to be verified via either the native Windows authentication or a custom forms-based authentication provided by the application.

❏ **Roles:** This obtains the roles an authenticated user has been assigned, which enables you to allow certain users access to different parts of the application. For example, additional administrative functions may be made available to admin users.

❏ **Web settings:** This stores per-user application settings on the server, which allows them to be shared across multiple computers and applications.

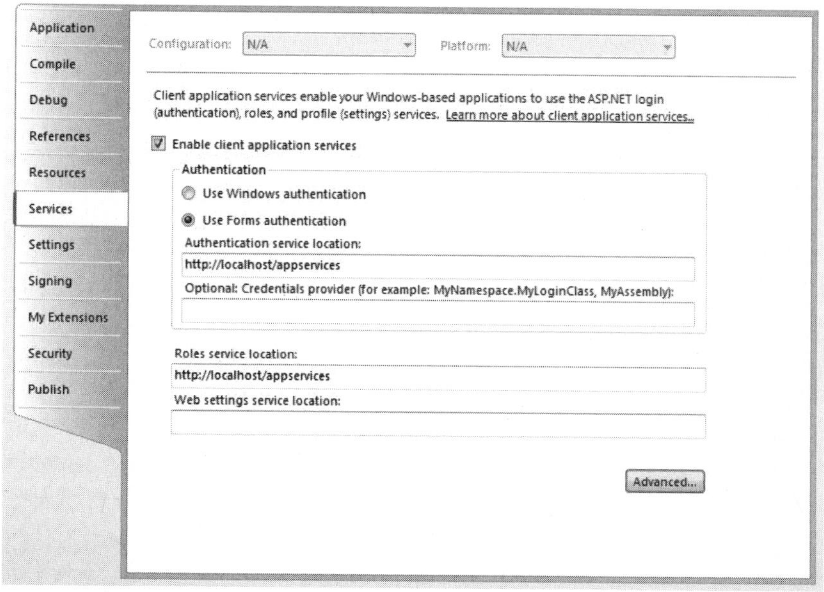

Figure 6-13

Client application services use a provider model for web services extensibility. The service providers include offline support that uses a local cache to ensure that it can still operate even when a network connection is not available.

Settings

Project settings can be of any type and simply reflect a name/value pair whose value can be retrieved at runtime. Settings can be scoped to either the application or the user, as shown in Figure 6-14. Settings are stored internally in the Settings.settings file and the app.config file. When the application is compiled these files are renamed according to the executable being generated — for example, SampleApplication.exe.config.

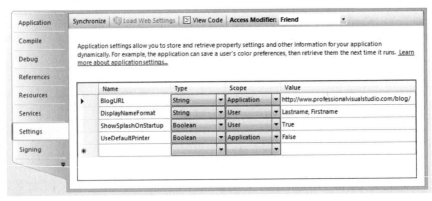

Figure 6-14

Application-scoped settings are read-only at runtime, and you can change them only by manually editing the config file. User settings can be dynamically changed at runtime, and may have a different value saved for each user who runs the application. The default values for user settings are stored in the app.config file, and the per-user settings are stored in a user.config file under the user's private data path.

Application and user settings are described in more detail in Chapter 36.

Signing

Figure 6-15 shows the Signing tab, which enables developers to determine how assemblies are signed in preparation for deployment. You can sign an assembly by selecting a key file. You can create a new key file by selecting <New . . . > from the file selector drop-down.

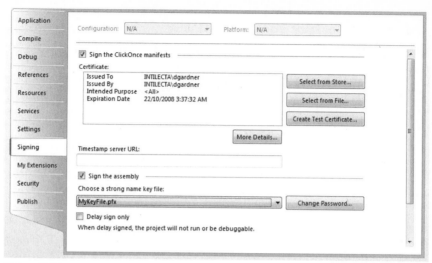

Figure 6-15

The ClickOnce deployment model for applications enables an application to be published to a web site where a user can click once to download and install the application. Because this model is supposed to support deployment over the Internet, an organization must be able to sign the deployment package. The Signing tab provides an interface for specifying the certificate to use to sign the ClickOnce manifests.

Chapter 46 provides more detail on assembly signing and Chapter 47 discusses ClickOnce deployments.

My Extensions (Visual Basic only)

The My Extensions tab, shown in Figure 6-16, enables you to add a reference to an assembly that extends the Visual Basic My namespace, using the new extension methods feature. Extension methods enable developers to add new methods to an existing class without having to use inheritance to create a sub-class or recompile the original type.

Extension methods were primarily introduced to enable LINQ to be shipped without requiring major changes to the base class library. However, extension methods can be used in a number of other interesting scenarios.

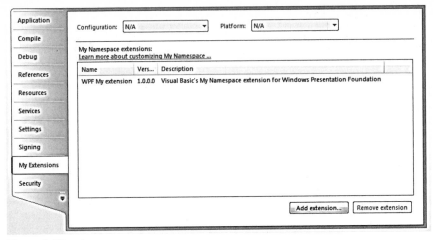

Figure 6-16

Security

Applications deployed using the ClickOnce deployment model may be required to run under limited or partial trust. For example, if a low-privilege user selects a ClickOnce application from a web site across the Internet, the application will need to run with partial trust as defined by the Internet zone. This typically means that the application can't access the local file system, has limited networking ability, and can't access other local devices such as printers, databases, and computer ports.

The Security tab, illustrated in Figure 6-17, has a "Calculate Permissions" button that will determine the permissions the application requires to operate correctly.

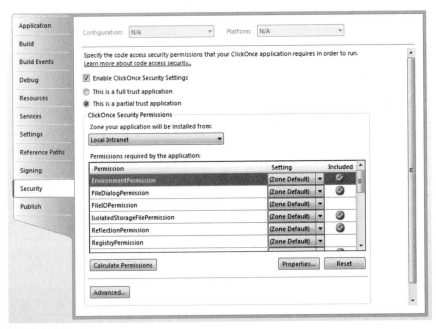

Figure 6-17

Modifying the permission set that is required for a ClickOnce application may limit who can download, install, and operate the application. For the widest audience, specify that an application should run in partial trust mode with security set to the defaults for the Internet zone. Alternatively, specifying that an application requires full trust will ensure that the application has full access to all local resources, but will necessarily limit the audience to local administrators.

Code Access Security and the implications for ClickOnce deployments are described in detail in Chapter 27.

Publish

The ClickOnce deployment model can be divided into two phases: the initial publication of the application and subsequent updates, and the download and installation of both the original application and subsequent revisions. You can deploy an existing application using the ClickOnce model by using the Publish tab, shown in Figure 6-18.

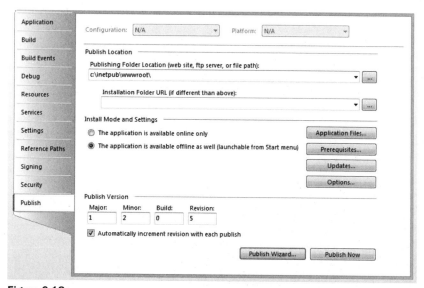

Figure 6-18

If the Install mode for a ClickOnce application is set to be available offline when it is initially downloaded from the web site, it will be installed on the local computer. This will place the application in the Start menu and the Add/Remove Programs list. When the application is run and a connection to the original web site is available, the application will determine whether any updates are available. If there are updates, users will be prompted to determine whether they want the updates to be installed.

The ClickOnce deployment model is explained more thoroughly in Chapter 47.

Web (Web Application Projects only)

The Web tab, shown in Figure 6-19, controls how Web Application Projects are launched when executed from within Visual Studio. Visual Studio ships with a built-in web server suitable for development purposes. The Web tab enables you to configure the port and virtual path that this server runs under. You may also choose to enable NTLM authentication.

> *The Enable Edit and Continue option enables editing of code-behind and stand-alone class files during a debug session. Editing of the HTML in an* `.aspx` *or* `.ascx` *page is enabled regardless of this setting; however, editing of inline code in an* `.aspx` *page or an* `.ascx` *file is never enabled.*

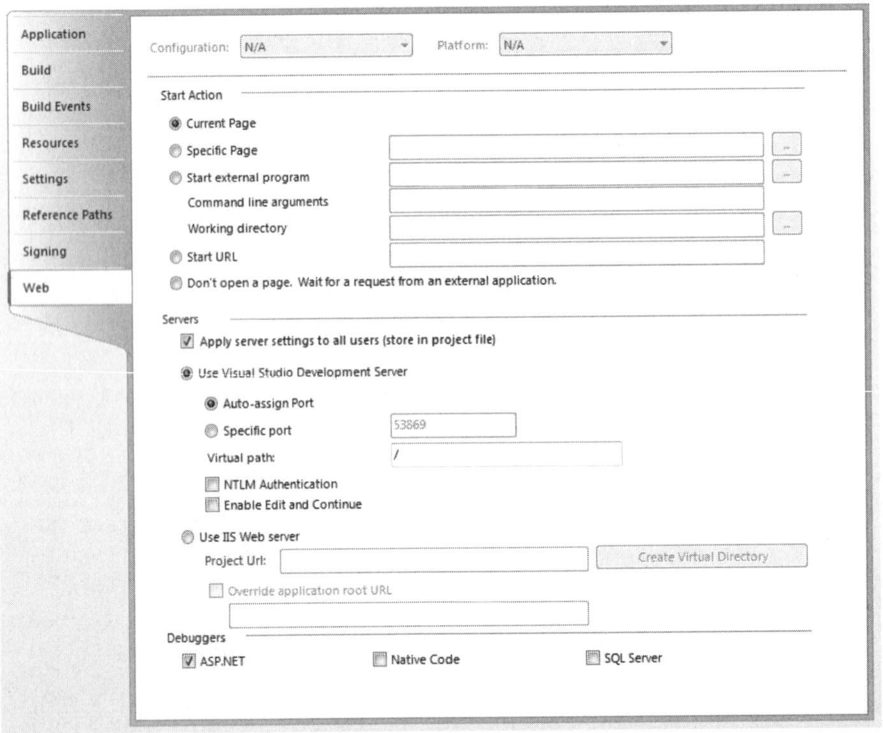

Figure 6-19

The debugging options for web applications are explored in Chapter 42.

Web Site Projects

The Web Site Project functions quite differently from other project types. Web Site Projects do not include a `.csproj` or `.vbproj` file, which means they have a number of limitations in terms of build options, project resources, and managing references. Instead, Web Site Projects use the folder structure to define the contents of the project. All files within the folder structure are implicitly part of the project.

Web Site Projects provide the advantage of dynamic compilation, which enables you to edit pages without rebuilding the entire site. The file can be saved and simply reloaded in the browser; therefore they enable extremely short code and debug cycles. Microsoft first introduced Web Site Projects with Visual Studio 2005; however, it was quickly inundated with customer feedback to reintroduce the Application Project model, which had been provided as an additional download. By the release of Service Pack 1, Web Application Projects were back within Visual Studio as a native project type.

Since Visual Studio 2005 an ongoing debate has been raging about which is better — Web Site Projects or Web Application Projects. Unfortunately, there is no simple answer to this debate. Each has its own pros and cons, and the decision comes down to your requirements and your preferred development workflow.

Further discussion of Web Site and Web Application Projects is included in Chapter 31.

Summary

In this chapter you have seen how a solution and projects can be configured via the user interfaces provided within Visual Studio 2008. In particular, this chapter showed you how to do the following:

- ❑ Create and configure solutions and projects
- ❑ Control how an application is compiled, debugged, and deployed
- ❑ Configure the many project-related properties
- ❑ Include resources and settings with an application
- ❑ Enforce good coding practices

In subsequent chapters, many of the topics, such as building and deploying projects and the use of resource files, will be examined in more detail.

7

Source Control

Many different methodologies for building software applications exist, and though the theories about team structure, work allocation, design, and testing often differ, one point that they agree on is that there should be a single repository for all source code for an application. Source control is the process of storing source code (referred to as checking code in) and accessing it again (referred to as checking code out) for editing. When we refer to source code, we mean any resources, configuration files, code files, or even documentation that is required to build and deploy the application.

Source code repositories also vary in structure and interface. Basic repositories provide a limited interface through which files can be checked in and out. The storage mechanism can be as simple as a file share, and no history may be available. Yet this repository still has the advantage that all developers working on a project can access the same file, with no risk of changes being overwritten or lost. Most sophisticated repositories not only provide a rich interface for checking in and out, such as merging and other resolution options, but can also be used from within Visual Studio to manage the source code. Other functionality that a source control repository can provide includes versioning of files, branching, and remote access.

Most organizations start using a source control repository to provide a mechanism for sharing source code between participants in a project. Instead of developers having to manually copy code to and from a shared folder on a network, the repository can be queried to get the latest version of the source code. When a developer finishes his or her work, any changes can simply be checked into the repository. This ensures that everyone in the team can access the latest code. Also, having the source code checked into a single repository makes it easy to perform regular backups.

Version tracking, including a full history of what changes were made and by whom, is one of the biggest benefits of using a source control repository. Although most developers would like to think that they write perfect code, the reality is that quite often a change might break something else. Being able to review the history of changes made to a project makes it possible to identify which change caused the breakage. Tracking changes to a project can also be used for reporting and reviewing purposes, because each change is date stamped and its author indicated.

Selecting a Source Control Repository

Visual Studio 2008 does not ship with a source control repository, but it does include rich support for checking files in and out, as well as merging and reviewing changes. To make use of a repository from within Visual Studio 2008, it is necessary to specify which repository to use. Visual Studio 2008 supports deep integration with Team Foundation Server (TFS), Microsoft's premier source control and project tracking system. In addition, Visual Studio supports any source control client that uses the Source Code Control (SCC) API. Products that use the SCC API include Microsoft Visual SourceSafe, and the free, open-source source-control repositories Subversion and CVS.

> *You would be forgiven for thinking that Microsoft Visual SourceSafe is no longer available, considering that all the press mentions is TFS. However, Microsoft Visual SourceSafe 2005 is still available and fully compatible with Visual Studio 2008. In fact, Visual SourceSafe is an ideal source control repository for individual developers or small development teams.*

To make Visual Studio 2008 easy to navigate and work with, any functionality that is not available is typically hidden from the menus. By default, Visual Studio 2008 does not display the source control menu item. In order to get this item to appear, you must configure the source control provider information under the Options item on the Tools menu. The Options window, with the Source Control tab selected, is shown in Figure 7-1.

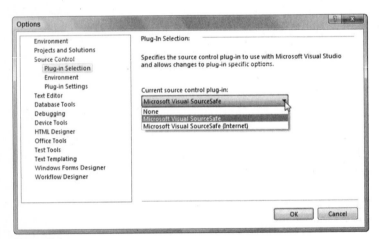

Figure 7-1

Initially very few settings for source control appear. However, once a provider has been selected, additional nodes are added to the tree to control how source control behaves. These options are specific to the source control provider that has been selected.

For the remainder of this chapter, we will focus on the use of Visual SourceSafe with Visual Studio 2008. In Chapter 58, we cover the use of Team Foundation, which offers much richer integration and functionality as a source control repository.

> *The Internet-based version of Visual SourceSafe uses a client-server model that runs over HTTP or HTTPS, instead of accessing the source code repository through a file share. Additional setup is required on the server side to expose this functionality.*

Once a source control repository has been selected from the plug-in menu, it is necessary to configure the repository for that machine. For Visual SourceSafe, this includes specifying the path to the repository, the user with which to connect, and the settings to use when checking files in and out of the repository.

Environment Settings

Most source control repositories define a series of settings that must be configured in order for Visual Studio 2008 to connect to and access information from the repository. These settings are usually unique to the repository, although some apply across most repositories.

In Figure 7-2 the Environment tab is shown, illustrating the options that control when files are checked in and out of the repository. These options are available for most repositories. The drop-down menu at the top of the pane defines a couple of profiles, which provide suggestions for different types of developers.

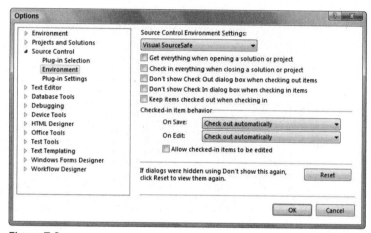

Figure 7-2

Plug-In Settings

Most source control repositories need some additional settings in order for Visual Studio 2008 to connect to the repository. These are specified in the Plug-in Settings pane, which is customized for each repository. Some repositories, such as SourceSafe, do not require specific information regarding the location of the repository until a solution is added to source control. At that point, SourceSafe requests the location of an existing repository or enables the developer to create a new repository.

Accessing Source Control

This section walks through the process of adding a solution to a new Visual SourceSafe 2008 repository, although the same principles apply regardless of the repository chosen. This process can be applied to any new or existing solution that is not already under source control. We also assume here that SourceSafe is not only installed, but that it has been selected as the source control repository within Visual Studio 2008.

Creating the Repository

The first step in placing a solution under source control is to create a repository in which to store the data. It is possible to place any number of solutions in the same repository, although this means that it is much harder to separate information pertaining to different projects. Furthermore, if a repository is corrupted, it may affect all solutions contained within that repository.

To begin the process of adding a solution to source control, navigate to the File menu and select Source Control ⇨ Add Solution to Source Control, as shown in Figure 7-3.

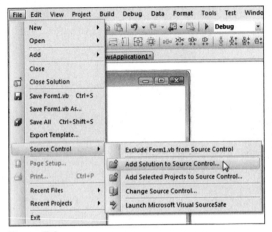

Figure 7-3

If this is the first time you have accessed SourceSafe, this will open a dialog box that lists the available databases, which at this stage will be empty. Clicking the Add button will initiate the Add SourceSafe Database Wizard, which will step you through either referencing an existing database, perhaps on a server or elsewhere on your hard disk, or creating a new database.

To create a new SourceSafe database you need to specify a location for the database and a name. You must also specify the type of locking that is used when checking files in and out. Selecting the Lock-Modify-Unlock model allows only a single developer to check out a file at any point in time. This prevents two people from making changes to the same file at the same time, which makes the check-in process very simple. However, this model can often lead to frustration if multiple developers need to adjust the same resource. Project files are a common example of a resource that multiple developers may need to be able to access at the same time. In order to add or remove files from a project, this file must be checked out. Unless developers are diligent about checking the project file back in after they add a new file, this can significantly slow down a team.

An alternative model, Copy-Modify-Merge, allows multiple developers to check out the same file. Of course, when they are ready to check the file back in, there must be a process of reconciliation to ensure that their changes do not overwrite any changes made by another developer. Merging changes can be a difficult process and can easily result in loss of changes or a final code set that neither compiles nor runs. This model offers the luxury of allowing concurrent access to files, but suffers from the operational overhead during check in.

Adding the Solution

Once a SourceSafe repository has been created, the Add to SourceSafe dialog will appear, which prompts you for a location for your application and a name to give it in the repository. SourceSafe works very similarly to a network file share — it creates folders under the root ($/) into which it places the files under source control.

> *Although it is no longer required with SourceSafe, many development teams align the SourceSafe folder structure to the directory structure on your computer. This is still considered a recommended practice because it encourages the use of good directory and folder structures.*

After specifying a name and location in the repository, SourceSafe will proceed to add each file belonging to the solution into the source control repository. This initiates the process of tracking changes for these files.

> *The Source Code Control (SCC) API assumes that the .sln solution file is located in the same folder or a direct parent folder to the project files. If you place the .sln solution file in a different folder hierarchy to the project files, then you should expect some "interesting" source control maintenance issues.*

Solution Explorer

The first difference that you will see after adding your solution to source control is that Visual Studio 2008 adjusts the icons within the Solution Explorer to indicate their source control status. Figure 7-4 illustrates three file states. When the solution is initially added to the source control repository, the files all appear with a little padlock icon next to the file type icon. This indicates that the file has been checked in and is not currently checked out by anyone. For example, the Solution file and Form1.vb have this icon.

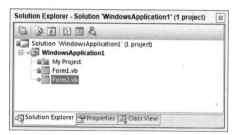

Figure 7-4

Once a solution is under source control, all changes are recorded, including the addition and removal of files. Figure 7-4 illustrates the addition of Form2.vb to the solution. The plus sign next to Form2.vb indicates that this is a new file. The tick next to the WindowsApplication1 project signifies that the file is currently checked out. In the scenario where two people have the same file checked out, this will be indicated with a double tick next to the appropriate item.

Checking In and Out

Files can be checked in and out using the right-click shortcut menu associated with an item in the Solution Explorer. When a solution is under source control, this menu expands to include the items shown on the left in Figure 7-5.

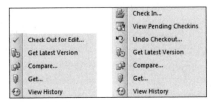

Figure 7-5

Before a file can be edited, it must be checked out. This can be done using the Check Out for Edit menu item. Once a file is checked out, the shortcut menu expands to include additional options, including Check In, View Pending Checkins, Undo Checkout, and more, as shown on the right in Figure 7-5.

Pending Changes

In a large application it can often be difficult to see at a glance which files have been checked out for editing, or recently added or removed from a project. The Pending Checkins window, shown in Figure 7-6, is very useful for seeing which files are waiting to be checked into the repository. It also provides a space into which a comment can be added. This comment is attached to the files when they are checked into the repository so that the reason for the change(s) can be reviewed at a later date.

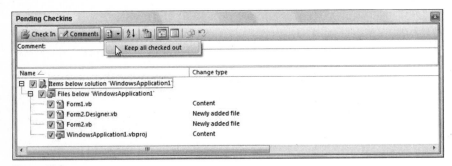

Figure 7-6

To check a file back in, you should ensure that there is a check against the file in the list, add an appropriate comment in the space provided, and then select the Check In button. Depending on the options you have specified, you may also receive a confirmation dialog prior to the item's being checked in.

One option that many developers prefer is to set Visual Studio to automatically check a file out when it is edited. This saves the often unnecessary step of having to check the file out before editing. However, it can result in files being checked out prematurely, for example if a developer accidentally makes a change in the wrong file. Alternatively, a developer may decide that changes made previously are no longer required and wish to revert to what is contained in the repository. The last button on the Toolbar contained within the Pending Checkins window is an Undo Checkout button. This will retrieve the current version from the repository, in the process overwriting the local changes that were made by the developer. This option is also available via the right-click shortcut menu.

Before checking a file into the repository, it is a good idea for someone to review any changes that have been made. In fact, some organizations have a policy requiring that all changes be reviewed before being checked in. Selecting the Compare Versions menu item brings up an interface that highlights any differences between two versions of a file. Figure 7-7 shows that a Form Load event handler has been added to Form1.vb. Although not evident in Figure 7-7, the type of change is also color coded; additions are highlighted in green text, while red and blue lines indicate deleted and changed lines.

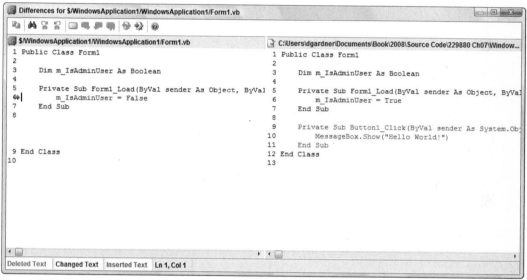

Figure 7-7

Because source files can often get quite large, this window provides some basic navigation shortcuts. The Find option can be used to locate particular strings. Bookmarks can be placed to ease navigation forward and backward within a file. The most useful shortcuts are the Next and Previous difference buttons. These enable the developer to navigate through the differences without having to manually scroll up and down the file.

Merging Changes

Occasionally, changes might be made to the same file by multiple developers. In some cases these changes can be automatically resolved if they are unrelated, such as the addition of a method to an existing class. However, when changes are made to the same portion of the file, there needs to be a process by which the changes can be mediated to determine the correct code.

Figure 7-8 illustrates the Merge dialog that is presented to developers when they attempt to check in a file that has been modified by another developer. The top half of the dialog shows the two versions of the file that are in conflict. Each pane indicates where that file differs from the original file that the developer checked out, which appears in the lower half of the screen. In this case, both versions had a message box inserted, and it is up to the developer to determine which of the messages is correct.

Unlike the Compare Versions dialog, the Merge dialog has been designed to facilitate developer interaction. From the top panes, changes made in either version can be accepted or rejected by simply clicking the change. The highlighting changes to indicate that a change has been accepted, and that piece of code is inserted into the appropriate place in the code presented in the lower pane. The lower pane also allows the developer to enter code, although it does not support IntelliSense or error detection.

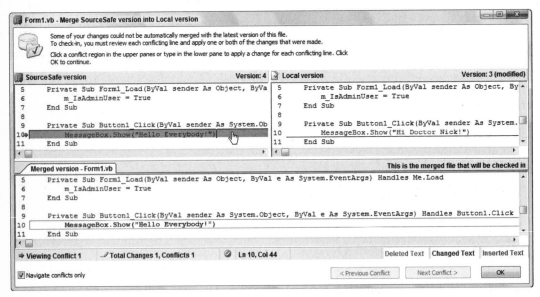

Figure 7-8

Once the conflicts have been resolved, clicking the OK button will save the changes to your local file. The merged version can then be checked into the repository.

History

Any time a file is checked in and out of the SourceSafe repository, a history is recorded of each version of the file. Use the View History option on the right-click shortcut menu from the Solution Explorer to review this history. Figure 7-9 shows a brief history of a file that had three revisions checked in. This dialog enables developers to view previous versions, look at details (such as the comments), get the particular version (overwriting the current file), and check out the file. Additional functionality is provided to compare different versions of the file, pin a particular version, roll the file back to a previous version (which will erase newer versions), and report on the version history.

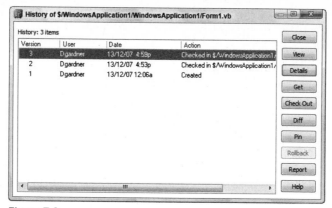

Figure 7-9

Pinning

The History window (refer to Figure 7-9) can be used to pin a version of the file. Pinning a version of a file makes that version the current version. When a developer gets the current source code from the repository, the pinned version is returned. Pinning a version of a file also prevents anyone from checking that file out. This can be useful if changes that have been checked are incomplete or are causing errors in the application. A previous version of the file can be pinned to ensure that other developers can continue to work while the problem is resolved.

Offline Support for Source Control

Visual Studio 2008 provides built-in offline support for Visual SourceSafe when the source code repository is not available. A transient outage could occur for many reasons — the server may be down, a network outage may have occurred, or you could be using your laptop at home.

If you open a solution in Visual Studio that has been checked into Visual SourceSafe, and the source code repository is not available, you will first be prompted to continue or select a different repository. You may also be asked if you want to try to connect using HTTP. Assuming you select No for both of these prompts, you will be presented with four options on how to proceed, as shown in Figure 7-10.

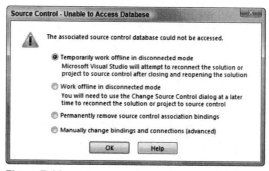

Figure 7-10

If the issue is transient, then you should select the first option: "Temporarily work offline in disconnected mode." This will allow you to check out files and continue editing source code.

The first time you attempt to check out a file while working in disconnected mode, you will be presented with a very large dialog box that displays a small essay. The basic gist of this message is that Visual Studio will actually be simulating a checkout on your behalf, and you may need to manually merge changes when you go to check code back in.

The next time you open the solution and the source code repository is available, Visual Studio will automatically check out any "simulated" checkouts that occurred while working in disconnected mode.

Many of the source control operations are not available while working in disconnected mode. These are operations that typically depend on direct access to the server, such as Check In, Merge Changes, View History, and Compare Versions.

Summary

This chapter demonstrated Visual Studio 2008's rich interface for using a source control repository to manage files associated with an application. Checking files in and out can be done using the Solution Explorer window, and more advanced functionality is available via the Pending Changes window.

Although SourceSafe is sufficient for individuals and small teams of developers, it has not been designed to scale for a large number of developers. It also doesn't provide any capability to track tasks or reviewer comments against a set of changes. Chapter 58 discusses the advantages and additional functionality that is provided by Team Foundation Server, an enterprise-class source control repository system.

8

Forms and Controls

Ever since its earliest days, Visual Studio has excelled at providing a rich visual environment for rapidly designing forms and windows. From simple drag-and-drop procedures for placing graphical controls onto the form, to setting properties that control advanced layout and behavior of controls, the form editor built into Visual Studio 2008 provides you with immense power without your having to dive into code.

This chapter walks you through these processes, bringing you up to speed with the latest additions to the toolset so that you can maximize your efficiency when creating Windows or web applications. While the examples and discussion in this chapter use only Windows Forms, many of the principles and techniques being discussed apply equally well to Web Forms applications.

The Windows Form

When you create a Windows application project, Visual Studio 2008 will automatically create a single blank form ready for your user interface design (see Figure 8-1). There are two common ways to modify the visual design of a Windows Form: either by using the mouse to change the size or position of the form or the control, or by changing the value of the control's properties in the Properties window.

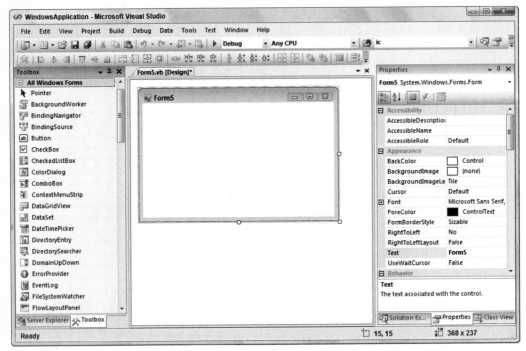

Figure 8-1

Almost every visual control, including the Windows Form itself, can be resized using the mouse. Resize grippers will appear when the form or control has focus in the Design view. For a Windows Form, these will be visible only on the bottom, the right side, and the bottom right corner. Use the mouse to grab the gripper and drag it to the size you want. As you are resizing, the dimensions of the form will be displayed on the bottom right of the status bar.

There is a corresponding property for the dimensions and positions of Windows Forms and controls. As you may recall from Chapter 2, the Properties window, shown on the right-hand side of Figure 8-1, shows the current value of many of the attributes of the form. This includes the Size property, a compound property made up of the Height and Width properties. Click on the + icon to display the individual properties for any compound properties. You can set the dimensions of the form in pixels by entering either an individual value in both the Height and Width properties, or a compound Size value in the format width, height.

The Properties window, shown in Figure 8-2, displays some of the available properties for customizing the form's appearance and behavior.

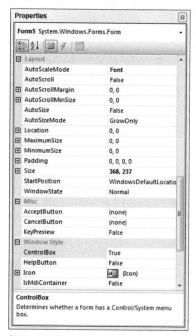

Figure 8-2

Properties are displayed in one of two views: either grouped together in categories, or in alphabetical order. The view is controlled by the first two icons at the top of the Properties window. The following two icons toggle the attribute list between displaying properties and events.

Three categories cover most of the properties that affect the overall look and feel of a form: Appearance, Layout, and Window Style. Many of the properties in these categories are also available on Windows controls.

Appearance Properties

The Appearance category covers the colors, fonts, and form border style. Many Windows Forms applications leave most of these properties as their defaults. The Text property is one that you will typically change, as it controls what is displayed in the forms caption bar.

If the form's purpose differs from its normal behavior, you may need a fixed-size window or a special border, as is commonly seen in tool windows. The FormBorderStyle property controls how this aspect of your form's appearance is handled.

Layout Properties

In addition to the Size properties discussed earlier, the Layout category contains the MaximumSize and MinimumSize properties, which control how small or large a window can be resized. The StartPosition and Location properties can be used to control where the form is displayed in the screen. The WindowState property can be used to initially display the form minimized, maximized, or normally, according to its default size.

Window Style Properties

The Window Style category includes properties that determine what is shown in the Windows Form's caption bar, including the Maximize, Minimize, and Form icons. The ShowInTaskbar property determines whether the form is listed in the Windows Taskbar. Other notable properties in this category include the TopMost property, which is used to ensure that the form always appears on top of other windows, even when it does not have focus, and the Opacity property, which can be used to make a form semitransparent.

Form Design Preferences

There are some Visual Studio IDE settings you can modify that will simplify your user interface design phase. In the Options dialog (shown in Figure 8-3) of Visual Studio 2008, two pages of preferences deal with the Windows Forms Designer.

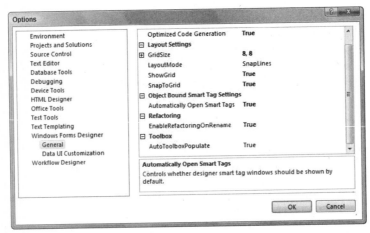

Figure 8-3

The main settings that affect your design are the layout settings. By default, Visual Studio 2008 uses a layout mode called SnapLines. Rather than position visible components on the form via an invisible grid, SnapLines helps you position them based on the context of surrounding controls and the form's own borders. You'll see how to use this new mode in a moment, but if you prefer the older style of form design that originated in Visual Basic 6 and was used in the first two versions of Visual Studio .NET, you can change the LayoutMode property to SnapToGrid.

> *The SnapToGrid layout mode is still used even if the LayoutMode is set to SnapLines. SnapLines becomes active only when you are positioning a control relative to another control. At other times, SnapToGrid will be active and will enable you to position the control on the grid vertex.*

The GridSize property is used for positioning and sizing controls on the form. As you move controls around the form, they will snap to specific points based on the values you enter here. Most of the time you'll find a grid of 8 × 8 (the default) too large for fine-tuning, so changing this to something such as 4 × 4 might be more appropriate.

Both SnapToGrid and SnapLines are aids for designing user interfaces using the mouse. Once the control has been roughly positioned, you can use the keyboard to fine-tune control positions by "nudging" the control with the arrow keys.

ShowGrid will display a network of dots on your form's design surface when you're in SnapToGrid mode so you can more easily see where the controls will be positioned when you move them. Finally, setting the SnapToGrid property to False will deactivate the layout aids for SnapToGrid mode and result in pure free-form form design.

While you're looking at this page of options, you may want to change the Automatically Open Smart Tags value to False. The default setting of True will pop open the smart tag task list associated with any control you add to the form, which can be distracting during your initial form design phase. Smart tags are discussed later in this chapter.

The other page of preferences that you can customize for the Windows Forms Designer is the Data UI Customization section. This will be discussed in Chapter 24.

Adding and Positioning Controls

You can add two types of controls to your Windows Forms: graphical components that actually reside on the form itself, and components that do not have a specific visual interface displaying on the form.

You add graphical controls to your form in one of two ways. The first is to locate the control you want to add in the Toolbox and double-click its entry. Visual Studio 2008 will place it in a default location on the form — the first control will be placed against the top and left borders of the form, with subsequent controls tiled down and to the right.

The second method is to click the entry on the list and drag it onto the form. As you drag over available space on the form, the mouse cursor will change to show you where the control will be positioned. This enables you to directly position the control where you want it, rather than first add it to the form and then move it to the desired location. Either way, once the control is on the form, you can move it as many times as you like, so it doesn't really matter how you get the control onto the form's design surface.

There is actually one other method to add controls to a form — copy and paste a control or set of controls from another form. If you paste multiple controls at once, the relative positioning and layout of the controls to each other will be preserved. Any property settings will also be preserved, although the control names may be changed.

When you design your form layouts in SnapLines mode (see previous section), a variety of guidelines will be displayed as you move controls around in the form layout. These guidelines are recommended "best practice" positioning and sizing markers, so you can easily position controls in relation to each other and the edge of the form.

Figure 8-4 shows a Button control being moved toward the top left corner of the form. As it gets near the recommended position, the control will snap to the exact recommended distance from the top and left borders, and small blue guidelines will be displayed.

Figure 8-4

These guidelines work for both positioning and sizing a control, enabling you to snap to any of the four borders of the form — but they're just the tip of the SnapLines iceberg. When additional components are present on the form, many more guidelines will begin to appear as you move a control around.

In Figure 8-5, you can see a second Button control being moved. The guideline on the left is the same as for the first button, indicating the ideal distance from the left border of the form. However, now three additional guidelines are displayed. A blue vertical line appears on either side of the control, confirming that the control is aligned with both the left and right sides of the other Button control already on the form (this is expected because the buttons are the same width). The other vertical line indicates the ideal gap between two buttons.

Figure 8-5

Vertically Aligning Text Controls

One problem with alignment of controls that, until recently, had persisted since the very early versions of Visual Basic was the vertical alignment of text within a control, such as a TextBox compared to a Label. The problem was that the text within each control was at a different vertical distance from the top border of the control, resulting in the text itself not aligning.

Many programmers went through the pain of calculating the appropriate number of pixels that one control or the other had to be shifted in order for the text portions to line up with each other (and more often than not it was a number of pixels that was smaller than the grid size, resulting in manual positioning via the Properties window or in code).

As shown in Figure 8-6, an additional guideline is now available for lining up controls that have text associated with them. In this example, the Cell Phone label is being lined up with the textbox containing the actual Cell Phone value. A line, colored magenta by default, appears and snaps the control in place. You can still align the label to the top or bottom border of the textbox by shifting it slightly and snapping it to its guideline, but this new guideline takes the often painful guesswork out of lining up text.

Note that the other guidelines show that the label is horizontally aligned with the Label controls above it, and that it is positioned the recommended distance from the textbox.

Figure 8-6

Automatic Positioning of Multiple Controls

Visual Studio 2008 gives you additional tools to automatically format the appearance of your controls once they are positioned approximately where you want them. The Format menu, shown in Figure 8-7, is normally accessible only when you're in the Design view of a form. From here you can have the IDE automatically align, resize, and position groups of controls, as well as set the order of the controls in the event that they overlap each other. These commands are also available via the design toolbar and keyboard shortcuts.

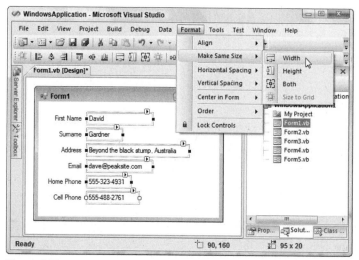

Figure 8-7

The form displayed in Figure 8-7 contains several TextBox controls, all with differing widths. This looks messy and we should clean it up by setting them all to the same width as the widest control. The Format menu enables you to automatically resize the controls to the same width, using the Make Same Size ⇨ Width command.

> *The commands in the Make Same Size menu use the first control selected as the template for the dimensions. You can first select the control to use as the template and then add to the selection by holding the Ctrl key down and clicking each of the other controls. Alternatively, once all controls are the same size, you can simply ensure they are still selected and resize the group at the same time with the mouse.*

Automatic alignment of multiple controls can be performed in the same way. First, select the item whose border should be used as a base, and then select all the other elements that should be aligned with it. Next select Format ⇨ Align and choose which alignment should be performed. In this example the Label controls have all been positioned with their right edges aligned. We could have done this using the guidelines, but sometimes it's easier to use this mass alignment option.

Two other handy functions are the Horizontal Spacing and Vertical Spacing commands. These will automatically adjust the spacing between a set of controls according to the particular option you have selected.

Locking Control Design

Once you're happy with your form design you will want to start applying changes to the various controls and their properties. However, in the process of selecting controls on the form you may inadvertently move a control from its desired position, particularly if you're not using either of the snap layout methods or if you are trying to align many controls with each other.

Fortunately, Visual Studio 2008 provides a solution in the form of the Lock Controls command, available in the Format menu. When controls are locked you can select them to set their properties, but you cannot use the mouse to move or resize them, or the form itself. The location of the controls can still be changed via the Properties grid.

Figure 8-8 shows how small padlock icons are displayed on controls that are selected while the Lock Controls feature is active.

Figure 8-8

You can also lock controls individually by setting the Locked property of the control to True in the Properties window.

Setting Control Properties

You can set the properties on controls using the Properties window, just as you would a form's settings. In addition to simple text value properties, Visual Studio 2008 has a number of property editor types, which aid you in setting the values efficiently by restricting them to a particular subset appropriate to the type of property.

Many advanced properties have a set of subordinate properties that you can individually access by expanding the entry in the Properties window. Figure 8-9 (left) displays the Properties window for a label, with the Font property expanded to show the individual properties available.

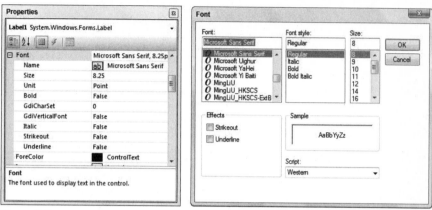

Figure 8-9

Many properties also provide extended editors, as is the case for Font properties. In Figure 8-9 (right), an extended editor button in the Font property has been selected, causing the Choose Font dialog to appear.

Some of these extended editors invoke full-blown wizards, such as in the case of the Data Connection on some data-bound components, while others have custom-built inline property editors. An example of this is the Dock property, for which you can choose a visual representation of how you want the property docked to the containing component or form.

Service-Based Components

As mentioned earlier in this chapter, two kinds of components can be added to your Windows Forms — those with visual aspects and those without. Service-based components, such as timers and dialogs, and extender controls, such as tooltip and error-provider components, can all be used to enhance the application.

Rather than place these components on the form, when you double-click one in the Toolbox, or drag and drop it onto the design surface, Visual Studio 2008 will create a tray area below the Design view of the form and put the new instance of the component type there, as shown in Figure 8-10.

Figure 8-10

To edit the properties of one of these controls, locate its entry in the tray area and open the Properties window.

> *In the same way that you can create your own custom visual controls by inheriting from* System.Windows.Forms.Control, *you can create nonvisual service components by inheriting from* System.ComponentModel.Component. *In fact,* System.ComponentModel.Component *is the base class for* System.Windows.Forms.Control.

Smart Tag Tasks

Smart tag technology was introduced in Microsoft Office. It provides inline shortcuts to a small selection of actions you can perform on a particular element. In Microsoft Word, this might be a word or phrase, while in Microsoft Excel it could be a spreadsheet cell. Visual Studio 2008 supports the concept of design-time smart tags for a number of the controls available to you as a developer.

Whenever a selected control has a smart tag available, a small right-pointing arrow will be displayed on the top right corner of the control itself. Clicking this smart tag indicator will open up a Tasks menu associated with that particular control.

Figure 8-11 shows the tasks for a newly added DataGridView control. The various actions that can be taken usually mirror properties available to you in the Properties window (such as the `Multiline` option for a TextBox control), but sometimes they provide quick access to more advanced settings for the component.

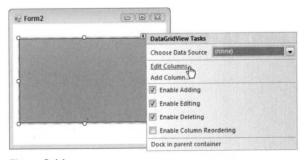

Figure 8-11

The Edit Columns and Add Column commands shown in Figure 8-11 are not listed in the DataGridView's Properties list, while the Choose Data Source and Enable settings directly correlate to individual properties (for example, Enable Adding is equivalent to the `AllowUserToAddRows` property).

Container Controls

Several controls, known as *container controls,* are designed specifically to help you with your form's layout and appearance. Rather than have their own appearance, they hold other controls within their bounds. Once a container houses a set of controls, you no longer need to move the child controls individually, but can instead just move the container. Using a combination of `Dock` and `Anchor` values, you can have whole sections of your form's layout automatically redesign themselves at runtime in response to the resizing of the form and the container controls that hold them.

Panel and SplitContainer

The Panel control is used to group components that are associated with each other. When placed on a form, it can be sized and positioned anywhere within the form's design surface. Because it's a container control, clicking within its boundaries will select anything inside it. In order to move it, Visual Studio 2008 places a move icon at the top left corner of the control. Clicking and dragging this icon enables you to reposition the Panel.

The SplitContainer control (shown in Figure 8-12) automatically creates two Panel controls when added to a form (or another container control). It divides the space into two sections, each of which you can control individually. At runtime, users can resize the two spaces by dragging the splitter bar that divides them. SplitContainers can be either vertical (as in Figure 8-12) or horizontal, and they can be contained with other SplitContainer controls to form a complex layout that can then be easily customized by the end user without your needing to write any code.

Sometimes it's hard to select the actual container control when it contains other components, such as in the case of the SplitContainer housing the two Panel controls. To gain direct access to the SplitContainer control itself, you can either locate it in the drop-down list in the Properties window, or right-click one of the Panel controls and choose the Select command that corresponds to the SplitContainer. This context menu will contain a Select command for every container control in the hierarchy of containers, right up to the form itself.

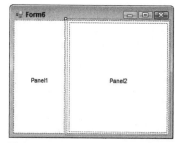

Figure 8-12

FlowLayoutPanel

The FlowLayoutPanel control enables you to create form designs with a behavior similar to that of web browsers. Rather than explicitly positioning each control within this particular container control, Visual Studio will simply set each component you add to the next available space. By default, the controls will flow from left to right, and then from top to bottom, but you can use the FlowDirection property to reverse this order in any configuration, depending on the requirements of your application.

Figure 8-13 displays the same form with six button controls housed within a FlowLayoutPanel container. The FlowLayoutPanel was set to fill the entire form's design surface, so that as the form is resized the container is also automatically resized. As the form gets wider and space becomes available, the controls begin to be realigned to flow left to right before descending down the form.

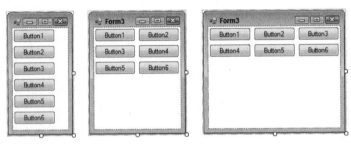

Figure 8-13

TableLayoutPanel

An alternative to the previously discussed container controls is the TableLayoutPanel container. It works much like a table in Microsoft Word or in a typical web browser, with each cell acting as an individual container for a single control.

Note that you cannot add multiple controls within a single cell directly. You can, however, place another container control such as a Panel within the cell, and then place the required components within that child container.

Placing a control directly into a cell will automatically position the control to the top left corner of the table cell. You can use the Dock property to override this behavior and position it as required. The Dock property is discussed further later in this chapter.

The TableLayoutPanel container enables you to easily create a structured, formal layout in your form with advanced features, such as the capability to automatically grow by adding more rows as additional child controls are added.

Figure 8-14 shows a form with a TableLayoutPanel added to the design surface. The smart tag tasks were then opened and the Edit Rows and Columns command executed. As a result, the Column and Row Styles dialog is displayed so you can adjust the individual formatting options for each column and row. The dialog displays several tips for designing table layouts in your forms, including spanning multiple rows and columns and how to align controls within a cell. You can change the way the cells are sized here, as well as add or remove additional columns and rows.

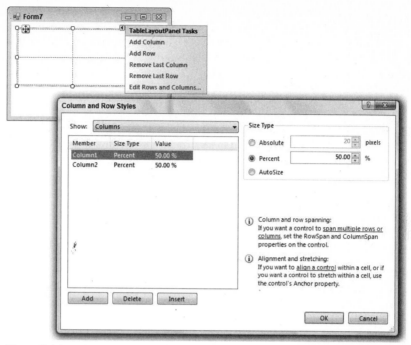

Figure 8-14

Docking and Anchoring Controls

It's not enough to design layouts that are nicely aligned according to the design-time dimensions. At runtime a user will likely resize the form, and ideally the controls on our form will resize automatically to fill the modified space. The control properties that have the most impact on this are Dock and Anchor. Figure 8-15 (left) and 8-15 (right) show how the controls on a Windows Form will properly resize once you have set the correct Dock and Anchor property values.

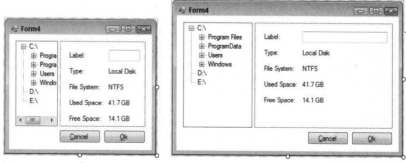

Figure 8-15

The Dock property controls which borders of the control are bound to the container. For example, in Figure 8-15 (left), the TreeView control Dock property has been set to fill the left panel of a SplitContainer, effectively docking it to all four borders. Therefore, no matter how large or small the left-hand side of the SplitContainer is made, the TreeView control will always resize itself to fill the available space.

The Anchor property defines the edges of the container to which the control is bound. In Figure 8-15 (left), the two button controls have been anchored to the bottom right of the form. When the form is resized, as shown in 8-15 (right), the button controls maintain the same distance to the bottom right of the form. Similarly, the TextBox control has been anchored to the left and right borders, which means that it will automatically grow or shrink as the form is resized.

Summary

In this chapter you developed a good understanding of how Visual Studio can help you to quickly design the layout of Windows Forms applications. The various controls and their properties enable you to quickly and easily create complex layouts that can respond to user interaction in many ways. In later chapters you will learn about the specifics of designing the user interfaces for other application platforms, including Office Add-Ins, Web, and WPF applications.

9

Documentation Using Comments and Sandcastle

Documentation is a critical, and often overlooked, feature of the development process. Without documentation, other programmers, code reviewers, and management have a more difficult time analyzing the purpose and implementation of code. You can even have problems with your own code once it becomes complex, and having good internal documentation can aid in the development process.

XML comments are a way of providing that internal documentation for your code without having to go through the process of manually creating and maintaining documents. Instead, as you write your code, you include *metadata* at the top of every definition to explain the intent of your code. Once the information has been included in your code, it can be consumed by Visual Studio to provide Object Browser and IntelliSense information.

Sandcastle is a set of tools that act as documentation compilers. These tools can be used to easily create very professional-looking external documentation in Microsoft-compiled HTML help (.CHM) or Microsoft Help 2 (.HxS) format from the XML comments you have added to your code.

Inline Commenting

All programming languages supported by Visual Studio provide a method for adding inline documentation. By default, all inline comments are highlighted in green.

Visual Basic .NET uses a single quote character to denote anything following it to be a comment, as shown in the following code listing:

```
Public Sub New(ByVal Username As String, ByVal Password As String)
    ' This call is required by the Windows Form Designer.
    InitializeComponent()
    ' Perform the rest of the class initialization, which for now
    ' means we just save the parameters to private data members
    _username = Username 'This includes the domain name
    _password = Password
End Sub
```

C# supports both single-line comments and comment blocks. Single-line comments are denoted by // at the beginning of the comment. Block comments typically span multiple lines and are opened by /* and closed off by */, as shown in the following code listing:

```
public UserRights(string Username, string Password)
{
    // This call is required by the Windows Form Designer.
    InitializeComponent();
    /*
     *  Perform the rest of the class initialization, which for now
     *  means we just save the parameters to private data members
     */
    _username = Username; //This includes the domain name
    _password = Password;
}
```

XML Comments

XML comments are specialized comments that you include in your code listings. When the project goes through the build process, Visual Studio can optionally include a step to generate an XML file based on these comments to provide information about user-defined types such as classes and individual members of a class (user-defined or not), including events, functions, and properties.

XML comments can contain any combination of XML and HTML tags. Visual Studio will perform special processing on a particular set of predefined tags, as you'll see throughout the bulk of this chapter. Any other tags will be included in the generated documentation file as is.

Adding XML Comments

XML comments are added immediately before the property, method, or class definition they are associated with. Visual Studio will automatically add an XML comment block when you type the shortcut code /// in C# before a member or class declaration. In some cases the XML comments will already be present in code generated by the supplied project templates, as you can see in Figure 9-1.

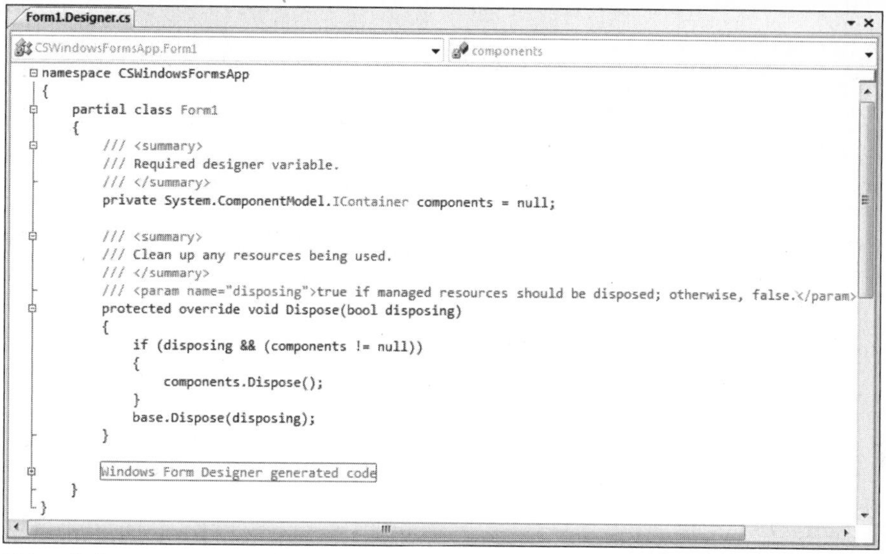

Figure 9-1

The automatic insertion of the summary section can be turned off on the Advanced page for C# in the Text Editor group of options.

Adding an XML comment block to Visual Basic is achieved by using the ''' shortcut code. In this way it replicates the way C# documentation is generated.

In both languages, once the comments have been added, Visual Studio will automatically add a collapsible region to the left margin so you can hide the documentation when you're busy writing code. Hovering over the collapsed area will display a tooltip message containing the first few lines of the comment block.

XML Comment Tags

Though you can use any kind of XML comment structure you like, including your own custom XML tags, Visual Studio's XML comment processor recognizes a number of predefined tags and will automatically format them appropriately. The Sandcastle document generator has support for a number of additional tags, and you can supplement these further with your own XML schema document.

If you need to use angle brackets in the text of a documentation comment, use the entity references < and >.

Because documentation is so important, the next section of this chapter details each of these predefined tags, their syntax, and how you would use them in your own documentation.

The <c> Tag

The <c> tag indicates that the enclosed text should be formatted as code, rather than normal text. It's used for code that is included in a normal text block. The structure of <c> is simple, with any text appearing between the opening and closing tags being marked for formatting in the code style:

```
<c>code-formatted text</c>
```

The following example shows how <c> might be used in the description of a subroutine in C#:

```
/// <summary>
/// The <c>sender</c> object is used to identify who invoked the procedure.
/// </summary>
private void MyLoad(object sender)
{
    //...code...
}
```

The <code> Tag

If the amount of text in the documentation you need to format as code is more than just a phrase within a normal text block, you can use the <code> tag instead of <c>. This tag marks everything within it as code, but it's a block-level tag, rather than a character-level tag. The syntax of this tag is a simple opening and closing tag with the text to be formatted inside, as shown here:

```
<code>
Code-formatted text
Code-formatted text
</code>
```

The <code> tag can be embedded inside any other XML comment tag. The following listing shows an example of how it could be used in the summary section of a property definition in Visual Basic:

```
''' <summary>
''' The <c>MyName</c> property is used in conjunction with other properties
''' to setup a user properly. Remember to include the <c>MyPassword</c> field too:
''' <code>
''' theObject.MyName = "Name"
''' theObject.MyPassword = "x4*@v"
''' </code>
''' </summary>
Public ReadOnly Property MyName() As String
    Get
        Return mMyName
    End Get
End Property
```

The <example> Tag

A common requirement for internal documentation is to provide an example of how a particular procedure or member can be used. The <example> tags indicate that the enclosed block should be treated as a discrete section of the documentation, dealing with a sample for the associated member.

Effectively, this doesn't do anything more than help organize the documentation, but used in conjunction with an appropriately designed XML style sheet or processing instructions, the example can be formatted properly.

The other XML comment tags, such as `<c>` and `<code>`, can be included in the text inside the `<example>` tags to give you a comprehensively documented sample. The syntax of this block-level tag is simple:

```
<example>
Any sample text goes here.
</example>
```

Using the example from the previous discussion, the following listing moves the `<code>` formatted text to an `<example>` section:

```
'''  <summary>
'''  The <c>MyName</c> property is the name of the user logging on to the system.
'''  </summary>
'''  <example>
'''  The <c>MyName</c> property is used in conjunction with other properties
'''  to setup a user properly. Remember to include the <c>MyPassword</c> field too:
'''  <code>
'''  theObject.MyName = "Name"
'''  theObject.MyPassword = "x4*@v"
'''  </code>
'''  </example>
Public ReadOnly Property MyName() As String
    Get
        Return mMyName
    End Get
End Property
```

The `<exception>` Tag

The `<exception>` tag is used to define any exceptions that could be thrown from within the member associated with the current block of XML documentation. Each exception that can be thrown should be defined with its own `<exception>` block, with an attribute of `cref` identifying the fully qualified type name of an exception that could be thrown. Note that the Visual Studio 2008 XML comment processor will check the syntax of the exception block to enforce the inclusion of this attribute. It will also ensure that you don't have multiple `<exception>` blocks with the same attribute value. The full syntax is as follows:

```
<exception cref="exceptionName">
Exception description.
</exception>
```

Extending the Visual Basic example from the previous tag discussions, the following listing adds two exception definitions to the XML comments associated with the `MyName` property: `System.TimeoutException` and `System.UnauthorizedAccessException`.

```
'''  <summary>
'''  The <c>MyName</c> property is the name of the user logging on to the system.
'''  </summary>
'''  <exception cref="System.TimeoutException">
'''  Thrown when the code cannot determine if the user is valid within a reasonable
'''  amount of time.
'''  </exception>
'''  <exception cref="System.UnauthorizedAccessException">
'''  Thrown when the user identifier is not valid within the current context.
'''  </exception>
'''  <example>
'''  The <c>MyName</c> property is used in conjunction with other properties
'''  to setup a user properly. Remember to include the <c>MyPassword</c> field too:
'''  <code>
'''  theObject.MyName = "Name"
'''  theObject.MyPassword = "x4*@v"
'''  </code>
'''  </example>
Public ReadOnly Property MyName() As String
    Get
        Return mMyName
    End Get
End Property
```

There is no way in .NET to force developers to handle a particular exception when they call a method or property. Adding the <exception> *tag to a method is a good way to indicate to developers using the method that they should handle certain exceptions.*

The <include> Tag

You'll often have documentation that needs to be shared across multiple projects. In other situations, one person may be responsible for the documentation while others are doing the coding. Either way, the <include> tag will prove useful. The <include> tag enables you to refer to comments in a separate XML file so they are brought inline with the rest of your documentation. Using this method, you can move the actual documentation out of the code listing, which can be handy when the comments are extensive.

The syntax of <include> requires that you specify which part of the external file is to be used in the current context. The path attribute is used to identify the path to the XML node, and uses standard XPath terminology:

```
<include file="filename" path="XPathQuery" />
```

The external XML file containing the additional documentation must have a path that can be navigated with the attribute you specify, with the end node containing an attribute of name to uniquely identify the specific section of the XML document to be included.

You can include files in either Visual Basic or C# using the same tag. The following listing takes the C# sample used in the <c> tag discussion and moves the documentation to an external file:

```
/// <include file="externalFile.xml" path="MyDoc/Procedures[@name='MyLoad']/*" />
private void MyLoad(object sender)
{
    ...code...
}
```

The external file's contents would be populated with the following XML document structure to synchronize it with what the <include> tag processing expects to find:

```
<MyDoc>
    <Procedures name="MyLoad">
        <summary>
            The <c>sender</c> object is used to identify who invoked the procedure.
        </summary>
    </Procedures>
</MyDoc>
```

The <list> Tag

Some documentation requires lists of various descriptions, and with the <list> tag you can generate numbered and unnumbered lists along with two-column tables. All three take two parameters for each entry in the list — a term and a description — represented by individual XML tags, but they instruct the processor to generate the documentation in different ways.

To create a list in the documentation, use the following syntax, where type can be one of the following values — bullet, numbered, or table:

```
<list type="type">
    <listheader>
        <term>termName</term>
        <description>description</description>
    </listheader>
    <item>
        <term>myTerm</term>
        <description>myDescription</description>
    </item>
</list>
```

The <listheader> block is optional, and is usually used for table-formatted lists or definition lists. For definition lists the <term> tag must be included, but for bullet lists, numbered lists, or tables the <term> tag can be omitted.

The XML for each type of list can be formatted differently using an XML style sheet. An example of how to use the `<list>` tag in Visual Basic appears in the following code. Note how the sample has omitted the `listheader` tag, because it was unnecessary for the bullet list:

```
''' <summary>
''' Some function.
''' </summary>
''' <returns>
''' This function returns either:
''' <list type="bullet">
''' <item>
''' <term>True</term>
''' <description>Indicates that the routine was executed successfully.
''' </description>
''' </item>
''' <item>
''' <term>False</term>
''' <description>Indicates that the routine functionality failed.</description>
''' </item>
''' </list>
''' </returns>
Public Function MyFunction() As Boolean
    '...code...
    Return False
End Function
```

The <para> Tag

Without using the various internal block-level XML comments such as `<list>` and `<code>`, the text you add to the main `<summary>`, `<remarks>`, and `<returns>` sections all just runs together. To break it up into readable chunks, you can use the `<para>` tag, which simply indicates that the text enclosed should be treated as a discrete paragraph. The syntax is simple:

```
<para>This text will appear in a separate paragraph.</para>
```

The <param> Tag

To explain the purpose of any parameters in a function declaration, you can use the `<param>` tag. This tag will be processed by the Visual Studio XML comment processor with each instance requiring a name attribute that has a value equal to the name of one of the properties. Enclosed within the opening and closing `<param>` tags is the description of the parameter:

```
<param name="parameterName">Definition of parameter.</param>
```

The XML processor will not allow you to create multiple `<param>` tags for the one parameter, or tags for parameters that don't exist, producing warnings that are added to the Error List in Visual Studio if you try. The following Visual Basic example shows how the `<param>` tag is used to describe two parameters of a function:

```
''' <param name="MyName">The Name of the user to log on.</param>
''' <param name="MyPassword">The Password of the user to log on.</param>
Public Function LoginProc(ByVal MyName As String, ByVal MyPassword As String) _
    As Boolean
```

```
    '...code...
    Return False
End Function
```

The <param> tag is especially useful for documenting preconditions for a method's parameters, such as if a null value is not allowed.

The <paramref> Tag

If you are referring to the parameters of the method definition elsewhere in the documentation other than the <param> tag, you can use the <paramref> tag to format the value, or even link to the parameter information depending on how you code the XML transformation. The compiler does not require that the name of the parameter exist, but you must specify the text to be used in the name attribute, as the following syntax shows:

```
<paramref name="parameterName" />
```

Normally, <paramref> tags are used when you are referring to parameters in the larger sections of documentation such as the <summary> or <remarks> tags, as the following C# example demonstrates:

```
/// <summary>
/// The <paramref name="sender" /> object is used to identify who
/// invoked the procedure.
/// </summary>
/// <param name="sender">Who invoked this routine</param>
/// <param name="e">Any additional arguments to this instance of the event.</param>
private void Form1_Load(object sender, EventArgs e)
{

}
```

The <permission> Tag

To describe the code access security permission set required by a particular method, use the <permission> tag. This tag requires a cref attribute to refer to a specific permission type:

```
''' <permission cref="permissionName">
''' description goes here
''' </permission>
```

If the function requires more than one permission, use multiple <permission> blocks, as shown in the following Visual Basic example:

```
''' <permission cref="System.Security.Permissions.RegistryPermission">
''' Needs full access to the Windows Registry.
''' </permission>
''' <permission cref="System.Security.Permissions.FileIOPermission">
''' Needs full access to the .config file containing application information.
''' </permission>
Public Function LoginProc(ByVal MyName As String, ByVal MyPassword As String) _
    As Boolean
    '...code...
    Return False
End Function
```

The <remarks> Tag

The <remarks> tag is used to add an additional comment block to the documentation associated with a particular method. Discussion on previous tags has shown the <remarks> tag in action, but the syntax is as follows:

```
<remarks>
Any further remarks go here
</remarks>
```

Normally, you would create a summary section, briefly outline the method or type, and then include the detailed information inside the <remarks> tag, with the expected outcomes of accessing the member.

The <returns> Tag

When a method returns a value to the calling code, you can use the <returns> tag to describe what it could be. The syntax of <returns> is like most of the other block-level tags, consisting of an opening and closing tag with any information detailing the return value enclosed within:

```
<returns>
Description of the return value.
</returns>
```

A simple implementation of <returns> in Visual Basic might appear like the following code:

```
''' <returns>
''' This function returns either:
''' <c>True</c> which indicates that the routine was executed successfully,
''' or <c>False</c> which indicates that the routine functionality failed.
''' </returns>
Public Function MyFunction() As Boolean
    '...code...
    Return False
End Function
```

In addition to the return value of a function, the <returns> tag is especially useful for documenting any post-conditions that should be expected.

The <see> Tag

You can add references to other items in the project using the <see> tag. Like some of the other tags already discussed, the <see> tag requires a cref attribute with a value equal to an existing member, whether it is a property, method, or class definition. The XML processor will produce a warning if a member does not exist. The <see> tag is used inline with other areas of the documentation such as <summary> or <remarks>. The syntax is as follows:

```
<see cref="memberName" />
```

When Visual Studio processes the <see> tag, it produces a fully qualified address that can then be used as the basis for a link in the documentation when transformed via style sheets. For example, referring to an application with a form containing a property named MyName would result in the following cref value:

```
<see cref="applicationName.formName.CheckUser"/>
```

The following example uses the <see> tag in a Visual Basic code listing to provide a link to another function called CheckUser. If this function does not exist, Visual Studio will use IntelliSense to display a warning and add it to the Error List:

```
''' <param name="MyName">The name of the user to log in.</param>
''' <param name="MyPassword">The password of the user to log in.</param>
''' <returns><c>True</c> if login attempt was successful, otherwise returns
''' <c>False</c>.</returns>
''' <remarks>
''' Use <see cref="CheckUser" /> to verify that the user exists
''' before calling LoginProc.
''' </remarks>
Public Function LoginProc(ByVal MyName As String, ByVal MyPassword As String) _
    As Boolean
    '...code...
    Return False
End Function
```

The <seealso> Tag

The <seealso> tag is used to generate a separate section containing information about related topics within the documentation. Rather than being inline like <see>, the <seealso> tags are defined outside the other XML comment blocks, with each instance of <seealso> requiring a cref attribute containing the name of the property, method, or class to link to. The full syntax appears like so:

```
<seealso cref="memberName" />
```

Modifying the previous example, the next listing shows how the <seealso> tag can be implemented in Visual Basic code:

```
''' <param name="MyName">The name of the user to log in.</param>
''' <param name="MyPassword">The password of the user to log in.</param>
''' <returns><c>True</c> if login attempt was successful, otherwise returns
''' <c>False</c>.</returns>
''' <remarks>
''' Use <see cref="CheckUser" /> to verify that the user exists
''' before calling LoginProc.
''' </remarks>
''' <seealso cref="MyName" />
''' <seealso cref="MyPassword" />
Public Function LoginProc(ByVal MyName As String, ByVal MyPassword As String) _
    As Boolean
    '...code...
    Return False
End Function
```

The <summary> Tag

The <summary> tag is used to provide the brief description that appears at the top of a specific topic in the documentation. As such it is typically placed before all public and protected elements. In addition, the `<summary>` area is used for Visual Studio's IntelliSense engine when using your own custom-built code. The syntax to implement `<summary>` is as follows:

```
<summary>
Text goes here.
</summary>
```

The `<typeparam>` Tag

The `<typeparam>` tag provides information about the type parameters when dealing with a generic type or member definition. The `<typeparam>` tag expects an attribute of `name` containing the type parameter being referred to:

```
<typeparam name="typeName">
Description.
</typeparam>
```

You can use `<typeparam>` in either C# or Visual Basic, as the following listing shows:

```
''' <typeparam name="T">
''' Base item type (must implement IComparable)
''' </typeparam>
Public Class myList(Of T As IComparable)
      ' code.
End Class
```

The `<typeparamref>` Tag

If you are referring to a generic type parameter elsewhere in the documentation other than the `<typeparam>` tag, you can use the `<typeparamref>` tag to format the value, or even link to the parameter information depending on how you code the XML transformation:

```
<typeparamref name="parameterName" />
```

Normally, `<typeparamref>` tags are used when you are referring to parameters in the larger sections of documentation such as the `<summary>` or `<remarks>` tags, as the following listing demonstrates:

```
''' <summary>
''' Creates a new list of arbitrary type <typeparamref name="T"/>
''' </summary>
''' <typeparam name="T">
''' Base item type (must implement IComparable)
''' </typeparam>
Public Class myList(Of T As IComparable)
      ' code.
End Class
```

The `<value>` Tag

Normally used to define a property's purpose, the `<value>` tag gives you another section in the XML where you can provide information about the associated member. The value tag is not used by IntelliSense.

```
<value>The text to display</value>
```

When used in conjunction with a property, you would normally use the `<summary>` tag to describe what the property is for, whereas the `<value>` tag is used to describe what the property represents:

```
/// <summary>
/// The Username property represents the currently logged on users logonid
/// </summary>
/// <value>
/// The Username property gets/sets the _username private data member
/// </value>
public string Username
{
    get { return _username; }
    set { _username = value; }
}
```

Using XML Comments

Once you have the XML comments inline with your code, you'll most likely want to generate an XML file containing the documentation. In Visual Basic this setting is on by default, with an output path and filename specified with default values. However, C# has the option turned off as its default behavior, so if you want documentation you'll need to turn it on manually.

To ensure that your documentation is being generated where you require, open the property pages for the project through the Solution Explorer's right-click context menu. Locate the project for which you want documentation, right-click its entry in the Solution Explorer, and select Properties. Alternatively, in Visual Basic you can simply double-click the My Project entry in the Solution Explorer.

The XML documentation options are located in the Build section (see Figure 9-2). Below the general build options is an Output section that contains a checkbox that enables XML-documentation file generation. When this checkbox is enabled, the text field next to it becomes available for you to specify the filename for the XML file that will be generated.

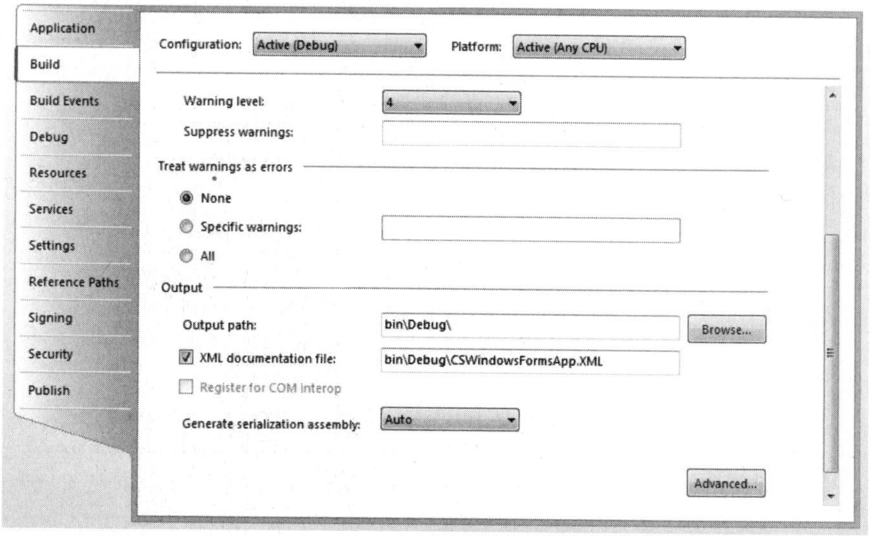

Figure 9-2

Once you've saved these options, the next time you perform a build, Visual Studio will add the `/doc` compiler option to the process so that the XML documentation is generated as specified.

The XML file that is generated will contain a full XML document that you can apply XSL transformations against, or process through another application using the XML Document Object Model. All references to exceptions, parameters, methods, and other "see also" links will be included as fully addressed information, including namespace, application, and class data. Later in this chapter you see how you can make use of this XML file to produce professional-looking documentation using Sandcastle.

IntelliSense Information

The other useful advantage of using XML comments is how Visual Studio 2008 consumes them in its own IntelliSense engine. As soon as you define the documentation tags that Visual Studio understands, it will generate the information into its IntelliSense, which means you can refer to the information elsewhere in your code.

IntelliSense can be accessed in two ways. If the member referred to is within the same project or is in another project within the same solution, you can access the information without having to build or generate the XML file. However, you can still take advantage of IntelliSense even when the project is external to your current application solution.

The trick is to ensure that when the XML file is generated by the build process, it has the same name as the .NET assembly being built. For example, if the compiled output is `myApplication.exe`, then the associated XML file should be named `myApplication.xml`. In addition, this generated XML file should be in the same folder as the compiled assembly so that Visual Studio can locate it.

Sandcastle Documentation Generation Tools

Sandcastle is a set of tools published by Microsoft that act as documentation compilers. These tools can be used to easily create very professional-looking external documentation in Microsoft-compiled HTML help (.CHM) or Microsoft Help 2 (.HxS) format. At the time of writing, Sandcastle was still beta software and had been released only as a Community Technology Preview (CTP).

> *NDoc, an open source project, is another well-known documentation generator. Although NDoc was widely used, it never gained much financial or contributor support as an open source project. In June 2006, the creator of NDoc, Kevin Downs, announced he was discontinuing work on the project.*

The primary location for information on Sandcastle is the Sandcastle blog at `http://blogs.msdn.com/sandcastle/`. There is also a project on CodePlex, Microsoft's open-source project hosting site, at `www.codeplex.com/Sandcastle/`. You can find a discussion forum and a link to download the latest Sandcastle installer package on this site.

By default, Sandcastle installs to `c:\Program Files\Sandcastle`. When it is run, Sandcastle creates a large number of working files and the final output file under this directory. Unfortunately all files and folders under Program Files require administrator permissions to write to, which can be problematic particularly if you are running on Windows Vista with UAC enabled. Therefore it is recommended that you install it to a location where your user account has write permissions.

Out of the box, Sandcastle is used from the command-line only. There are a number of third parties who have put together GUI interfaces for Sandcastle, which are linked to on the Wiki.

To begin, open a Visual Studio 2008 Command Prompt from Start Menu ⇨ All Programs ⇨ Microsoft Visual Studio 2008 ⇨ Visual Studio Tools, and change the directory to `<Sandcastle Install Directory>\Examples\sandcastle\`.

> *The Visual Studio 2008 Command Prompt is equivalent to a normal command prompt except that it also sets various environment variables, such as directory search paths, which are often required by the Visual Studio 2008 command-line tools.*

In this directory you will find an example class file, test.cs, and an MSBuild project file, build.proj. The example class file contains methods and properties that are commented with all of the standard XML comment tags that were explained earlier in this chapter. You can compile the class file and generate the XML documentation file by entering the command:

```
csc /t:library test.cs /doc:example.xml
```

Once that has completed, we are now ready to generate the documentation help file. The simplest way to do this is to execute the example MSBuild project file that ships with Sandcastle. This project file has been hard-coded to generate the documentation using `test.dll` and `example.xml`. Run the MSBuild project by entering the command:

```
msbuild build.proj
```

The MSBuild project will call several Sandcastle tools to build the documentation file, including MRefBuilder, BuildAssembler, and XslTransform.

You may be surprised at how long the documentation takes to generate. This is partly because the MRefBuilder tool uses reflection to inspect the assembly and all dependent assemblies to obtain information about all of the types, properties, and methods in the assembly and all dependent assemblies. In addition, anytime it comes across a base .NET Framework type, it will attempt to resolve it to the MSDN online documentation in order to generate the correct hyperlinks in the documentation help file.

> *The first time you run the MSBuild project, it will generate reflection data for all of the .NET Framework classes, so you can expect it to take even longer to complete.*

By default, the build.proj MSBuild project generates the documentation with the *vs2005* look-and-feel, as shown in Figure 9-3, in the directory `<Sandcastle Install Directory>\Examples\sandcastle\chm\`. You can choose a different output style by adding one of the following options to the command line:

```
/property:PresentationStyle=vs2005
/property:PresentationStyle=hana
/property:PresentationStyle=prototype
```

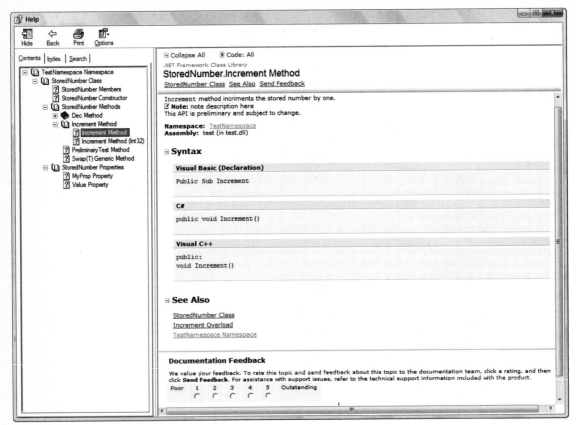

Figure 9-3

The following listing shows the source code section from the example class file, test.cs, which relates to the page of the help documentation shown in Figure 9-3:

```
/// <summary><c>Increment</c> method increments the stored number by one.
/// <note type="caution">
/// note description here
/// </note>
/// <preliminary/>
/// </summary>
public void Increment()
{
    number++;
}
```

The default target for the build.proj MSBuild project is "Chm", which builds a CHM-compiled HTML Help file for the test.dll assembly. You can also specify one of the following targets on the command line:

```
/target:Clean  - removes all generated files
/target:HxS    - builds HxS file for Visual Studio in addition to CHM
```

The Microsoft Help 2 (.HxS) is the format that the Visual Studio help system uses. You must install the Microsoft Help 2.x SDK in order to generate .HxS files. This is available and included as part of the Visual Studio 2008 SDK.

Task List Comments

The Task List window is a feature of Visual Studio 2008 that allows you to keep track of any coding tasks or outstanding activities you have to do. Tasks can be manually entered as User Tasks, or automatically detected from the inline comments. The Task window can be opened by selecting View ⇨ Task List, or by using the keyboard shortcut CTRL+\, CTRL+T. Figure 9-4 shows the Task List window with some User Tasks defined.

User Tasks are saved in the solution user options (.suo) file, which contains user-specific settings and preferences. It is not recommended that you check this file into source control, and as such, User Tasks cannot be shared by multiple developers working on the same solution.

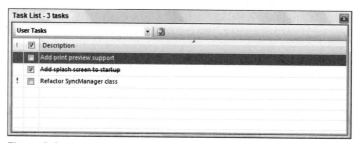

Figure 9-4

The Task List has a filter in the top-left corner that toggles the listing between Comment Tasks and manually entered User Tasks.

When you add a comment into your code with text that begins with a *comment token*, the comment will be added to the Task List as a Comment Task. The default comment tokens that are included with Visual Studio 2008 are TODO, HACK, UNDONE, and UnresolvedMergeConflict.

The following code listing shows a TODO comment. Figure 9-5 shows how this comment appears as a Task in the Task List window. You can double-click the Task List entry to go directly to the comment line in your code.

```
using System;
using System.Windows.Forms;

namespace CSWindowsFormsApp
{
    public partial class Form1 : Form
    {
        public Form1()
        {
```

(continued)

(continued)

```
        InitializeComponent();

        //TODO: The database should be intialized here
    }

  }
}
```

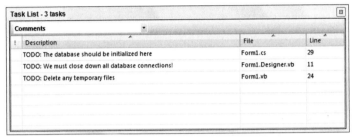

Figure 9-5

The list of comment tokens can be edited from an Options page under Tools ⇨ Options ⇨ Environment ⇨ Task List, as shown in Figure 9-6. Each token can be assigned a priority — Low, Normal, High. The default token is TODO and it cannot be renamed or deleted. You can, however, adjust its priority.

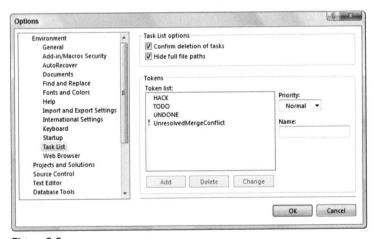

Figure 9-6

In addition to User Tasks and Comments, you can also add shortcuts to code within the Task List. To create a Task List Shortcut, place the cursor on the location for the shortcut within the code editor and select Edit ⇨ Bookmarks ⇨ Add Task List Shortcut. This will place an arrow icon in the gutter of the code editor, as shown in Figure 9-7.

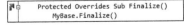

Figure 9-7

If you now go to the Task List window you will see a new category called Shortcuts listed in the drop-down list. By default the description for the shortcut will contain the line of code (see Figure 9-8); however, you can edit this and enter whatever text you like. Double-clicking an entry will take you to the shortcut location in the code editor.

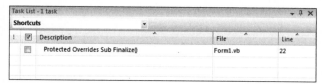

Figure 9-8

As with User Tasks, Shortcuts are stored in the .suo file, and therefore aren't checked into source control or shared among users. Therefore they are a great way to annotate your code with private notes and reminders.

Summary

XML comments are not only extremely powerful, but also very easy to implement in a development project. Using them will enable you to enhance the existing IntelliSense features by including your own custom-built tooltips and Quick Info data. Using Sandcastle, you can generate professional-looking comprehensive documentation for every member and class within your solutions. Finally, Task List comments are useful for keeping track of pending coding tasks and other outstanding activities.

10

Project and Item Templates

Most development teams build a set of standards that specify how they build applications. This means that every time you start a new project or add an item to an existing project, you have to go through a process to ensure that it conforms to the standard. Visual Studio 2008 enables you to create templates that can be reused without your having to modify the standard item templates that Visual Studio 2008 ships with. This chapter describes how you can create simple templates and then extend them using the `IWizard` interface. It also examines how you can create a multi-project template that can save you a lot of time when you're starting a new application.

Creating Templates

There are two types of templates: those that create new project items and those that create entire projects. Both types of templates essentially have the same structure, as you will see later, except that they are placed in different template folders. The project templates appear in the New Project dialog, whereas the item templates appear in the Add New Item dialog.

Item Template

Although it is possible to build a template manually, it is much quicker to create one from an existing sample and make changes as required. This section begins by looking at an item template — in this case, an About form that contains some basic information, such as the application's version number and who wrote it.

To begin, create a new Visual Basic Windows Forms application called StarterProject. Instead of creating an About form from scratch, you can customize the About Box template that ships with Visual Studio. Right-click the StarterProject project, select Add ➪ New Item, and add a new About

Box. Customize the default About screen by deleting the logo and first column of the TableLayoutPanel. The customized About screen is shown in Figure 10-1.

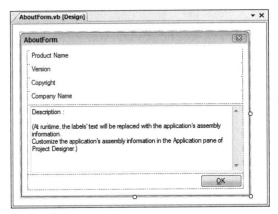

Figure 10-1

To make a template out of the About form, select the Export Template item from the File menu. This starts the Export Template Wizard, shown in Figure 10-2. If you have unsaved changes in your solution, you will be prompted to save before continuing. The first step is to determine what type of template you want to create. In this case, select the Item Template radio button and make sure that the project in which the About form resides is selected in the drop-down list.

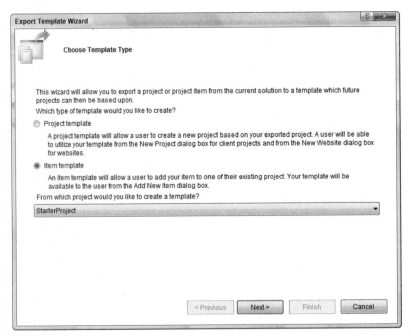

Figure 10-2

Click "Next>". You will be prompted to select the item on which you want to base the template. In this case, select the About form. The use of checkboxes is slightly misleading, as you can only select a single item on which to base the template. After you make your selection and click "Next>", the dialog shown in Figure 10-3 enables you to include any project references that you may require. This list is based on the list of references in the project in which that item resides. Because this is a form, include a reference to the System.Windows.Forms library. If you do not, and a new item of this type were added to a class library, it is possible that the project would not compile, as it would not have a reference to this assembly.

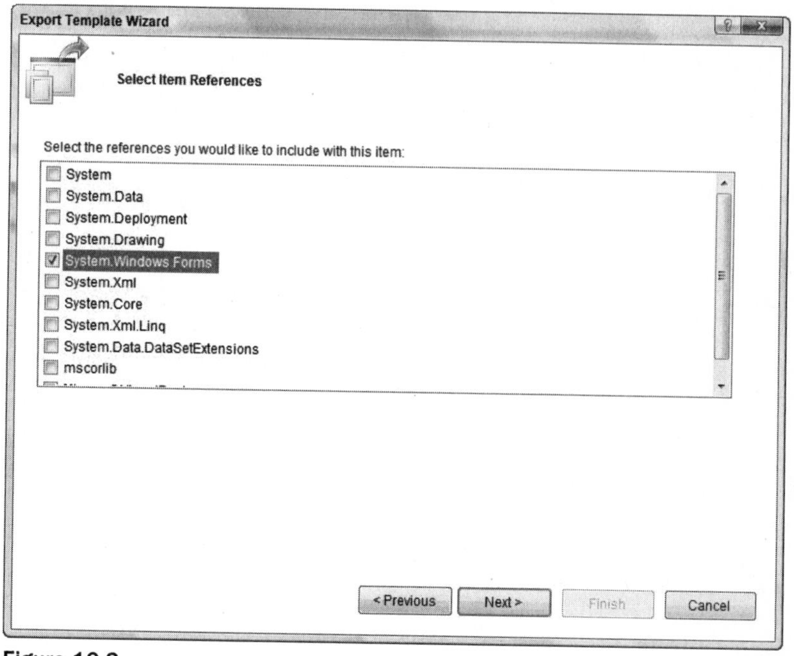

Figure 10-3

The final step in the Export Template Wizard is to specify some properties of the template to be generated, such as the name, description, and icon that will appear in the Add New Item dialog. Figure 10-4 shows the final dialog in the wizard. As you can see, it contains two checkboxes, one for displaying the output folder upon completion and one for automatically importing the new template into Visual Studio 2008.

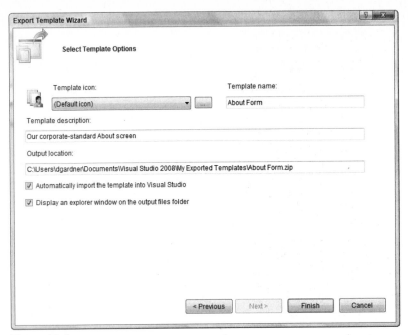

Figure 10-4

By default, exported templates are created in the My Exported Templates folder under the current user's Documents/Visual Studio 2008 folder. Inside this root folder are a number of folders that contain user settings about Visual Studio 2008 (as shown in Figure 10-5).

Figure 10-5

Also notice the Templates folder in Figure 10-5. Visual Studio 2008 looks in this folder for additional templates to display when you are creating new items. Not shown here are two sub-folders beneath the Templates folder that hold item templates and project templates, respectively. These, in turn, are divided by language. If you check the "Automatically import the template into Visual Studio" option on the final page of the Export Template Wizard, the new template will not only be placed in the output folder but will also be copied to the relevant location, depending on language and template type, within the

Templates folder. Visual Studio 2008 will automatically display this item template the next time you display the Add New Item dialog, as shown in Figure 10-6.

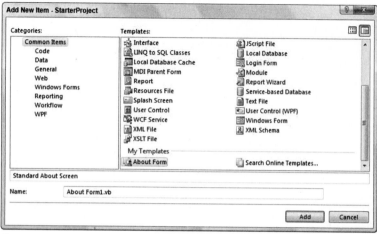

Figure 10-6

Project Template

You build a project template the same way you build an item template, with one difference. Whereas the item template is based on an existing item, the project template needs to be based on an entire project. For example, you might have a simple project, as shown in Figure 10-7, that has a main form, complete with menu bar, an About form, and a splash screen.

Figure 10-7

To generate a template from this project, you follow the same steps you took to generate an item template, except that you need to select Project Template when asked what type of template to generate. After you've completed the Export Template Wizard, the new project template will appear in the New Project dialog, shown in Figure 10-8.

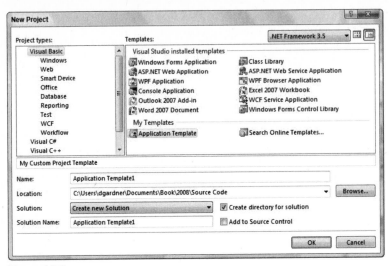

Figure 10-8

Template Structure

Before examining how to build more complex templates, you need to understand what is produced by the Export Template Wizard. If you look in the My Exported Templates folder, you will see that all the templates are exported as compressed zip folders. The zip folder can contain any number of files or folders, depending on whether they are templates for single files or full projects. However, the one common element of all template folders is that they contain a .vstemplate file. This file is an XML document that determines what happens when the template is used. The following listing illustrates the project template that was exported earlier.

```
<VSTemplate Version="2.0.0"
    xmlns="http://schemas.microsoft.com/developer/vstemplate/2005" Type="Project">
  <TemplateData>
    <Name>Application Template</Name>
    <Description>My Custom Project Template</Description>
    <ProjectType>VisualBasic</ProjectType>
    <ProjectSubType></ProjectSubType>
    <SortOrder>1000</SortOrder>
    <CreateNewFolder>true</CreateNewFolder>
    <DefaultName>Application Template</DefaultName>
    <ProvideDefaultName>true</ProvideDefaultName>
    <LocationField>Enabled</LocationField>

    <EnableLocationBrowseButton>true</EnableLocationBrowseButton>
    <Icon>__TemplateIcon.ico</Icon>
  </TemplateData>
  <TemplateContent>
    <Project TargetFileName="StarterProject.vbproj" File="StarterProject.vbproj"
      ReplaceParameters="true">
      <ProjectItem ReplaceParameters="true" TargetFileName="AboutForm.vb">
        AboutForm.vb</ProjectItem>
```

```
      <ProjectItem ReplaceParameters="true" TargetFileName="AboutForm.Designer.vb">
          AboutForm.Designer.vb</ProjectItem>
      <ProjectItem ReplaceParameters="true" TargetFileName="AboutForm.resx">
          AboutForm.resx</ProjectItem>
      <ProjectItem ReplaceParameters="true" TargetFileName="MainForm.vb">
          MainForm.vb</ProjectItem>
      <ProjectItem ReplaceParameters="true" TargetFileName="MainForm.Designer.vb">
          MainForm.Designer.vb</ProjectItem>
      <ProjectItem ReplaceParameters="true" TargetFileName="MainForm.resx">
          MainForm.resx</ProjectItem>
      <Folder Name="My Project" TargetFolderName="My Project">
        <ProjectItem ReplaceParameters="true" TargetFileName="Application.myapp">
            Application.myapp</ProjectItem>
        <ProjectItem ReplaceParameters="true"
            TargetFileName="Application.Designer.vb">
            Application.Designer.vb</ProjectItem>
        <ProjectItem ReplaceParameters="true" TargetFileName="AssemblyInfo.vb">
            AssemblyInfo.vb</ProjectItem>
        <ProjectItem ReplaceParameters="true" TargetFileName="Resources.resx">
            Resources.resx</ProjectItem>
        <ProjectItem ReplaceParameters="true"
            TargetFileName="Resources.Designer.vb">
            Resources.Designer.vb</ProjectItem>
        <ProjectItem ReplaceParameters="true" TargetFileName="Settings.settings">
            Settings.settings</ProjectItem>
        <ProjectItem ReplaceParameters="true"
            TargetFileName="Settings.Designer.vb">
            Settings.Designer.vb</ProjectItem>
      </Folder>
      <ProjectItem ReplaceParameters="true" TargetFileName="SplashForm.vb">
          SplashForm.vb</ProjectItem>
      <ProjectItem ReplaceParameters="true"
          TargetFileName="SplashForm.Designer.vb">
          SplashForm.Designer.vb</ProjectItem>
      <ProjectItem ReplaceParameters="true" TargetFileName="SplashForm.resx">
          SplashForm.resx</ProjectItem>
    </Project>
  </TemplateContent>
</VSTemplate>
```

At the top of the sample, the VSTemplate node contains a Type attribute that determines whether this is an item template (Item), a project template (Project), or a multiple project template (ProjectGroup). The remainder of the sample is divided into TemplateData and TemplateContent. The TemplateData block includes information about the template itself, such as its name and description and the icon that will be used to represent it in the New Project dialog, whereas the TemplateContent block defines the structure of the template.

In the preceding example, the content starts with a Project node, which indicates the project file to use. The files contained in this template are listed by means of the ProjectItem nodes. Each node contains a TargetFileName attribute that can be used to specify the name of the file as it will appear in the project created from this template. In the case of an item template, the Project node is missing and ProjectItems are contained within the TemplateContent node.

It's possible to create templates for a solution that contains multiple projects. These templates contain a separate .vstemplate file for each project in the solution. They also have a global .vstemplate file, which describes the overall template and contains references to each projects' individual .vstemplate files.

For more information on the structure of the .vstemplate file, see the full schema at C:\Program Files\Microsoft Visual Studio 9.0\Xml\Schemas\1033\vstemplate.xsd.

Template Parameters

Both item and project templates support parameter substitution, which enables replacement of key parameters when a project or item is created from the template. In some cases these are automatically inserted. For example, when the About form was exported as an item template, the class name was removed and replaced with a template parameter, as shown here:

```
Public Class $safeitemname$
```

There are 14 reserved template parameters that can be used in any project. These are listed in the following table.

Table 10-1: Template Parameters

Parameter	Description
clrversion	Current version of the common language runtime
GUID[1-10]	A GUID used to replace the project GUID in a project file. You can specify up to ten unique GUIDs (e.g., GUID1, GUID2, etc.).
itemname	The name provided by the user in the Add New Item dialog
machinename	The current computer name (e.g., computer01)
projectname	The name provided by the user in the New Project dialog
registeredorganization	The registry key value that stores the registered organization name
rootnamespace	The root namespace of the current project. This parameter is used to replace the namespace in an item being added to a project.
safeitemname	The name provided by the user in the Add New Item dialog, with all unsafe characters and spaces removed
safeprojectname	The name provided by the user in the New Project dialog, with all unsafe characters and spaces removed
time	The current time on the local computer
userdomain	The current user domain
username	The current user name
webnamespace	The name of the current web site. This is used in any web form template to guarantee unique class names.
year	The current year in the format YYYY

In addition to the reserved parameters, you can also create your own custom template parameters. You define these by adding a `<CustomParameters>` section to the `.vstemplate` file, as shown here:

```
<TemplateContent>
    ...
    <CustomParameters>
        <CustomParameter Name="$timezoneName $" Value="(GMT+8:00) Perth"/>
        <CustomParameter Name="$timezoneOffset $" Value="+8"/>
    </CustomParameters>
</TemplateContent>
```

You can refer to this custom parameter in code as follows:

```
string tzName = "$timezoneName$";
string tzOffset = "$timezoneOffset$";
```

When a new item or project containing a custom parameter is created from a template, Visual Studio will automatically perform the template substitution on both custom and reserved parameters.

Extending Templates

Building templates based on existing items and projects limits what you can do because it assumes that every project or scenario will require exactly the same items. Instead of creating multiple templates for each different scenario (for example, one that has a main form with a black background and another that has a main form with a white background), with a bit of user interaction you can accommodate multiple scenarios from a single template. Therefore, this section takes the project template created earlier and tweaks it so users can specify the background color for the main form. In addition, you'll build an installer for both the template and the wizard that you will create for the user interaction.

To add user interaction to a template, you need to implement the IWizard interface in a class library that is then signed and placed in the Global Assembly Cache (GAC) on the machine on which the template will be executed. For this reason, to deploy a template that uses a wizard you also need rights to deploy the wizard assembly to the GAC.

Template Project Setup

Before plunging in and implementing the IWizard interface, follow these steps to set up your solution so you have all the bits and pieces in the same location, which will make it easy to make changes, perform a build, and then run the installer:

1. Begin with the StarterProject solution that you created for the project template earlier in the chapter. Make sure that this solution builds and runs successfully before proceeding. Any issues with this solution will be harder to detect later, as the error messages that appear when a template is used are somewhat cryptic.

2. Into this solution add a Visual Basic Class Library project, called WizardClassLibrary, in which you will place the IWizard implementation.

3. Add to the WizardClassLibrary a new empty class file called MyWizard.vb, and a blank Windows Form called ColorPickerForm.vb. These will be customized later.

4. To access the `IWizard` interface, add references to the Class Library project to both `EnvDTE90.dll` and `Microsoft.VisualStudio.TemplateWizardInterface.dll`, both located at C:\Program Files\Microsoft Visual Studio 9.0\Common7\IDE\PublicAssemblies\.

5. Finally, you will also need to add a Setup project to the solution. To do this, select File ⇨ Add ⇨ New Project, expand the Other Project Types category, and then highlight Setup and Deployment. Select the Setup Wizard template and follow the prompts to include the Primary Output from WizardClassLibrary and Content Files from WizardClassLibrary.

This should result in a solution that looks similar to what is shown in Figure 10-9.

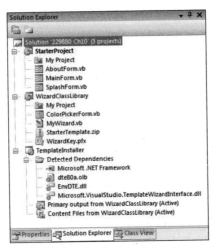

Figure 10-9

As shown in Figure 10-9, when you include the primary output and content files from the Class Library project to the installer it also adds a number of dependencies. Since the template will only be used on a machine with Visual Studio 2008, you don't need any of these dependencies. Exclude them by clicking the Exclude menu item on the right-click context menu. Then perform the following steps to complete the configuration of the Installer project.

1. By default, when you add project outputs to the installer, they are added to the Application folder. In this case, add the primary output of the class library to the GAC, and place the content files for the class library into the user's Visual Studio Templates folder. Before you can move these files, right-click the Installer project and select View ⇨ File System from the context menu to open the File System view.

2. By default, the File System view contains the Application folder (which can't be deleted), the User's Desktop folder, and the User's Programs Menu folder. Remove the two user folders by selecting Delete from the right-click context menu.

3. Add both the Global Assembly Cache (GAC) folder and the User's Personal Data folder (My Documents) to the file system by right-clicking the File System on Target Machine node and selecting these folders from the list.

4. Into the User's Personal Data folder, add a Visual Studio 2008 folder, followed by a Templates folder, followed by a ProjectTemplates folder. The result should look like what is shown in Figure 10-10.

Figure 10-10

5. To complete the installer, move the primary output from the Application folder into the Global Assembly Cache folder, and then move the content files from the Application folder to the ProjectTemplates folder. (Simply drag the files between folders in the File System view.)

IWizard

Now that you've completed the installer, you can work back to the wizard class library. As shown in Figure 10-9, you have a form, ColorPickerForm, and a class, MyWizard. The former is a simple form that can be used to specify the color of the background of the main form. To this form you will need to add a Color Dialog control, called ColorDialog1, a Panel called PnlColor, a Button called BtnPickColor with the label 'Pick Color', and a Button called BtnAcceptColor with the label 'Accept Color'.

Rather than use the default icon that Visual Studio uses on the form, you can select a more appropriate icon from the Visual Studio 2008 Image Library. The Visual Studio 2008 Image Library is a collection of standard icons, images, and animations that are used in Windows, Office, and other Microsoft software. You can use any of these images royalty-free to ensure that your applications are visually consistent with Microsoft software.

The image library is installed with Visual Studio as a compressed file called VS2008ImageLibrary.zip. By default, you can find this under <Program Files Path>\Microsoft Visual Studio 9\Common7\ VS2008ImageLibrary\. Extract the contents of this zip file to a more convenient location, such as a directory under your profile.

To replace the icon on the form, first go to the Properties window and the select the Form in the drop-down list at the top. On the Icon property click the ellipsis (. . .) to load the file selection dialog. Select the icon file you wish to use and click OK (for this example we've chosen VS2008ImageLibrary\Objects\ ico_format\WinVista\Settings.ico).

Once completed, the ColorPickerForm should look similar to the one shown in Figure 10-11.

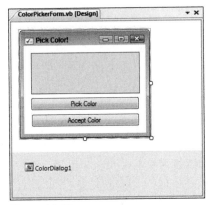

Figure 10-11

The following code listing can be added to this form. The main logic of this form is in the event handler for the 'Pick Color' button, which opens the ColorDialog that is used to select a color.

```
Public Class ColorPickerForm
    Private Sub BtnPickColor_Click(ByVal sender As System.Object, _
                      ByVal e As System.EventArgs) Handles BtnPickColor.Click
        Me.ColorDialog1.Color = Me.PnlColor.BackColor
        If Me.ColorDialog1.ShowDialog() = Windows.Forms.DialogResult.OK Then
            Me.PnlColor.BackColor = Me.ColorDialog1.Color
        End If
    End Sub

    Public ReadOnly Property SelectedColor() As Drawing.Color
        Get
            Return Me.PnlColor.BackColor
        End Get
    End Property

    Private Sub BtnAcceptColor_Click(ByVal sender As System.Object, _
                      ByVal e As System.EventArgs) Handles BtnAcceptColor.Click
        Me.DialogResult = Windows.Forms.DialogResult.OK
        Me.Close()
    End Sub
End Class
```

The MyWizard class implements the IWizard interface, which provides a number of opportunities for user interaction throughout the template process. In this case, add code to the RunStarted method, which will be called just after the project-creation process is started. This provides the perfect opportunity to select and apply a new background color for the main form:

```vb
Imports Microsoft.VisualStudio.TemplateWizard
Imports System.Collections.Generic
Imports System.Windows.Forms

Public Class MyWizard
    Implements IWizard

    Public Sub BeforeOpeningFile(ByVal projectItem As EnvDTE.ProjectItem) _
                                        Implements IWizard.BeforeOpeningFile
    End Sub

    Public Sub ProjectFinishedGenerating(ByVal project As EnvDTE.Project) _
                                Implements IWizard.ProjectFinishedGenerating
    End Sub

    Public Sub ProjectItemFinishedGenerating _
                        (ByVal projectItem As EnvDTE.ProjectItem) _
                            Implements IWizard.ProjectItemFinishedGenerating
    End Sub

    Public Sub RunFinished() Implements IWizard.RunFinished

    End Sub

    Public Sub RunStarted(ByVal automationObject As Object, _
                    ByVal replacementsDictionary As _
    Dictionary(Of String, String), _
                    ByVal runKind As WizardRunKind, _
                    ByVal customParams() As Object) _
    Implements IWizard.RunStarted
        Dim selector As New ColorPickerForm
        If selector.ShowDialog = DialogResult.OK Then
            Dim c As Drawing.Color = selector.SelectedColor
            Dim colorString As String = "System.Drawing.Color.FromArgb(" & _
    c.R.ToString & "," & _
    c.G.ToString & "," & _
    c.B.ToString & ")"
            replacementsDictionary.Add _
                        ("Me.BackColor = System.Drawing.Color.Silver", _
                        "Me.BackColor = " & colorString)
        End If
    End Sub

    Public Function ShouldAddProjectItem(ByVal filePath As String) As Boolean _
                            Implements IWizard.ShouldAddProjectItem
        Return True
    End Function
End Class
```

In the `RunStarted` method, you prompt the user to select a new color and then use that response to add a new entry into the replacements dictionary. In this case, you are replacing `"Me.BackColor = System.Drawing.Color.Silver"` with a concatenated string made up of the RGB values of the color specified by the user. The replacements dictionary is used when the files are created for the new project, as they will be searched for the replacement keys. Upon any instances of these keys being found, they will be replaced by the appropriate replacement values. In this case, you're looking for the line specifying that the `BackColor` is `Silver`, and replacing it with the new color supplied by the user.

The class library containing the implementation of the `IWizard` interface must contain a strongly named assembly capable of being placed into the GAC. To ensure this, use the Signing tab of the Project Properties dialog to generate a new signing key, as shown in Figure 10-12.

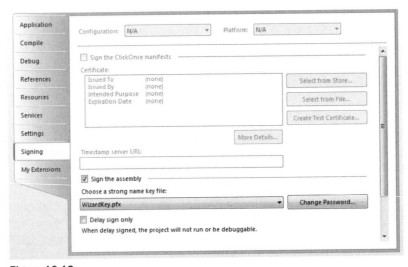

Figure 10-12

After you check the "Sign the assembly" checkbox, there will be no default value for the key file. To create a new key, select <New . . .> from the drop-down list. Alternatively, you can use an existing key file using the <Browse . . .> item in the drop-down list.

Starter Template

You're basing the template for this example on the StarterProject, and you need only make minor changes in order for the wizard you just built to work correctly. In the previous section you added an entry in the replacements dictionary, which searches for instances where the `BackColor` is set to `Silver`. If you want the `MainForm` to have the `BackColor` specified while using the wizard, you need to ensure that the replacement value is found. To do this, simply set the `BackColor` property of the `MainForm` to `Silver`. This will add the line `"Me.BackColor = System.Drawing.Color.Silver"` to the MainForm.Designer.vb file so that it is found during the replacement phase.

Instead of exporting the StarterProject as a new template each time and manually adding a reference to the wizard, use a command-line zip utility (in this case 7-zip, available at www.7-zip.org, was used, but any command-line zip utility will work) to build the template. This makes the process easier to automate from within Visual Studio 2008. If you were to manually zip the StarterProject folder you would have all the content files for the template, but you would be missing the `.vstemplate` file and the associated icon file. You can easily fix this by adding the `.vstemplate` file (created when you exported the project template) to the StarterProject folder. You can also add the icon file to this folder. Make sure that you do *not* include these files in the StarterProject itself; they should appear as excluded files, as shown in Figure 10-13.

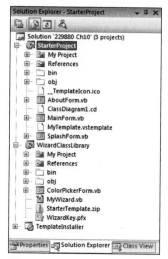

Figure 10-13

To have the wizard triggered when you create a project from this template, add some additional lines to the MyTemplate.vstemplate file:

```
<VSTemplate Version="2.0.0"
xmlns="http://schemas.microsoft.com/developer/vstemplate/2005" Type="Project">
  <TemplateData>
  ...
  </TemplateData>
  <TemplateContent>
  ...
  </TemplateContent>
  <WizardExtension>
    <Assembly>WizardClassLibrary, Version=1.0.0.0, Culture=neutral,
      PublicKeyToken=022e960e5582ca43, Custom=null</Assembly>
    <FullClassName>WizardClassLibrary.MyWizard</FullClassName>
  </WizardExtension>
</VSTemplate>
```

The `<WizardExtension>` node added in the sample indicates the class name of the wizard and the strong-named assembly in which it resides. You have already signed the wizard assembly, so all you need to do is determine the `PublicKeyToken` by opening the assembly using Lutz Roeder's Reflector for .NET (available at www.aisto.com/roeder/dotnet/). If you haven't already built the WizardLibrary, you will have to build the project so you have an assembly to open with Reflector. Once you have opened the assembly in Reflector, you can see the `PublicKeyToken` of the assembly by selecting the assembly in the tree, as shown in Figure 10-14. The `PublicKeyToken` value in the `.vstemplate` file needs to be replaced with the actual value found using Reflector.

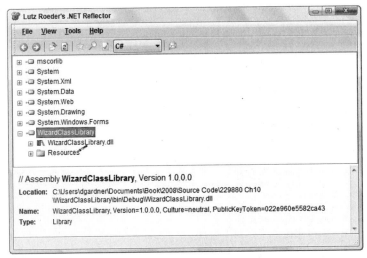

Figure 10-14

The last change you need to make to the StarterProject is to add a post-build event command that will zip this project into a project template. In this case, the command to be executed is a call to the 7-zip executable, which will zip the entire contents of the StarterProject folder, recursively, into StarterTemplate.zip, placed in the WizardClassLibrary folder. Note that you may need to supply the full path for your zip utility.

```
7z.exe a -tzip ..\..\..\WizardClassLibrary\StarterTemplate.zip ..\..\*.* -r
```

In Figure 10-13, notice that the generated zip file (StarterTemplate.zip) is included in the Class Library project. The Build Action property for this item is set to Content. This aligns with the installer you set up earlier, which will place the Content files from the class library into the Templates folder as part of the installation process.

You have now completed the individual projects required to create the project template (StarterProject), added a user interface wizard (WizardClassLibrary), and built an installer to deploy your template. One last step is to correct the solution dependency list to ensure that the StarterProject is rebuilt (and hence the template zip file recreated) prior to the installer being built. Because there is no direct dependency between the Installer project and the StarterProject, you need to open the solution properties and indicate that there is a dependency, as illustrated in Figure 10-15.

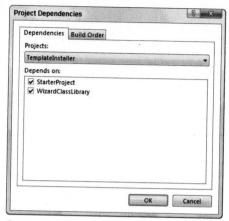

Figure 10-15

Your solution is now complete and can be used to install the StarterTemplate and associated IWizard implementation. Once the solution is installed, you can create a new project from the StarterTemplate you have just created.

Summary

This chapter provided an overview of how to create both item and project templates with Visual Studio 2008. Existing projects or items can be exported into templates that you can deploy to your colleagues. Alternatively, you can build a template manually and add a user interface using the IWizard interface. From what you learned in this chapter, you should be able to build a template solution that can create a template, build and integrate a wizard interface, and finally build an installer for your template.

Part III
Languages

11

Generics, Nullable Types, Partial Types, and Methods

When the .NET Framework was initially released, many C++ developers cited the lack of code templates as a primary reason for not moving to the .NET Framework. Generics, as introduced in version 2.0 of the .NET Framework, are more than simply design-time templates, because they have first-class support within the CLR. This chapter explores the syntax, in both C# and VB.NET, for consuming and creating generics. The chapter also looks at Nullable types, which help bridge the logical gap between database and object data; Partial types and methods, which help effectively partition code to promote code generation; and operator overloading.

Generics

For anyone unfamiliar with templates in C++ or the concept of a generic type, this section begins with a simple example that illustrates where a generic can replace a significant amount of coding, while also maintaining strongly typed code. This example stores and retrieves integers from a collection. As you can see from the following code snippet, there are two ways to do this: either using a non-typed ArrayList, which can contain any type, or using a custom-written collection:

```
'Option 1 - Non-typed Arraylist
'Creation - unable to see what types this list contain
Dim nonTypedList As New ArrayList
'Adding - no type checking, so can add any type
nonTypedList.Add(1)
nonTypedList.Add("Hello")
nonTypedList.Add(5.334)
'Retrieving - no type checking, must cast (should do type checking too)
Dim output As Integer = CInt(nonTypedList.Item(1))
```

(continued)

(continued)

```
'Option 2 - Strongly typed custom written collection
'Creation - custom collection
Dim myList As New IntegerCollection
'Adding - type checking, so can only add integers
myList.Add(1)
'Retrieving - type checking, so no casting required
output = myList.Item(0)
```

Clearly, the second approach is preferable because it ensures that you put only integers into the collection. However, the downside of this approach is that you have to create collection classes for each type you want to put in a collection. You can rewrite this example using the generic `List` class:

```
'Creation - generic list, specifying the type of objects it contains
Dim genericList As New List(Of Integer)
'Adding - type checking
genericList.Add(1)
'Retrieving - type checking
output = genericList.Item(0)
```

This example has the benefits of the strongly typed collection without the overhead of having to rewrite the collection for each type. To create a collection that holds strings, all you have to do is change the Type argument of the `List` — for example, `List(Of String)`.

In summary, generic types have one or more Type parameters that will be defined when an instance of the type is declared. From the example you just saw, the class `List` has a Type parameter, T, which, when specified, determines the type of items in the collection. The following sections describe in more detail how to consume, create, and constrain generic types.

Consumption

You have just seen a VB.NET example of how to consume the generic `List` to provide either a collection of integers or a collection of strings. You can accomplish this by supplying the Type parameter as part of the declaration. The following code snippets illustrate the consumption of generic types for both VB.NET and C#:

C#

```
Dictionary<String,double> scores = new Dictionary<String,double>();
```

VB.NET

```
Dim scores As New Dictionary(Of String, Double)
```

There are also generic methods, which also have a Type parameter that must be supplied when the method is invoked. This is illustrated in calling the `Choose` method, which randomly picks one of the two arguments passed in:

C#

```
newValue=Chooser.Choose<int>(5, 6);
newValue=Chooser.Choose(7, 8);
```

VB.NET

```
newValue = Chooser.Choose(of Integer)(5,6)
newValue = Chooser.Choose(7,8)
```

In these examples, you can see that a Type argument has been supplied in the first line but omitted in the second line. You're able to do this because type inferencing kicks in to automatically determine what the Type argument should be.

Creation

To create a generic type, you need to define the Type parameters that must be provided when the type is constructed, performed as part of the type signature. In the following example, the ObjectMapper class defines two Type parameters, TSource and TDestination, that need to be supplied when an instance of this class is declared:

C#

```
public class ObjectMapper<TSource, TDestination>
{
    private TSource source;
    private TDestination destination;

    public ObjectMapper(TSource src , TDestination dest )
    {
        source = src;
        destination = dest;
    }
}
```

VB.NET

```
Public Class ObjectMapper(Of TSource, TDestination)
    Private source As TSource
    Private destination As TDestination

    Public Sub New(ByVal src As TSource, ByVal dest As TDestination)
        source = src
        destination = dest
    End Sub
End Class
```

A naming convention for Type parameters is to begin them with the letter T, followed by some sort of descriptive name if there is more than one Type parameter. In this case, the two parameters define the type of Source and Destination objects to be provided in the mapping.

Generic methods are defined using a similar syntax as part of the method signature. Although generic methods may often be placed within a generic type, that is not a requirement; in fact, they can exist anywhere a non-generic method can be written. The following `CreateObjectMapper` method takes two objects of different types and returns a new `ObjectMapper` object, passing the Type arguments for the method through to the constructor:

C#

```
public static ObjectMapper<TCreateSrc, TCreateDest>
    CreateObjectMapper<TCreateSrc, TCreateDest>
                                    (TCreateSrc src, TCreateDest dest)
{
    return new ObjectMapper<TCreateSrc, TCreateDest>(src, dest);
}
```

VB.NET

```
Public Shared Function CreateObjectMapper(Of TCreateSrc, TCreateDest) _
                    (ByVal src As TCreateSrc, ByVal dest As TCreateDest) _
                        As ObjectMapper(Of TCreateSrc, TCreateDest)
    Return New ObjectMapper(Of TCreateSrc, TCreateDest)(src, dest)
End Function
```

Constraints

So far, you have seen how to create and consume generic types and methods. However, having Type parameters limits what you can do with the parameter because you only have access to the basic object methods such as `GetType`, `Equals`, and `ToString`. Without more information about the Type parameter, you are limited to building simple lists and collections. To make generics more useful, you can place constraints on the Type parameters to ensure that they have a basic set of functionality. The following example places constraints on both parameters:

C#

```
public class ObjectMapper<TSource, TDestination>
                        : IComparable<ObjectMapper<TSource,TDestination>>
                    where TSource: IComparable<TSource>
                    where TDestination: new()
{
    private TSource source;
    private TDestination destination;

    public ObjectMapper(TSource src)
    {
        source = src;
        destination = new TDestination();
    }
    public int
CompareTo(ObjectMapper<TSource,TDestination> mapper)
    {
        return source.CompareTo(mapper.source);
    }
}
```

VB.NET

```
Public Class ObjectMapper(Of TSource As IComparable(Of TSource), _
                     TDestination As New)
    Implements IComparable(Of ObjectMapper(Of TSource, TDestination))

    Private source As TSource
    Private destination As TDestination

    Public Sub New(ByVal src As TSource)
        source = src
        destination = new TDestination
    End Sub
    Public Function CompareTo _
            (ByVal other As ObjectMapper(Of TSource, TDestination)) As Integer _
            Implements System.IComparable(Of ObjectMapper _
                                (Of TSource, TDestination)).CompareTo
        Return source.CompareTo(other.source)
    End Function
End Class
```

The TSource parameter is required to implement the IComparable interface so that an object of that type can be compared to another object of the same type. This is used in the CompareTo, which implements the IComparable interface for the ObjectMapper class, to compare the two source objects. The TDestination parameter requires a constructor that takes no arguments. The constructor is changed so that instead of a Destination object being provided, it is created as part of the constructor.

This example covered interface and constructor constraints. The full list of constraints is as follows:

- ❑ **Base class:** Constrains the Type parameter to be, or be derived from, the class specified.

- ❑ **Class or Structure:** Constrains the Type parameter to be a class or a structure (a struct in C#).

- ❑ **Interface:** Constrains the Type parameter to implement the interface specified.

- ❑ **Constructor:** Constrains the Type parameter to expose a no-parameter constructor. Use the new keyword as the constraint.

Multiple constraints can be supplied by separating the constraints with a comma, as shown in these snippets:

C#

```
public class MultipleConstraintClass<T>
                        where T: IComparable, new()
    {...}
```

VB.NET

```
Public Class MultipleConstraintClass(Of T As {IComparable,new})
...
End Class
```

Nullable Types

Any developer who has worked with a database understands some of the pain that goes into aligning business objects with database schemas. One of the difficulties has been that the default value for a database column could be nothing (as in not specified), even if the column was an integer. In .NET, value types, such as integers, always have a value. When pulling information from the database, it was necessary to add additional logic that would maintain state for the database columns to indicate whether a value had been set. Two of the most prominent solutions to this problem were to either adjust the database schema to prevent nothing values, which can be an issue where a field is optional, or to add a Boolean flag for every field that could be nothing, which added considerable amounts of code to even a simple application.

Generic types provide a mechanism to bridge this divide in quite an efficient manner, using the generic Nullable type. The Nullable type is a generic structure that has a single Type parameter, which is the type it will be wrapping. It also contains a flag indicating whether a value exists, as shown in the following snippet:

```vb
Public Structure Nullable(Of T As Structure)
    Private m_hasValue As Boolean
    Private m_value As T

    Public Sub New(ByVal value As T)
        Me.m_value = value
        Me.m_hasValue = True
    End Sub

    Public ReadOnly Property HasValue() As Boolean
        Get
            Return Me.m_hasValue
        End Get
    End Property

    Public ReadOnly Property Value() As T
        Get
            If Not Me.HasValue Then
                Throw new Exception("...")
            End If
            Return Me.m_value
        End Get
    End Property

    Public Function GetValueOrDefault() As T
        Return Me.m_value
    End Function

    Public Function GetValueOrDefault(ByVal defaultValue As T) As T
        If Not Me.HasValue Then
            Return defaultValue
        End If
        Return Me.m_value
    End Function
```

```
        Public Shared Narrowing Operator CType(ByVal value As Nullable(Of T)) As T
            Return value.m_value
        End Operator

        Public Shared Widening Operator CType(ByVal value As T) As Nullable(Of T)
            Return New Nullable(Of T)(value)
        End Operator
End Structure
```

This code indicates how you can create a new Nullable type by specifying a Type argument and calling the constructor. However, the last two methods in this structure are operators that allow conversion between the Nullable type and the Type argument provided. Conversion operators are covered later in this chapter, but for now it is sufficient to understand that conversion from the Type argument to a Nullable type is allowed using implicit conversion, whereas the reverse requires explicit casting. You can also see that the Type parameter, T, is constrained to be a structure. Because class variables are object references, they are implicitly nullable.

The following example creates and uses a Nullable type. You can see that C# has additional support for Nullable types with an abbreviated syntax when working with the Nullable type:

C#

```
Nullable<int>x=5;
int? y,z;
if (x.HasValue)
    y=x.Value;
else
    y=8;
z=x?? + y??7;
int? w = x + y;
```

VB.NET

```
Dim x, y As Nullable(Of Integer)
Dim z as Integer?
x = 5
If x.HasValue Then
    y = x.Value
Else
    y = 8
End If
z = x.GetValueOrDefault + y.GetValueOrDefault(7)
Dim w as Integer = x + y
```

In these examples, both languages can use the HasValue property to determine whether a value has been assigned to the Nullable type. If it has, the Value property can be used to retrieve the underlying value. The Value property throws an exception if no value has been specified. Having to test before you access the Value property is rather tedious, so the GetValueOrDefault function was added. This retrieves the value if one has been supplied; otherwise, it returns the default value. There are two overloads to this method, with and without an alternative value. If an alternative value is supplied, this is the default value that is returned if no value has been supplied. Alternatively, the default value is defined as the zero-initialized underlying type. For example, if the underlying type were a `Point`, made up of two double values, the default value would be a `Point` with both values set to zero.

Both C# and VB.NET have abbreviations to make working with Nullable types easier. `Nullable<int>` or `Nullable(of Integer)` can be abbreviated as `int?` and `Integer?`, which defines a Nullable integer variable. The second abbreviation (C# only) is the null coalescing operator, `??`. This is used to abbreviate the `GetValueOrDefault` function. Finally the last line of both snippets shows an interesting feature, which is support for null propagation. If either x or y are null, the null value propagates to w. This is the equivalent of the following:

C#

```
int? w = x.HasValue && y.HasValue ? x.Value + y.Value : (int?)null;
```

VB.NET

```
Dim w as Integer? = CInt(If(x.HasValue and y.HasValue, x.Value + y.Value, Nothing))
```

Null propagation can lead to unexpected results and should be used with extreme caution. As a null value anywhere in an extended calculation can lead to a null result, it can be difficult to identify any errors.

Partial Types

Partial types are a simple concept that enable a single type to be split across multiple files. The files are combined at compile time into a single type. As such, Partial types cannot be used to add or modify functionality in existing types. The most common reason to use Partial types is to separate generated code. In the past, elaborate class hierarchies had to be created to add additional functionality to a generated class due to fear of that code being overwritten when the class was regenerated. Using Partial types, the generated code can be partitioned into a separate file, and additional code added to a file where it will not be overwritten by the generator.

Partial types are defined by using the `Partial` keyword in the type definition. The following example defines a `Person` class across two files:

```
'File 1 - fields and constructor
Partial Public Class Person
    Private m_Name As String
    Private m_Age As Integer
    Public Sub New(ByVal name As String, ByVal age As Integer)
        Me.m_Name = name
        Me.m_Age = age
    End Sub
End Class
```

```
'File 2 - public properties
Public Class Person
    Public ReadOnly Property Age() As Integer
        Get
            Return Me.m_Age
        End Get
    End Property
    Public ReadOnly Property Name() As String
        Get
            Return Me.m_Name
        End Get
    End Property
End Class
```

You will notice that the Partial keyword is used only in one of the files. This is specific to VB.NET, because C# requires all partial classes to use this keyword. The disadvantage there is that the Partial keyword needs to be added to the generated file. The other difference in C# is that the Partial keyword appears after the class accessibility keyword (in this case, Public).

Form Designers

Both the Windows and Web Forms designer make use of Partial types to separate the designer code from event handlers and other code written by the developer. The Windows Forms designer generates code into an associated designer file. For example, for Form1.vb there would also be Form1.designer.vb. In addition to protecting your code so that it isn't overwritten by the generated code, having the designer code in a separate file also trims down the code files for each form. Typically, the code file would only contain event handlers and other custom code.

In the previous version of Visual Studio, Web Forms were split across two files where controls had to be defined in both the designer file and the code-behind files so event handlers could be wired up. The designer file inherited from the code-behind file, which introduced another level of complexity. With Partial types, this has been simplified, with controls being defined in the designer file and only event handlers being defined in the code file. The code file is now a code-beside file, because both the code and designer information belong to the same class.

A technique often used by VB.NET developers is to use the Handles syntax for wiring event handlers to form control events. The controls are defined in the generated code while the event handler is left to the developer. C# developers have to manually wire and unwire the event handler, which normally needs to be done as part of the constructor. This is difficult if the code generator doesn't provide an appropriate mechanism for accessing the constructor — the WinForms code generator in Visual Studio 2008 generates the following stub in the developer code file:

```
public partial class MainForm : Form
{
    public MainForm()
    {
        InitializeComponent();
    }
}
```

Partial Methods

Partial types by themselves are only half the solution to separating generated code from the code you write. Take the following scenario: the generated code exposes a property, which can be used to set the eye color of the previously created `Person` class. In order to extend the functionality of the `Person` class you want to be able to execute additional code whenever this property is changed. Previously you would have had to create another class that inherits from `Person`, in which you override the `EyeColor` property, adding your own code. This leads to a very messy inheritance model that can adversely affect the performance of your application. Even if you don't override the generated methods or properties, because they will be defined as being virtual, the compiler will not inline them, adversely affecting performance.

Partial methods provide a much better model for generated code and your code to intertwine. Now, instead of code generators marking everything as virtual they can insert calls to partial methods:

```
Private mEyeColor As Color
Public Property EyeColor() As Color
    Get
        Return mEyeColor
    End Get
    Set(ByVal value As Color)
        EyeColorChanging()
        mEyeColor = value
        EyeColorChanged()
    End Set
End Property

Partial Private Sub EyeColorChanging()
End Sub

Partial Private Sub EyeColorChanged()
End Sub
```

In this snippet you can see the calls to the partial methods `EyeColorChanging` and `EyeColorChanged` as part of the `EyeColor` property. Below this property are the declarations for these partial methods. To insert additional code you just need to implement these methods in your code file:

```
Private Sub EyeColorChanging()
    MsgBox("About to change the eye color!")
End Sub

Private Sub EyeColorChanged()
    MsgBox("Eye color has been changed")
End Sub
```

So far you probably haven't seen any great savings over the previously mentioned inheritance model. The big advantage with partial methods is that if you choose not to implement any of the partial methods the compiler will remove the declaration and all calls to that partial method during compilation. This means that there are no runtime penalties associated with having thousands of these method declarations in the generated code file to make the generated code more extensible.

There are some limitations with partial methods, namely that the partial methods must be marked as private and cannot have return values. Both of these constraints are due to the implementation-dependent inclusion of the methods at compile time. If a method is not private, it would need to be accessible after compilation — otherwise changing the implementation would break any existing references. Similarly if a method has a return value, there may be code that depends on a value being returned from the method call, which makes excluding the method call at compilation time difficult.

Operator Overloading

Both VB.NET and C# now support operator overloading, which means that you can define the behavior for standard operators such as +, −, /, and *. You can also define type conversion operators that control how casting is handled between different types.

Operators

The syntax for operator overloading is very similar to a static method except that it includes the Operator keyword, as shown in the following example:

C#

```
public class OperatorBaseClass{
    private int m_value;

    public static OperatorBaseClass operator +(OperatorBaseClass op1 ,
                                               OperatorBaseClass op2 )
    {
        OperatorBaseClass obc =new OperatorBaseClass();
        obc.m_value = op1.m_value + op2.m_value;
        return obc;
    }
}
```

VB.NET

```
Public Class OperatorBaseClass
    Private m_value As Integer

    Public Shared Operator +(ByVal op1 As OperatorBaseClass, _
                             ByVal op2 As OperatorBaseClass) As OperatorBaseClass
        Dim obc As New OperatorBaseClass
        obc.m_value = op1.m_value + op2.m_value
        Return obc
    End Operator
End Class
```

In both languages, a binary operator overload requires two parameters and a return value. The first value, op1, appears to the left of the operator, with the second on the right side. Clearly, the return value is substituted into the equation in place of all three input symbols. Although it makes more sense to make both input parameters and the return value the same type, this is not necessarily the case, and this syntax can be used to define the effect of the operator on any pair of types. The one condition is that one of the input parameters must be of the same type that contains the overloaded operator.

Type Conversions

A type conversion is the process of converting a value of one type to another type. These can be broadly categorized into *widening* and *narrowing* conversions. In a widening conversion, the original type has all the necessary information to produce the new type. As such, this conversion can be done implicitly and should never fail. An example would be casting a derived type to its base type. Conversely, in a narrowing conversion, the original type may not have all the necessary information to produce the new type. An example would be casting a base type to a derived type. This conversion cannot be guaranteed, and needs to be done via an explicit cast.

The following example illustrates conversions between two classes, `Person` and `Employee`. Converting from a `Person` to an `Employee` is a well-known conversion, because an employee's initial wage can be defined as a multiple of their age (for example, when they are employed). However, converting an `Employee` to a `Person` is not necessarily correct, because an employee's current wage may no longer be a reflection of the employee's age:

C#

```
public class Employee
{
    ...
    static public implicit operator Employee(Person p)
    {
        Employee emp=new Employee();
        emp.m_Name=p.Name;
        emp.m_Wage = p.Age * 1000;
        return emp;
    }
    static public explicit operator Person(Employee emp)
    {
        Person p = new Person();
        p.Name = emp.m_Name;
        p.Age=(int)emp.m_Wage/1000;
        return p;
    }
}
```

VB.NET

```
Public Class Employee
    ...
    Public Shared Widening Operator CType(ByVal p As Person) As Employee
        Dim emp As New Employee
        emp.m_Name = p.Name
        emp.m_Wage = p.Age * 1000
        Return emp
    End Operator
    Public Shared Narrowing Operator CType(ByVal emp As Employee) As Person
        Dim p As New Person
        p.Name = emp.m_Name
        p.Age = CInt(emp.m_Wage / 1000)
        Return p
    End Operator
End Class
```

Why Static Methods Are Bad

Now that you know how to overload operators and create your own type conversions, this section serves as a disclaimer stating that static methods should be avoided at all costs. Because both type conversions and operator overloads are static methods, they are only relevant for the type for which they are defined. This can cause all manner of grief and unexpected results when you have complex inheritance trees. To illustrate how you can get unexpected results, consider the following example:

```vb
Public Class FirstTier
    Public Value As Integer
    Public Shared Widening Operator CType(ByVal obj As FirstTier) As String
        Return "First Tier: " & obj.Value.ToString
    End Operator
    Public Overrides Function ToString() As String
        Return "First Tier: " & Me.Value.ToString
    End Function
End Class

Public Class SecondTier
    Inherits FirstTier
    Public Overloads Shared Widening Operator CType(ByVal obj As SecondTier) _
                                        As String
        Return "Second Tier: " & obj.Value.ToString
    End Operator

    Public Overrides Function ToString() As String
        Return "Second Tier: " & Me.Value.ToString
    End Function
End Class

'Sample code to call conversion and tostring functions
Public Class Sample
    Public Shared Sub RunSampleCode
        Dim foo As New SecondTier
        foo.Value = 5
        Dim bar As FirstTier = foo

        Console.WriteLine("<SecondTier> ToString " & vbTab & foo.ToString)
        Console.WriteLine("<SecondTier> CStr " & vbTab & CStr(foo))

        Console.WriteLine("<FirstTier> ToString " & vbTab & bar.ToString)
        Console.WriteLine("<FirstTier> CStr " & vbTab & CStr(bar))
    End Sub
End Class
```

The output from this sample is as follows:

```
<SecondTier> ToString    Second Tier: 5
<SecondTier> CStr        Second Tier: 5
<FirstTier> ToString     Second Tier: 5
<FirstTier> CStr         First Tier: 5
```

As you can see from the sample, the last cast gives an unusual response. In the first two casts, you are dealing with a `SecondTier` variable, so both `ToString` and `CStr` operations are called from the `SecondTier` class. When you cast the object to a `FirstTier` variable, the `ToString` operation is still routed to the `SecondTier` class, because this overrides the functionality in the `FirstTier`. However, because the `CStr` operation is a static function, it is routed to the `FirstTier` class, because this is the type of variable. Clearly, the safest option here is to ensure that you implement and call the `ToString` method on the instance variable. This rule holds for other operators, such as equals, which can be overridden instead of defining the = operator. In cases where you need a +, −, / or * operator, consider using nonstatic Add, Subtract, Divide, and Multiply operators that can be run on an instance.

As the final word on operator overloading and type conversion, if you find yourself needing to write either type of static method you should reassess your design to see if there is an alternative that uses instance methods such as `Equals` *or* `ToString`*.*

Property Accessibility

Good coding practices state that fields should be private and wrapped with a property. This property should be used to access the backing field, rather than to refer to the field itself. However, one of the difficulties has been exposing a public read property so that other classes can read the value, but also making the write part of the property either private or at least protected, preventing other classes from making changes to the value of the field. The only workaround for this was to declare two properties, a public read-only property and a private, or protected, read-write, or just write-only, property. Visual Studio 2008 lets you define properties with different levels of accessibility for the read and write components. For example, the `Name` property has a public read method and a protected write method:

C#

```csharp
public string Name
{
    get { return m_Name; }
    protected set { m_Name = value; }
}
```

VB.NET

```vbnet
Public Property Name() As String
    Get
        Return Me.m_Name
    End Get
    Protected Set(ByVal value As String)
        Me.m_Name = value
    End Set
End Property
```

The limitation on this is that the individual read or write components cannot have an accessibility that is more open than the property itself. For example, if you define the property to be protected, you cannot make the read component public. Instead, you need to make the property public and the write component protected.

Custom Events

Both C# and VB.NET can declare custom events that determine what happens when someone subscribes or unsubscribes from an event, and how the subscribers list is stored. Note that the VB.NET example is more verbose, but it enables you to control how the event is actually raised. In this case, each handler is called asynchronously for concurrent access. The RaiseEvent waits for all events to be fully raised before resuming:

C#

```csharp
List<EventHandler> EventHandlerList = new List<EventHandler>();

public event EventHandler Click{
    add{EventHandlerList.Add(value);}
    remove{EventHandlerList.Remove(value);}
}
```

VB.NET

```vb
Private EventHandlerList As New ArrayList

Public Custom Event Click As EventHandler
    AddHandler(ByVal value As EventHandler)
        EventHandlerList.Add(value)
    End AddHandler
    RemoveHandler(ByVal value As EventHandler)
        EventHandlerList.Remove(value)
    End RemoveHandler
    RaiseEvent(ByVal sender As Object, ByVal e As EventArgs)
        Dim results As New List(Of IAsyncResult)
        For Each handler As EventHandler In EventHandlerList
            If handler IsNot Nothing Then
                results.Add(handler.BeginInvoke(sender, e, Nothing, Nothing))
            End If
        Next
        While results.Find(AddressOf IsFinished) IsNot Nothing
            Threading.Thread.Sleep(250)
        End While
    End RaiseEvent
End Event
Private Function IsFinished(ByVal async As IAsyncResult) As Boolean
    Return async.IsCompleted
End Function
```

Summary

This chapter explained how generic types, methods, and delegates can significantly improve the efficiency with which you can write and maintain code. You were also introduced to features — such as property accessibility and custom events — that give you full control over your code and the way it executes.

The following chapter examines some of the new language features that support the introduction of LINQ, namely implicit typing, object initialization, and extension methods.

12

Anonymous Types, Extension Methods, and Lambda Expressions

Although the introduction of generics in version 2.0 of the .NET Framework reduced the amount of code that you had to write, there were still a number of opportunities to simplify both C# and VB.NET, letting you write more efficient code. In this chapter you will see a number of new language features that have been introduced to not only simplify the code you write but also support LINQ, which is covered in more detail in Chapter 21.

Object and Array Initialization

With the introduction of the .NET Framework, Microsoft moved developers into the world of object-oriented design. However, as you no doubt will have experienced, there are always multiple class designs with quite often no one right answer. One such open-ended example is the question of whether to design your class to have a single parameterless constructor, multiple constructors with different parameter combinations, or a single constructor with optional parameters. This choice is often dependent on how an instance of the class will be created and populated. In the past this might have been done in a number of statements, as shown in the following snippet:

VB.NET

```vbnet
Dim p As New Person
With p
    .FirstName = "Bob"
    .LastName = "Jane"
    .Age = 34
End With
```

C#

```
Person p = new Person();
p.FirstName = "Bob";
p.LastName = "Jane";
p.Age = 34;
```

If you have to create a number of objects this can rapidly make your code unreadable, which often leads designers to introduce constructors that take parameters. Doing this will pollute your class design with unnecessary and often ambiguous overloads. Now you can reduce the amount of code you have to write by combining object initialization and population into a single statement:

VB.NET

```
Dim p As New Person With {.Firstname = "Bob", .LastName = "Jane", .Age = 34}
```

C#

```
Person p = new Person {FirstName="Bob", LastName="Jane", Age=34};
```

You can initialize the object with any of the available constructors, as shown in the following VB.NET snippet, which uses a constructor where the parameters are the first and second name of the Person object being created:

```
Dim p As New Person("Bob", "Jane") With {.Age = 34}
```

As you can see from this snippet, it is less clear what the constructor parameters represent. Using named elements within the braces makes it easier for someone else to understand what properties are being set. You are not limited to just public properties. In fact, any accessible property or field can be specified within the braces. This is illustrated in Figure 12-1, where the IntelliSense drop-down shows the available properties and fields. In this case Age is a public property and mHeight is a public member variable.

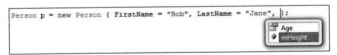

Figure 12-1

You will notice that the IntelliSense drop-down contains within the braces only the properties and fields that haven't already been used. This is only a feature of IntelliSense within C#. However, if you try to set a field or property multiple times in either language, you will get a build error.

As you have seen, object initialization is a shortcut for combining the creation and population of new objects. However, the significance of being able to create an object and populate properties in a single statement is that you can incorporate this ability into an expression tree. Expression trees are the foundation of LINQ, allowing the same syntax to be reused to query collections of objects, as well as XML and SQL data. Working directly with expression trees will be covered in more detail at the end of this chapter.

Object initialization can also be useful when you're populating arrays, collections, and lists. In the following snippet, an array of Person objects can be defined in a single statement.

VB.NET

```
Dim people As Person() = New Person() { _
                New Person With {.FirstName = "Bob", .LastName = "Jane"}, _
                New Person With {.FirstName = "Fred", .LastName = "Smith"}, _
                New Person With {.FirstName = "Sarah", .LastName = "Plane"}, _
                New Person With {.FirstName = "Jane", .LastName = "West"} _
                                    }
```

C#

```
Person[] people = new Person[]{
                    new Person {FirstName = "Bob", LastName = "Jane"},
                    new Person {FirstName = "Fred", LastName = "Smith"},
                    new Person {FirstName = "Sarah", LastName = "Plane"},
                    new Person {FirstName = "Jane", LastName = "West"}
                    };
```

In both languages you can omit the call to the array constructor (i.e. New Person() or new Person[]), as this is implicitly derived from the array initialization. If you are coding in C# you can apply this same syntax to the initialization of collections and lists, or any custom collection you may be creating.

```
List<Person> people = new List<Person>{
                    new Person {FirstName = "Bob", LastName = "Jane"},
                    new Person {FirstName = "Fred", LastName = "Smith"},
                    new Person {FirstName = "Sarah", LastName = "Plane"},
                    new Person {FirstName = "Jane", LastName = "West"}
                        };
```

In order for your custom collection to be able to use this syntax, it must both implement IEnumerable and have an accessible Add method (case-sensitive). The Add method must accept a single parameter that is the type, or a base class of the type, that you are going to be populating the list with. If there is a return parameter, it is ignored.

VB.NET developers can still use the IEnumerable constructor overload on a number of common collections and lists in order to populate them.

```
Dim people As New List(Of Person)(New Person() { _
            New Person With {.FirstName = "Bob", .LastName = "Jane"}, _
            New Person With {.FirstName = "Fred", .LastName = "Smith"}, _
            New Person With {.FirstName = "Sarah", .LastName = "Plane"}, _
            New Person With {.FirstName = "Jane", .LastName = "West"} _
                                })
```

Implicit Typing

One of the significant aspects of the .NET Framework is the Common Type System, which was introduced in order to separate the concept of a data type from any specific language implementation. This system is used as the basis for all .NET languages, guaranteeing type safety (although VB.NET developers can elect to disable Option Strict and/or Option Explicit, which both reduces the level of static, or "compile-time," type verification and can lead to undesirable runtime behavior).

More recently there has been a move away from statically typed languages toward more dynamic languages where the type checking is done at runtime. While this can improve developer productivity and increase flexibility so that an application can evolve, it also increases the probability that unexpected errors will be introduced.

In a concerted effort to ensure that the .NET Framework remains as the platform of choice, it was necessary for both C# and VB.NET to incorporate some of the productivity features of these more dynamic languages. One such feature is the ability to infer type information based on variable usage. This is often referred to as *type inferencing* or *implicit typing*. In Figure 12-2 you can see that we have not defined the type of the variable bob, yet when we use the variable it is clearly defined as a Person object. As this is a compiler feature, we get the added benefit of IntelliSense, which indicates what methods, properties, and fields are accessible, as well as designer indicators if we use a variable in a way that is not type-safe.

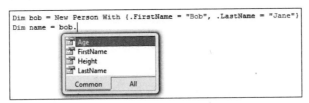

Figure 12-2

As you can see in Figure 12-2, implicit typing in VB.NET reuses the existing Dim keyword to indicate that a variable is being declared. In C#, the usual format for declaring a variable is to enter the variable type followed by the variable name. However, when using implicit typing you do not want to specify the variable type, as it will be inferred by the compiler; instead, you use the Var keyword.

```
var bob = new Person { FirstName = "Bob", LastName = "Jane" };
```

Implicit typing can be used in a number of places throughout your code. In fact, in most cases where you would define a variable of a particular type you can now use implicit typing. For example, the compiler can infer that For statements are of the iteration variable type.

```
For Each p In people
    MessageBox.Show(p.FirstName & " is " & p.Age & " years old")
Next
```

You might wonder why you would want to use this feature, as you could easily specify the variable types in these examples. In Chapters 21 to 23 you will be introduced to language-integrated queries, and there you will see the real benefits of implicit typing.

It is important to note that using implicit typing does not reduce the static type checking of your code. Behind the scenes the compiler still defines your variables with a specific type that is verifiable by the runtime engine.

VB.NET only: With its background in VB6, VB.NET has a number of options that can be toggled depending on how you want the compiler to enforce strong typing. These are Option Strict, Option Explicit, and Option Infer, and the following table contains a subset of the different combinations, showing how they affect the way you can write code.

Table 12-1: Toggling Options in VB.NET

Explicit	Strict	Infer	Allowed	Disallowed	Discussion
Off	Off	Off	w = 5		w is typed as an object, as it is not possible to infer the type.
On	Off	Off	Dim w = 5	w = 5	w is still typed as an object; the only condition is that w must be declared by means of the Dim syntax.
Off	Off	On	Dim w = 5 m = 6		In this case the type of w is inferred to be Integer but m remains an Object.
On	Off	On	Dim w = 5	w = 5	The type of w is inferred to be Integer.
On	On	Off	Dim w as Integer = 5	w = 5 Dim w = 5	The type of w is explicitly set to be Integer.
On	On	On	Dim w as Integer = 5 Dim w = 5	w = 5 Dim w	w must be declared and either a type specified or a value specified from which to infer the type.

Essentially, the rules are that Option Explicit requires the variable to be declared by means of the Dim keyword. Option Strict requires that either the type of the variable is specified or can be inferred by the compiler, and Option Infer determines whether type inferencing is enabled. Note that disabling Option Infer can make working with LINQ very difficult.

Anonymous Types

Often when you are manipulating data you may find that you need to record pairs of data. For example, when iterating through people in a database you might want to extract height and weight. You can either use a built-in type (in this case a Point or PointF might suffice) or create your own class or structure in which to store the information. If you do this only once within your entire application, it seems quite superfluous to have to create a separate file, think of an appropriate class or structure name, and define all the fields, properties, and constructors. Anonymous types give you an easy way to create these types using implicit typing, which you have just learned about.

VB.NET

```
Dim personAge = New With {.Name = "Bob", .Age = 55}
```

C#

```
var personAge=new {Name="Bob", Age=55};
```

In the preceding example, you can see that the `personAge` variable is being assigned a value that is made up of a `String` and an `Integer`. If you were to interrogate the type information of the `personAge` variable, you would see that it is named `"VB$AnonymousType_0`2[System.String,System.Int32]"` (or `"<>f__AnonymousType0`2[System.String,System.Int32]"` in C#) and that it has the properties `Name` and `Age`. One of the points of difference between C# and VB.NET is whether these properties are read-only (i.e., immutable) or not. In C# all properties of an anonymous type are immutable, as shown by the IntelliSense in Figure 12-3. This makes generating hash codes simpler. Essentially, if the properties don't change then they can all be used to generate the hash code for the object, which is used for accessing items within a dictionary.

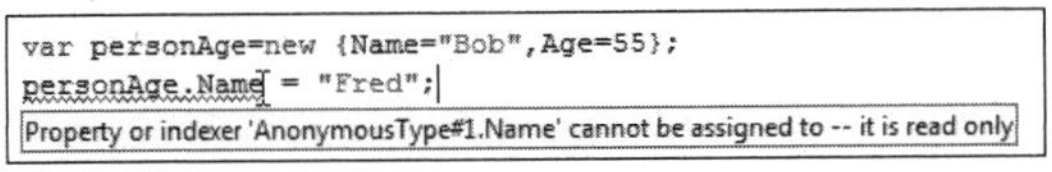

```
var personAge=new {Name="Bob",Age=55};
personAge.Name = "Fred";
Property or indexer 'AnonymousType#1.Name' cannot be assigned to -- it is read only
```

Figure 12-3

While the properties of the variable `personAge` are immutable, it is possible to assign a new object to `personAge`. The new object must have the anonymous type structure, which is determined by the names, types to, and order of the members.

In contrast, the properties in VB.NET by default are not read-only, but you can use the `Key` keyword to specify which properties should be immutable and thus used as part of the hash code. Figure 12-4 shows how you can make the `Name` property read-only by inserting the `Key` keyword before the property name. Again, this is indicated with appropriate IntelliSense when you attempt to assign a value to the `Name` property. The `Age` property, however, is still mutable.

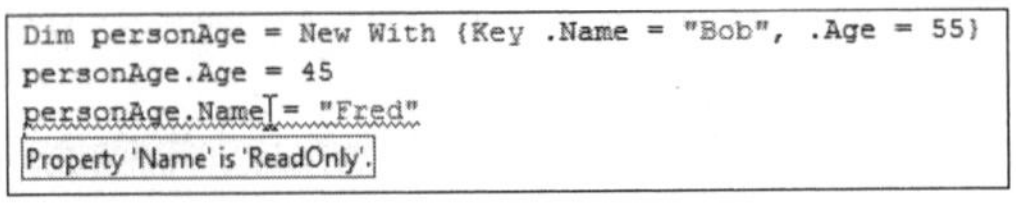

```
Dim personAge = New With {Key .Name = "Bob", .Age = 55}
personAge.Age = 45
personAge.Name = "Fred"
Property 'Name' is 'ReadOnly'.
```

Figure 12-4

It might appear that having only a single keyed property would give you the most flexibility. However, you should be aware that this might result in objects that are not equal and having same hash code. This happens when two objects have the same values for the keyed properties (in which case the hash code is identical) but different non-keyed properties.

Now that you have seen how you can create an anonymous type using the full syntax, it's time to look at how you can use the condensed form that doesn't require you to name all the properties. In the following example, the `Person` object, `p`, is projected into a new variable, `nameAge`. The first property uses the syntax you have already seen in order to rename the property from `FirstName` to just `Name`. There is no need to rename the `Age` property, so the syntax has been condensed appropriately. Note that when you're doing this, the anonymous type property can only be inferred from a single property with no arguments or expressions. In other words, you can't supply `p.Age + 5` and expect the compiler to infer `Age`.

VB.NET

```
Dim p As New Person With {.FirstName = "Bob", .LastName = "Jane", .Age = 55}
Dim nameAge = New With {.Name = p.FirstName, p.Age}
```

C#

```
Person p = new Person { FirstName = "Bob", LastName = "Jane", Age=55 };
var nameAge = new { Name = p.FirstName, p.Age };
```

Again, you might wonder where anonymous types would be useful. Imagine that you want to iterate through a collection of `Person` objects and retrieve just the first name and age as a duple of data. Instead of having to declare a class or structure, you can create an anonymous type to hold the information. The newly created collection might then be passed on to other operations in which only the first name and age of each person is required.

```
Dim ages = CreateList(New With {.Name = "", .Age = 0})
For Each p In people
    ages.Add(New With {.Name = p.FirstName, .Age = p.Age})
Next
```

This snippet highlights one of the key problems with anonymous types, which is that you don't have direct access to the type information. This is a problem when you want to combine anonymous types with generics. In the case above, the variable `ages` is actually a `List(of T)`, but in order to create the list we have to use a little magic to coerce the compiler into working out what type `T` should be. The `CreateList` method, shown in the following snippet, is a generic method that takes a single argument of type `T` and returns a new `List(of T)`. As the compiler can infer `T` from the example object passed into the method, you don't have to explicitly specify `T` when calling the method.

```
Public Function CreateList(Of T)(ByVal example As T) As List(Of T)
    Return New List(Of T)
End Function
```

While this might seem a bit of a hack, you will see later on that you will seldom have to explicitly create lists of anonymous types, as there is a simpler way to project information from one collection into another.

Extension Methods

A design question that often arises is whether to extend a given interface to include a specific method. Extending any widely used interface, for example `IEnumerable`, will not only break contracts where the interface has been implemented but will also force any future class that implements the interface to include the new method. Although there are scenarios where this is warranted, there are also numerous cases in which you simply want to create a method to manipulate an object that matches a particular interface.

One possible example involves a `Count` method that simply iterates through an `IEnumerable` and returns the number of elements. Adding this method to the `IEnumerable` interface would actually increase the amount of redundant code, as each class implementing the interface would have to implement the `Count` method. A solution to this problem is to create a helper class that has a static `Count` method that accepts an `IEnumerable` parameter.

```
Public Shared Function Count(ByVal items As IEnumerable) As Integer
    Dim i As Integer = 0
    For Each x In items
        i += 1
    Next
    Return i
End Function

Dim cnt = Count(people)
```

While this solution is adequate in most scenarios, it can lead to some terse-looking code when you use multiple static methods to manipulate a given object. Extension methods promote readability by enabling you to declare static methods that appear to modify the public type information for a class or interface. For example, in the case of the IEnumerable interface there are built-in extension methods that enable you to call people.Count in order to access the number of items in people, a variable declared as an IEnumerable. As you can see from the IntelliSense in Figure 12-5, the Count method appears as if it were an instance method, although it can be distinguished by the extension method icon to the left of the method name and the <Extension> prefix in the tooltip information.

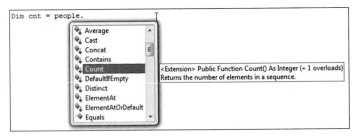

Figure 12-5

All extension methods are static, must be declared in a static class (or a module in the case of VB.NET), and must be marked with the Extension attribute. The Extension attribute informs the compiler that the method should be available for all objects that match the type of the first argument. In the following example, the extension method would be available in the IntelliSense list for Person objects, or any class that derives from Person. Note that the C# snippet doesn't explicitly declare the Extension attribute; instead, it uses the this keyword to indicate that it is an extension method.

VB.NET

```
Public Module PersonHelper
    <System.Runtime.CompilerServices.Extension()> _
    Public Function AgeMetric(ByVal p As Person) As Double
        Return p.Age / 2 + 7
    End Function
End Module
```

C#

```csharp
public static class PersonHelper
{
    public static double AgeMetric(this Person p)
    {
        return p.Age/2 +7;
    }
}
```

In order to make use of extension methods, the static class (or module in VB.NET) has to be brought into scope via a `using` statement (or `imports` in VB.NET). This is true even if the extension method is in the same code file in which it is being used.

VB.NET

```vbnet
imports PersonHelper
```

C#

```csharp
using PersonHelper;
```

When an extension method is invoked it is done almost the same way as for any conventional static method, the difference being that instead of all parameters being explicitly passed in, the first argument is inferred by the compiler from the calling context. In the preceding example, the collection `people` would be passed into the `Count` method. This, of course, means that there is one less argument to be specified when an extension method is being called.

Although extension methods are called in a similar way to instance methods, they are limited to accessing the public methods and properties of the arguments. Because of this it is common practice for extension methods to return new objects, rather than modifying the original argument. Following this practice means that extension methods can easily be chained. For example, the following code snippet takes persons 10 to 15, in reverse order from the `people` collection.

```vbnet
Dim somePeople = people.Skip(10).Take(5).Reverse()
```

Each of the three extension methods — `Skip`, `Take`, and `Reverse` — accepts an `IEnumerable` as its first (hidden) argument and returns a new `IEnumerable`. The returned `IEnumerable` is then passed into the subsequent extension method.

Lambda Expressions

Over successive versions of the .NET Framework, the syntax with which you can define and reference reusable functions has evolved. In the early versions, you had to explicitly declare a delegate and then create an instance of it in order to obtain a reference to a function. In version 2.0 of the .NET Framework, C# shipped with a new feature called *anonymous methods*, whereby you could declare a multiple-line reusable function within a method. *Lambda expressions* in their simplest form are just a reduced notation for anonymous methods. However, lambda expressions can also be specified as expression trees. This means that you can combine, manipulate, and extend them dynamically before invoking them.

To begin with, let's examine the following simple lambda function, which takes an input parameter, x, increments it, and returns the new value. When the function is executed with an input value of 5, the return value assigned to the variable y will be 6.

VB.NET

```
Dim fn As Func(Of Integer, Integer) = Function(x) x + 1
Dim y As Integer = fn(5)
```

C#

```
Func<int, int> fn = x => x + 1;
int y = fn(5);
```

You can see that in both languages the type of fn has been explicitly declared. Func is a generic delegate that is defined within the framework and has five overloads with a varying number of input parameters and a single return value. In this case there is a single input parameter, but because both input and return values are generic, there are two generic parameters. From the earlier discussion of implicit typing and anonymous types, you would expect that you could simplify this syntax by removing the explicit reference to the Func delegate. Unfortunately, this is only the case in VB.NET, and you will notice that we need to specify what type the input variable x is.

VB.NET

```
Dim fn = Function(x As Integer) x + 1
Dim y As Integer = fn(5)
```

Manipulating the input parameters has only limited benefits over the more traditional approach of creating a delegate to a method and then calling it. The lambda syntax also enables you to reference variables in the containing method. To do this without lambda expressions would require a lot of code to encapsulate the referenced variables. Take the following snippet, wherein the method-level variable inc determines how much to increment x by. The output values y and z will end up with the values 20 and 25 respectively.

```
Dim inc As Integer = 10
Dim fn = Function(x As Integer) x + inc
Dim y = fn(10)
inc = 15
Dim z = fn(10)
```

Although VB.NET has better support for implicit typing with lambdas, C# has a much richer functionality when it comes to what you can do within a lambda expression. So far we have only seen a lambda expression with a single expression that returns a value. An alternative syntax for this uses curly braces to indicate the beginning and end of the lambda expression. This means that C# can have multiple statements, whereas VB.NET is limited to only a single return expression.

```
int inc = 5;
Func<int, int> fn = x => {inc += 5;
                          return x + inc; };
```

Using this syntax (that is, using the curly braces to delimit the lambda body) means that the expression cannot be referenced as an expression tree.

It is also possible to create lambda expressions with no input parameters, and, with C#, lambda expressions with no return values. Because C# doesn't support implicit typing with lambda expressions, you have to either use one of the existing zero-argument, no-return values or delegates, or create your own. In the following snippet you can see that fn is a `MethodInvoker` delegate, but we could have also used the `Threadstart` delegate, as it has the same signature.

VB.NET

```
Dim inc as Integer = 5
Dim noInput = Function() inc + 1
```

C#

```
int inc = 5;
Func<int> noInput = () => inc + 1;
System.Windows.Forms.MethodInvoker noReturn = () => inc += 5;
```

All these scenarios are lambda expressions, but you may come across references to lambda functions *and* lambda statements. *Essentially, these terms refer to specific subsets of lambda expressions, those that return values and those that don't, respectively.*

Another aspect of lambda expressions is that they can be represented as expression trees. An expression tree is a representation of a single-line lambda expression that can be manipulated at runtime, compiled (during code execution), and then executed.

VB.NET

```
Imports System.Linq.Expressions
...
Dim fnexp As Expression(Of Func(Of Integer, Integer)) = Function(x) x + 1
Dim fnexp2 = Expression.Lambda(Of Func(Of Integer, Integer))( _
                        Expression.Add(fnexp.Body, Expression.Constant(5)), _
                        fnexp.Parameters)
Dim fn2 = fnexp2.Compile()
Dim result = fn2(5)
```

C#

```
using System.Linq.Expressions
...
Expression<Func<int, int>> fnexp = x => x + 1;
var fnexp2=Expression.Lambda<Func<int,int>>(
                        Expression.Add(fnexp.Body, Expression.Constant(5)),
                        fnexp.Parameters);
Func<int, int> fn2 = fnexp2.Compile();
int result = fn2(5);
```

As you can see from this example, we have taken a simple lambda expression, represented as an expression tree (by means of the `Expression` class), and then added a constant of 5 to it. The net effect is that we now have another expression tree that takes x, adds 1 to it, then adds 5 to it, giving a result of 11. As each operation typically has two operands, you end up with an in-memory binary tree of which the leaves represent the operands, which are linked by operators.

Expression trees are an important concept when you consider that LINQ was intended to be a query language independent of implementation technology. When a lambda expression is represented as a tree (and you will see later that LINQ statements can also be represented as expression trees), the work of evaluating the expression can be passed across language, technology, or even machine boundaries. For example, if you have an expression that selects rows from a database, this would be much better performed in T-SQL within the SQL Server engine, perhaps even on a remote database server, than in .NET, in memory on the local machine.

Summary

In order to draw together the points you have seen in this chapter, let's go back to an early example in which we were projecting the `first name` and `age` properties from the `people` collection into a newly created list. The following extension method enables us to not only supply a predicate for determining which objects to select, but also to specify a function for doing the output projection.

```
<System.Runtime.CompilerServices.Extension()> _
Public Function Retrieve(Of TInput, TResult)( _
                            ByVal source As IEnumerable(Of TInput), _
                            ByVal predicate As Func(Of TInput, Boolean), _
                            ByVal projection As Func(Of TInput, TResult) _
                                ) As IEnumerable(Of TResult)

    Dim outList As New List(Of TResult)
    For Each inputValue In source
        If predicate(inputValue) Then outList.Add(projection(inputValue))
    Next
    Return outList
End Function
```

Note that in this example we have been able to keep all the parameters, both input and output, generic enough that the method can be used across a wide range of `IEnumerable` collections and lists. When this method is invoked, we use the expressive power of extension methods so that it appears as an instance method on the `people` collection. As you saw earlier, we could chain the output of this method with another extension method for an `IEnumerable` object.

```
Dim peopleAges = people.Retrieve( _
    Function(inp As Person) inp.Age > 40, _
    Function(outp As Person) New With {.Name = outp.FirstName, outp.Age} _
        )
```

To determine which `Person` objects to return, a simple lambda function checks if the age is greater than 40. Interestingly, we use an anonymous type in the lambda function to project from a `Person` to the name-age duple. Doing this also requires the compiler to use type inferencing to determine the resulting `IEnumerable`, `peopleAges` — the contents of this `IEnumerable` all have properties `Name` (`String`) and `Age` (`Integer`).

Through this chapter you have seen a number of language improvements, syntactical shortcuts that contribute to the objective of creating expression trees that can be invoked. This is the foundation on which LINQ is based. You will see significant improvements in your ability to query data wherever it may be located.

13

Language-Specific Features

One of the hotly debated topics among developers is which .NET language is the best for performance, efficient programming, readability, and so on. Although each of the .NET languages has a different objective and target market, developers are continually seeing long-term feature parity. In fact, there are very few circumstances where it is possible to do something in one language that can't be done in another. This chapter examines some features that are specific to either C# or VB.NET.

C#

The C# language has always been at the forefront of language innovation, with a focus on writing efficient code. It includes features such as anonymous methods, iterators, automatic properties, and static classes that help tidy up your code and make it more efficient.

Anonymous Methods

Anonymous methods are essentially methods that do not have a name, and at surface level they appear and behave the same way as normal methods. A common use for an anonymous method is writing event handlers. Instead of declaring a method and adding a new delegate instance to the event, this can be condensed into a single statement, with the anonymous method appearing inline. This is illustrated in the following example:

```
private void Form1_Load(object sender, EventArgs e)
{
    this.button1.Click += new EventHandler(OldStyleEventHandler);

    this.button1.Click += delegate{
                            Console.WriteLine("Button pressed - new school!");
                                  };
}
private void OldStyleEventHandler(object sender, EventArgs e){
    Console.WriteLine("Button pressed - old school!");
}
```

The true power of anonymous methods is that they can reference variables declared in the method in which the anonymous method appears. The following example searches a list of employees, as you did in the previous chapter, for all employees who have salaries less than $40,000. The difference here is that instead of defining this threshold in the predicate method, the amount is held in a method variable. This dramatically reduces the amount of code you have to write to pass variables to a predicate method. The alternative is to define a class variable and use that to pass in the value to the predicate method.

```
private void ButtonClick(object sender, EventArgs e)
{
    List<Employee> employees = GetEmployees();
    int wage = 0;
    bool reverse = false;
    Predicate<Employee> employeeSearch = delegate(Employee emp)
    {
        if (reverse==false)
            return (emp.Wage < wage);
        else
            return !(emp.Wage < wage);
    };

    wage = 40000;
    List<Employee> lowWageEmployees = employees.FindAll(employeeSearch);
    wage=60000;
    List<Employee> mediumWageEmployees = employees.FindAll(employeeSearch);
    reverse = true;
    List<Employee> highWageEmployees = employees.FindAll(employeeSearch);
}
```

In this example, you can see that an anonymous method has been declared within the ButtonClick method. The anonymous method references two variables from the containing method: wage and reverse. Although the anonymous method is declared early in the method, when it is evaluated it uses the current values of these variables. One of the challenges with debugging anonymous methods is this delayed execution pattern. You can set breakpoints within the anonymous method, as shown in Figure 13-1, but these won't be hit until the method is evaluated.

```
List<Employee> employees = GetEmployees();
int wage = 0;
bool reverse = false;
Predicate<Employee> employeeSearch = delegate(Employee emp)
{
    if (reverse == false)
        return (emp.Wage < wage);
    else
        return !(emp.Wage < wage);
};

wage = 40000;
var lowWageEmployees = employees.FindAll(employeeSearch);
```

Figure 13-1

In this figure you can see that the last line is highlighted, which indicates it is part of the current call stack. Figure 13-2 further illustrates this with an excerpt from the call stack window.

Figure 13-2

Here you can see that it is the `ButtonClick` method that is executing. When the execution gets to the `FindAll` method it calls the anonymous method, as indicated by the top line in Figure 13-2, which is where the breakpoint is set in Figure 13-1.

Iterators

Prior to generics, you not only had to write your own custom collections, you also had to write enumerators that could be used to iterate through the collection. In addition, if you wanted to define an enumerator that iterated through the collection in a different order, you had to generate an entire class that maintained state information. Writing an iterator in C# dramatically reduces the amount of code you have to write in order to iterate through a collection, as illustrated in the following example:

```
public class ListIterator<T> : IEnumerable<T>
{
    List<T> myList;
    public ListIterator(List<T> listToIterate){
        myList=listToIterate;
    }

    public IEnumerator<T> GetEnumerator() {
        foreach (T x in myList) yield return x;
    }

    System.Collections.IEnumerator System.Collections.IEnumerable.GetEnumerator()
    {
        return GetEnumerator();
    }

    public IEnumerable<T> Top5OddItems {
        get {
            int cnt = 0;
            for (int i = 0; i < myList.Count - 1; i++){
                if (i % 2 == 0){
                    cnt += 1;
                    yield return myList[i];
                }
                if (cnt == 5) yield break;
            }
        }
    }
}
```

In this example, the keyword `yield` is used to return a particular value in the collection. At the end of the collection, you can either allow the method to return, as the first iterator does, or you can use `yield break` to indicate the end of the collection. Both the `GetEnumerator` and `Top5OddItems` iterators can be used to cycle through the items in the `List`, as shown in the following snippet:

```
public static void PrintNumbers()
{
    List<int> randomNumbers = GetNumbers();

    Console.WriteLine("Normal Enumeration");
    foreach (int x in (new ListIterator<int>(randomNumbers)))
    {
        Console.WriteLine("{0}", x.ToString());
    }

    Console.WriteLine("Top 5 Odd Values");
    foreach (int x in (new ListIterator<int>(randomNumbers)).Top5OddItems)
    {
        Console.WriteLine("{0}", x.ToString());
    }
}
```

The debugging experience for iterators can be a little confusing, especially while you are enumerating the collection — the point of execution appears to jump in and out of the enumeration method. Each time through the `foreach` loop the point of execution returns to the enumeration method at the previous yield statement, returning when it either exits the enumeration method or it encounters another yield statement.

Static Classes

At some stage most of you have written a class that contains only static methods. In the past there was always the possibility that someone would create an instance of this class. The only way to prevent this was to create a private constructor and make the class non-inheritable. In the future, however, an instance method might accidentally be added to this class, which of course could not be called, because an instance of the class could not be created. C# now permits a class to be marked as `static`, which not only prevents an instance of the class from being created, it also prevents any class from inheriting from it and provides design-time checking to ensure that all methods contained in the class are static methods:

```
public static class HelperMethods
{
    static Random rand = new Random();
    public static int RandomNumber(int min, int max)
    {
        return rand.Next(min, max);
    }
}
```

In this code snippet, the `static` keyword in the first line indicates that this is a static class. As such, it cannot contain instance variables or methods.

Naming Conflicts

An issue that crops up occasionally is how to deal with naming conflicts. Of course, good design practices are one of the best ways to minimize the chance of a conflict. However, this alone is not enough, because quite often you don't have control over how types in third-party libraries are named. This section covers three techniques to eliminate naming conflicts. To illustrate them, we'll start from the scenario in which you have a naming conflict for the class BadlyNamedClass in two namespaces:

```
namespace NamingConflict1
{
    public class BadlyNamedClass
    {
        public static string HelloWorld()
        {
            return "Hi everyone! - class2";
        }
    }
}

namespace NamingConflict2
{
    public class BadlyNamedClass
    {
        public static string HelloWorld()
        {
            return "Hi everyone! - class1";
        }
    }
}
```

Clearly, if you import both NamingConflict1 and NamingConflict2, you will end up with a naming conflict when you try to reference the class BadlyNamedClass, as shown in Figure 13-3.

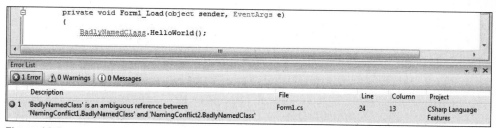

Figure 13-3

Namespace Alias Qualifier

When namespaces are imported into a source file with the using statement, the namespaces can be assigned an alias. In addition to minimizing the code you have to write when accessing a type contained within the referenced namespace, providing an alias means types with the same name in different imported namespaces can be distinguished using the alias. The following example uses a namespace alias to resolve the conflict illustrated in the opener to this section:

```
using NCF1 = NamingConflict2;
using NCF2 = NamingConflict1;
public class Naming
{
    public static string SayHelloWorldVersion1()
    {
        return NCF1.BadlyNamedClass.HelloWorld();
    }
    public static string SayHelloWorldVersion2()
    {
        return NCF2.BadlyNamedClass.HelloWorld();
    }
}
```

This resolves the current conflict, but what happens when you introduce a class called either NCF1 or NCF2? You end up with a naming conflict between the introduced class and the alias. The namespace alias qualifier :: was added so this conflict could be resolved without changing the alias. To fix the code snippet, you would insert the qualifier whenever you reference NCF1 or NCF2:

```
using NCF1 = NamingConflict2;
using NCF2 = NamingConflict1;
public class Naming
{
    public static string SayHelloWorldVersion1()
    {
        return NCF1::BadlyNamedClass.HelloWorld();
    }
}
public class NCF1 {/*...*/}
public class NCF2 {/*...*/}
```

The namespace alias qualifier can only be preceded by a using alias (as shown here), the global keyword, or an extern alias (both to be covered in the next sections).

Global

The global identifier is a reference to the global namespace that encompasses all types and namespaces. When used with the namespace alias qualifier, global ensures a full hierarchy match between the referenced type and any imported types. For example, you can modify the sample to use the global identifier:

```
public class Naming
{
    public static string SayHelloWorldVersion1()
    {
        return global::NamingConflict1.BadlyNamedClass.HelloWorld();
    }
}
public class NCF1 {/*...*/}
public class NCF2 {/*...*/}
```

Extern Aliases

Despite both the namespace alias qualifier and the global identifier, it is still possible to introduce conflicts. For example, adding a class called NamingConflict1 would clash with the namespace you were trying to import. An alternative is to use an *extern alias* to provide an alias to an external reference. When a reference is added to a project, by default it is assigned to the global namespace and is subsequently available throughout the project. However, this can be modified by assigning the reference to an alternative alias. In Figure 13-4, the conflicting assembly has been assigned an external alias of X.

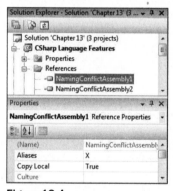

Figure 13-4

Types and namespaces that exist in references that are added to the Global namespace can be used without explicitly importing them into a source file using their fully qualified names. When an alternative alias is specified, as shown in Figure 13-4, this reference must be imported into every source file that needs to use types or namespaces defined within it. This is done with the extern alias statement, as shown in the following example:

```
extern alias X;

public class Naming
{
    public static string SayHelloWorldVersion1()
    {
        return X::NamingConflict1.BadlyNamedClass.HelloWorld();
    }
}
public class NCF1 {/*...*/}
public class NamingConflict1 {/*...*/}
```

This example added a reference to the assembly that contains the NamingConflict1 namespace, and set the Aliases property to X, as shown in Figure 13-4. To reference classes within this assembly, use the namespace alias qualifier, preceded by the extern alias defined at the top of the source file.

Pragma

Occasionally you would like to ignore compile warnings. This can be done for superficial reasons — perhaps you don't want a warning to appear in the build log. Occasionally, you have a legitimate need to suppress a compile warning; it might be necessary to use a method that has been marked obsolete during a transition phase of a project. Some teams have the compile process set to treat all warnings as errors; in this case, you can use the Pragma statement to disable and then restore warnings:

```
[Obsolete]
public static string AnOldMethod()
{ return "Old code...."; }
```

```
#pragma warning disable 168
public static string CodeToBeUpgraded()
{
    int x;
    #pragma warning disable 612
    return AnOldMethod();
    #pragma warning restore 612
}
#pragma warning restore 168
```

Two warnings are disabled in this code. The first, warning 168, is raised because you have not used the variable x. The second, warning 612, is raised because you are referencing a method marked with the Obsolete attribute. These warning numbers are very cryptic and your code would benefit from some comments describing each warning and why it is disabled. You may be wondering how you know which warnings you need to disable. The easiest way to determine the warning number is to examine the build output, as shown in Figure 13-5.

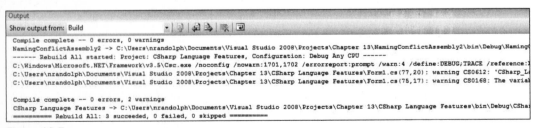

Figure 13-5

Here, the warnings CS0612 and CS0168 are visible in the middle of the build output window, with a description accompanying the warning.

Automatic Properties

Quite often when you define the fields for a class you will also define a property through which that field can be modified. This is the principle of encapsulation and allows us to easily change implementation details, for example the name of the field, without breaking other code. Though this is definitely good coding practice, it is a little cumbersome to write and maintain when all the property does is get and set the underlying field. For this reason C# now has Automatic Properties, where the backing field no longer has to be explicitly defined. As shown in Figure 13-6, the property snippet, prop, has been updated to use automatic[ally implemented] properties.

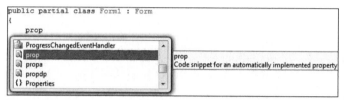

Figure 13-6

When you insert this snippet you get an expansion similar to Figure 13-7. Here the default expansion has been modified by setting the accessibility of the set operation to "protected" by adding in the appropriate keyword (the type and name of this property have also been updated to string and Summary).

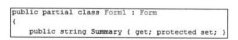

Figure 13-7

As you can see from this code, there is no defined backing field. If at a later stage you want to change the behavior of the property, or you want to explicitly define the backing field, you can simply complete the implementation details.

VB.NET

Very few new language features are available only in VB.NET, the most significant being the My namespace, which is covered in detail in the next chapter. This said, there are some small additions to the language that are worth knowing about.

IsNot

The IsNot operator is the counterpart to the Is operator that is used for reference equality comparisons. Whereas the Is operator will evaluate to True if the references are equal, the IsNot operator will evaluate to True if the references are not equal. Although a minor improvement, this keyword can save a considerable amount of typing, eliminating the need to go back to the beginning of a conditional statement and insert the Not operator:

```
Dim aPerson As New Person
Dim bPerson As New Person
If Not aPerson Is bPerson Then
    Console.WriteLine("This is the old way of doing this kind of check")
End If
If aPerson IsNot bPerson Then
    Console.WriteLine("This is the old way of doing this kind of check")
End If
```

Not only does the IsNot operator make it more efficient to write the code; it also makes it easier to read. Instead of the "Yoda-speak" expression If Not aPerson Is bPerson Then, you have the much more readable expression If aPerson IsNot bPerson Then.

Global

The VB.NET Global keyword is very similar to the C# identifier with the same name. Both are used to escape to the outermost namespace, and both are used to remove any ambiguity when resolving namespace and type names. In the following example the System class is preventing the code from compiling because there is no Int32. However, the definition of y uses the Global keyword to escape to the outermost namespace to correctly resolve the System.Int32 to the .NET Framework type.

```
Public Class System
End Class

Public Class Test
    Private Sub Example()
        'This won't compile as Int32 doesn't exist in the System class
        Dim x As System.Int32

        'Global escapes out so that we can reference the .NET FX System class
        Dim y As Global.System.Int32
    End Sub
End Class
```

TryCast

In an ideal world you would always work with interfaces and there would never be a need to cast between object types. However, the reality is that you build complex applications and often have to break some of the rules of object-oriented programming to get the job done. To this end, one of the most commonly used code snippets is the *test-and-cast technique*, whereby you test an object to determine whether it is of a certain type before casting it to that type so you can work with it. The problem with this approach is that you are in fact doing two casts, because the TypeOf expression attempts to convert the object to the test type. The result of the conversion is either nothing or an object that matches the test type, so the TypeOf expression then does a check to determine whether the result is nothing. If the result is not nothing, and the conditional statement is true, then the second cast is performed to retrieve the variable that matches the test type. The following example illustrates both the original syntax, using TypeOf, and the improved syntax, using TryCast, for working with objects of unknown type:

```
Dim fred As Object = New Person
If TypeOf (fred) Is Employee Then
    Dim emp As Employee = CType(fred, Employee)
    'Do actions with employee
End If

Dim joe As Object = New Person
Dim anotherEmployee As Employee = TryCast(joe, Employee)
If anotherEmployee IsNot Nothing Then
    'Do actions with another employee
End If
```

The `TryCast` expression, as illustrated in the second half of this example, maps directly to the `isinst` CLR instruction, which will return either nothing or an object that matches the test type. The result can then be compared with nothing before performing operations on the object.

Ternary If Operator

Unlike most other languages until recently, VB.NET did not have a single-line ternary `If` statement. To compensate for this there is the `IIf` function in the Visual Basic library. Unfortunately, because this is a simple function, it evaluates all arguments before calling into the function. For example, the following code would throw a `NullReferenceException` in the case that the company did not exist:

```
Dim address as String = IIf(company IsNot Nothing, company.Address, "")
```

The new ternary `If` statement is part of the Visual Basic language, which means that despite appearing as a function, it behaves slightly differently. It is similar to the `IIf` function in that it takes three arguments: a test expression, and return values for when the expression evaluates to true and false. However, unlike the `IIf` function, it evaluates the test expression first, and only then evaluates the corresponding return values.

Figure 13-8 illustrates the slightly misleading IntelliSense that appears for the `If` statement. From this figure it would appear that the return value from the `If` statement is an object. In fact the return value is inferred from the type of the two return value arguments.

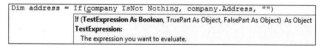

Figure 13-8

If you attempt to return two different types, the compiler will complain, saying that it cannot infer a common type and that you need to provide a conversion for one of the arguments.

Relaxed Delegates

One of the most powerful features of .NET is the concept of delegates, which essentially allows you to manipulate a reference to a function so as to dynamically invoke it. Delegates in VB.NET have been a source of frustration because they don't adhere to the same rules as other function calls when it comes to the compiler checking the calling syntax against the signature of the method. In order to call a delegate the signatures must match exactly; in the case of using a sub-class as an argument, you would have had to cast it to the type that was specified in the delegate signature. With relaxed delegates, introduced in VB9.0, delegates behave in the same way as other functions. For example, the following code illustrates how you can add event handlers with different signatures to the same event:

```vb.net
Public Class CustomerEventArgs
    Inherits EventArgs
    ...
End Class

Public Event DataChange As EventHandler(Of CustomerEventArgs)

Private Sub SignatureMatches(ByVal sender As Object, _
                    ByVal e As CustomerEventArgs) Handles Me.DataChange
End Sub

Private Sub RelaxedSignature(ByVal sender As Object, _
                    ByVal e As EventArgs) Handles Me.DataChange
End Sub

Private Sub NoArguments() Handles Me.DataChange
End Sub
```

The first method `SignatureMatches` exactly matches the delegate `DataChange` so there is no surprise that this is compiled. In the second method the second parameter is the base class `EventArgs`, from which `CustomerEventArgs` inherits. VB.NET now allows you to use both the `Handles` and `AddressOf` syntax to wire up delegates where the type of the parameters matches via inheritance.

In the last method, both arguments have been dropped and yet this still compiles. Using the `Handles` syntax, the VB.NET compiler will allow a partial match between the handler method and the delegate signature.

Summary

This chapter described the features that differentiate C# and VB.NET. It would appear that C#, with anonymous methods and iterators, is slightly ahead of the game. However, not being able to write anonymous methods and iterators does not limit the code that a VB.NET developer can write. The two primary .NET languages, C# and VB.NET, do have different objectives, but despite their best attempts to differentiate themselves they are constrained by the direction of the .NET Framework itself. In the long run there will be language parity, with differences only in the syntax and the functionality within Visual Studio.

The next chapter looks at the My namespace, which combines a rich class library with a powerful application model to deliver a framework with which developers can truly be more productive.

14

The My Namespace

The release of the .NET Framework was supposed to mark a revolution in the ability to rapidly build applications. However, for many Visual Basic programmers many tasks actually became more complex and a lot harder to understand. For example, where previously you could use a simple `Print` command to send a document to the default printer, you now needed to create a whole bunch of objects, and trap events to determine when and what those objects could print. Microsoft shipped the My namespace with version 2.0 of the .NET Framework, which gives Visual Basic developers shortcuts to common tasks.

This chapter examines the My namespace and describes how you can harness it to simplify the creation of applications. As you'll see, the My namespace actually encompasses web development as well, bringing the ease of development that Visual Basic 6 programmers were used to in Windows development to web applications and services. Even C# developers can take advantage of My, which can be handy for simple tasks that don't warrant the extra effort of writing masses of class-based code.

What Is the My Namespace?

The My namespace is actually a set of wrapper classes and structures that encapsulate complete sets of .NET classes and automated object instantiations and initializations. The structure of My, shown in Figure 14-1, shows that it is similar to a real namespace hierarchy. These classes mean that rather than creating an instance of a system class, initializing it with the values you need, and then using it for the specific purpose you need it for, you can simply refer to the corresponding My class and let .NET work out what needs to happen behind the scenes to achieve the same result. Consider more complex tasks that require you to create up to dozens of classes to do something simple, such as establish user credentials or navigate through the file system efficiently. Then consider the same one-class access that My provides for such functions, and you begin to see what can be achieved.

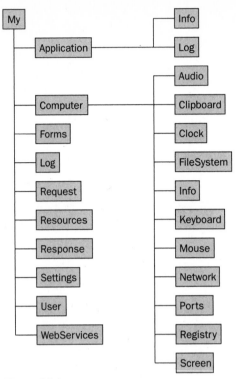

Figure 14-1

Ten major classes compose the top level of My. Each class has a number of methods and properties that you can use in your application, and two of them, My.Application and My.Computer, have additional subordinate classes in the namespace-like structure, which in turn have their own methods and properties. In a moment you'll see what each of them can do in detail, but here's a quick reference:

Table 14-1: Classes in the Top Level of My

My Object	Purpose
My.Application	Used to access information about the application, My.Application also exposes certain events that are application-wide. In addition, this class has two subordinate My classes: My.Application.Log and My.Application.Info.
My.Computer	Deals with the computer system in which the application is running, and is the most extensive My object. In fact, the My.Computer class has a total of 11 subordinate My classes, ranging from My.Computer.Audio to My.Computer.Screen, with classes in between that deal with things such as the file system and the network.
My.Forms	Provides quick access to the forms in the current application project

My Object	Purpose
`My.Log`	Gives you direct access to the application log so you can interact with it more easily than before
`My.Request`	Related to web page calls, the `My.Request` class, along with `My.Response` and `My.WebServices`, can be used to simplify your calls and interactions in web-based applications, and is the class used to hold the calls to the web service.
`My.Resources`	Enables you to easily access the various resources in your application
`My.Response`	Holds the web page response. See `My.Request` for more information.
`My.Settings`	Used to access both application-wide and user-specific settings
`My.User`	Used to determine the user's current login profile, including security information
`My.WebServices`	Gives you easy access to all the web services referenced in the current application project

Using My in Code

Using the `My` objects in your application code is straightforward in most Windows and web-based projects. Because the underlying real namespace is implicitly referenced and any necessary objects are created for you automatically, all you need to do is reference the object property or method you wish to use. As an example, consider the following code snippet that evaluates the user identity and role attached to the thread running an application:

```
Private Sub OK_Click(ByVal sender As System.Object, ByVal e As System.EventArgs) _
    Handles OK.Click
    If My.User.IsAuthenticated Then
        If My.User.IsInRole("Administrators") Then
            My.Application.Log.WriteEntry("User " & My.User.Name & _
                " logged in as Administrator", TraceEventType.Information)
        Else
            My.Application.Log.WriteEntry("User " & My.User.Name & _
                " does not have correct privileges.", TraceEventType.Error)
        End If
    End If
    ...
End Sub
```

The code is fairly straightforward, with the various `My` object properties and methods defined with readable terms such as `IsAuthenticated` and `WriteEntry`. However, before the introduction of My to the developer's toolbox, it was no trivial task to write the code to attach to the current principal, extract the authentication state, determine what roles it belongs to, and then write to an application log.

Every `My` object provides vital shortcuts to solve scenarios commonly faced by both Windows and web developers, as this example shows. Microsoft did a great job in creating this namespace for developers and has definitely brought the concept of ease of use back home to Visual Basic programmers in particular.

Using My in C#

Although My is widely available in Visual Basic projects, other languages such as C# can take advantage of some of the shortcuts as well. This is because the My namespace actually sits on a real .NET Framework 2.0 namespace called `Microsoft.VisualBasic.Devices` for most of its objects. For example, if you want to use the `My.Audio` or `My.Keyboard` objects in a Windows application being developed in C#, you can.

To access the My objects, you will first need to add a reference to the main Visual Basic library (which also contains other commonly used Visual Basic constructs such as enumerations and classes) in your project. The simplest way to do this is to right-click the References node in the Solution Explorer for the project to which you're adding My support, and choose Add Reference from the context menu.

After a moment the References dialog window will be displayed, defaulting to the .NET components. Scroll through the list until you locate `Microsoft.VisualBasic` and click "OK" to add the reference. At this point you're ready to use My, but you'll need to add the rather wordy `Microsoft.VisualBasic` `.Devices` namespace prefix to all your references to My objects. To keep your coding to a minimum, you can add a using statement to implicitly reference the objects. The result is code similar to the following listing:

```
using System;
...
using System.Windows.Forms;
using Microsoft.VisualBasic.Devices;

namespace WindowsApplication1
{
    public partial class Form1 : Form
    {
        ...
        private void Form1_Load(object sender, EventArgs e)
        {
            Keyboard MyKeyboard = new Keyboard();
            if (MyKeyboard.ScrollLock == true)
            {
                MessageBox.Show("Scroll Lock Is On!");
            }
        }
    }
}
```

Note that not all My objects are available outside Visual Basic. However, there is usually a way to access the functionality through other standard Visual Basic namespace objects. A prime example is the `FileSystemProxy`, which is used by the `My.Computer` object to provide more efficient access to the `FileSystem` object. Unfortunately for C# developers, this proxy class is not available to their code. Rather than using My for this purpose, C# programmers still can take advantage of Visual Basic's specialized namespace objects. In this case, C# code should simply use the `Microsoft.VisualBasic` `.FileIO.FileSystem` object to achieve the same results.

Contextual My

While ten My objects are available for your use, only a subset is ever available in any given project. In addition, some of the My classes have a variety of forms that provide different information and methods depending on the context.

By dividing application development projects into three broad categories, you can see how the My classes logically fit into different project types. The first category of development scenarios is Windows-based applications. Three kinds of projects fall into this area: Windows applications for general application development, Windows Control Libraries used to create custom user controls for use in Windows applications, and Windows Services designed to run in the services environment of Windows itself. The following table shows which classes these project types can access:

Table 14-2: Access to Windows-Based My Objects

My Class	Applications	Control Libraries	Services
My.Application	Available	Available	Available
My.Computer	Available	Available	Available
My.Forms	Available	Available	
My.Log			
My.Request			
My.Resources	Available	Available	Available
My.Response			
My.Settings	Available	Available	Available
My.User	Available	Available	Available
My.WebServices	Available	Available	Available

Some of the available classes are logical — for example, there's no reason why Windows Services applications need general access to a My.Forms *collection, as they do not have Windows Forms. However, it might appear strange that none of these application types has access to* My.Log. *This is because logging for Windows applications is done via* My.Application.Log.

All three project types use a variant of the My.Computer class related to Windows applications. It is modeled on the server-based version of My.Computer, which is used for web development but includes additional objects usually found on client machines, such as keyboard and mouse classes. The My.User class is also a Windows version, which is based on the current user authentication. (Well, to be accurate, it's actually based on the current *thread's* authentication.)

However, each of the three project types for Windows development uses different variations of the `My.Application` class. The lowest common denominator is the Library version of `My.Application`, which provides you with access to fundamental features in the application, such as version information and the application log. The Windows Control Library projects use this version.

Windows Services and application projects use a customized version of `My.Application` that inherits from this Library version and adds extra methods for accessing information such as command-line arguments.

Web development projects can use a very different set of `My` classes. It doesn't make sense for them to have `My.Application` or `My.Forms`, for instance, as they cannot have this Windows client-based information. Instead, you have access to the web-based `My` objects, as indicated in the following table:

Table 14-3: Access to Web-Based My Objects

My Class	Sites	Control Libraries
My.Application		
My.Computer	Available	Available
My.Forms		
My.Log	Available	
My.Request	Available	
My.Resources		Available
My.Response	Available	
My.Settings		Available
My.User	Available	Available
My.WebServices		Available

The web project styles use a different version of the `My.Computer` object. In these cases the information is quite basic and excludes all the normal Windows-oriented properties and methods. In fact, these two project types use the same `My.Computer` version as Windows Services. `My.User` is also different from the Windows version: It associates its properties with the identity of the application context.

Finally, some project types don't fit directly into either the Windows-based application development model or the web-based projects. Project types such as console applications and general class libraries fall into this category, and have access to a subset of `My` objects, as shown in the following table:

Table 14-4: Access to My Objects by Class Library and Console Apps

My Class	Class Library	Console App
My.Application	Available	Available
My.Computer	Available	Available
My.Forms		
My.Log		
My.Request		
My.Resources	Available	Available
My.Response		
My.Settings	Available	Available
My.User	Available	Available
My.WebServices	Available	Available

Projects that don't fit into any of the standard types do not have direct access to any of the My objects at all. This doesn't prevent you from using them in a similar fashion, as you saw with C# use of My.

The My.Computer object that is exposed to class libraries and console applications is the same version as the one used by the Windows project types — you get access to all the Windows properties and methods associated with the My.Computer object. The same goes for My.User, with any user information being accessed relating to the thread's associated user identity.

Which features are available to a specific project type is actually controlled by a conditional-compilation constant, _MYTYPE. For example, including /define:_MYTYPE=\"Console\" *in the call to the compiler will cause the My classes appropriate to a Console or Windows Service to be created. Alternatively, this property is set in the project file as* <MyType>Console</MyType>. *In both cases the value is case-sensitive.*

Default Instances

Several of the My objects use *default instances* of the objects in your project. A default instance is an object that is automatically instantiated by the .NET runtime and that you can then reference in your code. For example, instead of defining and creating a new instance of a form, you can simply refer to its default instance in the My.Forms form collection. My.Resources works in a similar way by giving you direct references to each resource object in your solution, while My.WebServices provides proxy objects for each web service reference added to your project, so you don't even need to create those. In each of these cases the Visual Basic compiler adds generated code to your assembly. Later you will see how to extend the My namespace to include your own code, as well as package it so that it is automatically available for any application you build.

Using the default instances is straightforward — simply refer to the object by name in the appropriate collection. To show a form named Form1, you would use `My.Forms.Form1.Show`, while you can call a web service named CalcWS by using the `My.WebServices.CalcWS` object.

A Namespace Overview

In this section you will get a flavor for the extent of the functionality available via the `My` namespace. As it is not possible to go through all the classes, methods, and overall functionality available, it is recommended that you use this as a starting point from which to explore further.

My.Application

The `My.Application` object gives you immediate access to various pieces of information about the application. At the lowest level, `My.Application` enables you to write to the application log through the subordinate `My.Application.Log`, as well as to add general information common to all Windows-based projects to the `My.Application.Info` object.

As mentioned earlier, if the context of `My.Application` is a Windows service, it also includes information related to the command-line arguments and the method of deployment. Windows Forms applications have all this information in the contextual form `My.Application` and enable the accessing of various forms-related data.

Prior to `My`, all of this information was accessible through a variety of methods, but it was difficult to determine where some of the information was. Now the information is all consolidated into one easy-to-use location. To demonstrate the kind of data you can access through `My.Application`, try the following sample task:

1. Start Visual Studio 2008 and create a Visual Basic Windows application. Add a button to the form. You'll use the button to display information about the application.

2. Double-click the My Project node in the Solution Explorer to access the Solution properties. In the Application page, click Assembly Information, set the Title, Copyright, and Assembly Version fields to something you'll recognize, and click "OK" to save the settings.

3. Return to the Form1 Design view and double-click the newly added button to have Visual Studio automatically generate a stub for the button's `Click` event. Add the following code:

```
Private Sub Button1_Click(ByVal sender As System.Object, _
                          ByVal e As System.EventArgs)
    Handles Button1.Click
    Dim message As New System.Text.StringBuilder
    With My.Application
        With .Info
            message.Append("Application Title:")
            message.AppendLine(vbTab & vbTab & vbTab & .Title)
            message.Append("Version:")
            message.AppendLine(vbTab & vbTab & vbTab & vbTab & .Version.ToString)
            message.Append("Copyright:")
            message.AppendLine(vbTab & vbTab & vbTab & .Copyright)
        End With
        message.Append("Number of Commandline Arguments:")
```

```
          message.AppendLine(vbTab & .CommandLineArgs.Count)
          message.Append("Name of the First Open Form:")
          message.AppendLine(vbTab & vbTab & .OpenForms(0).Name)
      End With
      MessageBox.Show(message.ToString)
  End Sub
```

This demonstrates the use of properties available to all My-compatible applications in the
My.Application.Info object, then the use of properties available to Windows Services and
Windows Forms applications with the CommandLineArgs property, and then finally the
OpenForms information that's only accessible in Windows Forms applications.

4. Run the application and click the button on the form and you will get a dialog similar to the one
shown in Figure 14-2.

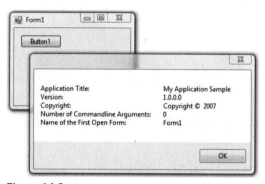

Figure 14-2

The information in My.Application is especially useful when you need to give feedback to your
users about what version of the solution is running. It can also be used internally to make logical
decisions about which functionality should be performed based on active forms and version information.

My.Computer

My.Computer is by far the largest object in the My namespace. In fact, it has ten subordinate objects that
can be used to access various parts of the computer system, such as keyboard, mouse, and network.
Besides these ten objects, the main property that My.Computer exposes is the machine name, through
the conveniently named Name property.

My.Computer.Audio

The My.Computer.Audio object gives you the capability to play system and user sound files without
needing to create objects and use various API calls. There are two main functions within this object:

❑ PlaySystemSound will play one of the five basic system sounds.

❑ Play will play a specified audio file. You can optionally choose to have the sound file play in the
background and even loop continuously. You can halt a background loop with the Stop method.

The following snippet of code illustrates how to use these functions:

```
My.Computer.Audio.PlaySystemSound(Media.SystemSounds.Beep)
My.Computer.Audio.Play("C:\MySoundFile.wav", AudioPlayMode.BackgroundLoop)
My.Computer.Audio.Stop()
```

My.Computer.Clipboard

The Windows clipboard has come a long way since the days when it could store only simple text. Now you can copy and paste images, audio files, and file and folder lists as well. The `My.Computer.Clipboard` object provides access to all of this functionality, giving you the ability to store and retrieve items of the aforementioned types as well as custom data specific to your application.

Three main groups of methods are used in `My.Computer.Clipboard`. These are `Contains`, `Get`, and `Set`. The `Contains` methods are used to check the clipboard for a specific type of data. For example, `ContainsAudio` will have a value of `True` if the clipboard contains audio data. `GetAudio` will retrieve the audio data in the clipboard (if there is some), and the other `Get` methods are similar in functionality for their own types. Finally, `SetAudio` stores audio data in the clipboard, while the other `Set` methods will do the same for the other types of data.

The only exceptions to these descriptions are the `ContainsData`, `GetData`, and `SetData` methods. These three methods enable you to store and retrieve custom data for your application in any format you like, taking a parameter which identifies the custom data type. The advantage of using these is that if you have sensitive data that you allow the user to copy and paste within your application, you can preclude it from being accidentally pasted into other applications by using your own format.

To reset the clipboard entirely, use the `Clear` method.

My.Computer.Clock

Previously, converting the current system time to a standard GMT time was an often frustrating task for some developers, but with `My.Computer.Clock` it's easy. This object exposes the current time in both local and GMT formats as `Date`-type variables with `LocalTime` and `GmtTime` properties.

In addition, you can retrieve the system timer of the computer with the `TickCount` property.

My.Computer.FileSystem

Accessing the computer file system usually involves creating multiple objects and having them refer to each other in ways that sometimes appear illogical. The `My.Computer.FileSystem` object does away with all the confusion with a central location for all file activities, whether it's just file manipulation (such as copying, renaming, or deleting files or directories) or reading and writing to a file's contents.

The following sample routine searches for files containing the word `loser` in the `C:\Temp` directory, deleting each file that's found:

```
Dim foundList As System.Collections.ObjectModel.ReadOnlyCollection (Of String)
foundList = My.Computer.FileSystem.FindInFiles("C:\Temp", "loser", True, _
    FileIO.SearchOption.SearchTopLevelOnly)

For Each thisFileName As String In foundList
    My.Computer.FileSystem.DeleteFile(thisFileName)
Next
```

My.Computer.Info

Similar to the `Info` object that is part of `My.Application`, the `My.Computer.Info` object exposes information about the computer system. Notably, it returns memory status information about the computer and the installed operating system. The important properties are listed in the following table:

Table 14-5: Computer Properties

Property	Description
AvailablePhysicalMemory	The amount of physical memory free on the computer
TotalPhysicalMemory	The total amount of physical memory on the computer
AvailableVirtualMemory	The amount of virtual addressing space available
TotalVirtualMemory	The total amount of virtual-addressable space
OSFullName	The full operating system, such as Microsoft Windows XP Professional
OSPlatform	The platform identifier, such as Win32NT
OSVersion	The full version of the operating system

My.Computer.Keyboard and My.Computer.Mouse

The `My.Computer.Keyboard` and `My.Computer.Mouse` objects return information about the currently installed keyboard and mouse on your computer, respectively. The `Mouse` object will let you know if there is a scroll wheel, how much the screen should scroll if it's used, and whether the mouse buttons have been swapped.

`My.Computer.Keyboard` provides information about the various control keys such as Shift, Alt, and Ctrl, as well as keyboard states such as caps lock, number lock, and scroll lock. You can use this information to affect the behavior of your application in response to a specific combination of keys.

The `My.Computer.Keyboard` object also exposes the `SendKeys` method that many Visual Basic programmers use to simulate keystrokes.

My.Computer.Network

At first glance, the `My.Computer.Network` object may look underwhelming. It has only a single property, which indicates whether the network is available or not — `IsAvailable`. However, in addition to this property, `My.Computer.Network` has three methods that can be used to send and retrieve files across the network or web:

❑　`Ping`: Use `Ping` to determine whether the remote location you intend to use is reachable with the current network state.

❑　`DownloadFile`: Specify the remote location and where you want the file to be downloaded to.

❑　`UploadFile`: Specify the file to be uploaded and the remote location's address.

Of course, networks can be unstable, particularly if you're talking about the web: that's where the
NetworkAvailabilityChanged event comes to the rescue. The My.Computer.Network object exposes
this event for you to handle in your application, which you can do by defining an event-handler routine
and attaching it to the event:

```
Public Sub MyNetworkAvailabilityChangedHandler( ByVal sender As Object, _
                                        ByVal e As Devices.NetworkAvailableEventArgs)
    ... do your code.
End Sub

Private Sub Form1_Load(ByVal sender As System.Object,ByVal e As System.EventArgs) _
    Handles MyBase.Load
    AddHandler
    My.Computer.Network.NetworkAvailabilityChanged, _
            AddressOf MyNetworkAvailabilityChangedHandler
End Sub
```

You can then address any network work your application might be doing when the network goes down,
or even kick off background transfers when your application detects that the network has become
available again.

> *The* NetworkAvailabilityChanged *event is only triggered by changes to the local connectivity
> status. It doesn't validate that a particular server is accessible and that your application is "connected."
> Therefore, your web service, or other, requests may still fail, so it is important you do your own network
> validation and error handling.*

My.Computer.Ports

The My.Computer.Ports object exposes any serial ports available on the computer through the
SerialPortNames property. You can then use OpenSerialPort to open a specific port and write to it
using standard I/O methods.

My.Computer.Registry

Traditionally, the Windows registry has been dangerous to play around with — so much so, in fact, that
Microsoft originally restricted Visual Basic programmers' access to only a small subset of the entire
registry key set.

My.Computer.Registry provides a reasonably safe way to access the entire registry. You can still mess
things up, but because its methods and properties are easy to use, it's less likely.

Each of the hives in the registry is referenced by a specific property of My.Computer.Registry, and
you can use GetValue and SetValue in conjunction with these root properties to give your application
access to any data that the end user can access.

For instance, to determine whether a particular registry key exists, you can use the following snippet:

```
If My.Computer.Registry.GetValue("HKEY_LOCAL_MACHINE\MyApp", "Value", Nothing) _
    Is Nothing Then
    MessageBox.Show("Value not there.")
End If
```

My.Forms and My.WebServices

`My.Forms` gives you access to the forms in your application. The advantage using this object has over the old way of using your forms is that it provides a default instance of each form so you don't need to define and instantiate them manually. Whereas before, if you wanted to display Form1 elsewhere in your application, you would write this:

```
Dim mMyForm As New Form1
mMyForm.Show
```

Now you can simply write this:

```
My.Forms.Form1.Show
```

Each form has a corresponding property exposed in the `My.Forms` object. You can determine which forms are currently open using the `My.Application.OpenForms` collection.

`My.WebServices` performs a similar function but for — you guessed it — the web services you've defined in your project. If you add a reference to a web service and name the reference `MyCalcWS`, you can use the `My.WebServices.MyCalcWS` instance of the web service proxy rather than instantiate your own each time you need to call it.

Accessing the web service default instance means that you don't need to recreate the service proxy each time, which is quite an expensive operation.

My for the Web

When building web applications, you can use the `My.Request` and `My.Response` objects to set and retrieve the HTTP request and HTTP response information, respectively. This is a godsend to any developer who has tried to maintain these objects and found it difficult to remember where the information was located. These objects are basically `System.Web.HTTPRequest` and `System.Web.HTTPResponse` classes, but you don't have to worry about which page has what data because they're referring to the current page.

My.Resources

.NET applications can have many types of embedded resource objects. Visual Studio 2008 has an easy way of adding resource objects in the form of the Resources page of My Project in Visual Basic, or the corresponding Properties area in C#. `My.Resources` makes using these resources in code just as easy.

Each resource added to the project has a unique name assigned to it (normally the filename for audio and graphic files that are inserted into the resource file), which you can refer to in code. These names are rendered to object properties exposed by the `My.Resources` object. For example, if you have an image resource called `MainFormBackground`, the shortcut for accessing it is `My.Resources.MainFormBackground`. More information on using Visual Studio 2008 to work with resource files can be found in Chapter 38.

Other My Classes

The other `My` classes are fairly basic in their use. The `My.User` class enables you to determine information about the current user. When you are using role-based security, this includes the current principal, but as you saw earlier in this chapter you can also retrieve the user's login name and whether he or she belongs to specific roles.

`My.Settings` exposes the `Settings` strings in your application, enabling you to edit or retrieve the information in the same way that `My.Forms` exposes the application form objects and `My.Resources` exposes the resource file contents. `Settings` can be scoped either as application (read-only) or per user, so that they can be persisted between sessions with the `My.Settings.Save` method.

Finally, `My.Log` is an alternative for addressing the application log within web site projects.

`My.Log` is only available for web site projects. For all other projects you should use `My.Application.Log`.

Your Turn

While the `My` namespace is already loaded with numerous productivity shortcuts, it has been put together with the average Visual Basic developer in mind. There are always going to be cases where you go looking for a shortcut that just isn't there. In these cases it's possible to extend the namespace in a couple of different ways.

Methods and Properties

The simplest way to extend the `My` namespace is to add your own methods or properties. These can be stand-alone, or they can belong to one of the existing `My` namespace classes. For example, the following function, which extracts name-value pairs from a string into a dictionary, is a stand-alone function and will appear at the top level of the `My` namespace.

```vb
Namespace My
    <HideModuleName()> _
    Module StringHelpers
        Friend Function ParseString(ByVal stringToParse As String, _
                                    ByVal pairSeparator As Char, _
                                    ByVal valueSeparator As Char) _
                                                As Dictionary(Of String, String)
            Dim dict As New Dictionary(Of String, String)
            Dim nameValues = From pair In stringToParse.Split(pairSeparator), _
                             values In pair.Split(valueSeparator) _
                        Select New With {.Name = values(0), _
                                         .Value = values(1)}

            For Each nv In nameValues
                dict.Item(nv.Name) = nv.Value
            Next
            Return dict
        End Function


    End Module
End Namespace
```

Figure 14-3 illustrates that the StringHelpers module is completely hidden when you're accessing this function.

Figure 14-3

As both My.Application and My.Computer return an instance of a generated partial class, you can extend them by adding properties and methods. To do so, you need to create the partial classes MyApplication and MyComputer in which to place your new functionality. As the following snippet shows, you can even maintain state, as My.Computer will return a single instance (per thread) of the MyComputer class.

```
Namespace My
    Partial Class MyComputer
        Private mCounter As Integer = 0
        Friend Property VeryAccessibleCounter() As Integer
            Get
                Return mCounter
            End Get
            Set(ByVal value As Integer)
                mCounter = value
            End Set
        End Property
    End Class
End Namespace
```

Extending the Hierarchy

So far, you have seen how you can add methods and properties to existing points in the My namespace. You'll be pleased to know that you can go further by creating your own classes that can be exposed as part of the My namespace. In the following example we have the MyStringHelper class (following the naming pattern used by the framework), which is exposed via the StringHelper property in the module.

```
Namespace My
    <HideModuleName()> _
    Module StringHelpers
        Private mHelper As New ThreadSafeObjectProvider(Of MyStringHelper)
        Friend ReadOnly Property StringHelper() As MyStringHelper
            Get
                Return mHelper.GetInstance()
            End Get
        End Property
    End Module

    <System.ComponentModel.EditorBrowsable(System.ComponentModel
.EditorBrowsableState.Never)> _
    Friend NotInheritable Class MyStringHelper
```

(continued)

(continued)

```
          Friend Function ParseString(ByVal stringToParse As String, _
                              ByVal pairSeparator As Char, _
                              ByVal valueSeparator As Char) _
                                          As Dictionary(Of String, String)
          Dim dict As New Dictionary(Of String, String)
          Dim nameValues = From pair In stringToParse.Split(pairSeparator), _
                          values In pair.Split(valueSeparator) _
                     Select New With {.Name = values(0), _
                              .Value = values(1)}

          For Each nv In nameValues
              dict.Item(nv.Name) = nv.Value
          Next
          mParseCount += 1
          Return dict
      End Function

      Private mParseCount As Integer = 0
      Friend ReadOnly Property ParseCount() As Integer
          Get
              Return mParseCount
          End Get
      End Property
  End Class
End Namespace
```

Unlike in the previous case, where we extended the `MyComputer` class, here we have had to use the `EditorBrowsable` attribute to ensure that the `MyStringHelper` class doesn't appear via IntelliSense. Figure 14-4 illustrates how `My.StringHelper` would appear within Visual Studio 2008.

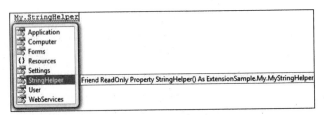

Figure 14-4

As with `My.Computer`, our addition to the `My` namespace is thread-safe, as we used the single-instance backing pattern with the `ThreadSafeObjectProvider(of T)` class. Like regular classes, your additions to the `My` namespace can raise events that you can consume in your application. If you wish to expose your event via `My.Application` (like the `Startup` and `Shutdown` events), you can either declare the event within the `MyApplication` partial class or use a custom event to reroute the event from your class through the `MyApplication` class.

Packaging and Deploying

Now that you have personalized the `My` namespace, you may wish either to share it with colleagues or make it available for other projects that you are working on. To do this you need to package what you have written using the Export Template feature of Visual Studio 2008. With some minor tweaks, this package will then be recognized by Visual Studio as an extension to the My namespace, allowing it to be added to other projects.

You can export your code with the Export Template Wizard, accessible via the Export Template item on the File menu. This wizard will guide you through the steps necessary in order to export your code as an Item template with any assembly references your code may require. Since you need to modify the template before importing it back into Visual Studio 2008, it is recommended that you uncheck the "Automatically import the template into Visual Studio" option on the final page of the wizard.

The compressed file created by this wizard contains your code file, an icon file, and a .vstemplate file that defines the structure of the template. To identify this template as an extension of the My namespace, you need to modify the .vstemplate file to include a CustomDataSignature element. As you can't modify the .vstemplate within the compressed file, you will need to either copy it out, modify it and replace the original file, or expand the whole compressed file. The last choice will make the next step, that of adding a new file to the compressed file, easier.

```
<VSTemplate Version="2.0.0"
xmlns="http://schemas.microsoft.com/developer/vstemplate/2005" Type="Item">
    <TemplateData>
        <DefaultName>My String Helper.vb</DefaultName>
        <Name>My String Helper</Name>
        <Description>&lt;No description available&gt;</Description>
        <ProjectType>VisualBasic</ProjectType>
        <SortOrder>10</SortOrder>
        <Icon>__TemplateIcon.ico</Icon>
        <CustomDataSignature>Microsoft.VisualBasic.MyExtension</CustomDataSignature>
    </TemplateData>
    <TemplateContent>
        <References />
        <ProjectItem SubType="Code" TargetFileName="$fileinputname$.vb"
            ReplaceParameters="true">StringHelperMyExtension.vb</ProjectItem>
    </TemplateContent>
</VSTemplate>
```

This snippet illustrates the new CustomDataSignature element in the .vstemplate file, which Visual Studio 2008 uses as a key to look for an additional .CustomData file. In order to complete the template you need to create a .CustomData file (the name of the file is actually irrelevant) that contains a single XML element.

```
<VBMyExtensionTemplate
    ID="Custom.My.Extension"
    Version="1.0.0.0"
    AssemblyFullName="System.Configuration"
/>
```

The Id and Version attributes are used to uniquely identify the extension so that it is not added to a project more than once. The AssemblyFullName attribute is optional and indicates that when an assembly is added to a project that has this name, this template should be invoked to extend the My namespace.

Once you have created this file you need to recompress all the files that make up the template. This file should then be added to the Documents\Visual Studio 2008\Templates\ItemTemplates\Visual Basic folder, which will import the template into Visual Studio 2008 the next time it is started. You can now add your extension to the My namespace to any project by clicking the "Add extension . . ." button on the My Extensions tab of the Project Properties dialog, as shown in Figure 14-5.

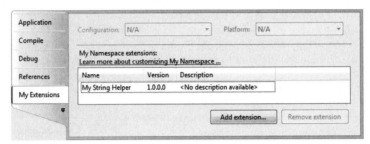

Figure 14-5

As mentioned earlier, you can set up your extension to be automatically added when an assembly with a specific name is added to a project. In the example the assembly was System.Configuration, and Figure 14-6 illustrates adding it to a project. Accepting this dialog will make the extension we just created available within this project.

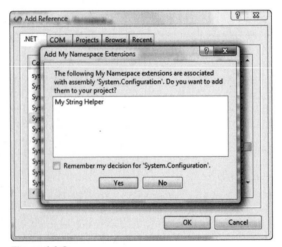

Figure 14-6

Summary

Although the My namespace was originally intended for Visual Basic programmers, C# developers can also harness some of the efficiencies it offers in the code they write. As you have seen, you can also create and share your own extensions to this namespace.

One of the themes of Visual Studio has always been to make developing applications more efficient — providing the right tools to get the job done with minimal effort. The My namespace helps defragment the .NET Framework by providing a context-driven breakdown of frequently used framework functionalities. By following this example, you can extend the My namespace so that your whole team can be more productive.

15

The Languages Ecosystem

The .NET language ecosystem is alive and well. With literally hundreds of languages (you can find a fairly complete list here: www.dotnetpowered.com/languages.aspx) targeting the .NET Framework, .NET developers have a huge language arsenal at their disposal. Because the .NET Framework was designed with language interoperability in mind, these languages are also able to talk to each other, allowing for a creative cross-pollination of languages across a cross-section of programming problems. You're literally able to choose the right language tool for the job.

This chapter explores some of the latest languages paradigms within the ecosystem, each with particular features and flavors that make solving those tough programming problems just a little bit easier. After a tour of some of the programming language paradigms, we use that knowledge to take a look at a new addition to Microsoft's supported language list: a functional programming language called F#.

Hitting a Nail with the Right Hammer

We need to be flexible and diverse programmers. The programming landscape requires elegance, efficiency, and longevity. Gone are the days of picking one language and platform and executing like crazy to meet the requirements of our problem domain. Different nails sometimes require different hammers.

Given that there are hundreds of available languages on the .NET platform, what makes them different from each other? Truth be told, most are small evolutions of each other, and are not particularly useful in an enterprise environment. However, it is easy to class these languages into a range of programming paradigms.

There are various ways to classify programming languages, but I like to take a broad-strokes approach, putting languages into four broad categories: imperative, declarative, dynamic, and functional. Let's take a quick look at these categories and what languages fit within them.

Imperative

Your classic all-rounder — imperative languages describe how, rather than what. Imperative languages were designed from the get-go to raise the level of abstraction of machine code. It's said that when Grace Hopper invented the first-ever compiler, the A-0 system, her machine code programming colleagues complained that she would put them out of a job.

It includes languages where language statements primarily manipulate program state. Object-oriented languages are classic state manipulators through their focus on creating and changing objects. The C and C++ languages fit nicely in the imperative bucket, as do our favorites Visual Basic.NET and C#.

They're great at describing real-world scenarios through the world of the type system and objects. They are strict — meaning the compiler does a lot of safety checking for you. Safety checking (or type soundness) means you can't easily change a Cow type to a Sheep type — so, for example, if you declare that you need a Cow type in the signature of your method, the compiler will make sure that you don't hand that method a Sheep instead. They usually have fantastic reuse mechanisms too — code written with polymorphism in mind can easily be abstracted away so that other code paths, from within the same module through to entirely different projects, can leverage the code that was written. They also benefit from being the most popular. So they're clearly a good choice if you need a team of people working on a problem.

Declarative

Declarative languages describe what, rather than how (in contrast to imperative, which describes the how through program statements that manipulate state). Your classic well-known declarative language is HTML. It describes the layout of a page: what font, text, and decoration are required, and where images should be shown. Parts of another classic, SQL, are declarative — it describes what it wants from a relational database. A recent example of a declarative language is XAML (eXtensible Application Markup Language), which leads a long list of XML-based declarative languages.

Declarative languages are great for describing and transforming data. And as such, we've invoked them from our imperative languages to retrieve and manipulate data for years.

Dynamic

The dynamic category includes all languages that exhibit "dynamic" features like late-bound binding and invocation (you learn about these in a couple of paragraphs or so), REPL (Read Eval Print Loops), duck typing (non-strict typing, that is, if an object looks like a duck and walks like a duck it must be a duck), and more.

Dynamic languages typically delay as much compilation behavior as they possibly can to runtime. Whereas your typical C# method invocation "Console.WriteLine()" would be statically checked and linked to at compile time, a dynamic language would delay all this to runtime. Instead, it will look up the "WriteLine()" method on the "Console" type while the program is actually running, and if it finds it, will invoke it at runtime. If it does not find the method or the type, the language may expose features for the programmer to hook up a "failure method," so that the programmer can catch these failures and programmatically "try something else."

Other features include extending objects, classes, and interfaces at runtime (meaning modifying the type system on the fly); dynamic scoping (for example, a variable defined in the GLOBAL scope can be accessed by private or nested methods); and more.

Compilation methods like this have interesting side effects. If your types don't need to be fully defined up front (because the type system is so flexible), you can write code that will consume strict interfaces (like COM, or other .NET assemblies, for example) and make that code highly resilient to failure and versioning of that interface. In the C# world, if an interface you're consuming from an external assembly changes, you typically need a recompile (and a fix-up of your internal code) to get it up and running again. From a dynamic language, you could hook the "method missing" mechanism of the language, and when a particular interface has changed simply do some "reflective" lookup on that interface and decide if you can invoke anything else. This means you can write fantastic glue code that glues together interfaces that may not be versioned dependently.

Dynamic languages are great at rapid prototyping. Not having to define your types up front (something you would do straightaway in C#) allows you concentrate on code to solve problems, rather than on the type constraints on the implementation. The REPL (Read Eval Print Loop) allows you to write prototypes line-by-line and immediately see the changes reflect in the program instead of wasting time doing a compile-run-debug cycle.

If you're interested in taking a look at dynamic languages on the .NET platform, you're in luck. Microsoft has released IronPython (`www.codeplex.com/IronPython`), which is a Python implementation for the .NET Framework. The Python language is a classic example of a dynamic language, and is wildly popular in the scientific computing, systems administration, and general programming space. If Python doesn't tickle your fancy, you can also download and try out IronRuby (`www.ironruby.net/`), which is an implementation of the Ruby language for the .NET Framework. Ruby is a dynamic language that's popular in the web space, and though it's still relatively young, it has a huge popular following.

Functional

The functional category focuses on languages that treat computation like mathematical functions. They try really hard to avoid state manipulation, instead concentrating on the result of functions as the building blocks for solving problems. If you've done any calculus before, the theory behind functional programming might look familiar.

Because functional programming typically doesn't manipulate state, the surface area of side effects generated in a program is much smaller. This means this is fantastic for implementing parallel and concurrent algorithms. The holy grail of highly concurrent systems is the avoidance of overlapping "unintended" state manipulation. Dead-locks, race conditions, and broken invariants are classic manifestations of not synchronizing your state manipulation code. Concurrent programming and synchronization through threads, shared memory, and locks is incredibly hard, so why not avoid it altogether? Because functional programming encourages the programmer to write stateless algorithms, the compiler can then reason about automatic parallelism of the code. And this means you can exploit the power of multi-core processors without the heavy lifting of managing threads, locks, and shared memory.

Functional programs are terse. There's usually less code required to arrive at a solution than with its imperative cousin. Less code typically means fewer bugs and less surface area to test.

What's It All Mean?

These categories are broad by design: languages may include features that are common to one or more of these categories. The categories should be used as a way to relate the language features that exist in them to the particular problems that they are good at solving.

Languages like C# and VB.NET are now leveraging features from their dynamic and functional counterparts. Linq (Language Integrated Query) is a great example of a borrowed paradigm. Consider the following C# 3.0 Linq query:

```
var query =    from c in customers
               where c.CompanyName == "Microsoft"
               select new { c.ID, c.CompanyName };
```

There are a few borrowed features here. The "var" keyword says "inference the type of the query specified," which looks a lot like something out of a dynamic language. The actual query itself "from c in . . ." looks and acts like the declarative language SQL, and the "select new { c.ID . . ." creates a new anonymous type, again something that looks fairly dynamic. The code-generated results of these statements are particularly interesting: they're actually not compiled into classic IL (intermediate language); they're instead compiled into what's called an expression tree and then interpreted at runtime — something that's taken right out of the dynamic language playbook.

The truth is, these categories don't particularly matter too much for deciding which tool to use to solve the right problem. Cross-pollination of feature sets from each category into languages is in fashion at the moment, which is good for a programmer, whose favorite language typically picks up the best features from each category.

And if you're a .NET programmer, you've got more to smile about. Language interoperation through the CLS (Common Language Specification) works seamlessly, meaning you can use your favorite imperative language for the majority of the problems you're trying to solve, then call into a functional language for your data manipulation, or maybe some hard-core math you need to solve a problem.

So now that we've learned a little bit about the various categories and paradigms of languages and their features, let's explore one of the newest members to the Microsoft Developer Division, a functional language called F#.

Introducing F#

F# (pronounced F Sharp) is a brand-new language incubated out of Microsoft Research in Cambridge, England, by the guy that brought generics to the .NET Framework, Don Syme. Microsoft's Developer Division recently welcomed F# to the Visual Studio range of supported languages. F# is a multi-paradigm functional language. This means it's primarily a functional language, but supports other flavors of programming, like imperative and object-oriented programming styles.

Downloading and Installing F#

You can download and install F# today from `http://research.microsoft.com/fsharp/fsharp.aspx`. Simply download the latest msi or zip file, and fire it up. This will invoke the installer as shown in Figure 15-1.

Figure 15-1

The F# installer will lay out the compiler and libraries into the directory you specify, and install the relevant F# Visual Studio template files. This allows you to use the compiler from both the command line and from Visual Studio. It also includes F# documentation and F# samples to help you get on your way.

Your First F# Program

Now, let's fire up Visual Studio 2008 and create a new F# project. As Figure 15-2 shows, the F# new project template is located in the Other Project Types node in the New Project dialog. Give it a name and click "OK."

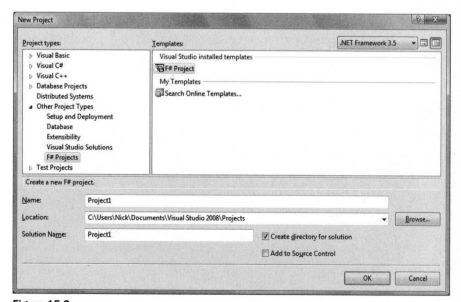

Figure 15-2

Unlike its C# and Visual Basic.NET cousins, F# doesn't create a default "Hello World" template file. You need to do the heavy lifting yourself. Right-click the Project in the Solution Explorer, and click Add New Item. Figure 15-3 shows the item templates that are installed for F#.

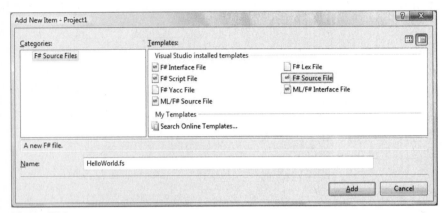

Figure 15-3

Click F# Source File and give it a name. This creates an F# file that's filled with all sorts of interesting F# language examples to get you started. Walking down that file and checking out what language features are available is an interesting exercise in itself. Instead, we'll quickly get the canonical "Hello World" example up and running to see the various options available for compilation and interactivity. So remove, or comment out, all the template code, and replace it with this:

```
#light

print_endline "Hello, F# World!"
```

The first statement, #light, is a compile flag to indicate that the code is written using the optional lightweight syntax. With this syntax, white-space indentation becomes significant, reducing the need for certain tokens such as "in" and ";;". The second statement simply prints out "Hello, F# World!" to the console.

There are two ways to run an F# program. The first is to simply run the application as you would normally (press F5 to Start Debugging). This will compile and run your program as shown in Figure 15-4.

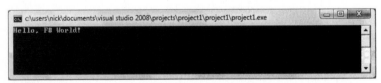

Figure 15-4

The other way to run an F# program is to use the F# Interactive Prompt from within Visual Studio. This allows you to highlight and execute code from within Visual Studio, and immediately see the result in your running program. It also allows you to modify your running program on the fly!

To use the F# Interactive Prompt, you must first enable it in Visual Studio 2008 from the Add-in Manager (Tools ⇨ Add-in Manager). Figure 15-5 shows the Add-in Manager where all you need to do is check all the checkboxes, because the F# Interactive Prompt add-in was installed as part of installing F#.

You may find that the checkboxes in the Startup and Command Line columns are disabled. If this is the case, you will need to restart Visual Studio 2008 as Administrator.

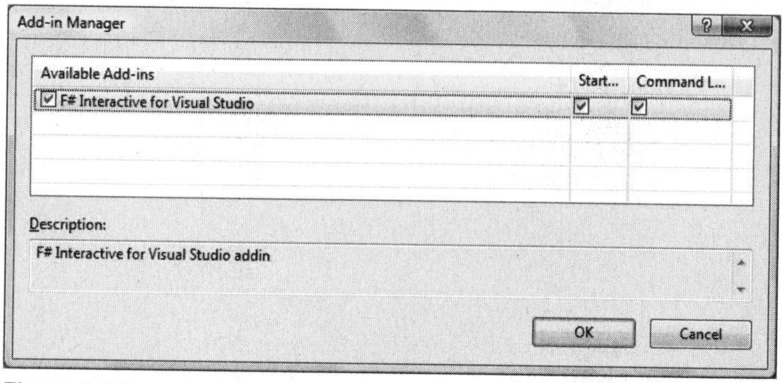

Figure 15-5

When you click "OK" this will immediately create the F# interactive window in Visual Studio, as shown in Figure 15-6.

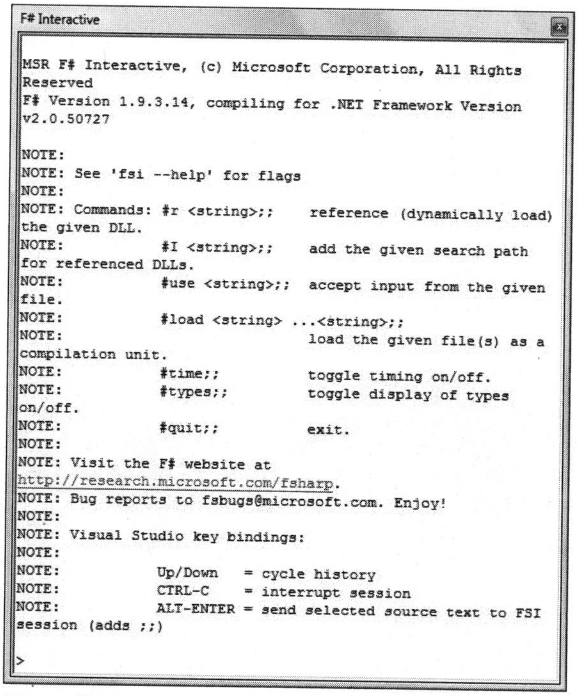

Figure 15-6

From that window, you can start interacting with the F# compiler through the REPL (Read Eval Print Loop) prompt. This means that for every line of F# you type it will compile and execute that line immediately. The experience is equivalent to what you would get at the command line with the fsi.exe (F# Interactive) executable, found in the F# installation directory. REPLs are great if you want to test ideas quickly and modify programs on the fly. They allow for quick algorithm experimentation, and rapid prototyping.

However, from the REPL prompt in the F# interactive window, you essentially miss out on the value that Visual Studio delivers through IntelliSense, code snippets, and so on. The best experience is that of both worlds: using the Visual Studio text editor to create your programs, and piping that output through to the Interactive Prompt. You can do this by hitting Alt+Enter on any highlighted piece of F# source code. In Figure 15-7 the code in the F# source file you created earlier has been selected.

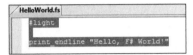

Figure 15-7

Pressing Alt+Enter will pipe the highlighted source code straight to the Interactive Prompt and execute it immediately, as shown in Figure 15-8.

```
F# Interactive
> Hello, F# World!
val it : unit = ()
>
```

Figure 15-8

And there you have it: your first F# program.

Exploring F# Language Features

A primer on the F# language is beyond the scope of this book, but it's worth exploring some of the cooler language features that it supports. If anything, it should whet your appetite for F#, and act as a catalyst to go and learn more about this great language.

A very common data type in the F# world is the list. It's a simple collection type with expressive operators. You can define empty lists, multi-dimensional lists, and your classic flat list. The F# list is immutable, meaning you can't modify it once it's created; you can only take a copy. F# exposes a feature called List Comprehensions to make creating, manipulating, and comprehending lists easier and more expressive. Consider the following:

```
#light

let countInFives = { for x in 1 .. 20 when x % 5 = 0 -> x }

print_any countInFives
System.Console.ReadLine()
```

The expression in curly braces does a classic "for" loop over a list that contains elements 1 through to 20 (the " . . " expression is shorthand for creating a new list with elements 1 through 20 in it). The "when" is a comprehension that the "for" loop executes for each element in the list. It says "when x module 5 equals 0, then return x." The curly braces are shorthand for "create a new list with all returned elements in it." And there you have it — a very expressive way of defining a new list on the fly in one line.

F#'s Pattern Matching feature is a flexible and powerful way to create control flow. In the C# world, we have the switch (or simply a bunch of nested "if else's"), but we're usually constrained to the type of what we're switching over. F#'s pattern matching is similar, but more flexible, allowing the test to be over whatever types or values you specify. For example, let's take a look at defining a Fibonacci function in F# using pattern matching:

```
let rec fibonacci = function
  | x when x < 0 -> failwith "Bzzt. Value can't be less than 0."
  | 0 | 1 as x -> x
  | x -> fibonacci(x - 1) + fibonacci(x - 2)

printfn "fibonacci 15 = %i" (fibonacci 15)
```

The pipe operator " | " specifies that you want to match the input to the function against an expression on the right side of the pipe. The first match line says fail when "x" is less than 0. The second says return the input of the function "x" when "x" matches either 0 or 1. The third line says return the recursive result of a call to Fibonacci with an input of x - 1, adding that to another recursive call where the input is x - 2. The last line writes the result of the Fibonacci function to the console.

Pattern matching in functions has an interesting side effect — it makes dispatch and control flow over different receiving parameter types much easier and cleaner. In the C#/VB.NET world, you would traditionally write a series of overloads based on parameter types, but in F# this is unnecessary, because the pattern matching syntax allows you to achieve the same thing within a single function.

Lazy evaluation is another neat language feature common to functional languages that F# also exposes. It simply means that the compiler can schedule the evaluation of a function or an expression only when it's needed, rather than pre-computing it up front. This means that you only have to run code you absolutely have to — fewer cycles spent executing and less working set means more speed.

Typically, when you have an expression assigned to a variable, that expression gets immediately executed in order to store the result in the variable. Leveraging the theory that functional programming has no side effects, there is no need to immediately express this result (because in-order execution is not necessary), and as a result, we should only execute when the variable result is actually required. Let's have a look at a simple case:

```
let lazyDiv = lazy ( 10 / 2 )
print_any lazyDiv
```

First, the lazy keyword is used to express a function or expression that will only be executed when forced. The second line prints whatever is in lazyDiv to the console. If you execute this example, what you actually get as the console output is "{status = Delayed;}". This is because under the hood the input to "print_any" is similar to a delegate. We actually need to force, or invoke, the expression before we'll get a return result, as in the following example:

```
let lazyDiv = lazy ( 10 / 2 )
let result = Lazy.force lazyDiv
print_any result
```

The "Lazy.force" function forces the execution of the lazyDiv expression.

This concept is very powerful when optimizing for application performance. Reducing the amount of working set, or memory, that an application needs is extremely important in improving both startup performance and runtime performance. Lazy evaluation is also a required concept when dealing with massive amounts of data. If you needed to iterate through terabytes of data stored on disk, you can easily write a Lazy evaluation wrapper over that data, so that you only slurp up the data when you actually need it. The Applied Games Group in Microsoft Research have a great write-up of using F#'s Lazy evaluation feature with exactly that scenario: http://blogs.technet.com/apg/archive/2006/11/04/dealing-with-terabytes-with-f.aspx.

Summary

This chapter provided an overview of programming language paradigms: imperative, dynamic, declarative, and functional, and how they can best solve programming problems and scenarios. It briefly described some of the Microsoft offerings in this space, including IronPython and IronRuby in the dynamic space, and XAML as an example of the declarative space. We also took a deeper look at the newest member of the Microsoft Developer Division language team: the functional language F#. We explored how F# integrates with the IDE, and also a few of the cooler language features it exposes.

Part IV
Coding

16

IntelliSense and Bookmarks

One thing that Microsoft has long been good at is providing automated help as you write your code. Older versions of Visual Basic had a limited subset of this automated intelligence known as IntelliSense, but with the introduction of Visual Studio .NET, Microsoft firmly established the technology throughout the whole application development environment. In Visual Studio 2008 it is even more pervasive than before, so much so that it has been referred to as IntelliSense Everywhere.

This chapter illustrates the many ways in which IntelliSense helps you write your code. Among the topics covered are code snippets, the use of XML commenting in your own projects to create more IntelliSense information, and other features as simple as variable-name completion. You will also learn how to set and use bookmarks in your code for easier navigation.

IntelliSense Explained

IntelliSense is the general term for automated help and actions in a Microsoft application. The most commonly encountered aspect of IntelliSense is those wavy lines you see under words that are not spelled correctly in Microsoft Word, or the small visual indicators in a Microsoft Excel spreadsheet that inform you that the contents of the particular cell do not conform to what was expected.

Even these basic indicators enable you to quickly perform related actions. Right-clicking a word with red wavy underlining in Word will display a list of suggested alternatives. Other applications have similar features.

The good news is that Visual Studio has had similar functionality for a long time. In fact, the simplest IntelliSense features go back to tools such as Visual Basic 6. The even better news is that Visual Studio 2008 has IntelliSense on overdrive, with many different features grouped under the

IntelliSense banner. From visual feedback for bad code and smart tags for designing forms to shortcuts that insert whole slabs of code, IntelliSense in Visual Studio 2008 provides greatly enhanced opportunities to improve your efficiency while creating applications.

General IntelliSense

The simplest feature of IntelliSense gives you immediate feedback about bad code in your module listings. Figure 16-1 shows one such example, in which an unknown data type is used to instantiate an object and then a second line of code tries to set a property. Because the data type is unknown in the context in which this code appears, Visual Studio draws a blue wavy line underneath it to indicate a problem.

The formatting of this color feedback can be adjusted in the Fonts and Colors group of Options.

Hovering the mouse pointer over the offending piece of code displays a tooltip to explain the problem. In this example the cursor was placed over the data type, with the resulting tooltip "Type 'Customer' is not defined."

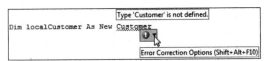

Figure 16-1

Visual Studio is able to look for this kind of error by continually precompiling the code you write in the background, and looking for anything that will produce a compilation error. If you were to add a reference to the class containing the `Customer` definition, Visual Studio would automatically process this and remove the IntelliSense marker.

Figure 16-1 also displays a smart tag associated with the error. This applies only to errors for which Visual Studio 2008 can offer you corrective actions. At the end of the problem code, a small yellow marker is displayed. Placing the mouse pointer over this marker will display the smart tag action menu associated with the type of error — in this case, it's an Error Correction Options list, which when activated will provide a list of data types that you may have meant to use.

The smart tag technology found in Visual Studio is not solely reserved for the code window. In fact, Visual Studio 2008 also includes smart tags on visual components when you're editing a form or user control in Design view (see Figure 16-2).

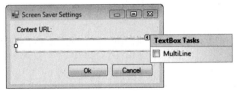

Figure 16-2

When you select a control that has a smart tag, a small triangle will appear at the top right corner of the control itself. Click this button to open the smart tag Tasks list — Figure 16-2 shows the Tasks list for a standard `TextBox` control.

Completing Words and Phrases

The power of IntelliSense in Visual Studio 2008 becomes apparent as soon as you start writing code. As you type, various drop-down lists are displayed to help you choose valid members, functions, and parameter types, thus reducing the number of potential compilation errors before you even finish writing your code. Once you become familiar with the IntelliSense behavior, you'll notice that it can greatly reduce the amount of code you actually have to write. This is a significant savings to developers using more verbose languages such as VB.NET.

In Context

In Visual Studio 2008, IntelliSense appears almost as soon as you begin to type within the code window. Figure 16-3 illustrates the IntelliSense displayed during the creation of a `For` loop in VB.NET. On the left side of the image IntelliSense appeared as soon as the *f* was entered, and the list of available words progressively shrank as each subsequent key was pressed. As you can see, the list is made up of all the alternatives, whether they be statements, classes, methods, or properties, that match the letters entered (in this case those beginning with the prefix `for`).

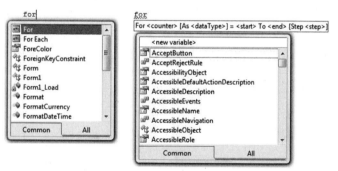

Figure 16-3

Notice the difference in the right-hand image of Figure 16-3, where a space has been entered after the word `for`. Now the IntelliSense list has expanded to include all the alternatives that could be entered at this position in the code. In addition, there is a tooltip that indicates the syntax of the `For` statement. Lastly, there is a <new variable> item just above the IntelliSense list. This is to indicate that it's possible for you to specify a new variable at this location.

While it can be useful that the IntelliSense list is reduced based on the letters you enter, this feature is a double-edged sword. Quite often you will be looking for a variable or member but won't quite remember what it is called. In this scenario, you might enter the first couple of letters of a guess and then use the scrollbar to locate the right alternative. Clearly, this won't work if the alternative doesn't begin with the letters you have entered. To bring up the full list of alternatives, simply hit the backspace key with the IntelliSense list visible.

If you find that the IntelliSense information is obscuring other lines of code, or you simply want to hide the list, you can press Esc. Alternatively, if you simply want to view what is hidden behind the IntelliSense list without closing it completely, you can hold down the Ctrl key. This will make the IntelliSense list translucent, enabling you to read the code behind it, as shown in Figure 16-4.

Figure 16-4

List Members

Because IntelliSense has been around for so long, most developers will be familiar with the member list that appears when you type the name of an object and immediately follow it by a period. This indicates that you are going to refer to a member of the object, and Visual Studio will automatically display a list of members available to you for that object (see Figure 16-5). If this is the first time you've accessed the member list for a particular object, Visual Studio will simply show the member list in alphabetic order with the top of the list visible. However, if you've used it before, it will highlight the last member you accessed to speed up the process for repetitive coding tasks.

Figure 16-5 also shows another helpful aspect of the member list for Visual Basic programmers. The Common and All tabs (at the bottom of the member list) enable you to view either just the commonly used members or a comprehensive list.

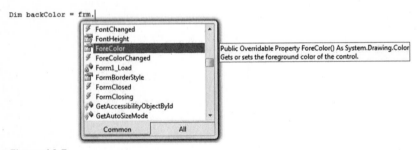

Figure 16-5

Only Visual Basic gives you the option to filter the member list down to commonly accessed properties, methods, and events.

Stub Completion

In addition to word and phrase completion, the IntelliSense engine has another feature known as *stub completion*. This feature can be seen in its basic form when you create a function by writing the declaration of the function and pressing Enter. Visual Studio will automatically reformat the line, adding the appropriate `ByVal` keyword for parameters that don't explicitly define their contexts, and also adding an `End Function` line to enclose the function code.

Visual Studio 2008 takes stub completion an extra step by enabling you to do the same for interface and method overloading. When you add certain code constructs such as an interface in a C# class definition, Visual Studio will give you the opportunity to automatically generate the code necessary to implement the interface. To show you how this works, the following steps outline a task in which the IntelliSense engine generates an interface implementation in a simple class.

1. Start Visual Studio 2008 and create a C# Windows Forms Application project. When the IDE has finished generating the initial code, open `Form1.cs` in code.

2. At the top of the file, add a `using` statement to provide a shortcut to the `System.Collections` namespace:

```
using System.Collections;
```

3. Add the following line of code to start a new class definition:

```
public class MyCollection : IEnumerable
```

As you type the `IEnumerable` interface, Visual Studio will first add a red wavy line at the end to indicate that the class definition is missing its curly braces, and then add a smart tag indicator at the beginning of the interface name (see Figure 16-6).

Figure 16-6

4. Hover your mouse pointer over the smart tag indicator. When the drop-down icon appears, click it to open the menu of possible actions. You should also see the tooltip explaining what the interface does, as shown in Figure 16-7.

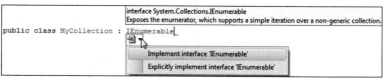

Figure 16-7

5. Click the "Explicitly implement interface 'IEnumerable'" command and Visual Studio 2008 will automatically generate the rest of the code necessary to implement the minimum interface definition. Because it detects that the class definition itself isn't complete, it will also add the braces to correct that issue at the same time. Figure 16-8 shows what the final interface will look like.

```
public class MyCollection : IEnumerable
{
    #region IEnumerable Members

    IEnumerator IEnumerable.GetEnumerator()
    {
        throw new NotImplementedException();
    }

    #endregion
}
```

Figure 16-8

Event handlers can also be automatically generated by Visual Studio 2008. The IDE does this much as it performs interface implementation. When you write the first portion of the statement (for instance, `myBase .OnClick +=`), Visual Studio gives you a suggested completion that you can select by simply pressing Tab.

Parameter Information

In old versions of Microsoft development tools, such as Visual Basic 6, as you created the call to a function, IntelliSense would display the parameter information as you typed. Thankfully, this incredibly useful feature is still present in Visual Studio 2008.

The problem with the old way parameter information was displayed was that it would only be shown if you were actually modifying the function call. Therefore, you could see this helpful tooltip as you created the function call or when you changed it but not if you were just viewing the code. The result was that programmers sometimes inadvertently introduced bugs into their code because they intentionally modified function calls so they could view the parameter information associated with the calls.

Visual Studio 2008 eliminates that risk by providing an easily accessible command to display the information without modifying the code. The keyboard shortcut Ctrl+Shift+Space will display the information about the function call, as displayed in Figure 16-9. You can also access this information through the Edit ⇨ IntelliSense ⇨ Parameter Info menu command.

```
Dim myList As New List(Of String)(500)
        ▲ 2 of 3 ▼  New (capacity As Integer)
        capacity: The number of elements that the new list can initially store.
```

Figure 16-9

Quick Info

In a similar vein, sometimes you want to see the information about an object or interface without modifying the code. The Ctrl+K, Ctrl+I keyboard shortcut will display a brief tooltip explaining what the object is and how it was declared (see Figure 16-10).

You can also display this tooltip through the Edit ⇨ IntelliSense ⇨ Quick Info menu command.

Figure 16-10

IntelliSense Options

Visual Studio 2008 sets up a number of default options for your experience with IntelliSense, but you can change many of these in the Options dialog if they don't suit your own way of doing things. Some of these items are specific to individual languages.

General Options

The first options to look at are found in the Environment section under the Keyboard group. Every command available in Visual Studio has a specific entry in the keyboard mapping list (see the Options dialog shown in Figure 16-11, accessible via Tools ⇨ Options).

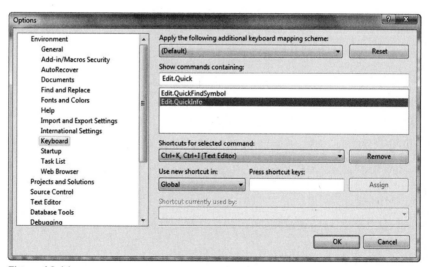

Figure 16-11

You can overwrite the predefined keyboard shortcuts, or add additional ones. The commands for the IntelliSense commands are as follows:

Table 16-1: IntelliSense Commands

Command Name	Default Shortcut	Command Description
Edit.QuickInfo	Ctrl+K, Ctrl+I	Displays the Quick Info information about the currently selected item
Edit.CompleteWord	Ctrl+Space	Attempts to complete a word if there is a single match, or displays a list to choose from if multiple terms match
Edit.ParameterInfo	Ctrl+Shift+Space	Displays the information about the parameter list in a function call
Edit.InsertSnippet	Ctrl+K, Ctrl+X	Invokes the Code Snippet dialog, from which you can select a code snippet to insert code automatically
Edit.GenerateMethodStub	Ctrl+K, Ctrl+M	Generates the full method stub from a template
Edit.ImplementAbstractClassStubs	None	Generates the abstract class definitions from a stub
Edit.ImplementInterfaceStubsExplicitly	None	Generates the explicit implementation of an interface for a class definition
Edit.ImplementInterfaceStubsImplicitly	None	Generates the implicit implementation of an interface for a class definition

Use the techniques discussed in Chapter 3 to add additional keyboard shortcuts to any of these commands.

Statement Completion

You can control how IntelliSense works on a global language scale (see Figure 16-12) or per individual language. In the General tab of the language group in the Options dialog, you want to change the "Statement completion" options to control how member lists should be displayed, if at all.

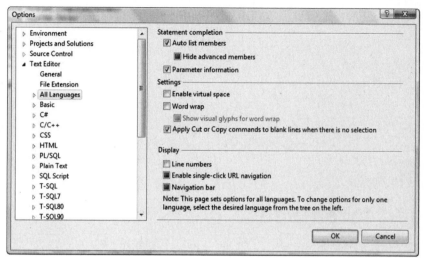

Figure 16-12

Note that the "Hide advanced members" option is only relevant to some languages, such as VB.NET, that make a distinction between commonly used members and advanced members.

C#-Specific Options

Besides the general IDE and language options for IntelliSense, some languages, such as C#, provide an additional IntelliSense tab in their own sets of options. Displayed in Figure 16-13, the IntelliSense for C# can be further customized to fine-tune how the IntelliSense features should be invoked and used.

First, you can turn off completion lists so they do not appear automatically, as discussed earlier in this chapter. Some developers prefer this because the member lists don't get in the way of their code listings. If the completion list is not to be automatically displayed but instead only shown when you manually invoke it, you can choose what is to be included in the lists in addition to the normal entries, including keywords and code snippet shortcuts.

To select an entry in a member list, you can use any of the characters shown in the Selection In Completion List section, or optionally after the space bar is pressed. Finally, as mentioned previously, Visual Studio will automatically highlight the member in a list that was last used. You can turn this feature off for these languages or just clear the history.

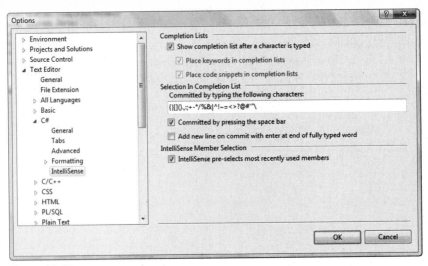

Figure 16-13

Extended IntelliSense

In addition to these aspects of IntelliSense, Visual Studio 2008 also implements extended IDE functionality that falls into the IntelliSense feature set. These features are discussed in detail in other chapters in this book, as referenced in the following discussion, but this chapter provides a quick summary of what's included in IntelliSense.

Code Snippets

Code snippets are sections of code that can be automatically generated and pasted into your own code, including associated references and Imports statements, with variable phrases marked for easy replacement. To invoke the Code Snippets dialog, press Ctrl+K, Ctrl+X. Navigate the hierarchy of snippet folders (shown in Figure 16-14) until you find the one you need. If you know the shortcut for the snippet, you can simply type it and press Tab, and Visual Studio will invoke the snippet without displaying the dialog. In Chapter 17, you'll see just how powerful code snippets are.

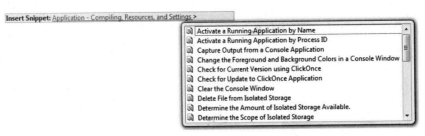

Figure 16-14

XML Comments

XML comments were discussed in Chapter 9 as a way of providing automated documentation for your projects and solutions. However, another advantage to using XML commenting in your program code is that Visual Studio can use it in its IntelliSense engine to display tooltips and parameter information beyond the simple variable-type information you see in normal user-defined classes.

A warning for VB.NET developers: Disabling the generation of XML documentation during compilation will also limit your ability to generate the XML comments in your code.

Adding Your Own IntelliSense

You can also add your own IntelliSense schemas, normally useful for XML and HTML editing, by creating a correctly formatted XML file and installing it into the Common7\Packages\schemas\xml sub-folder inside your Visual Studio installation directory (the default location is C:\Program Files\Microsoft Visual Studio 9.0). An example of this would be extending the IntelliSense support for the XML editor to include your own schema definitions. The creation of such a schema file is beyond the scope of this book, but you can find schema files on the Internet by searching for "IntelliSense schema in Visual Studio."

Bookmarks and the Bookmark Window

Bookmarks in Visual Studio 2008 enable you to mark places in your code modules so you can easily return to them later. They are represented by indicators in the left margin of the code, as shown in Figure 16-15.

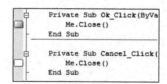

Figure 16-15

To toggle between bookmarked and not bookmarked on a line, use the shortcut Ctrl+K, Ctrl+K. Alternatively, you can use the Edit ⇨ Bookmarks ⇨ Toggle Bookmark menu command to do the same thing.

Remember that toggle *means just that. If you use this command on a line already bookmarked, it will remove the bookmark.*

Figure 16-15 shows a section of the code editor window with two bookmarks set. The top bookmark is in its normal state, represented by a shaded blue rectangle. The lower bookmark has been disabled and is represented by a solid white rectangle. Disabling a bookmark enables you to keep it for later use while excluding it from the normal bookmark-navigation functions.

To disable a bookmark, use the Edit ⇨ Bookmarks ⇨ Enable Bookmark toggle menu command. Use the same command to re-enable the bookmark. This seems counterintuitive because you actually want to disable an active bookmark, but for some reason the menu item isn't updated based on the cursor context.

You may want to set up a shortcut for disabling and enabling bookmarks if you plan on using them a lot in your code management. To do so, access the Keyboard Options page in the Environment group in Options and look for `Edit.EnableBookmark`*.*

Along with the ability to add and remove bookmarks, Visual Studio provides a Bookmarks tool window, shown in Figure 16-16. You can display this tool window by pressing Ctrl+K, Ctrl+W or via the View ⇨ Bookmark Window menu item. By default, this window is docked to the bottom of the IDE and shares space with other tool windows, such as the Task List and Find Results windows.

Figure 16-16

Figure 16-16 illustrates some useful features of bookmarks in Visual Studio 2008. The first feature is the ability it gives you to create folders that can logically group the bookmarks. In the example list, notice a folder named Old Bookmarks contains a bookmark named Bookmark3.

To create a folder of bookmarks, click the "new folder" icon in the toolbar along the top of the Bookmarks window (it's the second button from the left). This will create an empty folder (using a default name of Folder1, followed by Folder2, and so on) with the name of the folder in focus so that you can make it more relevant. You can move bookmarks into the folder by selecting their entries in the list and dragging them into the desired folder. Note that you cannot create a hierarchy of folders, but it's unlikely that you'll want to. Bookmarks can be renamed in the same way as folders, and for permanent bookmarks renaming can be more useful than accepting the default names of Bookmark1, Bookmark2, and so forth. Folders are not only a convenient way of grouping bookmarks; they also provide an easy way for you to enable or disable a number of bookmarks in one go, simply by using the checkbox beside the folder name.

To navigate directly to a bookmark, double-click its entry in the Bookmarks tool window. Alternatively, if you want to cycle through all of the enabled bookmarks defined in the project, use the Previous Bookmark (Ctrl+K, Ctrl+P) and Next Bookmark (Ctrl+K, Ctrl+N) commands. You can restrict this navigation to only the bookmarks in a particular folder by first selecting a bookmark in the folder and then using the Previous Bookmark in Folder (Ctrl+Shift+K, Ctrl+Shift+P) and Next Bookmark in Folder (Ctrl+Shift+K, Ctrl+Shift+N) commands.

The last two icons in the Bookmarks window are "toggle all bookmarks," which can be used to disable (or re-enable) all of the bookmarks defined in a project, and "delete," which can be used to delete a folder or bookmark from the list.

Deleting a folder will also remove all the bookmarks contained in the folder. Visual Studio will provide a confirmation dialog to safeguard against accidental loss of bookmarks. Deleting a bookmark is the same as toggling it off.

Bookmarks can also be controlled via the Bookmarks sub-menu, which is found in the Edit main menu. In Visual Studio 2008 bookmarks are also retained between sessions, making permanent bookmarks a much more viable option for managing your code organization.

Task lists are customized versions of bookmarks that are displayed in their own tool windows. The only connection that still exists between the two is that there is an Add Task List Shortcut command still in the Bookmarks menu. Be aware that this does not add the shortcut to the Bookmarks window but instead to the Shortcuts list in the Task List window.

Summary

IntelliSense functionality extends beyond the main code window. Various other windows, such as the Command and Immediate tool windows, can harness the power of IntelliSense through statement and parameter completion. Any keywords, or even variables and objects, known in the current context during a debugging session can be accessed through the IntelliSense member lists.

IntelliSense in all its forms enhances the Visual Studio experience beyond most other tools available to you. Constantly monitoring your keystrokes to give you visual feedback or automatic code completion and generation, IntelliSense enables you to be extremely effective at writing code quickly and correctly the first time. In the next chapter you'll dive into the details behind code snippets, a powerful addition to IntelliSense.

In this chapter you've also seen how you can set and navigate between bookmarks in your code. Becoming familiar with using the associated keystrokes will help you improve your coding efficiency.

17

Code Snippets and Refactoring

Code snippets are small chunks of code that can be inserted into an application's code base and then customized to meet the application's specific requirements. They do not generate full-blown applications or whole form definitions, unlike project and item templates. Instead, code snippets shortcut the programming task by automating frequently used code structures or obscure program code blocks that are not easy to remember. In the first part of this chapter you'll see how code snippets are a powerful tool that can improve coding efficiency enormously, particularly for programmers who perform repetitive tasks with similar behaviors.

One technique that continues to receive a lot of attention is refactoring, the process of reworking code to improve it without changing its functionality. This might entail simplifying a method, extracting a commonly used code pattern, or even optimizing a section of code to make it more efficient. The second part of this chapter reviews the refactoring support offered by Visual Studio 2008.

Unfortunately, because of the massive list of functionality that the VB.NET team tried to squeeze into Visual Studio 2005, support for a wide range of refactoring actions just didn't make the cut. Luckily for VB.NET developers, Microsoft came to an arrangement with Developer Express to license the VB version of its Refactor! product. This arrangement continues, giving VB.NET developers access to Refactor! for Visual Studio 2008. You can download it from the Visual Basic developer center at http://msdn.microsoft.com/vbasic/; follow the links to *Downloads*, then *Tools and Utilities*.

Refactor! provides a range of additional refactoring support that complements the integrated support available for C# developers. However, this chapter's discussion is restricted to the built-in refactoring support provided within Visual Studio 2008 (for C# developers) and the corresponding action in Refactor! (for VB.NET developers).

Code Snippets Revealed

Code snippets have been around in a variety of forms for a long time but generally required third-party add-ins for languages such as Visual Basic 6 and the early versions of Visual Studio. Visual Studio 2008 includes a full-fledged code snippet feature that not only includes blocks of code, but also allows multiple sections of code to be inserted in different locations within the module. In addition, replacement variables can be defined that make it easy to customize the generated snippet.

Original Code Snippets

The original code snippets from previous versions of Visual Studio were simple at best. These snippets can be used to store a block of plain text that can be inserted into a code module when desired. The process to create and use them is simple as well: select a section of code and drag it over to the Toolbox. This creates an entry for it in the Toolbox with a default name equal to the first line of the code. You can rename and arrange these entries like any other element in the Toolbox. To insert the snippet you simply drag the code to the desired location in the "Code view" as shown in Figure 17-1. Alternatively, positioning the cursor where you want the snippet to be inserted, holding Shift, and clicking the snippet will place the code at the cursor location.

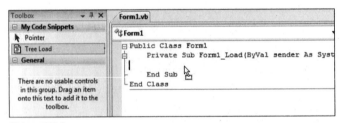

Figure 17-1

Many presenters used this simple technology to quickly generate large code blocks in presentations, but in a real-world situation it was not as effective as it could have been, because often you had to remember to use multiple items to generate code that would compile.

Unfortunately this model was too simple, as there was no way to share these so-called snippets, and equally hard to modify them. Nevertheless, this method of keeping small sections of code is still available to programmers in Visual Studio 2008, and it can prove useful when you don't need a permanent record of the code, but rather want to copy a series of code blocks for short-term use.

"Real" Code Snippets

In Visual Studio 2008, code snippets refer to something completely different. Code snippets are XML-based files containing sections of code that can include not only normal source code, but references, Imports statements, and replaceable parameters as well.

Visual Studio 2008 ships with many predefined code snippets for the three main languages, Visual Basic, C#, and J#. These snippets are arranged hierarchically in a logical fashion so that you can easily locate the appropriate snippet. Rather than locate the snippet in the Toolbox, you can use menu commands or keyboard shortcuts to bring up the main list of groups.

New code snippets can be created to automate almost any coding task and then can be stored in this code snippet library. Because each snippet is stored in a special XML file, you can even share them with other developers.

Using Snippets in Visual Basic

Code snippets are a natural addition to the Visual Basic developer's tool set. They provide a shortcut to insert code that either is difficult to remember or is used often with minor tweaks. One common problem some programmers have is remembering the correct references and Imports statements required to get a specific section of code working properly; code snippets in Visual Basic solve this problem by including all the necessary associations as well as the actual code.

To use a code snippet you should first locate where you want the generated code to be placed in the program listing and position the cursor at that point. You don't have to worry about the associated references and Imports statements; they will be placed in the correct location.

There are three scopes under which a snippet can be inserted:

❑ **Class Declaration:** The snippet will actually include a class declaration, so it should not be inserted into an existing class definition.

❑ **Member Declaration:** This snippet scope will include code that defines members, such as functions and event handler routines. This means it should be inserted outside an existing member.

❑ **Member Body:** This scope is for snippets that are inserted into an already defined member, such as an event handler routine.

Once you've determined where the snippet is to be placed, the easiest way to bring up the Insert Snippet dialog is to use the keyboard shortcut combination of Ctrl+K, Ctrl+X. There are two additional methods to start the Insert Snippet process. The first is to right-click at the intended insertion point in the code window and select Insert Snippet from the context menu that is displayed. The other option is to use the Edit ➪ IntelliSense ➪ Insert Snippet menu command.

The Insert Snippet dialog is a special kind of IntelliSense that appears inline in the code window. Initially it displays the words Insert Snippet along with a drop-down list of code snippet groups from which to choose. Once you select the group that contains the snippet you require (using up and down arrows, followed by the Tab key), it will show you a list of snippets, from which you simply double-click the one you need (alternatively, pressing Tab or Enter with the required snippet selected will have the same effect).

Because you can organize the snippet library into many levels, you may find that the snippet you need is multiple levels–deep in the Insert Snippet dialog. Figure 17-2 displays an Insert Snippet dialog in which the user has navigated through two levels of groups and then located a snippet named Draw a Pie Chart.

Figure 17-2

Figure 17-3 displays the result of selecting the Draw a Pie Chart snippet. This example shows a snippet with Member Declaration scope because it adds the definition of two subroutines to the code. To help you modify the code to your own requirements, the sections you would normally need to change are highlighted, with the first one conveniently selected.

```
Public Class Form1

    ' Shows how to call the DrawPieChart method
    Public Sub DrawPieChartHelper()
        Dim percents() As Integer = {10, 20, 70}
        Dim colors() As Color = {Color.Red, Color.CadetBlue, Color.Khaki}
        Dim graphics As Graphics = Me.CreateGraphics
        Dim location As Point = New Point(10, 10)
        Dim size As Size = New Size(150, 150)
        DrawPieChart(percents, colors, graphics, location, size)
    End Sub


    ' Draws a pie chart.
    Public Sub DrawPieChart(ByVal percents() As Integer, ByVal colors() As Color, _
    ByVal surface As Graphics, ByVal location As Point, ByVal pieSize As Size)
        ' Check if sections add up to 100.
        Dim sum As Integer = 0
        For Each percent As Integer In percents
            sum += percent
        Next
```

Figure 17-3

When changing the variable sections of the generated code snippet, Visual Studio 2008 helps you even further. Pressing the Tab key will move to the next highlighted value, ready for you to override the value with your own. Shift+Tab will navigate backward, so you have an easy way of accessing the sections of code that need changing without needing to manually select the next piece to modify. Some code snippets use the same variable for multiple pieces of the code snippet logic. This means changing the value in one place will result in it changing in all other instances.

You might have noticed in Figure 17-2 that the tooltip text includes the words "Shortcut: drawPie." This text indicates that the selected code snippet has a text shortcut that you can use to automatically invoke the code snippet behavior without bringing up the IntelliSense dialog. Of course, you need to know what the shortcut is before you can use this feature, but for those that you are aware of, all you need to do is type the shortcut into the code editor and press the Tab key. In Visual Basic the shortcut isn't even case-sensitive, so this example can be generated by typing the term "drawpie" and pressing Tab.

> Note that in some instances the IntelliSense engine may not recognize this kind of shortcut. If this happens to you, press Ctrl+Tab to force IntelliSense to intercept the Tab key.

Using Snippets in C# and J#

The code snippets in C# and J# are not as extensive as those available for Visual Basic but are inserted in the same way. Only Visual Basic supports the advanced features of the code snippet functionality, such as references and Imports statements. First, locate the position where you want to insert the generated code and then use one of the following methods:

❑   The keyboard chord Ctrl+K, Ctrl+X

❑   Right-click and choose Insert Snippet from the context menu

❑   Run the Edit ⇨ IntelliSense ⇨ Insert Snippet menu command

At this point, Visual Studio will bring up the Insert Snippet list for the current language, as Figure 17-4 shows. As you scroll through the list and hover the mouse pointer over each entry, a tooltip will be displayed to indicate what the snippet does and again the shortcut that can be used to invoke the snippet via the keyboard.

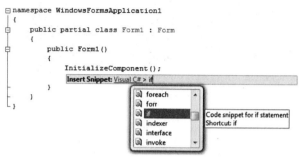

Figure 17-4

Although the predefined C# and J# snippets are limited in nature, you can create more functional and complex snippets for them.

Surround With Snippet

The last refactoring action, available in both C# and VB.NET, is the capability to surround an existing block of code with a code snippet. For example, to wrap an existing block with a conditional try-catch block, you would select the block of code and press Ctrl+K, Ctrl+S. This displays the Surround With dialog that contains a list of surrounding snippets that are available to wrap the selected line of code, as shown in Figure 17-5.

Figure 17-5

Selecting the `try` snippet results in the following code:

```
public void MethodXYZ(string name)
{
    try
    {
        MessageBox.Show(name);
    }
    catch (Exception)
    {
        throw;
    }
}
```

Code Snippets Manager

The Code Snippets Manager is the central library for the code snippets known to Visual Studio 2008. You can access it via the Tools ⇨ Code Snippet Manager menu command or the keyboard shortcut chord Ctrl+K, Ctrl+B.

When it is initially displayed, the Code Snippets Manager will show the snippets for the language you're currently using. Figure 17-6 shows how it will look when you're editing a Visual Basic project. The hierarchical folder structure follows the same set of folders on the PC by default, but as you add snippet files from different locations and insert them into the different groups, the new snippets slip into the appropriate folders.

If you have an entire folder of snippets to add to the library, such as when you have a corporate setup and need to import the company-developed snippets, you use the "Add" button. This brings up a dialog that you use to browse to the required folder. Folders added in this fashion will appear at the root level of the treeview — on the same level as the main groups of default snippets. However, you can add a folder that contains sub-folders, which will be added as child nodes in the treeview.

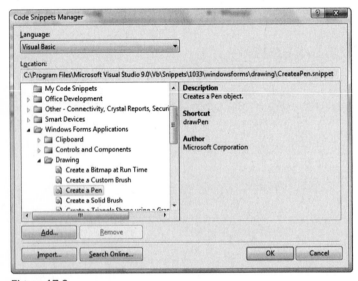

Figure 17-6

Removing a folder is just as easy — in fact, it's dangerously easy. Select the root node that you want to remove and click the "Remove" button. Instantly the node and all child nodes and snippets will be removed from the Snippets Manager without a confirmation window. You can add them back by following the steps explained in the previous walkthrough, but it can be frustrating trying to locate a default snippet folder that you inadvertently deleted from the list.

The location for the code snippets that are installed with Visual Studio 2008 is deep within the installation folder. By default, the code snippet library will be installed in C:\Program Files\ Microsoft Visual Studio 9.0\VB\Snippets\1033. Individual snippet files can be imported into the library using the "Import" button. The advantage of this method over the "Add" button is that you get the opportunity to specify the location of each snippet in the library structure.

Creating Snippets

Visual Studio 2008 does not ship with a code snippet creator or editor. However Bill McCarthy's VB Snippet Editor allows you to create, modify, and manage your snippets (supports VB, C#, XML, and J# snippets). Starting as an internal Microsoft project, the Snippet Editor was subsequently placed on GotDotNet where Bill fixed the outstanding issue and proceeded to add functionality. With the help of other MVPs it is now also available in a number of different languages. You can download the Visual Studio 2008 version from `http://BillMcCarthy.com/projects/Snippet_Editor`.

Creating code snippets by manually editing XML files can be tedious. It can also result in errors that are hard to track down, so it's recommended that you use the Snippet Editor where possible. When you start the Snippet Editor, it will display a welcome screen showing you how to browse and create new snippets. The left side of the screen is populated with a treeview containing all the Visual Basic snippets defined in your system and known to Visual Studio 2008. Initially the treeview is collapsed, but by expanding it you'll see a set of folders similar to those in the code snippet library (see Figure 17-7).

If you have other versions of Visual Studio installed, the Snippet Editor may have defaulted to manage the snippets for that installation. To select the Visual Studio edition to manage, use the Select Product drop-down on the Languages tab of the Options dialog. This dialog can be launched via the "Options" button in the top-right corner of the Snippet Editor.

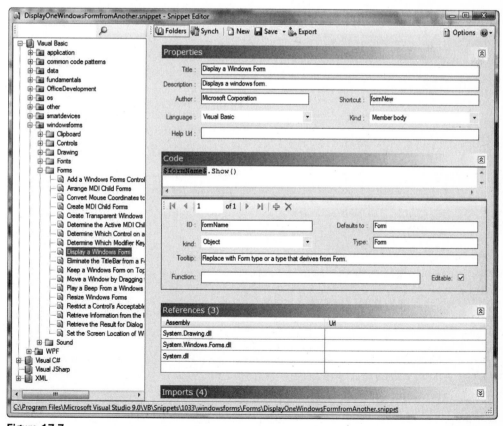

Figure 17-7

Reviewing Existing Snippets

An excellent feature of the Snippet Editor is the view it offers of the structure of any snippet file in the system. This means you can browse the default snippets installed with Visual Studio, which can provide insight into how to better build your own snippets.

Browse to the snippet you're interested in and double-click its entry to display it in the Editor window. Figure 17-7 shows a simple snippet to Display a Windows Form. Four main panes contain all the associated information about the snippet. From top to bottom, these panes are described in Table 17-1.

Table 17-1: Information Panes for Snippets

Pane	Function
Properties	The main properties for the snippet, including title, shortcut, and description.
Code	Defines the code for the snippet, including all `Literal` and `Object` replacement regions.
References	If your snippet will require assembly references, this tab allows you to define them.
Imports	Similar to the References tab, this tab enables you to define any `Imports` statements that are required in order for your snippet to function correctly.

Browsing through these tabs enables you to analyze an existing snippet for its properties and replacement variables. In the example shown in Figure 17-7, there is a single replacement region with an ID of `formName` and a default value of `"Form"`.

To demonstrate how the Snippet Editor makes creating your own snippets straightforward, follow this next exercise, in which you will create a snippet that creates three subroutines, including a helper subroutine:

1. Start the Snippet Editor and create a new snippet. To do this, select a destination folder in the treeview, right-click, and select Add New Snippet from the context menu that is displayed.

2. When prompted, name the snippet "Create A Button Sample" and click "OK". Double-click the new entry to open it in the Editor pane.

    Note that creating the snippet will not automatically open the new snippet in the Editor — don't overwrite the properties of another snippet by mistake!

3. The first thing you need to do is edit the `Title`, `Description`, and `Shortcut` fields (see Figure 17-8):

    ❑   `Title`: Create A Button Sample

    ❑   `Description`: This snippet adds code to create a button control and hook an event handler to it.

    ❑   `Shortcut`: CreateAButton

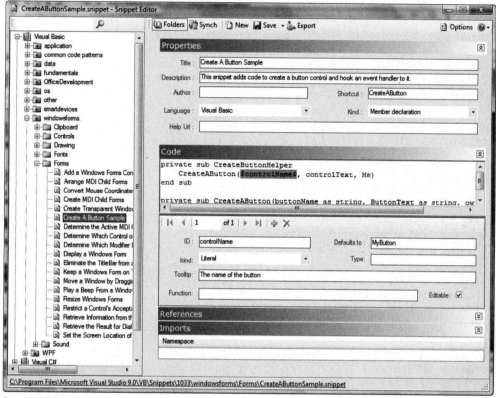

Figure 17-8

4. Because this snippet contains member definitions, set the Type to "Member Declaration."

5. In the Editor window, insert the code necessary to create the three subroutines:

```
Private Sub CreateButtonHelper
    CreateAButton(controlName, controlText, Me)
End Sub

Private Sub CreateAButton(ByVal ButtonName As String, ByVal ButtonText As String, _
                                          ByVal Owner As Form)

    Dim MyButton As New Button

    MyButton.Name = ButtonName
    MyButton.Text = ButtonName
    Owner.Controls.Add(MyButton)

    MyButton.Top = 0
    MyButton.Left = 0
    MyButton.Text = ButtonText
    MyButton.Visible = True

    AddHandler MyButton.Click, AddressOf ButtonClickHandler
```

(continued)

(continued)

```
End Sub

Private Sub ButtonClickHandler(ByVal sender As System.Object, _
                               ByVal e As System.EventArgs)
    MessageBox.Show("The " & sender.Name & " button was clicked")
End Sub
```

6. You will notice that your code differs from that shown in Figure 17-8 in that the word `controlName` does not appear highlighted. In Figure 17-8 this argument has been made a replacement region. You can do this by selecting the entire word, right-clicking, and selecting Add Replacement (or alternatively, clicking the "Add" button in the area below the code window).

7. Change the replacement properties like so:

    ❑ `ID:` `controlName`

    ❑ `Defaults to:` `"MyButton"`

    ❑ `Tooltip:` The name of the button

8. Repeat this for `controlText`:

    ❑ `ID:` `controlText`

    ❑ `Defaults to:` `"Click Me!"`

    ❑ `Tooltip:` The text property of the button

Your snippet is now done and ready to be used. You can use Visual Studio 2008 to insert the snippet into a code window.

Accessing Refactoring Support

Visual Studio 2008 makes use of both the main menu and the right-click context menu to invoke the refactoring actions. Refactor! uses only the context menu to invoke actions, although it does offer hints while you're working.

Refactoring support for C# developers is available via the Refactor menu or the right-click context menu, as shown in the left image of Figure 17-9. The full list of refactoring actions available to C# developers within Visual Studio 2008 includes Rename, Extract Method, Encapsulate Field, Extract Interface, Promote Local Variable to Parameter, Remove Parameters, and Reorder Parameters. You can also use Generate Method Stub, and Organize Usings, which can be loosely classified as refactoring.

Refactoring support for VB.NET developers, using Refactor!, is available via the right-click context menu, as shown in the right image of Figure 17-9. As you work with your code, Refactor! is busy in the background. The context menu dynamically changes so that only valid refactoring actions are displayed.

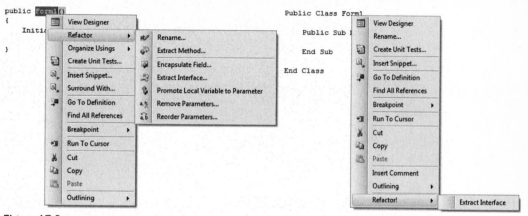

Figure 17-9

The refactoring support provided by Visual Studio 2008 for VB.NET developers is limited to the symbolic Rename. Refactor! adds support for much, much more: Create an Overload, Encapsulate a Field, Extract a Method, Extract a Property, Flatten Conditional Statement, Inline Temporary Variable, Introduce a Constant, Introduce Local Variable, Move Declaration Near Reference, Move Initialization to Declaration, Remove Assignments to Parameters, Rename, Reorder Parameters, Replace Temporary Variable with Method, Reverse Conditional Statement, Safe Rename, Simplify Conditional Statement, Split Initialization from Declaration, and Split Temporary Variable.

Refactoring Actions

The following sections describe each of the refactoring options and provide examples of how to use built-in support for both C# and Refactor! for VB.NET.

Extract Method

One of the easiest ways to refactor a long method is to break it up into several smaller methods. The Extract Method refactoring action is invoked by selecting the region of code you want moved out of the original method and selecting Extract Method from the context menu. In C#, this will prompt you to enter a new method name, as shown in Figure 17-10. If there are variables within the block of code to be extracted that were used earlier in the original method, they will automatically appear as variables in the method signature. Once the name has been confirmed, the new method will be created immediately after the original method. A call to the new method will replace the extracted code block.

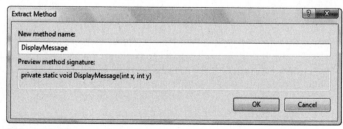

Figure 17-10

For example, in the following code snippet, if you wanted to extract the conditional logic into a separate method, then you would select the code, shown with a gray background, and choose Extract Method from the right-click context menu:

```
private void button1_Click(object sender, EventArgs e)
{
    string output = Properties.Settings.Default.AdventureWorksCS;
    if (output == null)
    {
        output = "DefaultConnectionString";
    }
    MessageBox.Show(output);
    /* ... Much longer method ... */
}
```

This would automatically generate the following code in its place:

```
Private void button1_Click(object sender, EventArgs e)
{
    string output = Properties.Settings.Default.AdventureWorksCS;
    output = ValidateConnectionString(output);
    MessageBox.Show(output);
    /* ... Much longer method ... */
}

private static string ValidateConnectionString(string output)
{
    if (output == null)
    {
        output = "DefaultConnectionString";
    }
    return output;
}
```

Refactor! handles this refactoring action slightly differently. After you select the code you want to replace, Refactor! prompts you to select a place in your code where you want to insert the new method. This can help developers organize their methods in groups, either alphabetically or according to functionality. Figure 17-11 illustrates the aid that appears to enable you to position, using the cursor keys, the insert location.

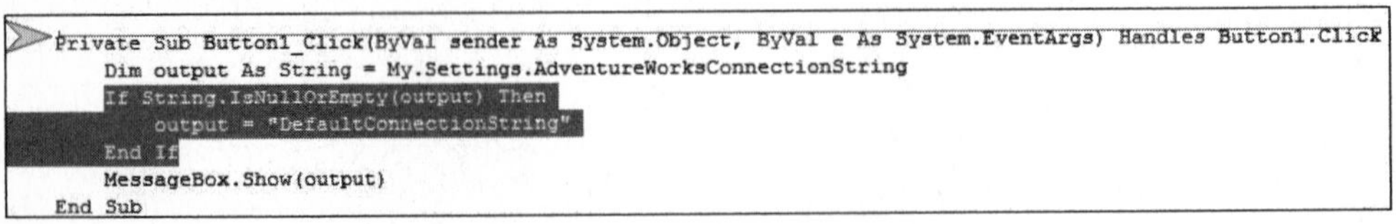

```
Private Sub Button1_Click(ByVal sender As System.Object, ByVal e As System.EventArgs) Handles Button1.Click
    Dim output As String = My.Settings.AdventureWorksConnectionString
    If String.IsNullOrEmpty(output) Then
        output = "DefaultConnectionString"
    End If
    MessageBox.Show(output)
End Sub
```

Figure 17-11

After selecting the insert location, Refactor! will insert the new method, giving it an arbitrary name. In doing so it will highlight the method name, enabling you to rename the method either at the insert location or where the method is called (see Figure 17-12).

```
Private Shared Sub Button1_ClickExtracted(ByRef output As String)
    If String.IsNullOrEmpty(output) Then
        output = "DefaultConnectionString"
    End If
End Sub
Private Sub Button1_Click(ByVal sender As System.Object, ByVal e As System.EventArgs) Handles Button1.Click
    Dim output As String = My.Settings.AdventureWorksConnectionString
    Button1_ClickExtracted(output)
    MessageBox.Show(output)
End Sub
```

Figure 17-12

Encapsulate Field

Another common task when refactoring is to encapsulate an existing class variable with a property. This is what the Encapsulate Field refactor action does. To invoke this action, select the variable you want to encapsulate and then choose the appropriate refactor action from the context menu. This will give you the opportunity to name the property and elect where to search for references to the variable, as shown in Figure 17-13.

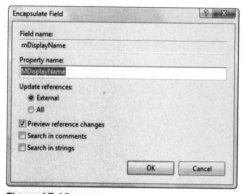

Figure 17-13

The next step after specifying the new property name is to determine which references to the class variable should be replaced with a reference to the new property. Figure 17-14 shows the preview window that is returned after the reference search has been completed. In the top pane is a tree indicating which files and methods have references to the variable. The checkbox beside each row indicates whether a replacement will be made. Selecting a row in the top pane brings that line of code into focus in the lower pane. Once each of the references has been validated, the encapsulation can proceed. The class variable is updated to be private, and the appropriate references are updated as well.

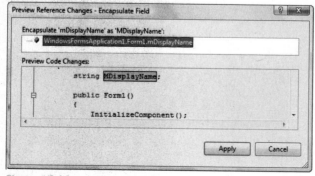

Figure 17-14

The Encapsulate Field refactoring action using Refactor! works in a similar way, except that it automatically assigns the name of the property based on the name of the class variable. The interface for updating references is also different, as shown in Figure 17-15. Instead of a modal dialog, Refactor! presents a visual aid that can be used to navigate through the references. Where a replacement is required, click the check mark. Unlike the C# dialog box, in which the checkboxes can be checked and unchecked as many times as needed, once you click the check mark, there is no way to undo this action.

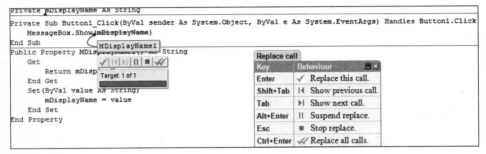

Figure 17-15

Extract Interface

As a project goes from prototype or early-stage development to a full implementation or growth phase, it's often necessary to extract the core methods for a class into an interface to enable other implementations or to define a boundary between disjointed systems. In the past you could do this by copying the entire method to a new file and removing the method contents so you were just left with the interface stub. The Extract Interface refactoring action enables you to extract an interface based on any number of methods within a class. When this refactoring action is invoked on a class, the dialog in Figure 17-16 is displayed, which enables you to select which methods are included in the interface. Once selected, those methods are added to the new interface. The new interface is also added to the original class.

Figure 17-16

In the following example, the first method needs to be extracted into an interface:

```
public class ConcreteClass
{
    public void ShouldBeInInterface()
    { /* ... */ }

    public void AnotherNormalMethod(int ParameterA, int ParameterB)
    { /* ... */ }

    public void NormalMethod()
    { /* ... */ }
}
```

Selecting Extract Interface from the right-click context menu will introduce a new interface and update the original class as follows:

```
interface IBestPractice
{
    void ShouldBeInInterface();
}
```

```
public class ConcreteClass : WindowsFormsApplication1.IBestPractice
{
    public void ShouldBeInInterface()
    { /* ... */ }

    public void NormalMethod(int ParameterA, int ParameterB)
    { /* ... */ }

    public void AnotherNormalMethod()
    { /* ... */ }
}
```

Extracting an interface is also available within Refactor! but doesn't allow you to choose which methods you wish to include in the interface. Unlike the C# interface extraction, which places the interface in a separate file and is recommended, Refactor! simply extracts all class methods into an interface in the same code file.

Reorder Parameters

Sometimes it's necessary to reorder parameters. This is often for cosmetic reasons, but it can also aid readability and is sometimes warranted when implementing interfaces. The Reorder Parameters dialog, shown in Figure 17-17, enables you to move parameters up and down in the list according to the order in which you wish them to appear.

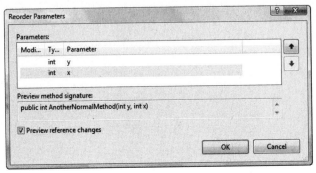

Figure 17-17

Once you establish the correct order, you're given the opportunity to preview the changes. By default, the parameters in every reference to this method will be reordered according to the new order. The Preview dialog, similar to the one shown in Figure 17-14, enables you to control which references are updated.

The Refactor! interface for reordering parameters is one of the most intuitive on the market. Again, the creators have opted for visual aids instead of a modal dialog, as shown in Figure 17-18. You can move the selected parameter left or right in the parameter list and navigate between parameters with the Tab key. Once the parameters are in the desired order, the search and replace interface, illustrated in Figure 17-15, enables the developer to verify all updates.

```
Public Sub NormalMethod(ByVal parameterA As Integer, ByVal parameterB As Integer)

End Sub
```

Reorder Parameters	
Key	Behaviour
Left	Move the parameter **left**.
Right	Move the parameter **right**.
Tab	Select the **next** parameter.
Shift+Tab	Select the **previous** parameter.
Enter or Num Enter	✓ **Commit** changes.
Esc	✗ **Cancel** changes.

Figure 17-18

Remove Parameters

It is unusual to have to remove a parameter while refactoring, because it usually means that the functionality of the method has changed. However, having support for this action considerably reduces the amount of searching that has to be done for compile errors that can occur when a parameter is removed. The other time this action is particularly useful is when there are multiple overloads for a method, and removing a parameter may not generate compile errors; in such a case, there may be runtime errors due to semantic, rather than syntactical, mistakes.

Figure 17-19 illustrates the Remove Parameters dialog that is used to remove parameters from the parameters list. If a parameter is accidentally removed, it can be easily restored until the correct parameter list is arranged. As the warning on this dialog indicates, removing parameters can often result in unexpected functional errors, so it is important to review the changes made. Again, the preview window can be used to validate the proposed changes.

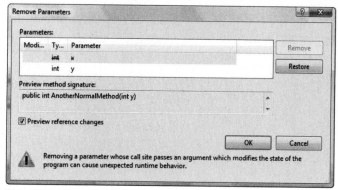

Figure 17-19

Refactor! only supports removing unused parameters, as shown in Figure 17-20. The other thing to note in Figure 17-20 is that Refactor! has been accessed via the smart tag that appeared when `parameterA` was given focus.

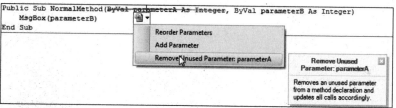

Figure 17-20

Rename

Visual Studio 2008 provides rename support in both C# and VB.NET. The Rename dialog for C# is shown in Figure 17-21; it is similar in VB.NET although it doesn't have the options to search in comments or strings.

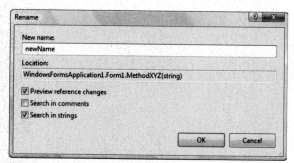

Figure 17-21

Unlike the C# rename support, which uses the preview window so you can confirm your changes, the rename capability in VB.NET simply renames all references to that variable.

Promote Variable to Parameter

One of the most common refactoring techniques is to adapt an existing method to accept an additional parameter. By promoting a method variable to a parameter, the method can be made more general. It also promotes code reuse. Intuitively, this operation would introduce compile errors wherever the method was referenced. However, the catch is that the variable you are promoting to a parameter must have an initial constant value. This constant is added to all the method references to prevent any changes to functionality. Starting with the following snippet, if the method variable output is promoted, then you end up with the second snippet:

```
public void MethodA()
{
    MethodB();
}
public void MethodB()
{
    string output = "Test String";
    MessageBox.Show( output);
}
```

After the variable is promoted, you can see that the initial constant value has been applied where this method is referenced:

```
public void MethodA()
{
    MethodB("Test String");
}
public void MethodB(string output)
{
    MessageBox.Show( output);
}
```

Promoting a variable to a parameter is not available within Refactor!, although you can promote a method variable to a class-level variable.

Generate Method Stub

As you write code, you may realize that you need a method that generates a value, triggers an event, or evaluates an expression. For example, the following snippet illustrates a new method that you need to generate at some later stage:

```
public void MethodA()
{
    string InputA;
    double InputB;
    int OutputC = NewMethodIJustThoughtOf(InputA, InputB);
}
```

Of course, the preceding code will generate a build error because this method has not been defined. Using the Generate Method Stub refactoring action (available as a smart tag in the code itself), you can generate a method stub. As you can see from the following sample, the method stub is complete with input parameters and output type:

```csharp
private int NewMethodIJustThoughtOf(string InputA, double InputB)
{
    throw new Exception("The method or operation is not implemented.");
}
```

Generating a method stub is not available within Refactor!.

Organize Usings

Over time you are likely to need to reference classes from different namespaces, and the `using` statement is a useful way to reduce the clutter in your code, making it easy for someone to read. However, the side effect is that the list of `using` statements can grow and become unordered as shown in Figure 17-22. C# has the ability to both sort these statements and remove statements that are no longer used, via the Organize Usings shortcut.

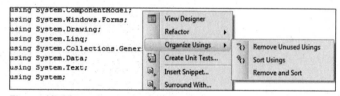

Figure 17-22

After selecting Remove and Sort, this list shrinks to include just `System` and `System.Windows.Forms`.

VB.NET developers don't have a way to sort and remove unused `Imports` statements. However, on the References tab on the Project Properties dialog, it's possible to mark namespaces to be imported into every code file. This can save significantly on the number of `Imports` statements. On this page there is also the ability to remove unused assembly references.

Summary

Code snippets are a valuable inclusion in the Visual Studio 2008 feature set. You learned in this chapter how to use them, and, more importantly, how to create your own, including variable substitution and `Imports` and reference associations for Visual Basic snippets. With this information you'll be able to create your own library of code snippets from functionality that you use frequently, saving you time in coding similar constructs later.

This chapter also provided examples of each of the refactoring actions available within Visual Studio 2008. Although VB.NET developers do not get complete refactoring support out of the box, Refactor! provides a wide range of refactoring actions that complement the editor the developer already has.

18

Modeling with the Class Designer

Traditionally, software modeling has been performed separately from coding, often during a design phase that is completed before coding begins. In many cases, the various modeling diagrams constructed during design are not kept up to date as the development progresses, and they quickly lose their value.

The Class Designer in Visual Studio 2008 brings modeling into the IDE, as an activity that can be performed at any time during a development project. Class diagrams are constructed dynamically from the source code, which means that they are always up to date. Any change made to the source code is immediately reflected in the class diagram, and any change to the diagram is also made to the code.

This chapter looks in detail at the Class Designer and explains how you can use it to design, visualize, and refactor your class architecture.

Creating a Class Diagram

The design process for an application typically involves at least a sketch of the classes that are going to be created and how they interact. Visual Studio 2008 provides a design surface, called the Class Designer, onto which classes can be drawn to form a class diagram. Fields, properties, and methods can then be added to the classes, and relationships can be established among classes. Although this design is called a class diagram, it supports classes, structures, enumeration, interfaces, abstract classes, and delegates.

Before you can start working with a class diagram, you need to add one to the project. This can be done by adding a new Class Diagram to a project as shown in Figure 18-1, selecting the View Class Diagram button from the toolbar in the Solution Explorer window, or right-clicking a project or class and selecting the View Class Diagram menu item. The new Class Diagram option will simply create a new blank class diagram within the project.

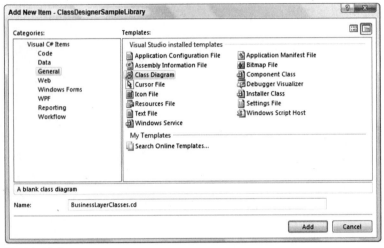

Figure 18-1

A class diagram using the menu items on the Solution Explorer can behave in different ways, depending on whether a project or a class was highlighted. If the project was selected and an existing diagram does not exist in the project, the Class Designer will automatically add all the types defined within a project to the initial class diagram. Although this may be desirable, for a project that contains a large number of classes, the process of creating and manipulating the diagram can be quite time consuming.

Unlike some tools that require all types within a project to be on the same diagram, the class diagram can include as many or as few of your types as you want. This makes it possible to add multiple class diagrams to a single solution.

> The scope of the Class Designer is limited to a single project. You cannot add types to a class diagram that are defined in a different project, even if it is part of the same solution.

The Class Designer can be divided into four components: the design surface, the Toolbox, the Class Details window, and the property grid. Changes made to the class diagram are saved in a .cd file, which works in parallel with the class code files to generate the visual layout shown in the Class Designer.

Design Surface

The design surface of the Class Designer enables the developer to interact with types using a drag-and-drop-style interface. Existing types can be added to the design surface by dragging them from either the class view or the Solution Explorer. If a file in the Solution Explorer contains more than one type, they are all added to the design surface.

Figure 18-2 shows a simple class diagram that contains two classes, Customer and Order, and an enumeration, OrderStatus. Each class contains fields, properties, methods, and events. There is an association between the classes, as a Customer class contains a property called Orders that is a list of Order objects, and the Order class implements the IDataErrorInfo interface. All this information is visible from this class diagram.

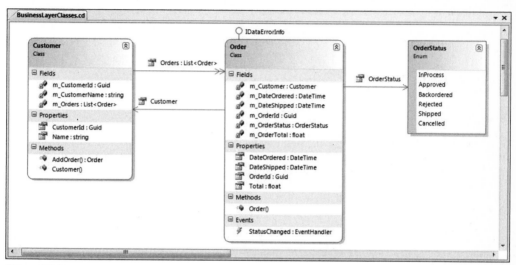

Figure 18-2

Each class appears as an entity on the class diagram, which can be dragged around the design surface and resized as required. A class is made up of fields, properties, methods, and events. In Figure 18-2, these components are grouped into compartments. Alternative layouts can be selected for the class diagram, which lists the components in alphabetical order or groups the components by accessibility.

The Class Designer is often used to view multiple classes to get an understanding of how they are associated. In this case, it is convenient to hide the components of a class to simplify the diagram. To hide all the components at once, use the toggle in the top right corner of the class on the design surface. If only certain components need to be hidden, they can be individually hidden, or the entire compartment can be hidden, by right-clicking the appropriate element and selecting the Hide menu item.

Toolbox

To facilitate items being added to the class diagram, there is a Class Designer tab in the Toolbox. To create an item, drag the item from the Toolbox onto the design surface or simply double-click it. Figure 18-3 shows the Toolbox with the Class Designer tab visible. The items in the Toolbox can be classified as either entities or connectors. Note the Comment item, which can be added to the Class Designer but does not appear in any of the code; it is there simply to aid documentation of the class diagram.

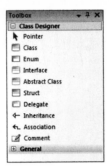

Figure 18-3

Entities

The entities that can be added to the class diagram all correspond to types in the .NET Framework. When a new entity is added to the design surface, it needs to be given a name. In addition, you need to indicate whether it should be added to a new file or an existing file.

Entities can be removed from the diagram by right-clicking and selecting the Remove From Diagram menu item. This will not remove the source code; it simply removes the entity from the diagram. In cases where it is desirable to delete the associated source code, select the Delete Code menu item.

The code associated with an entity can be viewed by either double-clicking the entity or selecting View Code from the right-click context menu.

The following list explains the entities in the Toolbox:

❑   **Class:** Fields, properties, methods, events, and constants can all be added to a class via the right-click context menu or the Class Details window. Although a class can support nested types, they cannot be added using the Designer surface. Classes can also implement interfaces. In Figure 18-2, the `Order` class implements the IDataErrorInfo interface.

❑   **Enum:** An enumeration can only contain a list of members that can have a value assigned to them. Each member also has a summary and remarks property, but these appear only as an XML comment against the member.

❑   **Interface:** Interfaces define properties, methods, and events that a class must implement. Interfaces can also contain nested types, but recall that adding a nested type is not supported by the Designer.

❑   **Abstract Class:** Abstract classes behave the same as classes except that they appear on the design surface with an italic name and are marked as `MustInherit`.

❑   **Struct:** A structure is the only entity, other than a comment, that appears on the Designer in a rectangle. Similar to a class, a structure supports fields, properties, methods, events, and constants. It, too, can contain nested types. However, unlike a class, a structure cannot have a destructor.

❑   **Delegate:** Although a delegate appears as an entity on the class diagram, it can't contain nested types. The only components it can contain are parameters that define the delegate signature.

Connectors

Two types of relationships can be established between entities. These are illustrated on the class diagram using connectors, and are explained in the following list:

❑ **Inheritance:** The inheritance connector is used to show the relationship between classes that inherit from each other.

❑ **Association:** Where a class makes reference to another class, there is an association between the two classes. This is shown using the association connector. If that relationship is based around a collection — for example, a list of Order objects — this can be represented using a *collection association*. A collection association called Orders is shown in Figure 18-2 connecting the Customer and Order classes.

A *class association* can be represented as either a field or property of a class, or as an association link between the classes. The right-click context menu on either the field, property, or the association can be used to toggle between the two representations.

In order to show a property as a collection association, you need to right-click the property in the class and select Show as Collection Association. This will hide the property from the class and display it as a connector to the associated class on the diagram.

Class Details

Components can be added to entities by right-clicking and selecting the appropriate component to add. Unfortunately, this is a time-consuming process and doesn't afford you the ability to add method parameters or return values. The Class Designer in Visual Studio 2008 includes a Class Details window, which provides a user interface that enables components to be quickly entered. This window is illustrated in Figure 18-4 for the Customer class previously shown in Figure 18-2.

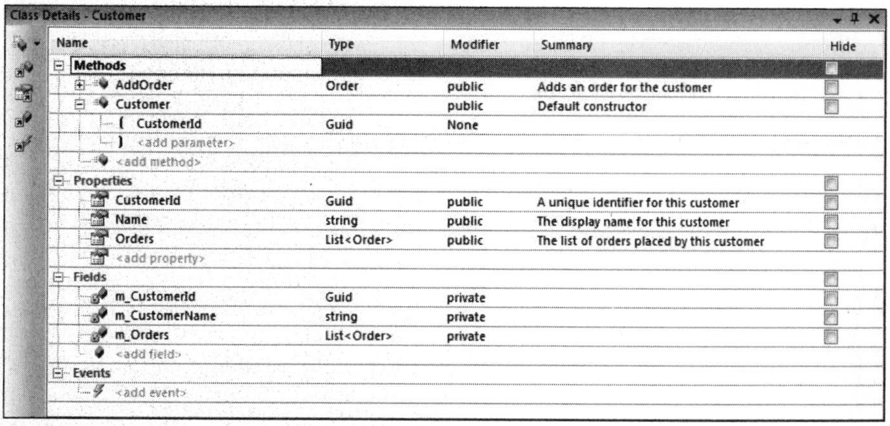

Figure 18-4

On the left side of the window are buttons that can aid in navigating classes that contain a large number of components. The top button can be used to add methods, properties, fields, or events to the class. The remaining buttons can be used to bring any of the component groups into focus. For example, the second button is used to navigate to the list of methods for the class. You can navigate between components in the list using the up and down arrow keys.

Because Figure 18-4 shows the details for a class, the main region of the window is divided into four alphabetical lists: Methods, Properties, Fields, and Events. Other entity types may have other components, such as Members and Parameters. Each row is divided into five columns that show the name, the return type, the modifier or accessibility of the component, a summary, and whether the item is hidden on the design surface. In each case, the Summary field appears as an XML comment against the appropriate component. Events differ from the other components in that the Type column must be a delegate. You can navigate between columns using the left and right arrow keys, Tab (next column), and Shift+Tab (previous column).

To enter parameters on a method, use the right arrow key to expand the method node so that a parameter list appears. Selecting the Add Parameter node will add a new parameter to the method. Once added, the new parameter can be navigated to by using the arrow keys.

Properties Window

Although the Class Details window is useful it does not provide all the information required for entity components. For example, properties can be marked as read-only, which is not displayed in the Class Details window. The Properties window in Figure 18-5 shows the full list of attributes for the `Orders` property of the `Customer` class.

Figure 18-5

Figure 18-5 shows that the `Orders` property is read-only and that it is not static. It also shows that this property is defined in the Customer.cs file. With partial classes, a class may be separated over multiple files. When a partial class is selected, the `File Name` property will show all files defining that class as a comma-delimited list. As a result of an arbitrary decision made when implementing the Class Designer, some of these properties are read-only in the Designer. They can, of course, be adjusted within the appropriate code file.

Layout

As the class diagram is all about visualizing classes, you have several toolbar controls at your disposal to create the layout of the entities on the Designer. Figure 18-6 shows the toolbar that appears as part of the Designer surface.

Figure 18-6

The first three buttons control the layout of entity components. From left to right, the buttons are Group by Kind, Group by Access, and Sort Alphabetically.

The next two buttons are used to automate the process of arranging the entities on the design surface. On the left is the Layout Diagram button, which will automatically reposition the entities on the design surface. It will also minimize the entities, hiding all components. The right button, Adjust Shapes Width, adjusts the size of the entities so that all components are fully visible.

Entity components, such as fields, properties, and methods, can be hidden using the Hide Member button.

The display style of entity components can be adjusted using the next three buttons. The left button, Display Name, sets the display style to show only the name of the component. This can be extended to show both the name and the component type using the Display Name and Type button. The right button, Display Full Signature, sets the display style to be the full component signature. This is often the most useful, although it takes more space to display.

The remaining controls on the toolbar enable you to zoom in and out on the Class Designer, and to display the Class Details window.

Exporting Diagrams

Quite often, the process of deciding which classes will be part of the system architecture is a part of a much larger design or review process. Therefore, it is a common requirement to export the class diagram for inclusion in reports.

You can export a class diagram either by right-clicking the context menu from any space on the Class Designer or via the Class Diagram menu. Either way, selecting the Export Diagram as Image menu item opens a dialog prompting you to select an image format and filename for saving the diagram.

Code Generation and Refactoring

One of the core goals of Visual Studio 2008 and the .NET Framework is to reduce the amount of code that developers have to write. There are two ways this goal is achieved: either reduce the total amount of code that has to be written or reduce the amount that actually has to be written manually. The first approach is supported through a very rich set of base classes included in the .NET Framework. The second approach, reduce the amount of code that is written manually, is supported by the code generation and refactoring tools included with the Class Designer.

Drag-and-Drop Code Generation

Almost every action performed on the class diagram results in a change in the underlying source code, and essentially provides some level of code generation. We've already covered a number of these changes, such as adding a property or method to a class in the Class Details window. However, there are some more advanced code generation actions that can be performed by manipulating the class diagram.

As we explained earlier in the chapter, you can use the inheritance connector to establish an inheritance relationship between a parent class and an inheriting class. When you do this, the code file of the derived class is updated to reflect this change. However, when the parent class is abstract, as in the case of the Product class in Figure 18-7, the Class Designer can perform some additional analysis and code generation. If the parent class is an abstract class and contains any abstract members, those members are automatically implemented in the inheriting classes. This is shown in Figure 18-7 (right) where the abstract properties Description, Price, and SKU have been added to the Book class. The method GetInventory() was not implemented because it was not marked as abstract.

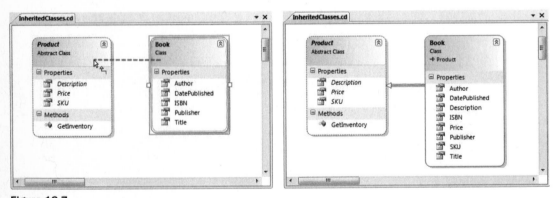

Figure 18-7

The inheritance connector can be used in one more way that results in automatic code generation. In Figure 18-8 (left) an interface, ICrudActions, has been added to the diagram. When the inheritance connector is dragged from the interface to a class, all the members of the interface are implemented on the class, as shown in Figure 18-8 (right).

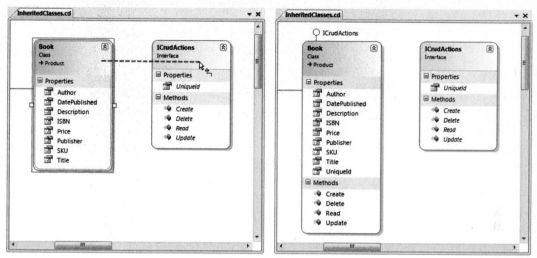

Figure 18-8

The following listing shows the code that was automatically generated when the ICrudActions interface was added to the Book class.

```csharp
#region ICrudActions Members
    public Guid UniqueId
    {
        get
        {
            throw new NotImplementedException();
        }
        set
        {
            throw new NotImplementedException();
        }
    }

    public void Create()
    {
        throw new NotImplementedException();
    }

    public void Update()
    {
        throw new NotImplementedException();
    }

    public void Read()
    {
        throw new NotImplementedException();
    }
```

(continued)

(continued)

```
        public void Delete()
        {
              throw new NotImplementedException();
        }
#endregion
```

IntelliSense Code Generation

The rest of the code-generation functions in the Class Designer are available under the somewhat unexpectedly named IntelliSense sub-menu. Since these code-generation functions apply only to classes, this menu is visible only when a class or abstract class has been selected on the diagram. The two code-generation functions included on this menu are Implement Abstract Class and Override Members.

The Implement Abstract Class function ensures that all abstract members from the base class are implemented in the inheriting class. To access this function, right-click the inheriting class, choose IntelliSense then choose Implement Abstract Class.

Somewhat related is the Override Members function, which is used to select public properties or methods from a base class that you would like to override. To access this function, right-click the inheriting class, choose IntelliSense, then choose Override Members. The dialog shown in Figure 18-9 will be displayed, populated with the base classes and any properties or methods that have not already been overridden.

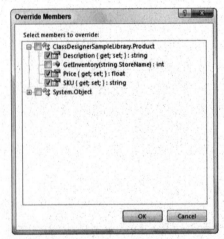

Figure 18-9

Refactoring with the Class Designer

In the previous chapter you saw how Visual Studio 2008 provides support for refactoring code from the code editor window. The Class Designer also exposes a number of these refactoring functions when working with entities on a class diagram.

The refactoring functions in the Class Designer are available by right-clicking an entity, or any of its members, and choosing an action from the Refactor sub-menu. The following refactoring functions are available:

❑ **Rename Types and Type Members**: Enables you to rename a type or a member of a type on the class diagram or in the Properties window. Renaming a type or type member changes it in all code locations where the old name appeared. You can even ensure that the change is propagated to any comments or static strings.

❑ **Encapsulate Field**: Provides the ability to quickly create a new property from an existing field, and then seamlessly update your code with references to the new property.

❑ **Reorder or Remove Parameters** (C# only): Enables you to change the order of method parameters in types, or to remove a parameter from a method.

❑ **Extract Interface** (C# only): You can extract the members of a type into a new interface. This function enables you to select only a subset of the members that you want to extract into the new interface.

You can also use the standard Windows Cut, Copy, and Paste actions to copy and move members between types.

PowerToys for the Class Designer

While the Class Designer is a very useful tool for designing and visualizing a class hierarchy, it can be cumbersome when trying to work with very large diagrams. To ease this burden you can either break up the diagram into multiple class diagrams, or install PowerToys for the Class Designer.

PowerToys for the Class Designer is a free add-in to Visual Studio that extends the functionality of the Class Designer in several ways. It includes enhancements that enable you to work more effectively with large diagrams including panning and zooming, improved scrolling, and diagram search. It also provides functions that address some of the limitations of the Class Designer such as the ability to create nested types and new derived classes and display XML comments.

The add-in, including source code, is available from `http://www.codeplex.com/modeling`. The download includes an MSI file for easy installation.

PowerToys actually consists of two add-ins: Design Tools Enhancements and Class Designer Enhancements. The Design Tools Enhancements provide common features for both the Class Designer and the Distributed System Designer, which is only available in Visual Studio Team System.

Visualization Enhancements

PowerToys for the Class Designer provides some very useful enhancements for visualizing and working with large class diagrams. The diagram search feature is one of the more useful; it allows you to search the entities on a diagram for a specific search term. The search dialog, shown in Figure 18-10, is invoked via the standard Find menu item or Ctrl+F shortcut.

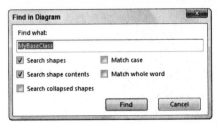

Figure 18-10

Another useful tool for large diagrams is the panning tool, which provides an easy way to see an overview of the entire diagram and navigate to different areas, without changing the zoom level. This tool is invoked by clicking a new icon that appears in the bottom right of the window, which will display the panning window, as shown in Figure 18-11.

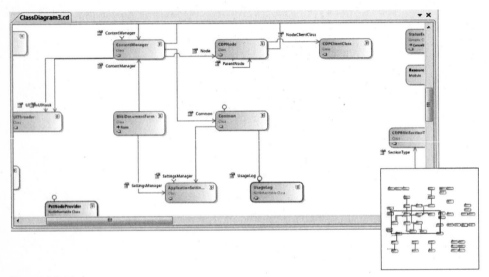

Figure 18-11

PowerToys also allows quite fine control over what is displayed on the diagram via the filtering options. These are available via the Class Diagram menu, and include:

❑ **Hide Inheritance Lines**: Hides all inheritance lines in selection

❑ **Show All Inheritance Lines**: Shows all hidden inheritance lines on the diagram

❑ **Show All Public Associations**: Shows all possibly public associations on the diagram

❑ **Show All Associations**: Shows all possible associations on the diagram

❑ **Show Associations as Members**: Shows all association lines as members

❑ **Hide Private**: Hides all private members

- ❏ **Hide Private and Internal**: Hides all private and/or internal members
- ❏ **Show Only Public**: Hides all members except for public; all hidden public members are shown
- ❏ **Show Only Public and Protected**: Hides all members except for public and protected; all hidden public and/or protected members are shown
- ❏ **Show All Members**: Shows all hidden members

Functionality Enhancements

PowerToys includes a number of enhancements that address some of the functional limitations of the Class Designer. While the Class Designer can display nested types, you cannot create them using the design surface.

This constraint is addressed by PowerToys by providing the ability to add nested types including classes, enumerations, structures, or delegates. You can also easily add several new member types, such as read-only properties and indexers.

There are also some improvements around working with interfaces. Often it is difficult to understand which members of a class have been used to implement an interface. PowerToys simplifies this by adding a Select Members menu item to the interface lollipop label on a type. For example, in Figure 18-12, the Select Members command is being invoked on the IStatus interface.

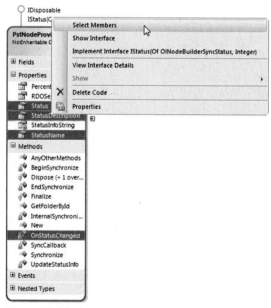

Figure 18-12

In addition to those we have mentioned here, there are many other minor enhancements and functionality improvements provided by PowerToys for the Class Designer that add up to make it a very useful extension.

Summary

This chapter focused on the Class Designer, one of the best tools built into Visual Studio 2008 for generating code. The design surface and supporting toolbars and windows provide a rich user interface with which complex class hierarchies and associations can be modeled and designed.

19

Server Explorer

The Server Explorer is one of the few tool windows in Visual Studio that is not specific to a solution or project. It allows you to explore and query hardware resources and services on local or remote computers. You can perform various tasks and activities with these resources, including adding them to your applications.

The Server Explorer, shown in Figure 19-1, has two sets of functionalities. The first, under the Data Connections node, enables you to work with all aspects of data connections, and includes the ability to create databases, add and modify tables, build relationships, and even execute queries. Chapter 22 covers the Data Connections functionality in detail. The second set of functionalities is under the Servers node and is explored in the remainder of this chapter.

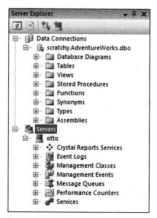

Figure 19-1

The Servers Node

The Servers node would be better named Computers, because it can be used to attach to and interrogate any computer to which you have access, regardless of whether it is a server or a desktop workstation. Each computer is listed as a separate node under the Servers node. Below each computer node is a list of the hardware, services, and other components that belong to that computer. Each of these contains a number of activities or tasks that can be performed. Several software vendors have components that plug into and extend the functionality provided by the Server Explorer.

To access Server Explorer, select Server Explorer on the View menu. By default, the local computer appears in the Servers list. To add computers, right-click the Servers node and select Add Server from the context menu. This opens the Add Server dialog shown in Figure 19-2.

Figure 19-2

Entering a computer name or IP address will initiate an attempt to connect to the machine using your credentials. If you do not have sufficient privileges, you can elect to connect using a different user name by clicking the appropriate link. The link appears to be disabled, but clicking it does bring up a dialog in which you can provide an alternative user name and password.

> *You will need Administrator privileges on any server that you want to access through the Server Explorer.*

Event Logs

The Event Logs node gives you access to the machine event logs. You can launch the Event Viewer from the right-click context menu. Alternatively, as shown in Figure 19-3, you can drill into the list of event logs to view the events for a particular application. Clicking on any of the events displays information about the event in the Properties window.

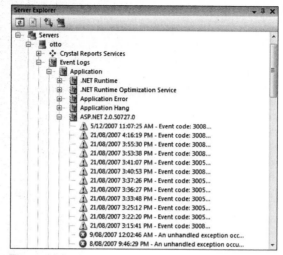

Figure 19-3

Although the Server Explorer is useful for interrogating a machine while writing your code, the true power comes with the component creation you get when you drag a resource node onto a Windows Form. For example, in this case, if you drag the Application node onto a Windows Form, you get an instance of the `System.Diagnostic.EventLog` class added to the nonvisual area of the designer. You can then write an entry to this event log using the following code:

```
Private Sub btnLogEvent_Click(ByVal sender As Object, ByVal e As EventArgs) _
    Handles btnLogEvent.Click
    Me.EventLog1.Source = "My Server Explorer App"
    Me.EventLog1.WriteEntry("Button Clicked", EventLogEntryType.Information)
End Sub
```

Because the preceding code creates a new Source in the Application Event Log, it will require administrative rights to execute. If you are running Windows Vista with User Account Control enabled, then you should create an application manifest. This is discussed Chapter 6.

You can also write exception information using the `WriteException` method, which accepts an exception and a string that may provide additional debugging information. Unfortunately, you still have to manually set the `Source` property before calling the `WriteEntry` method. Of course, this could also have been set using the Properties window for the `EventLog1` component.

For Visual Basic programmers, an alternative to adding an `EventLog` class to your code is to use the built-in logging provided by the My namespace. For example, you can modify the previous code snippet to write a log entry using the `Application.Log` property:

```
Private Sub btnLogMyEvent_Click(ByVal sender As Object, ByVal e As EventArgs) _
    Handles btnLogMyEvent.Click
    My.Application.Log.WriteEntry("Button Clicked", EventLogEntryType.Information)
End Sub
```

Using the My namespace to write logging information has a number of additional benefits. In the following configuration file, an EventLogTraceListener is specified to route log information to the event log. However, you can specify other trace listeners — for example, the FileLogTraceListener, which writes information to a log file by adding it to the SharedListeners and Listeners collections:

```xml
<?xml version="1.0" encoding="utf-8" ?>
<configuration>
    <system.diagnostics>
        <sources>
            <source name="DefaultSource" switchName="DefaultSwitch">
                <listeners>
                    <add name="EventLog"/>
                </listeners>
            </source>
        </sources>
        <switches>
            <add name="DefaultSwitch" value="Information" />
        </switches>
        <sharedListeners>
            <add name="EventLog"
                 type="System.Diagnostics.EventLogTraceListener"
                 initializeData="ApplicationEventLog"/>
        </sharedListeners>
    </system.diagnostics>
</configuration>
```

This configuration also specifies a switch called DefaultSwitch. This switch is associated with the trace information source via the switchName attribute and defines the minimum event type that will be sent to the listed listeners. For example, if the value of this switch were Critical, then events with the type Information would not be written to the event log. The possible values of this switch are shown in Table 19-1.

Table 19-1: Values for DefaultSwitch

DefaultSwitch	Event Types Written to Log
Off	No events
Critical	Critical events
Error	Critical and Error events
Warning	Critical, Error, and Warning events
Information	Critical, Error, Warning, and Information events
Verbose	Critical, Error, Warning, Information, and Verbose events
ActivityTracing	Start, Stop, Suspend, Resume, and Transfer events
All	All events

Note that there are overloads for both WriteEntry and WriteException that do not require an event type to be specified. These methods will default to Information and Error.

Management Classes

Figure 19-4 shows the full list of management classes available via the Server Explorer. Each node exposes a set of functionalities specific to that device or application. For example, right-clicking the Printers node enables you to add a new printer connection, whereas right-clicking the named node under My Computer enables you to add the computer to a domain or workgroup. The one thing common to all these nodes is that they provide a strongly typed wrapper around the Windows Management Instrumentation (WMI) infrastructure. In most cases, it is simply a matter of dragging the node representing the information in which you're interested across to the form. From your code you can then access and manipulate that information.

Figure 19-4

To give you an idea of how these wrappers can be used, this section walks through how you can use the management classes to retrieve information about a computer. Under the My Computer node, you will see a node with the name of the local computer. Selecting this node and dragging it onto the form will give you a ComputerSystem component in the nonvisual area of the form, as shown in Figure 19-5.

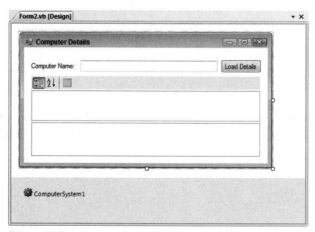

Figure 19-5

If you look in the Solution Explorer, you will see that it has also added a custom component called root.CIMV2.Win32_ComputerSystem.vb (or similar depending on the computer configuration). This custom component is generated by the Management Strongly Typed Class Generator (Mgmtclassgen.exe) and includes the ComputerSystem and other classes, which will enable you to expose WMI information.

If you click the ComputerSystem1 object on the form, you can see the information about that computer in the Properties window. In this application, however, you're not that interested in that particular computer; that computer was selected as a template to create the ComputerSystem class. The ComputerSystem object can be deleted, but before deleting it, take note of the Path property of the object. The Path is used, combined with the computer name entered in the form in Figure 19-5, to load the information about that computer. You can see this in the following code to handle the button click event for the "Load Details" button:

```vb
Public Class Form2
    Private Const CComputerPath As String = _

    "\\{0}\root\CIMV2:Win32_ComputerSystem.Name=""{0}"""

    Private Sub btnComputerDetails_Click(ByVal sender As System.Object, _
                                    ByVal e As System.EventArgs) _
                                            Handles btnComputerDetails.Click
        If Not Me.txtComputerName.Text = "" Then
            Dim computerName As String = Me.txtComputerName.Text
            Dim pathString As String = String.Format(CComputerPath, computerName)
            Dim path As New System.Management.ManagementPath(pathString)
            Dim cs As New ROOT.CIMV2.ComputerSystem(path)

            Me.ComputerPropertyGrid.SelectedObject = cs
        End If
    End Sub
End Class
```

In this example, the Path property is taken from the ComputerSystem1 object and the computer name component is replaced with a string replacement token, {0}. When the button is clicked, the computer name entered into the textbox is combined with this path using String.Format to generate the full WMI path. The path is then used to instantiate a new ComputerAccount object, which is in turn passed to a PropertyGrid called ComputerPropertyGrid. This is shown in Figure 19-6.

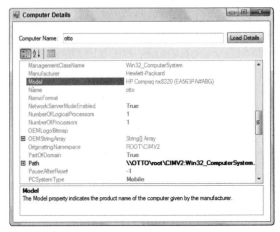

Figure 19-6

Though most properties are read-only, for those fields that are editable, changes made in this PropertyGrid are immediately committed to the computer. This behavior can be altered by changing the AutoCommit property on the ComputerSystem class.

Management Events

In the previous section you learned how you can drag a management class from the Server Explorer onto the form and then work with the generated classes. The other way to work with the WMI interface is through the Management Events node. A management event enables you to monitor any WMI data type and have an event raised if an object of that type is created, modified, or deleted. By default, this node will be empty, but you can create your own by selecting Add Event Query, which will invoke the dialog shown in Figure 19-7.

Use this dialog to locate the WMI data type in which you are interested. Because there are literally thousands of these, it is useful to use the Find box. In Figure 19-7, the search term "process" was entered, and the class CIM Processes was found under the root\CIMV2 node. Each instance of this class represents a single process running on the system. We are only interested in being notified when a new process is created, so ensure that the "Object creation" is selected from the drop-down menu.

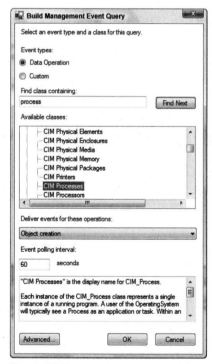

Figure 19-7

After clicking "OK", a CIM Processes Event Query node is added to the Management Events node. If you open a new instance of an application on your system, such as Notepad, you will see events being progressively added to this node. In the Build Management Event Query dialog shown in Figure 19-7, the default polling interval was set to 60 seconds, so you may need to wait up to 60 seconds for the event to show up in the tree once you have made the change.

When the event does finally show up, it will appear along with the date and time in the Server Explorer, and it will also appear in the Output window, as shown in the lower pane of Figure 19-8. If you select the event, you will notice that the Properties window is populated with a large number of properties that don't really make any sense. However, once you know which of the properties to query, it is quite easy to trap, filter, and respond to system events.

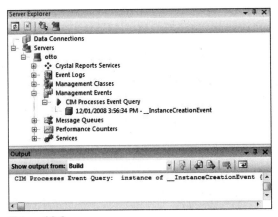

Figure 19-8

To continue the example, drag the CIM Processes Event Query node onto a form. This generates an instance of the `System.Management.ManagementEventWatcher` class, with properties configured so it will listen for the creation of a new process. The actual query can be accessed via the `QueryString` property of the nested `ManagementQuery` object. As with most watcher classes, the `ManagementEventWatch` class triggers an event when the watch conditions are met — in this case, the `EventArrived` event. To generate an event handler, add the following code:

```
Private Sub ManagementEventWatcher1_EventArrived(ByVal sender As System.Object, _
                    ByVal e As System.Management.EventArrivedEventArgs) _
                    Handles ManagementEventWatcher1.EventArrived
    For Each p As System.Management.PropertyData In e.NewEvent.Properties
        If p.Name = "TargetInstance" Then
            Dim mbo As System.Management.ManagementBaseObject = _
                    CType(p.Value, System.Management.ManagementBaseObject)
            Dim sCreatedProcess As String() = {mbo.Properties("Name").Value, _
                                    mbo.Properties("ExecutablePath").Value}
            Me.BeginInvoke(New LogNewProcessDelegate(AddressOf LogNewProcess), _
                    sCreatedProcess)

        End If
    Next
End Sub

Delegate Sub LogNewProcessDelegate(ByVal ProcessName As String, _
                    ByVal ExePath As String)
```

```
Private Sub LogNewProcess(ByVal ProcessName As String, ByVal ExePath As String)
    Me.lbProcesses.Items.Add(String.Format("{0} - {1}", ProcessName, ExePath))
End Sub

Private Sub chkWatchEvent_CheckedChanged(ByVal sender As System.Object, _
                                ByVal e As System.EventArgs) _
                                Handles chkWatchEvent.CheckedChanged

    If Me.chkWatchEvent.Checked Then
        Me.ManagementEventWatcher1.Start()
    Else
        Me.ManagementEventWatcher1.Stop()
    End If
End Sub
```

In the event handler, you need to iterate through the `Properties` collection on the `NewEvent` object. Where an object has changed, two instances are returned: `PreviousInstance`, which holds the state at the beginning of the polling interval, and `TargetInstance`, which holds the state at the end of the polling interval. It is possible for the object to change state multiple times within the same polling period. If this is the case, an event will only be triggered when the state at the end of the period differs from the state at the beginning of the period. For example, no event is raised if a process is started and then stopped within a single polling interval.

The event handler constructs a new `ManagementBaseObject` from a value passed into the event arguments to obtain the display name and executable path of the new process. Because the event is called on a background thread, we cannot directly update the ListBox. Instead we must call `Invoke` to execute the `LogNewProcess` function on the UI thread. Figure 19-9 shows the form in action.

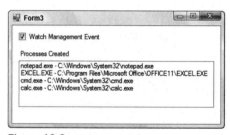

Figure 19-9

Notice also the addition of a checkbox to the form to control whether the form is watching for user events. The generated code for the event watcher does not automatically start the watcher.

Message Queues

The Message Queues node, expanded in Figure 19-10, gives you access to the message queues available on your computer. You can use three types of queues: private, which will not appear when a foreign computer queries your computer; public, which will appear; and system, which is used for unsent messages and other exception reporting. In order for the Message Queues node to be successfully expanded, you need to ensure that MSMQ is installed on your computer. This can be done via the Turn

Windows Features On or Off task menu item accessible from Start ⇨ Settings ⇨ Control Panel ⇨ Programs and Features. Some features of MSMQ are available only when a queue is created on a computer that is a member of a domain.

Figure 19-10

In Figure 19-10, the samplequeue has been added to the Private Queues node by selecting Create Queue from the right-click context menu. Once you have created a queue, you can create a properly configured instance of the MessageQueue class by dragging the queue onto your form. To demonstrate the functionality of the MessageQueue object, use the following code to add a couple of textboxes and a "Send" button. The "Send" button is wired up to use the MessageQueue object to send the message entered in the first textbox. In the Load event for the form, a background thread is created that continually polls the queue to retrieve messages, which will populate the second textbox:

```
Public Class Form4
    Private Sub btnSend_Click(ByVal sender As System.Object, _
                            ByVal e As System.EventArgs) Handles btnSend.Click
        Me.MessageQueue1.Send(Me.txtSendMsg.Text, "Message: " & _
                            Now.ToShortDateString & " " & Now.ToShortTimeString)
    End Sub

    Private Sub Form4_Load(ByVal sender As System.Object, _
                            ByVal e As System.EventArgs) Handles MyBase.Load
        Dim monitorThread As New Threading.Thread(AddressOf MonitorMessageQueue)
        monitorThread.IsBackground = True
        monitorThread.Start()
    End Sub

    Private Sub MonitorMessageQueue()
        Dim m As Messaging.Message
        While True
            Try
                m = Me.MessageQueue1.Receive(New TimeSpan(0, 0, 0, 0, 50))
                Me.ReceiveMessage(m.Label, m.Body)
            Catch ex As Messaging.MessageQueueException
                If Not ex.MessageQueueErrorCode = _
                                Messaging.MessageQueueErrorCode.IOTimeout Then
                    Throw ex
```

```
                End If
            End Try
            Threading.Thread.Sleep(10000)
        End While
    End Sub

    Private Delegate Sub MessageDel(ByVal lbl As String, ByVal msg As String)
    Private Sub ReceiveMessage(ByVal lbl As String, ByVal msg As String)
        If Me.InvokeRequired Then
            Me.Invoke(New MessageDel(AddressOf ReceiveMessage), lbl, msg)
            Return
        End If
        Me.txtReceiveMsg.Text = msg
        Me.lblMessageLabel.Text = lbl
    End Sub
End Class
```

Note in this code snippet that the background thread is never explicitly closed. Because the thread has the IsBackGround property set to True, it will automatically be terminated when the application exits. As with the previous example, because the message processing is done in a background thread, you need to switch threads when you update the user interface using the Invoke method. Putting this all together, you get a form like the one shown in Figure 19-11.

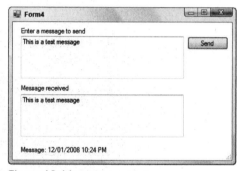

Figure 19-11

As messages are sent to the message queue, they will appear under the appropriate queue in Server Explorer. Clicking the message will display its contents in the Properties window.

Performance Counters

One of the most common things developers forget to consider when building an application is how it will be maintained and managed. For example, consider an application that was installed a year ago and has been operating without any issues. All of a sudden, requests start taking an unacceptable amount of time. It is clear that the application is not behaving correctly, but there is no way to determine the cause of the misbehavior. One strategy for identifying where the performance issues are is to use performance counters. Windows has many built-in performance counters that can be used to monitor operating system activity, and a lot of third-party software also installs performance counters so administrators can identify any rogue behavior.

The Performance Counters node in the Server Explorer tree, expanded in Figure 19-12, has two primary functions. First, it enables you to view and retrieve information about the currently installed counters. You can also create new performance counters, as well as edit or delete existing counters. As you can see in Figure 19-12, under the Performance Counters node is a list of categories, and under those is a list of counters.

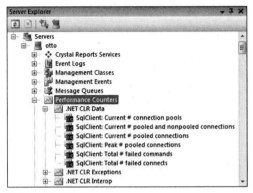

Figure 19-12

You must be running Visual Studio with Administrator rights in order to view the Performance Counters under the Server Explorer.

To edit either the category or the counters, select Edit Category from the right-click context menu for the category. To add a new category and associated counters, right-click the Performance Counters node and select Create New Category from the context menu. Both of these operations use the dialog shown in Figure 19-13. Here, a new performance counter category has been created that will be used to track a form's open and close events.

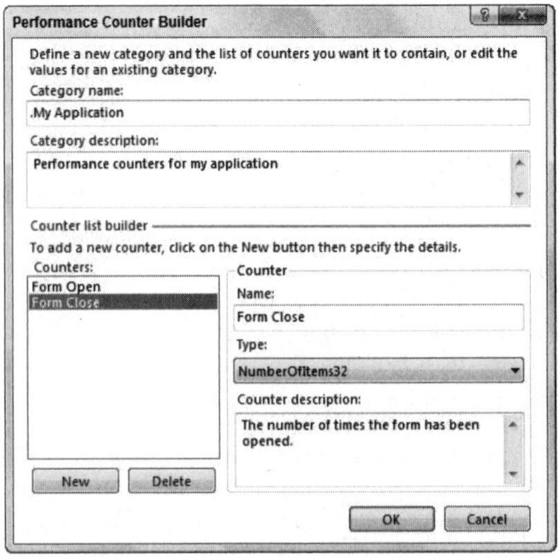

Figure 19-13

The second function of the Performance Counters section is to provide an easy way for you to access performance counters via your code. By dragging a performance counter category onto a form, you gain access to read and write to that performance counter. To continue with this chapter's example, drag the new .My Application performance counters, Form Open and Form Close, onto your form. Also add a couple of textboxes and a button so you can display the performance counter values. Finally, rename the performance counters so they have a friendly name. This should give you a form similar to the one shown in Figure 19-14.

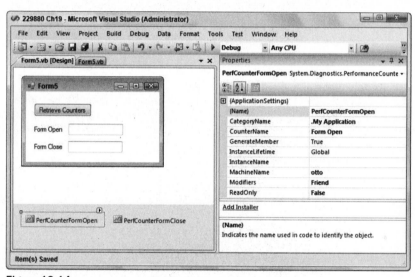

Figure 19-14

In the properties for the selected performance counter, you can see that the appropriate counter — in this case, Form Close — has been selected from the .My Application category. You will also notice a MachineName property, which is the computer from which you are retrieving the counter information, and a ReadOnly property, which needs to be set to False if you want to update the counter. (By default, the ReadOnly property is set to True.) To complete this form, add the following code to the "Retrieve Counters" button:

```
Private Sub btnRetrieveCounters_Click(ByVal sender As System.Object, _
                            ByVal e As System.EventArgs) _
                                       Handles btnRetrieveCounters.Click
    Me.txtFormOpen.Text = Me.PerfCounterFormOpen.RawValue
    Me.txtFormClose.Text = Me.PerfCounterFormClose.RawValue
End Sub
```

You also need to add code to the application to update the performance counters. For example, you might have the following code in the `Load` and `FormClosing` event handlers:

```
Private Sub Form5_Closing(ByVal sender As Object, _
                           ByVal e As System.Windows.Forms.FormClosingEventArgs) _
                                                         Handles Me.FormClosing
    Me.PerfCounterFormClose.Increment()
End Sub

Private Sub Form5_Load(ByVal sender As Object, _
                        ByVal e As System.EventArgs) Handles Me.Load
    Me.PerfCounterFormOpen.Increment()
End Sub
```

When you dragged the performance counter onto the form, you may have noticed a smart tag on the performance counter component that had a single item, Add Installer. When the component is selected, as in Figure 19-14, you will notice the same action at the bottom of the Properties window. Clicking this action in either place adds an `Installer` class to your solution that can be used to install the performance counter as part of your installation process. Of course, for this installer to be called, the assembly it belongs to must be added as a custom action for the deployment project. (For more information on custom actions, see Chapter 49.)

In the previous version of Visual Studio, you needed to manually modify the installer to create multiple performance counters. In the current version, you can simply select each additional performance counter and click Add Installer. Visual Studio 2008 will direct you back to the first installer that was created and will have automatically added the second counter to the `Counters` collection of the `PerformanceCounterInstaller` component, as shown in Figure 19-15.

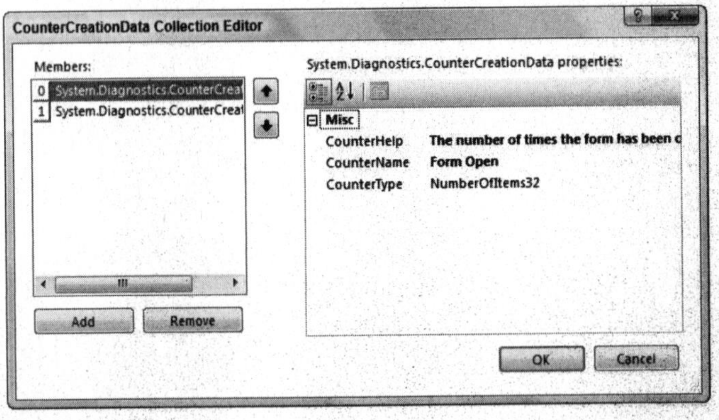

Figure 19-15

You can also add counters in other categories by adding additional `PerformanceCounterInstaller` components to the design surface. You are now ready to deploy your application with the knowledge that you will be able to use a tool such as perfmon to monitor how your application is behaving.

Services

The Services node, expanded in Figure 19-16, shows the registered services for the computer. Each node indicates the state of that service in the bottom-right corner of the icon. Possible states are stopped, running, or paused. Selecting a service will display additional information about the service, such as other service dependencies, in the Properties window.

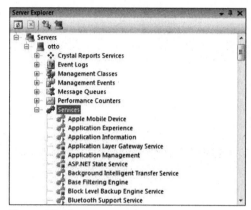

Figure 19-16

As with other nodes in the Server Explorer, each service can be dragged onto the design surface of a form. This generates a ServiceController component in the nonvisual area of the form. By default, the ServiceName property is set to the service that you dragged across from the Server Explorer, but this can be changed to access information and control any service. Similarly, the MachineName property can be changed to connect to any computer to which you have access. The following code shows some of the methods that can be invoked on a ServiceController component:

```
Private Sub Form6_Load(ByVal sender As Object, ByVal e As System.EventArgs) _
                                                Handles Me.Load
    Me.pgServiceProperties.SelectedObject = Me.ServiceController1
End Sub

Private Sub btnStopService_Click(ByVal sender As System.Object, _
                        ByVal e As System.EventArgs) _
                        Handles btnStopService.Click
    Me.ServiceController1.Refresh()
    If Me.ServiceController1.CanStop Then
        If Me.ServiceController1.Status = _
                ServiceProcess.ServiceControllerStatus.Running Then
            Me.ServiceController1.Stop()
            Me.ServiceController1.Refresh()
            MessageBox.Show("Service stopped", "Services")
        Else
            MessageBox.Show("This service is not currently running", "Services")
        End If
    Else
        MessageBox.Show("This service cannot be stopped", "Services")
```

(continued)

303

(continued)

```
        End If
    End Sub

    Private Sub btnStartService_Click(ByVal sender As System.Object, ByVal e As
        System.EventArgs) Handles btnStartService.Click
        Me.ServiceController1.Refresh()
        If Me.ServiceController1.Status = _
                ServiceProcess.ServiceControllerStatus.Stopped Then
            Me.ServiceController1.Start()
            Me.ServiceController1.Refresh()
            MessageBox.Show("Service started", "Services")
        Else
            MessageBox.Show("This service is not currently stopped", "Services")
        End If
    End Sub
```

In addition to the three main states — running, paused, or stopped — there are additional transition states: ContinuePending, PausePending, StartPending, and StopPending. If you are about to start a service that may be dependent on another service that is in one of these transition states, you can call the WaitForStatus method to ensure that the service will start properly.

Summary

In this chapter you learned how the Server Explorer can be used to manage and work with computer information. Chapter 22 completes the discussion on the Server Explorer, covering the Data Connections node in more detail.

20

Unit Testing

Application testing is one of the most time-consuming parts of writing software. Research into development teams and how they operate has revealed quite staggering results. Some teams employ a tester for every developer they have. Others maintain that the testing process can be longer than the initial development. This indicates that, contrary to the way development tools are oriented, testing is a significant portion of the software development life cycle. This chapter looks at a specific type of automated testing that focuses on testing individual components, or units, of a system.

Visual Studio 2008 has a built-in framework for authoring, executing, and reporting on test cases. Previously included only in the Team System Edition of Visual Studio, many of the testing tools are now available in the Professional Edition. This means a much wider audience can now more easily obtain the benefits of more robust testing. This chapter focuses on unit tests and adding support to drive the tests from a set of data.

Your First Test Case

Writing test cases is not a task that is easily automated, as the test cases have to mirror the functionality of the software being developed. However, at several steps in the process code stubs can be generated by a tool. To illustrate this, start with a fairly straightforward snippet of code to learn to write test cases that fully exercise the code. Setting the scene is a Subscription class with a private property called CurrentStatus, which returns the status of the current subscription as an enumeration value:

```
Public Class Subscription
    Public Enum Status
        Temporary
        Financial
        Unfinancial
        Suspended
```

(continued)

(continued)

```
        End Enum

        Private _PaidUpTo As Nullable(Of Date)

        Public Property PaidUpTo() As Nullable(Of Date)
            Get
                Return _PaidUpTo
            End Get
            Set(ByVal value As Nullable(Of Date))
                _PaidUpTo = value
            End Set
        End Property

        Public ReadOnly Property CurrentStatus() As Status
            Get
                If Not Me.PaidUpTo.HasValue Then Return Status.Temporary
                If Me.PaidUpTo.Value > Now Then
                    Return Status.Financial
                Else
                    If Me.PaidUpTo >= Now.AddMonths(-3) Then
                        Return Status.Unfinancial
                    Else
                        Return Status.Suspended
                    End If
                End If
            End Get
        End Property
    End Class
```

As you can see from the code snippet, four code paths need to be tested for the `CurrentStatus` property. If you were to perform the unit testing manually, you would have to create a separate `SubscriptionTest` class, either in the same project or in a new project, into which you would manually write code to instantiate a `Subscription` object, set initial values, and test the property. The last part would have to be repeated for each of the code paths through this property.

Fortunately, Visual Studio automates the process of creating a new test project, creating the appropriate `SubscriptionTest` class and writing the code to create the `Subscription` object. All you have to do is complete the test method. It also provides a runtime engine that is used to run the test case, monitor its progress, and report on any outcome from the test. Therefore, all you have to do is write the code to test the property in question. In fact, Visual Studio generates a code stub that executes the property being tested. However, it does not generate code to ensure that the `Subscription` object is in the correct initial state; this you must do yourself.

You can create empty test cases from the Test menu by selecting the New Test item. This prompts you to select the type of test to create, after which a blank test is created in which you need to manually write the appropriate test cases. However, you can also create a new unit test that contains much of the stub code by selecting the Create Unit Tests menu item from the right-click context menu of the main code window. For example, right-clicking within the `CurrentStatus` property and selecting this menu item brings up the Create Unit Tests dialog displayed in Figure 20-1. This dialog shows all the members of all the classes within the current solution and enables you to select the items for which you want to generate a test stub.

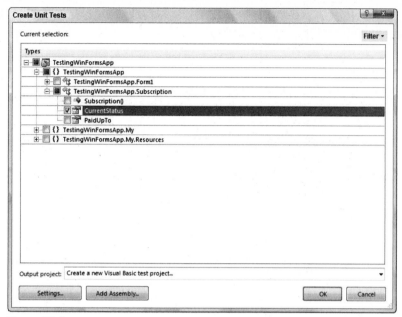

Figure 20-1

If this is the first time you have created a unit test, you will be prompted to create a new test project in the solution. Unlike alternative unit test frameworks such as NUnit, which allow test classes to reside in the same project as the source code, the testing framework within Visual Studio requires that all test cases reside in a separate test project. When test cases are created from the dialog shown in Figure 20-1, they are named according to the name of the member and the name of the class to which they belong. For example, the following code is generated when the "OK" button is selected (some comments and commented-out code have been removed from this listing):

```
Public Class SubscriptionTest

    Private testContextInstance As TestContext

    Public Property TestContext() As TestContext
        Get
            Return testContextInstance
        End Get
        Set(ByVal value As TestContext)
            testContextInstance = Value
        End Set
    End Property

    <TestMethod()> _
    Public Sub CurrentStatusTest()
        Dim target As Subscription = New Subscription
                'TODO: Initialize to an appropriate value
```

(continued)

(continued)

```
            Dim actual As Subscription.Status
            actual = target.CurrentStatus
            Assert.Inconclusive("Verify the correctness of this test method.")
        End Sub
    End Class
```

The test case generated for the `CurrentStatus` property appears in the final method of this code snippet. (The top half of this class is discussed later in this chapter.) As you can see, the test case was created with a name that reflects the property it is testing (in this case `CurrentStatusTest`) in a class that reflects the class in which the property appears (in this case `SubscriptionTest`). One of the difficulties with test cases is that they can quickly become unmanageable. This simple naming convention ensures that test cases can easily be found and identified.

If you look at the test case in more detail, you can see that the generated code stub contains the code required to initialize everything for the test. A `Subscription` object is created, and a test variable called `actual` is assigned the `CurrentStatus` property of that object. All that is missing is the code to actually test that this value is correct. Before going any further, run this test case to see what happens by opening the Test View window, shown in Figure 20-2, from the Test ➪ Windows menu.

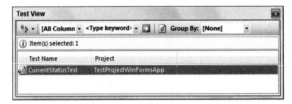

Figure 20-2

Selecting the `CurrentStatusTest` item and clicking the Run Selection button, the first on the left, invokes the test. This also opens the Test Results window, which initially shows the test as being either Pending or In Progress. Once the test has completed, the Test Results window will look like the one shown in Figure 20-3.

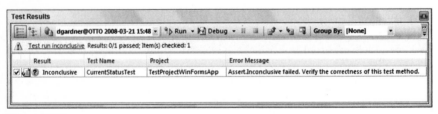

Figure 20-3

You can see from Figure 20-3 that the test case has returned an inconclusive result. Essentially, this indicates either that a test is not complete or that the results should not be relied upon, as changes may have been made that would make this test invalid. When test cases are generated by Visual Studio, they are all initially marked as inconclusive by means of the `Assert.Inconclusive` statement. In addition, depending on the test stub that was created, there may be additional TODO statements that will prompt you to complete the test case.

Returning to the code snippet generated for the `CurrentStatusTest` method, you can see both an `Assert.Inconclusive` statement and a TODO item. To complete this test case, remove the TODO comment and replace the `Assert.Inconclusive` statement with `Assert.AreEqual`, as shown in the following code:

```
<TestMethod()> _
Public Sub CurrentStatusTest()
    Dim target As Subscription = New Subscription
    Dim actual As Subscription.Status
    actual = target.CurrentStatus
    Assert.AreEqual(Subscription.Status.Temporary, actual, _
                    "Subscription.CurrentStatus was not set correctly.")
End Sub
```

Rerunning this test case will now produce a successful result, as shown in Figure 20-4.

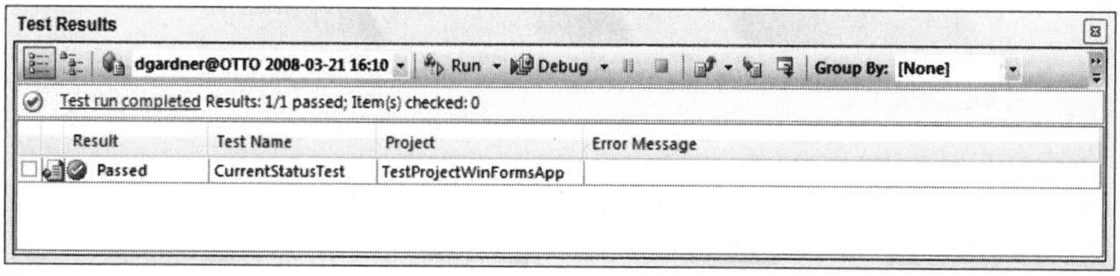

Figure 20-4

By removing the "inconclusive" warning from the test case, you are indicating that it is complete. Don't just leave it at this, because you have actually tested only one path through the code. Instead, add further test cases that fully exercise all code paths.

When you first created the unit test at the start of this chapter you may have noticed that, in addition to the new test project, two items were added under a new solution folder called Solution Items. These are a file with a `.vsmdi` extension and a LocalTestRun.testrunconfig file.

The `.vsmdi` file is a metadata file that contains information about the tests within the solution. When you double-click this file in Visual Studio it opens the Test List Editor, which is discussed at the end of this chapter.

LocalTestRun.testrunconfig is a Test Run Configuration file. This is an XML file that stores settings that control how a set of tests, called a *test run*, is executed. You can create and save multiple run configurations that represent different scenarios, and then make a specific run configuration active using the Test ➪ Select Active Test Run Configuration menu item. This will define which of the test run configurations should be used when tests are run.

When you double-click to open the LocalTestRun.testrunconfig file, it will launch a special-purpose editor. Within this editor you can configure a test run to copy required support files to a deployment directory, or link to custom startup and cleanup scripts. The editor also includes a Test Timeouts section, shown in Figure 20-5, which enables you to define a timeout after which a test will be aborted or marked as failed. This is useful if a global performance limit has been specified for your application (for example, if all screens must return within five seconds).

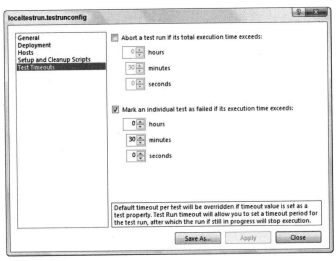

Figure 20-5

Most of these settings can be overridden on a per-method basis by means of test attributes, which are discussed in the next section.

Test Attributes

Before going any further with this scenario, take a step back and consider how testing is carried out within Visual Studio. As mentioned earlier, all test cases have to exist within test classes that themselves reside in a test project. But what really distinguishes a method, class, or project as containing test cases? Starting with the test project, if you look at the underlying XML project file, you will see that there is virtually no difference between a test project file and a normal class library project file. In fact, the only difference appears to be the project type: When this project is built it simply outputs a standard .NET class library assembly. The key difference is that Visual Studio recognizes this as a test project and automatically analyzes it for any test cases in order to populate the various test windows.

Classes and methods used in the testing process are marked with an appropriate attribute. The attributes are used by the testing engine to enumerate all the test cases within a particular assembly.

TestClass

All test cases must reside within a test class that is appropriately marked with the `TestClass` attribute. Although it may appear that there is no reason for this attribute other than to align test cases with the class and member that they are testing, you will later see some benefits associated with grouping test cases using a test class. In the case of testing the Subscription class, a test class called SubscriptionTest was created and marked with the TestClass attribute. Because Visual Studio uses attributes, the name of this class is irrelevant, although a suitable naming convention makes it easier to manage a large number of test cases.

TestMethod

Individual test cases are marked with the TestMethod attribute, which is used by Visual Studio to enumerate the list of tests that can be executed. The CurrentStatusTest method in the SubscriptionTest class is marked with the TestMethod attribute. Again, the actual name of this method is irrelevant, as Visual Studio only uses the attributes. However, the method name is used in the various test windows when the test cases are listed, so it is useful for test methods to have meaningful names.

Test Attributes

As you have seen, the unit-testing subsystem within Visual Studio uses attributes to identify test cases. A number of additional properties can be set to provide further information about a test case. This information is then accessible either via the Properties window associated with a test case or within the other test windows. This section goes through the descriptive attributes that can be applied to a test method.

Description

Because test cases are listed by test method name, a number of tests may have similar names, or names that are not descriptive enough to indicate what functionality they test. The description attribute, which takes a String as its sole argument, can be applied to a test method to provide additional information about a test case.

Owner

The Owner attribute, which also takes a String argument, is useful for indicating who owns, wrote, or is currently working on a particular test case.

Priority

The Priority attribute, which takes an Integer argument, can be applied to a test case to indicate the relative importance of a test case. While the testing framework does not use this attribute, it is useful for prioritizing test cases when you are determining the order in which failing, or incomplete, test cases are resolved.

Work Items

The WorkItem attribute can be used to link a test case to one or more work items in a work-item-tracking system such as Team Foundation Server. If you apply one or more WorkItem attributes to a test case, you can review the test case when making changes to existing functionality. You can read more about Team Foundation Server in Chapter 58.

Timeout

A test case can fail for any number of reasons. A performance test, for example, might require a particular functionality to complete within a particular time frame. Instead of the tester having to write complex multi-threading tests that stop the test case once a particular timeout has been reached, you can apply the `Timeout` attribute to a test case, as shown in the following shaded code. This ensures that the test case fails when that timeout has been reached.

```
<TestMethod()> _
<Description("Tests the functionality of the CurrentStatus method")> _
<Owner("David Gardner")> _
<Priority(3)> _
<Timeout(10000)> _
Public Sub CurrentStatusTest()
    Dim target As Subscription = New Subscription
    Dim actual As Subscription.Status
    actual = target.CurrentStatus
    Assert.AreEqual(Subscription.Status.Temporary, actual, _
                    "Subscription.CurrentStatus was not set correctly.")
End Sub
```

This snippet augments the original `CurrentStatusTest` method with these attributes to illustrate their usage. In addition to providing additional information about what the test case does and who wrote it, this code assigns the test case a priority of 3. Lastly, the code indicates that this test case should fail if it takes more than 10 seconds (10,000 milliseconds) to execute.

Asserting the Facts

So far, this chapter has examined the structure of the test environment and how test cases are nested within test classes in a test project. What remains is to look at the body of the test case and review how test cases either pass or fail. (When a test case is generated, you saw that an `Assert.Inconclusive` statement is added to the end of the test to indicate that it is incomplete.)

The idea behind unit testing is that you start with the system, component, or object in a known state, and then run a method, modify a property, or trigger an event. The testing phase comes at the end, when you need to validate that the system, component, or object is in the correct state. Alternatively, you may need to validate that the correct output was returned from a method or property. You do this by attempting to assert a particular condition. If this condition is not true, the testing system reports this result and ends the test case. A condition is asserted, not surprisingly, via the `Assert` class. There is also a `StringAssert` class and a `CollectionAssert` class, which provide additional assertions for dealing with `String` objects and collections of objects, respectively.

Assert

The `Assert` class in the UnitTesting namespace, not to be confused with the `Debug.Assert` or `Trace.Assert` method in the System.Diagnostics namespace, is the primary class used to make assertions about a test case. The basic assertion has the following format:

```
Assert.IsTrue(variableToTest, "Output message if this fails")
```

As you can imagine, the first argument is the condition to be tested. If this is true, the test case continues operation. However, if it fails, the output message is emitted and the test case exits with a failed result.

There are multiple overloads to this statement whereby the output message can be omitted or `String` formatting parameters supplied. Because quite often you won't be testing a single positive condition, several additional methods simplify making assertions within a test case:

❑ `IsFalse`: Tests for a negative, or false, condition

❑ `AreEqual`: Tests whether two arguments have the same value

❑ `AreSame`: Tests whether two arguments refer to the same object

❑ `IsInstanceOfType`: Tests whether an argument is an instance of a particular type

❑ `IsNull`: Tests whether an argument is nothing

This list is not exhaustive — there are several more methods, including negative equivalents of those listed. Also, many of these methods have overloads that allow them to be invoked in several different ways.

StringAssert

The `StringAssert` class does not provide any additional functionality that cannot be achieved with one or more assertions via the `Assert` class. However, it not only simplifies the test case code by making it clear that `String` assertions are being made; it also reduces the mundane tasks associated with testing for particular conditions. The additional assertions are as follows:

❑ `Contains`: Tests whether a `String` contains another `String`

❑ `DoesNotMatch`: Tests whether a `String` does not match a regular expression

❑ `EndsWith`: Tests whether a `String` ends with a particular `String`

❑ `Matches`: Tests whether a `String` matches a regular expression

❑ `StartsWith`: Tests whether a `String` starts with a particular `String`

CollectionAssert

Similar to the `StringAssert` class, `CollectionAssert` is a helper class that is used to make assertions about a collection of items. Some of the assertions are as follows:

❑ `AllItemsAreNotNull`: Tests that none of the items in a collection is a null reference

❑ `AllItemsAreUnique`: Tests that there are no duplicate items in a collection

❑ `Contains`: Tests whether a collection contains a particular object

❑ `IsSubsetOf`: Tests whether a collection is a subset of another collection

ExpectedException Attribute

Sometimes test cases have to execute paths of code that can cause exceptions to be raised. While exception coding should be avoided, there are conditions where this might be appropriate. Instead of writing a test case that includes a `Try-Catch` block with an appropriate assertion to test that an exception was raised, you can mark the test case with an `ExpectedException` attribute. For example, change the `CurrentStatus` property to throw an exception if the `PaidUp` date is prior to the date the subscription opened, which in this case is a constant:

```
Public Const SubscriptionOpenedOn As Date = #1/1/2000#
Public ReadOnly Property CurrentStatus() As Status
    Get
        If Not Me.PaidUpTo.HasValue Then Return Status.Temporary
        If Me.PaidUpTo.Value > Now Then
            Return Status.Financial
        Else
            If Me.PaidUpTo >= Now.AddMonths(-3) Then
                Return Status.Unfinancial
            ElseIf Me.PaidUpTo >= SubscriptionOpenedOn Then
                Return Status.Suspended
            Else
                Throw New
ArgumentOutOfRangeException("Paid up date is not valid as it is before the
subscription opened")
            End If
        End If
    End Get
End Property
```

Using the same procedure as before, you can create a separate test case for testing this code path, as shown in the following example:

```
<TestMethod()> _

<ExpectedException(GetType(ArgumentOutOfRangeException), _
        "Argument exception not raised for invalid PaidUp date")> _
Public Sub CurrentStatusExceptionTest()
    Dim target As Subscription = New Subscription

    target.PaidUpTo = Subscription.SubscriptionOpenedOn.AddMonths(-1)
    Dim val As Subscription.Status = Subscription.Status.Temporary

    Assert.AreEqual(val, target.CurrentStatus, _
        "This assertion should never actually be evaluated")
End Sub
```

The `ExpectedException` attribute not only catches any exception raised by the test case; it also ensures that the type of exception matches the type expected. If no exception is raised by the test case, this attribute will fail.

Initializing and Cleaning Up

Despite Visual Studio's generating the stub code for test cases you are to write, typically you have to write a lot of setup code whenever you run a test case. Where an application uses a database, that database should be returned to its initial state after each test to ensure that the test cases are completely repeatable. This is also true for applications that modify other resources such as the file system. Visual Studio provides support for writing methods that can be used to initialize and clean up around test cases. (Again, attributes are used to mark the appropriate methods that should be used to initialize and clean up the test cases.)

The attributes for initializing and cleaning up around test cases are broken down into three levels: those that apply to individual tests, those that apply to an entire test class, and those that apply to an entire test project.

TestInitialize and TestCleanup

As their names suggest, the `TestInitialize` and `TestCleanup` attributes indicate methods that should be run before and after each test case within a particular test class. These methods are useful for allocating and subsequently freeing any resources that are needed by all test cases in the test class.

ClassInitialize and ClassCleanup

Sometimes, instead of setting up and cleaning up after each test, it can be easier to ensure that the environment is in the correct state at the beginning and end of running an entire test class. Previously, we explained that test classes are a useful mechanism for grouping test cases; this is where you put that knowledge to use. Test cases can be grouped into test classes that contain one method marked with the `ClassInitialize` attribute and another marked with the `ClassCleanup` attribute.

> When you use the Create Unit Test menu to generate a unit test, it will generate stubs for the `TestInitialize`, `TestCleanup`, `ClassInitialize`, and `ClassCleanup` methods in a code region that is commented out.

AssemblyInitialize and AssemblyCleanup

The final level of initialization and cleanup attributes is at the assembly, or project, level. Methods for initializing before running an entire test project, and cleaning up after, can be marked with the `AssemblyInitialize` and `AssemblyCleanup` attributes, respectively. Because these methods apply to any test case within the test project, only a single method can be marked with each of these attributes.

For both the assembly-level and class-level attributes, it is important to remember that even if only one test case is run, the methods marked with these attributes will also be run.

Testing Context

When you are writing test cases, the testing engine can assist you in a number of ways, including by managing sets of data so you can run a test case with a range of data, and by enabling you to output additional information for the test case to aid in debugging. This functionality is available through the TestContext object that is generated within a test class.

Data

The CurrentStatusTest method generated in the first section of this chapter tested only a single path through the CurrentStatus property. To fully test this method, you could have written additional statements and assertions to set up and test the Subscription object. However, this process is fairly repetitive and would need to be updated if you ever changed the structure of the CurrentStatus property. An alternative is to provide a DataSource for the CurrentStatusTest method whereby each row of data tests a different path through the property. To add appropriate data to this method, use the following process:

1. Create a local database and database table to store the various test data. In this case, create a database called LoadTest with a table called Subscription_CurrentStatus. The table has an Identity column called Id, a nullable DateTime column called PaidUp, and an nvarchar(20) column called Status.

2. Add appropriate data values to the table to cover all paths through the code. Test values for the CurrentStatus property are shown in Figure 20-6.

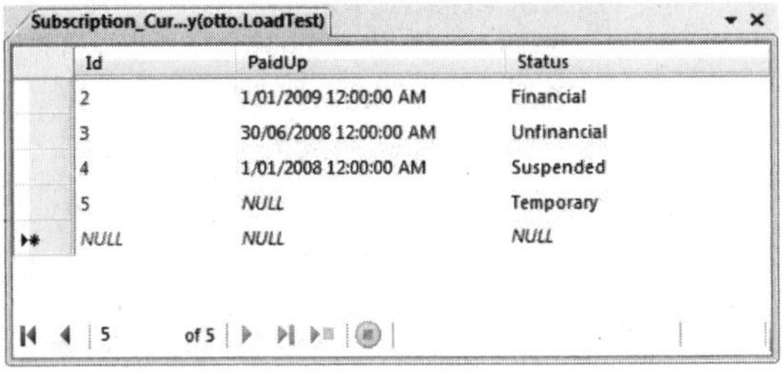

Subscription_Cur...y(otto.LoadTest)			
Id	PaidUp	Status	
2	1/01/2009 12:00:00 AM	Financial	
3	30/06/2008 12:00:00 AM	Unfinancial	
4	1/01/2008 12:00:00 AM	Suspended	
5	NULL	Temporary	
NULL	NULL	NULL	

Figure 20-6

3. Select the appropriate test case in the Test View window and open the Properties window. Select the Data Connection String property and click the ellipsis button to open the Connection Properties dialog.

4. Use the Connection Properties dialog to connect to the database created in Step 1. You should see a connection string similar to the following:

```
Data Source=localhost;Initial Catalog=LoadTest;Integrated Security=True
```

5. If the connection string is valid, a drop-down box appears when you select the DataTable property, enabling you to select the database table you created in Step 1.

6. To open the test case in the main window, return to the Test View window and select Open Test from the right-click context menu for the test case. Notice that a `DataSource` attribute has been added to the test case. This attribute is used by the testing engine to load the appropriate data from the specified table. This data is then exposed to the test case through the `TestContext` object.

7. Modify the test case to access data from the `TestContext` object and use the data to drive the test case, which gives you the following `CurrentStatusTest` method:

```
    <DataSource("System.Data.SqlClient", "Data Source=localhost;
 Initial Catalog=LoadTest;Integrated Security=True", "Subscription_CurrentStatus",
 DataAccessMethod.Sequential)> _
    <TestMethod()> _
    Public Sub CurrentStatusTest()
        Dim target As Subscription = New Subscription
        If Not
 IsDBNull(Me.TestContext.DataRow.Item("PaidUp")) Then
            target.PaidUpTo = CType(Me.TestContext.DataRow.Item("PaidUp"), Date)
        End If
        Dim val As Subscription.Status = _

 CType([Enum].Parse(GetType(Subscription.Status), _

 CStr(Me.TestContext.DataRow.Item("Status"))), Subscription.Status)
        Assert.AreEqual(val, target.CurrentStatus, _
                "Subscription.CurrentStatus was not set correctly.")
    End Sub
```

When this test case is executed, the `CurrentStatusTest` method is executed four times (once for each row of data in the database table). Each time it is executed, a `DataRow` object is retrieved and exposed to the test method via the `TestContext.DataRow` property. If the logic within the `CurrentStatus` property changes, you can add a new row to the `Subscription_CurrentStatus` to test any code paths that may have been created.

Before moving on, take one last look at the `DataSource` attribute that was applied to the `CurrentStatusTest`. This attribute takes four arguments, the first three of which are used to determine which `DataTable` needs to be extracted. The remaining argument is a `DataAccessMethod` enumeration, which determines the order in which rows are returned from the `DataTable`. By default, this is `Sequential`, but it can be changed to `Random` so the order is different every time the test is run. This is particularly important when the data is representative of end user data but does not have to be processed in any particular order.

Writing Test Output

Writing unit tests is all about automating the process of testing an application. Because of this, these test cases can be executed as part of a build process, perhaps even on a remote computer. This means that the normal output windows, such as the console, are not a suitable place for outputting test-related information. Clearly, you also don't want test-related information interspersed throughout the debugging or trace information being generated by the application. For this reason, there is a separate channel for writing test-related information so it can be viewed alongside the test results.

The `TestContext` object exposes a `WriteLine` method that takes a `String` and a series of `String.Format` arguments that can be used to output information to the results for a particular test. For example, adding the following line to the `CurrentStatusTest` method generates additional information with the test results:

```
TestContext.WriteLine("No exceptions thrown for test id {0}", _

    CInt(Me.TestContext.DataRow.Item(0)))
```

After the test run is completed, the Test Results window will be displayed, listing all the test cases that were executed in the test run along with their results. The Test Results Details window, shown in Figure 20-7, displays any additional information that was outputted by the test case. You can view this window by double-clicking the test case in the Test Results window.

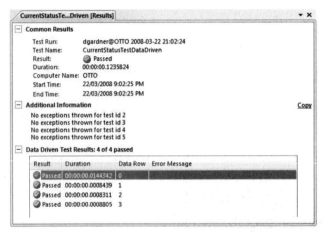

Figure 20-7

In Figure 20-7, you can see in the Additional Information section the output from the `WriteLine` method you added to the test method. Although you added only one line to the test method, the `WriteLine` method was executed for each row in the database table. The Data Driven Test Results section of Figure 20-7 provides more information about each of the test passes, with a row for each row in the table. Your results may differ from those shown in Figure 20-7, depending on the code you have in your `Subscription` class.

Advanced

Up until now, you have seen how to write and execute unit tests. This section goes on to examine how you can add custom properties to a test case, and how you can use the same framework to test private methods and properties.

Custom Properties

The testing framework provides a number of test attributes that you can apply to a method to record additional information about a test case. This information can be edited via the Properties window and updates the appropriate attributes on the test method. There are times when you want to drive your test methods by specifying your own properties, which can also be set using the Properties window. To do this, add `TestProperty` attributes to the test method. For example, the following code adds two attributes to the test method to enable you to specify an arbitrary date and an expected status. This might be convenient for ad hoc testing using the Test View and Properties window:

```
<TestMethod()> _
<TestProperty("SpecialDate", "1/1/2008")> _
<TestProperty("SpecialStatus", "Suspended")> _
Public Sub SpecialCurrentStatusTest()
    Dim target As Subscription = New Subscription

    target.PaidUpTo = CDate(Me.TestContext.Properties.Item("SpecialDate"))
    Dim val As Subscription.Status = _
    CType([Enum].Parse(GetType(Subscription.Status), _
    CStr(Me.TestContext.Properties.Item("SpecialStatus"))), _
            Subscription.Status)

    Assert.AreEqual(val, target.CurrentStatus, _
                    "Correct status not set for Paid up date {0}", target.PaidUpTo)
End Sub
```

By using the Test View to navigate to this test case and accessing the Properties window, you can see that this code generates two additional properties, `SpecialDate` and `SpecialStatus`, as shown in Figure 20-8.

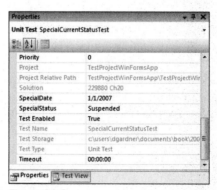

Figure 20-8

You can use the Properties window to adjust the `SpecialDate` and `SpecialStatus` values. Unfortunately, the limitation here is that there is no way to specify the data type for the values. As a result, the property grid displays and enables edits as if they were `String` data types.

Note one other limitation to using custom properties as defined for the `SpecialCurrentStatusTest` method. Looking at the code, you can see that you are able to access the property values using the Properties dictionary provided by the `TestContext`. Unfortunately, although custom properties automatically appear in the Properties window, they are *not* automatically added to this Properties dictionary. Therefore, you have to do a bit of heavy lifting to extract these properties from the custom attributes list and place them into the Properties dictionary. Luckily, you can do this in the `TestInitialize` method, as illustrated in the following code. Note that although this method will be executed for each test case in the class, and because of this will load all custom properties, it is not bound to any particular test case, as it uses the `TestContext` .Name property to look up the test method being executed.

```
<TestInitialize()> _
Public Sub Setup()
    Dim t As Type = Me.GetType
    Dim mi As Reflection.MethodInfo = t.GetMethod(Me.TestContext.TestName)
    Dim MyType As Type = GetType(TestPropertyAttribute)
    Dim attributes As Object() = mi.GetCustomAttributes(MyType, False)

    For Each attrib As TestPropertyAttribute In attributes
        Me.TestContext.Properties.Add(attrib.Name, attrib.Value)
    Next
End Sub
```

Testing Private Members

One of the selling points of unit testing is that it is particularly effective for testing the internals of your class to ensure that they function correctly. The assumption here is that if each of your classes works in isolation, then there is a better chance that they will work together correctly; and in fact, you can use unit testing to test classes working together. However, you might be wondering how well the unit-testing framework handles testing private methods.

One of the features of the .NET Framework is the capability to reflect over any type that has been loaded into memory and to execute any member regardless of its accessibility. This functionality does come at a performance cost, as the reflection calls obviously include an additional level of redirection, which can prove costly if done frequently. Nonetheless, for testing, reflection enables you to call into the inner workings of a class and not worry about the potential performance penalties for making those calls.

The other, more significant issue with using reflection to access nonpublic members of a class is that the code to do so is somewhat messy. Fortunately, Visual Studio 2008 does a very good job of generating a wrapper class that makes testing even private methods easy. To show this, return to the `CurrentStatus` property, change its access from `public` to `private`, and rename it `PrivateCurrentStatus`. Then regenerate the unit test for this property as you did earlier.

The following code snippet is the new unit-test method that is generated:

```
<TestMethod(), _
DeploymentItem("TestingWinFormsApp.exe")> _
Public Sub PrivateCurrentStatusTest()
    Dim target As Subscription_Accessor = New Subscription_Accessor
    Dim actual As Subscription.Status
    actual = target.PrivateCurrentStatus
    Assert.Inconclusive("Verify the correctness of this test method.")
End Sub
```

As you can see, the preceding example uses an instance of a new `Subscription_Accessor` class to access the `PrivateCurrentStatus` property. This is a class that was auto-generated and compiled into a new assembly by Visual Studio. A new file was also added to the test project, called TestingWinFormsApp.accessor, which is what causes Visual Studio to create the new accessor classes.

Managing Large Numbers of Tests

Visual Studio provides both the Test View window and the Test List Editor to display a list of all of the tests in a solution. The Test View window, which was shown earlier in the chapter in Figure 20-2, simply displays the unit tests in a flat list. However, if you have hundreds, or even thousands, of unit tests in your solution, then trying to manage them with a flat list will quickly become unwieldy.

The Test List Editor enables you to group and organize related tests into test lists. Since test lists can contain both tests and other test lists, you can further organize your tests by creating a logical, hierarchical structure. All the tests in a test list can then be executed together from within Visual Studio, or via a command-line test utility.

The Test List Editor can be opened from the Test ➪ Windows menu, or you can double-click the Visual Studio Test Metadata (`.vsmdi`) file for the solution. Figure 20-9 shows the Test List Editor for a solution with a number of tests organized into a hierarchical structure of related tests.

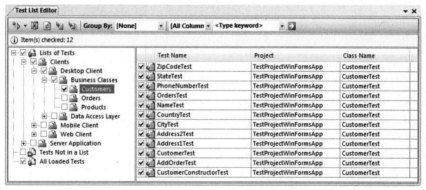

Figure 20-9

On the left in the Test List Editor window is a hierarchical tree of test lists available for the current solution. At the bottom of the tree are two project lists, one showing all the test cases (All Loaded Tests) and one showing those test cases that haven't been put in a list (Tests Not in a List). Under the Lists of Tests node are all the test lists created for the project.

To create a new test list, click Test ➪ Create New Test List. Test cases can be dragged from any existing list into the new list. Initially, this can be a little confusing because a test will be moved to the new list and removed from its original list. To add a test case to multiple lists, either hold the Ctrl key while dragging the test case or copy and paste the test case from the original list to the new list.

After creating a test list, you can run the whole list by checking the box next to the list in the Test Manager. The Run button executes all lists that are checked. Alternatively, you can run the list with the debugger attached using the Debug Checked Tests menu item.

Summary

This chapter described how you can use unit testing to ensure the correct functionality of your code. The unit-testing framework within Visual Studio is quite comprehensive, enabling you to both document and manage test cases.

You can fully exercise the testing framework using an appropriate data source to minimize the repetitive code you have to write. You can also extend the framework to test all the inner workings of your application.

The Test Edition of Visual Studio Team System contains even more functionality for testing, including the ability to track and report on code coverage, and support for load and web application testing. Chapter 56 provides more detail on Visual Studio Team System Test Edition.

Part V
Data

21

DataSets and DataBinding

A large proportion of applications use some form of data storage. This might be in the form of serialized objects or XML data, but for long-term storage that supports concurrent access by a large number of users, most applications use a database. The .NET Framework includes strong support for working with databases and other data sources. This chapter examines how to use DataSets to build applications that work with data from a database.

In the second part of this chapter you see how to use DataBinding to connect visual controls to the data they are to display. You see how they interact and how you can use the designers to control how data is displayed.

The examples in this chapter are based on the sample AdventureWorks database that is available as a download from www.codeplex.com (search for AdventureWorks).

DataSet Overview

The .NET Framework *DataSet* is a complex object that is approximately equivalent to an in-memory representation of a database. It contains *DataTables* that correlate to database tables. These in turn contain a series of *DataColumns* that define the composition of each *DataRow*. The DataRow correlates to a row in a database table. Of course, it is possible to establish relationships between DataTables within the DataSet in the same way that a database has relationships between tables.

One of the ongoing challenges for the object-oriented programming paradigm is that it does not align smoothly with the relational database model. The DataSet object goes a long way toward bridging this gap, because it can be used to represent and work with relational data in an object-oriented fashion. However, the biggest issue with a raw DataSet is that it is weakly typed. Although the type of each column can be queried prior to accessing data elements, this adds overhead and can make code very unreadable. Strongly typed DataSets combine the advantages of a DataSet with strong typing to ensure that data is accessed correctly at design time. This is done with the custom tool MSDataSetGenerator, which converts an XML schema into a strongly typed DataSet, essentially replacing a lot of runtime type checking with code generated at design time.

In the following code snippet, you can see the difference between using a raw DataSet, in the first half of the snippet, and a strongly typed DataSet, in the second half:

```
'Raw DataSet
Dim nontypedAwds As DataSet = RetrieveData()
Dim nontypedcontacts As DataTable = nontypedAwds.Tables("Contact")
Dim nontypedfirstContact As DataRow = nontypedcontacts.Rows(0)
MessageBox.Show(nontypedfirstContact.Item("FirstName"))

'Strongly typed DataSet
Dim awds As AdventureWorksDataSet = RetrieveData()
Dim contacts As AdventureWorksDataSet.ContactDataTable = awds.Contact
Dim firstContact As AdventureWorksDataSet.ContactRow = contacts.Rows(0)
MessageBox.Show(firstContact.FirstName)
```

Using the raw DataSet, both the table lookup and the column name lookup are done using string literals. As you are likely aware, string literals can be a source of much frustration and should be used only within generated code, and preferably not at all.

Adding a Data Source

You can manually create a strongly typed DataSet by creating an XSD using the XML schema editor. To create the DataSet, you set the custom tool value for the XSD file to be the MSDataSetGenerator. This will create the designer code file that is needed for strongly typed access to the DataSet.

Manually creating an XSD is difficult and not recommended unless you really need to; luckily in most cases, the source of your data will be a database, in which case Visual Studio 2008 provides a wizard that you can use to generate the necessary schema based on the structure of your database. Through the rest of this chapter, you will see how you can create data sources and how they can be bound to the user interface. To get started, create a new project called CustomerObjects, using the Visual Basic Windows Forms Application template. Then to create a strongly typed DataSet from an existing database, select Add New Data Source from the Data menu, and follow these steps:

> *Although this functionality is not available for ASP.NET projects, a workaround is to perform all data access via a class library.*

1. The first step in the Data Source Configuration Wizard is to select the type of data source to work with — a Database, Web Service, or an Object Data Source. In this case, you want to work with data from a database, so select the Database icon and click Next.

2. The next screen prompts you to select the database connection to use. To create a new connection, click the New Connection button, which opens the Add Connection dialog. The attributes displayed in this dialog are dependent on the type of database you are connecting to. By default the SQL Server provider is selected, which requires the Server name, authentication mechanism (Windows or SQL Server), and Database name in order to proceed. There is a Test Connection that you can use to ensure you have specified valid properties.

3. After you specify a connection, it will be saved as an application setting in the application configuration file.

When the application is later deployed, the connection string can be modified to point to the production database. This process can often take longer than expected to ensure that various security permissions line up. Because the connection string is stored in the configuration file as a string without any schema, it is quite easy to make a mistake when making changes to it. In Chapter 39 you learn more about connection strings and how you can customize them for different data sources.

A little-known utility within Windows can be used to create connection strings, even if Visual Studio is not installed. Known as the Data Link Properties dialog, you can use it to edit Universal Data Link files, files that end in .udl. *When you need to create or test a connection string, you can simply create a new text document, rename it to* something.udl *and then double-click it. This opens the Data Link Properties dialog, which enables you to create and test connection strings for a variety of providers. Once you have selected the appropriate connection, this information will be written to the UDL file as a connection string, which can be retrieved by opening the same file in Notepad. This can be particularly useful if you need to test security permissions and resolve other data connectivity issues.*

4. After specifying the connection, the next stage is to specify the data to be extracted. At this stage you will be presented with a list of tables, views, stored procedures, and functions from which you can select what to include in the DataSet. Figure 21-1 shows the final stage of the Data Source Configuration Wizard with a selection of columns from the Contact table in the AdventureWorks database.

You will probably want to constrain the DataSet so it doesn't return all the records for a particular table. You can do this after creating the DataSet, so for the time being simply select the information you want to return. The editor's design makes it easier to select more information here and then delete it from the designer, rather than create it afterwards.

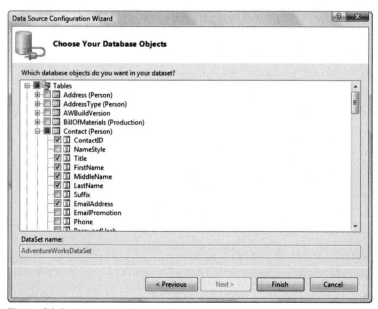

Figure 21-1

5. Click Finish to add the new DataSet to the Data Sources window, shown in Figure 21-2, where you can view all the information to be retrieved for the DataSet. Each column is identified with an icon that reflects the type of data. For example, the Contact ID field is numeric and ModifiedDate is datetime, whereas the other fields are all text.

Figure 21-2

The Data Sources window changes the icons next to each field depending on whether you are working in a code window or a design surface. This view shows the type of each field and is visible while working in the code window.

DataSet Designer

The Data Source Configuration Wizard uses the database schema to guess the appropriate .NET type to use for the DataTable columns. In cases where the wizard gets information wrong, it can be useful to edit the DataSet without the wizard. To edit without the wizard, right-click the DataSet in the Data Sources window and select Edit DataSet with Designer from the context menu. Alternatively, you can open the Data Sources window by double-clicking the XSD file in the Solution Explorer window. This will open the DataSet editor in the main window, as shown in the example in Figure 21-3.

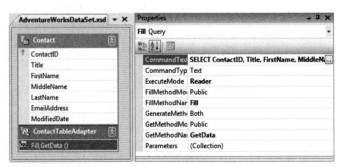

Figure 21-3

Here you start to see some of the power of using strongly typed DataSets. Not only has a strongly typed table (Contact) been added to the DataSet, you also have a ContactTableAdapter. This TableAdapter is used for selecting from and updating the database for the DataTable to which it is attached. If you have multiple tables included in the DataSet, you will have a TableAdapter for each. Although a single TableAdapter can easily handle returning information from multiple tables in the database, it becomes difficult to update, insert, and delete records.

As you can see in Figure 21-3, the ContactTableAdapter has been created with `Fill` and `GetData` methods, which are called to extract data from the database. The following code shows how you can use the `Fill` method to populate an existing strongly typed DataTable, perhaps within a DataSet. Alternatively, the `GetData` method creates a new instance of a strongly typed DataTable:

```
Dim ta As New AdventureWorksDataSetTableAdapters.ContactTableAdapter

'Option 1 - Create a new ContactDataTable and use the Fill method
Dim contacts1 As New AdventureWorksDataSet.ContactDataTable
ta.Fill(contacts1)

'Option 2 - Use the GetData method which will create a ContactDataTable for you
Dim contacts2 As AdventureWorksDataSet.ContactDataTable = ta.GetData
```

In Figure 21-3, the `Fill` and `GetData` methods appear as a pair because they make use of the same query. The Properties window can be used to configure this query. A query can return data in one of three ways: using a text command (as the example illustrates), a stored procedure, or TableDirect (where the contents of the table name specified in the `CommandText` are retrieved). This is specified in the CommandType field. Although the `CommandText` can be edited directly in the Properties window, it is difficult to see the whole query and easy to make mistakes. Clicking the ellipsis button (at the top right of Figure 21-3) opens the Query Builder window, shown in Figure 21-4.

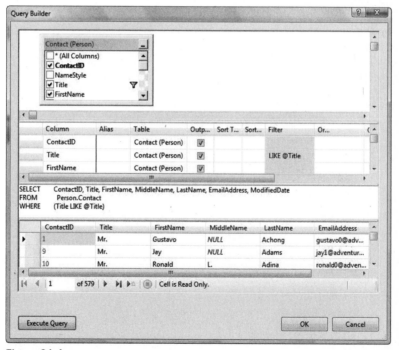

Figure 21-4

The Query Builder dialog is divided into four panes. In the top pane is a diagram of the tables involved in the query, and the selected columns. The second pane shows a list of columns related to the query. These columns are either output columns, such as FirstName and LastName, or a condition, such as the

Title field, or both. The third pane is, of course, the SQL command that is to be executed. The final pane includes sample data that can be retrieved by clicking the Execute Query button. If there are parameters to the SQL statement (in this case, @Title), a dialog will be displayed, prompting for values to use when executing the statement (see Figure 21-5).

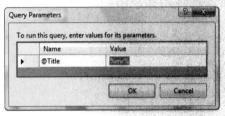

Figure 21-5

To change the query, you can make changes in any of the first three panes. As you move between panes, changes in one field are reflected in the others. You can hide any of the panes by unchecking that pane from the Panes item of the right-click context menu. Conditions can be added using the Filter column. These can include parameters (such as @Title), which must start with the at (@) symbol.

Returning to the DataSet designer, and the properties window associated with the Fill method, click the ellipsis to examine the list of parameters. This shows the Parameters Collection Editor, as shown in Figure 21-6. Occasionally, the Query Builder doesn't get the data type correct for a parameter, and you may need to modify it using this dialog.

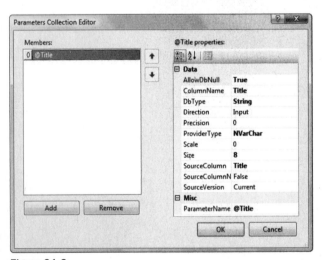

Figure 21-6

Also from the properties window for the query, you can specify whether the Fill and/or GetData methods are created, using the GenerateMethods property, which has values Fill, Get, or Both. You can also specify the names and accessibility of the generated methods.

Binding

The most common type of application is one that retrieves data from a database, displays the data, allows changes to be made, and then persists those changes back to the database. The middle steps that connect the in-memory data with the visual elements are what is referred to as DataBinding. DataBinding often becomes the bane a of developer's existence because it has been difficult to get right. Most developers at some stage or another have resorted to writing their own wrappers to ensure that data is correctly bound to the controls on the screen. Visual Studio 2008 dramatically reduces the pain of getting two-way DataBinding to work. The examples used in the following sections work with the AdventureWorks Lite sample database, and you saw earlier in this chapter that you will need to add this as a data source to your application. For simplicity, you'll work with a single Windows application, but the concepts discussed here can be extended over multiple tiers.

In this example, you build an application to assist you in managing the customers for AdventureWorks. To begin, you need to ensure that the AdventureWorksDataSet contains the Customer, SalesTerritory, Individual, Contact, and SalesOrderHeader tables. (You can reuse the AdventureWorksDataSet from earlier by clicking the "Configure Dataset with Wizard" icon in the Data Source window and editing which tables are included in the DataSet.) With the form designer (any empty form in your project will do) and Data Sources window open, set the mode for the Customer table to Details using the drop-down list. Before creating the editing controls, tweak the list of columns for the Customer table. You're not that interested in the CustomerID or rowguid fields, so set them to None (again using the drop-down list for those nodes in the Data Sources window). AccountNumber is a generated field, and ModifiedDate should be automatically set when changes are made, so both of these fields should appear as labels, preventing them from being edited.

Now you're ready to drag the Customer node onto the form design surface. This will automatically add controls for each of the columns you have specified. It will also add a BindingSource, a BindingNavigator, an AdventureWorksDataSet, a CustomerTableAdapter, and a TableAdapterManager to the form as shown in Figure 21-7.

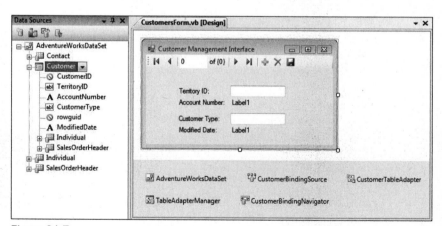

Figure 21-7

At this point you can build and run this application and navigate through the records using the navigation control, and you can also take the components apart to understand how they interact. Start with the AdventureWorksDataSet and the CustomerTableAdapter, because they carry out the

background grunt work of retrieving information and persisting changes to the database.
The AdventureWorksDataSet that is added to this form is actually an instance of the
AdventureWorksDataSet class that was created by the Data Source Configuration Wizard. This
instance will be used to store information for all the tables on this form. To populate the DataSet, call the
Fill method. If you open the code file for the form, you will see that the Fill command has been
added to the form's Load event handler. There is no requirement for this to occur while the form is
loading — for example, if parameters need to be passed to the SELECT command, then you might need
to input values before clicking a button to populate the DataSet.

```
Private Sub Form1_Load(ByVal sender As System.Object, _
                       ByVal e As System.EventArgs) Handles MyBase.Load
    Me.CustomerTableAdapter.Fill(Me.AdventureWorksDataSet.Customer)
End Sub
```

As you add information to this form, you'll also add TableAdapters to work with different tables
within the AdventureWorksDataSet.

BindingSource

The next item of interest is the CustomerBindingSource that was automatically added to the nonvisual
part of the form designer. This control is used to wire up each of the controls on the design surface with
the relevant data item. In fact, this control is just a wrapper for the CurrencyManager. However, using a
BindingSource considerably reduces the number of event handlers and custom code that you have to
write. Unlike the AdventureWorksDataSet and the CustomerTableAdapter — which are instances
of the strongly typed classes with the same names — the CustomerBindingSource is just an instance of
the regular BindingSource class that ships with the .NET Framework.

Take a look at the properties of the CustomerBindingSource so you can see what it does. Figure 21-8
shows the Properties window for the CustomerBindingSource. The two items of particular interest are
the DataSource and DataMember properties. The drop-down list for the DataSource property is
expanded to illustrate the list of available data sources. The instance of the AdventureWorksDataSet
that was added to the form is listed under CustomerForm List Instances. Selecting the
AdventureWorksDataSet type under the Project Data Sources node creates another instance on the
form instead of reusing the existing DataSet. In the DataMember field, you need to specify the table to
use for DataBinding. Later, you'll see how the DataMember field can be used to specify a foreign key
relationship so you can show linked data.

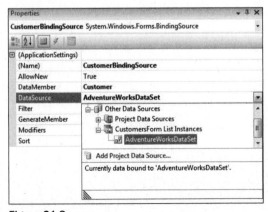

Figure 21-8

So far you have specified that the `CustomerBindingSource` will bind data in the Customer table of the `AdventureWorksDataSet`. What remains is to bind the individual controls on the form to the `BindingSource` and the appropriate column in the Customer table. To do this you need to specify a DataBinding for each control. Figure 21-9 shows the Properties grid for the TerritoryID textbox, with the DataBindings node expanded to show the binding for the `Text` property.

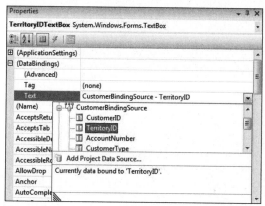

Figure 21-9

From the drop-down list you can see that the `Text` property is being bound to the TerritoryID field of the `CustomerBindingSource`. Because the `CustomerBindingSource` is bound to the Customer table, this is actually the TerritoryID column in that table. If you look at the designer file for the form, you can see that this binding is set up using a new `Binding`, as shown in the following snippet:

```
Me.TerritoryIDTextBox.DataBindings.Add( _
                    New System.Windows.Forms.Binding("Text", _
    Me.CustomerBindingSource, _
    "TerritoryID", True) _
                                    )
```

A `Binding` is used to ensure that two-way binding is set up between the Text field of the TerritoryID textbox and the TerritoryID field of the `CustomerBindingSource`. The controls for AccountNumber, CustomerType, and ModifiedDate all have similar bindings between their `Text` properties and the appropriate fields on the `CustomerBindingSource`.

Running the current application you will notice that the Modified Date value is displayed as in the default string representation of a date, for example, "13/10/2004 11:15." Given the nature of the application, it might be more useful to have it in a format similar to "Friday, 13 October 2004." To do this you need to specify additional properties as part of the DataBinding. In the Properties tool window, expand the DataBindings node and select the Advanced item. This will open up the Formatting and Advanced Binding dialog as shown in Figure 21-10.

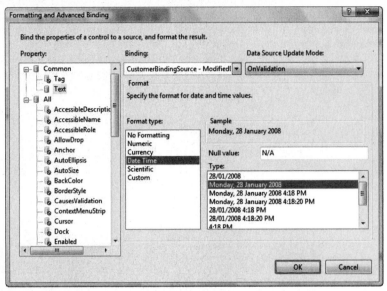

Figure 21-10

In the lower portion of Figure 21-10 you can see that we have selected one of the predefined formatting types, Date Time. This then presents another list of formatting options in which "Monday, 28 January 2008" has been selected — this is an example of how the value will be formatted. In this dialog we have also provided a Null value, "N/A," which will be displayed if there is no Modified Date value for a particular row. In the following code you can see that there are now three additional parameters that have been added to create the DataBinding for the Modified Date value:

```
Me.ModifiedDateLabel1.DataBindings.Add( _
        New System.Windows.Forms.Binding("Text", _
    Me.CustomerBindingSource, _
    "ModifiedDate", True, _
    DataSourceUpdateMode.OnValidation, _
                            "N/A", "D") _
        )
```

The OnValidation value simply indicates that the data source will be updated when the visual control has been validated. This is actually the default and is only specified here so that the next two parameters can be specified. The "N/A" is the value you specified for when there was no Modified Date value, and the "D" is actually a shortcut formatting string for the date formatting you selected.

BindingNavigator

Although the CustomerBindingNavigator component, which is an instance of the BindingNavigator class, appears in the nonvisual area of the design surface, it does have a visual representation in the form of the navigation toolstrip that is initially docked to the top of the form. As with regular toolstrips, this control can be docked to any edge of the form. In fact, in many ways the BindingNavigator behaves the same way as a toolstrip in that buttons and other controls can be added to the Items list. When the

BindingNavigator is initially added to the form, a series of buttons are added for standard data functionality, such as moving to the first or last item, moving to the next or previous item, and adding, removing, and saving items.

What is neat about the BindingNavigator is that it not only creates these standard controls, but also wires them up for you. Figure 21-11 shows the Properties window for the BindingNavigator, with the Data and Items sections expanded. In the Data section you can see that the associated BindingSource is the CustomerBindingSource, which will be used to perform all the actions implied by the various button clicks. The Items section plays an important role, because each property defines an action, such as AddNewItem. The value of the property defines the ToolStripItem to which it will be assigned — in this case, the "BindingNavigatorAddNewItem" button.

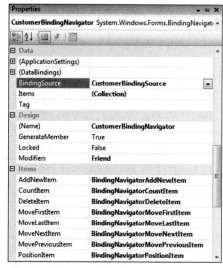

Figure 21-11

Behind the scenes, when this application is run and this button is assigned to the AddNewItem property, the OnAddNew method is wired up to the Click event of the button. This is shown in the following snippet, extracted using Reflector from the BindingNavigator class. The AddNewItem property calls the WireUpButton method, passing in a delegate to the OnAddNew method:

```
Public Property AddNewItem As ToolStripItem
    Get
        If ((Not Me.addNewItem Is Nothing) AndAlso Me.addNewItem.IsDisposed) Then
            Me.addNewItem = Nothing
        End If
        Return Me.addNewItem
    End Get
    Set(ByVal value As ToolStripItem)
        Me.WireUpButton(Me.addNewItem, value, _
                            New EventHandler(AddressOf Me.OnAddNew))
    End Set
```

(continued)

(continued)

```
        End Property

        Private Sub OnAddNew(ByVal sender As Object, ByVal e As EventArgs)
                If (Me.Validate AndAlso (Not Me.bindingSource Is Nothing)) Then
                        Me.bindingSource.AddNew
                        Me.RefreshItemsInternal
                End If
        End Sub

        Private Sub WireUpButton(ByRef oldButton As ToolStripItem, _
                                 ByVal newButton As ToolStripItem, _
                                 ByVal clickHandler As EventHandler)
                If (Not oldButton Is newButton) Then
                        If (Not oldButton Is Nothing) Then
                                RemoveHandler oldButton.Click, clickHandler
                        End If
                        If (Not newButton Is Nothing) Then
                                AddHandler newButton.Click, clickHandler
                        End If
                        oldButton = newButton
                        Me.RefreshItemsInternal
                End If
        End Sub
```

The OnAddNew method performs a couple of important actions. First, it forces validation of the active field, which is examined later in this chapter. Second, and the most important aspect of the OnAddNew method, it calls the AddNew method on the BindingSource. The other properties on the BindingNavigator also map to corresponding methods on the BindingSource, and it is important to remember that the BindingSource, rather than the BindingNavigator, does the work when it comes to working with the data source.

Data Source Selections

Now that you have seen how the BindingSource works, it's time to improve the user interface. At the moment, the TerritoryID is being displayed as a textbox, but this is in fact a foreign key to the SalesTerritory table. This means that if a user enters random text, an error will be thrown when you try to commit the changes. Because the list of territories is defined in the database, it would make sense to present a drop-down list that enables users to select the territory, rather than specify the ID. To add the drop-down, replace the textbox control with a ComboBox control, and bind the list of items in the drop-down to the SalesTerritory table in the database.

Start by removing the TerritoryID textbox. Next, add a ComboBox control from the toolbar. With the new ComboBox selected, note that a smart tag is attached to the control. Expanding this tag and checking the "Use data bound items" checkbox will open the Data Binding Mode options, as shown in Figure 21-12. Take this opportunity to rearrange the form slightly so the controls line up.

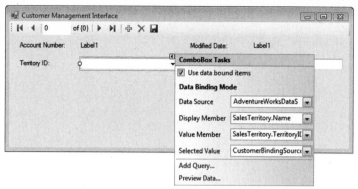

Figure 21-12

You need to define four things to get the DataBinding to work properly. The first is the data source. In this case, select the existing `AdventureWorksDataSet` that was previously added to the form, which is listed under Other Data Sources, CustomersForm List Instances. Within this data source, set the Display Member, the field that is to be displayed, to be equal to the Name column of the SalesTerritory table. The Value Member, which is the field used to select which item to display, is set to the TerritoryID column of the same table. These three properties configure the contents of the drop-down list. The last property you need to set determines which item will be selected and what property to update when the selected item changes in the drop-down list. This is the `SelectedValue` property; in this case, set it equal to the TerritoryID field on the existing `CustomerBindingSource` object.

In the earlier discussion about the `DataSet` and the `TableAdapter`, recall that to populate the Customer table in the `AdventureWorksDataSet`, you need to call the `Fill` method on the `CustomerTableAdapter`. Although you have wired up the TerritoryID drop-down list, if you run what you currently have, there would be no items in this list, because you haven't populated the DataSet with any values for the SalesTerritory table. To retrieve these items from the database, you need to add a `TableAdapter` to the form and call the `Fill` method when the form loads. When you added the `AdventureWorksDataSet` to the data source list, it not only created a set of strongly typed tables, it also created a set of table adapters. These are automatically added to the Toolbox under the Components tab. In this case, drag the `SalesTerritoryTableAdapter` onto the form and add a call to the `Fill` method to the Load event handler for the form. You should end up with the following:

```
Private Sub Form1_Load(ByVal sender As System.Object, _
                       ByVal e As System.EventArgs) Handles MyBase.Load
    Me.SalesTerritoryTableAdapter.Fill(Me.AdventureWorksDataSet.SalesTerritory)
    Me.CustomerTableAdapter.Fill(Me.AdventureWorksDataSet.Customer)
End Sub
```

Now when you run the application, instead of having a textbox with a numeric value, you have a convenient drop-down list from which to select the Territory.

New in Visual Studio 2008 generated code is the `TableAdapterManager` *that was automatically added to your form. This component is designed to simplify the loading and saving of data using table adapters. To simplify your example you can replace the data loading code with the following:*

```
Private Sub Form1_Load(ByVal sender As System.Object, _
                       ByVal e As System.EventArgs) Handles MyBase.Load
    Me.TableAdapterManager.SalesTerritoryTableAdapter.Fill _
                                (Me.AdventureWorksDataSet.SalesTerritory)
    Me.TableAdapterManager.CustomerTableAdapter.Fill _
                                (Me.AdventureWorksDataSet.Customer)
End Sub
```

BindingSource Chains

At the moment, you have a form that displays some basic information about a customer, such as Account Number, Sales Territory ID, and Customer Type. This information by itself is not very interesting, because it really doesn't tell you who the customer is or how to contact this person or entity. Before adding more information to this form, you need to limit the customer list. There are actually two types of customers in the database, Individuals and Stores, as indicated by the Customer Type field. For this example, you are only interested in Individuals, because Stores have a different set of information stored in the database. The first task is to open the `AdventureWorksDataSet` in the design window, click the `CustomerTableAdapter`, select the `SelectCommand` property, and change the query to read as follows:

```
SELECT    CustomerID, CustomerType, TerritoryID, rowguid,
          ModifiedDate, AccountNumber
FROM      Sales.Customer
WHERE     (CustomerType = 'I')
```

Now that you're dealing only with individual customers, you can remove the Customer Type information from the form.

To present more information about the customers, you need to add information from the Individual and Contact tables. The only column of interest in the Individual table is Demographics. From the Data Sources window, expand the Customer node, followed by the Individual node. Set the Demographics node to Textbox using the drop-down and then drag it onto the form. This will also add an `IndividualBindingSource` and an `IndividualTableAdapter` to the form.

When you run the application in this state, the demographics information for each customer is displayed. What is going on here to automatically link the Customer and Individual tables? The trick is in the new `BindingSource`. The `DataSource` property of the `IndividualBindingSource` is the `CustomerBindingSource`. In the DataMember field, you can see that the `IndividualBindingSource` is binding to the `FK_Individual_Customer_CustomerID` relationship, which of course is the relationship between the Customer table and the Individual table. This relationship will return the collection of rows in the Individual table that relate to the current customer. In this case, there will only ever be a single Individual record, but, for example, if you look at the relationship between an order and the OrderDetails table, there might be a number of entries in the OrderDetails table for any given order.

As you probably have noticed, the Individual table is actually a many-to-many joining table for the Customer and Contact tables. On the Customer side, this is done because a customer might be either an Individual or a Store; and similarly on the Contact side, not all contacts are individual customers.

The Data Sources window doesn't handle this many-to-many relationship very well, because it can only display parent-child (one-to-many) relationships in the tree hierarchy. Under the Contact node there is a link to the Individual table, but this won't help because dragging this onto the form will not link the BindingSources correctly. Unfortunately, there is no out-of-the-box solution to this problem within Visual Studio 2008. However, the following paragraphs introduce a simple component that you can use to give you designer support for many-to-many table relationships.

Begin by completing the layout of the form. For each of the fields under the Contact node, you need to specify whether or not you want it to be displayed. Then set the Contact node to Details, and drag the node onto the form. This will again add a ContactBindingSource and a ContactTableAdapter to the form.

To establish the binding between the IndividualBindingSource and the ContactBindingSource, you need to trap the ListChanged and BindingComplete events on the IndividualBindingSource. Then, using the current record of the IndividualBindingSource, apply a filter to the ContactBindingSource so only related records are displayed. Instead of manually writing this code every time you have to work with a many-to-many relationship, it's wise to create a component to do the work for you, as well as give you design-time support. The following code is divided into three regions. The opening section declares the fields, the constructor, and the Dispose method. This is followed by the Designer Support region, which declares the properties and helper methods that will be invoked to give you design-time support for this component. Lastly, the remaining code traps the two events and places the filter on the appropriate BindingSource:

```vb
Imports System.ComponentModel
Imports System.Drawing.Design

Public Class ManyToMany
    Inherits Component

    Private WithEvents m_LinkingBindingSource As BindingSource
    Private m_Relationship As String
    Private m_TargetBindingSource As BindingSource


    Public Sub New(ByVal container As IContainer)
        MyBase.New()
        container.Add(Me)
    End Sub

    Protected Overrides Sub Dispose(ByVal disposing As Boolean)
        If disposing Then
            Me.TargetBindingSource = Nothing
            Me.Relationship = Nothing
        End If
        MyBase.Dispose(disposing)
    End Sub

#Region "Designer Support"
    Public Property LinkingBindingSource() As BindingSource
        Get
            Return m_LinkingBindingSource
        End Get
```

(continued)

(continued)

```
            Set(ByVal value As BindingSource)
                If Not m_LinkingBindingSource Is value Then
                    m_LinkingBindingSource = value
                End If
            End Set
        End Property


        <RefreshProperties(RefreshProperties.Repaint), _
        Editor("System.Windows.Forms.Design.DataMemberListEditor, System.Design, _
    Version=2.0.0.0, Culture=neutral, PublicKeyToken=b03f5f7f11d50a3a", _
        GetType(UITypeEditor)), DefaultValue("")> _
        Public Property Relationship() As String
            Get
                Return Me.m_Relationship
            End Get
            Set(ByVal value As String)
                If (value Is Nothing) Then
                    value = String.Empty
                End If
                If Me.m_Relationship Is Nothing OrElse _
                                  Not Me.m_Relationship.Equals(value) Then
                    Me.m_Relationship = value
                End If
            End Set
        End Property


        <AttributeProvider(GetType(IListSource)), _
        RefreshProperties(RefreshProperties.Repaint), _
        DefaultValue(CType(Nothing, String))> _
        Public Property TargetBindingSource() As BindingSource
            Get
                Return Me.m_TargetBindingSource
            End Get
            Set(ByVal value As BindingSource)
                If (Me.m_TargetBindingSource IsNot value) Then
                    Me.m_TargetBindingSource = value
                    Me.ClearInvalidDataMember()
                End If
            End Set
        End Property


        <Browsable(False)> _
        Public ReadOnly Property DataSource() As BindingSource
            Get
                Return Me.TargetBindingSource
            End Get
        End Property


        Private Sub ClearInvalidDataMember()
            If Not Me.IsDataMemberValid Then
                Me.Relationship = ""
```

```vb
            End If
        End Sub

        Private Function IsDataMemberValid() As Boolean
            If String.IsNullOrEmpty(Me.Relationship) Then
                Return True
            End If
            Dim collection1 As PropertyDescriptorCollection = _
                        ListBindingHelper.GetListItemProperties(Me.TargetBindingSource)
            Dim descriptor1 As PropertyDescriptor = collection1.Item(Me.Relationship)
            If (Not descriptor1 Is Nothing) Then
                Return True
            End If
            Return False
        End Function
#End Region

#Region "Filtering"
    Private Sub BindingComplete(ByVal sender As System.Object, _
                        ByVal e As System.Windows.Forms.BindingCompleteEventArgs) _
                                    Handles m_LinkingBindingSource.BindingComplete
        BindNow()
    End Sub

    Private Sub ListChanged(ByVal sender As System.Object, _
                    ByVal e As System.ComponentModel.ListChangedEventArgs) _
                                Handles m_LinkingBindingSource.ListChanged
        BindNow()
    End Sub

    Private Sub BindNow()
        Dim src as DataView
        If Me.DesignMode Then Return

        If Me.TargetBindingSource Is Nothing Then Return
        Try
            src = CType(Me.TargetBindingSource.List, DataView)
        Catch ex as Exception
            'We can simply disable filtering if this isn't a List
            Return
        End Try
        Dim childColumn As String = _
                src.Table.ChildRelations(Me.Relationship).ChildColumns(0).ColumnName
        Dim parentColumn As String = _
                src.Table.ChildRelations(Me.Relationship).ParentColumns(0).ColumnName

        Dim filterString As String = ""
        For Each row As DataRowView In LinkingBindingSource.List

            If Not IsDBNull(row(parentColumn)) Then
                If Not filterString = "" Then filterString &= " OR "
                filterString &= childColumn & "= '" & row(parentColumn) & "'"
```

(continued)

(continued)

```
            End If
        Next
        Me.m_TargetBindingSource.Filter = filterString
        Me.m_TargetBindingSource.EndEdit()
    End Sub
#End Region

End Class
```

Adding this component to your solution will add it to the Toolbox, from which it can be dragged onto the nonvisual area on the designer surface. You now need to set the `LinkingBindingSource` property to be the `BindingSource` for the linking table — in this case, the `IndividualBindingSource`. You also have designer support for selecting the `TargetBindingSource` — the `ContactBindingSource` — and the `Relationship`, which in this case is `FK_Individual_Contact_ContactId`. The events on the `LinkingBindingSource` are automatically wired up using the `Handles` keyword, and when triggered they invoke the `BindNow` method, which sets the filter on the `TargetBindingSource`.

When you run this application, you can easily navigate between customer records. In addition, not only is the data from the Customer table displayed; you can also see the information from both the Individual table and the Contact table, as shown in Figure 21-13. Notice that the textbox for the Email Promotion column has been replaced with a checkbox. This can be done the same way that you replaced the TerritoryID textbox: by dragging the checkbox from the Toolbox and then using the DataBindings node in the Properties window to assign the EmailPromotion field to the checked state of the checkbox.

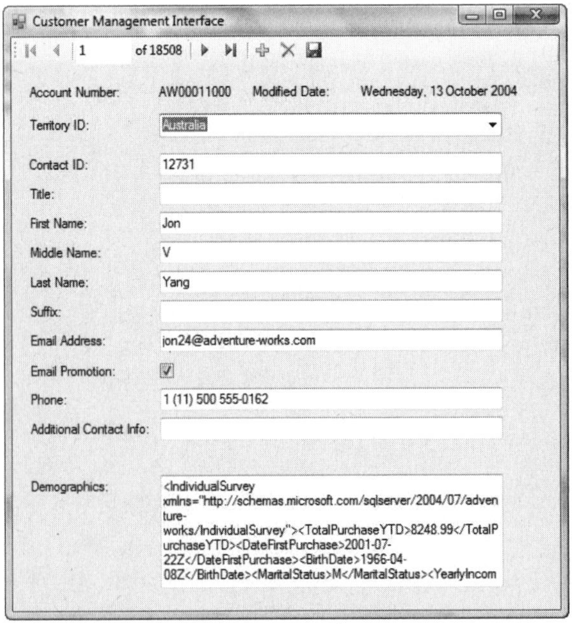

Figure 21-13

Saving Changes

Now that you have a usable interface, you need to add support for making changes and adding new records. If you double-click the Save icon on the `CustomerBindingNavigator` toolstrip, the code window opens with a code stub that would normally save changes to the Customer table. Unlike earlier, when the generated code didn't use the `TableAdapterManager`, the generated portion of this method does. As you can see in the following snippet, there are essentially three steps: the form is validated, each of the `BindingSources` have been instructed to end the current edit (you will need to add the lines of code for the Contact and Individual `BindingSources`), and then the `Update` method is called on the `TableAdapterManager` table adapters. Unfortunately the default `UpdateAll` method doesn't work with this example because it isn't intelligent enough to know that because Individual is a linking table between Customer and Contact, it needs to be saved last to ensure that there are no conflicts when changes are sent to the database:

In the following code, the lines

```
    Me.TableAdapterManager.CustomerTableAdapter.Update(Me.AdventureWorksDataSet
.Customer)
```

and

```
Me.TableAdapterManager.IndividualTableAdapter.Update(Me.AdventureWorksDataSet
.Individual)
```

appear on separate lines to allow for the width of the book page, but they must be entered as one line in your editor or the code will fail.

```
Private Sub CustomerBindingNavigatorSaveItem_Click(ByVal sender As System.Object, _
                                   ByVal e As System.EventArgs) _
                        Handles CustomerBindingNavigatorSaveItem.Click
    Me.Validate()
    Me.ContactBindingSource.EndEdit()
    Me.CustomerBindingSource.EndEdit()
    Me.IndividualBindingSource.EndEdit()
    Me.TableAdapterManager.CustomerTableAdapter.Update( _
                                  Me.AdventureWorksDataSet.Customer)
Me.TableAdapterManager.ContactTableAdapter.Update( _
                                  Me.AdventureWorksDataSet.Contact)
Me.TableAdapterManager.IndividualTableAdapter.Update( _
                                  Me.AdventureWorksDataSet.Individual)
End Sub
```

If you run this, make changes to a customer, and click the Save button, an exception will be thrown because you're currently trying to update calculated fields. You need to correct the `Update` and `Insert` methods used by the `CustomerTableAdapter` to prevent updates to the Account Number column, because it is a calculated field, and to automatically update the Modified Date field. Using the DataSet Designer, select the `CustomerTableAdapter`, open the Properties window, expand the UpdateCommand node, and click the ellipsis button next to the CommandText field. This opens the Query Builder dialog that you used in the previous chapter. Uncheck the boxes in the Set column for the rowguid and AccountNumber rows. In the New Value column, change `@ModifiedDate` to `getdate()`, to automatically set the modified date to the date on which the query was executed. This should give you a query similar to the one shown in Figure 21-14.

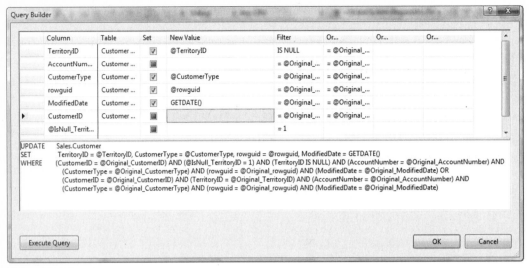

Figure 21-14

Unfortunately, the process of making this change to the Update command causes the parameter list for this command to be reset. Most of the parameters are regenerated correctly except for the IsNull_TerritoryId parameter, which is used to handle cases where the TerritoryID field can be null in the database. To fix this problem, open the Parameter Collection Editor for the Update command and update the settings for the @IsNull_TerritoryId parameter as outlined in Table 21-1.

Table 21-1: Settings for @IsNull_TerritoryId Parameter

Property	Value
AllowObNull	True
ColumnName	
DbType	Int32
Direction	Input
ParameterName	@IsNull_TerritoryID
Precision	0
ProviderType	Int
Scale	0
Size	0
SourceColumn	TerritoryID
SourceColumnNullMapping	False
SourceVersion	Original

Now that you've completed the Update command, not only can you navigate the customers, you can also make changes.

You also need to update the Insert command so it automatically generates both the modification date and the rowguid. Using the Query Builder, update the Insert command to match Figure 21-15.

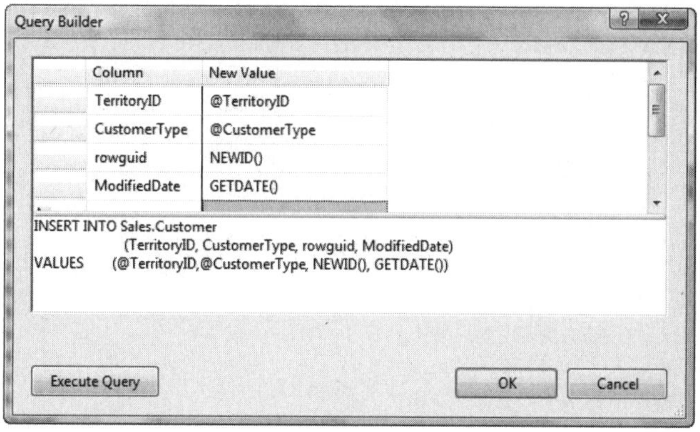

Figure 21-15

Unlike the Update method, you don't need to change any of the parameters for this query. Both the Update and Insert queries for the Individual and Customer tables should work without modifications.

Inserting New Items

You now have a sample application that enables you to browse and make changes to an existing set of individual customers. The one missing piece is the capability to create a new customer. By default, the Add button on the BindingNavigator is automatically wired up to the AddNew method on the BindingSource, as shown earlier in this chapter. In this case, you actually need to set some default values and create entries in both the Individual and Contact tables in addition to the record that is created in the Customer table. To do this, you need to write your own logic behind the Add button.

The first step is to double-click the Add button to create an event handler for it. Make sure that you also remove the automatic wiring by setting the AddNewItem property of the CustomerBindingNavigator to (None); otherwise, you will end up with two records being created every time you click the Add button. You can then modify the default event handler as follows to set initial values for the new customer, as well as create records in the other two tables:

```
Private Const cCustomerType As String = "I"
Private Sub BindingNavigatorAddNewItem_Click(ByVal sender As System.Object, _
                                        ByVal e As System.EventArgs) _
                                     Handles BindingNavigatorAddNewItem.Click

    Dim drv As DataRowView

    'Create record in the Customer table
    drv = TryCast(Me.CustomerBindingSource.AddNew, DataRowView)
    Dim customer = TryCast(drv.Row, AdventureWorksDataSet.CustomerRow)
```

(continued)

(continued)

```
            customer.rowguid = Guid.NewGuid
            customer.CustomerType = cCustomerType
            customer.ModifiedDate = Now
            Me.CustomerBindingSource.EndEdit

            'Create record in the Contact table
            drv = TryCast(Me.ContactBindingSource.AddNew, DataRowView)
            Dim contact = TryCast(drv.Row, AdventureWorksDataSet.ContactRow)
            contact.FirstName = "<first name>"
            contact.LastName = "<last name>"
            contact.EmailPromotion = 0
            contact.NameStyle = True
            contact.PasswordSalt = ""
            contact.PasswordHash = ""
            contact.rowguid = Guid.NewGuid
            contact.ModifiedDate = Now
            contact.rowguid = Guid.NewGuid
            Me.ContactBindingSource.EndEdit

            'Create record in the Individual table
            drv = TryCast(Me.IndividualBindingSource.AddNew, DataRowView)
            Dim individual = TryCast(drv.Row, AdventureWorksDataSet.IndividualRow)
            individual.CustomerRow = cr
            individual.ContactRow = ct
            individual.ModifiedDate = Now
            Me.IndividualBindingSource.EndEdit
    End Sub
```

From this example, it seems that you are unnecessarily setting some of the properties — for example, `PasswordSalt` and `PasswordHash` being equal to an empty string. This is necessary to ensure that the new row meets the constraints established by the database. Because these fields cannot be set by the user, you need to ensure that they are initially set to a value that can be accepted by the database. Clearly, for a secure application, the `PasswordSalt` and `PasswordHash` would be set to appropriate values.

Running the application with this method instead of the automatically wired event handler enables you to create a new Customer record using the Add button. If you enter values for each of the fields, you can save the changes.

Validation

In the previous section, you added functionality to create a new customer record. If you don't enter appropriate data upon creating a new record — for example, if you don't enter a first name — this record will be rejected when you click the Save button. In fact, an exception will be raised if you try to move away from this record. The schema for the `AdventureWorksDataSet` contains a number of constraints, such as `FirstName` can't be null, which are checked when you perform certain actions, such as saving or moving between records. If these checks fail, an exception is raised. You have two options. One, you can trap these exceptions, which is poor programming practice, because exceptions should not be used for execution control. Alternatively, you can pre-empt this by validating the data prior to the schema being checked. Earlier in the chapter, when you learned how the `BindingNavigator` automatically wires the `AddNew` method on the `BindingSource`, you saw that the `OnAddNew` method contains a call to a `Validate` method. This method propagates up and calls the `Validate` method on the active control, which returns a Boolean value that determines whether the action will proceed. This pattern is used by all the automatically wired events and should be used in the event handlers you write for the navigation buttons.

The `Validate` method on the active control triggers two events — Validating and Validated — that occur before and after the validation process, respectively. Because you want to control the validation process, add an event handler for the Validating event. For example, you could add an event handler for the Validating event of the FirstNameTextBox control:

```
Private Sub FirstNameTextBox_Validating(ByVal sender As System.Object, _
                          ByVal e As System.ComponentModel.CancelEventArgs) _
                                        Handles FirstNameTextBox.Validating
        Dim firstNameTxt As TextBox = TryCast(sender, TextBox)
        If firstNameTxt Is Nothing Then Return
        e.Cancel = firstNameTxt.Text = ""
End Sub
```

Though this prevents users from leaving the textbox until a value has been added, it doesn't give them any idea why the application prevents them from proceeding. Luckily, the .NET Framework includes an ErrorProvider control that can be dragged onto the form from the Toolbox. This control behaves in a manner similar to the tooltip control. For each control on the form, you can specify an Error string, which, when set, causes an icon to appear alongside the relevant control, with a suitable tooltip displaying the Error string. This is illustrated in Figure 21-16, where the Error string is set for the FirstNameTextBox.

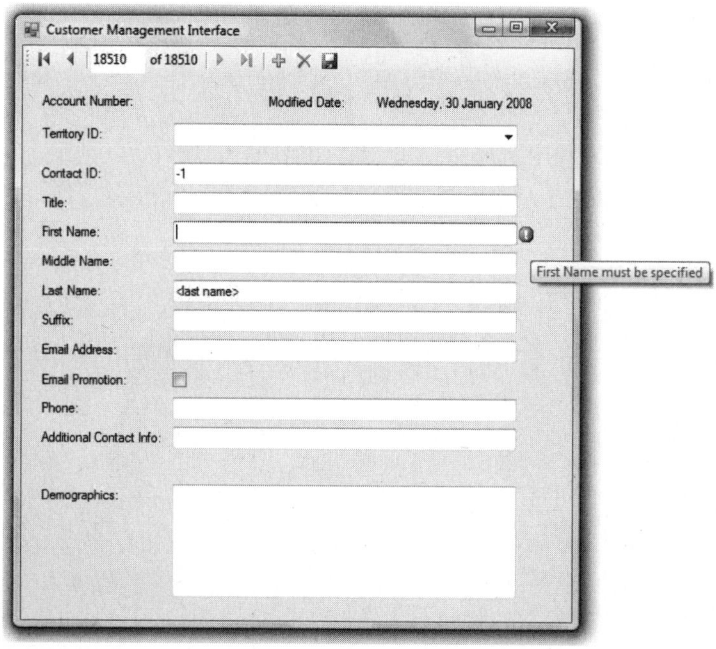

Figure 21-16

Clearly, you want only to set the Error string property for the FirstNameTextBox when there is no text. Following from the earlier example in which you added the event handler for the Validating event, you can modify this code to include setting the Error string:

```
Private Sub FirstNameTextBox_Validating(ByVal sender As System.Object, _
                        ByVal e As System.ComponentModel.CancelEventArgs) _
                                        Handles FirstNameTextBox.Validating
    Dim firstNameTxt As TextBox = TryCast(sender, TextBox)
    If firstNameTxt Is Nothing Then Return
    e.Cancel = firstNameTxt.Text = ""
    If firstNameTxt.Text = "" Then
        Me.ErrorProvider1.SetError(firstNameTxt, "First Name must be specified")
    Else
        Me.ErrorProvider1.SetError(firstNameTxt, Nothing)
    End If
End Sub
```

You can imagine that having to write event handlers that validate and set the error information for each of the controls can be quite a lengthy process, so the following component, for the most part, gives you designer support:

```
Imports System.ComponentModel
Imports System.Drawing.Design

<ProvideProperty("Validate", GetType(Control))> _
Public Class ControlValidator
    Inherits Component
    Implements IExtenderProvider

#Region "Rules Validator"
    Private Structure Validator
        Public Rule As Predicate(Of IRulesList.RuleParams)
        Public Information As ValidationAttribute
        Public Sub New(ByVal r As Predicate(Of IRulesList.RuleParams), _
                    ByVal info As ValidationAttribute)
            Me.Rule = r
            Me.Information = info
        End Sub
    End Structure
#End Region

    Private m_ErrorProvider As ErrorProvider
    Private rulesHash As New Dictionary(Of String, Validator)
    Public controlHash As New Dictionary(Of Control, Boolean)

    Public Sub New(ByVal container As IContainer)
        MyBase.New()
        container.Add(Me)
    End Sub

#Region "Error provider and Rules"

    Public Property ErrorProvider() As ErrorProvider
```

```vbnet
        Get
            Return m_ErrorProvider
        End Get
        Set(ByVal value As ErrorProvider)
            m_ErrorProvider = value
        End Set
    End Property

    Public Sub AddRules(ByVal ruleslist As IRulesList)
        For Each rule As Predicate(Of IRulesList.RuleParams) In ruleslist.Rules
            Dim attributes As ValidationAttribute() = _
                    TryCast(rule.Method.GetCustomAttributes _
                            (GetType(ValidationAttribute), True), _
                                        ValidationAttribute())
            If Not attributes Is Nothing Then
                For Each attrib As ValidationAttribute In attributes
                    rulesHash.Add(attrib.ColumnName.ToLower, _
                                        New Validator(rule, attrib))
                Next
            End If
        Next
    End Sub
#End Region

#Region "Extender Provider to turn validation on"
    Public Function CanExtend(ByVal extendee As Object) As Boolean _
                    Implements System.ComponentModel.IExtenderProvider.CanExtend
        Return TypeOf (extendee) Is Control
    End Function

    Public Sub SetValidate(ByVal control As Control, _
                        ByVal shouldValidate As Boolean)
        If shouldValidate Then
            AddHandler control.Validating, AddressOf Validating
        End If
        controlHash.Item(control) = shouldValidate
    End Sub

    Public Function GetValidate(ByVal control As Control) As Boolean
        If controlHash.ContainsKey(control) Then
            Return controlHash.Item(control)
        End If
        Return False
    End Function
#End Region

#Region "Validation"
    Private ReadOnly Property ItemError(ByVal ctrl As Control) As String
        Get
            Try
                If ctrl.DataBindings.Count = 0 Then Return ""
                Dim key As String = ctrl.DataBindings.Item(0).BindingMemberInfo
.BindingField
                Dim bs As BindingSource =
TryCast(ctrl.DataBindings.Item(0).DataSource, BindingSource)
```

(continued)

(continued)

```vb
                    If bs Is Nothing Then Return ""
                    Dim drv As DataRowView = TryCast(bs.Current, DataRowView)
                    If drv Is Nothing Then Return ""

                    Dim valfield As String = ctrl.DataBindings.Item(0).PropertyName
                    Dim val As Object = ctrl.GetType.GetProperty(valfield, _
                                            New Type() {}).GetValue(ctrl, Nothing)
                    Return ItemError(drv, key, val)
                Catch ex As Exception
                    Return ""
                End Try
            End Get
        End Property

        Private ReadOnly Property ItemError(ByVal drv As DataRowView, ByVal columnName _
    As String, ByVal newValue As Object) As String
            Get
                columnName = columnName.ToLower
                If Not rulesHash.ContainsKey(columnName) Then Return ""
                Dim p As Validator = rulesHash.Item(columnName)
                If p.Rule Is Nothing Then Return ""
                If p.Rule(New IRulesList.RuleParams(drv.Row, newValue)) Then Return ""

                If p.Information Is Nothing Then Return ""
                Return p.Information.ErrorString
            End Get
        End Property

        Private Sub Validating(ByVal sender As Object, ByVal e As CancelEventArgs)
            Dim err As String = InternalValidate(sender)
            e.Cancel = Not (err = "")
        End Sub

        Private Function InternalValidate(ByVal sender As Object) As String
            If Me.m_ErrorProvider Is Nothing Then Return ""
            Dim ctrl As Control = TryCast(sender, Control)
            If ctrl Is Nothing Then Return ""
            If Not Me.controlHash.ContainsKey(ctrl) OrElse Not Me.controlHash.Item(ctrl) _
    Then Return ""
            Dim err As String = Me.ItemError(ctrl)
            Me.m_ErrorProvider.SetError(ctrl, err)
            Return err
        End Function

        Private Sub ChangedItem(ByVal sender As Object, ByVal e As EventArgs)
            InternalValidate(sender)
        End Sub
#End Region

#Region "Validation Attribute"
    <AttributeUsage(AttributeTargets.Method)> _
```

```vb
    Public Class ValidationAttribute
        Inherits Attribute

        Private m_ColumnName As String
        Private m_ErrorString As String

        Public Sub New(ByVal columnName As String, ByVal errorString As String)
            Me.ColumnName = columnName
            Me.ErrorString = errorString
        End Sub

        Public Property ColumnName() As String
            Get
                Return m_ColumnName
            End Get
            Set(ByVal value As String)
                m_ColumnName = value
            End Set
        End Property

        Public Property ErrorString() As String
            Get
                Return m_ErrorString
            End Get
            Set(ByVal value As String)
                m_ErrorString = value
            End Set
        End Property
    End Class
#End Region

#Region "Rules Interface"
    Public Interface IRulesList

        Structure RuleParams
            Public ExistingData As DataRow
            Public NewData As Object
            Public Sub New(ByVal data As DataRow, ByVal newStuff As Object)
                Me.ExistingData = data
                Me.NewData = newStuff
            End Sub
        End Structure

        ReadOnly Property Rules() As Predicate(Of RuleParams)()

    End Interface
#End Region
End Class
```

The ControlValidator has a number of parts that work together to validate and provide error information. First, to enable validation of a control, the ControlValidator exposes an Extender Provider, which allows you to indicate whether the ControlValidator on the form should be used for validation.

The right pane in Figure 21-17 shows the Properties window for the FirstNameTextBox, in which the `Validate` property has been set to `True`. When the FirstNameTextBox is validated, the ControlValidator1 control will be given the opportunity to validate the `FirstName` property.

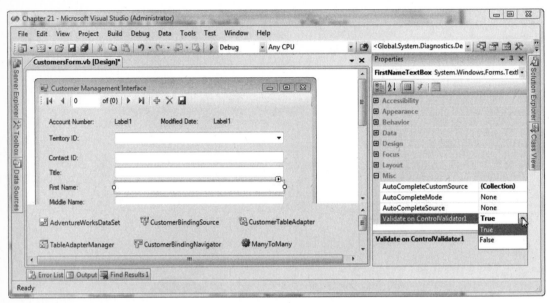

Figure 21-17

The ControlValidator has an `ErrorProvider` property that can be used to specify an ErrorProvider control on the form. This is not a requirement, however, and validation will proceed without one being specified. If this property is set, the validation process will automatically set the Error string property for the control being validated.

What you're currently missing is a set of business rules to use for validation. This is accomplished using a rules class that implements the `IRulesList` interface. Each rule is a predicate — in other words, a method that returns true or false based on a condition. The following code defines a `CustomerValidationRules` class that exposes two rules that determine whether the First Name and TerritoryID fields contain valid data. Each rule is attributed with the `ValidationAttribute`, which determines the column that the rule validates, and the Error string, which can be displayed if the validation fails. The column specified in the `Validation` attribute needs to match the field to which the control is data-bound:

```
Imports System
Imports CustomerBrowser.ControlValidator
Public Class CustomerValidationRules
    Implements IRulesList

    Public Shared ReadOnly Property Instance() As CustomerValidationRules
        Get
            Return New CustomerValidationRules
        End Get
```

```
            End Property

    Public ReadOnly Property Rules() As Predicate(Of IRulesList.RuleParams)() _
                                            Implements IRulesList.Rules
        Get
            Return New Predicate(Of IRulesList.RuleParams)() { _
                                        AddressOf TerritoryId, _
                                        AddressOf FirstName}
        End Get
    End Property

    <Validation("TerritoryID", "TerritoryID must be >0")> _
        Public Function TerritoryId(ByVal data As IRulesList.RuleParams) As Boolean
        Try
            If Not TypeOf (data.NewData) Is Integer Then Return False
            Dim newVal As Integer = CInt(data.NewData)
            If newVal > 0 Then Return True
            Return False
        Catch ex As Exception
            Return False
        End Try
    End Function

    <Validation("FirstName", "First Name must be specified")> _
    Public Function FirstName(ByVal data As IRulesList.RuleParams) As Boolean
        Try
            Dim newVal As String = TryCast(data.NewData, String)
            If newVal = "" Then Return False
            Return True
        Catch ex As Exception
            Return False
        End Try
    End Function
End Class
```

The last task that remains is to add the following line to the form's Load method to associate this rules class to the ControlValidator:

```
Me.ControlValidator1.AddRules(CustomerValidationRules.Instance)
```

To add more rules to this form, all you need to do is add the rule to the CustomerValidationRules class and enable validation for the appropriate control.

DataGridView

So far you've been working with standard controls, and you've seen how the BindingNavigator enables you to scroll through a list of items. Sometimes it is more convenient to display a list of items in a grid. This is where the DataGridView is useful, because it enables you to combine the power of the BindingSource with a grid layout.

Extending the Customer Management interface, add the list of orders to the form using the DataGridView. Returning to the Data Sources window, select the SalesOrderHeader node from under the Customer node. From the drop-down list, select DataGridView and drag the node into an empty area on the form. This adds the appropriate `BindingSource` and `TableAdapter` to the form, as well as a DataGridView showing each of the columns in the SalesOrderHeader table, as shown in Figure 21-18.

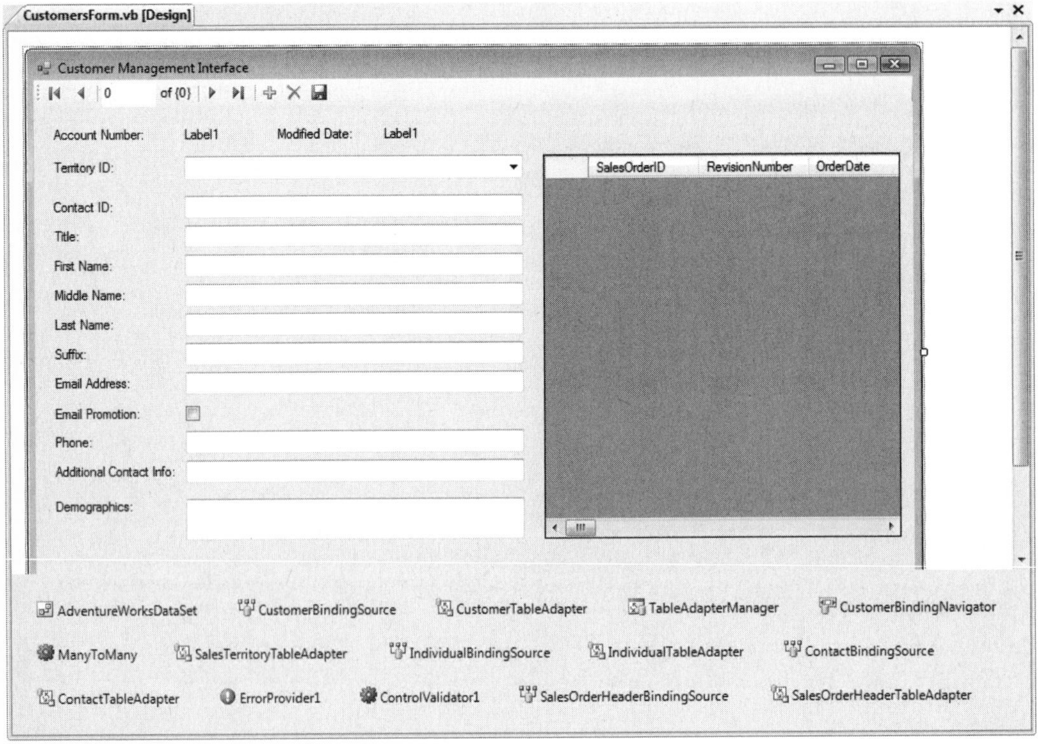

Figure 21-18

Unlike working with the Details layout, when you drag the DataGridView onto the form it ignores any settings you might have specified for the individual columns. Instead, every column is added to the grid as a simple text field. To modify the list of columns that are displayed, you can either use the smart tag for the newly added DataGridView or select Edit Columns from the right-click context menu. This will open the Edit Columns dialog (shown in Figure 21-19), in which columns can be added, removed, and reordered.

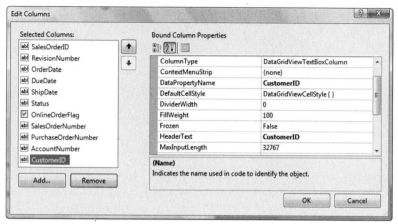

Figure 21-19

After specifying the appropriate columns, the finished application can be run, and the list of orders will be visible for each customer in the database.

Object Data Source

In a number of projects, an application is broken up into multiple tiers. Quite often it is not possible to pass around strongly typed DataSets, because they may be quite large, or perhaps the project requires custom business objects. In either case, it is possible to take the DataBinding techniques you just learned for DataSets and apply them to objects. For the purposes of this discussion, use the following Customer and SalesOrder classes:

```vb
Public Class Customer
    Private m_Name As String
    Public Property Name() As String
        Get
            Return m_Name
        End Get
        Set(ByVal value As String)
            m_Name = value
        End Set
    End Property

    Private m_Orders As New List(Of SalesOrder)
    Public Property Orders() As List(Of SalesOrder)
        Get
            Return m_Orders
        End Get
        Set(ByVal value As List(Of SalesOrder))
            m_Orders = value
        End Set
    End Property
End Class
```

(continued)

(continued)

```
Public Class SalesOrder
    Implements System.ComponentModel.IDataErrorInfo

    Private m_Description As String
    Public Property Description() As String
        Get
            Return m_Description
        End Get
        Set(ByVal value As String)
            m_Description = value
        End Set
    End Property

    Private m_Quantity As Integer
    Public Property Quantity() As Integer
        Get
            Return m_Quantity
        End Get
        Set(ByVal value As Integer)
            m_Quantity = value
        End Set
    End Property

    Private m_DateOrdered As Date
    Public Property DateOrdered() As Date
        Get
            Return m_DateOrdered
        End Get
        Set(ByVal value As Date)
            m_DateOrdered = value
        End Set
    End Property

    Public ReadOnly Property ErrorSummary() As String _
                            Implements System.ComponentModel.IDataErrorInfo.Error
        Get
            Dim summary As New System.Text.StringBuilder
            Dim err As String = ErrorItem("Description")
            If Not err = "" Then summary.AppendLine(err)
            err = ErrorItem("Quantity")
            If Not err = "" Then summary.AppendLine(err)
            err = ErrorItem("DateOrdered")
            If Not err = "" Then summary.AppendLine(err)
            Return summary.ToString
        End Get
    End Property

    Default Public ReadOnly Property ErrorItem(ByVal columnName As String) _
                    As String Implements System.ComponentModel.IDataErrorInfo.Item
        Get
            Select Case columnName
                Case "Description"
                    If Me.m_Description = "" Then _
```

```
                           Return "Need to order item description"
               Case "Quantity"
                   If Me.m_Quantity <= 0 Then _
                           Return "Need to supply quantity of order"
               Case "DateOrdered"
                   If Me.m_DateOrdered > Now Then _
                           Return "Need to specify a date in the past"
           End Select
           Return ""
        End Get
      End Property
   End Class
```

To use DataBinding with custom objects, follow roughly the same process as you did with DataSets. Add a new data source via the Data Sources window. This time, select an Object Data Source type. Doing so will display a list of available classes within the solution, as shown in Figure 21-20.

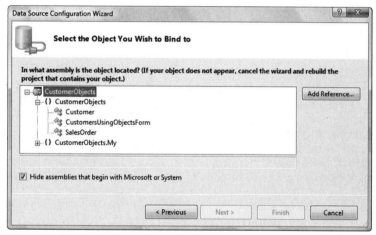

Figure 21-20

Select the Customer class and complete the wizard to add the Customer class, along with the nested list of orders, to the Data Sources window, as shown in Figure 21-21.

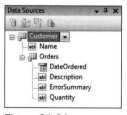

Figure 21-21

As you did previously, you can select the type of control you want for each of the fields before dragging the Customer node onto the form. Doing so adds a `CustomerBindingSource` and a `CustomerNavigator` to the form. If you set the Orders list to be a DataGridView and drag that onto the form, you will end up with the layout shown in Figure 21-22. As you did previously with the DataGridView, again opt to modify the default list of columns using the Edit Columns dialog accessible from the smart tag dialog.

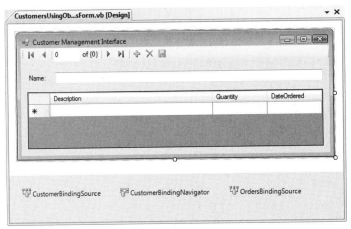

Figure 21-22

Unlike binding to a DataSet that has a series of TableAdapters to extract data from a database, there is no automatically generated fill mechanism for custom objects. The process of generating the customer objects is usually handled elsewhere in the application. All you have to do here is issue the following code snippet to link the existing list of customers to the `CustomerBindingSource` so they can be displayed:

```
Private Sub Form1_Load(ByVal sender As System.Object, _
                        ByVal e As System.EventArgs) Handles MyBase.Load
    Me.CustomerBindingSource.DataSource = GetCustomers()
End Sub

Public Function GetCustomers() As Customer()
    'Populate customers list..... eg from webservice
    Dim cust As Customer() = New Customer() { _
                            New Customer With {.Name = "Joe Blogs"}, _
                            New Customer With {.Name = "Sarah Burner"}, _
                            New Customer With {.Name = "Matt Swift"}, _
                            New Customer With {.Name = "Barney Jones"}}

    Return cust
End Function
```

Running this application provides a simple interface for working with customer objects.

IDataErrorInfo

You will notice in the code provided earlier that the `SalesOrder` object implements the `IDataErrorInfo` interface. This is an interface that is understood by the DataGridView and can be used to validate custom objects. As you did in the earlier application, you need to add an ErrorProvider to the form. Instead of manually wiring up events in the ErrorProvider control, in conjunction with the DataGridView use the `IDataErrorInfo` interface to validate the `SalesOrder` objects. The running application is shown in Figure 21-23, where an invalid date and no quantity have been specified for a `SalesOrder`.

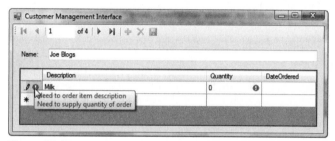

Figure 21-23

The icon at the end of the row provides a summary of all the errors. This is determined by calling the `Error` property of the `IDataError` interface. Each of the columns in turn provides an icon to indicate which cells are in error. This is determined by calling the `Item` property of the `IDataError` interface.

Working with Data Sources

At the beginning of the chapter you created a strongly typed DataSet that contains a number of rows from the Contact table, based on a `Title` parameter. The DataSet is contained within a class library, *ContactDataAccess*, that you are going to expose to your application via a web service. To do this, you need to add a Windows application, *ContactBrowser*, and an ASP.NET web service application, *ContactServices*, to your solution. This demonstrates how you can use Visual Studio 2008 to build a true multi-tier application.

> *Because this section involves working with ASP.NET applications, it is recommended that you run Visual Studio 2008 in Administrator mode if you are running Windows Vista. This will allow the debugger to be attached to the appropriate process.*

In the Web Service project, you will add a reference to the class library. You also need to modify the `Service` class file so it has two methods, in place of the default `HelloWorld` web method:

```
Imports System.Web.Services
Imports System.Web.Services.Protocols
Imports System.ComponentModel
Imports ContactDataAccess

<System.Web.Services.WebService(Namespace:="http://tempuri.org/")> _
<System.Web.Services.WebServiceBinding(ConformsTo:=WsiProfiles.BasicProfile1_1)> _
```

(continued)

(continued)

```
    <ToolboxItem(False)> _
    Public Class Service
        Inherits System.Web.Services.WebService

        <WebMethod()> _
        Public Function RetrieveContacts(ByVal Title As String) _
                        As AdventureWorksDataSet.ContactDataTable
            Dim ta As New AdventureWorksDataSetTableAdapters.ContactTableAdapter
            Return ta.GetData(Title)
        End Function

        <WebMethod()> _
        Public Sub SaveContacts(ByVal changes As Data.DataSet)
            Dim changesTable As Data.DataTable = changes.Tables(0)
            Dim ta As New AdventureWorksDataSetTableAdapters.ContactTableAdapter
            ta.Update(changesTable.Select)
        End Sub
    End Class
```

The first web method, as the name suggests, retrieves the list of contacts based on the `promotionalcategory` that is passed in. In this method, you create a new instance of the strongly typed TableAdapter and return the DataTable retrieved by the `GetData` method. The second web method is used to save changes to a DataTable, again using the strongly typed TableAdapter. As you will notice, the DataSet that is passed in as a parameter to this method is not strongly typed. Unfortunately, the generated strongly typed DataSet doesn't provide a strongly typed `GetChanges` method, which will be used later to generate a DataSet containing only data that has changed. This new DataSet is passed into the `SaveContacts` method so that only changed data needs to be sent to the web service.

Web Service Data Source

These changes to the web service complete the server side of the process, but your application still doesn't have access to this data. To access the data from your application, you need to add a data source to the application. Again, use the Add New Data Source Wizard, but this time select Service from the Data Source Type screen. To add a Web Service Data Source you then need to click Advanced, followed by Add Web Reference. Add the Web Service Data Source via the Add Web Reference dialog, as shown in Figure 21-24.

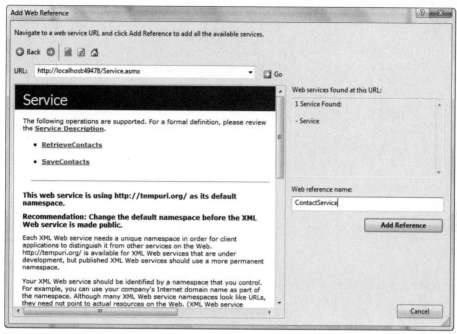

Figure 21-24

Clicking the "Web services in this solution" link displays a list of web services available in your solution. The web service that you have just been working on should appear in this list. When you click the hyperlink for that web service, the Add Reference button is enabled. Clicking the Add Reference button will add an AdventureWorksDataSet to the Data Sources window under the ContactService node. Expanding this node, you will see that the data source is very similar to the data source you had in the class library.

Browsing Data

To actually view the data being returned via the web service, you need to add some controls to your form. Open the form so the designer appears in the main window. In the Data Sources window, click the Contact node and select Details from the drop-down. This indicates that when you drag the Contact node onto the form, Visual Studio 2008 will create controls to display the details of the Contact table (for example, the row contents), instead of the default DataGridView. Next, select the attributes you want to display by clicking them and selecting the control type to use. For this scenario, select None for NameStyle, Suffix, and Phone. When you drag the Contact node onto the form, you should end up with the layout shown in Figure 21-25.

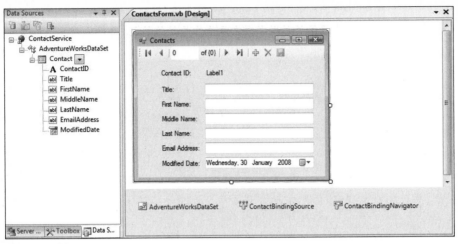

Figure 21-25

In addition to adding controls for the information to be displayed and edited, a Navigator control has also been added to the top of the form, and an `AdventureWorksDataSet` and a `ContactBindingSource` have been added to the nonvisual area of the form.

The final stage is to wire up the `Load` event of the form to retrieve data from the web service, and to add the Save button on the navigator to save changes. Right-click the save icon and select Enabled to enable the Save button on the navigator control, and then double-click the save icon to generate the stub event handler. Add the following code to load data and save changes via the web service you created earlier:

```vb
Public Class Form1

    Private Sub Form1_Load(ByVal sender As System.Object, _
                            ByVal e As System.EventArgs) Handles MyBase.Load
        Me.ContactBindingSource.DataSource = _
                            My.WebServices.Service.RetrieveContacts("%mr%")

    End Sub

    Private Sub ContactBindingNavigatorSaveItem_Click _
                (ByVal sender As System.Object, ByVal e As System.EventArgs) _
                            Handles ContactBindingNavigatorSaveItem.Click
        Me.ContactBindingSource.EndEdit()
        Dim ds = CType(Me.ContactBindingSource.DataSource, _
                            ContactService.AdventureWorksDataSet.ContactDataTable)
        Dim changesTable As DataTable = ds.GetChanges()
        Dim changes as New DataSet
        changes.Tables.Add(changesTable)
        My.WebServices.Service.SaveContacts(changes)
    End Sub
End Class
```

To retrieve the list of contacts from the web service, all you need to do is call the appropriate web method — in this case, RetrieveContacts. Pass in a parameter of %mr%, which indicates that only contacts with a Title containing the letters "mr" should be returned. The Save method is slightly more complex, because you have to end the current edit (to make sure all changes are saved), retrieve the DataTable, and then extract the changes as a new DataTable. Although it would be simpler to pass a DataTable to the SaveContacts web service, only DataSets can be specified as parameters or return values to a web service. As such, you can create a new DataSet and add the changes DataTable to the list of tables. The new DataSet is then passed into the SaveContacts method. As mentioned previously, the GetChanges method returns a raw DataTable, which is unfortunate because it limits the strongly typed data scenario.

This completes the chapter's coverage of the strongly typed DataSet scenario, and provides you with a two-tiered solution for accessing and editing data from a database via a web service interface.

Summary

This chapter provided an introduction to working with strongly typed DataSets. Support within Visual Studio 2008 for creating and working with strongly typed DataSets simplifies the rapid building of applications. This is clearly the first step in the process of bridging the gap between the object-oriented programming world and the relational world in which the data is stored.

It is hoped that this chapter has given you an appreciation for how the BindingSource, BindingNavigator, and other data controls work together to give you the ability to rapidly build data applications. Because the new controls support working with either DataSets or your own custom objects, they can significantly reduce the amount of time it takes you to write an application.

22

Visual Database Tools

Database connectivity is almost essential in every application you create, regardless of whether it's a Windows-based program or a web-based site or service. When Visual Studio .NET was first introduced, it provided developers with a great set of options to navigate to the database files on their file systems and local servers, with a Server Explorer, data controls, and data-bound components. The underlying .NET Framework included ADO.NET, a retooled database engine that works most efficiently in a disconnected world, which is becoming more prevalent today.

Visual Studio 2008 took those features and smoothed out the kinks, adding tools and functionality to the IDE to give you more direct access to the data in your application. This chapter looks at how you can implement data-based solutions with the tools provided in Visual Studio 2008, which can be collectively referred to as the Visual Database Tools.

Database Windows in Visual Studio 2008

A number of windows specifically deal with databases and their components. From the Data Sources window that shows project-related data files and the Data Connections node in the Server Explorer, to the Database Diagram Editor and the visual designer for database schemas, you'll find most of what you need directly within the IDE. In fact, it's unlikely that you'll need to venture outside of Visual Studio for most application solutions to editing database settings.

Figure 22-1 shows the Visual Studio 2008 IDE with a current database editing session. Notice how the windows, toolbars, and menus all update to match the particular context of editing a database table. In Figure 22-1, you can see the Table Designer menu, along with the Column Properties editing region below the list of columns. The normal Properties tool window contains the properties for the current table. The next few pages take a look at each of these windows and describe their purposes so you can use them effectively.

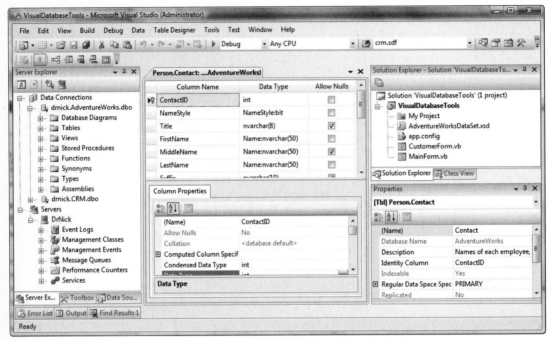

Figure 22-1

Server Explorer

In Chapter 19, you saw how the Server Explorer can be used to navigate the components that make up your system (or indeed the components of any server to which you can connect). One component of this tool window that was omitted from that discussion is the Data Connections node. Through this node Visual Studio 2008 provides a significant subset of the functionality that is available through other products, such as SQL Server Management Studio, for creating and modifying databases.

Figure 22-1 shows the Server Explorer window with an active database connection (`drnick` `.AdventureWorks.dbo`) and another database that Visual Studio is not currently connected to (`drnick` `.CRM.dbo`). The database icon displays whether or not you are actively connected to the database, and contains a number of child nodes dealing with the typical components of a modern database, such as Tables, Views, and Stored Procedures. Expanding these nodes will list the specific database components along with their details. For example, the Tables node contains a node for the Contact table, which in turn has nodes for each of the columns, such as FirstName, LastName, and Phone. Clicking these nodes enables you to quickly view the properties within the Properties tool window.

To add a new database connection to the Server Explorer window, click the Connect to Database button at the top of the Server Explorer, or right-click the Data Connections root node and select the Add Connection command from the context menu.

If this is the first time you have added a connection, Visual Studio will ask you what type of data source you are connecting to. Visual Studio 2008 comes packaged with a number of data source connectors, including Access, SQL Server, and Oracle, as well as a generic ODBC driver. It also includes a data source connector for Microsoft SQL Server Database File and Microsoft SQL Server Compact Edition databases.

The Database File option was introduced in SQL Server 2005 and borrows from the easy deployment model of its lesser cousins, Microsoft Access and MSDE. With SQL Server Database File, you can create a flat file for an individual database. This means you don't need to store it in the SQL Server database repository, and it's highly portable — you simply deliver the `.mdf` file containing the database along with your application. Alternatively, using a SQL Server Compact Edition (SSCE) database can significantly reduce the system requirements for your application. Instead of requiring an instance of SQL Server to be installed, the SSCE runtime can be deployed alongside your application.

Once you've chosen the data source type to use, the Add Connection dialog appears. Figure 22-2 shows this dialog for a SQL Server Database File connection, with the settings appropriate to that data source type. You are taken directly to this dialog if you already have data connections defined in Visual Studio.

Figure 22-2

The Change button returns you to the Data Sources page, enabling you to add multiple types of database connections to your Visual Studio session. Note how easy it is to create a SQL Server Database File. Just type or browse to the location where you want the file and specify the database name for a new database. If you want to connect to an existing database, use the Browse button to locate it on the file system.

Generally, the only other task you need to perform is to specify whether your SQL Server configuration is using Windows or SQL Server Authentication. The default installation of Visual Studio 2008 includes an installation of SQL Server 2005 Express, which uses Windows Authentication as its base authentication model.

The Test Connection button displays an error message if you try to connect to a new database. This is because it doesn't exist until you click OK, so there's nothing to connect to!

When you click OK, Visual Studio attempts to connect to the database. If successful, it adds it to the Data Connections node, including the children nodes for the main data types in the database, as discussed earlier.

If the database doesn't exist and you've chosen a connection type such as SQL Server Database File, Visual Studio 2008 will also attempt to create the database file for you.

Table Editing

The easiest way to edit a table in the database is to double-click its entry in the Server Explorer. An editing window is then displayed in the main workspace, consisting of two components. The top section is where you specify each field name, data type, and key information such as length for text fields, and whether the field is nullable.

Right-clicking a field gives you access to a set of commands that you can perform against that field, as shown in Figure 22-3. This context menu contains the same items as the Table Designer menu that is displayed while you're editing a table, but it is usually easier to use the context menu because you can easily determine which field you're referring to.

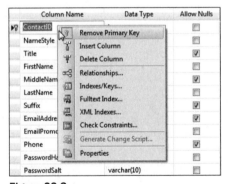

Figure 22-3

The lower half of the table editing workspace contains the Column Properties window for the currently selected column. Unlike the grid area that simply lists the Column Name, Data Type, and whether the column allows nulls, the column properties area allows you to specify all of the available properties for the particular data source type.

Figure 22-4 shows a sample Column Properties window for a field, ContactID, that has been defined with an identity clause that is automatically incremented by 1 for each new record added to the table.

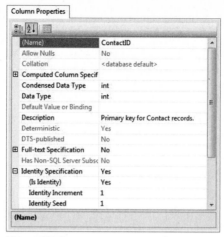

Figure 22-4

Relationship Editing

Most databases that are likely to be used by your .NET solutions are relational in nature, which means you connect tables together by defining relationships. To create a relationship, select one of the tables that you need to connect to and click the Relationships button on the toolbar, or use the Table Designer ⇨ Relationships menu command. The Foreign Key Relationships dialog is displayed (see Figure 22-5), containing any existing relationships that are bound to the table you selected.

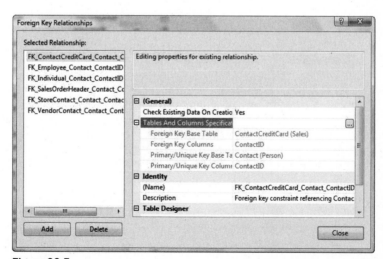

Figure 22-5

Click the Add button to create a new relationship, or select one of the existing relationships to edit. Locate the Tables and Columns Specification entry in the property grid and click its associated ellipsis to set the tables and columns that should connect to each other. In the Tables and Columns dialog, shown in Figure 22-6, first choose which table contains the primary key to which the table you selected will connect. Note that for new relationships the "Foreign key table" field is populated with the current table name and cannot be changed.

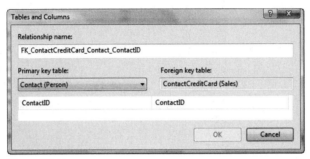

Figure 22-6

Once you have the primary key table, you then connect the fields in each table that should bind to each other. You can add multiple fields to the relationship by clicking the blank row that is added as you add the previous field. When you are satisfied with the relationship settings, click OK to save it and return to the Foreign Key Relationships dialog.

Views

Views are predefined queries that can appear like tables to your application and can be made up of multiple tables. Use the Data ⇨ Add New ⇨ View menu command or right-click the Views node in Server Explorer and choose Add New View from the context menu.

The first task is to choose which tables, other views, functions, and synonyms will be included in the current view. When you've chosen which components will be added, the View editor window is displayed (see Figure 22-7). This editor should be familiar to anyone who has worked with a visual database designer such as Access. The tables and other components are visible in the top area, where you can select the fields you want included. The top area also shows connections between any functions and tables. If you need to add additional tables, right-click the design surface and select Add Table.

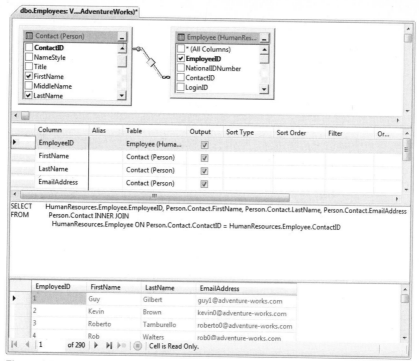

Figure 22-7

The middle area shows a tabular representation of your current selection, and adds columns for sorting and filtering properties, and the area directly beneath the tabular representation shows the SQL that is used to achieve the view you've specified. Changes can be made in any of these three panes with the other panes being dynamically updated with the changes.

The bottom part of the view designer can be used to execute the view SQL and preview the results. To execute this view, select Execute SQL from the right-click context menu on any of the panes, or the button with the same name from the View Designer toolbar.

Stored Procedures and Functions

To create and modify stored procedures and functions, Visual Studio 2008 uses a text editor such as the one shown in Figure 22-8. Although there is no IntelliSense to help you create your procedure and function definitions, Visual Studio doesn't allow you to save your code if it detects an error.

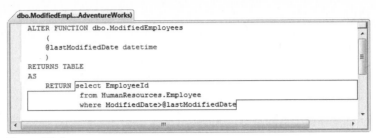

Figure 22-8

For instance, if the SQL function in Figure 22-8 were written as shown in the following code listing, Visual Studio would display a dialog upon an attempted save, indicating a syntax error near the closing parenthesis because of the extra comma after the parameter definition:

```
alter function dbo.ModifiedEmployees
    (
    @lastModifiedDate datetime,
    )
returns table
as
    return select EmployeeId
           from   HumanResources.Employee
           where  ModifiedDate > @lastModifiedDate
```

To help you write and debug your stored procedures and functions, there are shortcuts to insert SQL, Run Selection, and Execute from the right-click context menu for the text editor. Inserting SQL will display the Query Builder shown earlier in Figure 22-7 as a modal dialog. Run Selection will attempt to execute any selected SQL statements, displaying the results in the Output window. Finally, the Execute shortcut will run the entire stored procedure or function. If they accept input parameters a dialog similar to Figure 22-9 will be displayed, in which you can specify appropriate test values. Again, the results will be displayed in the Output window.

Run Function

The function <[dbo].[ModifiedEmployees]> requires the following parameters:

Type	Direction	Name	Value
datetime	In	@lastModifiedDate	<DEFAULT>

OK   Cancel

Figure 22-9

Database Diagrams

You can also create a visual representation of your database tables via database diagrams. To create a diagram, use the Data ⇨ Add New ⇨ Diagram menu command or right-click the Database Diagrams node in the Server Explorer and choose Add New Diagram from the context menu.

When you create your first diagram in a database, Visual Studio may prompt you to allow it to automatically add necessary system tables and data to the database. If you disallow this action, you won't be able to create diagrams at all; so it's just a notification, rather than an optional action to take.

The initial process of creating a diagram enables you to choose which tables you want in the diagram, but you can add tables later through the Database Diagram menu that is added to the IDE. You can use this menu to affect the appearance of your diagram within the editor too, with zoom and page break preview functionality as well as being able to toggle relationship names on and off.

Because database diagrams can be quite large, the IDE has an easy way of navigating around the diagram. In the lower right corner of the Database Diagram editor in the workspace is an icon displaying a four-way arrow. Click this icon and a thumbnail view of the diagram appears, as shown in Figure 22-10.

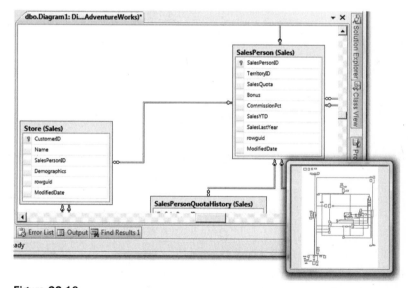

Figure 22-10

Just click and drag the mouse pointer around the thumbnail until you position the components you need to view and work with in the viewable area of the IDE.

Data Sources Window

One more window deserves explanation before you move on to actually using the database in your projects and solutions. The Data Sources window, which shares space with the Solution Explorer in the IDE, contains any active data sources known to the project (as opposed to the Data Connections in the Server Explorer, which are known to Visual Studio overall). To display the Data Sources tool window, use the Data ⇨ Show Data Sources menu command.

The Data Sources window has two main views, depending on the active document in the workspace area of the IDE. When you are editing code, the Data Sources window will display tables and fields with icons representing their types. This aids you as you write code because you can quickly reference the type without having to look at the table definition. This view is shown on the right image of Figure 22-11.

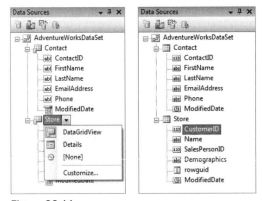

Figure 22-11

When you're editing a form in Design view, however, the Data Sources view changes to display the tables and fields with icons representing their current default control types (initially set in the Data UI Customization page of Options). The left image of Figure 22-11 shows that the text fields use TextBox controls, whereas the ModifiedDate field will use a DateTimePicker control. The icons for the tables indicate that all tables will be inserted as DataGridView components by default as shown in the drop-down list.

As you saw in the previous chapter, adding a data source is relatively straightforward. If the Data Sources window is currently empty, the main space will contain an Add a New Data Source link. Otherwise, click the Add New Data Source button at the top of the tool window, or use the Data ⇨ Add New Data Source menu command. In the Data Source Configuration Wizard that is displayed, you will be stepped through selecting the data source type, connection details, and finally what data elements you want to appear in the data source.

Editing Data Source Schemas

Once you have added a data source you can always go back and change it by selecting the Configure DataSet with Wizard item from the right-click context menu off the relevant node in the Data Sources window. However, in some cases the wizard doesn't give you the flexibility to customize the data source.

To do this you need to select Edit DataSet with Designer from the same shortcut menu. Shown in Figure 22-12, this designer displays a visual representation of each of the tables and views defined in the data source, along with any relationships that connect them.

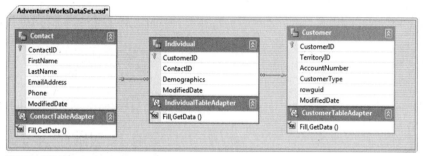

Figure 22-12

In this example, two tables named Contact and Individual are connected by the Contact.ContactID and Individual.ContactID fields. You can easily see which fields are the primary keys for each table; and to reduce clutter while you're editing the tables, you can collapse either the field list or the queries list in the `TableAdapter` defined for the table.

To perform actions against a table, either right-click the table or individual field and choose the appropriate command from the context menu, or use the main Data menu that is added to the menu bar of the IDE while you're editing the database schema.

To change the SQL for a query that you've added to the `TableAdapter`, first select the query you wish to modify and the use the Data ⇨ Configure menu command. The TableAdapter Configuration Wizard will appear, displaying a text representation of the existing query string (see Figure 22-13). You can either use the Query Builder to visually create a new query or simply overwrite the text with your own query.

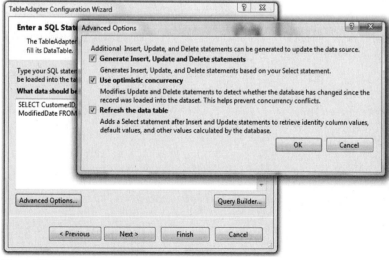

Figure 22-13

You can optionally have additional, associated queries for insert, delete, and update functionality generated along with the default Select query. To add this option, click the Advanced Options button and check the first option. The other options here enable you to customize how the queries will handle data during modification queries.

Figure 22-14 shows a sample Query Builder, which works in the same way as the view designer discussed earlier in this chapter (see Figure 22-7). You can add tables to the query by right-clicking the top area and choosing Add Table from the context menu, or by editing the Select statement in the text field.

To confirm that your query will run properly, click the Execute Query button to preview the results in the dialog before saving it. These functions also work when adding a new query to a `TableAdapter`, except that you can choose to use SQL statements or a stored procedure for the final query definition.

Figure 22-14 also shows how you can hide any of the panes via the context menu. Unchecking any of the panes will hide them, giving you more room to work with the remaining panes.

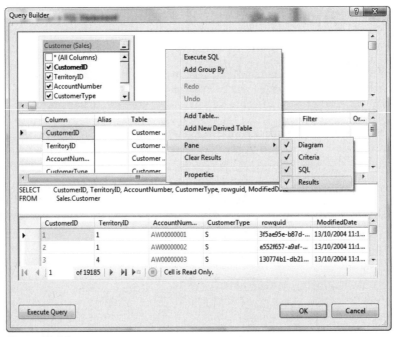

Figure 22-14

Data Binding Controls

Most Windows Forms controls can be bound to a data source once the data source has been added to the project. Add the control to the form and then access the Properties window for the control and locate the (Data Bindings) group. The commonly used properties for the particular field will be displayed, enabling you to browse to a field in your data source (or an existing `TableBindingSource` object). For example, a TextBox will have entries for both the `Text` and `Tag` properties.

When you click the drop-down arrow next to the property you want to bind to a data element, the Data Bindings property editor will be displayed (see Figure 22-15). Any data sources defined in your project appear under the Other Data Sources ⇨ Project Data Sources node. Expand the data source and table until you locate the field you want to bind to the property.

Figure 22-15

Visual Studio then automatically creates a `TableBindingSource` component and adds it to the form's designer view (it will be added to the tray area for nonvisual controls) along with the other data-specific components necessary to bind the data source to the form. This is a huge advance since the last version of Visual Studio, in which you had to first define the data adapters and connections on the form before you could bind the fields to controls.

If you need to bind a control to a property that is not listed as a common property for that control type, select the (Advanced) property from within the (Data Bindings) entry in the Properties window and click the ellipsis button to display the Formatting and Advanced Binding dialog, shown in Figure 22-16 for a TextBox control. This dialog also gives you control over the formatting that is used, which is particularly useful when you are displaying a numeric value and you want to control the number of decimal places, as well as defining a value to be bound when a null value is found in the underlying data source. The Data Source Update Mode allows you to choose between Never, OnPropertyChanged, and OnValidation. These roughly correspond to the control never updating, updating when the data value changes, or updating once the data has been validated.

The default update mode is OnValidation, which ties in with form validation, which in turn can be used to enable/disable the OK button. However, this can also be frustrating because it means the underlying data isn't updated until validation has been performed on a control — for example, if you change the value in a textbox, this value won't be propagated to the data source until validation occurs on the textbox, which is usually when the textbox loses focus. If you want to provide immediate feedback to the user it is recommended that you change the update mode to OnPropertyChanged.

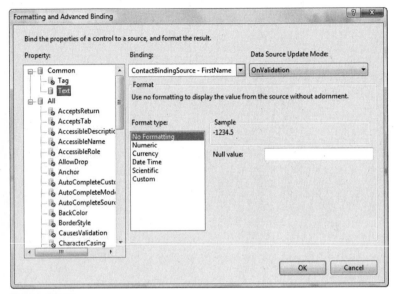

Figure 22-16

Locate the field you wish to bind and then select the corresponding binding setting from either a data source or existing `TableBindingSource` owned by the form. You can also customize the formatting of the data at this point, even for the common properties.

Changing the Default Control Type

You can change the default control for each data type by going into the Data UI Customization page in the Visual Studio Options dialog. This options page is located under the Windows Forms Designer group (see Figure 22-17).

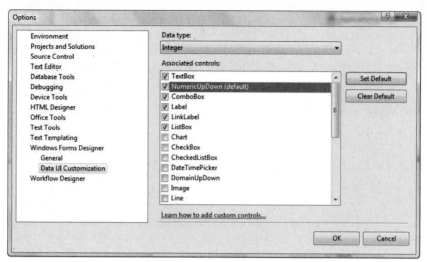

Figure 22-17

From the drop-down, select the data type you want to change and then pick which control type is to be associated with that kind of data. Note that you can select multiple control types to associate with the data type, but only one can be the default used by the data sources to set the initial control types for the fields and tables. In Figure 22-17, the default control type for Integer has been changed from the Visual Studio 2008 default of TextBox to an arguably better alternative, the NumericUpDown control.

Managing Test Data

Visual Studio 2008 also has the capability to view and edit the data contained in your database tables. To edit the information, use the Data ⇨ Show Table Data menu command after you highlight the table you want to view in the Server Explorer. You will be presented with a tabular representation of the data in the table as shown in Figure 22-18, enabling you to edit it to contain whatever default or test data you need to include. Using the buttons at the bottom of the table, you can navigate around the returned records and even create new rows. As you edit information, the table editor will display indicators next to fields that have changed.

ContactID	NameStyle	Title	FirstName	MiddleName	LastName	Suffix	Em.
1	False	Mr.	Gustavo	NULL	Achong	NULL	gust
2	False	Ms.	Catherine	R.	Abel	NULL	cath
3	False	Ms.	Kim	NULL	Abercrombie	NULL	kim
4	False	Sr.	Humberto	NULL	Acevedo	NULL	hum
5	False	Sra.	Pilar	NULL	Ackerman	NULL	pilar

Contact (Person):...k.AdventureWorks)

1 of 19972   Cell is Read Only.

Figure 22-18

You can also show the diagram, criteria, and SQL panes associated with the table data you're editing by right-clicking anywhere in the table and choosing the appropriate command from the Pane sub-menu. This can be useful for customizing the SQL statement that is being used to retrieve the data — for example, to filter the table for specific values, or just to retrieve the first 50 rows.

Previewing Data

You can also preview data for different data sources to ensure that the associated query will return the information you expect. In the database schema designer, right-click the query you want to test and choose Preview Data from the context menu. Alternatively, select Preview Data from the right-click context menu off any data source in the Data Sources tool window.

The Preview Data dialog is displayed with the object list defaulted to the query you want to test. Click the Preview button to view the sample data, shown in Figure 22-19. A small status bar provides information about the total number of data rows that were returned from the query, as well as how many columns of data were included.

If you want to change to a different query, you can do so with the "Select an object to preview" drop-down list. This list will contain other queries in the same data source, other data sources, and elsewhere in your solution. If the query you're previewing requires parameters, you can set their values in the Parameters list in the top right pane of the dialog. Clicking the Preview button will submit the query to the appropriate data source and display the subsequent results in the Results area on the Preview Data window.

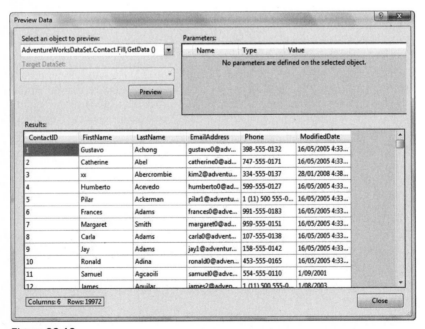

Figure 22-19

Summary

With the variety of tools and windows available to you in Visual Studio 2008, you can easily create and maintain databases without having to leave the IDE. You can manipulate data as well as define database schemas visually using the Properties tool window in conjunction with the Schema Designer view.

Once you have your data where you want it, Visual Studio keeps helping you by providing a set of drag-and-drop components that can be bound to a data source. These can be as simple as a checkbox or textbox, or as feature-rich as a DataGridView component with complete table views. The ability to drag whole tables or individual fields from the Data Sources window onto the design surface of a form and have Visual Studio automatically create the appropriate controls for you is a major advantage for rapid application development.

23

Language Integrated Queries (LINQ)

In Chapters 11 and 12 you saw a number of language features that have been added in order to facilitate a much more efficient programming style. Language Integrated Queries (LINQ) draws on these features to provide a common programming model for querying data. In this chapter you see how we can take some very verbose, imperative code and reduce it to a few declarative lines. You will see that this gives us the ability to make our code more descriptive rather than prescriptive. By this we mean that we are describing what we want to occur, rather than detailing how it should be done.

LINQ Providers

One of the key tenets of LINQ was the ability to abstract away the query syntax from the underlying data store. As you can see in Figure 23-1, LINQ sits below the various .NET languages such as C# and VB.NET. LINQ brings together various language features, such as extension methods, type inferences, anonymous types, and Lambda expressions, to provide a uniform syntax for querying data.

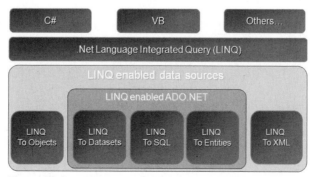

Figure 23-1

At the bottom of Figure 23-1 you can see that there are a number of LINQ-enabled data sources. Each data source has a LINQ provider that's capable of querying the corresponding data source. LINQ is not limited to just these data sources, and there are already providers available for querying all sorts of other data sources. For example, there is a LINQ provider for querying Sharepoint. In fact, the documentation that ships with Visual Studio 2008 includes a walk-through on creating your own LINQ provider.

In this chapter you'll see some of the standard LINQ query operations as they apply to standard .NET objects. Then in the following two chapters you'll see LINQ to XML, LINQ to SQL, and LINQ to Entities. As you will see, the syntax for querying the data remains constant, with only the underlying data source changing.

Old-School Queries

Instead of walking through exactly what LINQ is, let's start with an example that will demonstrate some of the savings that these queries offer. The scenario is one in which a researcher is investigating whether or not there is a correlation between the length of a customer's name and the customer's average order size. The relationship between a customer and the orders is a simple one-to-many as shown in Figure 23-2.

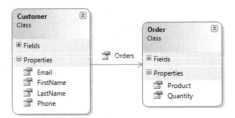

Figure 23-2

In the particular query we are examining, the researchers are looking for the average Milk order for customers with a first name greater than or equal to five characters, ordered by the first name:

```
Private Sub OldStyleQuery()
    Dim customers As Customer() = BuildCustomers()

    Dim results As New List(Of SearchResult)
    Dim matcher As New SearchForProduct("Milk")

    For Each c As Customer In customers
        If c.FirstName.Length >= 5 Then
            Dim orders As Order() = Array.FindAll(c.Orders, _
                                                  AddressOf matcher.ProductMatch)
            Dim cr As New SearchResult
            cr.Customer = c.FirstName & " " & c.LastName
            For Each o As Order In orders
                cr.Quantity += o.Quantity
                cr.Count += 1
```

```
            Next
            results.Add(cr)
        End If
    Next

    results.Sort(New Comparison(Of SearchResult)(AddressOf CompareSearchResults))

    ObjectDumper.Write(results)
End Sub
```

Before we jump in and show how LINQ can improve this snippet, let's examine how this snippet works. The opening line calls out to a method that simply generates `Customer` objects. This will be used throughout the snippets in this chapter. The main loop in this method iterates through the array of customers searching for those customers with a first name longer than five characters. Upon finding such a customer, we use the `Array.FindAll` method to retrieve all orders where the predicate is true. VB.NET doesn't have anonymous methods so in the past you couldn't supply the predicate function in line with the method. As as result, the usual way to do this was to create a simple class that could hold the query variable (in this case, the product, Milk) that we were searching for, and that had a method that accepted the type of object we were searching through, in this case an `Order`. With the introduction of Lambda expressions, we can now rewrite this line:

```
Dim orders = Array.FindAll(c.Orders, _
                           Function(o As Order) o.Product = mProductToFind)
```

Here we have also taken advantage of type inferencing in order to determine the type of the variable orders, which is of course still an array of orders.

Returning to the snippet, once we have located the orders we still need to iterate through them and sum up the quantity ordered and store this, along with the name of the customer and the number of orders. This is our search result, and as you can see we are using a `SearchResult` object to store this information. For convenience the `SearchResult` object also has a read-only `Average` property, which simply divides the total quantity ordered by the number of orders. Because we want to sort the customer list, we use the `Sort` method on the `List` class, passing in the address of a comparison method. Again, using Lambda expressions, this can be rewritten as an inline statement:

```
results.Sort(New Comparison(of SearchResult)( _
                        Function(r1 as SearchResult, r2 as SearchResult) _
                            String.Compare(r1.Customer, r2.Customer)))
```

The last part of this snippet is to print out the search results. Here we are using one of the samples that ships with Visual Studio 2008 called `ObjectDumper`. This is a simple class that iterates through a collection of objects printing out the values of the public properties. In this case the output would look like Figure 23-3.

Figure 23-3

385

As you can see from this relatively simple query, the code to do this in the past was quite prescriptive and required additional classes in order to carry out the query logic and return the results. With the power of LINQ we can build a single expression that clearly describes what the search results should be.

Query Pieces

This section introduces you to a number of the query operations that make up the basis of LINQ. If you have written SQL statements, these will feel familiar, although the ordering and syntax might take a little time to get used to. There are a number of query operations you can use, and there are numerous reference web sites that provide more information on how to use these. For the moment we will focus on those operations necessary to improve the search query introduced at the beginning of this chapter.

From

Unlike SQL, where the first statement is Select, in LINQ the first statement is typically From. One of the key considerations in the creation of LINQ was providing IntelliSense support within Visual Studio 2008. If you've ever wondered why there is no IntelliSense support in SQL Management Studio for SQL Server 2005 for writing queries, this is because, in order to determine what to select, you need to know where the data is coming from. By reversing the order of the statements, LINQ is able to generate IntelliSense as soon as you start typing.

As you can see from the tooltip in Figure 23-4, the From statement is made up of two parts, `<element>` and `<collection>`. The latter is the source collection from which you will be extracting data, and the former is essentially an iteration variable that can be used to refer to the items being queried. This pair can then be repeated for each source collection.

```
Private Sub LinqQueryFromOnly()
    Dim customers = BuildCustomers()

    Dim results = From c In customers, o In c.Orders|
                  From <element> In <collection>[, <element2> in <collection2>][, ...]

    ObjectDumper.Write(results, 1, log:=mOutStream)
End Sub
```

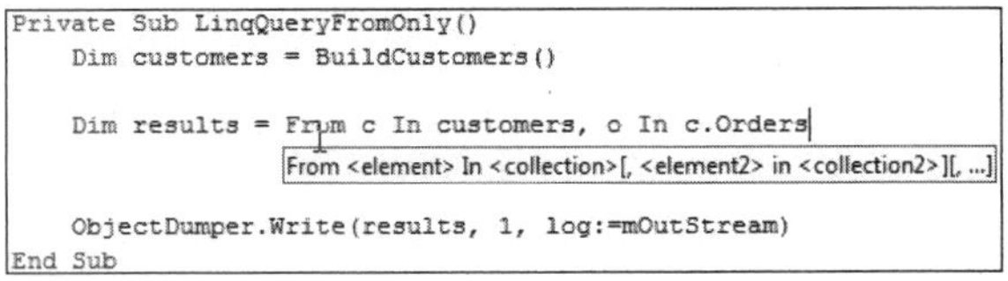

Figure 23-4

In this case you can see we are querying the customers collection, with an iteration variable `c`, and the orders collection `c.Orders` using the iteration variable `o`. There is an implicit join between the two source collections because of the relationship between a customer and that customer's orders. As you can imagine, this query will result in the cross-product of items in each source collection. This will lead to the pairing of a customer with each order that this customer has.

Note that we don't have a Select statement, because we are simply going to return all elements, but what does each result record look like? If you were to look at the tooltip for results, you would see that it is a generic IEnumerable of an anonymous type. The anonymous type feature is heavily used in LINQ so that you don't have to create classes for every result. If you recall from the initial code, we had to have a `SearchResult` class in order to capture each of the results. Anonymous types mean that we no longer have to create a class to store the results. During compilation, types containing the relevant properties are dynamically created, thereby giving us a strongly typed result set along with IntelliSense support. Though the tooltip for results may report only that it is an IEnumerable of an anonymous type, when you start to use the results collection you will see that the type has two properties, c and o, of type Customer and Order, respectively. Figure 23-5 displays the output of this code, showing the customer-order pairs.

Figure 23-5

Select

In the previous code snippet the result set was a collection of customer-order pairs, when in fact what we want to return is the customer name and the order information. We can do this by using a Select statement in a way similar to the way you would when writing a SQL statement:

```
Private Sub LinqQueryWithSelect()
    Dim customers = BuildCustomers()

    Dim results = From c In customers, o In c.Orders _
                Select c.FirstName, c.LastName, o.Product, o.Quantity

    ObjectDumper.Write(results)
End Sub
```

Now when we execute this code the result set is a collection of objects that have FirstName, LastName, Product, and Quantity properties. This is illustrated in the output shown in Figure 23-6.

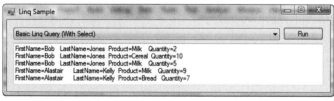

Figure 23-6

387

Where

So far all you have seen is how we can effectively flatten the customer-order hierarchy into a result set containing the appropriate properties. What we haven't done is filter these results so that they only return customers with a first name greater than or equal to five characters, and who are ordering Milk. In the following snippet we introduce a Where statement, which restricts the source collections on both these axes:

```
Private Sub LinqQueryWithWhere()
    Dim customers = BuildCustomers()

    Dim results = From c In customers, o In c.Orders _
                  Where c.FirstName.Length >= 5 And _
                        o.Product = "Milk" _
                  Select c.FirstName, c.LastName, o.Product, o.Quantity

    ObjectDumper.Write(results)
End Sub
```

One thing to be aware of here is the spot in which the Where statement appears relative to the From and Select statements. In Figure 23-7 you can see that you can place a Where statement after the Select statement.

Figure 23-7

The difference lies in the order in which the operations are carried out. As you can imagine, placing the Where statement after the Select statement causes the filter to be carried out after the projection. In the following code snippet you can see how the previous snippet can be rewritten with the Where statement after the Select statement. You will notice that the only difference is that there are no c or o prefixes in the Where clause. This is because these iteration variables are no longer in scope once the Select statement has projected the data from the source collection into the result set. Instead, the Where statement uses the properties on the generated anonymous type.

```
Dim results = From c In customers, o In c.Orders _
              Select c.FirstName, c.LastName, o.Product, o.Quantity _
              Where FirstName.Length >= 5 And _
                    Product = "Milk"
```

The output of this query is similar to the previous one in that it is a result set of an anonymous type with the four properties FirstName, LastName, Product, and Quantity.

Group By

We are getting close to our initial query, except that our current query returns a list of all the Milk orders for all the customers. For a customer who might have placed two orders for Milk, this will result in two records in the result set. What we actually want to do is to group these orders by customer and take an average of the quantities ordered. Not surprisingly, this is done with a Group By statement, as shown in the following snippet:

```
Private Sub LinqQueryWithGroupingAndWhere()
    Dim customers = BuildCustomers()

    Dim results = From c In customers, o In c.Orders _
                  Where c.FirstName.Length >= 5 And _
                        o.Product = "Milk" _
                  Group By c Into avg = Average(o.Quantity) _
                  Select c.FirstName, c.LastName, avg

    ObjectDumper.Write(results)
End Sub
```

What is a little confusing about the Group By statement is the syntax that it uses. Essentially what it is saying is "group by dimension X" and place the results "Into" an alias that can be used elsewhere. In this case the alias is `avg`, which will contain the average we are interested in. Because we are grouping by the iteration variable `c`, we can still use this in the Select statement, along with the Group By alias. Now when we run this we get the output shown in Figure 23-8, which is much closer to our initial query.

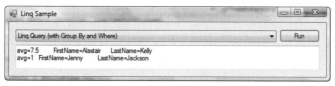

Figure 23-8

Custom Projections

We still need to tidy up the output so that we are returning a well-formatted customer name and an appropriately named average property, instead of the query results, `FirstName`, `LastName`, and `avg`. We can do this by customizing the properties that are contained in the anonymous type that is created as part of the Select statement projection. Figure 23-9 shows how you can create anonymous types with named properties.

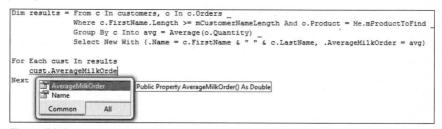

Figure 23-9

This figure also illustrates that the type of the `AverageMilkOrder` property is indeed a Double, which is what we would expect based on the use of the `Average` function. It is this strongly typed behavior that can really assist us in the creation and use of rich LINQ statements.

Order By

The last thing we have to do with the LINQ statement is to order the results. We can do this by ordering the customers based on their `FirstName` property, as shown in the following snippet:

```
Private Sub FinalLinqQuery()
    Dim customers = BuildCustomers()

    Dim results = From c In customers, o In c.Orders _
                  Order By c.FirstName _
                  Where c.FirstName.Length >= 5 And _
                      o.Product = "Milk" _
                  Group By c Into avg = Average(o.Quantity) _
                  Select New With {.Name = c.FirstName & " " & c.LastName, _
                                   .AverageMilkOrder = avg} _

    ObjectDumper.Write(results)
End Sub
```

One thing to be aware of is how you can easily reverse the order of the query results. Here this can be done either by supplying the keyword `Descending` (`Ascending` is the default) at the end of the Order By statement, or by applying the `Reverse` transformation on the entire results set:

```
Order By c.FirstName Descending
```

or

```
ObjectDumper.Write(results.Reverse)
```

As you can see from the final query we have built up, it is much more descriptive than the initial query. We can easily see that we are selecting the customer name and an average of the order quantities. It is clear that we are filtering based on the length of the customer name and on orders for Milk, and that the results are sorted by the customer's first name. We also haven't needed to create any additional classes to help perform this query.

Debugging and Execution

One of the things you should be aware of with LINQ is that the queries are not executed until they are used. In fact, each time you use a LINQ query you will find that the query is re-executed. This can potentially lead to some issues in debugging and some unexpected performance issues if you are executing the query multiple times. In the code you have seen so far, we have declared the LINQ statement and then passed the results object to the ObjectDumper, which in turn iterates through the query results. If we were to repeat this call to the ObjectDumper, it would again iterate through the results.

Unfortunately, this delayed execution can mean that LINQ statements are hard to debug. If you select the statement and insert a breakpoint, all that will happen is that the application will stop where you have declared the LINQ statement. If you step to the next line, the results object will simply state that it is an "In-Memory Query." In C# the debugging story is slightly better because you can actually set breakpoints within the LINQ statement. As you can see from Figure 23-10, the breakpoint on the conditional statement has been hit. From the call stack you can see that the current execution point is no longer actually in the `FinalQuery` method; it is in fact within the `ObjectDumper.Write` method.

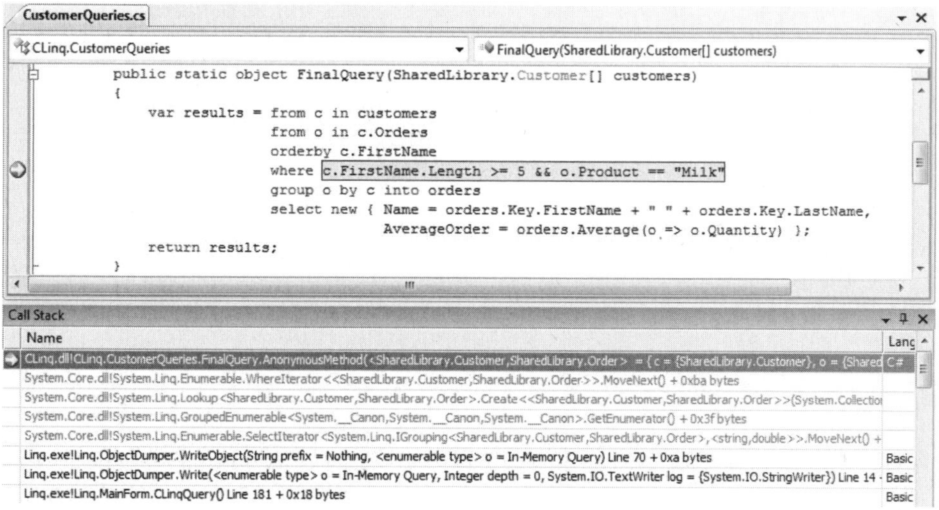

Figure 23-10

If you need to force the execution of a LINQ query, you can call ToArray or ToList on the results object. This will force the query to execute, returning an Array or List of the appropriate type. You can then use this array in other queries, reducing the need for the LINQ query to be executed multiple times.

Summary

In this chapter you have been introduced to Language Integrated Queries (LINQ), a significant step toward a common programming model for data access. You can see that LINQ statements help to make your code more readable, because you don't have to code all the details of how the data should be iterated, the conditional statements for selecting objects, or the code for building the results set.

The next two chapters go through LINQ to XML, LINQ to SQL, and LINQ to Entities. Although the query structure remains the same, there are unique features of each of these providers that make them relevant for particular scenarios.

24

LINQ to XML

In Chapter 23, you were introduced to Language Integrated Queries (LINQ) with an example that was able to query an object model for relevant customer-order information. While LINQ does provide an easy way to filter, sort, and project from an in-memory object graph, it is more common for the data source to be either a database or a file type, such as XML. In this chapter you will be introduced to LINQ to XML, which makes working with XML data dramatically simpler than with traditional methods such as using the document object model, XSLT, or XPath.

XML Object Model

If you have ever worked with XML in .NET, you will recall that the object model isn't as easy to work with as you would imagine. For example, in order to create even a single XML element you need to have an `XmlDocument`.

```
Dim x as New XmlDocument
x.AppendChild(x.CreateElement("Customer"))
```

As you will see when we start to use LINQ to query and build XML, this object model doesn't allow for the inline creation of elements. To this end, a new XML object model was created that resides in the System.Xml.Linq assembly presented in Figure 24-1.

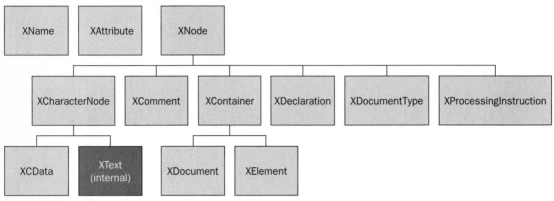

Figure 24-1

As you can see from Figure 24-1, there are classes that correspond to the relevant parts of an XML document: XComment, XAttribute, and XElements. The biggest improvement is that most of the classes can be instantiated by means of a constructor that accepts Name and Content parameters. In the following C# code, you can see that an element called Customers has been created that contains a single Customer element. This element, in turn, accepts an attribute, Name, and a series of Order elements.

```
XElement x = new XElement("Customers",
                    new XElement("Customer",
                            new XAttribute("Name","Bob Jones"),
                            new XElement("Order",
                                new XAttribute("Product", "Milk"),
                                new XAttribute("Quantity", 2)),
                            new XElement("Order",
                                new XAttribute("Product", "Bread"),
                                new XAttribute("Quantity", 10)),
                            new XElement("Order",
                                new XAttribute("Product", "Apples"),
                                new XAttribute("Quantity", 5))
                            )
                    );
```

While this code snippet is quite verbose and it's hard to distinguish the actual XML data from the surrounding .NET code, it is significantly better than with the old XML object model, which required elements to be individually created and then added to the parent node.

VB.NET XML Literals

One of the biggest innovations in the VB.NET language is the support for XML literals. As with strings and integers, an XML literal is treated as a first-class citizen when you are writing code. The following snippet illustrates the same XML generated by the previous C# snippet as it would appear using an XML literal in VB.NET.

```
Dim cust = <Customers>
                <Customer Name="Bob Jones">
                    <Order Product="Milk" Quantity="2"/>
                    <Order Product="Bread" Quantity="10"/>
                    <Order Product="Apples" Quantity="5"/>
                </Customer>
            </Customers>
```

Not only do you have the ability to assign an XML literal in code, you also get designer support for creating and working with your XML. For example, when you enter the > on a new element, it will automatically create the closing XML tag for you. Figure 24-2 illustrates how the Customers XML literal can be condensed in the same way as other code blocks in Visual Studio 2008.

```
Dim cust = <Customers>
                <Customer Name="Bob Jones"> ...
            </Customers>

Dim data = <Customers>
                <Customer >
            </Customers>
                                    End of statement expected.
```

Figure 24-2

You can also see in Figure 24-2 that there is an error in the XML literal being assigned to the data variable. In this case there is no closing tag for the Customer element. Designer support is invaluable for validating your XML literals, preventing runtime errors when the XML is parsed into XElement objects.

Paste XML as XElement

Unfortunately, C# doesn't have native support for XML literals, which makes generating XML a painful process, even with the new object model. Luckily, there is a time-saving add-in that will paste an XML snippet from the clipboard into the code window as a series of XElement objects. This can make a big difference if you have to create XML from scratch. The add-in, PasteXmlAsLinq in the LinqSamples folder, is available in the C# samples that ship with Visual Studio 2008. Simply open the sample in Visual Studio 2008, build the solution, navigate to the output folder, and copy the output files (namely PasteXmlAsLinq.Addin and PasteXmlAsLinq.dll) to the add-ins folder for Visual Studio 2008. When you restart Visual Studio 2008 you will see a new item, Paste XML as XElement, in the Edit menu when you are working in the code editor window, as you can see in Figure 24-3.

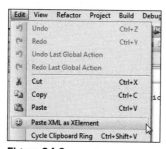

Figure 24-3

Visual Studio 2008 looks in a variety of places, defined in the Options dialog (Tools menu), for add-ins. Typically it looks in an add-ins folder located beneath the Visual Studio root documents directory. For example: C:\users\username\Documents\Visual Studio 2008\Addins.

To work with this add-in, all you need to do is to create the XML snippet in your favorite XML editor. In Figure 24-4 we have used XML Notepad, which is a freely available download from www.microsoft .com, but you can also use the built-in XML editor within Visual Studio 2008.

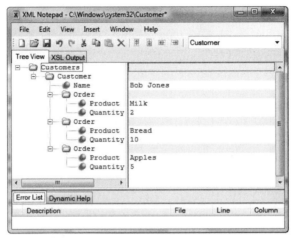

Figure 24-4

Once you have created the XML snippet, copy it to the clipboard (for example, by pressing Ctrl+C). Then place your cursor at the point at which you want to insert the snippet within Visual Studio 2008 and select Paste XML as XElement from the Edit menu. (Of course, if you use this option frequently you may want to assign a shortcut key to it so that you don't have to navigate to the menu.) The code generated by the add-in will look similar to what is shown in Figure 24-5.

```
XElement xml = new XElement("Customers",
                 new XElement("Customer",
                     new XAttribute("Name", "Bob Jones"),
                     new XElement("Order",
                         new XAttribute("Product", "Milk"),
                         new XAttribute("Quantity", "2")
                     ),
                     new XElement("Order",
                         new XAttribute("Product", "Bread"),
                         new XAttribute("Quantity", "10")
                     ),
                     new XElement("Order",
                         new XAttribute("Product", "Apples"),
                         new XAttribute("Quantity", "5")
                     )
                 )
             );
```

Figure 24-5

Creating XML with LINQ

While creating XML using the new object model is significantly quicker than previously possible, the real power of the new object model comes when you combine it with LINQ in the form of LINQ to XML (XLINQ). By combining the rich querying capabilities with the ability to create complex XML in a single statement, you can now generate entire XML documents in a single statement. Let's continue with the same example of customers and orders. In this case we have an array of customers, each of whom has any number of orders. What we want to do is create XML that lists the customers and their associated orders. We'll start by creating the customer list, and then introduce the orders.

To begin with, let's create an XML literal that defines the structure we want to create.

```
Dim customerXml = <Customers>
                    <Customer Name="Bob Jones">
                    </Customer>
                  </Customers>
```

Although we can simplify this code by condensing the `Customer` element into `<Customer Name="Bob Jones" />`, we're going to be adding the orders as child elements, so we will use a separate closing XML element.

Expression Holes

If we have multiple customers, the `Customer` element is going to repeat for each one, with Bob Jones being replaced by different customer names. Before we deal with replacing the name, we first need to get the `Customer` element to repeat. You do this by creating an expression hole, using a syntax familiar to anyone who has worked with ASP:

```
Dim customerXml = <Customers>
                    <%= From c In customers _
                        Select <Customer Name="Bob Jones">
                               </Customer> %>
                  </Customers>
```

Here you can see that `<%= %>` has been used to define the expression hole, into which a LINQ statement has been added. The `Select` statement creates a projection to an XML element for each customer in the `Customers` array, based on the static value `"Bob Jones"`. To change this to return each of the customer names we again have to use an expression hole. Figure 24-6 shows how Visual Studio 2008 provides rich IntelliSense support in these expression holes.

```
Dim customerXml = <Customers>
                    <%= From c In customers _
                        Select <Customer Name=<%= c.FirstName & " " & c.l %>>
                               </Customer> %>
                  </Customers>
```
LastName   Public Property LastName() As String

Figure 24-6

In the following snippet, you can see that we have used the loop variable Name so that we can order the customers based on their full names. This loop variable is then used to set the Name attribute of the customer node.

```
Dim customerXml = <Customers>
                    <%= From c In customers _
                        Let Name = c.FirstName & " " & c.LastName _
                        Order By Name _
                        Select <Customer Name=<%= Name %>>
                                    <%= From o In c.Orders _
                                        Select <Order
Product=<%= o.Product %>
Quantity=<%= o.Quantity %>
                                                          /> %>
                                </Customer> %>
                    </Customers>
```

The other thing to notice in this snippet is that we have included the creation of the Order elements for each customer. Although it would appear that the second, nested LINQ statement is independent of the first, there is an implicit joining through the customer loop variable c. Hence the second LINQ statement is iterating through the orders for a particular customer, creating an Order element with attributes Product and Quantity.

As you can imagine, the C# equivalent is slightly less easy to read but is by no means more complex. There is no need for expression holes, as C# doesn't support XML literals; instead, the LINQ statement just appears nested within the XML construction, as you can see in the following code.

```
var customerXml = new XElement("Customers",
                        from c in customers
                        select new XElement("Customer",
                                    new XAttribute("Name",
                                        c.FirstName + " " + c.LastName),
                                    from o in c.Orders
                                    select new XElement("Order",
                                        new XAttribute("Product",
                                                    o.Product),
                                        new XAttribute("Quantity",
                                                    o.Quantity)))));
```

In this code snippet the LINQ statement has been set to bold so that you can make it out. As you can see, for a complex XML document this would quite quickly become difficult to work with, which is one reason VB.NET now includes XML literals as a first-class language feature.

Querying XML

In addition to enabling you to easily create XML, LINQ can also be used to query XML. We will use the following Customers XML in this section to discuss the XLINQ querying capabilities:

```
<Customers>
    <Customer Name="Bob Jones">
        <Order Product="Milk" Quantity="2"/>
        <Order Product="Bread" Quantity="10"/>
```

```
        <Order Product="Apples" Quantity="5"/>
    </Customer>
    ...
</Customers>
```

The following two code snippets show the same query using VB.NET and C#, respectively. In both cases the `customerXml` variable (an `XElement`) is queried for all `Customer` elements, from which the `Name` attribute is extracted. The `Name` attribute is then split over the space between names, and the result is used to create a new `Customer` object.

VB.NET

```
Dim results = From cust In customerXml.<Customer> _
              Let nameBits = cust.@Name.Split(" "c) _
              Select New Customer() With {.FirstName = nameBits(0), _
                                          .LastName = nameBits(1)}
```

C#

```
var results = from cust in customerXml.Elements("Customer")
              let  nameBits = cust.Attribute("Name").Value.Split(' ')
              select new Customer() {FirstName = nameBits[0],
                                     LastName=nameBits[1] };
```

As you can see, the VB.NET XML language support extends to enabling you to query elements using `.<elementName>` and attributes using `.@attributeName`. Figure 24-7 shows the IntelliSense for the `customerXml` variable, which shows three XML query options.

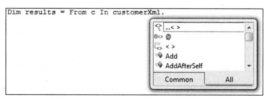

Figure 24-7

The second and third of these options you have seen in action in the previous query to extract attribute and element information, respectively. The third option enables you to retrieve all sub-elements that match the supplied element. For example, the following code retrieves all orders in the XML document, irrespective of which `customer` element they belong to:

```
Dim allOrders = From cust In customerXml...<Order> _
                Select New Order With {.Product = cust.@Product, _
                                       .Quantity = CInt(cust.@Quantity)}
```

Schema Support

Although VB.NET enables you to query XML using elements and attributes, it doesn't actually provide any validation that you have entered the correct element and attribute names. To reduce the chance of entering the wrong names, you can import an XML schema, which will extend the default IntelliSense support to include the element and attribute names. You import an XML schema as you would any other .NET namespace. First you need to add a reference to the XML schema to your project, and then you need to add an `Imports` statement to the top of your code file.

> *Unlike other import statements, an XML schema import can't be added in the Project Properties Designer, which means you need to add it to the top of any code file in which you want IntelliSense support.*

If you are working with an existing XML file but don't have a schema handy, manually creating an XML schema just so you can have better IntelliSense support seems like overkill. Luckily, the VB.NET team has made available the XML to Schema Inference Wizard for Visual Studio 2008, which you can download free from `www.microsoft.com`. Once installed, this wizard gives you the ability to create a new XML schema based on an XML snippet or XML source file, or from a URL that contains the XML source. In our example, we're going to start with an XML snippet that looks like the following:

```
<c:Customers xmlns:c="http://www.professionalvisualstudio.com/chapter24/customers">
    <c:Customer Name="Bob Jones">
        <c:Order Product="Milk" Quantity="2" />
        <c:Order Product="Cereal" Quantity="10" />
    </c:Customer>
    <c:Customer Name="Alastair Kelly">
        <c:Order Product="Milk" Quantity="9" />
        <c:Order Product="Bread" Quantity="7" />
    </c:Customer>
</c:Customers>
```

Note that unlike our previous XML snippets, this one includes a namespace — this is necessary, as the XML schema import is based upon importing a namespace (rather than importing a specific XSD file). To generate an XML schema based on this snippet, start by right-clicking your project in the Solution Explorer and selecting Add New Item. With the XML to Schema Inference Wizard installed, there should be an additional XML To Schema item template, as shown in Figure 24-8.

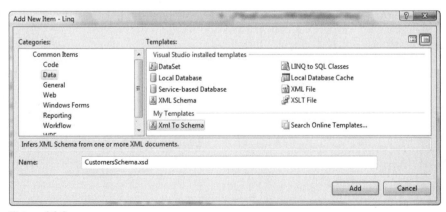

Figure 24-8

Selecting this item and clicking "OK" will prompt you to select the location of the XML from which the schema should be generated. In Figure 24-9, we have supplied an XML resource using the "Add as XM L . . ." button (i.e., click the button and paste the XML snippet into the supplied space).

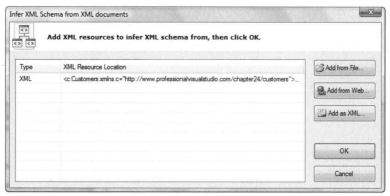

Figure 24-9

Once you click "OK", this will generate the CustomersSchema.xsd file containing a schema based upon the XML resources you have specified. The next step is to import this schema into your code file by adding an `Imports` statement to the XML namespace, as shown in Figure 24-10.

Figure 24-10

Figure 24-10 also contains an alias, c, for the XML namespace, which will be used throughout the code for referencing elements and attributes from this namespace. In your XLINQ queries you will now see that when you press < or @, the IntelliSense list will contain the relevant elements and attributes from the imported XML schema. In Figure 24-11, you can see these new additions when we begin to query the `customerXml` variable. If we were in a nested XLINQ statement (for example, querying orders for a particular customer), you would see only a subset of the schema elements (i.e., just the `c:Order` element).

Figure 24-11

It is important to note that importing an XML schema doesn't validate the elements or attributes you use. All it does is improve the level of IntelliSense available to you when you are building your XLINQ query.

Summary

In this chapter you have been introduced to the new XML object model and the XML language integration within VB.NET. You have also seen how LINQ can be used to query XML documents, and how Visual Studio 2008 IntelliSense enables a rich experience for working with XML in VB.NET.

The next chapter will cover LINQ to SQL and LINQ to Entities, two of the LINQ providers that can be used to query SQL data sources. As demonstrated in this chapter, it is important to remember that LINQ is not dependent on the data source's being a relational database, and that it can be extended to query all manner of data repositories.

25

LINQ to SQL and Entities

In the previous chapters you were introduced to Language Integrated Queries (LINQ) as it pertains to both your standard .NET objects and how it can be used to query XML data. Of course one of the primary sources of data for any application is typically a database. So, in this chapter you see both LINQ to SQL, a technology that shipped with Visual Studio 2008, and LINQ to Entities, which is likely to ship in conjunction with SQL Server 2008. Both of these technologies can be used for working with traditional databases, such as SQL Server. This allows you to write LINQ statements that will query the database, pull back the appropriate data, and populate .NET objects that you can work with. In essence, they are both object-relational mapping frameworks, attempting to bridge the gap between the .NET object model and the data-oriented relational model.

LINQ to SQL

You may be thinking that we are about to introduce you to yet another technology for doing data access. In fact, what you will see is that everything covered in this chapter extends the existing ADO.NET data access model. LINQ to SQL is much more than just the ability to write LINQ statements to query information from a database. It provides a true object to a relational mapping layer, capable of tracking changes to existing objects and allowing you to add or remove objects as if they were rows in a database.

Let's get started and look at some of the features of LINQ to SQL and the associated designers on the way. For this chapter we're going to use the AdventureWorksLT sample database (downloadable from the MSFTDBProdSamples project at www.codeplex.com). We're going to end up performing a similar query to that used in Chapter 23, which was researching customers with a first name greater than or equal to five characters and the average order size for a particular product. In Chapter 23 the product was Milk, but because we are dealing with a bike company we will use the "HL Road Frame — Red, 44" product instead.

Creating the Object Model

For the purpose of this chapter we will be using a normal Visual Basic Windows Forms application from the New Project dialog. You will also need to create a Data Connection to the AdventureWorksLT database (covered in Chapter 21), which for this example is `drnick.AdventureWorksLT.dbo`. The next step is to add a LINQ to SQL Classes item from the Add New Item dialog shown in Figure 25-1.

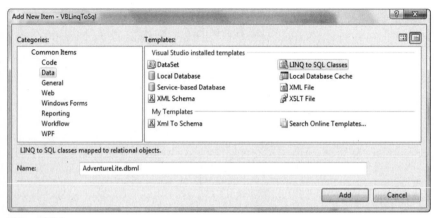

Figure 25-1

After providing a name, in this case AdventureLite, and accepting this dialog, three items will be added to your projects. These are AdventureLite.dbml, which is the mapping file; AdventureLite.dbml.layout, which like the class designer is used to lay out the mapping information to make it easier to work with; and finally AdventureLite.designer.vb, which contains the classes into which data is loaded as part of LINQ to SQL.

> *These items may appear as a single item, AdventureLite.dbml, if you don't have the Show All Files option enabled. Select the project and click the appropriate button at the top of the Solution Explorer tool window.*

Unfortunately, unlike some of the other visual designers in Visual Studio 2008 that have a helpful wizard to get you started, the LINQ to SQL designer initially appears as a blank design surface, as you can see in the center of Figure 25-2.

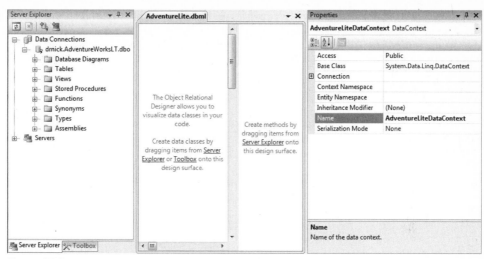

Figure 25-2

On the right side of Figure 25-2, you can see the properties associated with the main design area, which actually represents a DataContext. If you were to compare LINQ with ADO.NET, then a LINQ statement equates approximately to a command, whereas a DataContext roughly equates to the connection. It is only roughly because the DataContext actually wraps a database connection in order to provide object lifecycle services. For example, when you execute a LINQ to SQL statement it is the DataContext that ends up executing the request to the database, creating the objects based on the return data and then tracking those objects as they are changed or deleted.

If you have worked with the class designer you will be at home with the LINQ to SQL designer. As the instructions in the center of Figure 25-2 indicate, you can start to build your data mappings by dragging items from the Server Explorer (or manually creating them by dragging the item from the Toolbox). In our case we want to expand the Tables node, select the Customer, SalesOrderHeader, SalesOrderDetail, and Product tables, and drag them onto the design surface. You will notice from Figure 25-3 that a number of the classes and properties have been renamed to make the object model easier to read when we are writing LINQ statements. This is a good example of the benefits of separating the object model (for example, Order or OrderItem) from the underlying data (in this case, the SalesOrderHeader and SalesOrderDetail tables). Because we don't need all the properties that are automatically created, it is recommended that you select them, in the designer, and delete them. The end result should look like Figure 25-3.

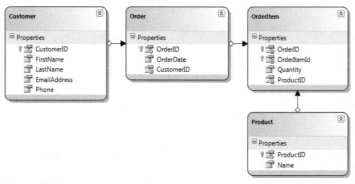

Figure 25-3

It is also worth noting that you can modify the details of the association between objects. Figure 25-4 shows the Properties tool window for the association between `Product` and `OrderItem`. Here we have set the generation of the `Child Property` to `False` because we won't need to track back from a `Product` to all the `OrderItems`. We have also renamed the `Parent Property` to `ProductInformation` to make the association more intuitive (although note that the name in the drop-down at the top of the Properties window uses the original SQL Server table names).

Figure 25-4

As you can see, you can control whether properties are created that can be used to navigate between instances of the classes. Though this might seem quite trivial, if you think about what happens if you attempt to navigate from an `Order` to its associated `OrderItems`, you can quickly see that there will be issues if the full object hierarchy hasn't been loaded into memory. For example, in this case if the `OrderItems` aren't already loaded into memory, LINQ to SQL intercepts the navigation, goes to the database, and retrieves the appropriate data in order to populate the `OrderItems`.

The other property of interest in Figure 25-4 is the `Participating Properties`. Editing this property will launch the Association Editor window (see Figure 25-5). You can also reach this dialog by right-clicking the association on the design surface and selecting Edit Association.

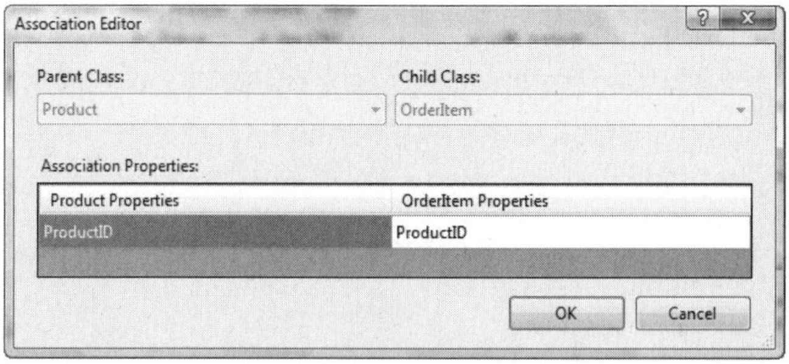

Figure 25-5

If you drag items from Server Explorer onto the design surface, you are unlikely to need the Association Editor. However, it is particularly useful if you are manually creating a LINQ to SQL mapping, because you can control how the object associations align to the underlying data relationships.

Querying with LINQ to SQL

In the previous chapters you will have seen enough LINQ statements to understand how to put together a statement that filters, sorts, aggregates, and projects the relevant data. With this in mind, examine the following LINQ to SQL snippet:

```
Using aw As New AdventureLiteDataContext
    Dim custs = From c In aw.Customers, o In c.Orders, oi In o.OrderItems _
                Where c.FirstName.Length >= 5 And _
                      oi.ProductInformation.Name = "HL Road Frame - Red, 44" _
                Group By c Into avg = Average(oi.Quantity) _
                Let Name = c.FirstName & " " & c.LastName _
                Order By Name _
                Select New With {Name, .AverageOrder = avg}

    For Each c In custs
        MsgBox(c.Name & " = " & c.AverageOrder)
    Next
End Using
```

The biggest difference here is that instead of the `Customer` and `Order` objects existing in memory before the creation and execution of the LINQ statement, now all the data objects are loaded at the point of execution of the LINQ statement. The AdventureLiteDataContext is the conduit for opening the connection to the database, forming and executing the relevant SQL statement against the database, and loading the return data into appropriate objects.

You will also note that the LINQ statement has to navigate through the Customers, Orders, OrderItems, and Product tables in order to execute the LINQ statement. Clearly if this were to be done as a series of SQL statements, it would be horrendously slow. Luckily the translation of the LINQ statement to SQL commands is done as a single unit.

> *There are some exceptions to this; for example, if you call ToList in the middle of your LINQ statement this may result in the separation into multiple SQL statements. Though LINQ to SQL does abstract you away from having to explicitly write SQL commands, you still need to be aware of the way your query will be translated and how it might affect your application performance.*

In order to view the actual SQL that is generated, we can use a debugging visualizer that was published by Scott Gutherie. Entitled the LINQ to SQL Debug Visualizer, you can download it from Scott's blog (`http://weblogs.asp.net/scottgu` and search for SQL Visualizer). The download includes both the source and the built visualizer `dll`. The latter should be dropped into your visualizers folder (typically `c:\Users\<username>\Documents\Visual Studio 2008\Visualizers`). When you restart Visual Studio 2008 you will be able to make use of this visualizer to view the actual SQL that is generated by LINQ to SQL for your LINQ statement. Figure 25-6 illustrates the default datatip for the same LINQ to SQL statement in C# (VB.NET is the same, except you don't see the generated SQL in the first line of the datatip).

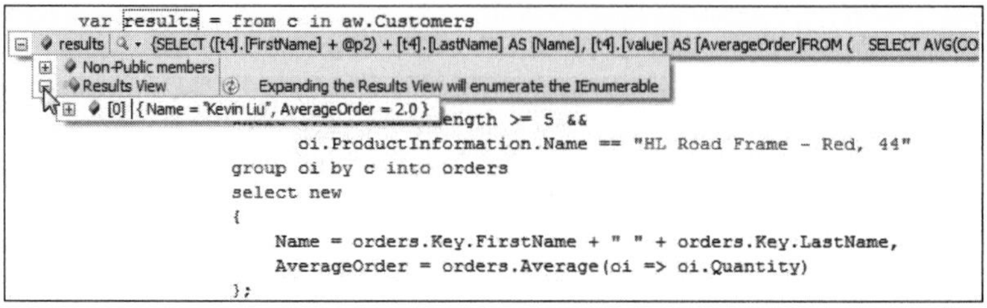

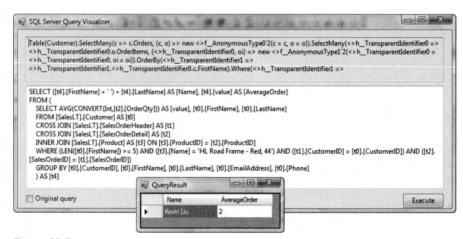

var results = from c in aw.Customers
results {SELECT ([t4].[FirstName] + @p2) + [t4].[LastName] AS [Name], [t4].[value] AS [AverageOrder]FROM (SELECT AVG(CO
Non-Public members
Results View
Expanding the Results View will enumerate the IEnumerable
[0] {Name = "Kevin Liu", AverageOrder = 2.0}
ength >= 5 &&
oi.ProductInformation.Name == "HL Road Frame - Red, 44"
group oi by c into orders
select new
{
Name = orders.Key.FirstName + " " + orders.Key.LastName,
AverageOrder = orders.Average(oi => oi.Quantity)
};

Figure 25-6

After adding the visualizer you will see the magnifying glass icon in the first line of the datatip, as in Figure 25-6. Clicking this will open up the LINQ to SQL Debug Visualizer so that you can see the way your LINQ to SQL statement is translated to SQL. Figure 25-7 illustrates this visualizer showing the way that the query is parsed by the compiler in the top half of the screen, and the SQL statement that is generated in the lower half of the screen. Clicking the "Execute" button will display the QueryResults window (inset into Figure 25-7) with the output of the SQL statement. Note that you can modify the SQL statement, allowing you to tweak it until you get the correct results set. This can quickly help you correct any errors in your LINQ statement.

SQL Server Query Visualizer
SELECT ([t4].[FirstName] + ' ') + [t4].[LastName] AS [Name], [t4].[value] AS [AverageOrder]
FROM (
SELECT AVG(CONVERT(Int,[t2].[OrderQty])) AS [value], [t0].[FirstName], [t0].[LastName]
FROM [SalesLT].[Customer] AS [t0]
CROSS JOIN [SalesLT].[SalesOrderHeader] AS [t1]
CROSS JOIN [SalesLT].[SalesOrderDetail] AS [t2]
INNER JOIN [SalesLT].[Product] AS [t3] ON [t3].[ProductID] = [t2].[ProductID]
GROUP BY [t0].[CustomerID], [t0].[FirstName], [t0].[LastName], [t0].[EmailAddress], [t0].[Phone]
) AS [t4]
QueryResult
Name
AverageOrder
Kevin Liu
2
Original query
Execute

Figure 25-7

Inserts, Updates, and Deletes

You can see from the earlier code snippet that the DataContext acts as the conduit through which LINQ to SQL queries are processed. To get a better appreciation of what the DataContext does behind the scenes, let's look at inserting a new product category into the AdventureWorksLT database. Before you can do this you will need to add the ProductCategory table to your LINQ to SQL design surface. In this case you don't need to modify any of the properties. Then to add a new category to your database, all you need is the following code:

```
Using aw As New AdventureLiteDataContext
    Dim cat As New ProductCategory
    cat.Name = "Extreme Bike"
    aw.ProductCategories.InsertOnSubmit(c)
    aw.SubmitChanges()
End Using
```

The highlighted lines insert the new category into the collection of product categories held in memory by the DataContext. When you then call SubmitChanges on the DataContext it is aware that you have added a new product category so it will insert the appropriate records. A similar process is used when making changes to existing items. In the following example we retrieve the product category we just inserted using the Like syntax. Because there is likely to be only one match, we can use the FirstOrDefault extension method to give us just a single product category to work with:

```
Using aw As New AdventureLiteDataContext
    Dim cat = (From pc In aw.ProductCategories _
                Where pc.Name Like "*Extreme*").FirstOrDefault
    cat.Name = "Extreme Offroad Bike"
    aw.SubmitChanges()
End Using
```

Once the change to the category name has been made, you just need to call SubmitChanges on the DataContext in order for it to issue the update on the database. Without going into too much detail the DataContext essentially tracks changes to each property on a LINQ to SQL object so that it knows which objects need updating when SubmitChanges is called. If you wish to delete an object, you simply need to obtain an instance of the LINQ to SQL object, in the same way as for doing an update, and then call DeleteOnSubmit on the appropriate collection. For example, to delete a product category you would call aw.ProductCategories.DeleteOnSubmit(categoryToDelete).

Stored Procedures

One of the questions frequently asked about LINQ to SQL is whether you can use your own stored procedures in place of the runtime-generated SQL. The good news is that for inserts, updates, and deletes you can easily specify the stored procedure that should be used. You can also use existing stored procedures for creating instances of LINQ to SQL objects. Let's start by adding a simple stored procedure to the AdventureWorksLT database. To do this, right-click the Stored Procedures node under the database connection in the Server Explorer tool window and select Add New Stored Procedure. This will open a code window with a new stored procedure template. In the following code we have selected to return the five fields that are relevant to our Customer object:

```
CREATE PROCEDURE dbo.GetCustomers
AS
BEGIN
    SET NOCOUNT ON
    SELECT c.CustomerID, c.FirstName, c.LastName, c.EmailAddress, c.Phone
    FROM SalesLT.Customer AS c
END;
```

Once you have saved this stored procedure it will appear under the Stored Procedures node. If you now open up the AdventureLite LINQ to SQL designer, you can drag this stored procedure across into the right-hand pane of the design surface. In Figure 25-8 you can see that the return type of the GetCustomers method is set to Auto-generated Type. This means that you will only be able to query information in the returned object. Ideally we would want to be able to make changes to these objects and be able to use the DataContext to persist those changes back to the database.

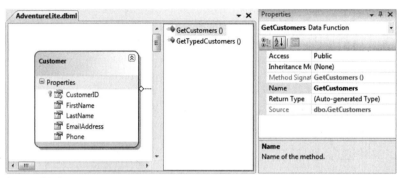

Figure 25-8

The second method, GetTypedCustomers, actually has the Return Type set as the Customer class. To create this method you can either drag the GetCustomers stored procedure to the right pane, and then set the Return Type to Customer, or you can drag the stored procedure onto the Customer class in the left pane of the design surface. The latter will still create the method in the right pane, but it will automatically specify the return type as the Customer type.

> *Note that you don't need to align properties with the stored procedure columns, because this mapping is automatically handled by the DataContext. This is a double-edged sword: clearly it works when the column names map to the source columns of the LINQ to SQL class but it may cause a runtime exception if there are missing columns or columns that don't match.*

Once you have defined these stored procedures as methods on the design surface, calling them is as easy as calling the appropriate method on the DataContext:

```
Using aw As New AdventureLiteDataContext
    Dim customers = aw.GetCustomers

    For Each c In customers
        MsgBox(c.FirstName)
    Next
End Using
```

Here you have seen how you can use a stored procedure to create instances of the LINQ to SQL classes. If you instead want to update, insert, or delete objects using stored procedures, you follow a similar process except you need to define the appropriate behavior on the LINQ to SQL class. To begin with, let's create an insert stored procedure for a new product category:

```
CREATE PROCEDURE dbo.InsertProductCategory
    (
    @categoryName nvarchar(50),
    @categoryId int OUTPUT
    )
AS
BEGIN
    INSERT INTO SalesLT.ProductCategory (Name) VALUES (@categoryName)
    SELECT @categoryId=@@identity
END;
```

Following the same process as before, you need to drag this newly created stored procedure from the Server Explorer across into the right pane of the LINQ to SQL design surface. Then in the Properties tool window for the `ProductCategory` class, modify the `Insert` property. This will open the dialog shown in Figure 25-9. Here you can select whether you want to use the runtime-generated code or customize the method that is used. In Figure 25-9 the `InsertProductCategory` method has been selected. Initially the Class Properties will be unspecified, because Visual Studio 2008 wasn't able to guess at which properties mapped to the method arguments. It's easy enough to align these to the `id` and `name` properties. Now when the DataContext goes to insert a ProductCategory it will use the stored procedure instead of the runtime-generated SQL statement.

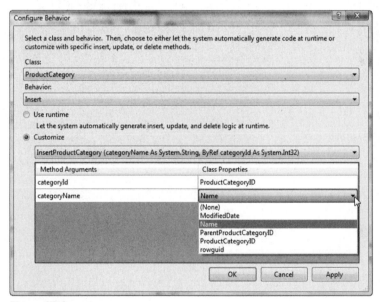

Figure 25-9

Binding LINQ to SQL Objects

The important thing to remember when using DataBinding with LINQ to SQL objects is that they are in fact normal .NET objects. This means that you can create a new object data source via the Data Sources tool window. In the case of the examples you have seen so far, you would go through the Add New Data

Source Wizard, selecting just the `Customer` object. Because the `Order` and `OrderItem` objects are accessible via the navigation properties `Orders` and then `OrderItems`, you don't need to explicitly add them to the Data Source window.

Once you have created the object data source (see the left side of Figure 25-10), you can then proceed to drag the nodes onto your form to create the appropriate data components. Starting with the Customer node, use the drop-down to specify that you want a DataGridView, then drag it onto your form. Next you need to specify that you want the Orders (a child node under Customer) to appear as details and then drag this to the form as well. You will notice that you don't get a binding navigator for this binding source, so from the Toolbox add a BindingNavigator to your form and set its `BindingSource` property to be the OrdersBindingSource that was created when you dragged over the Orders node. Lastly we want to display all the OrderItems in a DataGridView, so use the drop-down to set this and then drag the node onto the form. After doing all this you should end up with something similar to Figure 25-10. Note that we have also included a button that we will use to load the data and we have laid the Order information out in a panel to improve the layout.

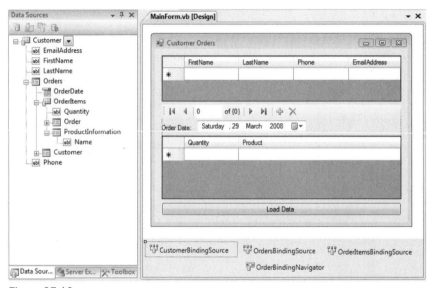

Figure 25-10

One of the things you will have noticed is that the columns on your OrderItems data grid don't match those in Figure 25-10. By default you will get Quantity, Order, and ProductInformation columns. Clearly the last two columns are not going to display anything of interest, but we don't really have an easy way to display the Name of the product in the order with the current LINQ to SQL objects. Luckily there is an easy way to effectively hide the navigation from OrderItem to ProductInformation so that the name of the product will appear as a property of OrderItem.

We do this by adding our own property to the `OrderItem` class. Each `LINQ to SQL` class is generated as a partial class, which means that extending the class is as easy as right-clicking on the class in the LINQ to SQL designer and selecting View Code. This will generate a custom code file, in our case AdventureLite.vb, and will include the partial class definition. You can then proceed to add your own code. In the following snippet we have added the `Product` property that will simplify access to the name of the product being ordered:

```
Partial Class OrderItem
    Public ReadOnly Property Product() As String
        Get
            Return Me.ProductInformation.Name
        End Get
    End Property
End Class
```

For some reason this property, perhaps because it is added to a second code file, will not be detected by the Data Sources tool window. However, you can still bind the Product column to this property by manually setting the `DataPropertyName` field in the Edit Columns dialog for the data grid.

The last thing to do is to actually load the data when the user clicks the button. To do this we can use the following code:

```
Private Sub btnLoad_Click(ByVal sender As System.Object, _
                ByVal e As System.EventArgs) Handles btnLoad.Click
    Using aw As New AdventureLiteDataContext
        Dim custs = From c In aw.Customers
        Me.CustomerBindingSource.DataSource = custs
    End Using
End Sub
```

You will notice that your application will now run and when the user clicks the button the customer information will be populated in the top data grid. However, no matter which customer you select, no information will appear in the Order information area. The reason for this is that LINQ to SQL uses lazy loading to retrieve information as it is required. Using the data visualizer you were introduced to earlier, if you inspect the query in this code you will see that it contains only the customer information:

```
SELECT [t0].[CustomerID], [t0].[FirstName], [t0].[LastName], [t0].[EmailAddress],
[t0].[Phone]
FROM [SalesLT].[Customer] AS [t0]
```

There are two ways to resolve this issue. The first is to force LINQ to SQL to bring back all the Order, OrderItem, and ProductInformation data as part of the initial query. To do this, modify the button click code to the following:

```
Private Sub btnLoad_Click(ByVal sender As System.Object, _
                    ByVal e As System.EventArgs) Handles btnLoad.Click
    Using aw As New AdventureLiteDataContext
        Dim loadOptions As New System.Data.Linq.DataLoadOptions
        loadOptions.LoadWith(Of Customer)(Function(c As Customer) c.Orders)
        loadOptions.LoadWith(Of Order)(Function(o As Order) o.OrderItems)
        loadOptions.LoadWith(Of OrderItem)(Function(oi As OrderItem) _
                        oi.ProductInformation)
        aw.LoadOptions = loadOptions

        Dim custs = From c In aw.Customers
        Me.CustomerBindingSource.DataSource = custs
    End Using
End Sub
```

Essentially what this code tells the DataContext is that when it retrieves `Customer` objects it should forcibly navigate to the `Orders` property. Similarly for the `Order` objects navigate to the `OrderItems` property, and so on. One thing to be aware of is that this solution could perform really badly if there are a large number of customers. In fact as the number of customers and orders increases, this will perform progressively worse, so this is not a great solution; but it does illustrate how you can use the `LoadOptions` property of the DataContext.

The other alternative is to not dispose of the DataContext. You need to remember what is happening behind the scenes with DataBinding. When you select a customer in the data grid, this will cause the OrderBindingSource to refresh. It tries to navigate to the `Orders` property on the customer. If you have disposed of the DataContext, there is no way that the `Orders` property can be populated. So the better solution to this problem is to change the code to the following:

```
Private aw As New AdventureLiteDataContext
Private Sub btnLoad_Click(ByVal sender As System.Object, _
                           ByVal e As System.EventArgs) Handles btnLoad.Click
    Dim custs = From c In aw.Customers
    Me.CustomerBindingSource.DataSource = custs
End Sub
```

Because the DataContext will still exist, when the binding source navigates to the various properties, LINQ to SQL will kick in, populating these properties with data. This is much more scalable than attempting to populate the whole customer hierarchy when the user clicks the button.

LINQ to Entities

At the time of writing, LINQ to Entities is still under development so some parts of the following discussion may vary in the final product. LINQ to Entities is a much larger set of technologies than LINQ to SQL. However, because it is still unreleased and likely to change, we will give only a rough overview of the technology in this chapter. Currently, to work with LINQ to Entities you need to download and install the ADO.NET Entity Framework and the ADO.NET Entity Framework Tools. It is likely that both of these will ship as a single update around the time of SQL Server 2008.

LINQ to Entities, like LINQ to SQL, is an object-relational mapping technology. However, unlike LINQ to SQL it is composed of a number of layers that define the database schema, entities schema, and a mapping between them. Although this adds quite a bit of additional complexity, it does mean that you have much richer capabilities when it comes to how you map your objects to tables in the database. For example, a customer entity might consist of information coming from the Customer and Individual tables in the database. Using LINQ to SQL you would have to represent this as two objects with a one-to-one association. With LINQ to Entities you can combine this information into a single `Customer` object that pulls data from both tables.

Let's walk through a simple example as an overview of this technology. Again we will use the AdventureWorksLT database and a Visual Basic Windows Forms application. In order to work with LINQ to Entities you need to add a new ADO.NET Entity Data Model, as you can see in Figure 25-11.

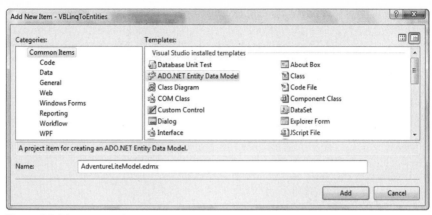

Figure 25-11

Unlike LINQ to SQL, where you were just presented with a designer, with LINQ to Entities you walk through a wizard where you can select either to generate the model from a database or just start with an empty model. Given that you want to base the model on the AdventureWorksLT database, you need to walk through the remainder of the wizard, select the appropriate database connection and then the database object you want to include. We want to use the same data we worked with earlier, so select the Customer, Product, SalesOrderDetail, and SalesOrderHeader tables. Figure 25-12 shows these four tables as entities in the LINQ to Entities designer.

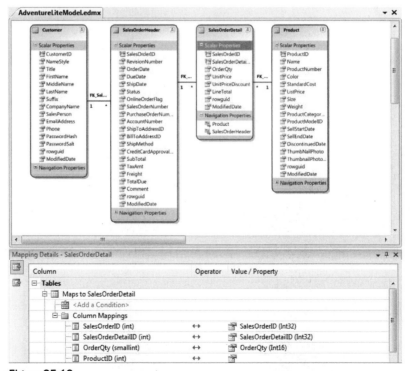

Figure 25-12

At the bottom of Figure 25-12, you can see the mappings for the SalesOrderDetail entity. As you can see, it is currently mapped to the SalesOrderDetail table and has mappings for the SalesOrderID, SalesOrderDetailID, and OrderQty columns. As with LINQ to SQL, you can easily modify the names of the entities, properties, and associations to make them easier to deal with in your code. Using the Mapping Details tool window, you can extend your entities to map to multiple tables, as well as overriding the insert, update, and delete functions.

To work with your entities you use similar code to LINQ to SQL, but instead of creating an instance of the DataContext, you need to create an instance of the object context, which in our case is the `AdventureWorksLTEntities` class. The following code queries all customers that have a first name longer than five characters:

```
Using alm As New AdventureWorksLTModel.AdventureWorksLTEntities
    Dim custs = From c In alm.Customer _
                Where c.FirstName.Length > 5
    For Each c In custs
        MsgBox(c.FirstName)
    Next
End Using
```

Other entity operations, such as inserting and deleting, are done slightly differently. Instead of calling InsertOnSubmit on the relevant collection, you need to call AddToCustomer to add a customer, AddToProduct to add a product, and so on. To delete an entity you need to call DeleteObject.

Summary

In this chapter you were introduced to LINQ to SQL and how you can use it as a basic object-relational mapping framework. Although you are somewhat limited in being able only to map an object to a single table, it can still dramatically simplify working with a database.

Here you have only just touched on the true power of LINQ to Entities. With much more sophisticated mapping capabilities, this technology will dramatically change the way you will work with data in the future.

26

Synchronization Services

Application design has gone through many extremes, ranging from stand-alone applications that don't share data to public web applications in which everyone connects to the same data store. More recently, we have seen a flurry in the number of peer-to-peer applications in which information is shared between nodes but no central data store exists. In the enterprise space, key buzzwords such as Software as a Service (SaaS) and Software and Services (S+S) highlight the transition from centralized data stores, through an era of outsourced data and application services, toward a hybrid model where data and services are combined within a rich application.

One of the reasons organizations have leaned toward web applications in the past has been the need to rationalize their data into a single central repository. Although rich client applications can work well across a low-latency network using the same data repository, they quickly become unusable if every action requires data to be communicated between the client and server over a slow public network. In order to reduce this latency, an alternative strategy is to synchronize a portion of the data repository to the client machine and to make local data requests. This will not only improve performance, as all the data requests happen locally, but it will also reduce the load on the server. In this chapter, you will discover how building applications that are only occasionally connected can help you build rich and responsive applications using the Microsoft Synchronization Services for ADO.NET.

Occasionally Connected Applications

An occasionally connected application is one that can continue to operate regardless of connectivity status. There are a number of different ways to access data when the application is offline. Passive systems simply cache data that is accessed from the server, so that when the connection is lost at least a subset of the information is available. Unfortunately, this strategy means that a very limited set of data is available and is really only suitable for scenarios where there is an unstable or unreliable connection, rather than completely disconnected applications. In the latter case, an active system that synchronizes data to the local system is required. The

Microsoft Synchronization Services for ADO.NET (Sync Services) is a synchronization framework that dramatically simplifies the problem of synchronizing data from any server to the local system.

Server Direct

To get familiar with the Sync Services, we will use a simple database that consists of a single table that tracks customers. You can create this using the Server Explorer within Visual Studio 2008. Right-click the Data Connections node and select Create New SQL Server Database from the shortcut menu. Figure 26-1 shows the Create New SQL Server Database dialog in which you can specify a server and a name for the new database.

Figure 26-1

When you click "OK", a database with the name CRM will be added to the local host SQL Server instance and a data connection added to the Data Connections node in the Server Explorer. From the Tables node, under the newly created data connection, select Add New Table from the right-click shortcut menu and create columns for CustomerId (primary key), Name, Email and Phone so that the table matches what is shown in Figure 26-2.

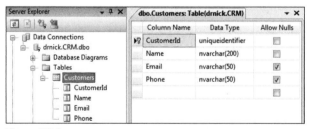

Figure 26-2

Now that you have a simple database to work with, it's time to create a new Visual Basic Windows Forms Application. In this case the application is titled QuickCRM, and in the Solution Explorer tool window of Figure 26-3 you can see that we have renamed Form1 to MainForm and added two additional forms, ServerForm and LocalForm.

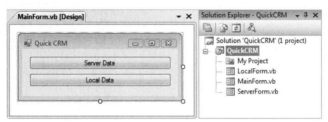

Figure 26-3

MainForm has two buttons, as shown in the editor area of Figure 26-3, and has the following code in order to launch the appropriate forms:

```
Public Class MainForm
    Private Sub btnServer_Click(ByVal sender As Object, _
                                ByVal e As EventArgs) Handles btnServer.Click
        My.Forms.ServerForm.Show()
    End Sub
    Private Sub btnLocal_Click(ByVal sender As Object, _
                                ByVal e As EventArgs) Handles btnLocal.Click
        My.Forms.LocalForm.Show()
    End Sub
End Class
```

Before we look at how you can use Sync Services to work with local data, let's see how you might have built an always-connected, or server-bound, version. From the Data menu select Add New Data Source and step through the Data Source Configuration Wizard, selecting the CRM database created earlier, saving the connection string to the application configuration file, and adding the Customers table to the CRMDataSet.

Open the ServerForm designer by double-clicking it in the Solution Explorer tool window. If the Data Sources tool window is not already visible, then select Show Data Sources from the Data menu. Using the drop-down on the Customers node, select Details and then select None from the CustomerId node. Dragging the Customers node across onto the design surface of the ServerForm will add the appropriate controls so that you can locate, edit, and save records to the Customers table of the CRM database, as shown in Figure 26-4.

Figure 26-4

You will recall from our table definition that the CustomerId can't be null, so we need to ensure that any new records are created with a new ID. To do this we tap into the `CurrentChanged` event on the `CustomersBindingSource` object. You can access this either directly in the code-behind of the ServerForm or by selecting `CustomersBindingSource` and finding the appropriate event in the Properties tool window.

```
Private Sub CustomersBindingSource_CurrentChanged _
                   (ByVal sender As System.Object, ByVal e As System.EventArgs) _
                                 Handles CustomersBindingSource.CurrentChanged
    Dim c As CRMDataSet.CustomersRow = _
    CType(CType(Me.CustomersBindingSource.CurrencyManager.Current, _
                        DataRowView).Row, _
                 CRMDataSet.CustomersRow)
    If c.RowState = DataRowState.Detached Then
        c.CustomerId = Guid.NewGuid
    End If
End Sub
```

This completes the part of the application that connects directly to the database to access the data. You can run the application and verify that you can access data while the database is online. If the database goes offline or the connection is lost, an exception will be raised by the application when you attempt to retrieve from the database or save new changes.

Getting Started with Synchronization Services

To get started with Sync Services you need to add a Local Database Cache item to your project via the Add New Item dialog. Following the CRM theme, we will name this `CRMDataCache.Sync`. As the name implies, this item is going to define the attributes of the cache in which the local data will be stored, as well as some of the synchronization properties. As the cache item is added to the project, this launches the Configure Data Synchronization dialog, shown in Figure 26-5.

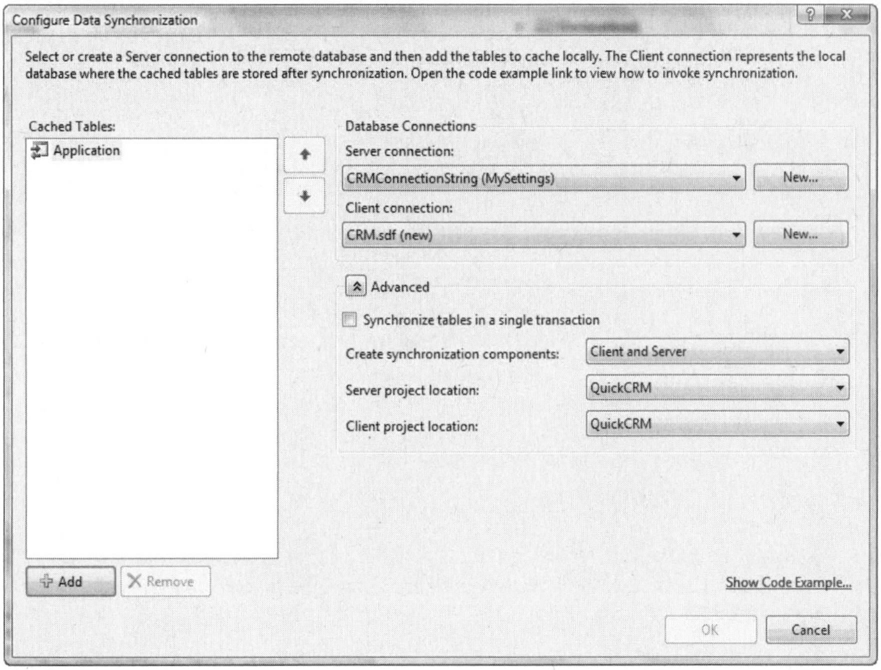

Figure 26-5

Unlike most dialogs, which generally work from left to right, this dialog starts in the middle with the definition of the database connections. The server connection drop-down should already include the connection string to the database that was created earlier. Once a server connection has been selected, a local database will be automatically created for the client connection if there are no SQL Server Compact 3.5 (SSCE) database files (.sdf) in the project. In Figure 26-5, the word "new" in parentheses after the client connection name indicates that the CRM.sdf has been newly created either automatically or via the "New" button within this dialog.

The next thing that needs to be decided is which of the server tables should be synchronized, or cached, in the client database. To begin with, the area at the left of Figure 26-5, entitled Cached Tables, is empty except for the Application node. You can add tables from the server with the "Add" button. This will launch the dialog shown in Figure 26-6.

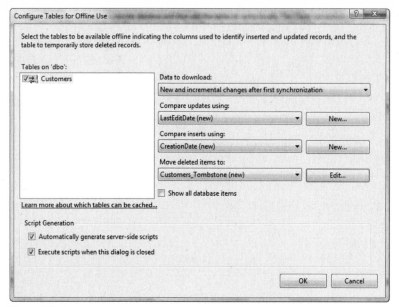

Figure 26-6

Before we look at the different fields in this dialog, you need to understand how most synchronization is coordinated. In most cases, an initial snapshot is taken of the data on the server and sent to the client. The next time the client synchronizes, the synchronization engine has to work out what has changed on both the client and the server since the last synchronization. Different technologies use different markers to track when things change and what changes need to be synchronized as a result. Sync Services takes quite a generic approach, one assuming that each table has a column that tracks when updates are made and when records are created. It also uses an additional backing table to track items that have been deleted. As you can imagine, if you have a large database, adding these additional columns and tables makes for significant overhead to support synchronization.

On the left of the Configure Tables for Offline Use dialog in Figure 26-6, you can see a list of all the tables that are available for synchronization. This list will include only tables that belong to the user's default schema (in this case dbo), have a primary key, and don't contain data types not supported by SSCE. Note that some of these limitations are imposed by the designer, not necessarily the synchronization framework itself. For example, you can manually configure Sync Services to synchronize tables from other schemas.

Selecting a table for synchronization will enable you to define the synchronization attributes for that table. In Figure 26-6, we have selected "New and incremental changes after first synchronization" to reduce network bandwidth. The trade-off is that more work is involved in tracking changes between synchronizations, which requires changes to the server database schema to track modifications. As the Customers table that we created earlier doesn't have columns for tracking when changes are made, the dialog has suggested that we create a LastEditDate, a CreationDate, and a new table, Customers_ Tombstone. By default, the additional columns are dates, but you can change these to be time stamps by clicking the "New" button and changing the data type.

In the lower area of Figure 26-6 are checkboxes with which you can control how the dialog behaves when you click "OK". If you're working on a database shared by others, you may want to review the generated scripts before allowing them to execute. In our case we will leave both checkboxes checked, which will create the database scripts (including undo scripts) and add them to our project, as well as execute them on the server database, to give us the additional change-tracking columns. The scripts will also add appropriate triggers to the Customers table to ensure the change-tracking columns are updated and to add deleted items to the Tombstone table. Clicking "OK" on this dialog will add the Customers node to the Configure Data Synchronization dialog so that it appears as in Figure 26-7.

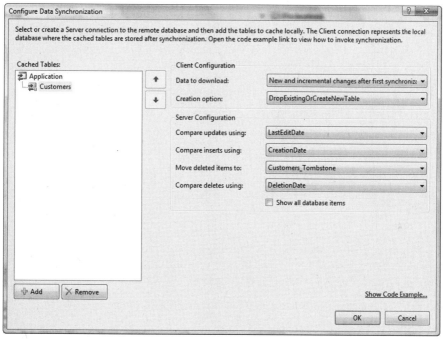

Figure 26-7

Selecting the Customers node enables you to change the options you just set, as well as use an additional Creation option. You can use this option to tailor how the synchronization framework will behave during the initial synchronization of data. For this example we will continue with the default value of `DropExistingOrCreateNewTable`. Clicking "OK" will both persist this configuration in the form of synchronization classes and invoke a synchronization between the server and the local data file, as shown in Figure 26-8.

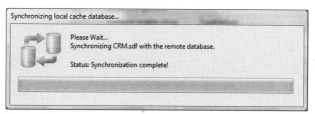

Figure 26-8

Forcing synchronization at this point means that the newly created SSCE database file is populated with the correct schema and any data available on the server. Once completed, the new database file is then added to the project. This in turn triggers the Dataset Configuration wizard. Step through this wizard, naming the new dataset LocalCRMDataSet, and include the Customers table.

If you now look at the Data Sources tool window, you will see that there is a LocalCRMDataSet node that contains a Customers node. As we did previously, set the Customers node to Details and the CustomerId, LastEditDate, and CreationDate nodes to None. Then drag the Customers node across onto the designer surface of the LocalForm. The result should be a form similar to the one shown in Figure 26-9.

Figure 26-9

Adding these components brings the same components to the design surface and the same code to the form as when we were connecting directly to the server. The difference here is that a CustomersTableAdapter will connect to the local database instead of the server. As we did before, we need to add the code to specify the CustomerId for new records.

```
Private Sub CustomersBindingSource_CurrentChanged _
                    (ByVal sender As System.Object, ByVal e As System.EventArgs) _
                                Handles CustomersBindingSource.CurrentChanged
    Dim c As LocalCRMDataSet.CustomersRow = _
    CType(CType(Me.CustomersBindingSource.CurrencyManager.Current, _
                        DataRowView).Row, _
                    LocalCRMDataSet.CustomersRow)
    If c.RowState = DataRowState.Detached Then
        c.CustomerId = Guid.NewGuid
    End If
End Sub
```

The last thing we need to add to this part of the project is a mechanism to invoke the synchronization process. Simply add a button, btnSynchronize, to the bottom of the LocalForm and double-click it to generate the click-event handler. Instead of our having to remember the syntax for working with the synchronization API, the team has given us a useful code snippet that we can drop into this event handler. Back in Figure 26-7, there was a link toward the lower right corner, just above the "OK" and "Cancel" buttons, titled "Show Code Example. . ." Clicking this will show a dialog that contains a code snippet you can copy and then paste into the click-event handler.

```
Private Sub btnSynchronize_Click(ByVal sender As System.Object, _
                      ByVal e As System.EventArgs) Handles btnSynchronize.Click
    ' Call SyncAgent.Synchronize() to initiate the synchronization process.
    ' Synchronization only updates the local database,
    ' not your project's data source.
    Dim syncAgent As CRMDataCacheSyncAgent = New CRMDataCacheSyncAgent()
    Dim syncStats As Microsoft.Synchronization.Data.SyncStatistics = _
    syncAgent.Synchronize()

    ' TODO: Reload your project data source from the local database
    '(for example, call the TableAdapter.Fill method).
    Me.CustomersTableAdapter.Fill(Me.LocalCRMDataSet.Customers)
End Sub
```

Pay particular attention to the next-to-last line of this snippet, in which we use the CustomersTableAdapter to fill the Customers table. This is important: Without this line the user interface will not reflect changes in the SSCE database that have been made by the synchronization process.

Synchronization Services over N-Tiers

So far, the entire synchronization process is conducted within the client application with a direct connection to the server. One of the objectives of an occasionally connected application is to be able to synchronize data over any connection, regardless of whether it is a corporate intranet or the public Internet. Unfortunately, with the current application you need to expose your SQL Server so that the application can connect to it. This is clearly a security violation, which you can solve by taking a more distributed approach. Sync Services has been designed with this in mind, allowing the server components to be isolated into a service that can be called during synchronization.

In this walkthrough we will create a new Local Database Cache that uses a WCF service to perform the server side of the synchronization process. To begin with, you need to add a new Visual Basic WCF Service Library project (under the WCF node of the Add New Project dialog) to your solution. We will call this project CRMServices. As we are going to use the Configure Data Synchronization dialog to create the service contract and implementation, you can remove the IService1.vb and Service1.vb files that are created by default.

You may have noticed in Figure 26-5 that there are options regarding which components will be created by the Configure Data Synchronization dialog. Previously, we wanted both client and server components to be located within the client application. However, we now want to create a new Local Database Cache object that places the server components into the CRMServices service library. As you did previously, add a new Local Database Cache object to the QuickCRM project, call it ServiceCRMDataCache.sync, and configure it to synchronize the Customers table. You will notice that when you go to select which tables you want to synchronize, the newly created Customers_Tombstone table is listed, and the columns for tracking when updates and inserts occur on the Customers table are not marked with the word "new." All you need to do is check the box next to the Customers node. As there are no changes to be made to the database schema, you can also uncheck both script-generation boxes. The main difference with the newly created cache object is that the location of the server components is the CRMServices service library, as indicated by the "Server project location" selection in Figure 26-10.

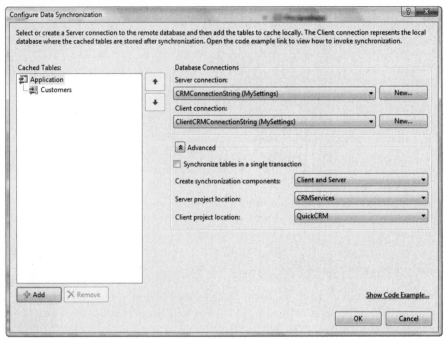

Figure 26-10

You will notice that when you click the "OK" button the new cache object, `ServiceCRMDataCache`
`.sync`, is added to the QuickCRM project. Two items also are added to the CRMServices project:
`ServiceCRMDataCache.Server.sync` and `ServiceCRMDataCache.Server.SyncContract.vb`.
The latter is where the service contract is defined.

```
<ServiceContractAttribute()>  _
Public Interface IServiceCRMDataCacheSyncContract
    <OperationContract()>  _
    Function ApplyChanges(ByVal groupMetadata As SyncGroupMetadata, _
                      ByVal dataSet As DataSet, _
                      ByVal syncSession As SyncSession) As SyncContext
    <OperationContract()>  _
    Function GetChanges(ByVal groupMetadata As SyncGroupMetadata, _
                      ByVal syncSession As SyncSession) As SyncContext
    <OperationContract()>  _
    Function GetSchema(ByVal tableNames As Collection(Of String), _
                      ByVal syncSession As SyncSession) As SyncSchema
    <OperationContract()>  _
    Function GetServerInfo(ByVal syncSession As SyncSession) As SyncServerInfo
End Interface
```

This file also declares an implementation for this contract that creates a
`ServiceCRMDataCacheServerSyncProvider` object (defined in `ServiceCRMDataCache.Server`
`.sync`), into which it forwards each request. Because of this, the WCF service is simply a proxy for the
server components. At the top of `ServiceCRMDataCache.Server.SyncContract.vb` are instructions

for adding the relevant service and behavior declarations to the `app.config` file. In our case we want to remove the service and behavior declarations for Service1 and replace them with these. This should give you a `system.serviceModel` section within the `app.config` file similar to the following:

```
<system.serviceModel>
    <services>
        <service name="CRMServices.ServiceCRMDataCacheSyncService"
behaviorConfiguration="CRMServices.ServiceCRMDataCacheSyncServiceBehavior">
            <host><baseAddresses>
                    <add baseAddress ="http://localhost:8080/
ServiceCRMDataCacheSyncService/"/>
            </baseAddresses></host>
            <endpoint address ="" binding="wsHttpBinding" contract="CRMServices
.IServiceCRMDataCacheSyncContract"/>
            <endpoint address="mex" binding="mexHttpBinding"
contract="IMetadataExchange" />
        </service>
    </services>
    <behaviors>
        <serviceBehaviors>
            <behavior name="CRMServices.ServiceCRMDataCacheSyncServiceBehavior">
                <serviceMetadata httpGetEnabled="True" />
                <serviceDebug includeExceptionDetailInFaults="False" />
            </behavior>
        </serviceBehaviors>
    </behaviors>
</system.serviceModel>
```

At this stage you should verify that your service declaration is correct by setting the CRMServices project to be your startup project and by launching your solution. Doing this will attempt to invoke the WCF Service Host and may result in the dialog in Figure 26-11 being displayed.

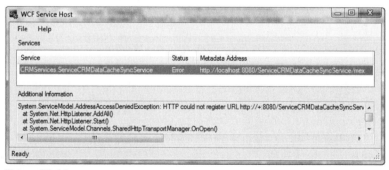

Figure 26-11

This is a well-documented error (see `http://go.microsoft.com/fwlink/?LinkId=70353`) that relates to the security involved in reserving portions of the `http` URL namespace. In Figure 26-11, you can see that it is attempting to register the address `http://localhost:8080/ServiceCRMDataCacheSyncService`. If you are running Windows Vista, you can overcome this issue using the `netsh` command (Windows XP or Windows Server 2003 uses the `httpcfg.exe` command) while running in Administrator mode.

```
>netsh http add urlacl url=http://+:8080/ServiceCRMDataCacheSyncService
user=MyDomain\nick
```

After reserving the appropriate URL namespace for when you run the CRMServices project, you should see the WCF Test Client dialog. Unfortunately, none of the service operations that we have defined is supported by the test client, but this dialog does verify that the service has been correctly set up.

The last thing we need to do is to configure the client application, QuickCRM, so that it knows to use the WCF service we have just defined. To do this, right-click the QuickCRM node on the Solution Explorer and select the Add Service Reference item. Using the Discover drop-down, shown in the upper right corner of Figure 26-12, you can easily find the WCF service in your solution.

There appears to be an issue with the Visual Studio 2008 Add Service Reference functionality. By default, it will attempt to reuse types that are defined in assemblies referenced by the consuming project. However, if you haven't built your project before adding the service reference, you may find that it creates unwanted type definitions. To resolve this you need to remove the service reference, close the solution, and delete the .suo file associated with your solution. (This file has the same name as your solution, except with the .suo extension, and will be located in the same folder as your solution.) Before attempting to add the service reference, ensure you have built all projects within your solution.

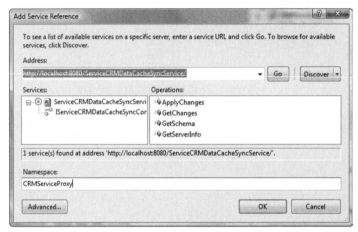

Figure 26-12

Adding a service reference this way also adds unnecessary security information to the app.config file in the QuickCRM project. In the following snippet you will see an Identity element. This element, not the entire snippet, needs to be removed in order for your project to be able to call the WCF service.

```
<client>
    <endpoint address="http://localhost:8080/ServiceCRMDataCacheSyncService/"
            binding="wsHttpBinding" bindingConfiguration="WSHttpBinding_
IServiceCRMDataCacheSyncContract"
        contract="CRMServiceProxy.IServiceCRMDataCacheSyncContract"
        name="WSHttpBinding_IServiceCRMDataCacheSyncContract">
        <identity>
            <userPrincipalName value="drnick\nick" />
        </identity>
    </endpoint>
</client>
```

Now that the application has a reference to the WCF service, you need to tell Sync Services to use the service as a proxy for the server side of the synchronization process. This involves overriding the default behavior of the `ServiceCRMDataCacheSyncAgent` that was created by the `Local Database Cache` object created earlier. To open the code window, right-click the `ServiceCRMDataCache.sync` item in Solution Explorer and select View Code.

```
Partial Public Class ServiceCRMDataCacheSyncAgent
    Private Sub OnInitialized()
        Dim proxy As New CRMServiceProxy.ServiceCRMDataCacheSyncContractClient
        Me.RemoteProvider = _
                    New Microsoft.Synchronization.Data.ServerSyncProviderProxy(proxy)
    End Sub
End Class
```

The two lines that make up the `OnInitialized` method create an instance of the WCF service proxy and then declare this as a proxy for the SyncAgent to use to perform the server components of the synchronization process.

This completes the steps necessary for setting up Sync Services to use a WCF service as a proxy for the server components. What remains is to add a "Synchronize Via Service" button to the LocalForm and then add the following code to the click-event handler in order to invoke the synchronization:

```
Private Sub btnSynchronizeViaService_Click(ByVal sender As System.Object, _
                                ByVal e As System.EventArgs) _
                            Handles btnSynchronizeViaService.Click
    ' Call SyncAgent.Synchronize() to initiate the synchronization process.
    ' Synchronization only updates the local database,
    ' not your project's data source.
    Dim syncAgent As ServiceCRMDataCacheSyncAgent = _
                            New ServiceCRMDataCacheSyncAgent()
    Dim syncStats As Microsoft.Synchronization.Data.SyncStatistics = _
                            syncAgent.Synchronize()

    ' TODO: Reload your project data source from the local database
    ' (for example, call the TableAdapter.Fill method).
    Me.CustomersTableAdapter.Fill(Me.LocalCRMDataSet.Customers)
End Sub
```

You will notice that this is the same code we used when synchronizing directly with the server. In fact, your application can monitor network connectivity, and depending on whether you can connect directly to the server, you can elect to use either of the two Sync Service implementations you have created in this walkthrough.

Background Synchronization

You will have noticed that when you click either of the synchronize buttons, the user interface appears to hang until the synchronization completes. Clearly this wouldn't be acceptable in a real-world application, so you need to synchronize the data in the background, thereby allowing the user to continue working. By adding a BackgroundWorker component (in the Components group in the Toolbox) to the LocalForm, we can do this with only minimal changes to our application. The following code illustrates how you can wire up the events of the BackgroundWorker, which has been named `bgWorker`, to use either of the Sync Service implementations:

```
Private Sub btnSynchronize_Click(ByVal sender As Object, ByVal e As EventArgs) _
    Handles btnSynchronize.Click
    Me.btnSynchronize.Enabled = False
    Me.btnSynchronizeViaService.Enabled = False

    Me.bgWorker.RunWorkerAsync(New CRMDataCacheSyncAgent())
End Sub

Private Sub btnSynchronizeViaService_Click(ByVal sender As System.Object, _
                                    ByVal e As System.EventArgs) _
                                Handles btnSynchronizeViaService.Click
    Me.btnSynchronize.Enabled = False
    Me.btnSynchronizeViaService.Enabled = False

    Me.bgWorker.RunWorkerAsync(New ServiceCRMDataCacheSyncAgent())
End Sub

Private Sub bgWorker_DoWork(ByVal sender As System.Object, _
                        ByVal e As System.ComponentModel.DoWorkEventArgs) _
                                        Handles bgWorker.DoWork
    Dim syncAgent As Microsoft.Synchronization.SyncAgent = _
                    TryCast(e.Argument, Microsoft.Synchronization.SyncAgent)
    If syncAgent Is Nothing Then Return
    syncAgent.Synchronize()
End Sub

Private Sub bgWorker_RunWorkerCompleted(ByVal sender As System.Object, _
                    ByVal e As System.ComponentModel.RunWorkerCompletedEventArgs) _
                                        Handles bgWorker.RunWorkerCompleted
    Me.CustomersTableAdapter.Fill(Me.LocalCRMDataSet.Customers)

    Me.btnSynchronize.Enabled = True
    Me.btnSynchronizeViaService.Enabled = True
End Sub
```

In this snippet we are not reporting any progress, but Sync Services does support quite a rich event model that you can hook into in order to report on progress. If you want to report progress via the BackgroundWorker component, you need to enable its `WorkerReportsProgress` property. The following code illustrates you how can hook into the `ApplyChanges` event on the client component of Sync Services in order to report progress (in this case to a label called "lblSyncProgress" added to the form). There are other events that correspond to different points in the synchronization process.

```
Private Sub bgWorker_DoWork(ByVal sender As System.Object, _
                        ByVal e As System.ComponentModel.DoWorkEventArgs) _
        Handles bgWorker.DoWork
    Dim syncAgent As Microsoft.Synchronization.SyncAgent = _
                    TryCast(e.Argument, Microsoft.Synchronization.SyncAgent)
    If syncAgent Is Nothing Then Return
```

```
        Dim clientProvider As _
            Microsoft.Synchronization.Data.SqlServerCe.SqlCeClientSyncProvider = _
            CType(syncAgent.LocalProvider, _
                Microsoft.Synchronization.Data.SqlServerCe.SqlCeClientSyncProvider)
        AddHandler clientProvider.ApplyingChanges, AddressOf ApplyingChanges
        syncAgent.Synchronize()
    End Sub
    Private Sub ApplyingChanges(ByVal sender As Object, _
                    ByVal e As Microsoft.Synchronization.Data.ApplyingChangesEventArgs)
        Me.bgWorker.ReportProgress(25, "Applying Changes")
    End Sub

    Private Sub bgWorker_ProgressChanged(ByVal sender As Object, _
                        ByVal e As System.ComponentModel.ProgressChangedEventArgs) _
                                            Handles bgWorker.ProgressChanged
        Me.lblSyncProgress.Text = e.UserState.ToString
    End Sub
```

Client Changes

Working through the example so far, you may have been wondering why none of the changes you have made on the client is being synchronized to the server. If you go back to Figure 26-6, you will recall that we selected "New and incremental changes after first synchronization" from the top drop-down, which might lead you to believe that changes from both the client and server will be synchronized. This is not the case and it is the wording above this control that gives it away. For whatever reason, this control only enables you to select options pertaining to "Data to download." In order to get changes to propagate in both directions, you have to override the default behavior for each table that is going to be synchronized. Again, right-click the CRMDataCache object in the Solution Explorer and select View Code. In the following code, we have set the SyncDirection property of the CustomersSyncTable to be bidirectional. You may also want to do this for the ServerCRMDataCache item so that both synchronization mechanisms will allow changes to propagate between client and server.

```
    Partial Public Class CRMDataCacheSyncAgent
        Partial Class CustomersSyncTable
            Private Sub OnInitialized()
                Me.SyncDirection = _
                            Microsoft.Synchronization.Data.SyncDirection.Bidirectional
            End Sub
        End Class
    End Class
```

If you were synchronizing other tables, you would need to set SyncDirection on each of the corresponding SyncTables. An alternative implementation would be to place this code in the OnInitialized method of the SyncAgent itself. Whichever way you choose, you still need to apply the Bidirectional value to all tables you want to synchronize in both directions.

```
    Partial Public Class CRMDataCacheSyncAgent
        Private Sub OnInitialized()
            Me.Customers.SyncDirection = _
                        Microsoft.Synchronization.Data.SyncDirection.Bidirectional
        End Sub
    End Class
```

Summary

In this chapter you have seen how to use the Microsoft Synchronization Services for ADO.NET to build an occasionally connected application. While you have other considerations when building such an application, such as how to detect network connectivity, you have seen how to perform synchronization as a background task and how to separate the client and server components into different application tiers. With this knowledge, you can begin to work with this new technology to build richer applications that will continue to work regardless of where they are being used.

The importance of Sync Services in building occasionally connected applications suggests that it would be perfectly suited for building applications for mobile devices such as those capable of running the .NET Compact Framework. As you have seen in this chapter, the initial release of Sync Services works with SQL Server Compact Edition on the client side, which again suggests this technology is suited for Windows Mobile devices. Unfortunately, the initial release of the Microsoft Synchronization Services for ADO.NET does not have support for running against the .NET Compact Framework. However, you can expect a subsequent release to include support for device applications.

Part VI
Security

27

Security in the .NET Framework

Application security is a consideration that is often put off until the end of a development project or, in all too many cases, ignored completely. As our applications become increasingly interconnected, the need to design and build secure systems is becoming increasingly important. Fortunately the .NET Framework provides a full suite of security features that make it easier than ever to build security into our applications.

In Chapter 28 you'll see how to secure your data by implementing cryptography, and in Chapter 29 protecting your source code is explained through the process of obfuscation. However, before you approach either feature within Visual Studio 2008 application programming, you should be familiar with the basic concepts that underpin how security works within the .NET environment.

Because security is such an important requirement for many applications, this chapter introduces these concepts, rather than examining any specific technical feature of the IDE.

Key Security Concepts

Security is best tackled in a holistic manner, by considering not just the application, but also the host and network environment where it is deployed. There's no use spending time encrypting your database connection strings if the administrator password is easy to guess!

One approach to implementing effective security is to consider the possible risks and threats to your application. Called *threat modeling*, this technique involves identifying threats, vulnerabilities, and most importantly, countermeasures for your specific application scenario.

> *When it comes to security threat modeling, it's a good idea to approach the world with a healthy dose of paranoia. As Kurt Cobain said, "Just because you're paranoid doesn't mean they aren't after you."*

Table 27-1 categorizes the areas that should be considered as part of a threat modeling exercise.

Table 27-1: Threat Modeling Considerations

Category	Considerations
Authentication	How do we verify a user and match this user with an identity in the system?
	Authentication is the process in which a user or system proves its identity. This is typically done either through something the user knows, such as a username and password, or has, such as a certificate or security token.
Authorization	What can a user do within the application?
	Authorization is how your application controls access to different resources and operations for different identities.
Data Input Validation	Is the data that has been entered both valid and safe?
	Input validation is the process of parsing and checking the data that was entered before it is saved or processed.
Data Protection	How does your application keep sensitive data from being accessed or modified?
	Data protection typically involves cryptography to ensure the integrity and confidentiality of sensitive data. This includes data that is in memory, being transferred over the network, or saved in a persistent store.
Source Code Protection	Can your application be easily reverse-engineered?
	Source code can contain information that could be used to bypass security, such as a hard-coded decryption key. Obfuscation is the most common technique for ensuring that a .NET application cannot be easily decompiled.
Configuration Management	How do you configure the application and are the settings stored securely?
	Configuration management must ensure that settings cannot be accessed or modified by unauthorized users. This is particularly important when the configuration contains sensitive information that could be used to bypass security, such as a database connection string.
Exception Management	What does your application do when it fails?
	Exception management should ensure that an application does not expose too much information to end users when an exception occurs. It should also ensure that the application fails gracefully, and is not left in an unknown state.
Auditing and Logging	Who did what and when did they do it?
	Auditing and logging refer to how your application records important actions and events. The location to which audit logs are written should ideally be tamper-proof.

By systematically identifying the security risks and putting in place appropriate countermeasures, we can begin to gain a level of trust that our applications and data can only be used in the manner that we intended.

The foundation of security is really all about trust and determining the scope and boundaries of our trust. For an application developer, this largely involves deciding to what degree you trust your users and external systems with which you interact, and what level of protection you need to put in place to guard against malicious users. You should ask questions such as, "Do I need to check the data that has been entered on this form, or can I simply assume that it is valid?"

However, as a system administrator or end user, you need to determine to what degree you trust that the applications you execute do not perform malicious actions. This is a fairly black-and-white decision when it comes to most non-.NET applications. If you don't fully trust an application, then you shouldn't execute it, because there is no way to limit the actions it performs. Even if you do trust that an application has good intentions, how sure are you that it does not contain a defect that causes it to inadvertently delete all of your personal files?

Built into the foundation of the .NET Framework is a policy-based security system called *code access security*, which can address these concerns by limiting the scope of actions that an application can perform. Because this is such an important part of security in the .NET Framework, it is discussed in detail in the following section.

Code Access Security

Code access security provides both developers and system administrators with a standardized mechanism to control and limit the actions that an application can perform. It allows applications to be trusted to varying degrees and to perform only the actions that are expected. Code access security also provides a formal process for applications to determine whether they have the necessary permissions to execute a particular function. This is a much more elegant solution than simply attempting the action, and handling an exception if it fails.

Code access security comes into play whenever an assembly is loaded, and provides the following functions:

❑ Defines permissions and permission sets that represent the right to access various system resources

❑ Defines different groups of assemblies, termed *code groups*, based on certain characteristics that the code shares

❑ Enables administrators to specify a security policy by associating sets of permissions with code groups

❑ Enables code to request the permissions it requires in order to run, as well as the permissions that would be useful to have, and specifies which permissions the code must never have

❑ Grants permissions to each assembly that is loaded, based on the permissions requested by the code and on the operations permitted by the security policy

Permission Sets

A permission set is a collection of related permissions, grouped together for administrative purposes. An individual permission expresses a specific level of authorization to access a protected resource. Nineteen distinct permissions are available for a permission set, covering resources such as the file system, registry, event log, printers, network sockets, and so on. As shown in Figure 27-1, each permission can either have unrestricted access to the resource, or be limited to a subset of actions or instances of the resource.

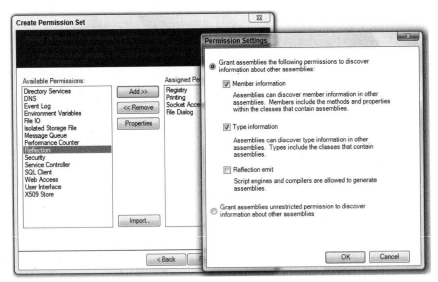

Figure 27-1

A number of predefined permission sets are created by default. These cover everything from *FullTrust*, which gives code unrestricted access to all protected resources, to *Nothing*, which denies access to all resources including the right to execute.

Evidence and Code Groups

Evidence is meta-information associated with an assembly that is gathered at runtime and used to determine what code group a particular assembly belongs to. A wide range of evidences is used by code access security:

❑ **Application Directory:** The directory in which an assembly resides.

❑ **GAC:** Whether or not the assembly has been added to the Global Assembly Cache (GAC).

❑ **Hash:** An MD5 or SHA1 cryptographic hash of the assembly.

❑ **Publisher:** The assembly's publisher's digital signature (requires the assembly to be signed).

❑ **Site:** The hostname portion of the URL from which the assembly was loaded.

❑ **Strong Name:** When an assembly has been digitally signed, the strong name consists of the public key, name, version, optional culture, and optional processor architecture.

❑ **URL:** The complete URL from which the assembly was loaded.

❑ **Zone:** The security zone from which the assembly was loaded (as defined by Internet Explorer on the local computer).

A code group associates a piece of evidence with a permission set. Administrators can create a code group for a specific set of evidence, such as all assemblies published by ACME Corporation. The relevant permission sets can then be applied to that code group. When an assembly published by ACME Corporation is loaded, the common language runtime will automatically associate it with that code group, and grant the assembly access to all the permissions in the permission set for that code group.

You cannot grant more than one permission set to a code group. However, you can create a copy of an existing code group and assign it a different permission set.

Security Policy

A security policy in .NET is a high-level grouping of related code groups and permission sets. There are four policies in .NET:

❑ **Enterprise:** Policy for a family of machines that are part of an Active Directory installation

❑ **Machine:** Policy for the current machine

❑ **User:** Policy for the logged-on user

❑ **AppDomain:** Policy for the executing application domain

The first three policies are configurable by system administrators. The final policy can only be administered through code for the current application domain.

By default, the Enterprise and User policies give all assemblies *FullTrust*. It is up to a system administrator to define the global security policy for an organization. However, the Machine policy is pre-populated with code groups based on the Internet Explorer Zones, as shown in Table 27-2.

Table 27-2: Default Machine Policy Code Groups

Code Group	Default Permission Set
My Computer Zone (code from the local computer)	FullTrust
Microsoft Strong Name (code signed with the Microsoft Strong Name)	
ECMA Strong Name (code signed with the ECMA strong name)	
Local Intranet Zone (code from a local network)	LocalIntranet
Internet Zone (code from the Internet)	Internet
Trusted Zone (code from trusted sites in Internet Explorer)	
Restricted Zone (code from untrusted sites in Internet Explorer)	Nothing

When the security policy is evaluated, Enterprise, Machine, and User levels are separately evaluated and intersected. This means that code is granted the minimum set of permissions that are common to all the code groups.

This multilevel, policy-based approach to code access security provides system administrators with a large degree of flexibility in defining a general security policy for an organization, and overriding it as necessary for an individual user or application.

Walkthrough of Code Access Security

The best way to fully appreciate how code access security works is to walk through an example of it in practice. We begin by creating a new Visual Basic console application with the following code:

```
Module Module1
    Sub Main()
        Console.WriteLine("About to access the registry")

        Try
            Dim regKey As Microsoft.Win32.RegistryKey
            regKey = Microsoft.Win32.Registry.LocalMachine.OpenSubKey( _
                            "SOFTWARE\Microsoft\Windows NT\CurrentVersion")

            Console.WriteLine(String.Format("This computer is running {0}", _
                                    regKey.GetValue("ProductName")))

            regKey.Close()

        Catch ex As Security.SecurityException
            Console.WriteLine("Security Exception: {0}", ex.Message)
        End Try

        Console.WriteLine("Completed. Press any key to continue")
        Console.ReadKey()

    End Sub
End Module
```

This console application simply reads a specific registry key — the product name of the local operating system version — and outputs its value to the console. If a security exception is thrown, this is caught and displayed to the console also.

If you build and run this application on your local machine you will see something like what is shown in Figure 27-2, depending on which version of Windows you're running.

```
About to access the registry
This computer is running Windows Vista (TM) Ultimate
Completed. Press any key to continue
```

Figure 27-2

However, if you copy the console application to a network share, and execute it from that share, it will generate a security exception as shown in Figure 27-3.

```
c:\Temp>\\homer\shared\cassample.exe
About to access the registry
Security Exception: Request for the permission of type 'System.Security.Permissi
ons.RegistryPermission, mscorlib, Version=2.0.0.0, Culture=neutral, PublicKeyTok
en=b77a5c561934e089' failed.
Completed. Press any key to continue
```

Figure 27-3

This fails and generates the security exception because, when you run the application from a network share, you are changing some of the evidence that code access security gathers. This changes the application from the Local Machine zone originally, to the Local Intranet zone. By default, assemblies that are in the Local Machine code group do not have the Registry permission set, and therefore cannot access the registry.

To execute this application from the network share you will need to create a custom code group that includes the Registry permission. Open the Microsoft .NET Framework Configuration from Control Panel ⇨ Administrative Tools. This useful tool allows you to adjust a number of configuration settings relating to the execution of .NET assemblies.

Expand the My Computer and the Runtime Security Policy nodes. You will see the three configurable security policies listed — Enterprise, Machine, and User. Expand the Machine node, followed by the Code Groups and then All_Code node. This is where you will see the default code groups listed, such as My_Computer_Zone, LocalIntranet_Zone, and so on. Though you could edit an existing default code group, it is highly recommended that you do not modify these, and instead, create a new custom code group.

Highlight the All_Code node and select Action ⇨ New from the menu. This will display the Create New Code Group Wizard. Enter a name for your new code group, such as My_Console_App, and click Next.

The Create Code Group screen is where you define the membership rules for this new code group based on the assembly evidence. Though you could use a very broad category such as Zone or Site, it is recommended that you keep the security policy as limited as you can and make the rule very specific to this assembly. Because the assembly has not been signed you cannot use the Strong Name or Publisher condition types. Instead use the Hash rule, which will use a cryptographic function to obtain a hash value of the contents of the assembly. Because even minor changes to the contents will result in a completely different hash value, you cannot edit or even rebuild the assembly without needing to recalculate the hash value.

Select Hash from the drop-down list of condition types, and click the Import button. After you select your assembly and click Open, the wizard will perform the hash function and save the value to the textbox, as shown in Figure 27-4.

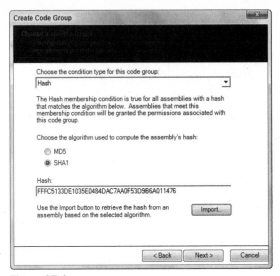

Figure 27-4

The next screen will allow you to choose the permission sets to grant to this code group. You could create a new permission set with just the Registry permission; however, because we have restricted this code group to a single assembly, it is safe to select the existing *FullTrust* permission set.

Once you have exited the wizard you will see your new code group listed. You can now go back to your network share and run the console application again. This time it will execute successfully.

Role-Based Security

Now that you understand how code access security works, we can turn our attention to a related feature included in the .NET Framework that can assist with authorization — role-based security. As you will remember from earlier in this chapter, authorization is how your application controls access to different resources and operations for different identities. At its most basic level, authorization answers the question, "What can a user do within this application?"

Role-based security approaches authorization by defining different application roles, and then building into your application security around those roles. Individual users are assigned to one or more roles, and inherit the rights assigned to those roles. The rights assigned to a role may allow access to certain functions within the application, or limit access to a subset of the data. For example, your application may need to provide full access to a database on sales tenders only to employees who are either managers or lead salespeople. However, the supporting employees involved in a tender may need access to a subset of the information, such as product specifications but not pricing information, which you want to be able to provide from within the same application.

Role-based security enables you to do this by explicitly specifying different levels of approval within the application functionality itself. You can even use this methodology to give different user roles access to the same functionality but with different behavior. For instance, managers may be able to approve all tenders, whereas lead salespeople can only approve tenders under a certain amount.

User Identities

You can implement role-based security in your application by retrieving information that Windows provides about the current user. It is important to note that this isn't necessarily the user who is currently logged on to the system, because Windows allows individuals to execute different applications and services via different user accounts as long as they provide the correct credentials. This means that when your application asks for user information, Windows returns the details relating to the specific user account being used for your application process.

Visual Studio 2008 applications use the .NET Framework, which gives them access to the *identity* of a particular user account through a `Principal` object. This object contains the access privileges associated with the particular identity, consisting of the roles to which the identity belongs.

Every role in the system consists of a group of access privileges. When an identity is created, a set of roles is associated with it, which in turn defines the total set of access privileges the identity has. For instance, you might have roles of ViewTenders, AuthorizeTenders, and RestrictTenderAmount in the example scenario used in this section. All employees associated with the sales process could be assigned the role of ViewTenders, while management and lead salespeople have the AuthorizeTenders roles as well. Finally, lead salespeople have a third role of RestrictTenderAmount, which your code can use later to determine whether they can authorize the particular tender being processed. Figure 27-5 shows how this could be represented visually.

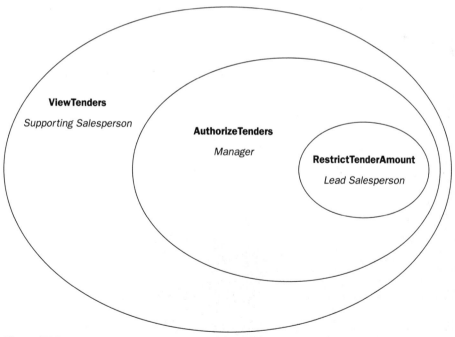

Figure 27-5

The easiest way to implement the role-based security functionality in your application is to use the `My.User` object. You can use the `IsAuthenticated` property to determine whether there is a valid user context under which your application is executing. If there isn't, your role-based security code will not work, so you should use this property to handle that situation gracefully.

If you're using this code in a C# application, you'll need to add the references to the My namespace, as explained in Chapter 14.

Once you've established that a proper user context is in use, use the IsInRole method to determine the methods to which the current user identity belongs. The actual underlying implementation of this depends on the current principal. If it is a Windows user principal (WindowsPrincipal), which means that we have authenticated the current principal against a Windows or Active Directory account, the function checks the user membership against Windows domain or local groups. If the current principal is any other principal, this function passes the name of the enumeration value in role to the principal's IsInRole method.

Walkthrough of Role-Based Security

As with code access security, the best way to understand role-based security is to walk through a simple example of it in practice. This time we will begin by creating a new Visual Basic Windows Forms application with a very simple layout of eight label controls as shown in Figure 27-6. The four labels on the right-hand side should be named lblIsAuthenticated, lblName, lblIsStandardUser, and lblIsAdminUser.

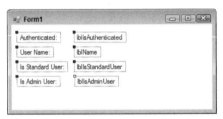

Figure 27-6

Add the following code behind this form:

```
Private Sub Form1_Load(ByVal sender As Object, ByVal e As System.EventArgs) _
                                                         Handles Me.Load
    With My.User
       Me.lblIsAuthenticated.Text = .IsAuthenticated
       If .IsAuthenticated Then
          Me.lblName.Text = .Name
          Me.lblIsStandardUser.Text = _
                  .IsInRole(ApplicationServices.BuiltInRole.User)
          Me.lblIsAdminUser.Text = _
                  .IsInRole(ApplicationServices.BuiltInRole.Administrator)
       Else
          Me.lblName.Text = ""
          Me.lblIsStandardUser.Text = "False"
          Me.lblIsAdminUser.Text = "False"
       End If
    End With
End Sub
```

When you run this code it should display your current username, and indicate whether the user is a member of the Users and Administrators group. If your computer is a member of a Windows domain, the actual groups it refers to are Domain Users and Domain Administrators. You can experiment with this form by using RunAs to execute it under different users' credentials.

> *In addition to using the built-in roles that Windows creates, you can also call the* IsInRole *method, passing in the role name as a string, in order to check the membership of your own custom-defined roles.*

Summary

Securing both your program code and your data is essential in today's computing environment. You need to inform the end users of your applications about what kind of access it requires to execute without encountering security issues. Once you understand the different types of security you can implement, you can use them to encrypt your data to protect your applications from unwanted use. Using a combination of role- and code-based security methodologies, you can ensure that the application runs only under the required permissions and that unauthorized usage will be blocked.

In the next chapter, you learn how to enhance the use of these concepts in a practical way by using the cryptography features of the .NET Framework to protect your data.

28

Cryptography

Anytime sensitive data is stored or transmitted across a network, it is at risk of being captured and used in an inappropriate or unauthorized way. Cryptography provides various mechanisms to protect against these risks. The .NET Framework includes support for several of the standard cryptographic algorithms, which can be combined to securely store data or transfer it between two parties.

General Principles

Cryptography focuses on four general principles to secure information that will be transferred between two parties. A secure application must apply a combination of these principles to protect any sensitive data:

❑   **Authentication:** Before information received from a foreign party can be trusted, the source of that information must be authenticated to prove the legitimacy of the foreign party's identity.

❑   **Non-Repudiation:** Once the identity of the information sender has been proven, there must be a mechanism to ensure that the sender did, in fact, send the information, and that the receiver received it.

❑   **Data Integrity:** Once the authentication of the sender and the legitimacy of the correspondence have been confirmed, the data must be verified to ensure that it has not been modified.

❑   **Confidentiality:** Protecting the information from anyone who may intercept the transmission is the last principle of cryptography.

Techniques

Cryptographic techniques fall into four broad categories. In each of these categories, a number of algorithms are implemented in the .NET Framework via an inherited provider model. For each category there is typically an abstract class that provides common functionality. The specific providers implement the details of the algorithm.

Hashing

To achieve the goal of data integrity, a *hashing algorithm* can be applied to the data being transferred. This will generate a byte sequence that has a fixed length, referred to as the *hash value.* To ensure data integrity the hash value has to be unique, and the algorithm should always produce the same hash value for a specific piece of data.

For example, if a piece of information is being sent from Julie to David, you can check the integrity of the information by comparing the hash value generated by Julie, from the original information, with the hash value generated by David, from the information he received. If the hash values match, the goal of data integrity has been achieved. Because the hash value cannot be converted back into the original information, both the information and the hash value have to be sent. This is clearly a risk, as the information can easily be read. In addition, the information cannot be guaranteed to come from Julie, because someone else could have used the same hashing algorithm before sending information to David.

The following hashing algorithms have been implemented in the .NET Framework:

❑ Triple DES

❑ MD5

❑ SHA-1

❑ SHA-2 (SHA-256, SHA-384, and SHA-512)

❑ RIPE-160

> *Both the MD5 and SHA-1 algorithms have been found to contain flaws, which means they are no longer considered secure by most security researchers. If possible, it is recommended that you use one of the other hashing algorithms.*

Each algorithm is implemented in several different classes that follow a distinct naming syntax. The native-managed code implementations are appended with the suffix *Managed*, and include:

❑ SHA1Managed

❑ SHA256Managed, SHA384Managed, SHA512Managed

❑ RIPEMD160Managed

The Message Authentication Code (MAC) implementations, which compute a hash for the original data and send both as a single message, are prefixed with *MAC*. The Hash-Based Message Authentication Code implementations, prefixed with *HMAC*, use a more secure process that mixes a secret key with the message data, hashes the result with the hash function, mixes that hash value with the secret key again, and then applies the hash function a second time. The following are the MAC and HMAC implementations:

❑   HMACMD5

❑   HMACSHA1

❑   HMACSHA256, HMACSHA384, HMACSHA512

❑   HMACRIPEMD160

❑   MACTripleDES

The Cryptographic Service Provider classes, identified with the suffix *CryptoServiceProvider*, provide a wrapper around the native Win32 Crypto API (CAPI), enabling this library to be easily accessed from managed code. The Cryptographic Service Provider wrapper classes are as follows:

❑ ▪ MD5CryptoServiceProvider

❑   SHA1CryptoServiceProvider

❑   SHA256CryptoServiceProvider, SHA384CryptoServiceProvider, SHA512CryptoServiceProvider

The Cryptographic Next Generation (CNG) classes are a new managed implementation of the Win32 Crypto API, which was introduced in version 3.5 of the .NET Framework. These classes include:

❑   MD5Cng

❑   SHA1Cng

❑   SHA256Cng, SHA384Cng, SHA512Cng

Symmetric (Secret) Keys

To protect the confidentiality of the information being transferred, it can be encrypted by the sender and decrypted by the recipient. Both parties can use the same key to encrypt and decrypt the data using a symmetric encryption algorithm. The difficulty is that the key needs to be securely sent between the parties, as anyone with the key can access the information being transmitted.

A piece of information being sent from Julie to David, both of whom have access to the same encryption key, can be encrypted by Julie. Upon receiving the encrypted information, David can use the same algorithm to decrypt the information, thus preserving the confidentiality of the information. But because of the risk of the key being intercepted during transmission, the authentication of the sender, and hence the integrity of the data, may be at risk.

The following symmetric algorithms included in the .NET Framework all inherit from the `SymmetricAlgorithm` abstract class:

❑   AesManaged

❑   DESCryptoServiceProvider

❑   RC2CryptoServiceProvider

❑   RijndaelManaged

❑   TripleDESCryptoServiceProvider

Asymmetric (Public/Private) Keys

Public-key, or *asymmetric,* cryptography algorithms can be used to overcome the difficulties associated with securely distributing a symmetric key. Instead of using the same key to encrypt and decrypt data, an asymmetric algorithm has two keys: one public and one private. The public key can be distributed freely to anyone, whereas the private key should be closely guarded. In a typical scenario, the public key is used to encrypt some information, and the only way that this information can be decrypted is with the private key.

Suppose Julie wants to ensure that only David can read the information she is transmitting. Using David's public key, which he has previously e-mailed her, she encrypts the information. Upon receiving the encrypted information, David uses his private key to decrypt the information. This guarantees data confidentiality. However, because David's public key can be easily intercepted, the authentication of the sender can't be confirmed.

The following asymmetric algorithms included in the .NET Framework all inherit from the `AsymmetricAlgorithm` abstract class:

- ❑ DSACryptoServiceProvider
- ❑ RSACryptoServiceProvider
- ❑ ECDiffieHellmanCng
- ❑ ECDsaCng

Signing

The biggest problem with using an asymmetric key to encrypt information being transmitted is that the authentication of the sender can't be guaranteed. When the asymmetric algorithm is used in reverse, the private key is used to encrypt data and the public key is used to decrypt the data, which guarantees authentication of the information sender. Of course, the confidentiality of the data is at risk, as anyone can decrypt the data. This process is known as *signing information.*

For example, before sending information to David, Julie can generate a hash value from the information and encrypt it, using her private key to generate a signature. When David receives the information, he can decrypt the signature using Julie's public key to get the hash value. Applying the hashing algorithm to the information and comparing the generated hash value with the value from the decrypted signature will guarantee the authentication of the sender and the integrity of the data. Because Julie must have sent the data, the goal of non-repudiation is achieved.

Signing information uses the same asymmetric algorithms that are used to encrypt data, and thus is supported in the .NET Framework with the same classes.

Summary of Goals

Individually, none of these four techniques achieves all the goals of cryptography. To be able to securely transmit data between two parties, you need to use them in combination. A common scheme is for each party to generate an asymmetric key pair and share the public keys. The parties can then generate a symmetric key that can be encrypted (using the public key of the receiving party) and signed (using the private key of the sending party). The receiving party needs to validate the signature (using the public key of the sending party) and decrypt the symmetric key (using the private key of the receiving party). Once the parties agree upon the symmetric key, it can be used to secure other information being transmitted.

Applying Cryptography

So far, you have seen the principles of cryptography and how they are achieved through the use of hashing, encryption, and signing algorithms. In this section, you'll walk through a sample that applies these algorithms and illustrates how the .NET Framework can be used to securely pass data between two parties.

Creating Asymmetric Key Pairs

Begin with a new Visual Basic Windows Forms application and divide the form into two vertical columns. You can do this using a `TableLayoutPanel` with docked Panel controls. Into each of the two vertical columns place a button, `btnCreateAsymmetricKey1` and `btnCreateAsymmetricKey2` respectively, which will be used to generate the asymmetric keys. Also add two textboxes to each column, which will be used to display the private and public keys. The textboxes in the left column should be named `TxtPublicKey1` and `TxtPrivateKey1`, and the textboxes in the right column should be named `TxtPublicKey2` and `TxtPrivateKey2`. The result should be something similar to Figure 28-1. For reference, add a name label to each of the vertical panels.

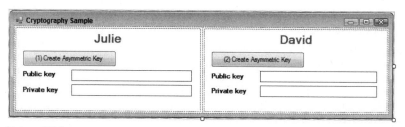

Figure 28-1

Double-clicking each of the buttons will create event handlers into which you need to add code to generate an asymmetric key pair. In this case use the `RSACryptoServiceProvider` class, which is an implementation of the RSA algorithm. Creating a new instance of this class automatically generates a new key pair that can be exported via the `ToXmlString` method, as shown in the following code. This method takes a Boolean parameter that determines whether the private key information should be exported:

```vb
Imports System
Imports System.IO
Imports System.Security.Cryptography
Imports System.Net.Sockets
Imports System.Text

Public Class Form1
#Region "Step 1 - Creating Asymmetric Keys"
    Private Sub BtnCreateAsymmetricKey1_Click(ByVal sender As System.Object, _
                                    ByVal e As System.EventArgs) _
                                    Handles btnCreateAsymmetricKey1.Click
        CreateAsymmetricKey(Me.TxtPrivateKey1, Me.TxtPublicKey1)
    End Sub

    Private Sub BtnCreateAsymmetricKey2_Click(ByVal sender As System.Object, _
                                    ByVal e As System.EventArgs) _
                                    Handles btnCreateAsymmetricKey2.Click
        CreateAsymmetricKey(Me.TxtPrivateKey2, Me.TxtPublicKey2)
    End Sub

    Private Sub CreateAsymmetricKey(ByVal txtPrivate As TextBox, _
                                    ByVal txtPublic As TextBox)
        Dim RSA As New RSACryptoServiceProvider()
        txtPrivate.Text = RSA.ToXmlString(True)
        txtPublic.Text = RSA.ToXmlString(False)
    End Sub
#End Region
End Class
```

In the preceding example you can see that a number of namespaces have been imported, which makes it much easier to work with the cryptography classes. When this application is run and the buttons are invoked, two new key pairs are created and displayed in the appropriate textboxes. Examining the text from one of the private key textboxes, you can see that it is an XML block broken up into a number of sections that represent the different components required by the RSA algorithm:

```xml
<RSAKeyValue>

  <Modulus>uUWTj5Ub+x+LN5xE63y8zLQf4JXNU0WAADsShaBK+jF/cDGd
Xc9VFcuDvRIX0oKLdUslpH
cRcFh3VLi7djU+oRKAZUfs+75mMCCnoybPEHWWCsRHoIk8s4BAZuJ7KCQ
O+Jb9DxYQbeeCI9bYm2yYWtHRvq7PJha5sbMvxkLOI1M=</Modulus>
  <Exponent>AQAB</Exponent>

  <P>79tcNXbc02ZVowH9qOuv3vrj6F009BSLdfSBtX6y8sosIAsLUfVqH+
UEPKQbZO/gLDAyf3U65Qkj 5QZE03CFeQ==</P>
```

```
      <Q>xb28iwn6BPHqCaDPhxtea6p/OnYNTtJ8f/3Y/zHE10Mc0aBjtY3Ci1
      ggnkUGvM4j/+BRTBwUOPKG NP9DUE94Kw==</Q>

      <DP>0IkkYytjlLyNSfsKIho/vxrcmYKn7moKUlRxjW2JgcM61+ViQzCew
      vonM93uH1TazzBcRyqSON0 4gv9vSXGz6Q==</DP>

      <DQ>j3bFICswlf2dyzZ82o0kyAB/Ji8YIKPd6A6ILT4yX3wloHE5ZjNff
      jGGGM4DwV/eBnr9ALcuhNK QREsez1mY2Q==</DQ>

      <InverseQ>hSlygkBiiYWyE7DjFgO1eOFhFQxOaLlvPoqlAxw0YepbSQA
      DBGmP8IB1ygzJjP3dmMEvQ Zhwsbs6MAfPIe/gYQ==</InverseQ>

      <D>r4WC7pxNDfQsaFrb0F00YJqlOJezFhjZ014jhgT+A1mxahEXDTDHYw
      aToCPr/bs/c7flyZIkK1Mk
      elcpAiwfT8ssNgx2H97zhcHkcvCBO8yCgc0r+cSYlRNKLa+UPwsoXcc5N
      XGT0SHQG+GCVl7bywrtrWRryaWOIpSwuHmjZYE=</D>
    </RSAKeyValue>
```

In actual fact, this block shows both the public- and private-key components, which you can see if you look at the corresponding public-key textbox:

```
    <RSAKeyValue>

      <Modulus>uUWTj5Ub+x+LN5xE63y8zLQf4JXNU0WAADsShaBK+jF/cDGd
      Xc9VFcuDvRIX0oKLdUslpH
      cRcFh3VLi7djU+oRKAZUfs+75mMCCnoybPEHWWCsRHoIk8s4BAZuJ7KCQ
      O+Jb9DxYQbeeCI9bYm2yYWtHRvq7PJha5sbMvxkLOI1M=</Modulus>
        <Exponent>AQAB</Exponent>
    </RSAKeyValue>
```

As you will learn later, this public key can be distributed so that it can be used to encrypt and sign information. Of course, the private key should be kept in a secure location.

Creating a Symmetric Key

In the example, only David is going to create a symmetric key (that will be shared with Julie after being encrypted and signed using a combination of their asymmetric keys). A more secure approach would be for both parties to generate symmetric keys and for them to be shared and combined into a single key.

Before adding code to generate the symmetric key, expand the dialog so the key can be displayed. Figure 28-2 shows two textboxes, named TxtSymmetricIV and TxtSymmetricKey, that will contain the IV (Initialization Vector) and the Key. The data being encrypted is broken down into a series of individually encrypted input blocks. If two adjacent blocks are identical, the process of encrypting a stream of data using a simple key would result in two identical blocks in the encrypted output. Combined with the knowledge of the input data, this can be used to recover the key. A solution to this problem is to use the previous input block as a seed for the encryption of the current block. Of course, at the beginning of the data there is no previous block, and it is here that the initialization vector is used. This vector can be as important as the key itself, so it should also be kept secure.

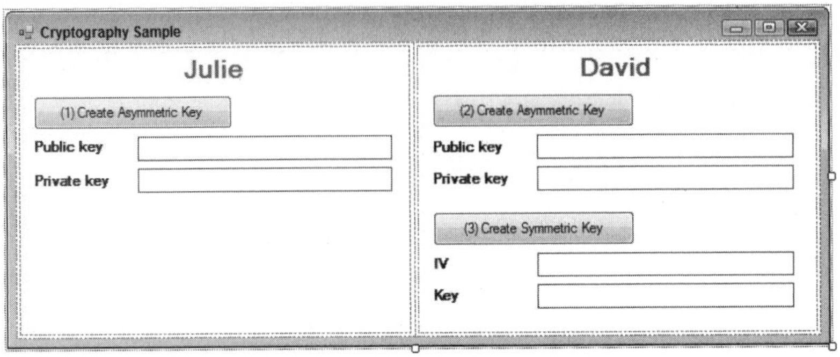

Figure 28-2

Add a new button named BtnCreateSymmetric to the form, and label it Create Symmetric Key. In the event handler for this button, you need to create an instance of the TripleDESCryptoServiceProvider class, which is the default implementation of the TripleDES algorithm. Create a new instance of the class and then call the GenerateIV and GenerateKey methods to randomly generate a new key and initialization vector. Because these are both byte arrays, convert them to a base-64 string so they can be displayed in the textbox:

```
Public Class Form1
#Region "Step 1 - Creating Asymmetric Keys"
'...
#End Region
#Region "Step 2 - Creating Symmetric Keys"
    Private Sub BtnCreateSymmetric_Click(ByVal sender As System.Object, _
                                ByVal e As System.EventArgs) _
                                        Handles BtnCreateSymmetric.Click

        Dim TDES As New TripleDESCryptoServiceProvider()
        TDES.GenerateIV()
        TDES.GenerateKey()
        Me.TxtSymmetricIV.Text = Convert.ToBase64String(TDES.IV)
        Me.TxtSymmetricKey.Text = Convert.ToBase64String(TDES.Key)
    End Sub
#End Region
End Class
```

Encrypting and Signing the Key

Now that we have the symmetric key, we need to encrypt it using Julie's public key and generate a hash value that can be signed using David's private key. The encrypted key and signature can then be transmitted securely to Julie. Three TextBox controls named TxtEncryptedKey, TxtHashValue, and TxtSymmetricSignature, as well as a button named BtnEncryptKey, have been added to the dialog in Figure 28-3, so you can create and display the encrypted key, the hash value, and the signature.

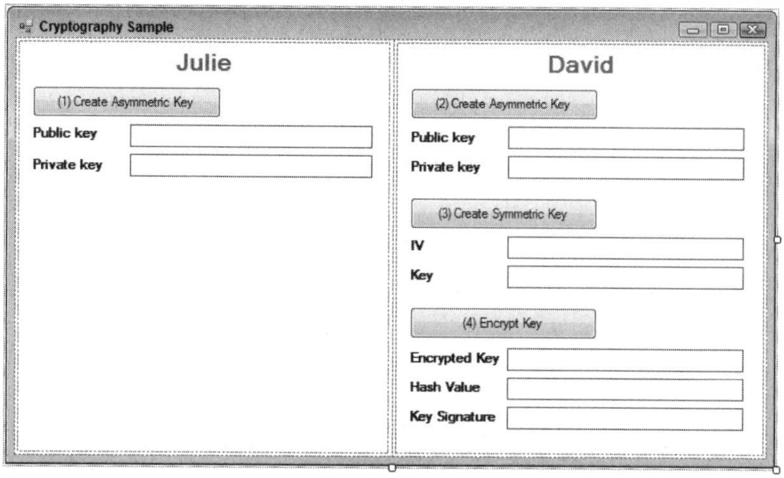

Figure 28-3

As we discussed earlier, this step involves three actions: encrypting the symmetric key, generating a hash value, and generating a signature. Encrypting the symmetric key is again done using an instance of the RSACryptoServiceProvider class, which is initialized using Julie's public key. It is then used to encrypt both the initialization vector and the key into appropriate byte arrays. Because you want to create only a single hash and signature, these two byte arrays are combined into a single array, which is prepended with the lengths of the two arrays. This is done so the arrays can be separated before being decrypted.

The single-byte array created as part of encrypting the symmetric key is used to generate the hash value with the SHA1Managed algorithm. This hash value is then signed again using an instance of the RSACryptoServiceProvider, initialized this time with David's private key. An instance of the RSAPKCS1SignatureFormatter class is also required to generate the signature from the hash value:

```
Public Class Form1
#Region "Step 1 & 2"
'...
#End Region
#Region "Step 3 - Encrypt, Hash and Sign Symmetric Key"
    Private Sub BtnEncryptKey_Click(ByVal sender As System.Object, _
                              ByVal e As System.EventArgs) _

Handles BtnEncryptKey.Click
        EncryptSymmetricKey()
        Me.TxtHashValue.Text = Convert.ToBase64String _

(CreateSymmetricKeyHash(Me.TxtEncryptedKey.Text))
SignSymmetricKeyHash()
End Sub
```

(continued)

(continued)

```vb
Private Sub EncryptSymmetricKey()
Dim iv, key As Byte()
Dim encryptedIV, encryptedkey As Byte()

        iv = Convert.FromBase64String(Me.TxtSymmetricIV.Text)
        key = Convert.FromBase64String(Me.TxtSymmetricKey.Text)

        'Load the RSACryptoServiceProvider class using
        'only the public key
        Dim RSA As New RSACryptoServiceProvider()
        RSA.FromXmlString(Me.TxtPublicKey1.Text)

        'Encrypt the Symmetric Key
        encryptedIV = RSA.Encrypt(iv, False)
        encryptedkey = RSA.Encrypt(key, False)

        'Create a single byte array containing both the IV and Key
        'so that we only need to encrypt and distribute a single value
        Dim keyOutput(2 * 4 - 1 + encryptedIV.Length + encryptedkey.Length) As Byte

Array.Copy(BitConverter.GetBytes(encryptedIV.Length), 0,keyOutput, 0, 4)

Array.Copy(BitConverter.GetBytes(encryptedkey.Length), 0, keyOutput, 4, 4)
        Array.Copy(encryptedIV, 0, keyOutput, 8, encryptedIV.Length)
        Array.Copy(encryptedkey, 0, keyOutput, 8 + encryptedIV.Length, _

encryptedkey.Length)

        Me.TxtEncryptedKey.Text = Convert.ToBase64String(keyOutput)
        End Sub

        Private Function CreateSymmetricKeyHash(ByVal inputString As String) As
Byte()

        'Retrieve the bytes for this string
        Dim UE As New UnicodeEncoding()
        Dim MessageBytes As Byte() = UE.GetBytes(inputString)

        'Use the SHA1Managed provider to hash the input string
        Dim SHhash As New SHA1Managed()
        Return SHhash.ComputeHash(MessageBytes)
    End Function

    Private Sub SignSymmetricKeyHash()
        'The value to hold the signed value.
        Dim SignedHashValue() As Byte

        'Load the RSACryptoServiceProvider using the
        'private key as we will be signing
        Dim RSA As New RSACryptoServiceProvider
        RSA.FromXmlString(Me.TxtPrivateKey2.Text)
```

```
        'Create the signature formatter and generate the signature
        Dim RSAFormatter As New RSAPKCS1SignatureFormatter(RSA)
        RSAFormatter.SetHashAlgorithm("SHA1")
        SignedHashValue = RSAFormatter.CreateSignature _

(Convert.FromBase64String(Me.TxtHashValue.Text))

        Me.TxtSymmetricSignature.Text = Convert.ToBase64String(SignedHashValue)
    End Sub
#End Region
End Class
```

At this stage, the encrypted key and signature are ready to be transferred from David to Julie.

Verifying Key and Signature

To simulate the encrypted key and signature being transferred, create additional controls on Julie's side of the dialog. Shown in Figure 28-4, the "Retrieve Key" button will retrieve the key, signature, and public key from David and populate the appropriate textboxes. In a real application, information could potentially be e-mailed, exported as a file and copied, or sent via a socket connection to a remote application. Essentially, it doesn't matter how the key and signature are transferred, as they are encrypted to prevent any unauthorized person from accessing the information.

Because the key and signature might have been sent via an unsecured channel, it is necessary to validate that the sender is who this person claims to be. You can do this by validating the signature using the public key from the sender. Figure 28-4 shows what the form will look like if the "Validate Key" button is pressed and the signature received is successfully validated against the public key from the sender.

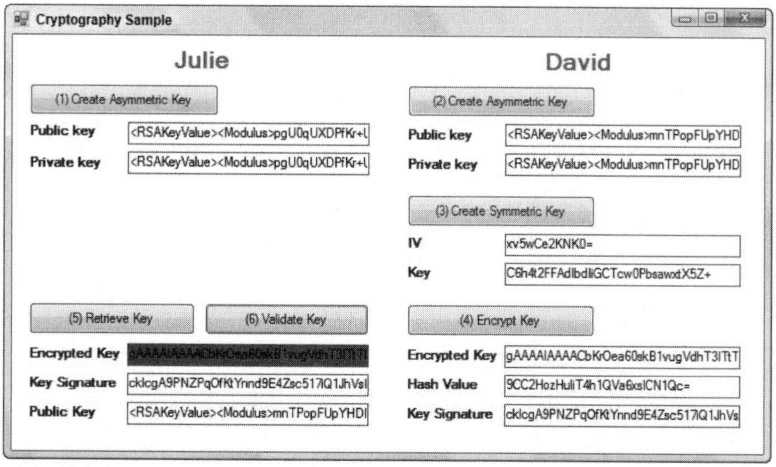

Figure 28-4

The code to validate the received signature is very similar to that used to create the signature. A hash value is created from the encrypted key. Using the same algorithm that was used to create the received signature, a new signature is created. Finally, the two signatures are compared via the `VerifySignature` method, and the background color is adjusted accordingly. To build this part of the form, add a button named `BtnRetrieveKeyInfo` and a button named `BtnValidate`. Next, add three new TextBox controls named `TxtRetrievedKey`, `TxtRetrievedSignature`, and `TxtRetrievedPublicKey`. Finally, add the following button-event handlers to the code:

```
Public Class Form1
#Region "Step 1 - 3"
'...
#End Region
#Region "Step 4 - Transfer and Validate Key Information"

    Private Sub BtnRetrieveKeyInfo_Click(ByVal sender As System.Object, _
                                         ByVal e As System.EventArgs) _
                                            Handles BtnRetrieveKeyInfo.Click
        Me.TxtRetrievedKey.Text = Me.TxtEncryptedKey.Text
        Me.TxtRetrievedSignature.Text = Me.TxtSymmetricSignature.Text
        Me.TxtRetrievedPublicKey.Text = Me.TxtPublicKey2.Text
    End Sub

    Private Sub BtnValidate_Click(ByVal sender As System.Object, _
                                  ByVal e As System.EventArgs) _

Handles BtnValidate.Click
        'Create the expected hash from the retrieved public key
        Dim HashValue, SignedHashValue As Byte()
        HashValue = CreateSymmetricKeyHash(Me.TxtRetrievedKey.Text)

        'Generate the expected signature
        Dim RSA As New RSACryptoServiceProvider()
        RSA.FromXmlString(Me.TxtRetrievedPublicKey.Text)
        Dim RSADeformatter As New RSAPKCS1SignatureDeformatter(RSA)
        RSADeformatter.SetHashAlgorithm("SHA1")
        SignedHashValue = Convert.FromBase64String(Me.TxtRetrievedSignature.Text)

        'Validate against received signature
        If RSADeformatter.VerifySignature(HashValue, SignedHashValue) Then
            Me.TxtRetrievedKey.BackColor = Color.Green
        Else
            Me.TxtRetrievedKey.BackColor = Color.Red
        End If
    End Sub
#End Region
End Class
```

Now that you have received and validated the encrypted key, the last remaining step before you can use the symmetric key to exchange data is to decrypt the key.

Decrypting the Symmetric Key

Decrypting the symmetric key will return the initialization vector and the key required to use the symmetric key. In Figure 28-5, the dialog has been updated to include the appropriate textboxes to display the decrypted values. These should match the initialization vector and key that were originally created by David. The button has been named `BtnDecryptKeyInformation`, and the two textboxes `TxtDecryptedIV` and `TxtDecryptedKey`.

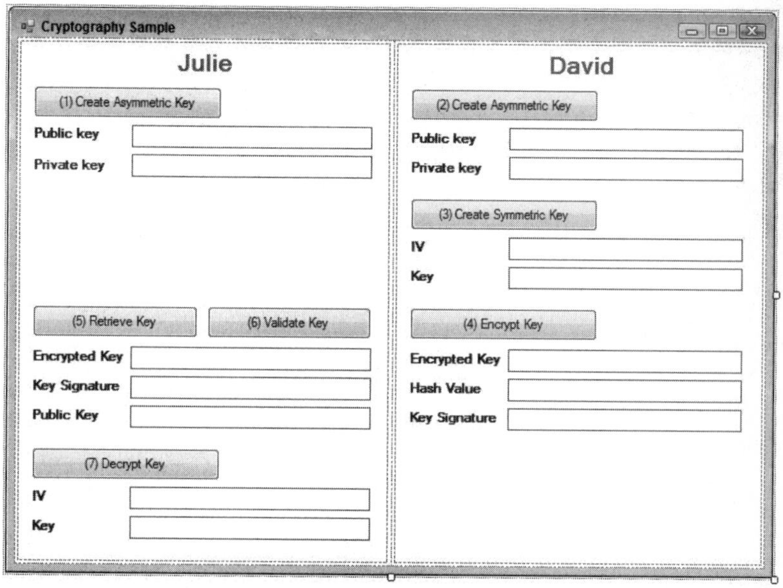

Figure 28-5

To decrypt the symmetric key, reverse the process for encrypting the symmetric key. Start by breaking up the single encrypted byte array into the `iv` and `key` byte arrays. To decrypt the key, you again need to create an instance of the `RSACryptoServiceProvider` class using Julie's private key. Because the data was encrypted using Julie's public key, the corresponding private key needs to be used to decrypt the data. This instance is then used to decrypt the initialization vector and the key:

```
Public Class Form1
#Region "Step 1 - 4"
'...
#End Region
#Region "Step 5 - Decrypt Symmetric key"
    Private Sub BtnDecryptKeyInformation_Click(ByVal sender As System.Object, _
                                    ByVal e As System.EventArgs) _
                                Handles BtnDecryptKeyInformation.Click

        Dim iv, key As Byte()

        'Retrieve the iv and key arrays from the single array
        Dim keyOutput As Byte() = Convert.FromBase64String(Me.TxtRetrievedKey.Text)
        ReDim iv(BitConverter.ToInt32(keyOutput, 0) - 1)
        ReDim key(BitConverter.ToInt32(keyOutput, 4) - 1)
        Array.Copy(keyOutput, 8, iv, 0, iv.Length)
        Array.Copy(keyOutput, 8 + iv.Length, key, 0, key.Length)

        'Load the RSACryptoServiceProvider class using Julie's private key
```

(continued)

(continued)

```
            Dim RSA As New RSACryptoServiceProvider()
            RSA.FromXmlString(Me.TxtPrivateKey1.Text)

            'Decrypt the symmetric key and IV.
            Me.TxtDecryptedIV.Text = Convert.ToBase64String(RSA.Decrypt(iv, False))
            Me.TxtDecryptedKey.Text = Convert.ToBase64String(RSA.Decrypt(key, False))
        End Sub
    #End Region
    End Class
```

Sending a Message

Both Julie and David have access to the symmetric key, which they can now use to transmit secure data. In Figure 28-6, the dialog has been updated one last time to include three new textboxes and a send button on each side of the form. Text can be entered in the first textbox. Pressing the send button will encrypt the text and place the encrypted data in the second textbox. The third textbox will be used to receive information from the other party. The button on the left is called btnSendAToB, and the associated textboxes are TxtMessageA, TxtMessageAEncrypted, and TxtReceivedMessageFromB. The corresponding button on the right is called BtnSendBToA, and the associated textboxes are TxtMessageB, TxtMessageBEncrypted, and TxtReceivedMessageFromA.

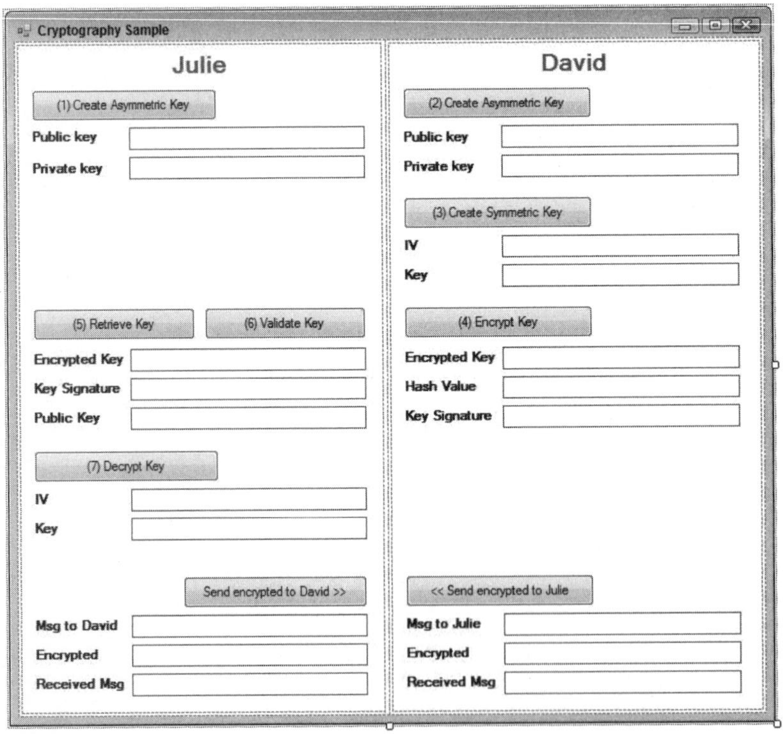

Figure 28-6

In the following code, the symmetric key is used to encrypt the text entered in the first textbox, placing the encrypted output in the second textbox. You will notice from the code that the process by which the data is encrypted is different from the process you used with an asymmetric algorithm. Asymmetric algorithms are useful for encrypting short amounts of data, which means that they are typically used for keys and pass phrases. On the other hand, symmetric algorithms can chain data together, enabling large amounts of data to be encrypted. For this reason, they are suitable for a streaming model. During encryption or decryption, the input data can come from any stream, be it a file, the network, or an in-memory stream. Here is the code:

```
Public Class Form1
#Region "Step 1 - 5"
'...
#End Region
#Region "Step 6 - Sending a Message"
    Private Sub btnSendAToB_Click(ByVal sender As System.Object, _
                                  ByVal e As System.EventArgs) _

Handles btnSendAToB.Click
        Me.TxtMessageAEncrypted.Text = EncryptData(Me.TxtMessageA.Text, _

        Me.TxtDecryptedIV.Text, _

        Me.TxtDecryptedKey.Text)
    End Sub
    Private Sub BtnSendBToA_Click(ByVal sender As System.Object, _
                                  ByVal e As System.EventArgs) _

Handles BtnSendBToA.Click
        Me.TxtMessageBEncrypted.Text = EncryptData(Me.TxtMessageB.Text, _

        Me.TxtSymmetricIV.Text, _

        Me.TxtSymmetricKey.Text)
    End Sub


    Private Function EncryptData(ByVal data As String, ByVal iv As String, _
                                          ByVal key As String) As String
        Dim KeyBytes As Byte() = Convert.FromBase64String(key)
        Dim IVBytes As Byte() = Convert.FromBase64String(iv)

        'Create the output stream
        Dim strm As New IO.MemoryStream

        'Create the TripleDES class to do the encryption
        Dim Triple As New TripleDESCryptoServiceProvider()

        'Create a CryptoStream with the output stream and encryption algorithm
        Dim CryptStream As New CryptoStream(strm, _

Triple.CreateEncryptor(KeyBytes, IVBytes), _

CryptoStreamMode.Write)
```

(continued)

(continued)

```
                'Write the text to be encrypted
                Dim SWriter As New StreamWriter(CryptStream)
                SWriter.WriteLine(data)
                SWriter.Close()

                Return Convert.ToBase64String(strm.ToArray)
        End Function
    #End Region
    End Class
```

To encrypt the text message to be sent, create another instance of the `TripleDESCryptoServiceProvider`, which is the same provider you used to create the symmetric key. This, combined with the memory output stream, is used to create the `CryptStream`. A `StreamWriter` is used to provide an interface for writing the data to the stream. The content of the memory stream is the encrypted data.

Receiving a Message

The final stage in this application is for the encrypted data to be transmitted and decrypted. To wire this up, trap the `TextChanged` event for the encrypted data textboxes. When this event is triggered, the encrypted data will be copied to the receiving side and decrypted, as shown in Figure 28-7. This simulates the information being sent over any unsecured channel.

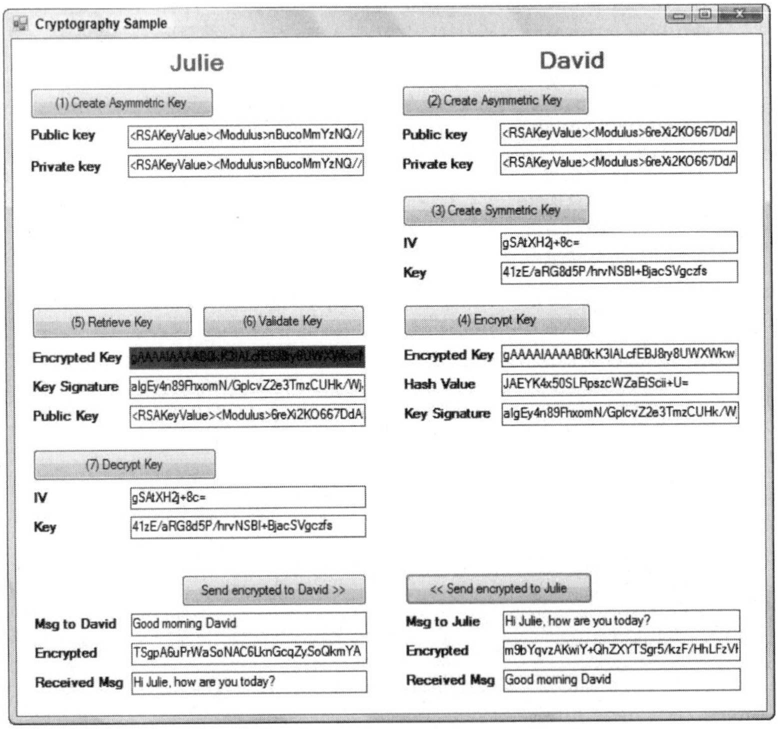

Figure 28-7

Decryption of the encrypted data happens the same way as encryption. An instance of the `TripleDESCryptoServiceProvider` is used in conjunction with the memory stream, based on the encrypted data, to create the `CryptoStream`. Via a `StreamReader`, the decrypted data can be read from the stream:

```
Public Class Form1
#Region "Step 1 - 6"
'...
#End Region
#Region "Step 7 - Receiving a Message"
    Private Sub TxtMessageAEncrypted_TextChanged(ByVal sender As Object, _
                                                 ByVal e As System.EventArgs) _
                                    Handles TxtMessageAEncrypted.TextChanged
        Me.TxtReceivedMessageFromA.Text = DecryptData( _

        Me.TxtMessageAEncrypted.Text, _

        Me.TxtSymmetricIV.Text, _

        Me.TxtSymmetricKey.Text)
    End Sub

    Private Sub TxtMessageBEncrypted_TextChanged(ByVal sender As Object, _
                                                 ByVal e As System.EventArgs) _
                                    Handles TxtMessageBEncrypted.TextChanged
        Me.TxtReceivedMessageFromB.Text = DecryptData( _

        Me.TxtMessageBEncrypted.Text, _

        Me.TxtDecryptedIV.Text, _

        Me.TxtDecryptedKey.Text)
    End Sub

    Private Function DecryptData(ByVal data As String, ByVal iv As String, _
                                             ByVal key As String) As String
        Dim KeyBytes As Byte() = Convert.FromBase64String(key)
        Dim IVBytes As Byte() = Convert.FromBase64String(iv)

        'Create the input stream from the encrypted data
        Dim strm As New IO.MemoryStream(Convert.FromBase64String(data))

        'Create the TripleDES class to do the decryption
        Dim Triple As New TripleDESCryptoServiceProvider()

        'Create a CryptoStream with the input stream and decryption algorithm
        Dim CryptStream As New CryptoStream(strm, _

    Triple.CreateDecryptor(KeyBytes, IVBytes), _
```

(continued)

(continued)

```
                                    CryptoStreamMode.Read)

            'Read the stream.
            Dim SReader As New StreamReader(CryptStream)
            Return SReader.ReadToEnd
        End Function
    #End Region
    End Class
```

As demonstrated in this example, you can use asymmetric keys to authenticate the communicating parties and securely exchange a symmetric key. This ensures non-repudiation, as only the authenticated parties have access to the key, and the information is securely encrypted to achieve confidentiality and data integrity. Using a combination of algorithms, you have protected your data and achieved the goals of cryptography.

Miscellaneous

So far, this chapter has covered the principles and algorithms that make up the primary support for cryptography within the .NET Framework. To round out this discussion, the following sections describe both how to use the SecureString class and how to use a key container to store a private key.

SecureString

It's often necessary to prompt users for a password, which is typically held in a String variable. Any information held in this variable will be contained within the String table. Because the information is stored in an unencrypted format, it can potentially be extracted from memory. To compound the problem, the immutable nature of the String class means that there is no way to programmatically remove the information from memory. Using the String class to work with private encryption keys can be considered a security weakness.

An alternative is to use the SecureString class. Unlike the String class, the SecureString class is not immutable, so the information can be modified and cleared after use. The information is also encrypted, so it can be retrieved from memory. Because you never want the unencrypted form of the information to be visible, there is no way to retrieve a String representation of the encrypted data. The following sample code inherits from the standard TextBox control to create the SecureTextbox class that will ensure that the password entered is never available as an unencrypted string in memory. This code should be placed into a new class file called SecureTextBox.vb.

```
Imports System.Security
Imports System.Windows.Forms

Public Class SecureTextbox
    Inherits TextBox

    Private Const cHiddenCharacter As Char = "*"c
    Private m_SecureText As New SecureString
```

```
Public Property SecureText() As SecureString
    Get
        Return m_SecureText
    End Get
    Set(ByVal value As SecureString)
        If value Is Nothing Then
            Me.m_SecureText.Clear()
        Else
            Me.m_SecureText = value
        End If
    End Set
End Property

Private Sub RefreshText(Optional ByVal index As Integer = -1)
    Me.Text = New String(cHiddenCharacter, Me.m_SecureText.Length)
    If index < 0 Then
        Me.SelectionStart = Me.Text.Length
    Else
        Me.SelectionStart = index
    End If
End Sub

Private Sub SecureTextbox_KeyPress(ByVal sender As Object, _
                                   ByVal e As KeyPressEventArgs) _
Handles Me.KeyPress
    If Not Char.IsControl(e.KeyChar) Then
        If Me.SelectionStart >= 0 And
Me.SelectionLength > 0 Then
            For i As Integer = Me.SelectionStart To _
                               (Me.SelectionStart +
Me.SelectionLength) - 1

Me.m_SecureText.RemoveAt(Me.SelectionStart)
            Next
        End If
    End If

    Select Case e.KeyChar
        Case Chr(Keys.Back)
            If Me.SelectionLength = 0 and
Me.SelectionStart > 0 Then
                'If nothing selected, then just backspace a single character

Me.m_SecureText.RemoveAt(Me.SelectionStart - 1)
            End If
        Case Chr(Keys.Delete)
            If Me.SelectionLength = 0 and _
                               Me.SelectionStart <
Me.m_SecureText.Length Then
Me.m_SecureText.RemoveAt(Me.SelectionStart)
            End If
```

(continued)

(continued)

```
            Case Else
                Me.m_SecureText.InsertAt(Me.SelectionStart, e.KeyChar)
        End Select
        e.Handled = True
        RefreshText(Me.SelectionStart + 1)
    End Sub
End Class
```

To make the SecureTextbox control available for use, you must first build the solution. Then, add a new Windows Form to your project and open it in the Designer. In the Toolbox window you will see a new tab group for your solution that contains the SecureTextbox control, as shown in Figure 28-8. The SecureTextbox control can be dragged onto a form like any other control.

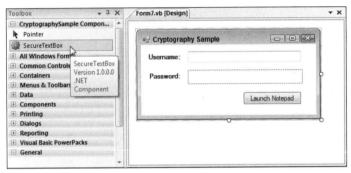

Figure 28-8

SecureTextbox works by trapping each `KeyPress` and adding any characters to the underlying `SecureString`. The `Text` property is updated to contain a `String` of asterisks (*) that is the same length as the `SecureString`. Once the text has been entered into the textbox, the `SecureString` can be used to initiate another process, as shown in the following example:

```
Private Sub btnStartNotepad_Click(ByVal sender As System.Object, _
                            ByVal e As System.EventArgs) _
                                        Handles btnStartNotePad.Click

    Dim psi As New ProcessStartInfo()
    psi.Password = Me.SecureTextbox1.SecureText
    psi.UserName = Me.txtUsername.Text
    psi.UseShellExecute = False
    psi.FileName = "notepad"

    Dim p As New Process()
    p.StartInfo = psi
    p.Start()
End Sub
```

Key Containers

In the example application you have just worked through, both Julie and David have an asymmetric key pair, of which the public key is shared. Using this information, they share a symmetric key that is used as a session key for transmitting data between parties. Given the limitations involved in the authentication of a symmetric key once it has been shared to multiple parties, maintaining the same key for an extended period is not a good idea. Instead, a new symmetric key should be established for each transmission session.

Asymmetric key pairs, on the other hand, can be stored and reused to establish each new session. Given that only the public key is ever distributed, the chance of the private key falling into the wrong hands is greatly reduced. However, there is still a risk that the private key might be retrieved from the local computer if it is stored in an unencrypted format. This is where a *key container* can be used to preserve the key pair between sessions.

Working with a key container is relatively straightforward. Instead of importing and exporting the key information using methods such as ToXMLString and FromXMLString, you indicate that the asymmetric algorithm provider should use a key container by specifying a CspParameters class in the constructor. The following code snippet retrieves an instance of the AysmmetricAlgorithm class by specifying the container name. If no existing key pair exists in a container with that name, a new pair will be created and saved to a new container with that name:

```
Private Sub btnLoadKeyPair_Click(ByVal sender As System.Object, _
                                 ByVal e As System.EventArgs) _

Handles BtnLoadKeyPair.Click
        Dim algorithm As AsymmetricAlgorithm = _

LoadAsymmetricAlgorithm(Me.TxtKeyContainerName.Text)
End Sub

Private Function LoadAsymmetricAlgorithm(ByVal container As String) _

As AsymmetricAlgorithm
    'Create the CspParameters object using the container name
    Dim cp As New CspParameters()
    cp.KeyContainerName = container

    'Create or load the key information from the container
    Dim rsa As New RSACryptoServiceProvider(cp)
    Return rsa
End Function
```

If you need to remove a key pair from a key container, follow the same process to create the AsymmetricAlgorithm. You then need to set PersistKeyInCsp to False and execute the Clear method. This will ensure that the key is removed from both the key container and the AsymmetricAlgorithm object.

Summary

This chapter demonstrated how cryptography can be used to establish a secure communication channel between multiple parties. Multiple steps are required to set up this channel, involving a combination of symmetric and asymmetric algorithms. When you're deciding on a security scheme for your application, it is important to remember the four goals of cryptography: authentication, non-repudiation, integrity, and confidentiality. Not all applications require that all of these goals be achieved, and a piecemeal approach might be necessary to balance performance and usability against security.

Now that you have seen how to protect the data in your application, the next chapter shows you how to use the technique of obfuscation to protect the embedded logic within your application from being reverse-engineered.

29

Obfuscation

If you've peeked under the covers at the details of how .NET assemblies are executed, you will have picked up on the fact that instead of compiling to machine language (and regardless of the programming language used), all .NET source code is compiled into the Microsoft Intermediary Language (MSIL, or just IL, for short). The IL is then *just-in-time* — compiled when it is required for execution. This two-stage approach has a number of significant advantages, such as allowing you to dynamically query an assembly for type and method information, using reflection. However, this is a double-edged sword, because this same flexibility means that once-hidden algorithms and business logic can easily be reverse-engineered, legally or otherwise. This chapter introduces obfuscation and how it can be used to protect your application logic. Be forewarned, however. Obfuscation provides no guarantees, because the IL must still be executable and can thus be analyzed and potentially decompiled.

MSIL Disassembler

Before looking at how you can protect your code from other people, this section describes a couple of tools that can help you build better applications. The first tool is the MSIL Disassembler, or IL Dasm, which is installed with both the .NET Framework SDK and the Microsoft Windows SDK v6.0A. If you have the .NET Framework SDK installed, you will find IL Dasm by choosing Start ➪ All Programs ➪ Microsoft .NET Framework SDK v2.0 ➪ Tools. If you have only the Windows SDK installed, it will be found under Start ➪ All Programs ➪ Microsoft Windows SDK v6.0A ➪ Tools. In Figure 29-1, a small class library has been opened using this tool, and you can immediately see the namespace and class information contained within this assembly.

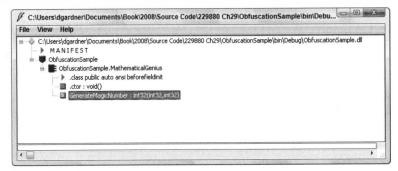

Figure 29-1

To compare the IL that is generated, the original source code for the `MathematicalGenius` class is as follows:

```
namespace ObfuscationSample
{
    public class MathematicalGenius
    {
        public static Int32 GenerateMagicNumber(Int32 age, Int32 height)
        {
            return age * height;
        }
    }
}
```

Double-clicking the `GenerateMagicNumber` method in IL Dasm will open up an additional window that shows the IL for that method. Figure 29-2 shows the IL for the `GenerateMagicNumber` method, which represents your patented algorithm. In actual fact, as you can roughly make out from the IL, the method expects two int32 parameters, `age` and `height`, and multiplies them.

```
ObfuscationSample.MathematicalGenius::GenerateMagicNumber : int32(int32,int32)
Find   Find Next
.method public hidebysig static int32  GenerateMagicNumber(int32 age,
                                                           int32 height) cil managed
{
  // Code size       9 (0x9)
  .maxstack  2
  .locals init ([0] int32 CS$1$0000)
  IL_0000:  nop
  IL_0001:  ldarg.0
  IL_0002:  ldarg.1
  IL_0003:  mul
  IL_0004:  stloc.0
  IL_0005:  br.s       IL_0007
  IL_0007:  ldloc.0
  IL_0008:  ret
} // end of method MathematicalGenius::GenerateMagicNumber
```

Figure 29-2

Anyone with a background in assembly programming will be at home reading the IL. For everyone else, a decompiler can convert this IL back into one or more .NET languages.

Decompilers

One of the most widely used decompilers is Reflector for .NET by Lutz Roeder (available for download at www.aisto.com/roeder/dotnet/). Reflector can be used to decompile any .NET assembly into C#, Visual Basic, Managed C++, and even Delphi. In Figure 29-3, the same assembly you just accessed is opened using IL Dasm, in Reflector.

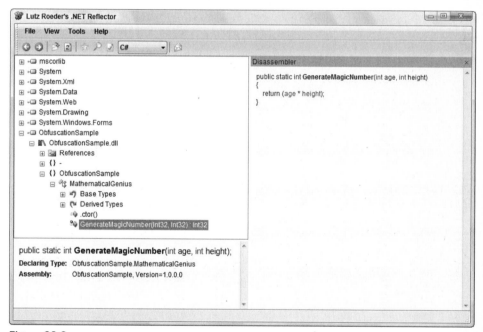

Figure 29-3

In the pane on the left of Figure 29-3, you can see the namespaces, type, and method information in a layout similar to IL Dasm. Double-clicking a method should open the Disassembler pane on the right, which will display the contents of that method in the language specified in the Toolbar. In this case, you can see the Visual Basic code that generates the magic number, which is almost identical to the original code.

You may have noticed in Figure 29-3 that some of the .NET Framework base class library assemblies are listed, including System, System.Data, and System.Web. Because obfuscation has not been applied to these assemblies, they can be decompiled just as easily using Reflector. However, in early 2008, Microsoft made large portions of the actual .NET Framework source code publically available, which means you can browse the original source code of these assemblies including the inline comments. This is shown in Chapter 43.

If the generation of the magic number were a real secret on which your organization made money, the ability to decompile this application would pose a significant risk. This is made worse when you add the File Disassembler add-in, written by Denis Bauer (available at `www.denisbauer.com/NETTools/FileDisassembler.aspx`). With this add-in, an entire assembly can be decompiled into source files, complete with a project file.

Obfuscating Your Code

So far, this chapter has highlighted the need for better protection for the logic that is embedded in your applications. Obfuscation is the art of renaming symbols in an assembly so that the logic is unintelligible and can't be easily understood if decompiled. Numerous products can obfuscate your code, each using its own tricks to make the output less likely to be understood. Visual Studio 2008 ships with the Community edition of Dotfuscator, which this chapter uses as an example of how you can apply obfuscation to your code.

Obfuscation does not prevent your code from being decompiled; it simply makes it more difficult for a programmer to understand the source code if it is decompiled. Using obfuscation also has some consequences that need to be considered if you need to use reflection or strong-name your application.

Dotfuscator

Although Dotfuscator can be launched from the Tools menu within Visual Studio 2008, it is a separate product with its own licensing. The Community edition contains only a subset of the functionality of the Standard and Professional versions of the product. If you are serious about trying to hide the functionality embedded in your application, you should consider upgrading.

After starting Dotfuscator from the Tools menu, it prompts you to either create a new project or use an existing one. Because Dotfuscator uses its own project format, create a new project that will be used to track which assemblies you are obfuscating and any options that you specify. Into the blank project, add the .NET assemblies that you want to obfuscate. Unlike other build activities that are typically executed based on source files, obfuscating takes existing assemblies, applies the obfuscation algorithms, and generates a set of new assemblies. Figure 29-4 shows a new Dotfuscator project into which has been added the assembly for the ObfuscationSample application.

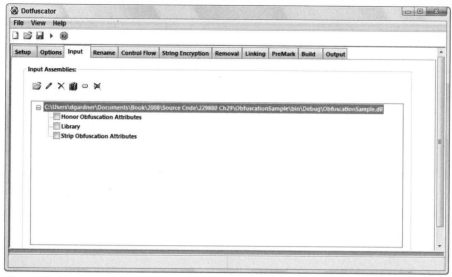

Figure 29-4

Without needing to adjust any other settings, you can select Build from the File menu, or click the "play" Button (fourth from the left) on the Toolbar, to obfuscate this application. The obfuscated assemblies will typically be added to a Dotfuscated folder. If you open this assembly using Reflector, as shown in Figure 29-5, you will notice that the GenerateMagicNumber method has been renamed, along with the input parameters. In addition, the namespace hierarchy has been removed and classes have been renamed. Although this is a rather simple example, you can see how numerous methods with the same, or similar, non-intuitive names could cause confusion and make the source code very difficult to understand when decompiled.

Figure 29-5

Unfortunately, this example obfuscated a public method. If you were to reference this assembly in another application, you would see a list of classes that have no apparent structure, relationship, or even naming convention. This would make working with this assembly very difficult. Luckily, Dotfuscator enables you to control what is renamed. Before going ahead, you will need to refactor the code slightly to pull the functionality out of the public method. If you didn't do this and you excluded this method from being renamed, your secret algorithm would not be obfuscated. By separating the logic into another method, you can obfuscate that while keeping the public interface. The refactored code would look like the following:

```
namespace ObfuscationSample
{
    public class MathematicalGenius
    {
        public static Int32 GenerateMagicNumber(Int32 age, Int32 height)
        {
            return CalculateMagicNumber(age, height);
        }

        private static int32 CalculateMagicNumber(Int32 age, Int32 height)
        {
            return age * height;
        }
    }
}
```

After rebuilding the application and refreshing the Dotfuscator project (because there is no Refresh button, you need to reopen the project by selecting it from the Recent Projects list), the Rename tab will look like the one shown in Figure 29-6.

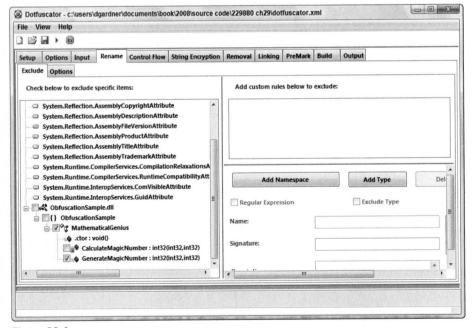

Figure 29-6

In the left pane you can see the familiar tree view of your assembly, with the attributes, namespaces, types, and methods listed. As the name of the tab suggests, this tree enables you to exclude symbols from being renamed. In Figure 29-6, the `GenerateMagicNumber` method, as well as the class that it is contained in, is excluded (otherwise, you would have ended up with something like `b. GenerateMagicNumber`, where `b` is the renamed class). As you can see in Figure 29-6, within the Rename tab there are two sub-tabs; Exclude and Options. On the Options sub-tab you will need to check the Keep Namespace checkbox. When you build the Dotfuscator project and look in the Output tab, you will see that the `MathematicalGenius` class and the `GenerateMagicNumber` method have not been renamed, as shown in Figure 29-7.

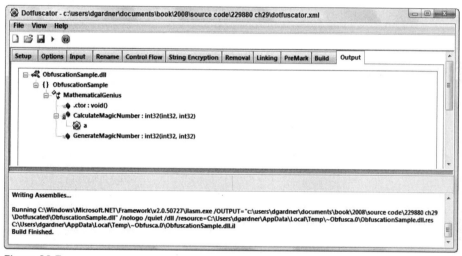

Figure 29-7

The `CalculateMagicNumber` method has been renamed to `a`, as indicated by the sub-node with the Dotfuscator icon.

Words of Caution

There are a couple of places where it is worth considering what will happen when obfuscation occurs, and how it will affect the workings of the application.

Reflection

The .NET Framework provides a rich reflection model through which types can be queried and instantiated dynamically. Unfortunately, some of the reflection methods use string lookups for type and method names. Clearly, the use of obfuscation will prevent these methods from working, and the only solution is not to mangle any symbols that may be invoked using reflection. Dotfuscator will attempt to determine a limited set of symbols to exclude based on how the reflection objects are used. For example, let's say that you dynamically create an object based on the name of the class, and you then cast that object to a variable that matches an interface the class implements. In that case, Dotfuscator would be able to limit the excluded symbols to include only types that implemented that interface.

Strongly Named Assemblies

One of the purposes behind giving an assembly a strong name is that it prevents the assembly from being tampered with. Unfortunately, obfuscating relies on being able to take an existing assembly and mangle the names and code flow, before generating a new assembly. This would mean that the assembly is no longer strongly named. To allow obfuscation to occur you need to delay signing of your assembly by checking the "Delay sign only" checkbox on the Signing tab of the Project Properties window, as shown in Figure 29-8.

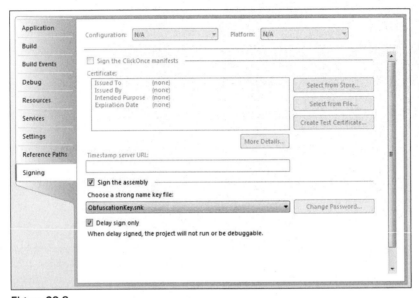

Figure 29-8

After building the assembly, you can then obfuscate it in the normal way. The only difference is that after obfuscating you need to sign the obfuscated assembly, which can be done manually using the Strong Name utility, as shown in this example:

```
sn -R ObfuscationSample.dll ObfuscationKey.snk
```

The Strong Name utility is not included in the default path, so you will either need to run this from a Visual Studio 2008 Command Prompt (Start ⇨ All Programs ⇨ Microsoft Visual Studio 2008 ⇨ Visual Studio Tools), or enter the full path to sn.exe.

Debugging with Delayed Signing

According to the Project Properties window, checking the "Delay sign only" box will prevent the application from being able to be run or debugged. This is because the assembly will fail the strong-name verification process. To enable debugging for an application with delayed signing, you can register the appropriate assemblies for verification skipping. This is also done using the Strong Name utility. For example, the following code will skip verification for the MyApplication.exe application:

```
sn -Vr MyApplication.exe
```

Similarly, the following will reactivate verification for this application:

```
sn -Vu MyApplication.exe
```

This is a pain for you to have to do every time you build an application, so you can add the following lines to the post-build events for the application:

```
"$(DevEnvDir)..\..\SDK\v2.0\Bin\sn.exe" -Vr "$(TargetPath)"
"$(DevEnvDir)..\..\SDK\v2.0\Bin\sn.exe" -Vr
   "$(TargetDir)$(TargetName).vshost$(TargetExt)"
```

The first line skips verification for the compiled application. However, Visual Studio 2008 uses an additional vshost file to bootstrap the application when it executes. This also needs to be registered to skip verification.

Attributes

In the previous example you saw how to choose which types and methods to obfuscate within Dotfuscator. Of course, if you were to start using a different obfuscating product you would have to configure it to exclude the public members. It would be more convenient to be able to annotate your code with attributes indicating whether a symbol should be obfuscated. You can do this by using the `Obfuscation` and `ObfuscationAssemblyAttribute` attributes.

The default behavior in Dotfuscator is to ignore the obfuscation attributes in favor of any exclusions specified in the project. In Figure 29-4 there are a series of checkboxes for each assembly added to the project, of which the top checkbox is Honor Obfuscation Attributes. A limitation with the Community edition of Dotfuscator is that you can't control this feature for each assembly. You can apply this feature to all assemblies using the second button from the right on the Toolbar.

ObfuscationAssemblyAttribute

The `ObfuscationAssemblyAttribute` attribute can be applied to an assembly to control whether it should be treated as a class library or as a private assembly. The distinction is that with a class library it is expected that other assemblies will be referencing the public types and methods it exposes. As such, the obfuscation tool needs to ensure that these symbols are not renamed. Alternatively, as a private assembly, every symbol can be potentially renamed. The following is the Visual Basic syntax for `ObfuscationAssemblyAttribute`:

```
[assembly: Reflection.ObfuscateAssemblyAttribute(false, StripAfterObfuscation=true)]
```

The two arguments that this attribute takes indicate whether it is a private assembly and whether to strip the attribute off after obfuscation. The preceding snippet indicates that this is not a private assembly, and that public symbols should not be renamed. In addition, the snippet indicates that the obfuscation attribute should be stripped off after obfuscation — after all, the less information available to anyone wishing to decompile the assembly, the better.

Adding this attribute to the assemblyinfo.vb file will automatically preserve the names of all public symbols in the ObfuscationSample application. This means that you can remove the exclusion you created earlier for the `GenerateMagicNumber` method.

Within Dotfuscator you can specify that you want to run all assemblies in library mode. Enabling this option has the same effect as applying this attribute to the assembly.

ObfuscationAttribute

The downside of the `ObfuscationAssemblyAttribute` attribute is that it will expose all the public types and methods regardless of whether they existed for internal use only. On the other hand, the `ObfuscationAttribute` attribute can be applied to individual types and methods, so it provides a much finer level of control over what is obfuscated. To illustrate the use of this attribute, extend the example to include an additional public method, `EvaluatePerson`, and place the logic into another class, `HiddenGenius`:

```
namespace ObfuscationSample
{
    [System.Reflection.ObfuscationAttribute(ApplyToMembers=true, Exclude=true)]
    public class MathematicalGenius
    {
        public static Int32 GenerateMagicNumber(Int32 age, Int32 height)
        {
            return HiddenGenius.CalculateMagicNumber(age, height);
        }

        private static Boolean EvaluatePerson(Int32 age, Int32 height)
        {
            return HiddenGenius.QualifyPerson(age, height);
        }
    }

    [System.Reflection.ObfuscationAttribute(ApplyToMembers=false, Exclude=true)]
    public class HiddenGenius
    {
        public static Int32 CalculateMagicNumber(Int32 age, Int32 height)
        {
            return age * height;
        }

        [System.Reflection.ObfuscationAttribute(Exclude=true)]
        public static Boolean QualifyPerson(Int32 age, Int32 height)
        {
            return (age / height) > 3;
        }
    }
}
```

In this example, the MathematicalGenius class is the class that you want to expose outside of this library. As such, you want to exclude this class and all its methods from being obfuscated. You do this by applying the ObfuscationAttribute attribute with both the Exclude and ApplyToMembers parameters set to True.

The second class, HiddenGenius, has mixed obfuscation. As a result of some squabbling among the developers who wrote this class, the QualifyPerson method needs to be exposed, but all other methods in this class should be obfuscated. Again, the ObfuscationAttribute attribute is applied to the class so that the class does not get obfuscated. However, this time you want the default behavior to be such that symbols contained in the class are obfuscated, so the ApplyToMembers parameter is set to False. In addition, the Obfuscation attribute is applied to the QualifyPerson method so that it will still be accessible.

Summary

In addition to learning about how to use obfuscation to protect your embedded application logic, this chapter reviewed two tools, IL Dasm and Reflector, which enable you to analyze and learn from what other developers have written. Although reusing code written by others without licensing their work is not condoned behavior, these tools can be used to learn techniques from other developers.

30

Client Application Services

A generation of applications built around services and the separation of user experience from backend data stores has seen requirements for occasionally connect applications emerge. Introduced in Chapter 26 on Microsoft Synchronization Services, occasionally connected applications are those that will continue to operate regardless of network availability. Chapter 26 discusses how data can be synchronized to a local store to allow the user to continue to work when the application is offline. However, this scenario leads to discussions (often heated) about security. As security (that is, user authentication and role authorization) is often managed centrally, it is difficult to extend so that it incorporates occasionally connected applications.

In this chapter you will become familiar with the client application services that extend ASP.NET Application Services for use in client applications. ASP.NET Application Services is a provider-based model for performing user authentication, role authorization, and profile management that has in the past been limited to web services and web sites. In Visual Studio 2008, you can configure your application to make use of these services throughout your application to validate users, limit functionality based on what roles users have been assigned, and save personal settings to a central location.

Client Services

Over the course of this chapter you will be introduced to the different application services via a simple Windows Forms application. In this case it is an application called ClientServices, which you can create by selecting the Visual Basic Windows Forms Application template from the File ⇨ New ⇨ Project menu item. You can also add the client application services to existing applications via the Visual Studio 2008 Project Properties Designer in the same way as for a new application.

The client application services include what is often referred to as an application framework for handling security. VB.NET has for a long time had its own Windows application framework that is enabled and disabled via the Application tab on the project properties designer. This framework already includes limited support for handling user authentication, but it conflicts with the client application services. Figure 30-1 shows how you can elect to use an application-defined authentication mode so that you can use both the Windows application framework and the client application services in your application.

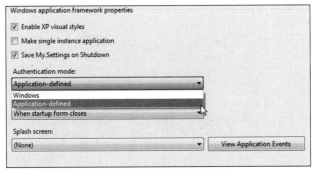

Figure 30-1

To begin using the client application services, you need to enable the checkbox on the Services tab of the project properties designer, as shown in Figure 30-2. The default authentication mode is to use Windows authentication. This is ideal if you are building your application to work within the confines of a single organization and you can assume that everyone has domain credentials. Selecting this option will ensure that those domain credentials are used to access the roles and settings services. Alternatively, you can elect to use Forms authentication, in which case you have full control over the mechanism that is used to authenticate users. We will return to this topic later in the chapter.

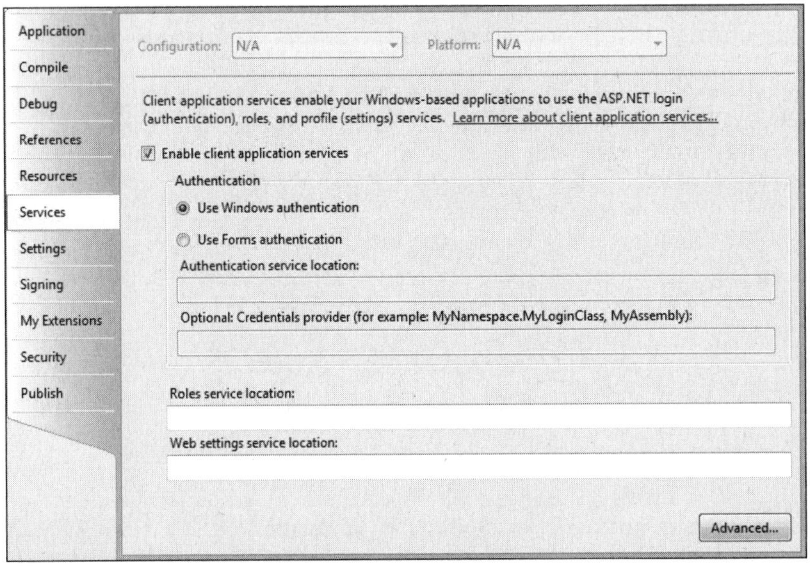

Figure 30-2

You will notice that when you enabled the client application services, an app.config file was added to your application if one did not already exist. Of particular interest is the `<system.web>` section, which should look similar to the following snippet:

```
<system.web>
    <membership defaultProvider="ClientAuthenticationMembershipProvider">
        <providers>
            <add name="ClientAuthenticationMembershipProvider"
type="System.Web.ClientServices.Providers.ClientWindowsAuthenticationMembershipProvider,
System.Web.Extensions, Version=3.5.0.0, Culture=neutral,
PublicKeyToken=31bf3856ad364e35" serviceUri="" connectionStringName=
"DefaultConnection" credentialsProvider="" />
        </providers>
    </membership>
    <roleManager defaultProvider="ClientRoleProvider" enabled="true">
        <providers>
            <add name="ClientRoleProvider"
type="System.Web.ClientServices.Providers.ClientRoleProvider, System.Web.Extensions,
Version=3.5.0.0, Culture=neutral, PublicKeyToken=31bf3856ad364e35"
serviceUri="" cacheTimeout="86400" connectionStringName="DefaultConnection" />
        </providers>
    </roleManager>
</system.web>
```

Here you can see that providers have been defined for membership and role management. You can extend the client application services framework by building your own providers that can talk directly to a database or to some other remote credential store such as Active Directory. Essentially, all the project properties designer does is modify the app.config file to define the providers and other associated properties. In order to validate the user, you need to add some code to your application to invoke these services. You can do this via the `ValidateUser` method on the `System.Web.Security.Membership` class, as shown in the following snippet:

```
Private Sub Form1_Load(ByVal sender As System.Object, _
                       ByVal e As System.EventArgs) Handles MyBase.Load
    If Membership.ValidateUser(Nothing, Nothing) Then
        MessageBox.Show ("User is valid")
    Else
        MessageBox.Show("Unable to verify user, application exiting")
        Application.Exit()
        Return
    End If
End Sub
```

Interestingly, there is no overload of the `ValidateUser` method that accepts no arguments; instead, when using Windows authentication, you should use `Nothing` (or `null` in C#) for the username and password arguments. In this case, `ValidateUser` does little more than prime the `CurrentPrincipal` of the application to use the client application services to determine which roles the user belongs to. You will see later that using this method is the equivalent of logging the user into the application.

The preceding code snippet, and others throughout this chapter, may require you to import the System. Web.Security namespace into this class file. You may also need to manually add a reference to System.Web.Extensions.dll in order to resolve type references.

Role Authorization

So far, you have seen how to enable the client application services, but they haven't really started to add value because the user has already been authenticated by the operating system when you were using Windows authentication for the client application. What isn't handled by the operating system is specifying which roles a user belongs to and thus what parts or functions within an application the user has access to. While this could be handled by the client application itself, it would be difficult to account for all permutations of users and the system would be impractical to manage, because every time a user was added or changed roles a new version of the application would have to be deployed. Instead, it is preferable to have the correlations between users and roles managed on the server, allowing the application to work with a much smaller set of roles through which to control access to functionality.

The true power of the client application services becomes apparent when you combine the client-side application framework with the ASP.NET Application Services. To see this you should add a new project to your solution using the Visual Basic ASP.NET Web Application template (under the Web node in the New Project dialog), calling it ApplicationServices. As we are not going to create any web pages, you can immediately delete the default page, default.aspx, that is added by the template. You could also use the ASP.NET Web Service Application template, as it differs only in the initial item, which is service1.asmx.

Right-clicking the newly created project in Solution Explorer, select Properties to bring up the project properties designer. As we will be referencing this web application from other parts of the solution, it is preferable to use a predefined port and virtual directory with the Visual Studio Development Server. On the Web tab, set the specific port to 12345 and the virtual path to /ApplicationServices.

ASP.NET Application Services is a provider-based model for authenticating users, managing roles, and storing profile (a.k.a. settings) information. Each of these components can be engaged independently, and you can either elect to use the built-in providers or create your own. To enable the role management service for access via client application services, add the following snippet before the `<system.web>` element in the web.config file in the ApplicationServices project:

```
<system.web.extensions>
    <scripting>
        <webServices>
            <roleService enabled="true"/>
        </webServices>
    </scripting>
</system.web.extensions>
```

As we want to perform some custom logic to determine which roles a user belongs to, you will need to create a new class, called `CustomRoles`, to take the place of the default role provider. Here you can take advantage of the `RoleProvider` abstract class, greatly reducing the amount of code you have to write. For this role provider we are interested only in returning a value for the `GetRolesForUser` method; all other methods can be left as method stubs.

```
Public Class CustomRoles
    Inherits RoleProvider

    Public Overrides Function GetRolesForUser(ByVal username As String) As String()
        If username.ToLower.Contains("Nick") Then
            Return New String() {"All Nicks"}
        Else
            Return New String() {}
        End If
    End Function
End Function
```

You now have a custom role provider and have enabled role management. The only thing missing is the glue that lets the role management service know to use your role provider. You provide this by adding the following roleManager node to the `<system.web>` element in the web.config file:

```xml
<roleManager enabled="true" defaultProvider=" CustomRoles">
    <providers>
        <add name=" CustomRoles" type="AuthenticationServices.CustomRoles"/>
    </providers>
</roleManager>
```

The last thing to do is to make use of this role information in your application. You can do this by adding a call to `IsUserInRole` to the `Form_Load` method:

```
Private Sub Form1_Load(ByVal sender As System.Object, _
                       ByVal e As System.EventArgs) Handles MyBase.Load
    If Membership.ValidateUser(Nothing, Nothing) Then
        '... Commented out for brevity ...
    End If
    If Roles.IsUserInRole("All Nicks") Then
        MessageBox.Show("User is a Nick, so should have Admin rights....")
    End If
End Sub
```

In order to see your custom role provider in action, set a breakpoint in the `GetRolesForUser` method. For this breakpoint to be hit, you have to have both the client application and the web application running in debug mode. To do this, right-click the Solution node in the Solution Explorer window and select Properties. From the Startup Project node, select Multiple Startup Projects and set the action of both projects to Start. Now when you run the solution you will see that the `GetRolesForUser` method is called with the Windows credentials of the current user, as part of the validation of the user.

User Authentication

In some organizations it would be possible to use Windows authentication for all user validation. Unfortunately, in many cases this is not possible, and application developers have to come up with their own solutions for determining which users should be able to access a system. This process is loosely referred to as *forms-based authentication,* as it typically requires the provision of a username and password combination via a login form of some description. Both ASP.NET Application Services and the client application services support forms-based authentication as an alternative to Windows authentication.

To begin with, you will need to enable the membership management service for access by the client application services. Adding the `<authenticationService>` element to the `<system.web .extensions>` element in the web.config file will do this. Note that we have disabled the SSL requirement, which is clearly against all security best practices and not recommended for production systems.

```
<system.web.extensions>
    <scripting>
        <webServices>
            <authenticationService enabled="true" requireSSL="false"/>
            <roleService enabled="true"/>
```

The next step is to create a custom membership provider that will determine whether a specific username and password combination is valid for the application. To do this, add a new class, `CustomAuthentication`, to the ApplicationServices application and set it to inherit from the `MembershipProvider` class. As with the role provider we created earlier, we are just going to provide a minimal implementation that validates credentials by ensuring the password is the reverse of the supplied username, and that the username is in a predefined list.

```
Public Class CustomAuthentication
    Inherits MembershipProvider

    Private mValidUsers As String() = {"Nick"}

    Public Overrides Function ValidateUser(ByVal username As String, _
                                        ByVal password As String) As Boolean
        Dim reversed As String = New String(password.Reverse.ToArray)
        Return (From user In mValidUsers _
                Where String.Compare(user, username, true) = 0 And _
                    user = reversed).Count > 0
    End Function

    ...
End Class
```

As with the role provider you created, you will also need to inform the membership management system that it should use the membership provider you have created. You do this by adding the following snippet to the `<system.web>` element in the web.config file:

```
<membership defaultProvider="CustomAuthentication">
    <providers>
        <add name="CustomAuthentication"
type="ApplicationServices.CustomAuthentication"/>
    </providers>
</membership>
```

You need to make one additional change to the web.config file by specifying that Forms authentication should be used for incoming requests. You do this by changing the `<authentication>` element in the web.config file to the following:

```
<authentication mode="Forms"/>
```

Back on the client application, only minimal changes are required to take advantage of the changes to the authentication system. On the Services tab of the project properties designer, select "Use Forms authentication." This will enable both the "Authentication service location" textbox and the "Optional: Credentials provider" textbox. For the time being, just specify the authentication service location as http://localhost:12345/ApplicationServices.

Previously, using Windows authentication, you performed the call to `ValidateUser` to initiate the client application services by supplying `Nothing` as each of the two arguments. You did this because the user credentials could be automatically determined from the current user context in which the application was running. Unfortunately, this is not possible for Forms authentication, so we need to supply a username and password.

```
Private Sub Form1_Load(ByVal sender As System.Object, _
                       ByVal e As System.EventArgs) Handles MyBase.Load
    If Membership.ValidateUser("Nick", "kciN") Then
        MessageBox.Show ("User is valid")
```

If you specify a breakpoint in the `ValidateUser` method in the ApplicationServices project, you will see that when you run this solution the server is contacted in order to validate the user. You will see later that this information can then be cached locally to facilitate offline user validation.

Settings

In the .NET Framework v2.0, the concept of settings with a User scope was introduced to allow per-user information to be stored between application sessions. For example, window positioning or theme information might have been stored as a user setting. Unfortunately, there was no way to centrally manage this information. Meanwhile, ASP.NET Application Services had the notion of profile information, which was essentially per-user information, tracked on a server, that could be used by web applications. Naturally, with the introduction of the client application services, it made sense to combine these ideas to allow settings to be saved via the Web. These settings have a scope of User (Web).

As with the membership and role services, you need to enable the profile service for access by the client application services. You do this by adding the `<profileService>` element to the `<system.web.extensions>` element in the web.config file.

```
<system.web.extensions>
        <scripting>
                <webServices>
                        <profileService enabled="true"

readAccessProperties="Nickname"

writeAccessProperties="Nickname" />
                        <authenticationService enabled="true" requireSSL="false"/>
```

Following the previous examples, we will build a custom profile provider that will use an in-memory dictionary to store user nicknames. Note that this isn't a good way to track profile information, as it would be lost every time the web server recycled and would not scale out to multiple web servers. Nevertheless, you need to add a new class, `CustomProfile`, to the ApplicationServices project and set it to inherit from `ProfileProvider`.

```
Imports System.Configuration

Public Class CustomProfile
    Inherits ProfileProvider

    Private nicknames As New Dictionary(Of String, String)

    Public Overrides Function GetPropertyValues(ByVal context As SettingsContext, _
                            ByVal collection AsSettingsPropertyCollection) _
                                        As SettingsPropertyValueCollection
        Dim vals As New SettingsPropertyValueCollection
        For Each setting As SettingsProperty In collection
            Dim value As New SettingsPropertyValue(var)
            If nicknames.ContainsKey(setting.Name) Then
                value.PropertyValue = nicknames.Item(setting.Name)
            End If
            vals.Add(value)
        Next
        Return vals
    End Function

    Public Overrides Sub SetPropertyValues(ByVal context As SettingsContext, _
                        ByVal collection As SettingsPropertyValueCollection)
        For Each setting As SettingsPropertyValue In collection
            nicknames.Item(setting.Name) = setting.PropertyValue.ToString
        Next
    End Sub

    ...
End Class
```

The difference with the profile service is that when you specify the provider to use in the `<system.web>` element in the web.config file, you also need to declare what properties can be saved via the profile service (see the following snippet). In order for these properties to be accessible via the client application services, they must have a corresponding entry in the `readAccessProperties` and `writeAccessProperties` attributes of the `<profileService>` element, shown earlier.

```
<profile enabled="true" defaultProvider="CustomProfile">
    <providers>
        <add name="CustomProfile" type="ApplicationServices.CustomProfile"/>
    </providers>
    <properties>
        <add name="Nickname" type="string"
                readOnly="false" defaultValue="{nickname}"
                serializeAs="String" allowAnonymous="false" />
    </properties>
</profile>
```

As an aside, the easiest way to build a full profile service is to use the utility aspnet_regsql.exe (typically found at C:\Windows\Microsoft.NET\Framework\v2.0.50727\aspnet_regsql.exe) to populate an existing SQL Server database with the appropriate table structure. You can then use the built-in `SqlProfileProvider` (`SqlMembershipProvider` and `SqlRoleProvider` for membership and role providers, respectively) to store and retrieve profile information. To use this provider, change the profile element you added earlier to the following:

```
<profile enabled="true" defaultProvider="CustomProfile">
    <providers>
        <add name="SqlProvider"
            type="System.Web.Profile.SqlProfileProvider"
            connectionStringName="SqlServices"
            applicationName="SampleApplication"
            description="SqlProfileProvider for SampleApplication" />
```

Note that the `connectionStringName` attribute needs to correspond to the name of a SQL Server connection string located in the `connectionStrings` section of the web.config file.

Returning to the custom profile provider you have created, to use this in the client application you just need to specify the web settings service location on the Services tab of the project properties designer. This location should be the same as for both the role and authentication services, `http://localhost:12345/ApplicationServices`.

This is where the Visual Studio 2008 support for application settings is particularly useful. If you now go to the Settings tab of the project properties designer and hit the "Load Web Settings" button, you will initially be prompted for credential information, as you need to be a validated user in order to access the profile service. Figure 30-3 shows this dialog with the appropriate credentials supplied.

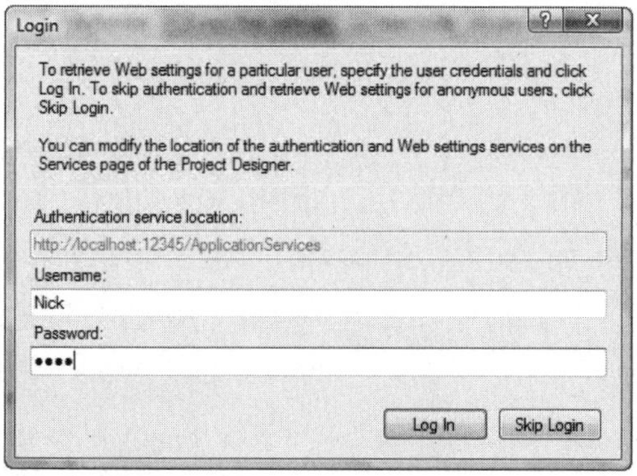

Figure 30-3

After a valid set of credentials is entered, the profile service will be interrogated and a new row added to the settings design surface, as shown in Figure 30-4. Here you can see that the scope of this setting is indeed User (Web) and that the default value, specified in the web.config file, has been retrieved.

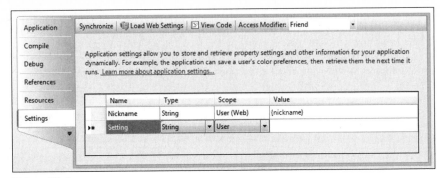

Figure 30-4

If you take a look at the app.config file for the client application, you will notice that a new `sectionGroup` has been added to the `configSections` element. This simply declares the class that will be used to process the custom section that has been added to support the new user settings.

```
<configSections>
    <sectionGroup name="userSettings"
type="System.Configuration.UserSettingsGroup, System, Version=2.0.0.0,
Culture=neutral, PublicKeyToken=b77a5c561934e089" >
        <section name="ClientServices.My.MySettings" type="System.Configuration
.ClientSettingsSection, System, Version=2.0.0.0, Culture=neutral,
PublicKeyToken=b77a5c561934e089" allowExeDefinition="MachineToLocalUser"
requirePermission="false" />
    </sectionGroup>
</configSections>
```

Toward the end of the app.config file you will see the custom section that has been created. As you would expect, the name of the setting is `Nickname` and the value corresponds to the default value specified in the web.config file in the ApplicationServices project.

```
<userSettings>
    <ClientServices.My.MySettings>
        <setting name="Nickname" serializeAs="String">
            <value>{nickname}</value>
        </setting>
    </ClientServices.My.MySettings>
</userSettings>
```

To make use of this in code you can use the same syntax as for any other setting. Here we simply retrieve the current value, request a new value, and then save this new value:

```
Private Sub Form1_Load(ByVal sender As System.Object, _
                        ByVal e As System.EventArgs) Handles MyBase.Load
    '... Commented out for brevity ...
    MessageBox.Show(My.Settings.Nickname)
    My.Settings.Nickname = InputBox("Please specify a nickname:", "Nickname")
    My.Settings.Save()
End Sub
```

If you run this application again, the nickname you supplied the first time will be returned.

Login Form

Earlier, when you were introduced to Forms authentication, we used a hard-coded username and password in order to validate the user. While it would be possible for the application to prompt the user for credentials before calling `ValidateUser` with the supplied values, there is a better way that uses the client application services framework. Instead of calling `ValidateUser` with a username/password combination, we go back to supplying `Nothing` as the argument values and define a credential provider: then the client application services will call the provider to determine the set of credentials to use.

```
Private Sub Form1_Load(ByVal sender As System.Object, _
                        ByVal e As System.EventArgs) Handles MyBase.Load
    If Membership.ValidateUser(Nothing, Nothing) Then
        MessageBox.Show ("User is valid")
```

This probably sounds more complex than it is, so let's start by adding a login form to the client application. Do this by selecting the Login Form template from the Add New Item dialog and calling it LoginForm. While you have the form designer open, click the "OK" button and change the `DialogResult` property to `OK`.

In order to use this login form as a credential provider, we will modify it to implement the `IClientFormsAuthenticationCredentialsProvider` interface. An alternative strategy would be to have a separate class that implements this interface and then displays the login form when the `GetCredentials` method is called. The following code snippet contains the code-behind file for the `LoginForm` class, showing the implementation of the `IClientFormsAuthenticationCredentialsProvider` interface.

```
Imports System.Web.ClientServices.Providers

Public Class LoginForm
    Implements IClientFormsAuthenticationCredentialsProvider

    Public Function GetCredentials() As ClientFormsAuthenticationCredentials _
            Implements IClientFormsAuthenticationCredentialsProvider.GetCredentials
        If Me.ShowDialog() = DialogResult.OK Then
            Return New ClientFormsAuthenticationCredentials(UsernameTextBox.Text, _
                                                            PasswordTextBox.Text, _
                                                            False)

        Else
            Return Nothing
        End If
    End Function
End Class
```

As you can see from this snippet, the `GetCredentials` method returns `ClientFormsAuthenticationCredentials` if credentials are supplied, or `Nothing` if "Cancel" is clicked. Clearly this is only one way to collect credentials information, and there is no requirement that you prompt the user for this information. (The use of dongles or employee identification cards are common alternatives.)

With the credentials provider created, it is just a matter of informing the client application services that they should use it. You do this via the "Optional: Credentials provider" field on the Services tab of the project properties designer, as shown in Figure 30-5.

Now when you run the application, you will be prompted to enter a username and password in order to access the application. This information will then be passed to the membership provider on the server to validate the user.

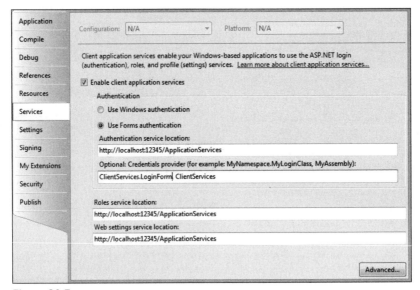

Figure 30-5

Offline Support

In the previous steps, if you had a breakpoint in the role provider code on the server, you may have noticed that it hit the breakpoint only the first time you ran the application. The reason for this is that it is caching the role information offline. If you click the "Advanced. . . " button on the Services tab of the project properties designer, you will see that there are a number of properties that can be adjusted to control this offline behavior, as shown in Figure 30-6.

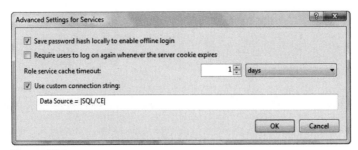

Figure 30-6

It's the role service cache timeout that determines how frequently the server is queried for role information. As this timeout determines the maximum period it will take for role changes to be propagated to a connected client, it is important that you set this property according to how frequently you expect role information to change. Clearly, if the application is running offline, the changes will be retrieved the next time the application goes online (assuming the cache timeout has been exceeded while the application is offline).

Clicking the "Save password hash" checkbox means that the application doesn't have to be online in order for the user to log in. The stored password hash is used only when the application is running in offline mode, in contrast to the role information, for which the cache is queried unless the timeout has been exceeded.

Whether the application is online or offline is a property maintained by the client application services, as it is completely independent of actual network or server availability. Depending on your application, it might be appropriate to link the two as shown in the following example, where offline status is set during application startup or when the network status changes. From the project properties designer, click the "View Application Events" button on the Application tab. This will display a code file in which the following code can be inserted:

```
Namespace My
    Partial Friend Class MyApplication
        Private Sub MyApplication_Startup(ByVal sender As Object, _
            ByVal e As Microsoft.VisualBasic.ApplicationServices.StartupEventArgs) _
                                                        Handles Me.Startup
            UpdateConnectivity()
        End Sub

        Private Sub MyApplication_NetworkAvailabilityChanged( _
            ByVal sender As Object, _
            ByVal e As Microsoft.VisualBasic.Devices.NetworkAvailableEventArgs) _
                                    Handles Me.NetworkAvailabilityChanged
            UpdateConnectivity()
        End Sub

        Private Sub UpdateConnectivity()
            System.Web.ClientServices.ConnectivityStatus.IsOffline = Not My.Computer
.Network.IsAvailable
        End Sub
    End Class
End Namespace
```

You should note that this is a very rudimentary way of detecting whether an application is online, and that most applications require more complex logic to determine if it is, in fact, connected or not. The other thing to consider is that when the application comes back online, you may wish to confirm that the user information is still up to date using the RevalidateUser method on the ClientFormsIdentity object (only relevant to Forms authentication):

```
CType(System.Threading.Thread.CurrentPrincipal.Identity, _
                                ClientFormsIdentity).RevalidateUser()
```

The last property in the Advanced dialog determines where the cached credential and role information is stored. This checkbox has been enabled because we chose to use Windows authentication earlier in the example. If you are using Forms authentication you can clear this checkbox. The client application services will use `.clientdata` files to store per-user data under the `Application.UserAppDataPath`, which is usually something like C:\Users\Nick\AppData\Roaming\ClientServices\1.0.0.0 under Windows Vista (slightly different under Windows XP). Using a custom connection string enables you to use a SQL Server Compact Edition (SSCE) database file to store the credentials information. This is required for offline support of Windows authentication.

> *Unfortunately, the designer is limited in that it doesn't enable you to specify any existing connections you may have. If you modify the app.config file, you can tweak the application to use the same connection.*

> *This might be a blessing in disguise, because the* |SQL/CE| *datasource property (which is the default) actually lets the client application services manage the creation and setup of the SSCE database file (otherwise you have to ensure that the appropriate tables exist).*

> *You will notice that the files that are created are* .spf *instead of the usual* .sdf *file extension — they are still SSCE database files that you can explore with Visual Studio 2008 (note that SQL Server Management Studio will not work with them, as they are SSCE v3.5, which is currently not supported).*

Summary

In this chapter, you have seen how the ASP.NET Application Services can be extended for use with client applications. With built-in support for offline functionality, the client application services will enable you to build applications that can seamlessly move between online and offline modes. Combined with the Microsoft ADO.NET Synchronization Services, they provide the necessary infrastructure to build quite sophisticated occasionally connected applications.

31

Device Security Manager

One of the challenges faced by developers building applications for the Windows Mobile platform is the uncertainty around the security profile of the target devices. Within a corporate environment it may be commonplace for the IT department to prescribe a given set of security settings for the company's mobile devices. Unfortunately in the consumer space this is quite often dictated by phone carriers or manufacturers.

With earlier versions of Visual Studio, an associated power toy would allow developers to manage the security settings on the device they were working with in order to test their application behavior. Now in Visual Studio 2008 this same functionality is available via the Device Security Manager. In this chapter you learn how to work with the Device Security Manager not only to manage your device security profile, but also to manage certificates and aid in validating your mobile application.

Security Configurations

The Device Security Manager (DSM) is found on the Tools menu alongside Connect to Device and the Device Emulator Manager. As an integrated part of Visual Studio 2008, the DSM will open in the main editor space, as shown in Figure 31-1.

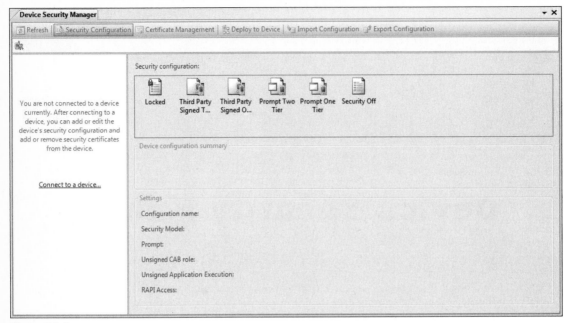

Figure 31-1

There are two main aspects to managing security on the Windows Mobile platform. These are Security Configuration and Certificate Management. Before you can use the DSM you must first connect to a device. The DSM is also capable of connecting to any of the device emulators that come with Visual Studio 2008, which is discussed later in the chapter. To get started, click the "Connect to a device" link in the left pane of the DSM. This will prompt you to select a device, or emulator, to connect to, as shown in Figure 31-2.

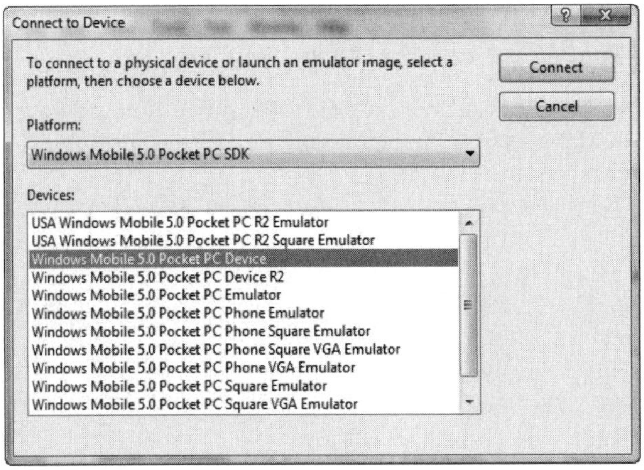

Figure 31-2

In Figure 31-2 a real Windows Mobile 5 device has been selected to connect to. In order to connect to a device, you need to ensure the device is correctly attached to your computer via the Windows Mobile Device Center (WMDC). Though basic connectivity is included in Windows Vista, you will need to download the update for the WMDC from the Microsoft web site. In the left image of Figure 31-3 you can see how the WMDC detects when a device is connected, allowing you to establish a partnership or connect in guest mode. From a development point of view it doesn't make any difference which option you choose, because both give you the functionality presented in the right image of Figure 31-3.

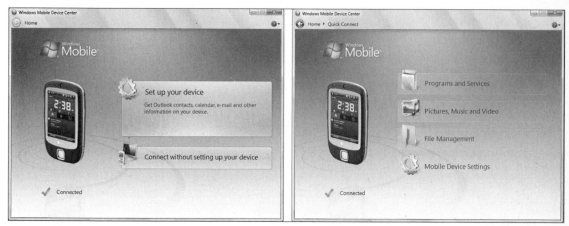

Figure 31-3

If you are using Windows XP, you need to use the latest version of ActiveSync, which provides comparable functionality to the Windows Mobile Device Center.

With your device attached to your computer via either the WMDC or ActiveSync, you can proceed with connecting the DSM to your device. Once attached, the DSM will add your device to the left-hand tree that lists Connected Devices. In Figure 31-4 you can see that the DSM is connected both to a real Windows Mobile 5 device and a Windows Mobile 6 emulator. Connecting to multiple devices and/or emulators can help you compare security configurations, which can help if you are trying to identify why your application behaves differently on one device than another.

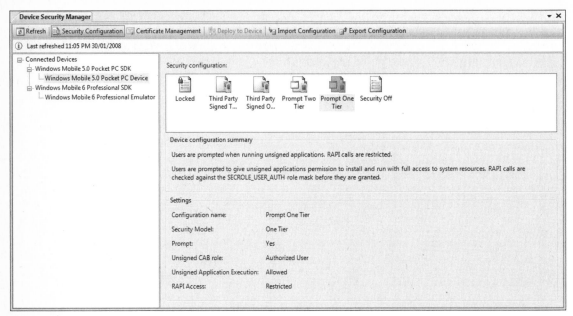

Figure 31-4

In Figure 31-4 you can see that on the Windows Mobile 5 device, which is currently selected, the current security configuration is Prompt One Tier. As the explanation indicates, this means that device users will be prompted if they attempt to run unsigned applications. In Figure 31-5 an attempt to run an unsigned application has been made on this device, and as you can see the user has been prompted to confirm this action.

Figure 31-5

Note that if this application references other non-signed components, the user will be prompted to allow access to each of these in turn. For most applications this might involve a number of components, which can be very frustrating for the user.

In Figure 31-4, the application was being run in debug mode from Visual Studio 2008. Selecting No to the prompt, or simply not selecting a response, will prevent application execution. Visual Studio is able to trap this error and indicate that this might be a security-related issue, as shown in Figure 31-6. This is important because some devices may come with a security profile that doesn't prompt the user, simply cancelling the execution of any unsigned applications.

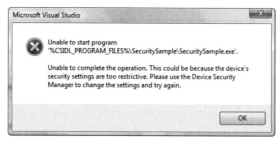

Figure 31-6

There are two ways to address this issue, which involve either signing your application or changing the security configuration of your device. To change the security configuration all you need do is select a different configuration, either from the list of predefined configurations or by loading your own xml configuration file, and then hitting the Deploy to Device button (see top of Figure 31-4). For example, the Security Off configuration will allow any application, signed or unsigned, to execute without prompts.

The other alternative is to sign your application so that it meets the conditions of execution. Figure 31-7 shows the Devices tab of the Project Properties dialog. In the Authenticode Signing section you can select a certificate with which to sign your application.

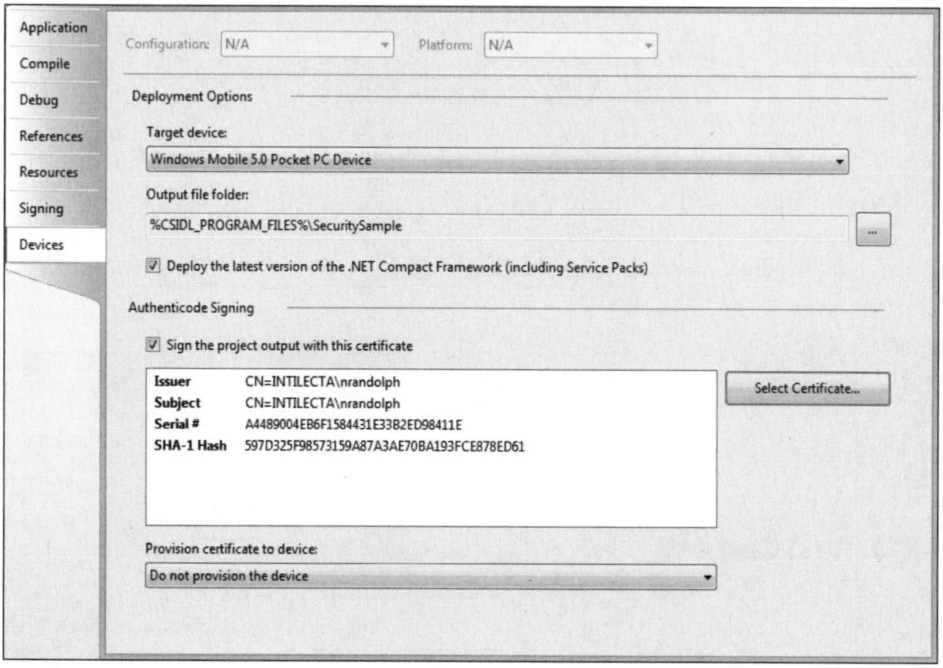

Figure 31-7

Here we have elected to use one of the developer certificates that were created by Visual Studio 2008. Unfortunately, even having the application signed with this certificate doesn't guarantee that it will execute without prompting the user. This is because the certificate hasn't come from one of the trusted certificate authorities and as such can't be verified.

To remove the prompts you have a couple of options. The best long-term solution is to acquire a real certificate that can be traced to a well-trusted authority, for example, VeriSign. However, during development it is easiest simply to deploy the developer certificate to the device. At the bottom of the dialog in Figure 31-7 you can elect to provision the certificate to the device. This is not recommended because it is easy to fall into a false sense of comfort that your application is working correctly — the certificate will automatically be deployed to any device on which you attempt to run your application.

Instead you should use the Certificate Management capabilities of the DSM as shown in Figure 31-8. In this case you can see that there is no certificate matching the developer certificate selected in the dialog of Figure 31-7.

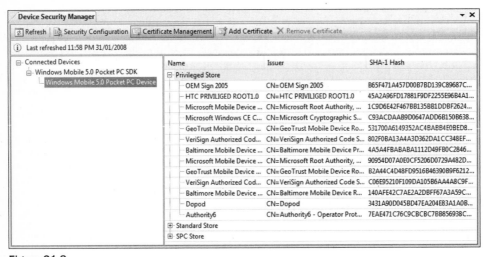

Figure 31-8

Clicking the Add Certificate button will allow you to add the developer certificate to the selected store. With this done, your application will run without prompting the user.

Note that reducing the security configuration on the device during development is the equivalent of doing all your development in administrator mode; it makes development very easy but leaves open the potential for your application to fail when you deploy it out to consumer devices. If you do this it is recommended that you do your testing on a device with a much stronger security configuration.

Device Emulation

With so many mobile devices on the market, it is not always economical for you to go out and purchase a new device in order to develop your application. Luckily, Microsoft has released a series of device emulators for each version of Windows Mobile. This allows you to compare functionality across different versions of the platform and even between emulators with different screen sizes and orientation.

Device Emulator Manager

In the previous version of Visual Studio, working with the device emulator was quite painful. If you didn't have your computer set up exactly right, Visual Studio would refuse to talk to the emulator. Unlike debugging your application on a real device via the WMDC (or ActiveSync), debugging on an emulator used its own communication layer, which was unreliable. This was addressed with the inclusion of the Device Emulator Manager.

The Device Emulator Manager gives you much better control over the state of emulators installed on your computer. Figure 31-9 shows the Device Emulator Manager with the Windows Mobile 5.0 Pocket PC Emulator running, which is evident from the play symbol next to the emulator.

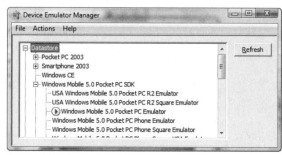

Figure 31-9

When you run your application from Visual Studio and elect to use an emulator, the Device Emulator Manager (DEM) is also started. If you try to close the DEM using the close button it will actually minimize itself into the system tray, because it is useful to have open while you work with the emulators.

Connecting

If an emulator is not currently active (that is, it appears without an icon beside it), you can start it by selecting Connect from the right-click context menu for that item in the tree. Once the emulator has been started, Visual Studio 2008 can use that emulator to debug your application.

After connecting to a device, the DEM can be used to shut down, reset, or even clear the saved state of the device. Clearing the saved state restores the device to the default state and may require Visual Studio to reinstall the .NET Compact Framework before you debug your application again (this depends on which emulator you are using and what version of the .NET Compact Framework you are targeting). This might be necessary if you get the emulator into an invalid state.

Cradling

The only remaining difference between running your application on a real device versus on the emulator is the communication layer involved. As mentioned previously, real devices use the WMDC to connect to the desktop. The communication layer provided by the WMDC is not only used by Visual Studio 2008 to debug your application, but it can also be the primary channel through which you synchronize data.

The ideal scenario is to have Visual Studio 2008 debug the emulator via the same communication layer. This has been achieved using the Device Emulator Manager to effectively cradle the emulator. From the right-click context menu for a running emulator, you can elect to cradle the device. This launches the WMDC, which may prompt you to set up a partnership between the emulator and the host computer — the same way you would for a real device. You can either set this up (if you are going to be doing a lot of debugging using the emulator) or just select the guest partnership.

Remember that once you have cradled the emulator, it is as if it were a real device at the end of the WMDC communication layer. As such, when you select which device you want to debug on, you need to select the Windows Mobile device, rather than any of the emulators. Using this technique, the interaction between Visual Studio 2008 and the emulator will mirror what you would get with a real device.

> *The Windows Mobile Device Center allows you to connect over a range of protocols including COM ports, Bluetooth, InfraRed, and DMA. The latter was introduced to improve performance when debugging applications — you need to select this communication method when debugging applications via the WMDC to an emulator.*

Summary

In this chapter you have seen how you can use the Device Security Manager to effectively manage the security settings on your device. With the ability to view and manage both the security configuration and the certificate stores, the DSM is a useful tool for profiling different devices to isolate behavior, and for testing your application on devices with a range of security settings.

You have also seen the Device Emulator Manager, which is used to connect, cradle, and administer the device emulators that are installed with Visual Studio 2008. As new versions of Windows Mobile become available, you can download and install new device emulators to help you build better, more reliable device applications.

Part VII
Platforms

32

ASP.NET Web Applications

When Microsoft released the first version of ASP.NET, one of the most talked-about features was the capability to create full-blown web applications much as Windows applications do. This release introduced the concept of developing feature-rich applications that can run over the Web in a wholly integrated way.

ASP.NET version 2.0, which was released in 2005, was a significant upgrade that included new features such as a provider model for everything from menu navigation to user authentication, more than 50 new server controls, a web portal framework, and built-in web site administration, to name but a few. These enhancements made it even easier to build complex web applications in less time.

The latest version of ASP.NET has continued this trend with several new components and server controls. Perhaps more significant, however, are the improvements that have been added to Visual Studio to make the development of web applications easier. These include enhancements to the HTML Designer, new CSS editing tools, and IntelliSense support for JavaScript. Visual Studio 2008 also includes out-of-the-box support for both Web Application projects and ASP.NET AJAX, which were not available when the previous version was released.

In this chapter you'll learn how to create ASP.NET web applications in Visual Studio 2008, as well as look at many of the web components that Microsoft has included to make your development life a little (and in some cases a lot) easier.

Web Application vs. Web Site Projects

With the release of Visual Studio 2005, a radically new type of project was introduced — the Web Site project. Much of the rationale behind the move to a new project type was based on the premise that web sites, and web developers for that matter, are fundamentally different from other types of applications (and developers), and would therefore benefit from a different model. Although Microsoft did a good job extolling the virtues of this new project type, many developers found it difficult to work with, and clearly expressed their displeasure to Microsoft.

Fortunately, Microsoft listened to this feedback, and a short while later released a free add-on download to Visual Studio that provided support for a new Web Application project type. It was also included with Service Pack 1 of Visual Studio 2005.

The major differences between the two project types are fairly significant. The most fundamental change is that a Web Site project does not contain a Visual Studio project file (`.csproj` or `.vbproj`), whereas a Web Application project does. As a result, there is no central file that contains a list of all the files in a Web Site project. Instead, the Visual Studio solution file contains a reference to the root folder of the Web Site project, and the content and layout are directly inferred from its files and sub-folders. If you copy a new file into a sub-folder of a Web Site project using Windows Explorer, then that file, by definition, belongs to the project. In a Web Application project you must explicitly add all files to the project from within Visual Studio.

The other major difference is in the way the projects are compiled. Web Application projects are compiled in much the same way as any other project under Visual Studio. The code is compiled into a single assembly that is stored in the \bin directory of the web application. As with all other Visual Studio projects, you can control the build through the property pages, name the output assembly, and add pre- and post-build action rules.

On the contrary, in a Web Site project all the classes that aren't code-behind-a-page or user control are compiled into one common assembly. Pages and user controls are then compiled dynamically as needed into a set of separate assemblies.

The big advantage of more granular assemblies is that the entire web site does not need to be rebuilt every time a page is changed. Instead, only those assemblies that have changes (or have a down-level dependency) are recompiled, which can save a significant amount of time, depending on your preferred method of development.

Microsoft has pledged that it will continue to support both the Web Site and Web Application project types in all future versions of Visual Studio.

So which project type should you use? The official position from Microsoft is "it depends," which is certainly a pragmatic, although not particularly useful, position to take. All scenarios are different, and you should always carefully weigh each alternative in the context of your requirements and environment. However, the anecdotal evidence that has emerged from the .NET developer community over the past few years, and the experience of the authors, is that in most cases the Web Application project type is the best choice.

> Unless you are developing a very large web project with hundreds of pages, it is actually not too difficult to migrate from a Web Site project to a Web Application project and vice versa. So don't get too hung up on this decision. Pick one project type and migrate it later if you run into difficulties.

Creating Web Projects

In addition to the standard ASP.NET Web Application and Web Site projects, Visual Studio 2008 provides support and templates for several specialized web application scenarios. These include web services, WCF services, server control libraries, and reporting applications. However, before we discuss these you should understand how to create the standard project types.

Creating a Web Site Project

As mentioned previously, creating a Web Site project in Visual Studio 2008 is slightly different from creating a regular Windows-type project. With normal Windows applications and services, you pick the type of project, name the solution, and click "OK". Each language has its own set of project templates and you have no real options when you create the project. Web Site project development is different because you can create the development project in different locations, from the local file system to a variety of FTP and HTTP locations that are defined in your system setup, including the local IIS server or remote FTP folders.

Because of this major difference in creating these projects, Microsoft has separated out the Web Site project templates into their own command and dialog. Selecting New Web Site from the File ⇨ New sub-menu will display the New Web Site dialog, where you can choose the type of project template you want to use (see Figure 32-1).

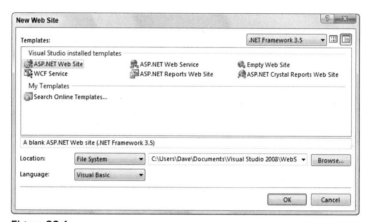

Figure 32-1

Most likely, you'll select the ASP.NET Web Site project template. This creates a web site populated with a single default web form and a basic Web.config file that will get you up and running quickly. The Empty Web Site project template creates nothing more than an empty folder and a reference in a solution file. The remaining templates, which are for the most part variations on the Web Site template, are discussed later in this chapter. Regardless of which type of web project you're creating, the lower section of the dialog enables you to choose where to create the project as well as what language should be used as a base for the project.

The more important choice you have to make is where the web project will be created. By default, Visual Studio expects you to develop the web site or service locally, using the normal file system. The default location is under the Documents/Visual Studio 2008/WebSites folder for the current user, but you can change this by overtyping the value, selecting an alternative location from the drop-down list, or clicking the "Browse" button.

The Location drop-down list also contains HTTP and FTP as options. Selecting HTTP or FTP will change the value in the filename textbox to a blank `http://` or `ftp://` prefix ready for you to type in the destination URL. You can either type in a valid location or click the "Browse" button to change the intended location of the project.

The Choose Location dialog (shown in Figure 32-2) enables you to specify where the project should be stored. Note that this isn't necessarily where the project will be deployed, as you can specify a different destination for that when you're ready to ship, so don't expect that you are specifying the ultimate destination here.

Figure 32-2

The File System option enables you to browse through the folder structure known to the system, including the My Network Places folders, and gives you the option to create sub-folders where you need them. This is the easiest way of specifying where you want the web project files, and the way that makes the files easiest to locate later.

Although you can specify where to create the project files, by default the solution file will be created in a new folder under the Documents/Visual Studio 2008/Projects folder for the current user. You can move the solution file to a folder of your choice without affecting the projects.

If you are using a local IIS server to debug your Web Site project, you can select the File System option and browse to your wwwroot folder to create the web site. However, a much better option is to use the local IIS location type and drill down to your preferred location under the Default Web Site folders. This interface enables you to browse virtual directory entries that point to web sites that are not physically located within the wwwroot folder structure, but are actually aliases to elsewhere in the file system or network. You can create your application in a new Web Application folder or create a new virtual directory entry in which you browse to the physical file location and specify an alias to appear in the web site list.

The FTP site location type is shown in Figure 32-2, which gives you the option to log into a remote FTP site anonymously or with a specified user. When you click "Open", Visual Studio saves the FTP settings for when you create the project, so be aware that it won't test whether the settings are correct until it attempts to create the project files and save them to the specified destination.

You can save your project files to any FTP server to which you have access, even if that FTP site doesn't have .NET installed. However, you will not be able to run the files without .NET, so you will only be able to use such a site as a file store.

The last location type is a remote site, which enables you to connect to a remote server that has FrontPage extensions installed on it. If you have such a site, you can simply specify where you want the new project to be saved, and Visual Studio 2008 will confirm that it can create the folder through the FrontPage extensions.

Once you've chosen the intended location for your project, clicking "OK" tells Visual Studio 2008 to create the project files and propagate them to the desired location. After the web application has finished initializing, Visual Studio opens the Default.aspx page and populates the Toolbox with the components available to you for web development.

The Web Site project has only a small subset of the project configuration options available under the property pages of other project types, as shown in Figure 32-3. To access these options right-click the project and select Property Pages.

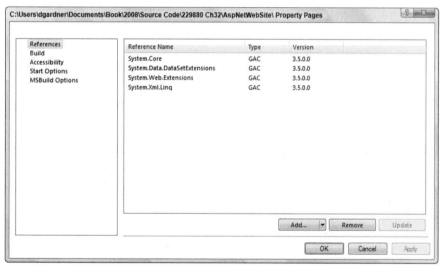

Figure 32-3

The References property page, shown in Figure 32-3, enables you to define references to external assemblies or web services. If you add a reference to an assembly that is not in the Global Application Cache (GAC), the assembly is copied to the \bin folder of your web project along with a .refresh file, which is a small text file that contains the path to the original location of the assembly. Every time the web site is built, Visual Studio will compare the current version of the assembly in the \bin folder with the version in the original location and, if necessary, update it. If you have a large number of external references, this can slow the compile time considerably. Therefore, it is recommended that you delete the associated .refresh file for any assembly references that are unlikely to change frequently.

The Build, Accessibility, and Start Options property pages provide some control over how the web site is built and launched during debugging. The accessibility validation options are discussed later in this chapter and the rest of the settings on those property pages are reasonably self-explanatory.

The MSBuild Options property page provides a couple of interesting advanced options for web applications. If you uncheck the "Allow this precompiled site to be updatable" option, all the content of the .aspx and .ascx pages is compiled into the assembly along with the code-behind. This can be useful if you want to protect the user interface of a web site from being modified. Finally, the "Use fixed naming and single page assemblies" option specifies that each page be compiled into a separate assembly rather than the default, which is an assembly per folder.

Creating a Web Application Project

Creating a Web Application project with Visual Studio 2008 is much the same as creating any other project type. Select File ➪ New ➪ Project and you will be presented with the New Project dialog box, shown in Figure 32-4. By filtering the project types by language and then by using Web, you will be given a selection of templates that is partially similar to those available for Web Site projects.

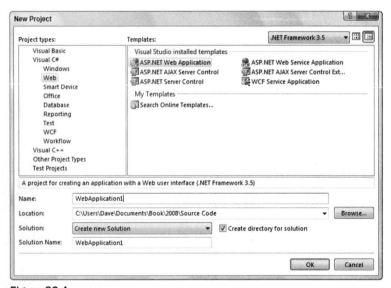

Figure 32-4

The notable difference in available project templates is that the empty site and reporting templates are not available as Web Application projects. However, the Web Application project type includes templates for creating several different types of server controls.

Once you click "OK" your new Web Application project will be created with a few more items than the Web Site projects. It includes an AssemblyInfo file, a References folder, and a My Project item under the Visual Basic or Properties node under C#.

You can view the project properties pages for a Web Application project by double-clicking the Properties or My Project item. The property pages include an additional Web page, as shown in Figure 32-5.

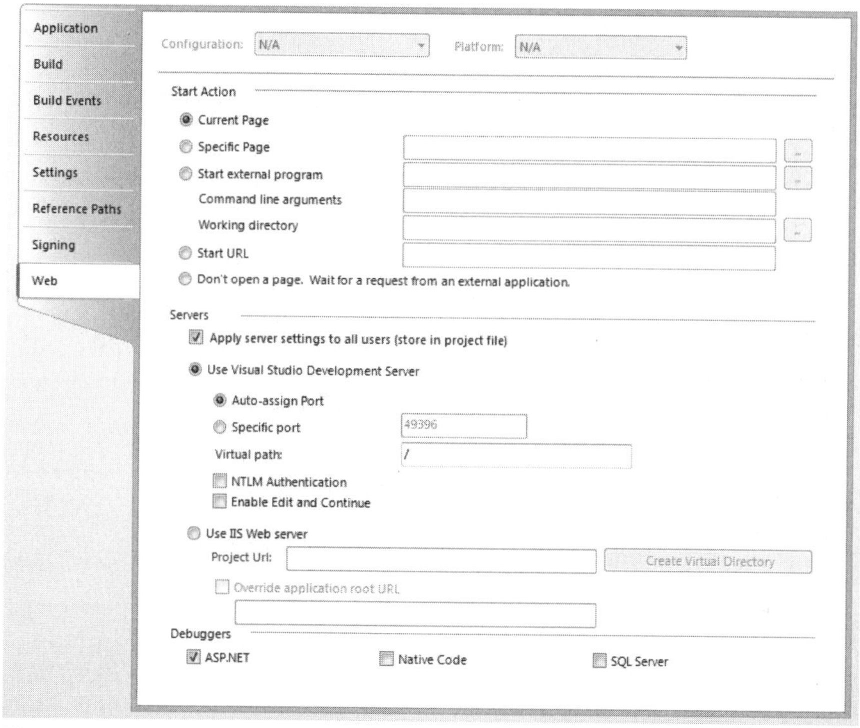

Figure 32-5

The options on the Web page are all related to debugging an ASP.NET web application and are covered in Chapter 45, "Advanced Debugging Techniques."

Other Web Projects

In addition to the standard ASP.NET Web Site and Web Application project templates, there are templates that provide solutions for more specific scenarios.

❑ **ASP.NET Web Service:** This creates a default web service called Service.asmx, which contains a sample Web method. This is available for both Web Site and Web Application projects.

❑ **WCF Service:** This creates a new Windows Communication Foundation (WCF) service, which contains a sample service endpoint. This is available for both Web Site and Web Application projects.

❑ **Reporting Web Site:** This creates an ASP.NET web site with a report (.rdlc) and a ReportViewer control bound to the report. This is only available as a Web Site project.

❑ **Crystal Reports Web Site:** This creates an ASP.NET web site with a sample Crystal Report. This is only available as a Web Site project.

❑ **ASP.NET Server Control:** Server controls include standard elements such as buttons and textboxes, and also special-purpose controls such as a calendar, menus, and a treeview control. This is only available as a Web Application project.

❑ **ASP.NET AJAX Server Control**: This contains the ASP.NET web server controls that enable you to add AJAX functionality to an ASP.NET web page. This is only available as a Web Application project.

❑ **ASP.NET AJAX Server Control Extender:** ASP.NET AJAX extender controls improve the client-side behavior and capabilities of standard ASP.NET web server controls. This is only available as a Web Application project.

There are further project templates available through add-on downloads. Good examples are the ASP.NET MVC and Silverlight 2.0 project types, which are discussed in Chapter 37.

Starter Kits, Community Projects, and Open-Source Applications

One of the best ways to learn any new development technology is to review a sample application. The Microsoft ASP.NET web site contains a list of starter kits and community projects at `http://www.asp.net/community/projects`. These web applications are excellent reference implementations for demonstrating best practices and good use of ASP.NET components and design.

At the time of writing, the starter kits had not been updated to version 3.5 of the .NET Framework. However, they are still very useful as they demonstrate a wide range of more advanced ASP.NET technologies and techniques including multiple CSS themes, master-detail pages, and user management.

The Microsoft ASP.NET site also contains a list of popular open-source projects that have been built on ASP.NET. By far the most up-to-date and comprehensive is the DinnerNow.net sample application, available at `http://www.dinnernow.net/`. Although it is categorized as an open-source application, it is really a reference implementation of many of the latest technologies from Microsoft.

The DinnerNow.net application is a fictitious marketplace where customers can order food from local restaurants for delivery to their homes or offices. In addition to the latest ASP.NET components, it demonstrates the use of IIS7, ASP.NET AJAX Extensions, LINQ, Windows Communication Foundation, Windows Workflow Foundation, Windows Presentation Foundation, Windows Powershell, and the .NET Compact Framework.

Another great place to find a large number of excellent open-source examples is CodePlex, Microsoft's open-source project-hosting web site. Located at `http://www.codeplex.com/`, CodePlex is a veritable wellspring of the good, the bad, and the ugly in Microsoft open-source applications.

Designing Web Forms

One of the biggest areas of improvement in Visual Studio 2008 for web developers is the visual design of web applications. The HTML Designer has been overhauled with a new split view that enables you to simultaneously work on the design and markup of a web form. You can also change the positioning, padding, and margins in Design view, using visual layout tools. Finally, Visual Studio 2008 now supports rich Cascading Style Sheet (CSS) editing tools for designing the layout and styling of web content.

The HTML Designer

The HTML Designer in Visual Studio has always been one of the reasons it is so easy to develop ASP.NET applications. Because it understands how to render HTML as well as server-side ASP.NET controls, you can simply drag and drop components from the Toolbox onto the designer surface in order to quickly build up a web user interface. You can also quickly toggle between viewing the HTML markup and the visual design of a web page or user control.

The modifications made to the View menu of the IDE are a great example of what Visual Studio does to contextually provide you with useful features depending on what you're doing. When you're editing a web page in Design view, additional menu commands become available for adjusting how the design surface appears (see Figure 32-6).

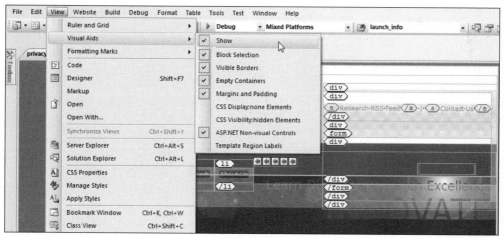

Figure 32-6

The three sub-menus at the top of the View menu — Ruler and Grid, Visual Aids, and Formatting Marks — provide you with a whole bunch of useful tools to assist with the overall layout of controls and HTML elements on a web page.

For example, when the Show option is toggled on the Visual Aids sub-menu, it will draw gray borders around all container controls and HTML tags such as `<table>` and `<div>` so you can easily see where each component resides on the form. It will also provide color-coded shading to indicate the margins and padding around HTML elements and server controls. Likewise, on the Formatting Marks sub-menu you can toggle options to display HTML tag names, line breaks, spaces, and much more. The impact of these options in the Designer can be seen in action in Figure 32-6.

In Visual Studio 2008 the HTML Designer supports a new split view, shown in Figure 32-7, which shows your HTML markup and visual design at the same time. You activate this view by opening a page in design mode and clicking the "Split" button on the bottom left of the Designer window.

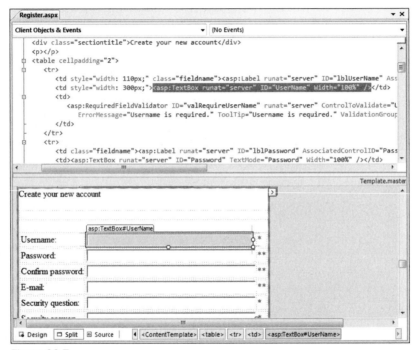

Figure 32-7

When you select a control or HTML element on the design surface, the Designer will highlight it in the HTML markup. Likewise, if you move the cursor to a new location in the markup, it will highlight the corresponding element or control on the design surface.

If you make a change to anything on the design surface, that change will immediately be reflected in the HTML markup. However, changes to the markup are not always shown in the Designer right away. Instead, you will be presented with an information bar at the top of the Design view stating that it is out of sync with the Source view (see Figure 32-8). You can either click the information bar or press Ctrl+Shift+Y to synchronize the views. Saving your changes to the file will also synchronize it.

Design view is out of sync with Source view. Click here to synchronize views.

Figure 32-8

If you have a widescreen monitor you can orient the split view vertically to take advantage of your screen resolution. Select Tools ➪ Options and then click the HTML Designer node in the treeview. There are a number of settings here to configure how the HTML Designer behaves, including an option called "Split views vertically."

Another feature worth pointing out in the HTML Designer is the tag navigator breadcrumb that appears at the bottom of the design window. This feature, which is also in the WPF Designer, displays the hierarchy of the current element or control and all its ancestors. The breadcrumb will display the type of the control or element and the ID or CSS class if it has been defined. If the tag path is too long to fit in the width of the Designer window, the list will be truncated and a couple of arrow buttons displayed so you can scroll through the tag path.

The tag navigator breadcrumb will display the path only from the current element to its top-level parent. It will not list any elements outside that path. If you want to see the hierarchy of all the elements in the current document you should use the Document Outline window, shown in Figure 32-9. Select View ➪ Other Windows ➪ Document Outline to display the window. When you select an element or control in the Document Outline, it will be highlighted in the Design and Source views of the HTML Designer. However, selecting an element in the HTML Designer does not highlight it in the Document Outline window.

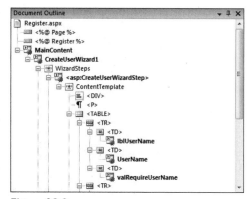

Figure 32-9

Positioning Controls and HTML Elements

One of the trickier parts of building web pages is the positioning of HTML elements. Several attributes can be set that control how an element is positioned, including whether it is using a relative or absolute position, the float setting, the z-index, and the padding and margin widths.

Fortunately, you don't need to learn the exact syntax and names of all of these attributes and manually type them into the markup. As with most things in Visual Studio, the IDE is there to assist with the specifics. Begin by selecting the control or element that you want to position in Design view. Then choose Format ⇨ Position from the menu to bring up the Position window shown in Figure 32-10.

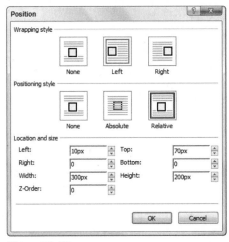

Figure 32-10

After you click "OK," the wrapping and positioning style you have chosen and any values you have entered for location and size will be saved to a style attribute on the HTML element.

If an element has relative or absolute positioning, you will be able to reposition it in the Design view. Beware, though, of how you drag elements around the designer, as you may be doing something you didn't intend! Whenever you select an element or control in Design view, a white tag will appear at the top left corner of the element. This will display the type of element, as well as the ID and class name if they are defined.

If you wish to reposition an element with relative or absolute positioning, drag it to the new position *using the white control tag*. If you drag the element using the control itself, it will not modify the HTML positioning, but will instead *move it to a new line of code in the source*.

Figure 32-11 shows a button that has relative positioning and has been repositioned. The actual location of the element in the normal flow of the document is shown with an empty blue rectangle. However, this control has been repositioned 45px down and 225px to the right of its original position. The actual control is shown in its new position, and blue horizontal and vertical guidelines are displayed, which indicate that the control is relatively positioned. The guidelines and original position of the element are shown only while it is selected.

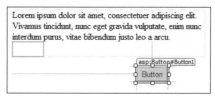

Figure 32-11

If a control uses absolute positioning, the positioning container is highlighted, and two additional guidelines are displayed that extend from the bottom and right of the control to the edge of the container.

The final layout technique that we will discuss here is setting the padding and margins of a HTML element. Many web developers are initially confused about the difference between these display attributes — which is not helped by the fact that different browsers render elements with these attributes differently. While not all HTML elements display a border, you can *generally* think of padding as the space inside the border, and of margins as the space outside.

If you look very closely within the HTML Designer, you may notice some gray lines extending a short way horizontally and vertically from all four corners of a control. These are only visible when the element is selected in the Design view. These are called *margin handles* and they allow you to set the width of the margins. Hover the mouse over the handle until it changes to a resize cursor, and then drag it to increase or decrease the margin width (see Figure 32-12).

Finally, within the HTML Designer you can set the padding around an element. If you select an element and then hold down the Shift key, the margin handles will become padding handles. Keeping the Shift key pressed, you can drag the handles to increase or decrease the padding width. When you release the Shift key they will revert to margin handles again. Figure 32-12 shows how an HTML image element looks in the Designer when the margin and padding widths have been set on all four sides.

Figure 32-12

At first, this means of setting the margins and padding can feel counterintuitive, because it does not behave very consistently. To increase the top and left margins you must drag the handlers into the element, while to increase the top and left padding you must drag the handlers away. However, just to confuse things, dragging the bottom and right handlers away from the element will increase both margin and padding widths.

Once you have your HTML layout and positioning the way you want them, you can follow good practices by using the new CSS tools to move the layout off the page and into an external style sheet. These tools are discussed in the section after next.

Formatting Controls and HTML Elements

In addition to the Position dialog window discussed in the previous section, Visual Studio 2008 provides a toolbar and a range of additional dialog windows that enable you to edit the formatting of controls and HTML elements on a web page.

The Formatting toolbar, shown in Figure 32-13, provides easy access to most of the formatting options. The leftmost drop-down list includes all the common HTML elements that can be applied to text, including the `<h1>` through `<h6>` headers, `<ul>`, `<ol>`, and `<blockquote>`.

Figure 32-13

Most of the other formatting dialog windows are listed as entries on the Format menu. These include windows for setting the foreground and background colors, font, paragraph, bullets and numbering, and borders and shading. These dialog windows are similar to those available in any word processor or WYSIWYG interface and their uses are immediately obvious.

The Insert Table dialog window, shown in Figure 32-14, provides a way for you to easily define the layout and design of a new HTML table. Open it by positioning the cursor on the design surface where you wish the new table to be placed and selecting Table ⇨ Insert Table.

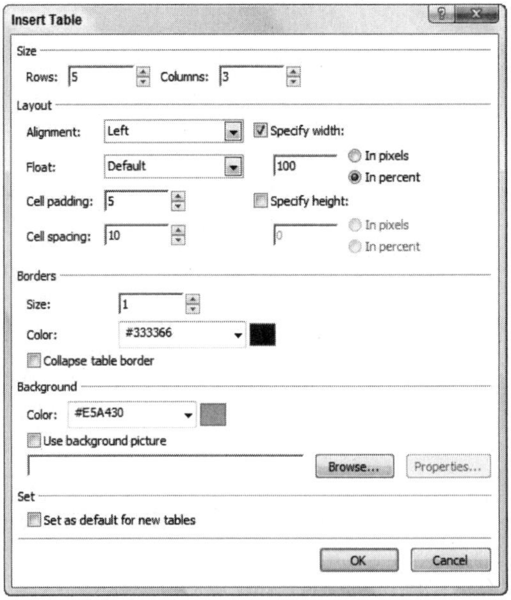

Figure 32-14

One final quite useful feature on the Insert Table and Font dialog windows is under the color selector. In addition to the list of Standard Colors, there is also the Document Colors list, shown in Figure 32-15. This lists all the colors that have been applied in some way or another to the current page, for example as foreground, background, or border colors. This saves you from having to remember custom RGB values for the color scheme that you have chosen to apply to a page.

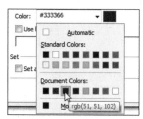

Figure 32-15

CSS Tools

Once upon a time, the HTML within a typical web page consisted of a mishmash of both content and presentation markup. Web pages made liberal use of HTML tags that defined *how* the content should be rendered, such as <font>, <center>, and <big>. Nowadays, designs of this nature are frowned upon — best practice dictates that HTML documents should specify only the content of the web page, wrapped in semantic tags such as <h1>, <ul>, and <div>. Elements requiring special presentation rules should be assigned a class attribute, and all style information should be stored in external Cascading Style Sheets (CSS).

Visual Studio 2008 has introduced new features that provide a rich CSS editing experience in an integrated fashion. As you saw in the previous section, you can do much of the work of designing the layout and styling the content in Design view. This is supplemented by the new Manage Styles and Apply Styles windows, a CSS Properties window, and the Style Application toolbar.

The Manage Styles window lists all the CSS styles that are internal, inline, or in an external CSS file linked through to the current page. The objective of this tool window is to provide you with an overall view of the CSS rules for a particular page, and to enable you to edit and manage those CSS classes.

All the styles are listed in a treeview with the style sheet forming the top-level nodes, as shown in Figure 32-16. The styles are listed in the order in which they appear in the style sheet file, and you can drag and drop to rearrange the styles, or even move styles from one style sheet to another.

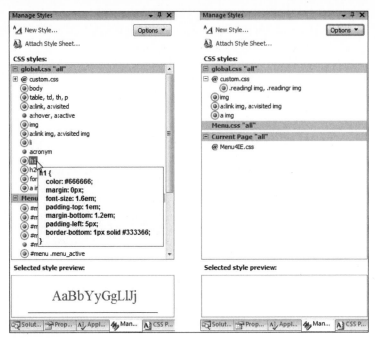

Figure 32-16

When you hover over a style the tooltip will show the CSS properties in that style, as shown in Figure 32-16 (left). The "Options" menu button enables you to filter the list of styles to show only those that are applicable to elements on the current page or, if you have an element selected in the HTML designer, only those that are relevant to the selected element. The right side of Figure 32-16 shows a filtered list of styles.

> *The selected style preview, which is at the bottom of the Manage Styles window, is generally not what will actually be displayed in the web browser. This is because the preview does not take into account any CSS inheritance rules that might cause the properties of the style to be overridden.*

The Manage Styles window uses a set of icons to provide further visual information about the type of each style. The icons next to the style names have different colors: a red dot indicates an ID-based style, a green dot a class-based style, a blue dot an element-based style, and a yellow dot an inline style.

A circle around a dot indicates that the style is used on the current page. For example, on the left side of Figure 32-16 you can quickly see that the h1 element is used on the active web page, while the acronym element is not. Finally, the @ symbol is used to indicate an imported external cascading style sheet.

When you right-click a style in the Manage Styles window you are given the option to create a new style from scratch, create a new style based on the selected style, or modify the selected style. Any of these three options will launch the Modify Style dialog box, shown in Figure 32-17. This dialog provides an intuitive way to define or modify a CSS style. Style properties are grouped into familiar categories, such as Font, Border, and Position, and a useful preview is displayed towards the bottom of the window.

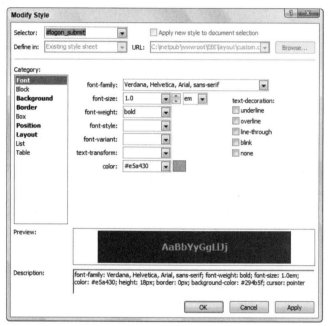

Figure 32-17

The second of the CSS windows is the Apply Styles window. While this has a fair degree of overlap with the Manage Styles window, its purpose is to enable you to easily apply styles to elements on the web page. Select View ➪ Apply Styles to open the window, shown in Figure 32-18. As in the Manage Styles window, all the available styles are listed in the window and you can filter the list to show only the styles that are applicable to the current page or the currently selected element. The window uses the same icons to indicate whether the style is ID-based, class-based, element-based, or inline. You can also hover over a style to display all the properties in the CSS rule.

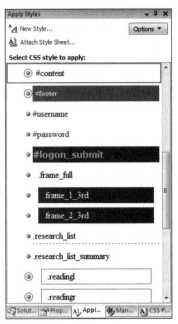

Figure 32-18

However, the Apply Styles window displays a much more visually accurate representation of the style than the Manage Styles window. It includes the font color and weight, background colors or images, borders, and even text alignment.

When you select an HTML element in the designer, the styles applied to that element are surrounded by a blue border in the Apply Styles window. This can be seen in Figure 32-18, where the `#content` style is active for the selected element. When you hover the mouse over any of the styles a drop-down button will appear over it, providing access to a context menu. This menu has options for applying that style to the selected element or, if the style has already been applied, for removing it. Simply clicking the style will also apply it to the current HTML element.

The third of the new CSS windows in Visual Studio 2008 is the CSS Properties window, shown in Figure 32-19. This displays a property grid with all the styles used by the HTML element that is currently selected in the Designer. In addition, the window gives you a comprehensive list of all of the available CSS properties. This enables you to add properties to an existing style, modify properties that you have already set, and create new inline styles.

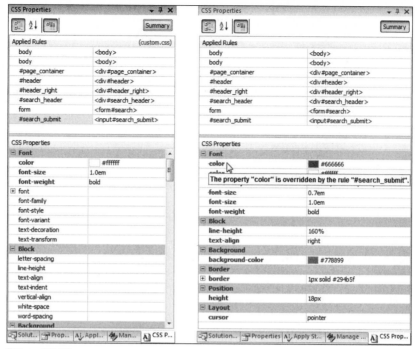

Figure 32-19

Rather than display the details of an individual style, as was the case with the Apply Styles and Manage Styles windows, the CSS Properties window instead shows a cumulative view of all the styles applicable to the current element, taking into account the order of precedence for the styles. At the top of the CSS Properties window is the Applied Rules section, which lists the CSS styles in the order in which they are applied. Styles that are lower on this list will override the styles above them.

Selecting a style in the Applied Rules section will show all the CSS properties for that style in the lower property grid. In Figure 32-19 (left) the #search_submit CSS rule has been selected, which has a definition for the color, font-size, and font-weight CSS properties. You can edit these properties or define new ones directly in this property grid.

The CSS Properties window also has a "Summary" button, which displays all the CSS properties applicable to the current element. This is shown in Figure 32-19 (right). CSS properties that have been overridden are shown with a red strikethrough, and hovering the mouse over the property will display a tooltip with the reason for the override.

Visual Studio 2008 also includes a new Style Application toolbar, shown in Figure 32-20, which enables you to control where style changes that you made using the formatting toolbars and dialog windows are saved. These include the Formatting toolbar and the dialog windows under the Format menu, such as Font, Paragraph, Bullets and Numbering, Borders and Shading, and Position.

Style Application: Manual
Target Rule: .readingtitle (custom.

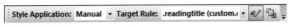

Figure 32-20

The Style Application toolbar has two modes: Auto and Manual. In Auto mode Visual Studio will automatically choose where the new style is applied. In Manual mode you can control where the resulting CSS properties are created via the Target Rule drop-down of the toolbar. Visual Studio 2008 defaults to Manual mode, and any changes to this mode are remembered for the current user.

The Target Rule drop-down is populated with a list of styles that have already been applied to the currently selected element. Inline styles are displayed with an entry that reads `< inline style >`. Styles defined inline in the current page have `(Current Page)` appended, and styles defined in an external style sheet have the filename appended.

Finally, in Visual Studio 2008 there is now IntelliSense support for CSS in both the CSS editor and HTML editor. The CSS editor, which is opened by default when you double-click a CSS file, provides IntelliSense prompts for all the CSS attributes and valid values, as shown in Figure 32-21. After the CSS styles are defined, the HTML editor will subsequently detect and display a list of valid CSS class names available on the web page when you add the `class` attribute to a HTML element. An invalid class reference in the HTML markup will be marked with a green squiggly line underneath the class name, and will generate a warning in the Error List window.

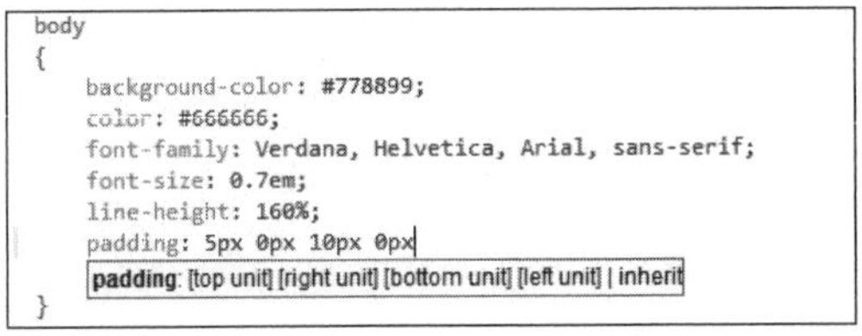

body
{
background-color: #778899;
color: #666666;
font-family: Verdana, Helvetica, Arial, sans-serif;
font-size: 0.7em;
line-height: 160%;
padding: 5px 0px 10px 0px
padding: [top unit] [right unit] [bottom unit] [left unit] | inherit
}

Figure 32-21

Validation Tools

Web browsers are remarkably good at hiding badly formed HTML code from end users. Invalid syntax that would cause a fatal error if it were in an XML document, such as out-of-order or missing closing tags, will often render fine in your favorite web browser. However, if you view that same malformed HTML code in a different browser, it may look totally different. This is one good reason to ensure that your HTML code is standards-compliant.

The first step to validating your standards compliance is to set the target schema for validation. You can do this from the HTML Source Editing toolbar shown in Figure 32-22.

XHTML 1.1
Internet Explorer 6.0
Internet Explorer 3.02 / Netscape Navigator 3.0
Netscape Navigator 4.0
HTML 4.01
XHTML 1.0 Transitional (Netscape 7, Opera 7, Internet Explorer 6)
XHTML 1.0 Frameset
XHTML 1.1

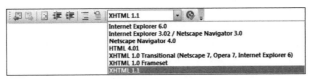

Figure 32-22

Your HTML markup will be validated against the selected schema. Validation works like a background spell-checker, examining the markup as it is entered and adding wavy green lines under the elements or attributes that are not valid based on the current schema. As shown in Figure 32-23, when you hover over an element marked as invalid a tooltip will appear showing the reason for the validation failure. A warning entry will also be created in the Error List window.

```
<html xmlns="http://www.w3.org/1999/xhtml">
<head>
    <title>Contact Us</title>
    <link rel="stylesheet" href="layout/global.css" type="text/css" media="all" />
</head>
<body>
    <img src="images\logo.png">
    Validation (XHTML 1.1): Empty elements such as 'img' must end with />.
</body>
</html>
```

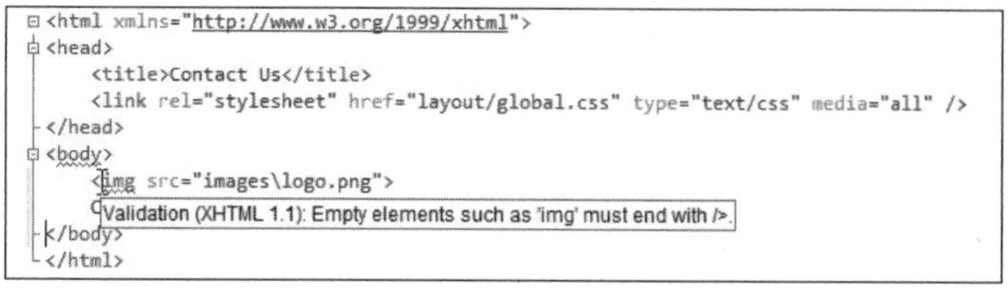

Figure 32-23

Schema validation will go a long way toward helping your web pages render the same across different browsers. However, it does not ensure that your site is accessible to everyone. There may be a fairly large group of people with some sort of physical impairment who find it extremely difficult to access your site due to the way the HTML markup has been coded.

The World Health Organization has estimated that 161 million people worldwide have a visual impairment (World Health Organization, 2000). In the United States, it is estimated that approximately 12 million people have some form of vision impairment that cannot be corrected by glasses (National Advisory Eye Council, 1998). That's a large body of people by anyone's estimate, especially given that it doesn't include those with other physical impairments.

In addition to reducing the size of your potential user base, if you do not take accessibilities into account you may run the risk of being on the wrong side of a lawsuit. A number of countries have introduced legislation that requires web sites and other forms of communication to be accessible to people with disabilities.

Fortunately, Visual Studio 2008 includes an accessibility-validation tool that checks HTML markups for compliance with accessibility guidelines. The Web Content Accessibility Checker, launched from Tools ⇨ Check Accessibility, enables you to check an individual page for compliance against several accessibility guidelines, including Web Content Accessibility Guidelines (WCAG) version 1.0 and the Americans with Disabilities Act Section 508 Guidelines, commonly referred to as Section 508.

Select the guidelines to check for compliance and click "Validate" to begin. Once the web page has been checked, any issues will be displayed as errors or warnings in the Error List window, as shown in Figure 32-24.

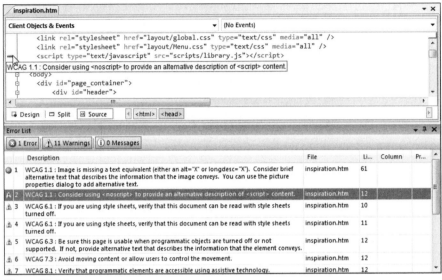

Figure 32-24

Web Controls

When ASP.NET version 1.0 was first released, a whole new way of building web applications was enabled for Microsoft developers. Instead of using strictly server-based components in ASP or similar languages, and having to deal with the sequential way page code was processed, ASP.NET introduced the concept of feature-rich controls for web pages that acted in ways similar to their Windows counterparts.

Web controls such as button and textbox components have familiar properties such as `Text`, `Left`, and `Width`, along with just as recognizable methods and events such as `Click` and `TextChanged`. In addition to these, ASP.NET 1.0 provided a limited set of web-specific components, some dealing with data-based information, such as the DataGrid control, and others providing common web tasks, such as an ErrorProvider to give feedback to users about problems with information they entered into a web form.

ASP.NET version 2.0 introduced over 50 web server controls including new navigation components, user authentication, web parts, and improved data controls. The latest version of ASP.NET has introduced several new highly functional data components including the ListView, DataPager, and LinqDataSource controls.

Unfortunately, we don't have room in this book to explore all the server controls available to web applications in much detail. In fact, many of the components, such as TextBox, Button, and Checkbox, are simply the web equivalents of the basic user interface controls that you are no doubt very familiar with already. However, it will be useful to provide an overview of some of the more specialized and functional server controls that reside in the ASP.NET web developers' toolkit.

Navigation Components

ASP.NET includes a simple way to add site-wide navigation to your web applications with the sitemap provider and associated controls. In order to implement sitemap functionality into your projects, you must manually create the site data, by default in a file called web.sitemap, and keep it up to date as you add or remove web pages from the site. Sitemap files can be used as a data source for a number of web controls, including SiteMapPath, which automatically keeps track of where you are in the site hierarchy, as well as the Menu and TreeView controls, which can present a custom subset of the sitemap information.

Once you have your site hierarchy defined in a web.sitemap file, the easiest way to use it is to drag and drop a SiteMapPath control onto your web page design surface (see Figure 32-25). This control automatically binds to the default sitemap provider, as specified in the Web.config file, to generate the nodes for display.

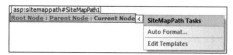

Figure 32-25

While the SiteMapPath control displays only the breadcrumb trail leading directly to the currently viewed page, at times you will want to display a list of pages in your site. The ASP.NET Menu control can be used to do this, and has modes for both horizontal and vertical viewing of the information. Likewise, the TreeView control can be bound to a sitemap and used to render a hierarchical menu of pages in a web site. Figure 32-26 shows a web page with a SiteMapPath, Menu, and TreeView that have each been formatted with one of the built-in styles.

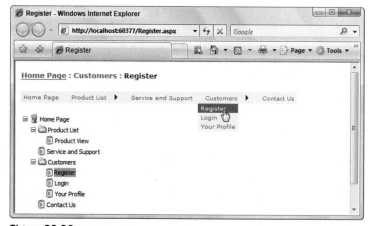

Figure 32-26

User Authentication

Perhaps the most significant additions to the web components in ASP.NET version 2.0 were the new user authentication and login components. Using these components, you can quickly and easily create the user-based parts of your web application without having to worry about how to format them or what controls are necessary.

Every web application has a default data source added to its ASP.NET configuration when it is first created. The data source is a SQL Server Express database with a default name pointing to a local file system location. This data source is used as the default location for your user authentication processing, storing information about users and their current settings.

The benefit of having this automated data store generated for each web site is that Visual Studio can have an array of user-bound web components that can automatically save user information without your needing to write any code.

Before you can sign in as a user on a particular site, you first need to create a user account. Initially, you can do that in the administration and configuration of ASP.NET, which is discussed later in this chapter, but you may also want to allow visitors to the site to create their own user accounts. The CreateUserWizard component does just that. It consists of two wizard pages with information about creating an account, and indicates when account creation is successful.

Once users have created their accounts they need to be able to log into the site, and the Login control fills this need. Adding the Login component to your page creates a small form containing User Name and Password fields, along with the option to remember the login credentials, and a "Log In" button (see Figure 32-27).

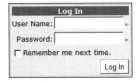

Figure 32-27

The trick to getting this to work straightaway is to edit your Web.config file and change the authentication to Forms. The default authentication type is Windows, and without the change the web site authenticates you as a Windows user because that's how you are currently logged in. Obviously, some web applications require Windows authentication, but for a simple web site that you plan to deploy on the Internet, this is the only change you need to make in order for the Login control to work properly.

You can also use several controls that will detect whether the user has logged on, and display different information to an authenticated user as opposed to an anonymous user. The LoginStatus control is a simple bi-state component that displays one set of content when the site detects that a user is currently logged in, and a different set of content when there is no logged-in user. The LoginName component is also simple, as it just returns the name of the logged-in user.

There are also controls that allow end users to manage their own passwords. The ChangePassword component works in conjunction with the other automatic user-based components to enable users to change their passwords. However, sometimes users forget their passwords, which is where the PasswordRecovery control comes into play. This component, shown in Figure 32-28, has three views: UserName, Question, and Success. The idea is that users first enter their usernames so the application can determine and display the security question, and then wait for an answer. If the answer is correct, then the component moves to the Success page and sends an e-mail to the registered e-mail address.

Figure 32-28

The last component in the Login group on the Toolbox is the LoginView object. LoginView enables you to create whole sections on your web page that are visible only under certain conditions related to who is (or isn't) logged in. By default, you have two views: the AnonymousTemplate, which is used when no user is logged in, and the LoggedInTemplate, used when any user is logged in. Both templates have an editable area that is initially completely empty.

However, because you can define specialized roles and assign users to these roles, you can also create templates for each role you have defined in your site (see Figure 32-29). The Edit RoleGroups command on the smart-tag Tasks list associated with LoginView displays the typical collection editor and enables you to build role groups that can contain one or multiple roles. When the site detects that the user logs in with a certain role, the display area of the LoginView component will be populated with that particular template's content.

Figure 32-29

See the "ASP.NET Web Site Administration" section later in this chapter for information on how to create and manage roles.

What's amazing about all of these controls is that with only a couple of manual property changes and a few extra entries in the Web.config file, you can build a complete user-authentication system into your web application. In fact, as you'll see in the "ASP.NET Web Site Administration" section later in this chapter, you can edit all these settings without needing to edit the Web.config file directly. Now that's efficient coding!

Data Components

Data controls were introduced to Microsoft web developers with the first version of Visual Studio .NET and have evolved to be even more powerful with each subsequent release of Visual Studio. Each data control has a smart-tag Tasks list associated with it that enables you to edit the individual templates for each part of the displayable area. For example, the DataList has seven templates in all, which can be individually customized (see Figure 32-30).

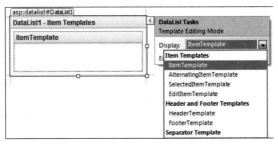

Figure 32-30

Visual Studio 2008 ships with three new data-related controls. These are LinqDataSource, ListView, and DataPager.

LinqDataSource

The data source control architecture in ASP.NET provides a really simple way for UI controls to bind to data. The data source controls that were released with ASP.NET 2.0 include SqlDataSource and AccessDataSource for binding to SQL Server or Access databases, ObjectDataSource for binding to a generic class, XmlDataSource for binding to XML files, and SiteMapDataSource for the site navigation tree for the web application.

Visual Studio 2008 ships with a new LinqDataSource control that enables you to directly bind UI controls to data sources using Language-Integrated Query (LINQ). This provides you with a designer-driven approach that automatically generates most of the code necessary for interacting with the data.

Before you can use LinqDataSource, you must already have a `DataContext` class created. The data context wraps a database connection in order to provide object lifecycle services. (Chapter 25 explains how to create a new `DataContext` class in your application.)

You can then create a LinqDataSource control instance by dragging it from the Toolbox onto the design surface. To configure the control, launch the Configure Data Source wizard under the smart tag for the control. Select the data context class, and then chose the data selection details you wish to use. Figure 32-31 shows the screen within the Configure Data Source wizard that enables you to choose the tables and columns to generate a LINQ to SQL query. It is then a simple matter to bind this data source to a UI server control, such as the ListView control, in order to provide read-only access to your data.

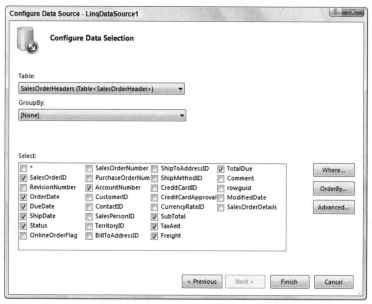

Figure 32-31

You can easily take advantage of more advanced data access functionality supported by LINQ, such as allowing inserts, updates, and deletes, by setting the `EnableInsert`, `EnableUpdate`, and `EnableDelete` properties on LinqDataSource to `true`. You can do this either programmatically in code or through the property grid.

More information on LINQ can be found in Chapters 23 through 25.

ListView and DataPager

A common complaint about the ASP.NET server controls is that developers have very little control over the HTML markups that they generate. This is especially true of the data access controls such as GridView, which always uses a HTML table to format the data it outputs, even though in some situations an ordered list would be more suitable.

The ListView control provides a good solution to the shortcomings of other data controls in this area. Instead of surrounding the rendered markup with superfluous `<table>` or `<span>` elements, it enables you to specify the exact HTML output that is rendered. The HTML markup is defined in the 11 templates that ListView supports:

❑   AlternatingItemTemplate

❑   EditItemTemplate

❑   EmptyDataTemplate

❑   EmptyItemTemplate

❑   GroupSeparatorTemplate

- ❑ GroupTemplate
- ❑ InsertItemTemplate
- ❑ ItemSeparatorTemplate
- ❑ ItemTemplate
- ❑ LayoutTemplate
- ❑ SelectedItemTemplate

The two most useful templates are LayoutTemplate and ItemTemplate. LayoutTemplate specifies the HTML markup that surrounds the output, while ItemTemplate specifies the HTML used to format each record that is bound to the ListView.

When you add a ListView control to the design surface, you can bind it to a data source and then open the Configure ListView dialog box shown in Figure 32-32, via smart-tag actions. This provides a code-generation tool that will automatically produce HTML code based on a small number of predefined layouts and styles.

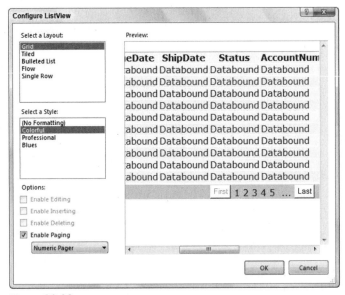

Figure 32-32

Because you have total control over the HTML markup, the Configure ListView dialog box does not even attempt to parse any existing markup. Instead, if you reopen the window it will simply show the default layout settings.

In addition to supporting edit, insert, and delete operations, the ListView control supports sorting and paging. The paging functionality in ListView is provided by the new DataPager control.

The DataPager control is used to split the data that is displayed by a UI control into multiple pages — necessary when you're working with very large data sets. It natively supports paging via either a `NumericPagerField` object, which lets users select a page number, or a `NextPreviousPagerField` object, which lets users navigate to the next or previous page. As with the ListView control, you can also write your own custom HTML markup for paging by using the `TemplatePagerField` object.

Web Parts

Another excellent feature in ASP.NET is the ability to create Web Parts controls and pages. These allow certain pages on your site to be divided into chunks that either you or your users can move around, and show and hide, to create a unique viewing experience. Web Parts for ASP.NET are loosely based on custom web controls but owe their inclusion in ASP.NET to the huge popularity of Web Parts in SharePoint Portals.

With a Web Parts page, you first create a WebPartManager component that sits on the page to look after any areas of the page design that are defined as parts. You then use WebPartZone containers to set where you want customizable content on the page, and then finally place the actual content into the WebPartZone container.

While these two components are the core of Web Parts, you need only look at the WebParts group in the Toolbox to discover a whole array of additional components (see Figure 32-33). You use these additional components to enable your users to customize their experience of your web site.

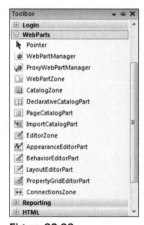

Figure 32-33

Unfortunately, there is not enough space in this book to cover the ASP.NET web controls in any further detail. If you want to learn more, we recommend you check out the massive *Professional ASP.NET 3.5: In C# and VB* by Bill Evjen, Scott Hanselman, and Devin Rader.

Master Pages

A very useful feature of web development in Visual Studio is the ability to create *master pages* that define sections that can be customized. This enables you to define a single page design that contains the common elements that should be shared across your entire site, specify areas that can house individualized content, and inherit it for each of the pages on the site.

To add a master page to your Web Application project, use the Add New Item command from the web site menu or from the context menu in the Solution Explorer. This displays the Add New Item dialog, shown in Figure 32-34, which contains a large number of item templates that can be added to a web application. You'll notice that besides Web Forms (.aspx) pages and Web User Controls, you can also add plain HTML files, style sheets, and other web-related file types. To add a master page, select the Master Page template, choose a name for the file, and click "Add."

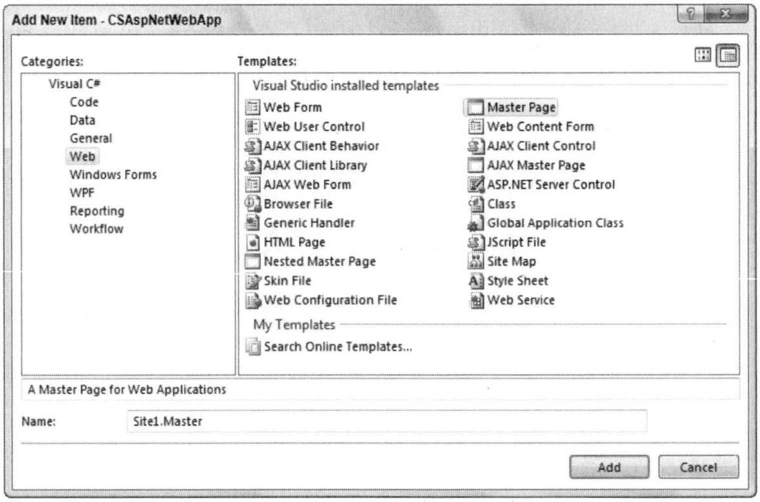

Figure 32-34

When a master page is added to your web site, it starts out as a minimal web page template with two empty ContentPlaceHolder components — one in the body of the web page and one in the head. This is where the detail information can be placed for each individual page. You can create the master page as you would any other web form page, complete with ASP.NET and HTML elements, CSS style sheets, and theming.

If your design requires additional areas for detail information, you can either drag a new ContentPlaceHolder control from the Toolbox onto the page, or switch to Source view and add the following tags where you need the additional area:

```
<asp:ContentPlaceHolder id="aUniqueId" runat="server">
</asp:ContentPlaceHolder>
```

Once the design of your master page has been finalized, you can use it for the detail pages for new web forms in your project.

Unfortunately, the process to add a form that uses a master page is slightly different depending on whether you are using a Web Application or Web Site project. For a Web Application project, rather than adding a new Web Form you should add a new Web Content Form. This will display the Select a Master Page dialog box shown in Figure 32-35. In a Web Site project, the Add New Item window contains a checkbox titled "Select master page." If you check this, the Select a Master Page dialog will be displayed.

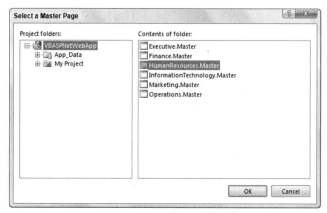

Figure 32-35

Select the master page to be applied to the detail page and click "OK." The new web form page that is added to the project will include one or more Content controls, which map to the ContentPlaceHolder controls on the master page.

It doesn't take long to see the benefits of master pages and understand why they have become a very popular feature. However, the one thing that has limited their usefulness has been the lack of support for nested master pages. While it has always been possible to nest master pages in ASP.NET, Visual Studio 2005 did not provide any support for it. Fortunately, this has been fixed in Visual Studio 2008.

Working with nested master pages is not much different from working with normal master pages. To add one, select Nested Master Page from the Add New Item window. You will be prompted to select the parent master page via the Select a Master Page window that was shown in Figure 32-35. When you subsequently add a new content web page, any nested master pages are also shown in the Select a Master Page window.

Rich Client-Side Development

In the last couple of years the software industry has seen a fundamental shift toward emphasizing the importance of the end-user experience in application development. Nowhere has that been more apparent than in the development of web applications. Fueled by technologies such as AJAX and an increased appreciation of JavaScript, we are now expected to provide web applications that approach the richness of their desktop equivalents.

Microsoft has certainly recognized this and has released a range of tools and enhancements in Visual Studio 2008 that support the creation of rich client-side interactions. There is now integrated debugging and IntelliSense support for JavaScript. ASP.NET AJAX, previously available only as a separate download, is shipped with Visual Studio 2008, and there is support in the IDE for AJAX Control Extenders. These tools make it much easier for you to design, build, and debug client-side code that provides a much richer user experience.

Developing with JavaScript

Writing JavaScript client code has long had a reputation for being difficult, even though the language itself is quite simple. Because JavaScript is a dynamic, loosely-typed programming language — very different from the strong typing enforced by Visual Basic and C# — JavaScript's reputation is even worse in some .NET developer circles.

Thus, one of the most anticipated new features of Visual Studio 2008 is IntelliSense support for JavaScript. You will notice the IntelliSense beginning immediately as you start typing, with prompts for native JavaScript functions and keywords such as `var`, `alert`, and `eval`.

Furthermore, the JavaScript IntelliSense in Visual Studio 2008 automatically evaluates and infers variable types to provide more accurate IntelliSense prompts. For example, in Figure 32-36 you can see that IntelliSense has determined that `optSelected` is an HTML object, as a call to the `document.getElementByID` function will return that type.

Figure 32-36

In addition to displaying IntelliSense within web forms, Visual Studio also supports IntelliSense in external JavaScript files. It will also provide IntelliSense help for referenced script files and libraries, such as the Microsoft AJAX library.

Microsoft has extended the XML commenting system in Visual Studio to recognize comments on JavaScript functions. IntelliSense will detect these XML code comments and display the summary, parameters, and return type information for the function.

A couple of limitations could prevent the JavaScript IntelliSense from displaying information in certain circumstances, including:

❑ A syntax or other error in an external referenced script file

❑ Invoking a browser-specific function or object. Most web browsers provide a set of objects that is proprietary to that browser. You can still use these objects, and in fact many popular JavaScript frameworks do; however, you won't get IntelliSense support for them.

❑ Referencing files that are outside the current project

❑ XML comments in the current document. Only XML comment data from external referenced script files will be displayed.

Visual Studio will constantly monitor changes to files in the project and update the IntelliSense as they happen. If for some reason you find that Visual Studio isn't displaying the latest information, you can force it to update the IntelliSense by selecting Edit ➪ IntelliSense ➪ Update JScript IntelliSense.

The new JavaScript IntelliSense, combined with the improved client-side debugging support, will significantly reduce the difficulty of developing JavaScript code with Visual Studio 2008.

Working with ASP.NET AJAX

Microsoft ASP.NET AJAX, which was previously available only as a separate download, now ships with Visual Studio 2008. The ASP.NET AJAX framework provides web developers with a familiar server-control programming approach for building rich client-side AJAX interactions.

ASP.NET AJAX includes both server-side and client-side components. A set of server controls, including the popular UpdatePanel and UpdateProgess controls, can be added to web forms to enable asynchronous partial-page updates without your needing to make changes to any existing code on the page. The client-side Microsoft AJAX Library is a JavaScript framework that can be used in any web application, such as PHP on Apache, and not just ASP.NET or IIS.

The following walkthrough will demonstrate how to enhance an existing web page by adding the ASP.NET AJAX UpdatePanel control to perform a partial-page update. In this scenario we have a very simple web form with a DropDownList server control, which has an AutoPostBack to the server enabled. The web form handles the `DropDownList.SelectedIndexChanged` event and saves the value that was selected in the DropDownList to a TextBox server control on the page. The code listing for this page is as follows:

AjaxSampleForm.aspx

```
<%@ Page Language="vb" AutoEventWireup="false"
    CodeBehind="AjaxSampleForm.aspx.vb"
    Inherits="ASPNetWebApp.AjaxSampleForm" %>
<!DOCTYPE html PUBLIC "-//W3C//DTD XHTML 1.0
    Transitional//EN"
    "http://www.w3.org/TR/xhtml1/DTD/xhtml1-transitional.dtd">
<html xmlns="http://www.w3.org/1999/xhtml" >
```

(continued)

(continued)

```
<head runat="server">
    <title>ASP.NET AJAX Sample</title>
</head>
<body>
    <form id="form1" runat="server">
        <div>
        Select an option:
        <asp:DropDownList ID="DropDownList1" runat="server" AutoPostBack="True">
            <asp:ListItem Text="Option 1" Value="Option 1" />
            <asp:ListItem Text="Option 2" Value="Option 2" />
            <asp:ListItem Text="Option 3" Value="Option 3" />
        </asp:DropDownList>
        <br />
        Option selected:
        <asp:TextBox ID="TextBox1" runat="server"></asp:TextBox>
        </div>
    </form>
</body>
</html>


AjaxSampleForm.aspx.vb

Public Partial Class AjaxSampleForm
    Inherits System.Web.UI.Page
    Protected Sub DropDownList1_SelectedIndexChanged(ByVal sender As Object, _
                                        ByVal e As EventArgs) _
                            Handles DropDownList1.SelectedIndexChanged
        System.Threading.Thread.Sleep(2000);
        Me.TextBox1.Text = Me.DropDownList1.SelectedValue
    End Sub
End Class
```

Notice that in the `DropDownList1_SelectedIndexChanged` method we have added a statement to sleep for two seconds. This will exaggerate the server processing time, thereby making it easier to see the effect of the changes we will make. When you run this page and change an option in the drop-down list, the whole page will be refreshed in the browser.

The first AJAX control that you need to add to your web page is a ScriptManager. This is a nonvisual control that's central to ASP.NET AJAX and is responsible for tasks such as sending script libraries and files to the client and generating any required client proxy classes. You can have only one ScriptManager control per ASP.NET web page, which can pose a problem when you're using master pages and user controls. In that case, you should add the ScriptManager to the topmost parent page, and a ScriptManagerProxy control to all child pages.

After you add the ScriptManager control, you can add any other ASP.NET AJAX controls. In this case add an UpdatePanel control to the web page, as shown in the following listing. Notice that `TextBox1` is now contained within the new UpdatePanel control.

```
<%@ Page Language="vb" AutoEventWireup="false"
    CodeBehind="AjaxSampleForm.aspx.vb"
    Inherits="ASPNetWebApp.AjaxSampleForm" %>
<!DOCTYPE html PUBLIC "-//W3C//DTD XHTML 1.0
    Transitional//EN"
    "http://www.w3.org/TR/xhtml1/DTD/xhtml1-transitional.dtd">
<html xmlns="http://www.w3.org/1999/xhtml" >
<head runat="server">
    <title>ASP.NET AJAX Sample</title>
</head>
<body>
    <form id="form1" runat="server">
    <asp:ScriptManager ID="ScriptManager1"
    runat="server"></asp:ScriptManager>
    <div>
        Select an option:
        <asp:DropDownList ID="DropDownList1" runat="server" AutoPostBack="True">
            <asp:ListItem Text="Option 1" Value="Option 1" />
            <asp:ListItem Text="Option 2" Value="Option 2" />
            <asp:ListItem Text="Option 3" Value="Option 3" />
        </asp:DropDownList>
        <br />
        Option selected:
        <asp:UpdatePanel ID="UpdatePanel1" runat="server">
            <ContentTemplate>
                <asp:TextBox ID="TextBox1" runat="server"></asp:TextBox>
            </ContentTemplate>
            <Triggers>
                <asp:AsyncPostBackTrigger ControlID="DropDownList1"
                                          EventName="SelectedIndexChanged" />
            </Triggers>
        </asp:UpdatePanel>
    </div>
    </form>
</body>
</html>
```

The web page now uses AJAX to provide a partial-page update. When you now run this page and change an option in the drop-down list, the whole page is no longer refreshed. Instead just the text within the textbox is updated. In fact, if you run this page you will notice that AJAX is *too* good at just updating part of the page. There is no feedback and if you didn't know any better you would think that nothing is happening. This is where the UpdateProgress control becomes useful. You can place an UpdateProgress control on the page, and when an AJAX request is invoked the HTML within the ProgressTemplate section of the control is rendered. The following listing shows an example of an UpdateProgress control for our web form.

```
<asp:UpdateProgress ID="UpdateProgress1" runat="server">
    <ProgressTemplate>
        Loading...
    </ProgressTemplate>
</asp:UpdateProgress>
```

The final server control in ASP.NET AJAX that hasn't been mentioned is the Timer control, which enables you to perform asynchronous or synchronous client-side postbacks at a defined interval. This can be useful for scenarios such as checking with the server to see if a value has changed.

Once you have added some basic AJAX functionality to your web application, you can further improve the client user experience by adding one or more elements from the AJAX Control Toolkit, which is discussed in the following section.

Using AJAX Control Extenders

AJAX Control Extenders provide a way to add AJAX functionality to a standard ASP.NET server control. The best-known set of control extenders is the AJAX Control Toolkit, a free open-source library of client behaviors that includes almost 40 control extenders. These either provide enhancements to existing ASP.NET web controls or provide completely new rich client UI elements. Figure 32-37 shows a Calendar Extender that has been attached to a TextBox control.

Figure 32-37

The ASP.NET AJAX Control Toolkit is available for download via a link from `http://www.asp.net/ajax/ajaxcontroltoolkit`. The download includes a sample web site that demonstrates the controls. Within the /bin directory of the sample web site is an assembly called `AjaxControlToolkit.dll`. Copy this to a directory where you won't accidentally delete it.

> *The download includes a Visual Studio Installer (VSI) file that contains templates for creating new AJAX Server Controls and AJAX Server Control Extenders. These templates are included by default in Visual Studio 2008 Professional Edition.*

To add the controls to the Visual Studio Control Toolbox, you should first create a new tab to house them. Right-click anywhere in the Toolbox window, choose Add Tab, and then rename the new tab something meaningful, such as AJAX Control Toolkit. Next, drag and drop `AjaxControlToolkit.dll` onto the new Control Toolbox tab. After a few moments the tab will be populated with all the controls in the AJAX Control Toolkit.

Visual Studio 2008 provides designer support for any AJAX Control Extenders, including the AJAX Control Toolkit. Once you have added the controls to the Toolbox, Visual Studio will add an entry to the smart-tag Tasks list of any web controls with extenders, as shown in Figure 32-38.

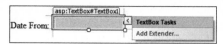

Figure 32-38

When you select the Add Extender task it will launch the Extender Wizard, shown in Figure 32-39. Choose an extender from the list and click "OK" to add it to your web form. In most cases the Extender Wizard will also automatically add a reference to the AJAX Control Toolkit library. However, if it does not you can manually add a binary reference to the `AjaxControlToolkit.dll` assembly.

> *As the Extender Controls are built on top of ASP.NET AJAX, you will need to ensure that a ScriptManager control is on your web form.*

Figure 32-39

As shown in Figure 32-40, Visual Studio 2008 includes all the properties for the control extender in the property grid, under the control to which the extender is attached.

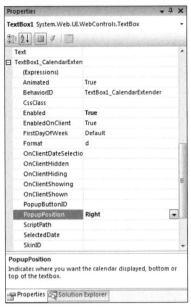

Figure 32-40

Since the AJAX Control Toolkit is open-source, you can customize or further enhance any of the control extenders it includes. Visual Studio 2008 also ships with Visual Basic and C# project templates to create your own AJAX Control Extenders and ASP.NET AJAX Controls. This makes it easy to build rich web applications with UI functionality that can be easily reused across your web pages and projects.

ASP.NET Web Site Administration

Although running your web application with default behavior will work in most situations, sometimes you'll need to manage the application settings beyond simply setting the properties of components and page items. The Web Site Administration Tool provides you with a web-based configuration application that enables you to define various security-related settings, such as users and roles, as well as application-wide settings that can come in handy, such as a default error page, and global SMTP mail settings that are used by various components, such as the PasswordRecovery control.

To start the Administration Tool, use the Project ➪ ASP.NET Configuration menu command for Web Application projects, or Website ➪ ASP.NET Configuration for Web Site projects. When the tool is launched, Visual Studio 2008 will instantiate a temporary web server on a unique port and open a web browser to the Administration Tool home page for the application you're currently administering.

You can determine whether the web server is active by looking in the notification area of your taskbar and finding the development server icon connected to the port that Visual Studio 2008 allocated when it was started up. You can stop an active web server by right-clicking its icon in the notification area and selecting Show Details. When the server information is displayed (see Figure 32-41), click the "Stop" button to stop the specific instance of the development web server.

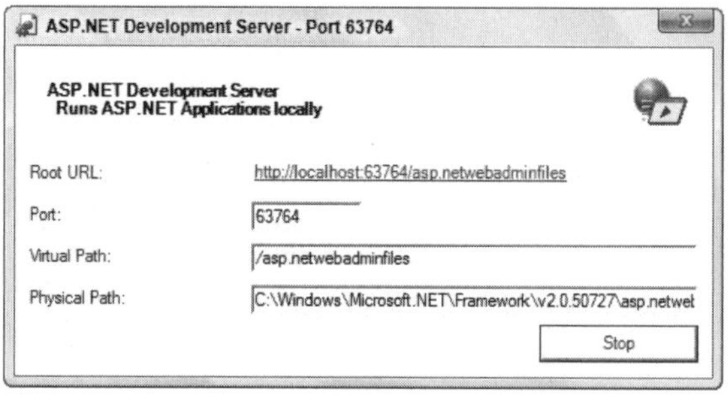

Figure 32-41

Note that stopping an active web server won't affect any other development servers that are currently running.

When the Administration Tool is displayed in your web browser, it will show the application name, accompanied by the name of the current Windows-based authenticated user. There are three main sections to the tool: security for the creation and maintenance of users, roles, and authentication; application configuration to control application-specific key-value pairs, SMTP settings, and debug configurations; and provider configuration to control the way the user administration data is stored for the site.

Security

The security section of the tool provides you with a summary of the users and roles defined in the site, and the authentication mode. You can change individual settings from this summary page by clicking their associated links, or use the Security Setup Wizard to step through each section of the security settings in turn.

The authentication mode is controlled by the access method page (shown in the wizard in Figure 32-42). If you choose "From the internet," the tool sets the authentication mode to Forms, while the "From a local area network" option results in an authentication mode of Windows.

The most useful part of this tool is the ability it gives you to add and edit roles. In the wizard you'll first need to enable role management by checking the Enable Roles for this Web Site option. Once roles are active you can define them either through the wizard or from the summary page. Each role is defined by a single string value, and it's up to you to control how that role will be used in your web application (with the exception of access rules, which we'll discuss in a moment).

The next step in the wizard is to create user accounts. The information on this page is a replication of the CreateUserAccount component, and enables you to create an initial user who can serve as administrator for your web site.

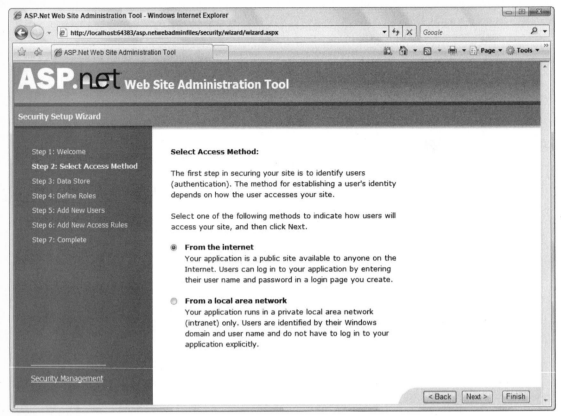

Figure 32-42

The access rules page (shown in Figure 32-43) enables you to restrict access to certain parts of your site to a specific role or user, or to grant access only when any user is logged in. As Figure 32-43 shows, by default there is a single rule (which is actually implicitly defined and inherited from the server) that defines full access to the entire site for all users.

Web site processing will look at the rules in the order in which they are defined, stopping at the first rule that applies to the particular context. For example, if you define first a rule that allows access to the Admin folder for anyone belonging to the Administrator's role, and then define a subsequent rule that denies access to the same folder for all users, it will effectively block access to the Admin folder for all users who do not belong to the Administrator's role.

Once you've got users, roles, and rules defined in your site, you can then start applying the access by clicking the Manage Users link from the summary security page. This will present you with a list of all users defined in the system. Click the Edit User or Edit Roles link to specify the roles to which each user belongs.

This information can be used to customize the content in your web pages with the LoginView component discussed earlier in this chapter.

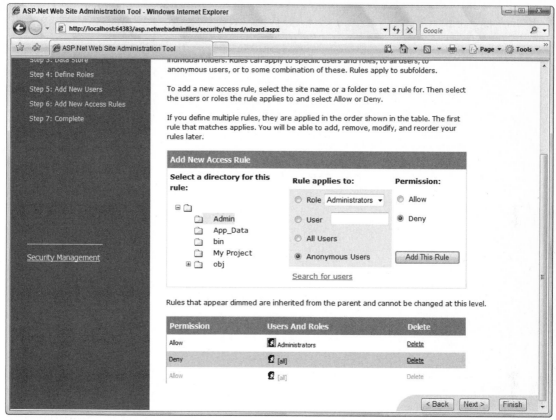

Figure 32-43

Application Settings

The application section of the Web Site Administration Tool enables you to define and edit application-specific settings in the form of key-value pairs, as well as to configure SMTP e-mail settings, including the default SMTP mail server and senders e-mail address.

You can also specify what level of debugging you want to perform on the application, and customize the tracing information being kept as you run the application.

ASP.NET Configuration in IIS

If you have already deployed an ASP.NET application to a production server, you can edit the configuration settings directly within Internet Information Services (IIS), located in the Administrative Tools section of the Control Panel. When ASP.NET is installed on a machine, you'll find that each web site (including virtual directories) will have a set of configuration tools in IIS under the property pages, as shown in Figure 32-44.

Figure 32-44

The tools included in IIS enable you to manage all the settings you saw earlier, including the creation and management of users, roles, application settings, and SMTP settings. You are also given access to more powerful administration tools that enable you to configure advanced settings such as the .NET compilation behavior, .NET trust level, and session state configuration. These tools enable you to maintain a web application running on any IIS server without needing to resort to editing the Web.config configuration file.

Summary

In this chapter you learned how to create ASP.NET applications using the Web Site and Web Application projects. The improvements to the HTML designer and the new CSS tools in Visual Studio 2008 provide you with great power over the layout and visual design of web pages. The vast number of web controls included in ASP.NET enables you to quickly put together highly functional web pages. Through the judicious use of JavaScript, ASP.NET AJAX, and control extenders in the AJAX Control Toolkit, you can provide a very rich user experience in your web applications.

Of course, there's much more to web development than we covered here. Chapter 37 continues the discussion on building rich web applications by exploring the latest web technologies from Microsoft: ASP.NET MVC and Silverlight 2.0. Chapter 44 provides detailed information about the tools and techniques available for effective debugging of web applications. Finally, Chapter 50 will walk you through the deployment options for web applications. If you are looking for more information after this then you should check out *Professional ASP.NET 3.5: In C# and VB* by Bill Evjen, Scott Hanselman, and Devin Rader. Weighing in at over 1,600 pages, this is the best and most comprehensive resource available to web developers who are building applications on the latest version of ASP.NET.

33

Office Applications

Microsoft Office applications have always been extensible via add-ins and various automation techniques. Even Visual Basic for Applications (VBA), which was widely known for various limitations in accessing system files, had the capability to write applications that used an instance of an Office application to achieve certain tasks, such as Word's spell-checking feature.

When Visual Studio .NET was released in 2002, Microsoft soon followed with the first release of Visual Studio Tools for Office (known by the abbreviation VSTO, pronounced *visto*). This initial version of VSTO didn't really produce anything new except for an easier way of creating application projects that would use Microsoft Word or Microsoft Excel. However, subsequent versions of VSTO quickly evolved and became more powerful, allowing you to build more functional applications that ran on the Office platform.

The latest version of VSTO was shipped as part of Visual Studio 2008. It provides significant enhancements over the previous version, including support for Office 2007 and the new Ribbon user interface, the ability to create application-level add-ins for Word, Excel, PowerPoint, Project, and Visio, and tools for building SharePoint workflows.

This chapter begins with a look at the types of applications you can build with VSTO. It then guides you through the process of creating a document-level customization to a Word document, including a custom Actions Pane. Following this, the chapter provides a walkthrough, showing how to create an Outlook add-in complete with an Outlook Form region. Finally, the chapter provides some important information regarding the debugging and deployment of Office applications.

Choosing an Office Project Type

The types of applications you can create using VSTO under Visual Studio have come a long way with the latest version. You now have the ability to create add-in applications for almost every product in the Office suite. Furthermore, these solutions can either be attached to a single document, or be loaded every time that application is launched.

You can create a new Office application by selecting File ⇨ New ⇨ Project. Select your preferred language (Visual Basic or Visual C#), and then select the Office project category, as shown in Figure 33-1.

> *It is technically possible to create Office applications using .NET languages besides Visual Basic or Visual C#. However, you will lose the benefits of the project and item templates and designer support provided by Visual Studio. Though it might be a good academic exercise to try creating an Outlook add-in using IronRuby, it will also be a lot more work.*

Visual Studio 2008 provides templates for both Office 2003 and Office 2007. The same projects can be created under both versions of Office, with the addition of SharePoint and InfoPath under Office 2007.

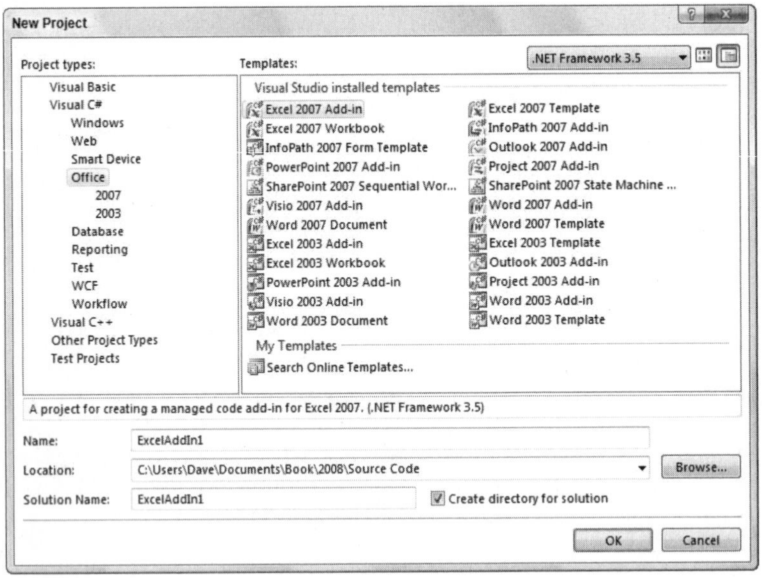

Figure 33-1

The project templates can be broadly categorized into four types of Office applications: document-level customizations, application-level add-ins, SharePoint workflows, and InfoPath forms.

Document-Level Customizations

A document-level customization is a solution that is based on a single document. To load the customization, an end user must open a specific document. Events in the document, such as loading the document or clicking buttons and menu items, can invoke event handler methods in the attached assembly. Document-level customizations can also be included with an Office template, which ensures that the customization is included when you create a new document from that template.

Visual Studio 2008 allows you to create document-level customizations for the following types of documents:

❑ Microsoft Excel Workbook

❑ Microsoft Excel Template

❑ Microsoft Word Document

❑ Microsoft Word Template

Using a document-level customization, you can modify the user interface of Word or Excel to provide a unique solution for your end users. For example, you can add new controls to the Office 2007 Ribbon or display a customized *Actions Pane* window.

Microsoft Word and Microsoft Excel also include a technology called *smart tags*, which enable developers to track the user's input and recognize when text in a specific format has been entered. Your solution can use this technology by providing feedback or even actions that the user could take in response to certain recognized terms, such as a phone number or address.

Visual Studio also provides a set of custom controls that are specific to Microsoft Word 2007. Called *content controls*, they allow you to do a number of useful things such as providing a rich user interface for entering data in the document or displaying data that is bound to those controls. You will see content controls in action later in this chapter.

Application-Level Add-In

Unlike a document-level customization, an application-level add-in is always loaded regardless of the document that is currently open. In fact, application-level add-ins will run even if the application is running with no documents open.

Previous versions of VSTO had significant limitations when it came to application-level add-ins. First, you could create add-ins only for Microsoft Outlook, and even then you could not customize much of the user interface.

Fortunately in Visual Studio 2008 such restrictions no longer exist, and you can create application-level add-ins for almost every product in the Microsoft Office suite, including Excel, InfoPath, Outlook, PowerPoint, Project, Visio, and Word. This applies equally to version 2003 and version 2007 of Office. You can create the same UI enhancements as you can with a document-level customization, such as adding new controls to the Office Ribbon.

You can also create a custom *Task Pane* as part of your add-in. Task Panes are very similar to the Action Panes that are available in document-level customization projects. However, custom Task Panes are associated with the application, not a specific document, and as such can be created only within an application-level add-in.

An Actions Pane, on the other hand, is a specific type of Task Pane that is customizable and is attached to a specific Word document or Excel workbook. You cannot create an Actions Pane in an application-level add-in.

Also new to Visual Studio 2008 is the ability to create custom Outlook form regions in Outlook add-in projects. Form regions are the screens that are displayed when an Outlook item is opened, such as a Contact or Appointment. You can either extend the existing form regions or create a completely custom Outlook form. Later in this chapter you walk through the creation of an Outlook 2007 add-in that includes a custom Outlook form region.

SharePoint Workflow

SharePoint workflows are used to define and control a process lifecycle for documents stored in a Microsoft SharePoint Server 2007 repository. Visual Studio 2008 provides support for two types of workflows: a *sequential* workflow and a *state machine* workflow.

A sequential workflow represents the workflow as a set of steps that are executed in order. For example, a document is submitted that generates an e-mail to an approver. The approver opens the document in SharePoint and either approves or rejects it. If approved, the document is published. If rejected, an e-mail is sent back to the submitter with the details of why it was rejected.

A state machine workflow represents the workflow as a set of states, transitions, and events. You define the start state for the workflow and it will transit to a new state when an event occurs. For example, you may have states such as Document Created and Document Published, and events that control the transition to these states such as Document Submitted and Document Approved.

When you first create a SharePoint workflow in Visual Studio 2008, it will launch the New Office SharePoint Workflow Wizard, which is used to select a SharePoint server and site for debugging and to define the debug configuration settings. Once the wizard is completed, you can use the Workflow Designer to design the SharePoint workflow schedule.

You can also use Visual Studio to design a form that gathers information from users at specific points in a workflow. These forms can be created as either ASP.NET web pages or InfoPath forms.

> *You cannot use the SharePoint workflow project templates in Visual Studio unless you are running an operating system that supports SharePoint Server, such as Windows Server 2003 or 2008. You cannot use a client operating system such as Windows Vista. You will also need to install SharePoint Server 2007 on that machine.*

InfoPath Form Template

When Microsoft first released InfoPath, it was seen as an excellent option for enabling organizations to build forms easily without having to resort to writing code. Though it was indeed the answer for many (providing the capability to create complex form designs with a robust graphical user interface and easy connection to data sources, all bound up in XML), it was difficult to create a form that was backed by code.

With the release of Visual Studio 2005, Microsoft also released the *InfoPath 2003 Toolkit for Visual Studio 2005* as an additional download. The Toolkit integrated with InfoPath 2003 SP1 to provide a managed code solution for creating and managing InfoPath forms that rely on program code to perform part of their functionality.

InfoPath 2007 has made it even easier to develop rich forms with the inclusion of a much cleaner managed-code object model. Forms with code written using this new object model work the same way regardless of whether you open them using the InfoPath–rich client or a web browser via Microsoft Office Forms Server 2007.

> *You must have InfoPath 2007 installed on your local computer in order to create InfoPath form templates using Visual Studio.*

Visual Studio 2008 includes native support for InfoPath form templates, including a project template and designer support for customizing the layout and design of your InfoPath forms. You can either design a new template from scratch, or based on a set of predefined templates that use external resources, such as a SQL database or web service. Additionally, you can create a template part that can be inserted in multiple form templates.

> *Though it's not obvious from the available project templates, you can use Visual Studio 2008 to create new form templates that work with InfoPath 2003. To maintain backward compatibility, create a new form template, click Tools ⇨ Form Options, and then in the Programming category click the Remove Code button. You will then be able to choose either C# (InfoPath 2003 Compatible) or Visual Basic (InfoPath 2003 Compatible) as the form template code language.*

Creating a Document-Level Customization

This section walks through the creation of a Word document customization. This demonstrates how to create a document-level customization complete with Word 2007 Content Controls and a custom Actions Pane.

> *Although this example uses Word 2007, if you do not have that version installed, you can still follow most of the instructions and create a document-level customization for Word 2003. Some features are not available in Word 2003, such as the Content Controls and the Ribbon.*

Your First VSTO Project

When you create a document-level customization with Visual Studio 2008, you can either create the document from scratch, or jump-start the design by using an existing document or template. A great source of templates, particularly for business-related forms, is the free templates available from Microsoft Office Online at `http://office.microsoft.com/templates/`.

This example uses the Absence request form that is available under the Forms, Employment category. When you download a template from the Office Online web site using Internet Explorer, it will open a new document based on the template in Word. Save this document as a Word Template to a convenient location on your computer, as shown in Figure 33-2.

Next launch Visual Studio 2008 and select File ➪ New ➪ Project. Filter the project types by selecting Visual C# followed by Office, and then choose a new Word 2007 Template. You will be presented with a screen that prompts you to create a new document or copy an existing one. Select the option to copy an existing document and then navigate to and select the document template you saved earlier. When you click OK, the project will be created and the document will open in the Designer as shown in Figure 33-3.

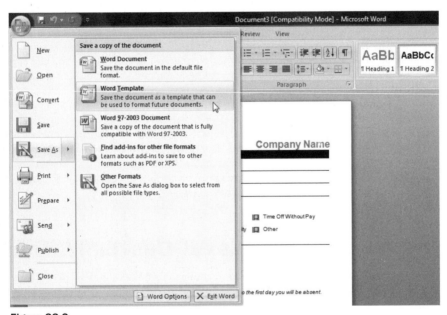

Figure 33-2

There are a few things worth pointing out in Figure 33-3. First, you'll notice that along the top of the Designer is the Office Ribbon. This is the very same Ribbon that is displayed in Word, and you can use it to modify the layout and design of the Word document. Second, in the Solution Explorer to the right, the file that is currently open is called ThisDocument.cs. You can right-click this file and select either View Designer to display the design surface for the document, currently shown in Figure 33-3, or View Code to open the source code behind this document in the Code Editor. Finally, in the Toolbox to the left, there is a tab group called Word Controls, which contains a set of controls that allow you to build rich user interfaces for data input and display.

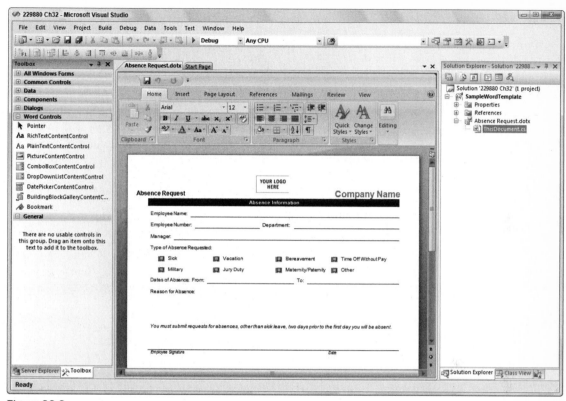

Figure 33-3

To customize this form, first drag three PlainTextContentControl controls onto the design surface for the *Employee Name, Employee Number,* and *Manager.* Rename these controls to txtEmpName, txtEmpNumber, and txtManager, respectively.

Next drag a DropDownListContentControl next to the Department field, and rename it ddDept.

Rather than use a set of checkboxes for the Type of Absence Requested, we will use a ComboBoxContentControl. Delete all the checkboxes from the document and in their place drag this ComboBoxContentControl and rename it cboType.

Following this, drag two DatePickerContentControls for the *From* and *To* dates, and rename these to be dtDateFrom and dtDateTo. Then drag a RichTextContentControl under the Reason for Absence label and rename it to txtReason.

Finally, to clean up the document a little, remove all the text that is below the RichTextContentControl. Once you have done this, your form should look similar to what is shown in Figure 33-4.

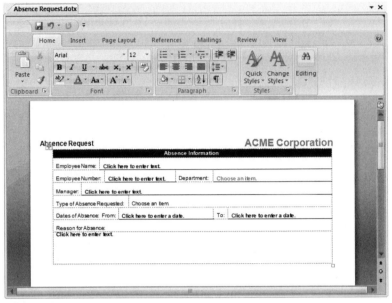

Figure 33-4

Before you run this project you will need to populate the Department and Type of Absence Requested drop-down lists. Although this can be done declaratively via the Properties field, we will perform it programmatically. Right-click the ThisDocument.cs file in the Solution Explorer and select View Code to display the managed code that is behind this document. Two methods will be predefined: a function that is run during startup when the document is opened, and a function that is run during shutdown when the document is closed.

Add the following code for the `ThisDocument_Startup` method to populate the Department and Type of Absence Requested drop-down lists:

```
private void ThisDocument_Startup(object sender, System.EventArgs e)
{
    ddDept.PlaceholderText = "Select your department";
    ddDept.DropDownListEntries.Add("Finance", "Finance", 0);
    ddDept.DropDownListEntries.Add("HR", "HR", 1);
    ddDept.DropDownListEntries.Add("IT", "IT", 2);
    ddDept.DropDownListEntries.Add("Marketing", "Marketing", 3);
    ddDept.DropDownListEntries.Add("Operations", "Operations", 4);

    cboType.PlaceholderText = "Select a reason, or enter your own";
    cboType.DropDownListEntries.Add("Sick", "Sick", 0);
    cboType.DropDownListEntries.Add("Vacation", "Vacation", 1);
    cboType.DropDownListEntries.Add("Bereavement", "Bereavement", 2);
    cboType.DropDownListEntries.Add("Leave Without Pay", "Leave Without Pay", 3);
    cboType.DropDownListEntries.Add("Military", "Military", 4);
    cboType.DropDownListEntries.Add("Jury Duty", "Jury Duty", 5);
    cboType.DropDownListEntries.Add("Maternity ", "Maternity ", 6);
}
```

You can now run the project in debug mode by pressing F5. This will compile the project and open the document in Microsoft Word. You can test out entering data in the various fields to obtain a feel for how they behave.

Protecting the Document Design

While you have the document open you may notice that in addition to entering text in the control fields that you added, you can also edit the surrounding text and even delete some of the controls. This is obviously not ideal in this scenario. Fortunately, Office 2007 and VSTO provide a way to prevent the document from undesirable editing.

Within Word 2007, click the Office button and click the Word Options button on the bottom of the screen. In the Word Options dialog window, check the box next to the "Show Developer tab in the Ribbon" option.

When you stop debugging and return to Visual Studio, you will see a new tab on the Toolbar above the Ribbon, as shown in Figure 33-5. This provides some useful functions for Office development-related tasks.

Figure 33-5

To prevent the document from being edited, you must perform a couple of steps. First, ensure that the Designer is open and then press Ctrl+A to select everything in the document (text and controls). On the Developer tab click Group ⇨ Group. This will allow you to treat everything on the document as a single entity, and easily apply properties to all elements in one step.

With this new group selected, open the Properties window and set the `Lock Content Control` property to `True`. Now when you run the project you will find that the standard text on the document cannot be edited or deleted, and you can only input data into the content controls that you have added.

Adding an Actions Pane

The final customization we will add to this document is an Actions Pane window. An Actions Pane is typically docked to one side of a window in Word, and can be used to display related information or provide access to additional information. For example, you could add an Actions Pane that retrieved and displayed the current employees' available leave balance.

An Actions Pane, and custom Task Pane in the case of application-level add-ins, is nothing more than a standard user control. In the case of an Actions Pane, Visual Studio has included an item template; however, this does little more than add a standard user control to the project with the Office namespace imported. For application-level add-ins there is no custom Task Panes item template, so you can simply add a standard user control to the project.

To add an Actions Pane to this document customization, right-click the project in the Solution Explorer, then select Add ⇨ New Item. Select Actions Pane Control, provide it with a meaningful name, and click Add. The Actions Pane will open in a new designer window. You are simply going to add a button that retrieves the user name of the current user and adds it to the document. Drag a button control onto the form and rename it btnGetName. Then double-click the control to register an event handler and add the following code for the button click event:

```
private void btnGetName_Click(object sender, EventArgs e)
{
    System.Security.Principal.WindowsIdentity myIdent =
        System.Security.Principal.WindowsIdentity.GetCurrent();
    Globals.ThisDocument.txtEmpName.Text = myIdent.Name;
}
```

The Actions Pane components are not added automatically to the document because you may want to show different Actions Panes, depending on the context users find themselves in when editing the document. However, if you have a single Actions Pane component and simply want to add it immediately when the document is opened, add the component to the `ActionsPane.Controls` collection of the document at startup, as demonstrated in the following code:

```
private void ThisDocument_Startup(object sender, System.EventArgs e)
{
    this.ActionsPane.Controls.Add(new NameOfActionsPaneControl)
}
```

For application-level add-ins, add the user control to the `CustomTaskPanes` *collection.*

When you next run the project it will display the document in Word with the Actions Pane window shown during startup, as shown in Figure 33-6.

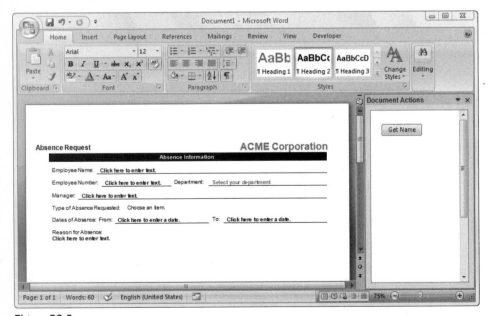

Figure 33-6

Creating an Application Add-In

This section walks through the creation of an add-in to Microsoft Outlook 2007. This will demonstrate how to create an application-level add-in that includes a custom Outlook form region for a Contact item.

> Never *develop Outlook add-ins using your production e-mail account! There's too much risk that you will accidently do something that you will regret later, such as accidentally deleting all of the e-mail in your Inbox. With Outlook you can create a separate* mail profile; *one for your normal mailbox, and one for your test mailbox.*

Some Outlook Concepts

Before creating an Outlook add-in, it is worth understanding some basic concepts that are specific to Outlook development. Though there is a reasonable degree of overlap, Outlook has always had a slightly different programming model from the rest of the products in the Office suite.

The Outlook object model is a heavily collection-based API. The `Application` class is the highest-level class and represents the Outlook application. This can be directly accessed from code as a property of the add-in; `this.Application` in C# or `Me.Application` in Visual Basic. With the `Application` class you can access classes that represent the *Explorer* and *Inspector* windows.

An Explorer window in Outlook is the main window that is displayed when Outlook is first opened and displays the contents of a folder, such as the Inbox or Calendar. Figure 33-7 (left) shows the Calendar in the Explorer window. The `Explorer` class represents this window, and includes properties, methods, and events that can be used to access the window and respond to actions.

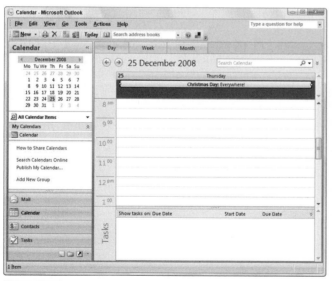

Figure 33-7

An Inspector window displays an individual item such as an e-mail message, contact, or appointment. Figure 33-7 right shows an Inspector window displaying an appointment item. The `Inspector` class includes properties and methods to access the window, and events that can be handled when certain actions occur within the window. Outlook form regions are hosted within Inspector windows.

The `Application` class also contains a `Session` object, which represents everything to do with the current Outlook session. This object provides you with access to the available address lists, mail stores, folders, items, and other Outlook objects. A mail folder, such as the Inbox or Calendar, is represented by a `MAPIFolder` class and contains a collection of items. Within Outlook every item has a `message class` property that determines how it is presented within the application. For example, an e-mail message has a message class of `IPM.Note` and an appointment has a message class of `IPM.Appointment`.

Creating an Outlook Form Region

Now that you understand the basics of the Outlook object model, you can create your first Outlook add-in. In Visual Studio 2008 select File ⇨ New ⇨ Project. Filter the project types by selecting Visual C# followed by Office, and then choose a new Outlook 2007 add-in project.

Unlike a document-level customization, an application-level add-in is inherently code-based. In the case of a Word or Excel add-in, there may not even be a document open when the application is first launched. An Outlook add-in follows a similar philosophy; when you first create an Outlook add-in project, it will consist of a single nonvisual class called `ThisAddIn.cs` (or `ThisAddIn.vb`). You can add code here that performs some actions during startup or shutdown.

To customize the actual user interface of Outlook you can add an Outlook form region. This is a user control that is hosted in an Outlook Inspector window when an item of a certain message class is displayed.

To add a new Outlook form region, right-click the project in the Solution Explorer, then select Add ⇨ New Item. From the list of available items select Outlook Form Region, provide it with a meaningful name, and click Add. Visual Studio will then open the New Outlook Form Region Wizard that will obtain some basic properties needed to create the new item.

The first step of the wizard asks you to either design a new form, or import an Outlook Form Storage (`.ofs`) file, which is a form designed in Outlook. Select "Design a new form region" and click Next.

The second step in the wizard allows you to select what type of form region to create. The wizard provides a handy visual representation of each type of form region, as shown in Figure 33-8. Select the Separate option and click Next.

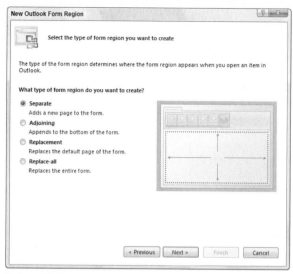

Figure 33-8

The next step in the wizard allows you to enter a friendly name for the form region, and, depending on the type of form region you've chosen, a title and description. This step also allows you to choose the display mode for the form region. *Compose* mode is displayed when an item is first being created, such as when you create a new e-mail message. *Read* mode is displayed when you subsequently open an e-mail message that has already been sent or received. Ensure that both of these checkboxes are ticked, enter "Custom Details" as the name, and click Next.

The final step in the wizard allows you to choose what message classes will display the form region. You can select from any of the standard message classes, such as mail message or appointment, or specify a custom message class. Select the `Contact message` class as shown in Figure 33-9 and click Finish to close the wizard.

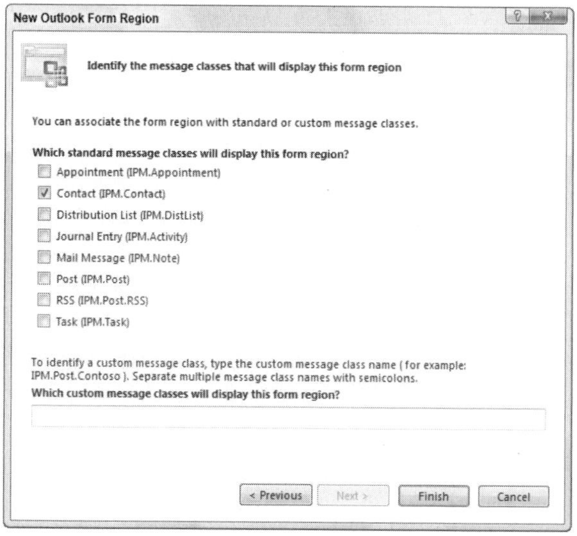

Figure 33-9

Once the wizard exits, the new form region will be created and opened in the designer. As mentioned earlier, an Outlook form region, like an Actions Pane and a Task Pane, is simply a user control. However, unlike an Actions Pane, it contains an embedded manifest that defines how the form region appears in Outlook. To access the manifest, ensure that the form is selected in the designer and open the Properties window. This will show a property called `Manifest`, under which you can set various properties to how it appears. This property can also be accessed through code at runtime.

In this scenario we will use the Outlook form region to display some additional useful information about a Contact. The layout of an Outlook form region is created in the same way as any other user control. Drag four Label controls and four textbox controls onto the design surface and align them as shown in Figure 33-10. Rename the textbox controls txtPartner, txtChildren, txtHobbies, and txtMet, and change the text on the labels to match these fields.

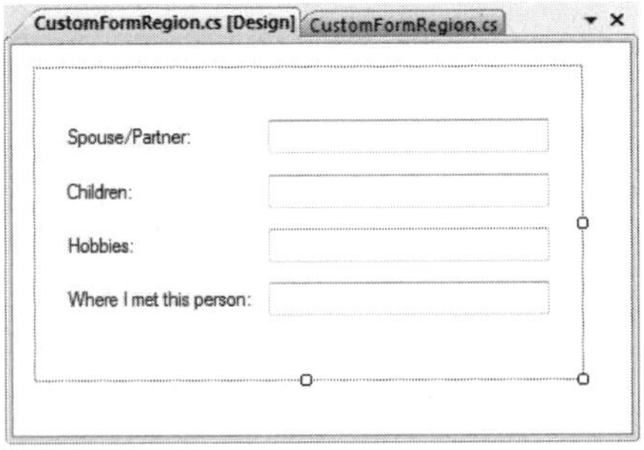

Figure 33-10

The `ContactItem` class contains a surprisingly large number of properties that are not obviously displayed in a standard Contact form in Outlook. In fact, with well over 100 contact-specific fields, there is a high chance that any custom property you want to display for a contact is already defined. In our case, the first three fields displayed on this form (spouse/partner, children, and hobbies) are available as existing properties.

There are also four properties called `User1` to `User4` that can be used to store custom properties. The "Where I met this person" field on this Outlook form region can be stored in one of those properties. The code behind the form region will already have stubs for the FormRegionShowing and FormRegionClosed event handlers. Add the following code to those properties to access the current Contact item and retrieve and save these custom properties:

```
private void CustomFormRegion_FormRegionShowing(object sender, System.EventArgs e)
{
    Outlook.ContactItem myContact = (Outlook.ContactItem)this.OutlookItem;
    this.txtPartner.Text = myContact.Spouse;
    this.txtChildren.Text = myContact.Children;
    this.txtHobbies.Text = myContact.Hobby;
    this.txtMet.Text = myContact.User1;
}

private void CustomFormRegion_FormRegionClosed(object sender, System.EventArgs e)
```

```
    {
        Outlook.ContactItem myContact = (Outlook.ContactItem)this.OutlookItem;
        myContact.Spouse = this.txtPartner.Text;
        myContact.Children = this.txtChildren.Text;
        myContact.Hobby = this.txtHobbies.Text;
        myContact.User1 = this.txtMet.Text;
    }
```

Press F5 to build and run the add-in in debug mode. If the solution compiled correctly, Outlook will open with your add-in registered. Open the Contacts folder and create a new Contact item. To view your custom Outlook form region, click the Custom Details button in the Show tab group of the Office Ribbon. Figure 33-11 shows how the Outlook form region should appear in the Contact Inspector window.

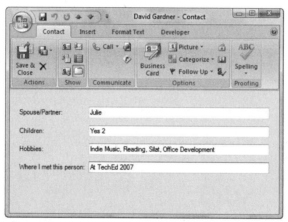

Figure 33-11

Debugging Office Applications

You can debug Office applications by using much the same process as you would with any other Windows application. All the standard Visual Studio debugger features, such as the ability to insert breakpoints and watch variables, are available when debugging Office applications.

The VSTO runtime, which is responsible for loading add-ins into their host applications, can display any errors that occur during startup in a message box, or write them to a log file. By default these options are disabled, and they can be enabled through environment variables.

To display any errors in a message box, create an environment variable called VSTO_SUPPRESSDISPLAYALERTS and assign it a value of 0. Setting this environment variable to 1, or deleting it altogether, will prevent the errors from being displayed.

To write the errors to a log file, create an environment variable called VSTO_LOGALERTS and assign it a value of 1. The VSTO runtime will create a log file called <manifestname>.manifest.log in the same folder as the application manifest. Setting the environment variable to 0, or deleting it altogether, will stop errors from being logged.

Unregistering an Add-In

When an application-level add-in is compiled in Visual Studio 2008, it will automatically register the add-in to the host application. Visual Studio will not automatically unregister the add-in from your application unless you run Build ⇨ Clean Solution. Therefore, you may find your add-in will continue to be loaded every time you launch the application. Rather than reopen the solution in Visual Studio, you can unregister the add-in directly from Office.

To unregister the application you will need to open the Add-Ins window. Under Outlook 2007, select Tools ⇨ Trust Center from the menu and then click Add-ins to bring up the window shown in Figure 33-12. For all the other Microsoft Office applications, open the Office menu and then click the Application Options button on the bottom of the menu screen.

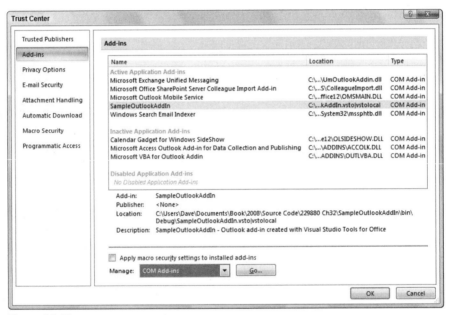

Figure 33-12

If it is registered and loaded, your application will be listed under the Active Application Add-ins list. Select COM Add-ins from the drop-down list at the bottom of the window and click the Go button. This will bring up the COM Add-Ins window shown in Figure 33-13 that will allow you to remove your add-in from the application.

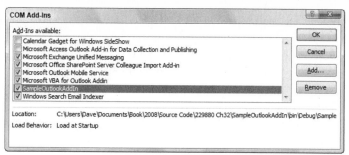

Figure 33-13

You can also disable your add-in by clearing the checkbox next to the add-in name in this window.

Disabled Add-Ins

When developing Office applications, you will inevitably do something that will generate an unhandled exception and cause your add-in to crash. If your add-in happens to crash when it is being loaded, the Office application will disable it. This is called *soft disabling*.

A soft-disabled add-in will not be loaded and will appear in the Trust Center (see Figure 33-12) under the Inactive Application Add-ins list. Visual Studio 2008 will automatically re-enable a soft disabled add-in when it is recompiled. You can also use the COM Add-Ins window that was displayed earlier in Figure 33-13 to re-enable the add-in by ticking the checkbox next to the add-in name.

An add-in will be flagged to be *hard disabled* when it causes the host application to crash, or when you stop the debugger, while the constructor or the Startup event handler is executing. The next time the Office application is launched, you will be presented with a dialog box similar to the one shown in Figure 33-14. If you select Yes the add-in will be hard disabled.

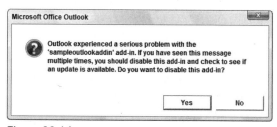

Figure 33-14

When an add-in is hard disabled it cannot be re-enabled from Visual Studio. If you attempt to debug a hard-disabled add-in, you will be presented with a warning message that the add-in has been added to the Disabled Items list and will not be loaded.

To remove the application from the Disabled Items list, start the Office application and open the Add-Ins window that was shown earlier in Figure 33-12 (Tools ➪ Trust Center from Outlook 2007, or open the Office menu and click the *ApplicationName* Options button from any of the other Office applications). Select Disabled Items from the drop-down list at the bottom of the window and click the Go button. This will display the Disabled Items window shown in Figure 33-15. Select your add-in and click Enable to remove it from this list.

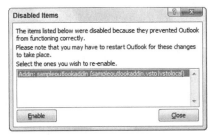

Figure 33-15

Deploying Office Applications

The two main ways to deploy Office applications are either using a traditional MSI setup project, or using the support for ClickOnce deployment that is built into Visual Studio 2008. ClickOnce is available only for Office 2007 solutions, although it can be used with both document-level customizations and application-level add-ins.

In previous versions of VSTO, configuring code access security was a manual process. Although VSTO hides much of the implementation details from you, in the background it needs to invoke COM+ code to communicate with Office. Because the CLR cannot enforce code access security for non-managed code, the CLR requires any applications that invoke COM+ components to have full trust to execute.

Fortunately, the ClickOnce support for Office applications that is built into Visual Studio 2008 automatically deploys with full trust. As with other ClickOnce applications, each time it is invoked it automatically checks for updates.

When an Office application is deployed it must be packaged with the required prerequisites. For Office 2007 applications, the following prerequisites are required:

❑   Windows Installer 3.1

❑   .NET Framework 3.5

❑   Visual Studio Tools for Office 3.0 runtime

❑   Microsoft Office 2007 primary interop assemblies (PIAs)

A primary interop assembly is an assembly that contains type definitions of types implemented with COM. A redistributable package of the Microsoft Office PIAs is available for download from Microsoft at no charge. The licensing agreement for the PIAs states that each end user must accept the Microsoft Software License Terms.

Because ClickOnce is not supported for Office 2003 solutions, you must use a setup project to deploy a solution. The prerequisites for Office 2003 are .NET Framework 2.0 or later, VSTO 2.0 runtime, and the Microsoft Office 2003 PIAs. You must also create and set security policies that grant the application full trust. More information on ClickOnce and MSI setup projects is available in Chapter 49.

Summary

This chapter introduced you to the major features in Visual Studio Tools for Office. It is now very easy to build feature-rich applications using Microsoft Office applications because the development tools are fully integrated into Visual Studio 2008. You can create .NET solutions that customize the appearance of the Office user interface with your own components at both the application level and the document level. This enables you to have unprecedented control over how end users interact with all of the products in the Microsoft Office suite.

34

Mobile Applications

In the past, building applications for mobile phones or PDAs was not for the fainthearted. It required not only a special set of tools but also a great deal of patience to get everything to work properly. The .NET Compact Framework — a smaller, limited-feature subset of the full .NET Framework available for Windows Mobile devices, and the associated designer support within Visual Studio — opened up the world of mobile application development to the general developer community. Once it was released, developers could build, test, and deploy applications just as they did Windows applications.

In Visual Studio 2008 and the .NET Compact Framework 3.5 this experience continues to improve, with richer designer support and a complete set of controls for building applications. This chapter shows you how easy it is to build and test device applications within Visual Studio 2008. In this chapter you'll notice references to the .NET Framework — zunless we specify otherwise, we're referring to the .NET Compact Framework.

Programming for mobile applications is all about optimizing the small-form factor, the mobility, and the unique functionality offered by these devices. The second part of this chapter looks at some more advanced techniques for building mobile applications, including rich support for building data applications and the new functionality offered by the Windows Mobile API.

Getting Started

The first thing you need to do to get started building a device application is to create a smart device project. You can either create this in a new solution or, if you are adding a device component to a larger application, add it to an existing solution. You create a smart device project the same way you would any other project type. You can select the File ⇨ New ⇨ Project menu command, or you can select Add ⇨ New Project from the right-click context menu in the Solution Explorer window. Figure 34-1 shows the New Project dialog with the Visual Basic, Smart Device node expanded. Notice that there is only one installed template, the Smart Device Project.

In previous versions this screen listed the different project types along with the different platform and framework versions. Unfortunately, this list was growing at an alarming rate with each new version of both Windows Mobile and the .NET Compact Framework.

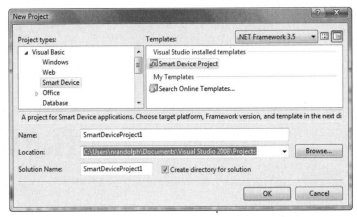

Figure 34-1

Selecting the Smart Device Project will invoke the Add New Smart Device Project dialog, shown in Figure 34-2, where you can select the target platform and the version of the .NET Compact Framework. Note that selecting the framework version in the top right corner of the New Project dialog doesn't affect the version of the .NET Compact Framework that your device application will be targeting.

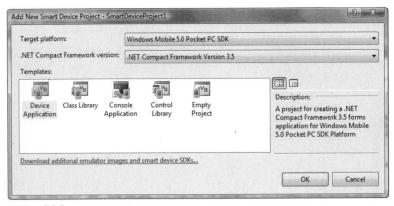

Figure 34-2

After selecting the target platform, framework version, and project type, click "OK" to generate the device application — in this case a Device Application for Windows Mobile 5 on version 3.5 of the framework.

You will notice that by default only Windows Mobile 5 is listed as a target platform. As new versions of the Windows Mobile platform become available you'll need to download the relevant SDK from the Microsoft web site, http://www.microsoft.com/, *in order for those platforms to be listed in the Add New Smart Device Project dialog.*

When the device project is created, it will appear in the Solution Explorer window with the same layout as a full .NET Framework project. The only difference is that the device project is distinguished from other projects by the icon used. Figure 34-3 shows a single VB.NET device project in the Solution Explorer window.

Figure 34-3

Selecting the SmartDeviceProject1 node brings up additional information about the project in the properties grid. This includes the version of the .NET Framework and the platform for which this project is being written.

The Design Skin

One of the significant improvements that was made back in Visual Studio 2005 was the inclusion of design skins for device applications. In the past, developers building forms for devices laid out controls using the standard form designer, which approximated what the form would look like when it was run on the device. In most cases this layout had to be tweaked, and in some cases redesigned, to fit the target device. Figure 34-4 shows two forms: Form1 with the design skin turned on, and Form2 with the design skin turned off.

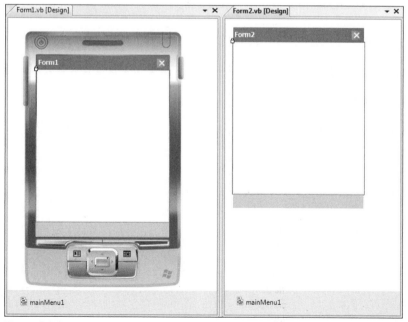

Figure 34-4

The design skin can be toggled on and off via the right-click context menu off the form design surface. You might be wondering why you would want to turn off the design skin. Other than giving you a better illustration of what the form is going to look like, the design skin does not add very much functionality. It also adds overhead every time the form is rendered in the designer. For this reason, Visual Studio 2008 is more responsive with the design skin disabled. Although the examples in this chapter show the design skin, there is no reason why you can't work with the design skin disabled.

You toggle the design skin on a per-form basis. Whether it is enabled or disabled is tracked along with other user settings. The default behavior for forms that you haven't opened can be controlled via the Tools ⇨ Options dialog. On the Device Tools ⇨ General page you can toggle the "Show skin in the Windows Forms Designer" checkbox.

Orientation

Windows Mobile 2003 Second Edition added the capability to change the orientation on a Pocket PC from portrait to landscape. Visual Studio 2008 supports switching the orientation of the design surface. This automatically resizes the form to the appropriate dimensions, enabling you to confirm that all of your controls are correctly positioned for both orientations.

To alter the orientation of the design surface you can select Rotate Left or Rotate Right from the right-click context menu off the design surface. If you have the design skin enabled, it will be rotated in the direction specified, while the form you are working on will remain upright. Without the design skin, the form will be resized as if the skin were present, so you can still see the effect on your visual layout.

Buttons

The one bit of functionality that the design skin does add is the ability to automatically generate a code stub for handling hardware button events. As you move your mouse over the hardware buttons on the design skin, a tooltip appears, letting you know which button it is (such as Soft Key 1). Clicking a button takes you to an event handler for the KeyDown event of the Form shown in the following code:

```
Public Class Form1
    Private Sub Form1_KeyDown(ByVal sender As Object, ByVal e As KeyEventArgs)_
                                              Handles MyBase.KeyDown
        If (e.KeyCode = System.Windows.Forms.Keys.Up) Then
            'Rocker Up
            'Up
        End If
        If (e.KeyCode = System.Windows.Forms.Keys.Down) Then
            'Rocker Down
            'Down
        End If
        If (e.KeyCode = System.Windows.Forms.Keys.Left) Then
            'Left
        End If
        If (e.KeyCode = System.Windows.Forms.Keys.Right) Then
            'Right
        End If
```

```
        If (e.KeyCode = System.Windows.Forms.Keys.Enter) Then
            'Enter
        End If
    End Sub
End Class
```

Note a few important points in this code snippet. First, the event handler actually handles the `KeyDown` event of the form. Because the keys may have different functions depending on which form of your application is open, it makes sense for them to map to the form. Second, note that this event handler handles only the directional keys, the rocker, and the Enter key.

Most devices have a number of additional hardware buttons, referred to as *application keys*. These keys do not have a set function and can appear anywhere (if at all) on the device. Unfortunately, there is no automatic mapping to the form events for any of the application keys, although use of the HardwareButton control (which provides this functionality) is covered later in this chapter.

The last point to take away from this snippet is that it is generated code, and you should probably replace the entire contents of the event handler with your own code that uses a more efficient syntax, such as a Select (VB.NET) or Switch (C#) statement.

> *The code generated for a Smartphone project also includes conditional statements for function keys and the number pad.*

The Toolbox

Device applications have their own set of tabs within the Toolbox window. These are essentially the same as the tabs shown for building normal applications, except that they are prefixed with the word "Device." Any developer who has worked with controls for a Windows application will feel at home using the device controls. Some are specific to particular device applications and enable you to take advantage of some of their device-specific functionality.

Common Controls

The standard controls, such as textboxes, checkboxes, labels, and buttons, are all available from the Common Device Controls tab. Figure 34-5 illustrates a simple form with a number of controls visible for both Pocket PC (left image) and Smartphone (right image). Note that device developers benefit from the same set of designer features as Windows developers. These include the alignment guides, shown in the image on the left.

Figure 34-5

The first version of the .NET Compact Framework was missing not only several of the standard controls, such as a DateTimePicker, but also basic layout functionality such as anchoring and docking. However, starting with version 2 the .NET Compact Framework has supported a wide range of controls, including splitters and status bars, as well as anchoring, docking, and auto-scrolling for panels and forms.

Mobile Controls

When you're building device applications, it is important to design them with the user interface in mind. Simply taking an existing Windows application and rebuilding it for the device is unlikely to work. The best device applications not only have intuitive form designs but also make use of available device-specific functionality, including the hardware buttons, the input panel, and the notification bubble.

The Hardware Button

The discussion of the design skin noted that although the forms KeyDown event handler could be used to trap some of the hardware buttons, it doesn't trap application key events. To handle one or more application keys you need to add a HardwareButton control to the form. This control does not have a visual component, so it appears in the nonvisual area of the designer.

Figure 34-6 shows the associated properties for a HardwareButton control that has been added to Form1. HardwareButton redirects the hardware button events to an AssociatedControl. The AssociatedControl must be a Form, Panel, or CustomControl; otherwise a NotSupportedException will be raised when the application is run. Any of the six application keys can be selected as the HardwareKey. Unfortunately, these are not flags, so they cannot be concatenated to allow a single HardwareButton to wire up all the application keys.

Figure 34-6

Once the HardwareButton control has been added to the form and the appropriate properties set, you still need to handle the click events. You can do this using an event handler for either the `KeyPress` or `KeyUp` event for the AssociatedControl. For example, if you were to use Form1 as the AssociatedControl, the event handler might look like the following:

```
Private Sub Form1_KeyUp(ByVal sender As Object, _
                        ByVal e As System.Windows.Forms.KeyEventArgs) _
                                                        Handles MyBase.KeyUp
    If e.KeyCode = Microsoft.WindowsCE.Forms.HardwareKeys.ApplicationKey1 Then
        MessageBox.Show("Hardware Key event")
    End If
End Sub
```

The Input Panel

Most device applications require some form of text input, and this is usually provided through the Soft Input Panel, or SIP as it is more commonly known. The SIP is a visual keyboard that can be used to tap out words. Alternative input methods such as the Letter Recognizer use the same input panel for text entry. Figure 34-7 shows an emulator for a Windows Mobile 5.0 Pocket PC device with the SIP showing. In this case the SIP is displaying the keyboard.

Figure 34-7

The SIP takes up valuable screen real estate both when it is open (as in Figure 34-7) and when it is closed (that is, when only the bottom bar is visible). Because of this it should be added to a form only when required. However, the default behavior when a menu is added to the form is for the SIP to become visible, so that you can open and close it at will. Hence it is important for you to be able to control what happens when the SIP changes status.

The first step in working with the SIP is to add an InputPanel control to the form. Again, this control appears in the nonvisual area of the form designer and has a single property, `Enabled`, which determines whether the SIP is open or closed. This control also exposes an `EnabledChanged` event, which is raised when the status of the SIP changes.

Double-clicking the newly created InputPanel generates an event handler for the `EnabledChanged` event. This handler needs to reposition the controls to optimize the layout for the reduced real estate. Because the SIP appears as if it were a control that sits on top of the form, when it changes state it does not resize the form. This means that there is no resize event on the form, so any repositioning of controls needs to be done via the `EnabledChanged` event handler.

At this stage, it is worth noting that the standard controls all support anchoring and docking. On applications designed for a desktop computer, these layout options make sense. However, on a mobile device, where screen real estate is already limited, allowing the controls to automatically resize often results in a clunky and difficult-to-use interface. For example, take a simple screen layout that contains a client list and two buttons. If the device is in portrait mode, the list should be positioned above the two buttons so the maximum number of items can be displayed. However, in landscape mode, instead of the controls being repositioned so that the list takes up the full width of the device, the list should be repositioned alongside the two buttons.

You could do this by defining multiple screen layouts based on the size and orientation of the screen. The following code snippet shows how you can toggle among a number of screen layouts depending on the screen orientation:

```vb
Imports Microsoft.WindowsCE.Forms
Public Class Form1

    <Flags()> _
    Private Enum FormLayout
        None = 0
        SIP_Open = 1
        SIP_Closed = SIP_Open << 1
        Portrait = SIP_Closed << 1
        Landscape = Portrait << 1
    End Enum

    Private Sub LayoutChanged(ByVal sender As Object, _
                              ByVal e As System.EventArgs) _
                         Handles MyBase.Resize, InputPanel1.EnabledChanged
        Layout()
    End Sub

    Private Sub InputPanel1_EnabledChanged(ByVal sender As System.Object, _
                                    ByVal e As System.EventArgs) _
                                        Handles InputPanel1.EnabledChanged
        Layout()
    End Sub

    Private Function DetermineCurrentLayout() As FormLayout
        Dim currentLayout As FormLayout
        'Determine whether it is landscape or portrait
        Select Case SystemSettings.ScreenOrientation
            Case ScreenOrientation.Angle0, ScreenOrientation.Angle180
                currentLayout = FormLayout.Portrait
            Case Else
                currentLayout = FormLayout.Landscape
        End Select

        'Determine whether the SIP is Open or Closed
        If Me.InputPanel1.Enabled Then
            currentLayout = currentLayout Or FormLayout.SIP_Open
        Else
            currentLayout = currentLayout Or FormLayout.SIP_Closed
        End If
        Return currentLayout
    End Function

    Private Sub Layout()
        Dim newLayout As FormLayout = DetermineCurrentLayout()

        Select Case newLayout
            Case FormLayout.Portrait Or FormLayout.SIP_Open
                Layout_PortraitWithInput()
```

(continued)

(continued)

```
                Case FormLayout.Portrait Or FormLayout.SIP_Closed
                    Layout_PortraitWithOutInput()
                Case FormLayout.Landscape Or FormLayout.SIP_Open
                    Layout_LandscapeWithInput()
                Case FormLayout.Landscape Or FormLayout.SIP_Closed
                    Layout_LandscapeWithOutInput()
            End Select

        End Sub

        Private Sub Layout_PortraitWithOutInput()
            'Position list control above the two buttons
        End Sub

        Private Sub Layout_PortraitWithInput()
            'Position list control above the two buttons
            'Reduce the height of the list and move the buttons up
            '    so that they are both visible above the SIP
        End Sub

        Private Sub Layout_LandscapeWithOutInput()
            'Position list control along side the two buttons
        End Sub

        Private Sub Layout_LandscapeWithInput()
            'Position list control along side the two buttons
            'Reduce the height of the list control so that all
            '    items are visible above the SIP
        End Sub
    End Class
```

This code snippet defines an enumeration that can be used to specify the current screen orientation. Two factors warrant consideration: the orientation of the screen and whether the SIP is visible. It may be that other form factors, such as a square screen, could be added to this list.

When an event is triggered that alters the orientation of the screen (such as the form resize event) or the status of the SIP (such as the InputPanel EnabledChanged event), the new screen configuration is detected via the DetermineCurrentLayout method, and the contents of the form are rearranged.

Notification

There are times when a background application might want to notify a user about a particular event, or get user feedback, without coming to the foreground. This can be done with a *notification bubble*. The contents of the bubble are essentially an HTML document that can use form input controls such as textboxes and buttons to retrieve user input.

Like both the HardwareButton and the InputPanel, when a Notification control is added to the form it appears in the nonvisual section of the designer. A number of properties can be set on a Notification control that determine the caption, icon, and text of the notification. There is also a Critical property, which can be set to heighten the importance of the notification, and an InitialDuration property, which controls how long the notification is shown. The Text property is where the HTML content is added to the notification bubble. While it is possible to use the property grid to enter this property, you will likely need to dynamically build the HTML content based on the status of your application. The following code snippet creates and displays the notification bubble illustrated in Figure 34-8:

```
Private Sub NotifyUser()
    'Build the HTML content for the Notification Bubble
    Dim htmlContent As System.Text.StringBuilder

    htmlContent = New System.Text.StringBuilder("<html><body>")
    htmlContent.Append("<a href=""Reference.htm"">Test Link</a>")
    htmlContent.Append("<p><form method=""GET"" action=mybubble>")
    htmlContent.Append("<p>This is an <font color=""#0000FF""><b>HTML</b></font>")
    htmlContent.Append("notification stored in a  <font color=""#FF0000"">")
    htmlContent.Append("<i>string</i></font> table!</p>")
    htmlContent.Append("<p><input type=text name=textinput ")
    htmlContent.Append("value=""Input Sample""><input type='submit'></p>")
    htmlContent.Append("<p align=right><input type=button name=OK value='Ok'>")
    htmlContent.Append("<input type=button name='cmd:2' value='Cancel'></p>")
    htmlContent.Append("</body></html>")

    'Set the Notification content
    Notification1.Text = htmlContent.ToString

    'Set the title and make this a critical bubble (red border)
    Notification1.Caption = "Title"
    Notification1.Critical = True
    Notification1.Icon = My.Resources.NotificationIcon

    'Display the Notification bubble
    Notification1.Visible = True
End Sub

Private Sub Notification_ResponseSubmitted(ByVal sender as Object, _
    ByVal e as ResponseSubmittedEventArgs) Handles Notification1.ResponseSubmitted
    'Make sure you clear away the notification bubble
    Notification1.Visible = False
    'Parse the response value string that is accessible via e.Response
End Sub
```

In addition to building the HTML content for the notification bubble, this code also sets the caption, or title, for the bubble, makes it Critical, which will make the border appear red, and finally displays the bubble. Instead of using the more common Show method that is used for forms, to display the notification bubble, set the Visible property to True. In Figure 34-8, you can see that the notification bubble is made up of three distinct parts. The icon is placed in the main menu bar at the top of the screen (to the left of the G icon), and this icon remains visible while the notification remains active. At the bottom of the screen there is a new soft key, "Hide," that the user can use to hide, but not dismiss, the notification. The actual notification bubble expands to include a title bar and the main notification window, where the HTML controls are displayed.

Figure 34-8

Double-clicking the Notification control attaches an event handler to the `ResponseSubmitted` event. This is one of two key events raised by the Notification control, and it is raised whenever a user clicks a button or link within the notification bubble. For the user to be able to dismiss a notification bubble, there must be at least one control, such as a hyperlink or a button, that can submit information. Failing to include one of these controls results in users being unable to get rid of the notification bubble.

The event handler for the `ResponseSubmitted` event has a `ResponseSubmittedEventArgs` type as a parameter. This class has a single `String` property, which is the `Response`. The contents of this string will vary depending on the type of response given. In this example, three types of responses might be received from the user:

❑ Clicking Test Link will set the response string to be equal to the URL specified for the link. In this case the URL is `Reference.htm`. It is up to the application to determine how this is processed, as it does not automatically navigate to this URL.

❑ The "Submit" button is actually a form Input control of type Submit, and as such submits the data collected by the form. In this case you have a textbox, so the response will appear as follows:

```
mybubble?textinput=Input+Sample
```

Notice that the name of the form being submitted is at the beginning of the string, and then all input controls are appended after the question mark in a `name=value` pattern. This pattern is useful when parsing the response string for form data.

❑ The last form of response is the value of any form button. In this case, clicking "OK" generates a response equal to the `value` property of the button, which would be `OK`.

The user can perform one other action on the form, which is to click the "Cancel" button. Clicking this button does not raise the ResponseSubmitted event, but instead minimizes the notification bubble so that only the icon appears in the menu bar. What makes this button special is the use of cmd:2 as the name of the button. This is actually an undocumented feature, but you can use cmd:0 through cmd:4 as identifiers for buttons with which you want to simply close the bubble and not send a response.

> You will notice that the last line in the event handler for the ResponseSubmitted event sets the Visible property of the notification to false. If you don't do this, the notification bubble will simply be hidden as it is by the "Hide" soft key, rather than being dismissed permanently.

The other event is the BubbleChanged event, which is triggered when the visibility of the notification bubble changes. In most cases the application will have displayed the bubble and will receive notification when the bubble is dismissed, via the ResponseSubmitted event. On some occasions, however, a user is not quick enough to interact with the notification, or perhaps chooses to ignore it. Once the InitialDuration has expired, the notification bubble automatically hides itself. In this case, it is important for the application to be notified when the visibility of the bubble changes, because a timer may need to be started to re-prompt the user.

Debugging

In the past, writing applications for mobile devices was a time-consuming process. The release of the Compact Framework brought with it a new wave of interactive debugger support for building device applications. Now, developers wanting to build mobile applications have the same support for debugging applications as for desktop or web applications. Subsequent chapters in this book cover the debugging features within Visual Studio 2008. Most of these apply equally to debugging device applications.

As you saw in Chapter 31 on the Device Security Manager, Visual Studio 2008 comes with a feature-rich device emulator that you can use to debug your application in place of a real device. While this is a convenience, it is highly recommended that you do your final round of application testing on a real device to ensure compatibility. In Chapter 31 you were also introduced to the Device Emulator Manager that, combined with the Windows Mobile Device Center (or ActiveSync on earlier versions of Windows), enables you to work with the emulator in much the same way as you would with a real device.

The Device Emulator Manager that ships with Visual Studio 2008 also enables you to dynamically adjust some features of the emulator. For example, you can adjust the battery level to see how your application will behave when the system is running low on power, or you might want to simulate plugging in a headset or car kit. You can do all this from the Emulator Properties window, accessible from the File menu of the running emulator itself. The Device Emulator Manager also supports automation so that device testing using an emulator can be integrated into your testing process.

> Some of the new features of the Device Emulator Manager will only work with the latest emulator images, downloadable from www.microsoft.com.

Project Settings

As you would imagine, there are additional project settings that pertain specifically to device projects. There are only a few, and they mainly pertain to setting additional debugging settings required for device applications. Figure 34-9 shows the Devices tab of the Project Settings window for a device project.

The "Target device" field is used to specify the device that is the default when your application is run from within Visual Studio 2008. You can also nominate the output file folder and whether the latest version of the .NET Compact Framework should be installed as part of the debugging process.

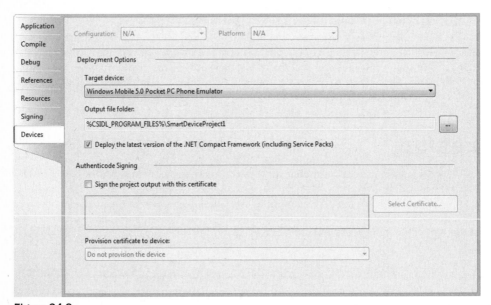

Figure 34-9

The last part of this tab enables you to sign your application so it can be executed on an appropriately provisioned device. Essentially, provisioning a device entails installing the appropriate digital certificates. As we mentioned in Chapter 31, it is not recommended that you use the "Provision certificate to device" option; rather, use the Device Security Manager to administer what certificates exist on the device.

The Data Source

Visual Studio 2008 includes designer support for building mobile data-bound applications that is similar to what it provides for full framework applications. This includes support for building mobile applications where it is useful to have a portable database that resides on the device. As with other project types, to add a data source to your application, select Add New Data Source from the Data Sources window. Select Database as the data source type and you will be prompted to select the database connection to use.

Mobile applications can connect directly to a SQL Server database using the same classes as desktop or web applications. However, this can limit the mobility of such a device, as it will require connectivity to the database to function. A better solution is to change the data source to be a SQL Server Compact

Edition (SSCE) database. By default, the Add Connection dialog shows connection properties for a SQL Server connection. Selecting Change, next to the Data Source label, enables you to change the data source to be SQL Server Compact 3.5, as shown in Figure 34-10.

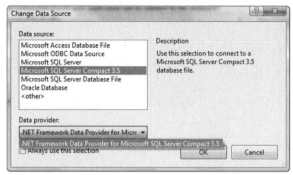

Figure 34-10

Accepting this change prompts you to select the parameters for the SSCE database to connect to. Here you can select either an existing database, as shown in Figure 34-11 (where the Northwind database that ships with Visual Studio 2008 has been selected), or create a new database. If you have an existing database on your mobile device, you can select that as well. To do so you need to select "ActiveSync connected device" (even if you are connected via the Windows Mobile Device Center) and then click "Browse."

Unless you are running Visual Studio 2008 as an administrator, you may see an error if you attempt to connect to the sample Northwind database in its default location. It's a good idea to copy the database to a different location before trying to access it.

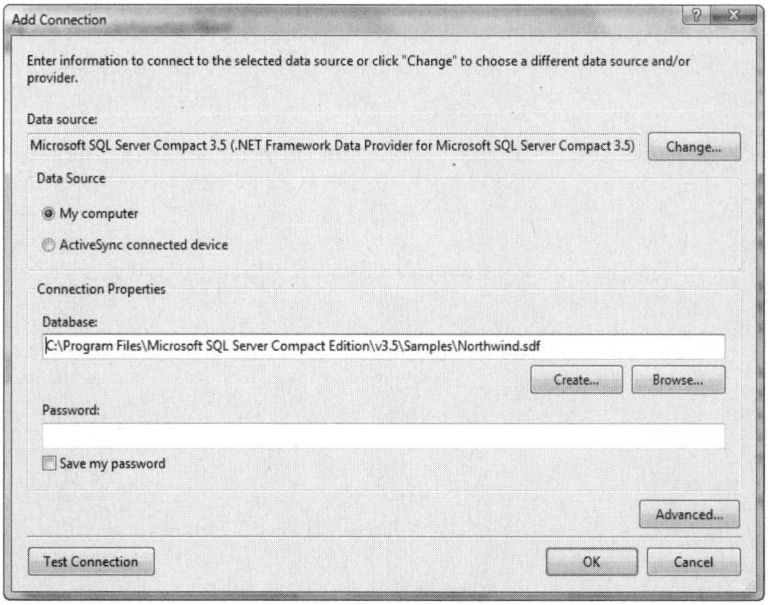

Figure 34-11

If you select a database that is not in the project folder, upon accepting the connection properties you will be asked if you want a copy to be made and included in your solution. This is a good idea, as it ensures that you can easily deploy your application without verifying whether the database already exists on the device. For debugging purposes, you can define when the database will be deployed with your application. Select the database file that has been added to your solution and use the Copy to Output Directory property to specify whether the database is always copied, never copied, or copied if newer than what is on the device.

When the data source is added to the solution, it is added both to the Data Sources window and to the Solution Explorer as an XSD file. Other files are also added to the project to support strongly typed access to the data via a DataSet. These are created by the custom tool MSDataSetGenerator, which is specified in the property grid for the XSD file. Later in this chapter you will look at an alternative tool that generates a SQLCeResultSet instead of a DataSet.

The DataSet

Once the data source has been added to the project, the Data Sources window can be used to add data-bound controls to the design surface for the device. This is the same process described earlier in the book when you were working with DataSets for a desktop application. This section shows you how easily you can build a user interface to not only view the data but also add and edit records. For this purpose, consider a limited scenario that works with the Northwind sample database that ships with Visual Studio 2008. This database is located in the SmartDevices SDK folder (C:\Program Files\Microsoft SQL Server Compact Edition\v3.5\Samples\Northwind.sdf) and can be added to the project as outlined in the previous section.

The scenario involves providing an interface for managing Customers and Orders. When adding the Northwind Data Source, you need to include these two tables, plus the Employees table for selecting the employee who took the order. This adds them to the NorthwindDataSet and ensures that you have appropriate table adapters for retrieving and updating information in the database. The Northwind Data Source appears in the Data Sources window and has nodes for Customers, Orders, and Employees. Because there is a relationship among these tables when you expand the Customers node, you will see a subnode for Orders.

For this scenario, add a new form, CustomersForm, to the project to lay out Customer information. From the Data Sources window, select the Customers node and ensure that the drop-down field is set to DataGrid. You also want to prevent the Customer ID from being added to the DataGrid, so select None from the Display Type drop-down for this field. Now drag the Customers node onto the form. This adds a DataGrid to the form, along with a NorthwindDataSet, a CustomersBindingSource, and a CustomersTableAdapter to the nonvisual area of the designer, as shown in Figure 34-12.

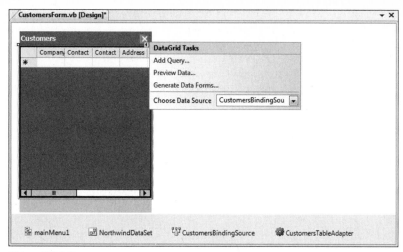

Figure 34-12

In Figure 34-12 you can see that the Company column is relatively narrow, and it is unlikely that many company names are going to be that short. To change the width of this column, you need to edit the column styling information. When building applications using the full .NET Framework, use the property called `Columns` for the DataGridView to control how the columns are arranged. This property is also accessible from the smart tag associated with this control. The DataGrid for mobile applications does not have this property; here the column layout information is buried in the `TableStyles` property. Selecting this property from the Property grid opens the Table Style Collection Editor, from which you need to select the `GridColumnStyles` property to open the DataGridColumnStyle Collection Editor, as shown in Figure 34-13.

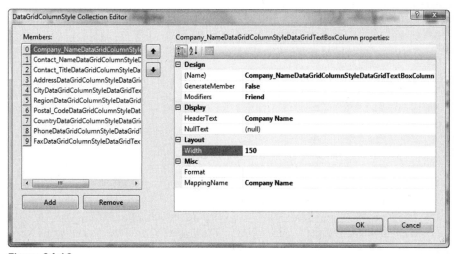

Figure 34-13

Selecting the Company entry in the Members list, adjust the Width to 150, as shown in Figure 34-13, which is more reasonable for this field. The `MappingName` property is also important, as it is used to associate a field in the data source with this column. In this case the `MappingName` property is linked to the Company Name field. The editor has some built-in smarts that determine what fields are available from the associated data source. Selecting the `MappingName` property reveals a drop-down list of the available fields. While on this screen you can remove several of the Customer fields, as they don't need to be visible on the opening screen.

Going back to Figure 34-12, you can see a couple of smart-tag tasks for the DataGrid. Of importance here is Generate Data Forms. Selecting this option automatically generates forms for viewing and editing information for Customers selected from the DataGrid. Before generating the forms, you need to configure the Data Sources window so you get only the fields you want available for editing.
In this case you don't want the Company Name to be changed, so select Label from the display type drop-down for that item. Now you can generate the data forms using the smart tag on the DataGrid. Depending on the number of fields in the table, this process might take a few minutes, but eventually it will not only generate the forms, with appropriate controls rendered to display and edit data fields, but will also wire up appropriate event handlers. Figure 34-14 illustrates the three customer forms you now have. On the left is the Customers list, in the middle is the summary information form for a customer, and on the right is the customer edit form. You will notice that for the Company Name field a label was generated instead of a textbox, thereby preventing this field from being edited.

Figure 34-14

The one problem introduced in making the Company Name field read-only for editing is that the same form is used for creating a new record. Because of this you need to provide a mechanism for assigning a company name to a new record. You can do this in the `Click` event handler for the New menu item. Double-clicking this menu item takes you to the generated event handler, where you can call an InputBox to get the company name for the new record. Notice in the following code snippet that you also need to provide the Customer ID field for this new record. Here you make a call to a method that ensures that the ID will be unique. Pass in the company name as a seed for the unique ID:

```
Private Sub NewMenuItemMenuItem_Click(ByVal sender As Object, _
                                      ByVal e As EventArgs) _
                    Handles NewMenuItemMenuItem.Click
    Dim newCompanyName As String = InputBox("Please enter the new company name:")
    If newCompanyName = "" Then Return

    Dim customer As NorthwindDataSet.CustomersRow = _
            CType(CType(CustomersBindingSource.AddNew, Data.DataRowView).Row, _
                                        NorthwindDataSet.CustomersRow)
    customer.Company_Name = newCompanyName
    customer.Customer_ID = GenerateUniqueCustomerID(newCompanyName)
    Dim customerEditDialog As CustomersEditViewDialog = _
                    CustomersEditViewDialog.Instance(Me.CustomersBindingSource)
    customerEditDialog.ShowDialog()
End Sub
```

So far, you have an application that enables you to browse the summary list of customers using a DataGrid, view the full information about a customer using the summary form, and add or edit a customer using the edit form. The next part in this scenario involves linking Order information so orders for a particular customer appear on the customer summary page. This information could also be added to the edit page using this process, but for brevity's sake we'll only add it to the summary page.

From the Data Sources window, drag the Orders node to the customer summary form. This requires some fiddling, as the existing controls are docked, but eventually you should be able to get it laid out with the DataGrid at the bottom of the list of customer attributes. (Hint: Set the Dock property to Top and then use the Document Outline tool window to help position the control.) Notice that it has again added a NorthwindDataSet, a table adapter, and a binding source to the nonvisual area of the design surface. Unfortunately, the generated bindings will not link the orders with the customer you're viewing, because they are referencing a new instance of the NorthwindDataSet.

Before correcting the issue with the data binding, you need to inject a step here to create the summary and edit forms for the Order information. Unfortunately, when you correct the data binding, you lose the ability to generate these forms. In the same way in which you created the customer summary and edit forms, select the Generate Data Forms smart-tag task from the Orders DataGrid. As before, this adds a New item to the existing menu, which you can name New Order to prevent confusion with the Edit menu item.

To correct the issue with the data binding, you need to open the CustomersSummaryViewDialog designer file and change the DataSource property of the OrdersBindingSource.

```
Me.OrdersBindingSource.DataMember = "Orders"
Me.OrdersBindingSource.DataSource = GetType(SmartDeviceProject1.NorthwindDataSet)
```

Setting the DataSource to a type is useful for design-time manipulation. However, at runtime you must change this DataSource to point to an actual data source so there is data to bind to. Therefore, you need to set the DataSource property to be equal to the NorthwindDataSet that is populated on the Customers form, by modifying the auto-generated Instance method, highlighted in the following code snippet.

Although this method appears in the CustomersSummaryViewDialog.Designer.vb file, which you should normally avoid modifying, this particular method will not be overwritten by subsequent changes to the layout of the form:

```
Public Shared Function Instance(ByVal bindingSource As BindingSource) _
                                             As CustomersSummaryViewDialog
     System.Windows.Forms.Cursor.Current = Cursors.WaitCursor
     If (defaultInstance Is Nothing) Then
          defaultInstance = New SmartDeviceProject1.CustomersSummaryViewDialog
          defaultInstance.CustomerssBindingSource.DataSource = bindingSource
          defaultInstance.OrdersBindingSource.DataSource = _
                                   defaultInstance.CustomerssBindingSource
          defaultInstance.OrdersBindingSource.DataMember = "Orders_FK00"
     End If
     defaultInstance.AutoScrollPosition = New System.Drawing.Point(0, 0)
     defaultInstance.CustomersBindingSource.Position = bindingSource.Position
     System.Windows.Forms.Cursor.Current = System.Windows.Forms.Cursors.Default
     Return defaultInstance
End Function
```

When you return to the form design you should also remove the additional NorthwindDataSet and TableAdapter, leaving the form looking like the one shown in Figure 34-15.

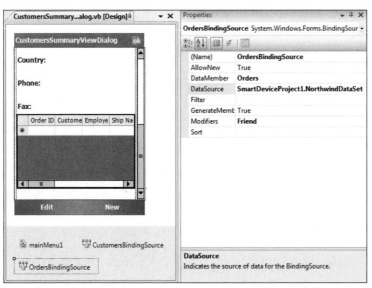

Figure 34-15

The last thing you need to do to display the list of orders for a customer is to retrieve the orders from the database by creating a second TableAdapter for the NorthwindDataSet that will be used to fill the Orders table. Return to the Customers form and you can easily add an OrdersTableAdapter by dragging it onto the form from the Toolbox. When you added the NorthwindDataSet these strongly typed adapters were added to the solution, and they were subsequently added to the Components tab of the Toolbox. To activate the TableAdapter, call the `Fill` method as part of the `Load` event for the form:

```
Private Sub CustomersForm_Load(ByVal sender As System.Object, _
                       ByVal e As System.EventArgs)
Handles MyBase.Load
      If NorthwindDataSetUtil.DesignerUtil.IsRunTime Then
          Me.CustomersTableAdapter.Fill(Me.NorthwindDataSet.Customers)
          Me.OrdersTableAdapter1.Fill(Me.NorthwindDataSet.Orders)
          Me.EmployeesTableAdapter1.Fill(me.NorthwindDataSet.Employees)
      End If
   End Sub
```

In this code snippet, notice that the TableAdapter for Employees has been filled. This adapter also needs to be added to the CustomersForm form, just as you did for Orders.

The order summary and order edit forms currently list all the attributes of the Order, including the Customer ID and Employee ID. Because you have arrived at this order via the Customer summary page, you don't need that field displayed. The Employee ID field is not very useful unless you have committed all these IDs to memory. It would be more useful if it displayed a name instead of an ID. To arrange this, you can combine the information from the Employees table.

You already have the information from the Employees table loaded into the NorthwindDataSet, so all you need to do is select the correct record from that table based on the Employee ID of the Order and display the name of the employee. Unfortunately, the Employees table currently returns First and Last Name fields, which makes it difficult to display, as you need to bind to a single field. To correct this, edit the Employee information via the NorthwindDataSet by double-clicking NorthWindDataSet.XSD in the Solution Explorer. This opens the DataSet designer. Right-click the Employees entity and select Configure to open the TableAdapter Configuration Wizard. Here you can change the information retrieved from the database to include a concatenated Name field, for displaying information, and the Employee ID field, for data binding. You can remove all the other fields, resulting in a SQL statement that should appear as shown in Figure 34-16.

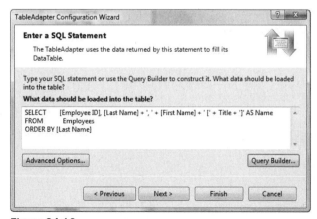

Figure 34-16

In Figure 34-16, the return values are ordered by last name so they are easier to identify. Clicking Finish regenerates the NorthwindDataSet with only these two fields in the Employees table.

The next step in the process is to add a data-bound field to both the summary and edit dialogs for Order information. Ideally, you want a label on the summary dialog and a drop-down list for the edit dialog. Begin with the edit dialog because it is the easier of the two to implement. This dialog, as it was automatically generated, contains text fields for Order ID, Customer ID, and Employee ID. Because the first two of these are not editable, remove both the Order ID and Customer ID fields and their associated labels from the dialog. In addition, remove the text field under the Employee ID label, rename the label to read Employee, and finally add a combobox to the form. The final result, after a bit of rearranging, should look similar to what is shown in Figure 34-17.

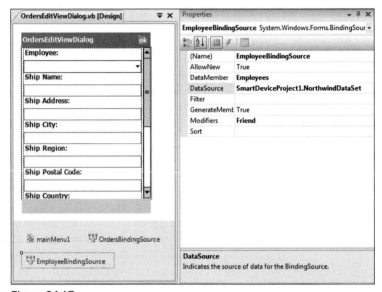

Figure 34-17

Figure 34-17 also shows a new EmployeeBindingSource, which will be used to populate the Employees drop-down list. You create this new EmployeeBindingSource by dragging a new BindingSource component from the Toolbox onto the form and renaming it EmployeeBindingSource. As you did previously, you need to edit the designer file for the OrdersEditViewDialog to set the `DataMember` and `DataSource` properties of the EmployeeBindingSource.

```
Me.EmployeesBindingSource.DataMember = "Employees"
Me.EmployeesBindingSource.DataSource = GetType(DeviceApplication1.NorthwindDataSet)
```

And again, at runtime the binding source has to be directed to a real data source.

```
Public Shared Function Instance(ByVal bindingSource As BindingSource) _
                                              As OrdersEditViewDialog
    System.Windows.Forms.Cursor.Current = Cursors.WaitCursor
    If (defaultInstance Is Nothing) Then
        defaultInstance = New DeviceApplication1.OrdersEditViewDialog
        defaultInstance.OrdersBindingSource.DataSource = bindingSource
        defaultInstance.EmployeesBindingSource.DataSource = _
                            My.Forms.CustomersForm.NorthwindDataSet
    End If
    defaultInstance.Employee_IDComboBox.Focus()
    defaultInstance.AutoScrollPosition = New System.Drawing.Point(0, 0)
    defaultInstance.OrdersBindingSource.Position = bindingSource.Position
    System.Windows.Forms.Cursor.Current = System.Windows.Forms.Cursors.Default
    Return defaultInstance
End Function
```

The last things you need to do to wire up the Employees drop-down list are to set the `DataSource` property in order to populate the drop-down, and to bind the `SelectedValue` property in order to provide two-way binding for the Order. Select the drop-down list and configure the `Data` properties so they match Figure 34-18.

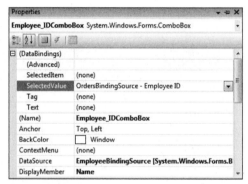

Figure 34-18

In Figure 34-18 the drop-down list is populated with the EmployeesBindingSource being used as the `DataSource`, the `Name` attribute being displayed in the list, and the `Employee ID` attribute being used for the value of the items in the list. The drop-down list is also data-bound to the `Employee ID` attribute on the OrdersBindingSource.

This completes the edit dialog for Order information. The Orders summary dialog is done in a similar manner, so begin by copying both the EmployeeBindingSource and the Employees drop-down from the edit dialog and pasting them onto the summary dialog. Again, the summary dialog presents the Order ID and Customer ID, which are not really required and can be removed. Because this is a summary dialog, you don't really want the Employee information to be presented in a drop-down list. A simple option here is to disable the drop-down list. However, this makes the interface look a little untidy. To fix this issue, you can change the employee field to be a label instead of a drop-down box.

This completes the scenario for working with Customers and Orders. Clearly, this example could be extended to work with OrderDetails, which requires a Product list lookup, by means of the same process we just walked through.

The ResultSet

So far this chapter has focused on using automatically generated DataSets to work with data from a SQL Mobile database. This was generated by MSDataSetGenerator, which was the custom tool assigned to the NorthwindDataSet.xsd file. A much lighter-weight alternative is available via a SQLCeResultSet. A little-documented fact is that you can again get Visual Studio 2008 to do the heavy lifting by using the MSResultSetGenerator to automatically generate strongly typed result sets.

To create a ResultSet, begin as you would to create a DataSet — by adding a new `DataSource`. This will, in fact, add a DataSet to your solution, but this is a result of the MSDataSetGenerator being used instead of the MSResultSetGenerator. Once you have created the `DataSource`, select the XSD file in the Solution Explorer and bring up the Properties window. Change the custom tool property to be MSResultSetGenerator in order to update your solution to include a strongly typed ResultSet. Once generated, the ResultSet can be used much like the DataSet.

Windows Mobile APIs

The most recent versions of Windows Mobile have given mobile developers access to the next generation of APIs for accessing device information. The improvements include managed APIs for existing functionality as well as a Notification Broker that enables developers to tap into system events. This section shows you how you can get started with these APIs.

To access the Windows Mobile managed APIs, you need to add references to the WindowsMobile assemblies. You can do this using the Add Reference item from the project's right-click context menu off the Solution Explorer. Seven assemblies are listed with the prefix Microsoft.WindowsMobile in the .NET tab of the Add Reference dialog. The functionality can be broken down according to the namespaces that are included (with the exception of the DirectX library, which for the sake of brevity is not included here).

Configuration

The configuration namespace includes a single class, the `ConfigurationManager`, which is used to test and process an XML configuration file that can be used to configure a device. For example, the following code adds the Microsoft web site to the list of favorites:

```
Imports Microsoft.WindowsMobile
Imports System.Xml
Public Class Form1
    Private Sub configurationExample(ByVal sender As System.Object, _
                                     ByVal e As System.EventArgs) _
                                              Handles SampleButton.Click
        Dim configDoc As XmlDocument = New XmlDocument()
        configDoc.LoadXml( _
            "<wap-provisioningdoc>" + _
            "<characteristic type=""BrowserFavorite"">" + _
```

```
            "<characteristic type=""Microsoft"">" + _
            "<parm name=""URL"" value=""http://www.microsoft.com""/>" + _
            "</characteristic>" + _
            "</characteristic>" + _
            "</wap-provisioningdoc>" _
            )
        Configuration.ConfigurationManager.ProcessConfiguration(configDoc, False)

    End Sub
End Class
```

In addition to the `ProcessConfiguration` method, which applies changes on the device, there is also a `TestConfiguration` method that can be used to validate a particular configuration file without any impact on the device on which the code is being run.

Forms

The Forms namespace has managed wrappers for three forms that can be used to collect an image from a camera (`CameraCaptureDialog`), select a contact (`ChooseContactDialog`), and select an image (`SelectPictureDialog`). The following code snippet makes use of each of the dialogs:

```
Imports Microsoft.WindowsMobile
Public Class Form1
    Private Sub Example(ByVal sender As System.Object, _
                        ByVal e As System.EventArgs) Handles SampleButton.Click

        Dim camera As New Forms.CameraCaptureDialog
        camera.Mode = Forms.CameraCaptureMode.Still
        camera.StillQuality = Forms.CameraCaptureStillQuality.High
        camera.Title = "Get me a picture!!!"
        If camera.ShowDialog() = Windows.Forms.DialogResult.OK Then
            MsgBox("Photo taken.....stored as" & camera.FileName)
        End If

        Dim picture As New Forms.SelectPictureDialog
        picture.CameraAccess = True
        picture.SortOrder = Forms.SortOrder.DateDescending
        If picture.ShowDialog() = Windows.Forms.DialogResult.OK Then
            MsgBox("Found that picture - " & picture.FileName)
        End If

        Dim contact As New Forms.ChooseContactDialog
        contact.RequiredProperties = New PocketOutlook.ContactProperty() _
                                    {PocketOutlook.ContactProperty.Email1Address}
        contact.ChooseContactOnly = True
        If contact.ShowDialog Then
            MsgBox("Contact selected - " & contact.SelectedContactName)
        End If
    End Sub
End Class
```

PocketOutlook

The PocketOutlook namespace includes a series of classes that make sending and receiving e-mail and SMS messages straightforward. As the following sample shows, writing an e-mail is as easy as starting an Outlook session, putting the e-mail together, and sending it:

```
Imports Microsoft.WindowsMobile
Public Class Form1
    Private Sub POOMExample(ByVal sender As System.Object, _
                            ByVal e As System.EventArgs) Handles
SampleButton.Click
        Using poom As New PocketOutlook.OutlookSession
            Dim email As New PocketOutlook.EmailMessage
            email.To.Add(New PocketOutlook.Recipient("destination@randomaccount.com"))
            email.Subject = "Sample Email"
            email.BodyText = "This email contains sample text to show how easy
email is..."
            poom.EmailAccounts(0).Send(email)
        End Using
    End Sub
End Class
```

Status

The Status namespace contains a wealth of information about the status of the device, including static attributes, such as whether there is a camera on the device, and dynamic attributes, such as the ActiveSync status. The following example shows how these two attributes can be queried:

```
Imports Microsoft.WindowsMobile
Public Class Form1
    Private Sub StatusExample(ByVal sender As System.Object, _
                              ByVal e As System.EventArgs) Handles
SampleButton.Click
        If Status.SystemState.ActiveSyncStatus = _
                Status.ActiveSyncStatus.Synchronizing Then _
                        MsgBox("Active sync is synchronising now, don't go away!")
        If Status.SystemState.CameraPresent = True Then _
                        MsgBox("There is a camera, why not take a photo")
    End Sub
End Class
```

You can also query entries using the RegistryState class in this namespace.

Telephony

The Telephony namespace contains a single class, Phone, which has a single static method called Talk, which can be used to initiate a phone call. An optional parameter, showPrompt, determines whether the user is prompted to proceed with the call or not. In the following code, the user is not prompted before the call is initiated:

```
Imports Microsoft.WindowsMobile
Public Class Form1
    Private Sub TelephonyExample(ByVal sender As System.Object, _
                                    ByVal e As System.EventArgs) _
                                            Handles SampleButton.Click

        Dim t As New Telephony.Phone
        t.Talk("0412413425", False)
    End Sub
End Class
```

The Notification Broker

One of the significant improvements in Windows Mobile 5.0 and above is the Notification Broker, which can be used to notify an application of a particular system event. This may be a change in any of the status states or it may be an incoming SMS or e-mail. The following example shows how you can register your application to intercept an SMS containing a particular string (in this case, "::"). If an incoming SMS is found to contain this string, the application is notified via the appropriate event handler and given an opportunity to process the SMS, after which the SMS is deleted. The other InterceptionAction is to just notify the application, without deleting the SMS after processing:

```
Imports Microsoft.WindowsMobile.PocketOutlook
Imports Microsoft.WindowsMobile.PocketOutlook.MessageInterception

Public Class Form1
    'Create the Interceptor
    Dim SMSProcessor As New MessageInterceptor( _
                                    InterceptionAction.NotifyAndDelete, True)
    Private Sub NotificationExample(ByVal sender As System.Object, _
                                    ByVal e As System.EventArgs) _
                                            Handles SampleButton.Click

        'Define the search condition, in this case must contain ::
        Dim msgCondition As New MessageCondition()
        msgCondition.Property = MessageProperty.Body
        msgCondition.ComparisonType = MessagePropertyComparisonType.Contains
        msgCondition.ComparisonValue = "::"
        SMSProcessor.MessageCondition = msgCondition

        'Attach an event handler
        AddHandler SMSProcessor.MessageReceived, _
                                    AddressOf SMSProcessor_MessageReceived
    End Sub

    'Event handler for when a matching SMS is received
    Private Sub SMSProcessor_MessageReceived _
                    (ByVal sender As Object, ByVal e As MessageInterceptorEventArgs)
        Dim theSMS As SmsMessage = CType(e.Message, SmsMessage)
        MsgBox("Message: " & theSMS.Body)
        Me.BringToFront()
    End Sub
End Class
```

Note that there is a trick to writing these types of SMS-intercepting applications using the emulators. Some of the emulators have built-in radio stacks, which means that they can simulate sending and receiving SMS messages. If you want to test the SMS interceptor, you can send an SMS, using Pocket Outlook or another application on the emulator, to the emulator's built-in test number, which is +1 425 001 0001. The SMS is delayed so that it doesn't appear immediately, enabling you to navigate back to your application if you need to.

Summary

This chapter introduced you to building device applications using Visual Studio 2008. Desktop developers will feel right at home with the familiar environment and all the necessary tools at hand to rapidly build, test, and deploy a mobile application. As you have seen, you can build quite complex mobile applications using Visual Studio 2008. The data-binding capabilities, combined with the rich functionality provided in the Windows Mobile APIs, enable you to harness the power of these devices.

Over the next several years, you are going to see a massive growth in mobile technologies as the lines dividing mobile phones, cameras, PDAs, laptops, and tablets begin to fade. Soon you will be writing applications that can reside on a device of any form factor, have the capability to record and display data, and can access an arbitrary set of device-specific features, such as the ability to take a photo or make a phone call. With Visual Studio 2008, you are able to start the journey and begin developing for what will become the devices of the future.

35

WPF Applications

The Windows Presentation Foundation (WPF) is one of the most significant pieces of technology to be released when it comes to building rich user interface applications. Unlike previous revisions of Windows Forms, WPF has been written entirely from the ground up to make use of vector graphics and overcome some of the limitations so often encountered with Windows Forms development.

This chapter won't attempt to cover in any detail the WPF framework. Instead, what you will see is an overview of Visual Studio 2008 capabilities to help you rapidly build user interfaces.

Getting Started

As with all other types of applications that you can build with Visual Studio 2008, the place to start is the New Project dialog. In the past, support for WPF required the installation of additional tooling that bolted onto Visual Studio 2005. As you can see from the New Project dialog in Figure 35-1, a number of built-in project types for WPF ship with Visual Studio 2008: WPF Application, WPF Browser Application, WPF Custom Control Library, and WPF User Control Library.

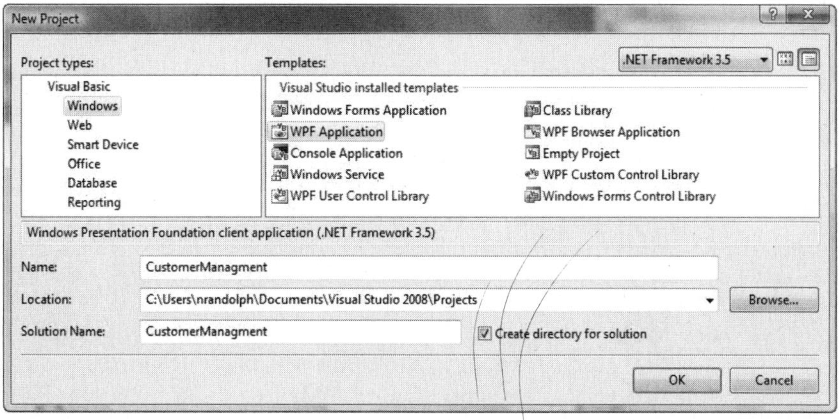

Figure 35-1

You will notice that these projects are for the most part a direct parallel to the Windows Forms equivalent. The exception is the WPF Browser Application, which will generate an XBAP application, which uses the browser as the container for your rich client application. Although you still need the .NET Framework v3.5 installed on the user's computer, the user can now run an XBAP application via either Internet Explorer or Firefox.

In this case we will work with a WPF Application, but most of the features of Visual Studio 2008 discussed herein apply equally to the other project types. As with other application types, when you select a WPF Application, Visual Studio 2008 goes ahead and prepares a new project (and new solution if specified) with the appropriate file structure. In this respect there is nothing unique to WPF and it makes use of the same project template system discussed in Chapter 10. The end result should look similar to Figure 35-2.

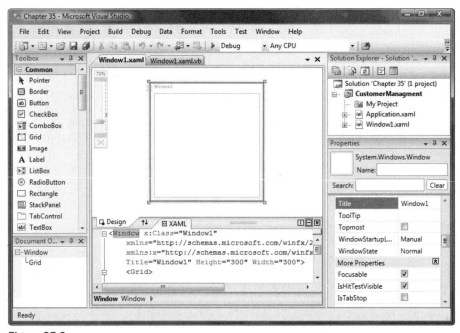

Figure 35-2

Here you can see that the project structure consists of an Application.xaml and a Window1.xaml. In fact these both have associated code-behind files, Application.xaml.vb and Window1.xaml.vb, which you can view if you expand out the relevant project items. At this stage the Application.xaml contains a single Application xaml element, which is used to define the StartupUri, in this case Window1.xaml. For those familiar with Windows Forms, this is the equivalent of the startup form. You can either set this manually in the XAML code or use the project properties dialog. In fact for the most part the project properties dialog is the same as for any Windows Forms application, allowing you to define settings, resources, and other properties.

Working around the layout of Figure 35-2, you can see that the familiar Toolbox tool window, attached to the left side of the screen, has been populated with WPF controls that are similar to what you would be used to when building a Windows Forms application. Below this window, still on the left side, is the

Document Outline tool window. As with both Windows Forms and Web Applications, this gives you a hierarchical view of the elements on the current window. Selecting any of these nodes in this window will highlight the appropriate control in the main editor window, making it easier to navigate more complex documents. An interesting feature of the Document Outline when working with WPF is that as you hover over an item you will get a mini-preview of the control. This will help you identify the correct control.

If the Document Outline or any other tool window is not visible, it might be collapsed against one of the edges. Alternatively you may need to force it to be displayed by selecting it from the View menu.

Across on the other side of Figure 35-2 is the Properties tool window. However, this window has been reworked to provide a richer experience when editing WPF windows and controls. Lastly, in the middle of the screen, is of course the main editor space, which is currently split so as to show both the visual layout of the window and the XAML code that defines the layout.

WPF Designer

The new designer that has been created for working with WPF windows and controls has a number of unique features that will aid you in building rich user interface applications. Let's just examine in more detail the main editor window mentioned earlier. Figure 35-3 isolates this window so you can see in more detail the various components.

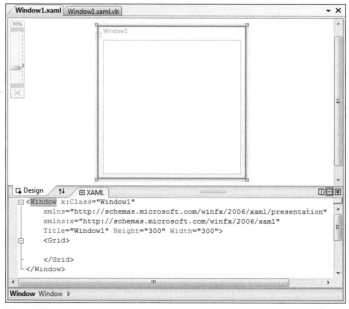

Figure 35-3

First you will notice that the window is clearly split into a visual designer at the top and a code window at the bottom. If you prefer the other way around you can simply click on the up/down arrows between the Design and XAML tabs. In Figure 35-3 the second icon in on the right side is highlighted to indicate that the screen is being split horizontally. Selecting the icon to its left will instead split the screen vertically.

If you prefer not to work in split screen mode, you can double-click either the Design or XAML tab. This will make the relevant tab fill the entire editor window, as shown in Figure 35-4. To return to split screen mode you just need to click the Expand Pane icon, which is the first icon in on the right of the splitter bar.

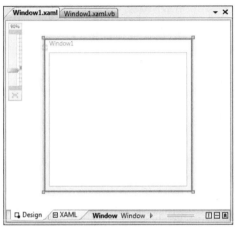

Figure 35-4

In Figure 35-4 you can clearly see the zoom control in the visual designer portion of the editor space. With the increased sophistication of the WPF designer, it can be really difficult to make precise changes with the window at 10 percent. The zoom control allows you to easily zoom in or out on the windows or control being edited. In this case the screen is zoomed out to 90 percent. There is a dark mark where 100 percent is on the zoom scale and the button at the bottom of the zoom control allows you to easily zoom the control so that it fits in the current window with a minimal amount of white space surrounding it.

The last thing worth noting is the cookie-crumb tracker that is at the bottom of the visual designer window, to the right of the Design and XAML tabs. In this case it only has the single Window element, but you will see that as we add more elements to the window this feature will become quite useful in determining the current control hierarchy.

Manipulating Controls

As you will see as you start to work with the WPF designer, there are areas where it is much better than the Windows Forms designer. One such area is in the ability to manipulate controls. Figure 35-5 shows the rules that are added when you resize a control.

Figure 35-5

By default the Windows1.xaml was created with a single grid element. Before you commence adding elements you might want to define some rows and columns, which can be used to control the layout of other controls. To do this, select the grid by selecting in the blank area in the middle of the window, selecting the relevant node from the Document Outline tool window, or selecting the corresponding grid element in the xaml file itself.

> *Although the Grid control provides the most flexibility in laying out your controls, there are occasions when a different layout pattern is required. Other layout panels include the StackPanel, DockPanel, and FlowPanel.*

When the grid element is selected, a border appears around the top and left edges of the grid, highlighting both the actual area occupied by the grid and the relative sizing of each of the rows and columns, as shown in Figure 35-6. This figure currently shows a grid with two rows and two columns. Additional rows or columns can be added by simply clicking at a location within the border.

Figure 35-6

Once added, the row or column markers can be selected and dragged to get the correct sizing, as shown in Figure 35-6 with the column that is being repositioned. You will notice that when you are initially placing the markers you won't get any sizing indicators until you have actually placed the marker. Unfortunately, if you then want to remove a marker, you will need to remove the appropriate element from the XAML file.

In Figure 35-7 you can see that a number of new rows have been added, which will be used to align the children controls. The left image shows the textbox that has been added to the right cell as it is positioned within the cell. You can see that the bottom of the text in the textbox is aligned with the text in the label in the left-hand cell. Once you have positioned the textbox you will see different indicators, as seen in the right image, which indicate how the control will be stretched as the parent control is resized. In this case the control is anchored to the left, top, and bottom. Clicking the small circle to the right of the textbox will toggle it to the same small triangle that is on the other three sides, and in doing so, will anchor the textbox to the right.

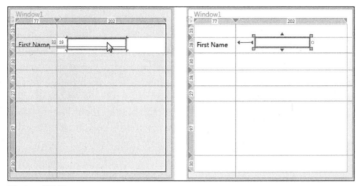

Figure 35-7

Properties and Events

As you can see, the visual indicators allow you to do quite a bit of control layout and positioning using the designer. However, there are always going to be times when you want more control. Instead of immediately dropping into the XAML file, you can use the Properties tool window instead. The WPF Properties window has been given a bit of a facelift, as shown on the right of Figure 35-8.

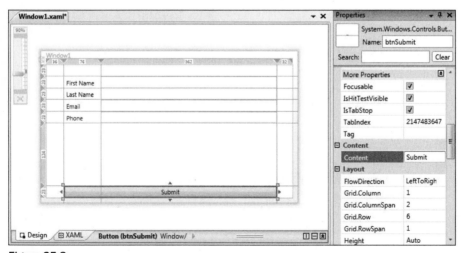

Figure 35-8

From Figure 35-8, the most noticeable feature of the Properties tool window is the new header area. In the Properties tool window for Windows Forms development, you normally have a selector that allows you to specify the control you want to set the properties for. Here, that option, despite being quite useful, has been dropped in favor of providing a small visual guide to the control and its name. Also absent from the Properties is the ability to switch between group and alphabetic sort order — the only saving grace is the search function introduced into the header area.

If you have not had the opportunity to work with WPF, one of the differences that you need to overcome is that there is no longer a Text property. Instead it has been effectively replaced by a Content property. In the case of a button, a label, or a textbox, you can for the most part treat this as you would the Text property for a Windows Forms control. However, the distinction is that the Content property can in fact accept any WPF element, allowing almost limitless ability to customize the layout of a control without necessarily having to create a custom control.

Because we have gotten the first pass of a form that can accept a customer's name and contact details, we just need to add some functionality to the Submit button. As you would expect, you can double-click the button control to automatically create the appropriate event handler. Once created, if you want to navigate from the XAML definition of the control through to the corresponding event handler, you can select the Navigate to Event Handler item from the right-click shortcut menu, as shown in Figure 35-9.

Figure 35-9

For VB.NET developers, double-clicking the button control will wire up the event using the Handles syntax. This is unfortunate because it then breaks the Navigate to Event Handler shortcut.

Styling Your Application

Although the WPF designer built into Visual Studio 2008 provides a significant amount of functionality for laying out controls, you will find that it really only supports a small subset of the full capabilities of WPF. You will also note that there are significant limitations in the Properties tool windows, such as the inability to be able to select a font from an existing list, that make it hard to be effective when building WPF user interfaces. To overcome these limitations it is recommended that you use a complementary product called Expression Blend (Blend). Because both Blend and Visual Studio 2008 share a common solution format, it is easy to work between the two products, making design changes in Blend and programmatic changes in Visual Studio. Figure 35-10 shows the same solution open within Blend.

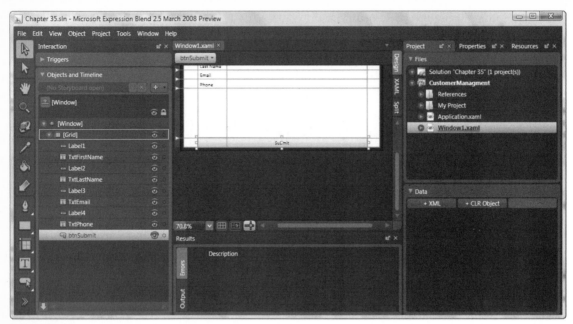

Figure 35-10

You will notice in Figure 35-10 that this is Expression Blend 2.5 March 2008 Preview. At the time of writing the next version of Blend was in beta, so there may be some minor variations between the content herein and the final product.

To demonstrate how you can use Blend to style your application, let's examine how you can apply a template to the Submit button that is at the bottom of the window. Start by right-clicking the btnSubmit element in the Objects and Timeline tool window, as shown in Figure 35-11.

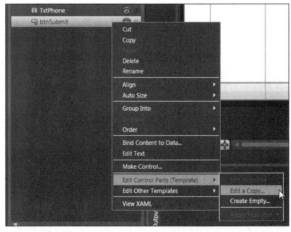

Figure 35-11

In the next dialog you can keep the default Name, but change where the template is defined by selecting New and accepting the prompts to create a new resource dictionary for the application. Once this is done, you will see that a new ResourceDictionary1.xaml file has been added to your project (this will automatically be picked up by Visual Studio 2008 when you go back to it in a couple of minutes), and it has been opened for editing with the initial button layout, as shown in Figure 35-12.

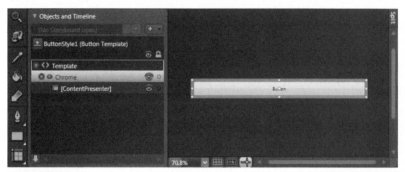

Figure 35-12

You are going to replace the default "Chrome" with a flat style layout. To do this, select the [ContentPresenter] node and copy it to the clipboard by right-clicking and selecting Copy. Then delete the Chrome node. Because you are going to add a rectangle, which will be your background, and then the [ContentPresenter], you are going to want a grid, so double-click the Grid icon, which is the bottom icon on Figure 35-12. This will add the grid to the main area of the template. Next double-click the Grid item in the Objects and Timelines tool window to make sure it has focus, before double-clicking the Rectangle icon (second from the bottom) to add a rectangle. The last item to be added is the [ContentPresenter] you copied earlier. You can do this by right-clicking the Grid node and selecting Paste. Once you have done this, you will have something similar to Figure 35-13.

Figure 35-13

Clearly this needs to be tidied up by stretching the rectangle to cover the entire width of the button template. You can also modify the shape by selecting the corner handles and rotating. Figure 35-14 illustrates how you can round the corners by selecting just inside the corner. This can be a bit fiddly to get right because you can only perform this operation when the mouse is in the correct location. The easiest way is to slowly move the mouse around the vicinity of the corner until it changes the cursor to that shown in Figure 35-14.

Figure 35-14

The last thing you are going to do to the button is add a splash of color. To do this you use the Brushes tool window, typically on the right side of the screen, as shown in Figure 35-15. In this figure a gradient has already been applied across the button by first selecting the gradient brush (the middle icon right beneath the `OpacityMask` property) and then selecting appropriate colors for the gradient.

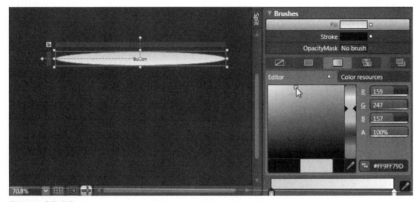

Figure 35-15

Once you are happy with the changes you have made, you can simply save what you have done and return to Visual Studio 2008. You will be prompted to reload the project because Blend added the resource dictionary, but once this is done you should be able to open the window you were working on, with the end result looking something like Figure 35-16 (better if you have more of an artistic streak).

Figure 35-16

Windows Forms Interoperability

Up until now you have seen how you can build a WPF application that consists of a single window. However, it is unlikely that you are going to be able to migrate any existing applications across to WPF in one go. From the experience of trying to convince people to upgrade from VB6 to .NET using a "big-bang" approach, Microsoft has acknowledged that few organizations are likely to accept this as a viable upgrade path. So Microsoft has provided bi-directional interoperability support between WPF and Windows Forms applications through what is colloquially called Crossbow. In essence this is really about providing a hosting element with a Windows Forms application so that a WPF control can be inserted. Let's show this with a bit of an example based on the work you have done so far.

To begin with, let's create a WPF control that contains the same controls and layout as the window you have been working with so far. From the Add New Item dialog (see Figure 35-17), select the User Control (WPF) item. This will add the XAML and xaml.vb files necessary to create a WPF user control. If you examine the XAML you will see that it is essentially the same as the original XAML for the window we started with at the beginning of the chapter except that the root XAML element is UserControl instead of Window.

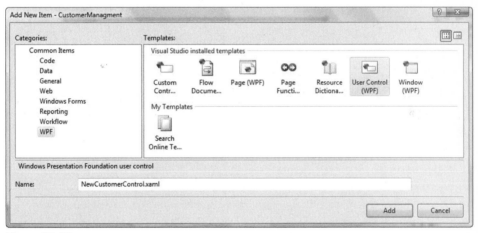

Figure 35-17

To copy the control layout across from the window into the user control, you can either select the controls in the designer or just select the relevant XAML. In this case you want to copy across the entire contents of the grid element. Because the Windows Forms application will be providing the Submit button, you can remove that and you can resize the rows and columns so that the new control looks like Figure 35-18.

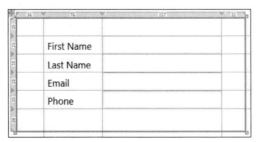

Figure 35-18

Because you are going to be hosting this control in a Windows Forms application, you will need to create a new project to contain the host application. In this case you are going to create a new project, Customers, based on the Visual Basic Windows Forms Application project template. The first thing you need to do is to reference your existing WPF project. Right-click the new Windows Forms project and select Add Reference. From the Projects tab select the WPF project and click OK to proceed.

In Figure 35-19 you can see that there is a WPF Interoperability tab in the Toolbox, under which there is a single item called the ElementHost. This is the control that you will be using to host the WPF control you have just created. Drag this onto the form, as shown in the visual designer of Figure 35-19, and you will see that there is a smart tag that prompts you to select the WPF control that you want to be hosted. Note that you may need to build your project in order for the WPF control from the referenced project to appear in the drop-down.

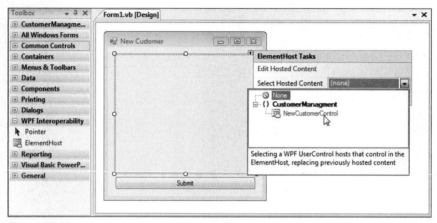

Figure 35-19

Once you have selected the WPF control to host, added a Submit button, and tidied up the form, you now need a way to interact with the WPF control so as to extract the new customer data when the Submit button is clicked. To do this you will use DataBinding, which is one of the most powerful features of WPF. Here you will bind a simple customer class, created in the Windows Forms application, to the WPF control you created earlier. You will need to go ahead and add a new class in the Windows Forms project called Customer with four string properties, FirstName, LastName, Email, and Phone.

You can now bind the Customer class directly to the WPF control that you have already built, with only minor changes to take advantage of the built-in data-binding capabilities in WPF. In the control XAML you just need to add the Text attribute with the Binding Path syntax in the following snippet:

```
<TextBox Grid.Row="1" Name="TxtFirstName" Grid.Column=."2"
        Text="{Binding Path=FirstName}"/>
<TextBox Grid.Row="2" Name="TxtLastName" Grid.Column="2"
        Text="{Binding Path=LastName}"/>
<TextBox Grid.Row="3" Name="TxtEmail" Grid.Column="2"
        Text="{Binding Path=Email}"/>
<TextBox Grid.Row="4" Name="TxtPhone" Grid.Column="2"
        Text="{Binding Path=Phone}"/>
```

In this snippet you can see that the Binding Path has been set to the corresponding property name. At runtime the WPF control will do all the heavy lifting between a customer object and the textboxes. The last thing you need to do is to specify what customer you are binding to. This is done dynamically at runtime by setting the `DataContext` property on the WPF control:

```
Private mNewCustomer As Customer
Private Sub Form1_Load(ByVal sender As Object,
                        ByVal e As System.EventArgs) Handles Me.Load
    mNewCustomer = New Customer
    CType(Me.hostCustomer.Child, CustomerManagment.NewCustomerControl)
.DataContext = mNewCustomer
End Sub
```

Finally, you need to add the event handler for the "Submit" button:

```
Private Sub btnSubmit_Click(ByVal sender As Object, ByVal e As System.EventArgs)
Handles btnSubmit.Click
    MsgBox(String.Format("Adding the new customer '{0} {1}' with email address
{2} and phone number {3}", mNewCustomer.FirstName, _
                        mNewCustomer.LastName, _
                        mNewCustomer.Email, _
                        mNewCustomer.Phone))
    'Call webservice or WCF service to add the new customer or kick off a workflow
    'AddCustomerService()
End Sub
```

Summary

In this chapter you have seen how you can work with Visual Studio 2008 to build applications with the Windows Presentation Foundation. In addition to being able to easily style an application, similar to the way CSS allows styling of a web application, you can also integrate WPF components into existing applications.

WCF and WF Applications

In the last chapter you saw an overview of Windows Presentation Foundation (WPF), which you can use to build the user interface for your applications. Now you'll see how you can use Visual Studio 2008 to work with the Windows Communication Foundation (WCF) and the Windows Workflow Foundation (WF). Released in conjunction with WPF as part of version 3.0 of the .NET Framework, WCF provides a consistent interface for working across a variety of communication technologies, while WF provides a solid platform for building workflow applications.

Windows Communication Foundation

Within the .NET Framework there are a variety of ways that you can communicate among applications, such as Remoting, Web Services, and a myriad of networking protocols. This has often frustrated application developers who not only had to pick the appropriate technology to use, but also had to write plumbing code that would allow their applications to use different technologies depending on the runtime environment. For example, when users are connected directly to the intranet it is better for them to use a Remoting or direct TCP/IP connection. However, this would cause security issues if done from outside the corporate firewall, in which case a secured web service would be preferable, despite being slower.

The Windows Communication Foundation (WCF) provides a uniform way to build messaging applications that are technology-agnostic. Clearly there will still be application requirements, such as that the message should be set asynchronously, or that a return value is expected, or that the message should or should not be part of a transaction. However, WCF abstracts the choice of technology away from the application so that it can be defined at runtime via configuration files.

Without going into too much detail, since one could write an entire book on WCF alone, there are three main components in a WCF service: the A(ddress), B(inding) and C(ontract) of WCF. In the context of a traditional web service, the address would be the web service URL, the binding would be SOAP, and the contract would be the web service method signature. This is a very simplistic interpretation of these three components, and as you start to work with WCF you will see that it really is a powerful communication framework.

You will see through the following example how you can use the visual designers in Visual Studio 2008 to define the ABCs of WCF for a particular service. Let's start by creating a new WCF project using the Visual Basic WCF Service Library template, as shown in Figure 36-1.

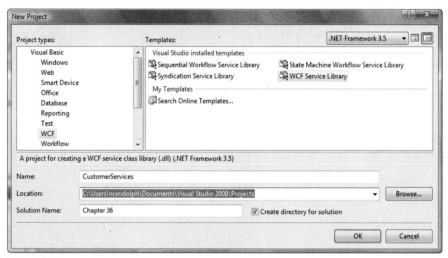

Figure 36-1

If you look in the Web folder, you will see that there is also a WCF Service Application template that allows you to define a WCF service that is already configured to be hosted within an ASP.NET web application. Doing this is a lot like creating a more traditional ASP.NET web service application, except that it uses the WCF framework.

By default, a new WCF Service Library will include IService1.vb and Service1.vb, which define the interface and the implementation of a basic service, respectively. We will start by replacing the contents of IService1.vb with the following code:

```vb
<ServiceContract()> _
Public Interface IService1

    <OperationContract()> _
    Function CreateNewCustomer(ByVal c As Customer) As Guid

End Interface

<DataContract()> _
Public Class Customer
    Private mFirstName As String
    Private mLastName As String
    Private mEmail As String
    Private mPhone As String
    <DataMember()> _
    Public Property Phone() As String
        Get
            Return mPhone
```

```
            End Get
            Set(ByVal value As String)
                mPhone = value
            End Set
        End Property
        <DataMember()> _
        Public Property Email() As String
            Get
                Return mEmail
            End Get
            Set(ByVal value As String)
                mEmail = value
            End Set
        End Property
        <DataMember()> _
        Public Property LastName() As String
            Get
                Return mLastName
            End Get
            Set(ByVal value As String)
                mLastName = value
            End Set
        End Property
        <DataMember()> _
        Public Property FirstName() As String
            Get
                Return mFirstName
            End Get
            Set(ByVal value As String)
                mFirstName = value
            End Set
        End Property
    End Class
```

What you can see from this code is that we are defining a service called IService1 (we will rename it in a minute) that exposes the operation CreateNewCustomer. IService1 and CreateNewCustomer are identified by the ServiceContract and OperationContract attributes, respectively. In addition, there is a Customer class that is marked with a DataContract attribute and that contains properties marked with the DataMember attribute. This class represents, as the attribute name suggests, a data contract that is to be shared, along with the service contract, between the caller and the service. In this case, the class will be used to marshal the argument for the CreateNewCustomer method call from the caller into the service.

Although this is not strictly required, we recommend that you keep your data contract classes separate from your other application classes and that you use them only for passing data in and out of services. This way you minimize the dependencies between your application and the services that it exposes or calls.

In Service1.vb you will also have to replace the initial code with the appropriate implementation of IService1. For simplicity, we are just going to return a new GUID that might represent the ID of the customer once he or she has been approved and added to the company database.

```
Public Class Service1
    Implements IService1

    Public Function CreateNewCustomer(ByVal c As Customer) _
                            As Guid Implements IService1.CreateNewCustomer
        'for the moment return a new guid to indicate the id of the added customer
        Return Guid.NewGuid
    End Function
End Class
```

With these changes made, build and run the WCF Service Library. Unlike a normal class library, a WCF Service Library can be "run," because Visual Studio 2008 ships with the WcfSvcHost utility. This is an application that can be used to host WCF services for the purpose of debugging. Figure 36-2 shows this utility appearing in the taskbar.

Figure 36-2

As the balloon in Figure 36-2 indicates, clicking the balloon or the taskbar icon will bring up a dialog showing more information about the service that is running. In actuality, this dialog will not be very informative about a correctly running WCF service, but as you will see later, when the service doesn't start correctly the dialog can help you work out what is going wrong.

As part of running the WCF Service Library, in addition to hosting your WCF service Visual Studio 2008 also launches the WCF Test Client utility, as you can see in Figure 36-3. This utility automatically detects the running services and provides a simple tree representation of them and their corresponding operations.

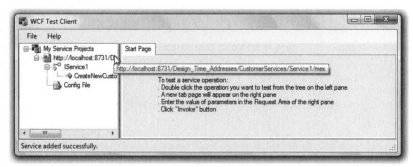

Figure 36-3

When you click a service operation you will see that the tab on the right-hand side of the dialog changes to indicate request and response values. Unlike the very basic test page for ASP.NET Web Services, the WCF Test Client can help you simulate calls to relatively complex WCF Services. In Figure 36-4, you can see that in the Request section the input argument, c, has been broken down into its respective elements — Email, FirstName, LastName, and Phone, as defined by the DataMember attributes seen earlier. You can edit any of these elements via this dialog before hitting the "Invoke" button. Figure 36-4 also shows that any return value will be displayed in a similar layout in the Response section of the tab.

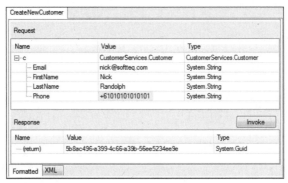

Figure 36-4

If you are trying to isolate an issue, it may be important to see exactly what information is traveling down the wire for each service request. You can do this using third-party tools such as Fiddler, but for a simple XML representation of what was sent and received you can simply click the XML tab. Figure 36-5 shows the body XML for both the request and the response. You will notice that, particularly for the response, there is a lot of additional XML that can significantly degrade the performance of the service request.

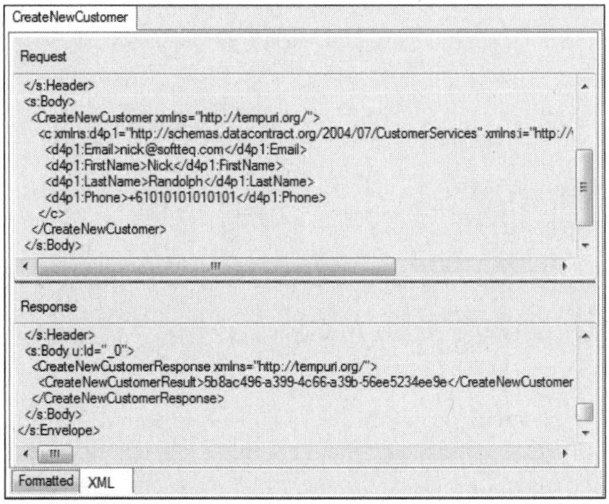

Figure 36-5

At this stage, we still have a service contact called IService1. In the interest of writing more maintainable and understandable code, we should go ahead and rename this ICustomerService, and rename the corresponding implementation CustomerService. To do this, select the IService1.vb item in the Solution Explorer tool window, press F2, and rename the file. This will not only rename the file but also the interface name and any other references. Repeat this procedure with Service1.vb.

You read earlier about the ABCs of WCF services. Well, the interface class with the `ServiceContract` attributes defines the service contract. The remaining elements, `Address` and `Binding`, are defined in the application configuration file, which is used by the WCF runtime when it exposes the service. In the previous step where you renamed the service interface, you will have broken the application configuration, as it is now referencing a nonexistent service contract, IService1. To fix this you can use the new WCF Service Configuration Editor. This editor can be launched from the Tools ➪ WCF Service Configuration Editor menu item. After selecting this menu item you will have to browse to open the app. config file in your WCF Service Library. Alternatively, you can right-click the app.config file in the Solution Explorer and select Edit WCF Configuration. In either case, a configuration editor will be launched that looks similar to what is shown in Figure 36-6.

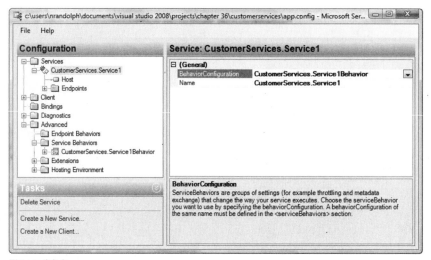

Figure 36-6

The items that you need to change are:

- Services — CustomerServices.Service1: Change `Name` to CustomerServices.CustomerService

- Services — CustomerServices.CustomerService — Host: Change `BaseAddress` to `http://localhost:90/CustomerServices/CustomerService/`

- Services — CustomerServices.CustomerService — Endpoints — (Empty Name) (first item): Change `Contact` to CustomerServices.ICustomerService

- Advanced — Service Behaviors — CustomerServices.Service1Behavior: Change `Name` to CustomerServices.CustomerServiceBehavior

Essentially, all you have done here is fix the application configuration file to use the adjusted service contact and change the address to use a different port and base directory. Now when you run the WCF

Service it will have the correct configuration information to be able to configure the necessary WCF service endpoints. Depending on your computer configuration you may end up with the WCF Service Host (which you were introduced to earlier when it was running silently in the taskbar), prompting you with an error relating to the registration of the URL you specified in the configuration file, as seen in Figure 36-7.

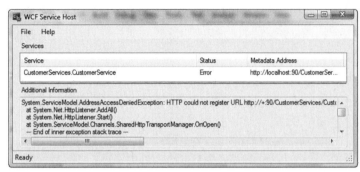

Figure 36-7

Although you can't see the full error message in Figure 36-7, there is actually a help URL that provides additional information on how you can resolve this issue. The issue is a result of security policies on the computer that are preventing the WCF Service Host from registering the URL you have specified. In this case, you can resolve this by executing the following command using an elevated permissions command prompt (i.e., while running as administrator).

```
netsh http add urlacl url=http://+:90/CustomerServices user=<username>
```

This command will allow the specified user to register URLs that match the URL prefix. When you again try to run your WCF Service Library, it should start successfully, and the WCF Test Client utility should be presented as before.

Consuming a WCF Service

Now that you have successfully created your WCF service, it is time to use it within an application. To do this, let's begin by adding the rich client application we built in Chapter 35. If you recall, this is a Windows Forms application that uses a WPF control bound to a `Customer` object. In order to add this application, you need to use the File ⇨ Add ⇨ Existing Project menu item to add first the WPF project, CustomerManagement, and then the Windows Forms project, Customers, to your solution.

The next thing is to add a reference to the WCF service to the Windows Forms application. Right-click the project node in the Solution Explorer tool window and select Add Service Reference. This will open the dialog shown in Figure 36-8, in which you can specify the WCF service you want to add a reference to. As you can see, there is a very convenient "Discover" button that you can use to quickly locate services contained within the current solution.

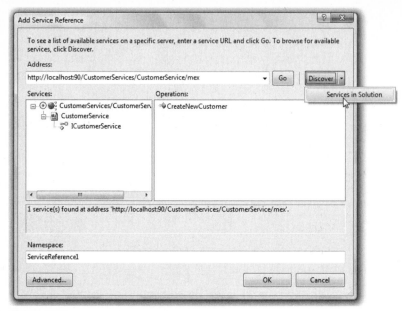

Figure 36-8

Select the ICustomerService node in the Services tree, change the namespace to CustomerServices, and press "OK" to complete the process of adding a service reference to your application. With this reference added, we simply need to modify the code of the "Submit" button so that it creates an instance of the WCF service and then calls the CreateNewCustomer operation. This is illustrated in the following code snippet.

```
Private Sub btnSubmit_Click(ByVal sender As Object, _
                            ByVal e As System.EventArgs)
    Handles btnSubmit.Click
      MsgBox(String.Format("Adding the new customer '{0} {1}'
    with email address {2} and phone number {3}",
    mNewCustomer.FirstName, mNewCustomer.LastName, _
                        mNewCustomer.Email,
    mNewCustomer.Phone))
      'Call webservice or WCF service to add the new customer
    or kick off a workflow
      Dim customerservice As New
    CustomerServices.CustomerServiceClient
      Dim serviceC = PopulaterServiceCustomer(mNewCustomer)
      Dim newCustomerId As Guid =
    customerservice.CreateNewCustomer(serviceC)
      MsgBox("New customer added with Id '" &
    newCustomerId.ToString & "'")
    End Sub

    Private Function PopulaterServiceCustomer(ByVal c As Customer) _
                                            As CustomerServices.Customer
        Dim serviceC As New CustomerServices.Customer
```

```
        serviceC.FirstName = c.FirstName
        serviceC.LastName = c.LastName
        serviceC.Email = c.Email
        serviceC.Phone = c.Phone
        Return serviceC
    End Function
```

You now have a rich client application that can be used to specify the details of a new customer, which will be passed to a WCF service. Although the WCF service currently simply returns a new GUID, it could potentially do data validation, request approval, and any other steps that are required before the insertion of a new customer record.

When you added a reference to the WCF service to your rich client application, you will have noticed that an app.config file was added to the project if it didn't already exist. In either case, if you take a look at this file you'll see that it now contains a `system.serviceModel` element that contains bindings and client elements. Within the bindings element you can see that there is a `wsHttpBinding` element — this is the default WCF binding, which defines how to communicate with the WCF service. Here you can see that the sub-elements override some of the default values. The other element, `Client`, contains an endpoint element. This element defines the `Address`, which in this case is a URL; `Binding`, which references the customized `wsHttpBinding` defined in the bindings element; and `Contract`, which is the CustomerServices.ICustomerService interface of the WCF service that is to be called. Because this information is all defined in the configuration file, if any of these elements changes (for example, the URL of the endpoint), instead of having to recompile the entire application you can just modify the configuration file.

Windows Workflow Foundation

Over time, organizations try to keep improving their internal processes for menial tasks such as expense reporting and timesheeting. This results in their defining a series of steps, or activities, that make up a process, or workflow. The Windows Workflow Foundation (WF) builds on this concept to allow the rapid development of such workflows. Although it has been built as an engine on which developers can build their own applications, there are already commercial products, such as Sharepoint, that make use of this engine to allow non-developers to build business workflows.

Again, we will not go into much detail about WF itself, instead providing a walkthrough of how you can get started with building a workflow application using Visual Studio 2008 and linking it with the WCF service you have just created. In this example, we will start by adding a new project based on the Sequential Workflow Console Application. As you can see in Figure 36-9, you have a number of different WF project types to choose from depending on whether you want a sequential or a state machine workflow, and whether you want a console application or workflow library. In this case we want a sequential workflow because we want a workflow that has a start, goes through a series of activities, and then ends, and we want a console application so that we don't have to worry about hosting the workflow. The console application template contains the necessary code to host the workflow, so we can focus on building the workflow itself.

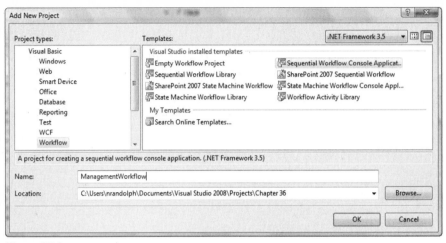

Figure 36-9

You will notice that once you have created the Workflow project the workflow designer appears in the main editor space. As you can see from Figure 36-10, the sequential workflow has a start (the green circle with a down arrow), an end (the red square with a white octagon), and a space in the middle where you can drop activities in order to form a workflow sequence.

Figure 36-10

As you can see from Figure 36-10, the WF team has done a lot of work to support the design-time experience of building workflows — so much so that you can actually host the WF designer within your application. This means that WF can be used not only for building predefined workflows for your application, but also to allow the users of your application to build workflows of their own, perhaps based on a subset of the WF activities that are specific to your application.

The metaphor for building workflows is very similar to that for building Windows or web applications using Visual Studio 2008. In the Toolbox are a series of activities, which you can drag across onto your workflow. At the top of the Toolbox is a tab (in Figure 36-11 this is the CustomerManagement tab) in which any activities that you have created, either from scratch or to override one of the default activities, will appear. The next tab shows the Windows Workflow v3.0 activities, which form the bulk of the standard activities and include many more that are not visible in Figure 36-11. Lastly are two tasks that have been included in Windows Workflow v3.5 and are the output of a project entitled Silver, which was created to make the integration between WF and WCF much simpler.

Figure 36-11

In our example, you are going to make use of one of the new WF v3.5 activities, sendActivity1, in order to call out to the WCF service you created earlier in the chapter. Once you have dragged this item from the Toolbox into the center of the workflow designer, you will see that it has appeared in the workflow as a new rounded rectangle, as shown in Figure 36-12. Although you can't see the colors here, in the top right-hand corner of this rectangle is a red circle with a white exclamation mark — this is a smart tag that, when you expand it, will indicate what you need to do in order to fix the validation error on the activity. In the case of the activity you just added in this example, it has failed to validate because you haven't defined a WCF service to call. If you click on the warning it will take you to the relevant property, in this case ServiceOperationInfo, in the Properties tool window for the sendActivity1 activity.

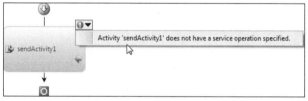

Figure 36-12

Before you can specify the WCF service created earlier, you must add a reference to the WCF service to this project. You can do this by selecting Add Service Reference from the Solution Explorer right-click shortcut menu. This will open the Add Service Reference window that you used earlier in this chapter to add the WCF service reference to the Windows Forms application. Again, you want to select Discover to locate the service in the current solution, then select the ICustomerService service and update the namespace to CustomerServices.

Now that you have a reference to the WCF service, you can use the Choose Operation dialog to select the WCF service for the sendActivity1 activity. You can open this dialog by selecting the ServiceOperationInfo property in the Properties tool window and then clicking the ellipsis button. Initially, the Choose Operation dialog will be empty, so you will have to click "Import" and then select the ICustomerService service from under the <Current Project> element in the Type tab. Once selected, this will populate the `ServiceOperationInfo` property in the Properties tool window, as you can see in Figure 36-13.

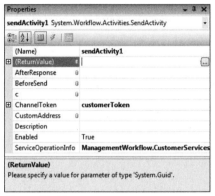

Figure 36-13

Having specified the `ServiceOperationInfo` property, you will notice that the validation error has not gone away. Instead, it is highlighting that you haven't specified a `ChannelToken`. In Figure 36-13 you can see that a channel token called `customerToken` has been defined. The name is irrelevant; what is important is the `EndpointName`. This name has to match the endpoint that was added to the app.config file when you added the reference to the WCF service to your workflow application. If you open this file you will see that there is an endpoint element (at system.serviceModel/client/endpoint) that contains a name attribute, most likely `WSHttpBinding_ICustomerService`. The `EndpointName` of the `ChannelToken` has to exactly match the name attribute so that the WCF service can be called by the workflow.

Now that we have fixed the validation errors, we can run this workflow. However, in order to make it useful we need a way of defining the customer to be set to the WCF service and a way of reporting on the return value, which in this case is the ID of the new customer. In Figure 36-13 you can see that there are properties for `(ReturnValue)` and for `c`, which is the input to the ICustomerService service. At this stage neither of these is bound to anything, which makes it hard for any other activity in the workflow to work with them. You will also notice that next to each property is a little icon indicating that it is capable of being bound. Using a concept called *dependency properties*, these properties can effectively be bound fields or properties of the workflow itself, making them accessible from any activity in the workflow. Start by double-clicking the binding icon next to the `c` property. This will open the dialog shown in Figure 36-14.

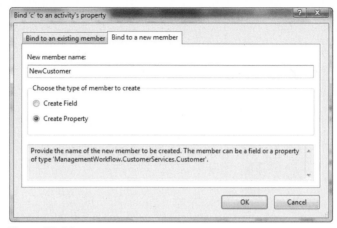

Figure 36-14

Although you can bind to an existing member, in this case we are going to define new properties for both the argument, c, and the return value. In Figure 36-14 you can see that we are defining a property called NewCustomer, which will be passed into the WCF service call. Similarly, we will also define a property called NewCustomerId as the return value from the call.

Now that we have these properties, which can be used by other activities in the workflow, we need additional activities that will be used to define the new customer and report the new customer ID. In our case we will use two instances of the codeActivity activity, but you could use any of the predefined activities or your own. Dragging these from the Toolbox and placing one on either side of the WCF service call activity will create a workflow similar to the one shown in Figure 36-15.

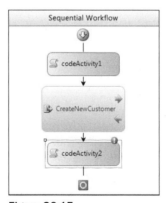

Figure 36-15

Again you will notice that there is a validation error on codeActivity2. This time we can simply double-click the activity, and it will fix the validation error by creating the necessary event handler for the ExecuteCode event. In the following code, we are creating a new customer in codeActivity1 that will be passed into the WCF service. Then, in codeActivity2, we are simply writing the return value out to the console.

```vbnet
Private Sub codeActivity1_ExecuteCode(ByVal sender As System.Object, _
                                  ByVal e As System.EventArgs)
    newCustomer = New CustomerServices.Customer
    newCustomer.FirstName = "Bob"
    newCustomer.LastName = "Jones"
    newCustomer.Email = "bob@random.com"
    newCustomer.Phone = "+61 011 011 100"
End Sub

Private Sub codeActivity2_ExecuteCode(ByVal sender As System.Object, _
                                  ByVal e As System.EventArgs)
    Console.WriteLine("Customer created with Id '" & NewCustomerId.ToString & "'")
End Sub
```

Before you go ahead and debug this application, you will want to make sure that both the WCF Service Library and the WF console application are launched, in that order. Do this by selecting Properties from the right-click shortcut menu on the Solution node in the Solution Explorer. On the Startup Project node select "Multiple startup projects" and set the Action on the WCF Service Library and WF Console application to Start. Also make sure that the WCF Service Library is higher on the list to ensure that it starts before the workflow application.

In addition to having a rich designer support for building workflows, WF also includes debugging capabilities. Figure 36-16 shows how you can define a breakpoint (set on both the code activities) and how the activity is highlighted when it is the current execution item. To define a breakpoint, simply select the activity and press F9, or select Insert Breakpoint from the right-click shortcut menu.

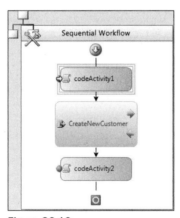

Figure 36-16

As in a normal debugging session, in a workflow you step through code using shortcut keys. Pressing F10 will step through the workflow, while F11 will step into the current activity. For example, in Figure 36-16 pressing F11 will drop in the code for the ExecuteCode event handler.

Summary

In this chapter you have seen an overview of the Windows Communication Foundation (WCF) and Windows Workflow Foundation (WF) in Visual Studio 2008. While this only skims the surface of the full potential of each of these technologies, you can see that Visual Studio 2008 can be used to rapidly build applications that consume and expose WCF services or contain WF workflows. Coupled with a rich WPF user interface, these technologies will forge a new generation of service-oriented applications.

Next Generation Web: Silverlight and ASP.NET MVC

There's no doubt that users are expecting richer and more sophisticated user interfaces in web applications. High-profile web applications such as Google Maps, Windows Live Local, and Gmail have captured the imagination of web developers and led to an increased interest in pushing the boundaries of what is possible to build using HTML.

Unfortunately, web applications that are as rich and functional as these are notoriously complex to build and maintain. The tangle of technologies that is used by these applications, such as Ajax, DHTML, and JavaScript, is such that you need specialist development expertise that focuses purely on client-side web technologies.

Silverlight solves this problem by bringing the managed code to client-side development. Silverlight is a cross-platform, cross-browser plug-in that includes a lightweight version of the .NET Framework and delivers advanced functionality such as vector graphics, animation, and streaming media.

At the same time that client-side demands have increased, the complexity of the ASP.NET code on the server side has also increased. Enter the ASP.NET MVC framework. ASP.NET MVC applies the Model-View-Controller (MVC) architectural pattern, which allows you to separate an application into three components: the Model, the View, and the Controller. This provides better testability of the front-end code and gives you full control over the behavior and output produced by your web application.

In this chapter, you learn how to build the next generation of web applications using Silverlight 2 and the ASP.NET MVC framework. In the first half of the chapter you walk through the process to build a new Silverlight component and integrate it into an existing web page. The second half explains the details and benefits of the Model-View-Controller pattern and shows you how to build a new ASP.NET MVC application.

This chapter covers products that were in beta at the time of writing. As such, some of the content and screenshots may have changed in subsequent releases. When the products are released in their final version, we will offer a download of the new version of this chapter at wrox.com. Just search for this book by the ISBN number 978-0-4702-2988-0, and look in the Chapter 37 folder under "errata."

Silverlight

The first version of Silverlight focused on delivering the fundamentals needed to build Rich Internet Applications (RIAs). This included support for the rendering of raster and vector graphics, text, and animation, tracking and handling input, and streaming media (both audio and video). In a Silverlight 1.0 application, the user interface is defined using the XAML markup language and JavaScript is used to initialize the Silverlight plug-in instance.

Silverlight exposes a DOM API to the browser, which allows JavaScript code to manipulate the Silverlight UI and respond to events. This provides an easy way for those familiar with JavaScript to build Silverlight applications. However, at the same time, you are limited to the interactions and functions that you can build with JavaScript.

Silverlight 2 is a significant upgrade to version 1.0 and enables you to build Silverlight applications, including the code that drives their UI, using managed code that runs under the CLR. It does not require end users to have a full version of the .NET Framework installed on their computers; in fact even if you have a full version of .NET installed it won't be used by Silverlight. Instead, when you install the Silverlight 2 runtime, it will install a lightweight version of the .NET Framework and base classes. Lightweight means that not every class that is available in the full version is included; however, a surprising number of classes are available given the small 4.3MB size of the runtime.

You can use any .NET language to build Silverlight 2 applications, including Visual Basic and C#. This provides cross-browser, cross-platform development of RIAs that leverages all the power of the .NET Framework.

Silverlight — Is It Really a Cross-Browser, Cross-Platform Solution?

Microsoft does not have the best track record for ensuring its technologies work on platforms other than Windows and Internet Explorer. So it would be understandable if you were skeptical about what Microsoft really means when it says Silverlight is "*cross-browser, cross-platform.*"

In this case the rhetoric is backed up by actions. At the time of writing, Microsoft had released the Silverlight 1.0 and 2.0 beta runtimes for both Windows and Mac. This enables support for IE, Firefox, and Safari on Windows, and Firefox and Safari on the Mac. Opera has also announced that it is working with Microsoft to build Silverlight support into its browser (at the time of writing it was *unofficially* available on Opera).

As for Linux, you may have heard of a project called Mono, which is an open-source implementation of the .NET Framework on Linux that is led by Novell. Microsoft has

---

made an agreement with Novell to officially support and provide assistance for an implementation of the Silverlight runtime on Linux. This has been named Moonlight, and will target both version 1.0 and 2.0 of Silverlight.

As for the mobile platform, Microsoft has announced upcoming support of the Silverlight 1.0 runtime for Windows Mobile 6. Nokia has also announced that it will build support for Silverlight into its S60 software running Symbian OS, as well as for Series 40 devices and Nokia Internet tablets.

Though there's not 100 percent coverage of all browsers and platforms, the most popular operating systems and browsers are fully supported. So you can deploy Silverlight with confidence that the vast majority of your potential audience will be able to access your web site.

Getting Started with Silverlight 2

To develop Silverlight applications using Visual Studio you will first need to install the Microsoft Silverlight Tools for Visual Studio 2008. You will find a link to this free download off the Silverlight community site at `http://silverlight.net/GetStarted/`. The download includes everything you need to build Silverlight applications, including project templates for Visual Basic and C#, IntelliSense and debugger support, and an SDK.

The Silverlight Tools for Visual Studio 2008 and the Silverlight 2 SDK were at Beta 1 release at the time of writing. At the start of this chapter are instructions on how you can obtain an updated version of this chapter once the final version of Silverlight 2 has been released.

The Silverlight Tools for Visual Studio download consists of an executable setup program called `silverlight_chainer.exe`. After you have downloaded and installed it, you will be able to create your first Silverlight application. Open Visual Studio and select File ⇨ New ⇨ Project to open the New Project dialog box. Under both Visual Basic and Visual C# in the project types, there will be a new entry called Silverlight, which is where the new templates can be found. Select the Silverlight Application project template under the C# project types and click OK.

Before the new project is created, Visual Studio will prompt you to create an HTML page to host the Silverlight application for testing. You can generate a new web site or web application project, or simply add a static HTML page to the Silverlight project. If you are adding the project to an existing solution that already contains a web project, you can choose to add an HTML page to that and have Visual Studio configure the necessary project references. For now, instruct Visual Studio to generate an HTML test page in this project as shown in Figure 37-1. Later in this chapter we look at how your Silverlight applications can be added to an existing ASP.NET Web Form.

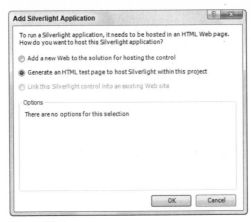

Figure 37-1

Once you click OK, Visual Studio will create the project and open the designer. If you've already read Chapter 35, then you'll immediately notice how similar Silverlight applications are to Windows Presentation Foundation applications. In fact the initial codename for Silverlight was WPF/E, which should give you some idea as to how closely they are related. Silverlight implements the same programming model as WPF, and shares many of the same UI controls.

When you first create a Silverlight application, the project will contain two XAML files, App.xaml and Page.xaml. These are files containing XML that describe the layout and design of the UI in the same way that HTML describes a web page. Associated with these XAML files are two code-behind files that contain the source code to perform actions and respond to UI events.

The code behind the App.xaml file provides event handlers for application-level events, such as Application_Startup, Application_Exit, and Application_UnhandledException. You can add your own custom code to perform actions in the event handlers. Application-wide resources and styles are also declared in the XAML of the App.xaml file, although there is no designer support for this.

The Page.xaml file defines the UI that is shown when the application is loaded. This is where you will design your Silverlight application by adding controls to the form and handling events in the code-behind.

The Silverlight Controls

Silverlight 2 ships with a range of useful controls for constructing rich user interfaces. These include the Canvas, Grid, and StackPanel layout controls, as well as the usual standard UI controls such as Button, TextBox, ListBox, and RadioButton. In addition, there are a range of more functional user controls including Calendar, DataGrid, and MediaElement, which can be used to build even richer user interfaces.

> *In Beta 1 of the Silverlight Tools for Visual Studio you can only drag-and-drop a control onto the XAML. Dragging a control onto the design surface of a Silverlight application is not supported. However, this will likely be fixed in a subsequent release.*

To begin designing your Silverlight application you should first create some rows for the default Grid control that was added to the page. Add three rows to the grid with varying heights, as shown in the following XAML listing:

```xml
<UserControl x:Class="SampleSilverlightApp.Page"
    xmlns="http://schemas.microsoft.com/client/2007"
    xmlns:x="http://schemas.microsoft.com/winfx/2006/xaml"
    Width="400" Height="300">
    <Grid x:Name="LayoutRoot" Background="White">
        <Grid.RowDefinitions>
            <RowDefinition Height="30"/>
            <RowDefinition Height="40"/>
            <RowDefinition Height="*"/>
        </Grid.RowDefinitions>
    </Grid>
</UserControl>
```

In the third row we have specified an asterisk (*) for the height. This means that the last row should use all the remaining space.

Next you can begin to add controls to build up the layout of the application. Add a TextBlock control, followed by a DatePicker control and then another TextBlock control. Position the first TextBlock control into the first row by adding the attribute `Grid.Row="0"` to it. In the same way position the DataPicker in the second row, and the other TextBlock control into the third row.

Finally, add the text **Enter your date of birth:** to the first TextBlock so the user has some instructions when this application is run. Once you have finished, your application should look similar to Figure 37-2.

Figure 37-2

Handling Events

Before you add any event handler code it is a good idea to specify a name for any of the controls that you're going to need to access from code. You can specify a name by adding an x:Name attribute to the control (the "x" simply refers to one of the namespaces that is added to the XAML by default). Give the DatePicker a name of x:Name="dpDOB", and the bottom TextBlock a name of x:Name="tbResults".

All controls support a range of standard events that you can register event handlers for. The source code for an event handler is stored in the code-behind file — in this case Page.xaml.cs. However, you must also wire up the event handler to the control. This is done from within the XAML by typing the name of the event and letting IntelliSense generate the stub for the handler. Add a new handler to the dbDOB control for the DateSelected event, as shown in Figure 37-3.

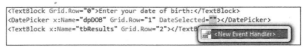

Figure 37-3

This event will fire whenever a date is selected from the picker, or when one is manually entered and the user presses Enter. Add the following code to the dpDOB_DateSelected function in the Page.xaml.cs file:

```
private void dpDOB_DateSelected(object sender, DatePickerDateChangedEventArgs e)
{
  if (dpDOB.SelectedDate.HasValue)
  {
    DateTime dob = dpDOB.SelectedDate.Value;
    int age = CalculateAge(dob);
    System.Text.StringBuilder results = new System.Text.StringBuilder();
    results.AppendFormat("You were born on a {0}.\n", dob.DayOfWeek.ToString());
    results.AppendFormat("You are {0} years old.\n", age);
    results.AppendFormat("You are {0} days old.\n",
                         DateTime.Now.Subtract(dob).Days);
    results.AppendFormat("Your next birthday will be a {0}.\n",
                  dob.AddYears(age + 1).DayOfWeek.ToString());
    tbResults.Text = results.ToString();
  }
}

private int CalculateAge(DateTime dob)
{
  if (DateTime.Now.Month < dob.Month ||
          (DateTime.Now.Month == dob.Month && DateTime.Now.Day < dob.Day))
  {
    return (DateTime.Now.Year - dob.Year) - 1;
  }
  else
  {
    return DateTime.Now.Year - dob.Year;
  }
}
```

This code will take the date that was entered into the dpDOB DatePicker control, and calculate the age in years and days, the day of birth, and the day of the next birthday.

You can now run this solution by pressing F5. Visual Studio will generate an HTML test page to host the Silverlight application, and open this in Internet Explorer as shown in Figure 37-4. Within Visual Studio you can perform the usual debugging tasks such as setting breakpoints and viewing object properties. Chapter 44 contains more information on Silverlight debugging.

Silverlight 2 applications compile into a single file with a `.xap` *extension (pronounced "zap"). This is a compressed archive that contains the application assembly, a manifest, any dependant assemblies, and embedded resources. You can even rename this file to have a* `.zip` *extension and open it to view the files inside. A basic "Hello World" Silverlight application is only 4 kB in size. As long as you stick with the standard Silverlight controls and don't require any embedded resources, more complex applications will still only be in the order of 6–8 kB.*

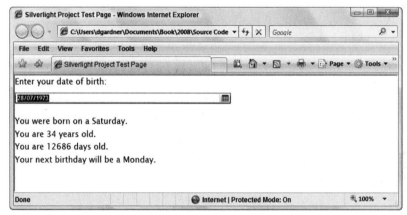

Figure 37-4

Interacting with Your Web Page

Though there are some scenarios where Silverlight can be used for an entire web application, it generally works best when it is used to meet a specific function on a web page. This ensures you don't lose any of the benefits of traditional web pages, such as addressable URLs and accessibility support, while at the same time making important parts of your web page visually richer and more functional.

Silverlight 2 allows you to interact with the web page on which a Silverlight control is hosted in a number of ways. You can access the HTML DOM elements and call JavaScript code on a web page from managed code in the Silverlight application. Additionally, you can invoke an access method or property that is in a Silverlight application from JavaScript.

To access the web page that is hosting a Silverlight control you should first add an import to the System. Windows.Browser namespace. You can then obtain a reference to an `HtmlDocument` class that represents the current page from the `HtmlPage.Document` property. For example, suppose you have a web page that contains a standard HTML textbox:

```
<input type="text" id="txtExample" name="txtExample" value="" />
```

631

You can add a *using* statement for System.Windows.Browser to the App.xaml.cs file, and add the following code to the `Application_Startup` method. When the Silverlight application is loaded with the page, it will find the textbox and set its value to "Hello from Silverlight".

```
private void Application_Startup(object sender, StartupEventArgs e)
{
    // Load the main control
    this.RootVisual = new Page();

    HtmlDocument doc = HtmlPage.Document;
    HtmlElement elem = doc.GetElementById("txtExample");
    if (elem != null)
    {
        elem.SetAttribute("value", "Hello from Silverlight");
    }
}
```

Invoking a managed code method or property in a Silverlight application from JavaScript is a little more involved. First add a new class called `SilverlightCallableClass.cs` to the Silverlight application. As the name suggests, this will contain our functions that can be invoked from JavaScript. Within this class add the following method:

```
[System.Windows.Browser.ScriptableMember()]
public string HelloWorld(string sName)
{
    return string.Format("HELLO {0}!", sName.ToUpper());
}
```

The `ScriptableMember` attribute must be explicitly added to any properties or methods that you wish to access from the web page.

Next you must register this class as a scriptable object by making a call to BrowserRegisterScriptableObject from the `Application_Startup` method in App.xaml.cs:

```
SilverlightCallableClass scc = new SilverlightCallableClass();
HtmlPage.RegisterScriptableObject("myScc", scc);
```

You can now call this method from JavaScript by obtaining a reference to the Silverlight object on the web page and calling the method off the `Content` property. For example, the snippet of HTML will invoke the `HelloWorld` method and display a message box with "HELLO DAVE!" when you click on the button:

```
<object id="myApp" data="data:application/x-silverlight,"
        type="application/x-silverlight-2-b1" Width="400" Height="300">
        <param name="source" value="ClientBin/SampleSilverlightApp.xap"/>
</object>
<input id="Button1" type="button" value="Hello" onclick="callHelloWorld()" />
<script type="text/javascript">
    function callHelloWorld(){
        var slCtl = document.getElementById("myApp");
        alert(slCtl.Content.myScc.HelloWorld("dave"));
    }
</script>
```

One important point to note in the preceding code is that you must add an `id` attribute to the Silverlight object element. When you use Visual Studio to automatically generate an HTML test page, as shown in the next section, it will not include this attribute.

The preceding code will only work with Beta 1 of Silverlight 2. If you are running a newer beta or the final release, you will need to update the `type="application/x-silverlight-2-b1"` *attribute of the Silverlight object element to match your current version.*

Hosting Silverlight Applications

Silverlight applications can be hosted on a web page in a number of ways. You can simply use the HTML object tag to embed the Silverlight control on a page, or you can use the ASP.NET Silverlight web controls to add it to an ASP.NET Web Form.

Begin by adding a new ASP.NET Web Site project to your solution. Then right-click the new Web Site project in the Solution Explorer and select Add Silverlight Link. This will display the dialog box shown in Figure 37-5. Select the defaults on this dialog box and click Add.

Figure 37-5

This will create a reference to the Silverlight application and generate two files: a static HTML page and an ASP.NET Web Form. Open the static HTML page and view the markup. You will see that an HTML object element has been added to the page that references your Silverlight control. Visual Studio also adds some basic error-handling script and a link to download and install Silverlight if the page is accessed from a browser that does not have it. You can copy this object element, with or without the error-handling script, to any other web page.

The advantage of hosting a Silverlight control using the object tag is that it is loaded purely on the client side, and therefore has no dependency on the web server platform that is used. For example, your Silverlight control could be hosted on a PHP web page that is being served from an Apache web server on Linux.

The second approach for hosting a Silverlight application is to use the new Silverlight ASP.NET server controls, called MediaPlayer and Silverlight. These controls allow you to use the familiar server control programming model to host Silverlight applications on an ASP.NET web page.

When you installed the Silverlight Tools for Visual Studio, it also registered these new controls. The Silverlight control allows you to embed a Silverlight application on a web page, similar to hosting via the object tag. However, it also allows you to specify the source of the Silverlight application and various properties and methods that control how it is rendered at runtime from code. You also have access to various events such as Init, Load, and PreRender, which you can handle on the server.

The MediaPlayer control inherits from the Silverlight control, and displays a Silverlight application skinned with media controls (play, pause, stop, and so on). This allows you to integrate streaming media including audio (WMA) and video (WMV) through a web page without needing to code an XAML or JavaScript.

> *Any web page that uses the Silverlight or MediaPlayer controls must also include the ASP.NET AJAX ScriptManager control.*

When you added the Silverlight link to the web site earlier, it also generated a sample ASPX page. This page uses a Silverlight control to host the Silverlight application, and provides a quick way for you to test it out. Right-click the Web Site project and select Set as Default Project, and then right-click the ASPX page and select Set as Start Page, and then press F5 to run the page.

ASP.NET MVC

Since the late 1990s the most common architectural pattern employed to build large web applications has been the *n*-tier architectural pattern. Most implementations of *n*-tier applications use three tiers: a presentation tier that contains the user interface code, a business logic tier that provides the core processing logic for the application, and a data access tier that is responsible for retrieving and saving information to a backend data store.

One of the problems with this architecture is that there can be a tendency for business-logic and data-access code to migrate up through the tiers until it is irrevocably intertwined with the user interface code. With ASP.NET Web Forms, which support the *n*-tier architecture, you do need a degree of discipline to ensure that this does not happen. It is all too common to see ASP.NET applications where SQL queries are hardcoded as strings and embedded into data access code within an event handler of a web control.

An alternate architectural pattern that has been growing in popularity over the past few years is Model-View-Controller (MVC). The MVC architectural pattern does a much better job of encouraging and enforcing a clear separation of components into application control, business logic, and UI presentation.

ASP.NET MVC provides a framework that enables you to easily create applications that use the MVC architectural pattern on the ASP.NET platform. First announced at the ALT.NET conference in late 2007, ASP.NET MVC is a good example of the more open and transparent side of Microsoft that has emerged in recent years. The source code for the framework has been published at CodePlex (http://codeplex.com/aspnet), and the features supported by the framework have been shaped through community feedback on frequent preview releases.

The ASP.NET MVC framework provides the following benefits:

❑ It makes it easier to manage complexity by dividing an application into the Model, the View, and the Controller.

❑ It does not use view state, server controls, or postbacks, which give you a programming model that is less of an abstraction of the way HTTP actually works. A related benefit is that this allows much more control over the HTML that your application generates.

❑ It supports a custom routing infrastructure, which provides you with more control over the URLs that you publish. This makes it search engine– and REST-friendly.

❑ It provides better support for test-driven development (TDD).

As Microsoft has been careful to state, ASP.NET MVC is not a replacement for Web Forms. It's simply an alternate way of building web applications on the ASP.NET platform that some people will find preferable. Microsoft has made it very clear that it will fully support both ASP.NET Web Forms and ASP.NET MVC into the future.

Model-View-Controller

If you've never come across it before, you might be surprised to learn that this "new" Model-View-Controller architecture was first described in 1979, which means it's older than some of you reading this book!

In the MVC architecture, applications are separated into the following components:

❑ **Model:** The Model consists of classes that implement domain-specific logic for the application. Although the MVC architecture does not concern itself with the specifics of the data access layer, it is understood that the model should encapsulate any data access code. Generally, the model will call separate data access classes responsible for retrieving and storing information in a database.

❑ **View:** The Views are the classes that take the model and render it into a format where the user can interact with it.

❑ **Controller:** The Controller is responsible for bringing everything all together. A Controller processes and responds to events, such as a user clicking on a button. The Controller maps these events onto the Model and invokes the appropriate View.

These descriptions aren't really helpful until you understand how they interact together. The request life cycle of an MVC application normally consists of the following:

1. The user performs an action that triggers an event, such as entering a URL or clicking a button. This generates a request to the Controller.

2. The Controller receives the request and invokes the relevant action on the Model. Often this will cause a change in the Model's state, although not always.

3. The Controller retrieves any necessary data from the Model and invokes the appropriate View, passing it the data from the Model.

4. The View renders the data and sends it back to the user.

The most important thing to note here is that both the View and Controller depend on the Model. However, the Model has no dependencies, which is one of the key benefits of the architecture. This separation is what provides better testability and makes it easier to manage complexity.

Different MVC framework implementations have minor variations in the preceding life cycle. For example, in some cases the View will query the Model for the current state, instead of receiving it from the Controller.

Now that you understand the Model-View-Controller architectural pattern, you can begin to apply this newfound knowledge by building your first ASP.NET MVC application.

Getting Started with ASP.NET MVC

You can download the ASP.NET MVC framework from a link on the ASP.NET community site at `http://asp.net/mvc/`. The installer contains the Visual Studio 2008 project and item templates and three new assemblies: System.Web.Abstractions.dll, System.Web.MVC.dll, and System.Web.Routing.dll.

This chapter was written using ASP.NET MVC Preview 2 and some details will definitely have changed in subsequent releases since the time of writing. At the start of this chapter are instructions on how you can obtain an updated version of this chapter once the final version of ASP.NET MVC has been released.

Once you've installed ASP.NET MVC, open Visual Studio and select File ➪ New ➪ Project. In the Web project category of both Visual Basic and Visual C# you will see a new project template called *ASP.NET MVC Web Application*. Select the C# version of this project template and click OK.

Before the new project is created, Visual Studio will prompt you to generate a unit test project for the application as shown in Figure 37-6. Though this is not required, it is highly recommended, because improved testability is one of the core advantages of MVC. You can also add a test project later by selecting the *ASP.NET MVC Test* project template under the Test category in the New Project dialog box. Select the option to generate a unit test project and click OK.

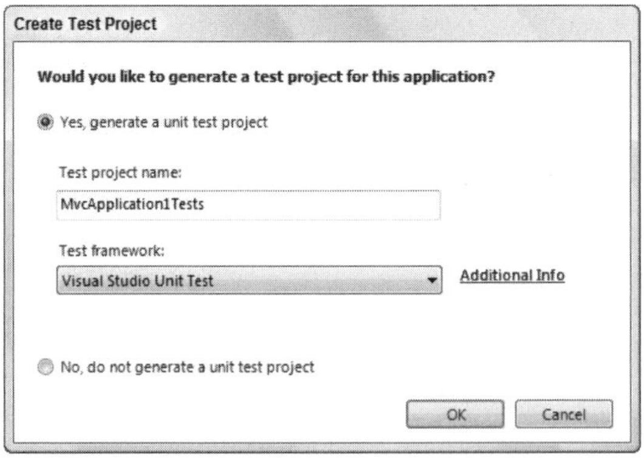

Figure 37-6

When an ASP.NET MVC application is first created, it will generate a number of files and folders — quite a lot more than are found in other project templates when you first create them. In actual fact, the MVC application that is generated from the project template is a complete application that can be immediately run.

The folder structure that is automatically generated by Visual Studio is shown in Figure 37-7 and includes the following folders:

❏ **Content:** A location to store static content files such as CSS files and images

❏ **Controllers:** Contains the Controller files. A sample Controller called `HomeController` is created by the project template.

❏ **Models:** Contains Model files. This is also a good place to store any data access classes that are encapsulated by the Model. The MVC project template does not create an example Model.

❏ **Views:** Contains the View files. The MVC project template creates two folders and three files in the Views. The Home sub-folder contains two example View files that are invoked by the `HomeController`. The Shared folder contains a master page that is used by these Views.

Visual Studio also creates a Default.aspx file, which is simply a placeholder that is needed to ensure IIS loads the MVC application correctly. There is also a Global.asax file, which is used to configure the routing rules (more on that later).

Finally, if you elected to create a test project this will be created with a Controllers folder that contains a unit test stub for the `HomeController` class.

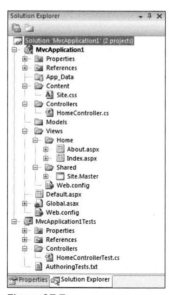

Figure 37-7

Although it doesn't do much yet, you can run the MVC application by pressing F5. When it opens in Internet Explorer it will first render the Index view, with a link that allows you to navigate to the About view. Neither of these views is particularly interesting, because they just render static content.

The next section explains how you can build your own Controller, followed by some more interesting Views that render a dynamic user interface.

Controllers and Action Methods

This section and the next walk through how to add a new Controller class and associated Views. This will provide an alternative implementation of the birthday calculator that was created earlier in this chapter as a Silverlight application.

Begin by right-clicking the Controllers folder in the Solution Explorer and selecting Add ➪ New Item. This will display the Add New Item dialog, shown in Figure 37-8. Under the Web category, there is a new entry called MVC, which contains the item templates specific to this project type. Select the MVC Controller class template and enter **BirthdayController.cs** as the name. The MVC framework requires all Controller names to end with "Controller".

You may be wondering why there is no template for creating an MVC Model. That's because a Model is an ordinary class that happens to implement some domain-specific functionality. Because there is no base class to inherit from, or a specific interface to implement, there is no item template to create a Model class.

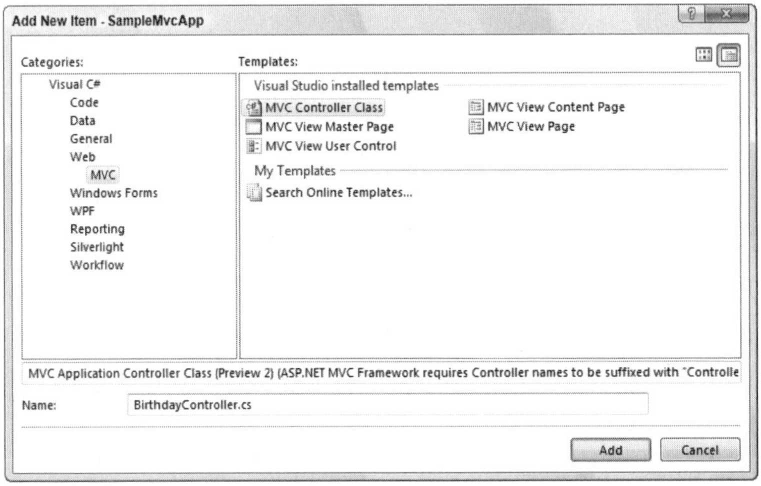

Figure 37-8

Controller classes inherit from the System.Web.Mvc.Controller class, which performs all of the heavy lifting in terms of determining the relevant method to call for an action and mapping URL parameter values. This means that you can concentrate on the implementation details of your Actions, which typically involves invoking a method on a Model class and then selecting the View to render.

A newly created Controller class will be populated with a default Action method called `Index`. You can add a new Action simply by adding a public method to the class. If a method is public, it will be visible as an Action on the Controller. You can stop a public method from being exposed as an Action by adding the `System.Web.Mvc.NonAction` attribute to the method. The following listing contains the Controller class with the default Action that simply renders the `Index` view, and a public method that is not visible as an Action:

```
public class BirthdayController : Controller
{
    public void Index()
    {
        RenderView("Index");
    }

    [System.Web.Mvc.NonAction()]
    public void NotAnAction()
    {
            // This is not visible as an Action
    }
}
```

Before you go any further you will need to create a class for the Model. In the Models folder of the solution, add a new class file called Birthday.cs. Within this class, add the following code:

```
public class Birthday
{
    private DateTime mDoB;

    public Birthday(DateTime DoB)
    {
      mDoB = DoB;
    }

    public int AgeInYears
    {
        get
        {
            if (DateTime.Now.Month < mDoB.Month ||
                (DateTime.Now.Month == mDoB.Month && DateTime.Now.Day < mDoB.Day))
            {
                return (DateTime.Now.Year - mDoB.Year) - 1;
            }
            else
            {
                return DateTime.Now.Year - mDoB.Year;
            }
        }
    }

    public int AgeInDays
    {
        get
        {
```

(continued)

(continued)

```
                return DateTime.Now.Subtract(mDoB).Days;
        }

    }

    public string BornOn
    {
        get
        {
            return mDoB.DayOfWeek.ToString();
        }
    }

    public string NextBirthdayOn
    {
        get
        {
            return mDoB.AddYears(AgeInYears + 1).DayOfWeek.ToString();
        }
    }
}
```

This code is basically a copy of the logic that was used in the Silverlight application that was created earlier in this chapter. However, you have now encapsulated it in its own class, rather than having it mixed up with the user interface code. The Birthday class consists of a constructor that takes a DateTime representing the Date of Birth, and four public properties that calculate the age, day of birth, and day of the next birthday.

Now you are ready to implement a new Controller Action. Within the BirthdayController.cs file add the Age method, as shown in the following code listing:

```
public class BirthdayController : Controller
{
    public void Index()
    {
        RenderView("Index");
    }

    public void Age(DateTime DoB)
    {
        Models.Birthday birthday = new Models.Birthday(DoB);
        ViewData["AgeInYears"] = birthday.AgeInYears;
        ViewData["AgeInDays"] = birthday.AgeInDays;
        ViewData["BornOn"] = birthday.BornOn;
        ViewData["NextBirthdayOn"] = birthday.NextBirthdayOn;
        RenderView("Age");
    }

    [System.Web.Mvc.NonAction()]
    public void NotAnAction()
    {
        // This is not visible as an Action
    }
}
```

As mentioned earlier, you don't need to do anything to expose this method as an Action. Simply declaring it as public is sufficient to make it accessible. As you will see in the following section, the DateTime parameter is specified on the View that invokes this Controller Action, and is automatically mapped by the MVC framework.

This Action method begins by instantiating the `Birthday` class, which is functioning as the Model, and passing in the DoB parameter. The ViewData is a dictionary object that can store any object or variable and is accessible by the Views. This is how the Controller passes data from the Model onto the Views. Finally the Action method calls the `RenderView` method, passing in the name of the View to be invoked as a string parameter.

Now that you have created your Model and Controller, all that's needed is to create the Views to display the UI.

Rendering a UI with Views

Views are added in much the same way as Controllers, except they must be placed in a specific folder so that the ASP.NET MVC framework can find them. Within the Views folder of the project, create a new folder that matches the name of the Controller. For example, the Controller class that was added earlier was called `BirthdayController`; therefore the folder you create under Views should be called Birthday.

Master/Detail View pages are supported in ASP.NET MVC. Because the example Views created by the project template use Master/Detail pages, we won't demonstrate them here.

Right-click this new folder, select Add ⇨ New Item, and add an MVC View Page item called Index.aspx. The file that is created is very similar to a standard Web Forms page; for example, it contains a page directive where you can specify the usual attributes such as cache settings and whether ViewState is enabled. There is also a code-behind file for the page. However, there are some important differences that need to be highlighted.

First, instead of inheriting from `System.Web.UI.Page`, an MVC View inherits from `System.Web.Mvc.ViewPage`. Secondly, in the markup you will notice that there is no server-based form by default. No server form means that there is no ViewState emitted with the page.

The majority of the ASP.NET server controls must be placed inside a server form. Some controls such as a Literal or Repeater control will work fine outside a form; however, if you try to use a Button or DropDownList control, your page will throw an exception at runtime.

Many people will prefer to simply implement the view using standard HTML elements, because it provides the way to get the most control and produce the cleanest markup. However, if you are a developer who prefers the convenience of server controls, you can use the HTML helpers that are included with the framework. Previously referred to as the MVC Toolkit, the helpers provide a quick way to automatically generate HTML elements such as buttons and drop-down lists. These can be thought of as server controls for MVC; however, unlike server controls, they don't use ViewState or generate postbacks and they render much cleaner HTML.

The following HTML listing is for the Index.aspx View. The shaded lines are the markup that we have modified or added:

```
<%@ Page Language="C#" AutoEventWireup="true" CodeBehind="Index.aspx.cs" Inherits="
MvcApplication1.Views.Birthday.Index" %>
<!DOCTYPE html PUBLIC "-//W3C//DTD XHTML 1.0 Transitional//EN" "http://www.w3.org/
TR/xhtml1/DTD/xhtml1-transitional.dtd">

<html xmlns="http://www.w3.org/1999/xhtml" >
<head runat="server">
    <title>Birthday Calculator</title>
</head>
<body>
    <form id="myForm" action="/birthday/age" method="post">
    <div>
        Enter your Date of Birth:
        <input type="text" name="DoB" />
    </div>
    </form>
</body>
</html>
```

There are a couple of important things to point out about this View. First, the `action` attribute of the form has been formatted to match the initial routing rules. By default, the MVC framework will map a URL based on the Controller name followed by the Action method name. In the preceding example, when the form is submitted it will post the form to the URL `/birthday/age`, which will be mapped to the `age` method on the `BirthdayController` class. Routing rules are discussed further in the next section.

Secondly the ASP.NET MVC framework automatically maps any fields that are in the form post-data, or have been added as query parameters, into parameters on the Action method. In the preceding example, the input textbox has been given a name of DoB. Because this name matches the DoB DateTime parameter on the `age` method it will be automatically mapped.

If the user enters an invalid date into this form, it will throw an exception. It is possible (and good practice) for you to handle this exception and render the view again indicating the error.

Next, add another View called Age.aspx. As you saw in a previous listing, the Controller will call this View to display the results of the `age` Action method. The following listing uses shading to show the markup that has been modified on this page. The ViewData dictionary object, which was populated by the Controller Action method, contains the results of the action from the Model.

```
<%@ Page Language="C#" AutoEventWireup="true" CodeBehind="Age.aspx.cs"
Inherits="MvcApplication1.Views.Birthday.Age" %>
<!DOCTYPE html PUBLIC "-//W3C//DTD XHTML 1.0
    Transitional//EN" "http://www.w3.org/TR/xhtml1/DTD/xhtml1-transitional.dtd">

<html xmlns="http://www.w3.org/1999/xhtml" >
<head runat="server">
    <title>Birthday Calculator</title>
</head>
```

```
<body>
    <div>
        You are <%= ViewData["AgeInYears"] %> years old.<br />
        You are <%= ViewData["AgeInDays"] %> days old.<br />
        You were born on a <%= ViewData["BornOn"] %>.<br />
        Your next birthday will be on a <%= ViewData["NextBirthdayOn"] %>.
    </div>
</body>
</html>
```

You are now ready to run the MVC application. Press F5, and the project will compile and open in Internet Explorer. The default page that is loaded belongs to a View on the `HomeController` Action that was first created with the project. To navigate to the `BirthdayController` add `/Birthday` to the end of the URL. Figure 37-9 (left) shows the `Index` Action and View, which is first displayed when the `BirthdayController` is invoked. Figure 37-9 (right) shows the results of submitting this form, which is the Age Action and View.

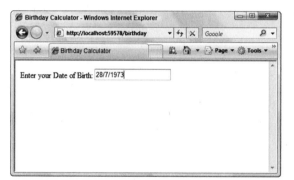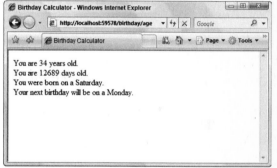

Figure 37-9

In addition to passing the ViewData as a late-bound, weak-typed dictionary object, you can use an alternate method to pass a strongly-typed class. This will give you IntelliSense and type checking from within the View. For example, rather than query the Model in the Controller Action and pass the results into the View, you could simply pass the entire `Models.Birthday` object through to the View, as shown in the following modified listing:

```
public void Age(DateTime DoB)
{
    Models.Birthday birthday = new Models.Birthday(DoB);
    RenderView("Age2", birthday);
}
```

In addition to the `ViewPage` base class that we have been using so far, the ASP.NET MVC framework also includes a `ViewPage<T>` class that uses generics. In the code-behind file, Age.aspx.cs, update the class to inherit from `ViewPage<Models.Birthday>`, as shown in the following listing:

```
public partial class Age : ViewPage<Models.Birthday>
{
}
```

643

The `ViewData` property will now be strongly typed using the `Birthday Model` class. This will provide you with IntelliSense as shown in Figure 37-10, as well as type checking at compile time.

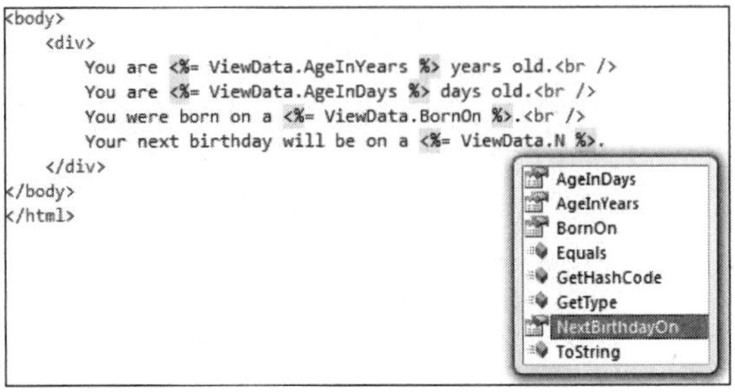

```
<body>
    <div>
        You are <%= ViewData.AgeInYears %> years old.<br />
        You are <%= ViewData.AgeInDays %> days old.<br />
        You were born on a <%= ViewData.BornOn %>.<br />
        Your next birthday will be on a <%= ViewData.N %>.
    </div>
</body>
</html>
```

- AgeInDays
- AgeInYears
- BornOn
- Equals
- GetHashCode
- GetType
- NextBirthdayOn
- ToString

Figure 37-10

Custom URL Routing

As mentioned previously, the ASP.NET MVC framework uses custom URL routing rules to map URLs to Controller classes and Actions. Each rule is defined according to a URL pattern that you define.

> *Although it is shipped along with ASP.NET MVC, the URL routing is implemented in a separate namespace and assembly called System.Web.Routing. This means that you can use it to create custom URL routing in an ASP.NET Web Forms application without introducing any dependency on MVC.*

The following code listing shows the default routing rules that are created when the ASP.NET MVC project is created by Visual Studio:

```
public class GlobalApplication : System.Web.HttpApplication
{
    public static void RegisterRoutes(RouteCollection routes)
    {
        // Note: Change the URL to "{controller}.mvc/{action}/{id}" to enable
        //       automatic support on IIS6 and IIS7 classic mode

        routes.Add(new Route("{controller}/{action}/{id}", new MvcRouteHandler())
        {
            Defaults = new RouteValueDictionary(new {action="Index", id=""}),
        });

        routes.Add(new Route("Default.aspx", new MvcRouteHandler())
        {
            Defaults = new RouteValueDictionary(
                        new {controller="Home", action="Index", id = "" }),
        });
    }

    protected void Application_Start(object sender, EventArgs e)
    {
        RegisterRoutes(RouteTable.Routes);
    }
}
```

You can modify the preceding to ensure that the new `BirthdayController` is used by default when the application is first opened by replacing the `controller="Home"` with `controller="Birthday"`.

Routing rules are added by adding them to the `System.Web.Mvc.RouteTable.Routes` collection. This is a static collection of `System.Web.Mvc.Route` objects.

The order in which Route objects are added to the Routes collection is important. Rules are evaluated in order starting with the first route that was added to the collection. When a match is found, no more routes are evaluated. This means that typically routes are added starting with the strictest rule first, with a general catch-all route as the last route.

In addition to the default route, the ASP.NET MVC application project template creates a default rule based on the pattern {controller}/{action}/{id}. For example, assuming that the MVC application had been deployed to the root of a web server, this routing rule would match the URL `http://servername/products/list/monitors`, and subsequently call the Action `list` on the Controller `products`, passing in the parameter id=monitors. If no Action or Id was specified, for example in the URL `http://servername/products/`, the default action called `Index` would be called.

You can also add validation rules to a route that can be used to further control URL routing. These validation rules can use regular expressions. For example, the following route enables a URL like `/news/item/123456`, but not `/news/item/12345678` or `/news/item/1234`:

```
routes.Add(new Route("news/item/[id]", new MvcRouteHandler())
{
    Defaults = new { controller="News", action="Item" },
    Validation = new { id =  @" ^\d{6}$ " }
});
```

The URL routing classes are very powerful and flexible, and allow you to easily create "pretty" URLs. Though this appeals to some developers' senses of aesthetics, there are other good reasons to have URLs formatted in this way, such as making your application search engine–friendly or exposing a REST API.

Summary

In this chapter you learned how to build the next generation of web applications using Silverlight 2 and the ASP.NET MVC framework. Though these technologies don't replace traditional ASP.NET Web Forms, they do open up new ways to build web applications that may better suit the objectives of your solution.

The Microsoft Silverlight Tools for Visual Studio 2008 enable you to develop Rich Internet Applications with Silverlight 2 that are written in the language of your choice and leverage the power of the .NET Framework. The ASP.NET MVC framework provides a way to cleanly separate your application into Model, View, and Controller parts, thus enabling better testability and giving you more control over the behavior and output produced by your web application.

This chapter only scratched the surface of what is possible with Silverlight and ASP.NET MVC. If you are looking for more information, a great starting point is the Silverlight community site at `http://silverlight.net/` and the ASP.NET MVC home page at `http://asp.net/mvc/`.

Part VIII

Configuration and Internationalization

Configuration Files

One of the challenges of building applications is adjusting the way the application functions on the fly without having to rebuild it. There's a long history of applications using configuration files to control the way an application runs. .NET applications use a series of XML configuration files that can be adjusted to determine application behavior. This chapter explores the structure of these configuration files and demonstrates how you can store custom information using a configuration section handler.

Config Files

The .NET Framework configuration system consists of several configuration files (discussed in the following sections) that can be used to adjust one or more applications on a computer system. Part of this system is an inheritance model that ensures that configurations can be applied at the appropriate level.

Machine.Config

At the root of the inheritance model is the machine.config file (located in the *systemroot*\Microsoft .NET\Framework*versionNumber*\CONFIG\ folder), which defines configuration settings for the entire system. All configuration files inherit from this file and can override these settings. It is worth noting that although Visual Studio 2008 ships with version 3.5 of the .NET Framework, it is still based on version 2.0 of the CLR, which means that the configuration files are located in a v2.*x.x.x* sub-folder.

Web.Config

Web applications are configured via the web.config file. This file can be located in a number of locations, depending on the scope to which the settings need to be applied. To apply a configuration to all web applications on a machine, place the web.config file in the same directory as the machine.config file. In most cases the settings need to be applied at a much finer granularity. As such, the web.config file can also be placed in any virtual directory or subdirectory to control web applications at that level. If it is placed in the root folder for a web site, the configuration will be applied to all ASP.NET applications in that web site.

A word of caution: When you are working with virtual directories that do not align with the directory structure on the computer, it's possible to have an application that has different configurations depending on how it is referenced. For example, consider C:\inetpub\wwwroot\MainApplication\ Contacts\Contact.aspx, which has been set up with both MainApplication and Contacts as virtual directories. You can reference the contact page as either:

```
http://localhost/MainApplication/Contacts/Contact.aspx
```

or:

```
http://localhost/Contacts/Contact.aspx
```

In the first case, the configuration settings that are applied are inherited from the MainApplication folder and may be overridden by a configuration file in the Contacts folder. However, in the second case, settings are applied only from the configuration file within the Contacts folder.

Making changes to a web.config file will cause the ASP.NET application to be restarted. This is quite an effective way to force a web application to flush its cache and behave as if it were being accessed for the first time, without having to restart the entire server.

App.Config

Windows applications can be configured via an application configuration file, which also inherits from machine.config. As the output assembly name is known only when an application is compiled, this file starts off as app.config and is renamed to *application*.exe.config as part of the build process. For example, an application with AccountingApplication.exe as the main executable would have a configuration file entitled AccountingApplication.exe.config. This configuration file is automatically loaded based on its name when the application is loaded.

Security.Config

In conjunction with the application configuration files are a number of security configuration files. These also follow an inheritance path but across a different dimension. Instead of being application-focused, the security configuration files are broken down into enterprise (Enterprisesec.config), machine (Security. config), and user (Security.config). The enterprise- and machine-level files are both stored in the same location as the Machine.config file, while the user-level file is stored under the user-specific application data folder.

Configuration Schema

A configuration file, whether it is a machine.config, a web.config, or an application configuration file, needs to adhere to the configuration schema that determines which elements should be included. The schema can be found at C:\Program Files\Microsoft Visual Studio 9.0\Xml\Schemas\DotNetConfig. xsd and is broken down into a number of sections.

Section: configurationSections

Configuration files can be customized to contain any structured XML data. In order to do this, you must define a custom section in the configurationSections block within the configuration file. This defines both the name of the configuration section and the class that is to be called in order to process the section.

The first configurationSections section in the machine.config file defines the handlers for each of the standard configuration sections discussed here. For example, the following code snippet defines the section handler for the ConfigurationApplication.My.MySettings configuration section, along with the corresponding section. The schema of this section must correspond to what the System.Configuration.ClientSettingsSection class expects, rather than the normal configuration file schema.

```
<configuration>
    <configSections>
        <section name="ConfigurationApplication.My.MySettings"
                type="System.Configuration.ClientSettingsSection,
System, Version=2.0.0.0, Culture=neutral, PublicKeyToken=b77a5c561934e089"
                requirePermission="false" />
    </configSections>
    ...
    <ConfigurationApplication.My.Settings>
        <setting name="PrimaryServer" serializeAs="String">
         <value>www.softteq.com</value>
        </setting>
    </ConfigurationApplication.My.Settings>
</configuration>
```

It is also possible to include configSections in a sectionGroup element that can be used to help lay out configuration information. The previous example can be extended as follows:

```
<configuration>
    <configSections>
        <sectionGroup name="applicationSettings"
                    type="System.Configuration.ApplicationSettingsGroup,
System, Version=2.0.0.0, Culture=neutral, PublicKeyToken= b77a5c561934e089" >
            <section name="ConfigurationApplication.My.MySettings"
                    type="System.Configuration.ClientSettingsSection,
System, Version=2.0.0.0, Culture=neutral, PublicKeyToken=b77a5c561934e089"
                    requirePermission="false" />
            <section name="ReferencedAssembly.My.MySettings"
                    type="System.Configuration.ClientSettingsSection,
System, Version=2.0.0.0, Culture=neutral, PublicKeyToken=b77a5c561934e089"
```

(continued)

(continued)

```
                      requirePermission="false" />
        </sectionGroup>
    </configSections>
    ...
    <applicationSettings>
        <ConfigurationApplication.My.Settings>
            <setting name="PrimaryServer" serializeAs="String">
              <value>www.softteq.com</value>
          </setting>
        </ConfigurationApplication.My.Settings>
        <ReferencedAssembly.My.Settings>
            <setting name="SecondaryServer" serializeAs="String">
              <value>www.peaksite.com</value>
          </setting>
        </ReferencedAssembly.My.Settings>
    </applicationSettings>
</configuration>
```

Where used, the `configSections` element must appear as the first child of the configuration element.

Section: startup

The `startup` configuration section determines the version of the framework that is either required (`requiredRuntime`) or supported (`supportedRuntime`) by the framework. By default, a .NET application will attempt to execute using the same version of the framework on which it was built. Any application being built with support for multiple versions of the framework should indicate this with the `supportedRuntime` element, defining the most preferred framework version first:

```
<configuration>
    <startup>
        <supportedRuntime version="v2.0.50727"/>
        <supportedRuntime version="v1.1.4322"/>
    </startup>
</configuration>
```

This configuration section would be used by an application that has been tested for both version 2.0 and 1.1 of the .NET Framework. Anomalies were detected in the testing for version 1.0 of the .NET Framework, so it has been omitted from the `supportedRuntime` list. The version number must correspond exactly to the installation directory for that framework version (for example, version 2.0 of the .NET Framework typically installs to C:\WINDOWS\Microsoft.NET\Framework\v2.0.50727\).

Section: runtime

Garbage collection is a feature of the .NET Framework that distinguishes it from non-managed environments. The process of collecting and disposing of unreferenced objects is usually done in parallel with the main application on a separate thread. This means that the user should not see any performance issues as a result of this process being run. However, there may be circumstances when this process should be run inline with the main application. The `runtime` section of the configuration file can be used to provide limited control over how the .NET runtime engine operates. Among other things, you can specify whether the garbage collection should be done concurrently with the main application.

This section can also be used to specify a location in which to search for assemblies that may be required by an application. This attribute can be useful if an application references assemblies. The following code illustrates the use of the `codeBase` attribute to locate the ImportantAssembly.dll, as well as to dictate that garbage collection be done inline with the main application thread:

```
<configuration>
    <runtime>
        <assemblyBinding xmlns="urn:schemas-microsoft-com:asm.v1">
            <dependentAssembly>
                <assemblyIdentity name="ImportantAssembly"
                                  publicKeyToken="32ab4ba45e0a69a1"
                                  culture="neutral" />
                <codeBase version="2.0.0.0" href="../ImportantAssembly.dll"/>
            </dependentAssembly>
        </assemblyBinding>
        <gcConcurrent enabled="false"/>
    </runtime>
</configuration>
```

Section: system.runtime.remoting

The `remoting` section of the configuration file can be used to specify information about remote objects and channels required by the application. For example, the default HTTP channel can be directed to listen to port 8080 by means of the following configuration snippet:

```
<configuration>
    <system.runtime.remoting>
        <application>
            <channels>
                <channel port="8080" ref="http"/>
            </channels>
        </application>
    </system.runtime.remoting>
</configuration>
```

Section: system.net

Because of the current demand for more secure operating environments, organizations often use proxies to monitor and protect traffic on their networks. This can often result in applications not functioning correctly unless they have been configured to use the appropriate proxies. The networking section of the configuration files can be used to adjust the proxy that an application uses when making HTTP requests.

The .NET Framework ships with an `SmtpClient` class that can be used to send mail from within an application. Obviously, doing this requires information such as the server and the credentials to use when sending mail. Although such information can be hard-coded within an application, a more flexible approach would be to specify it in a configuration file that can be adjusted when the application is deployed. The following configuration snippet illustrates the use of the default proxy (although it bypasses the proxy for local addresses and the DeveloperNews web site) and specifies the default SMTP settings to be used by the SMTP client:

```
<configuration>
    <system.net>
        <defaultProxy>
            <proxy usesystemdefaults="true"
                    proxyaddress="http://192.168.200.222:3030"
                    bypassonlocal="true" />
            <bypasslist>
                <add address="[a-z]+\.developernews\.com" />
            </bypasslist>
        </defaultProxy>
        <mailSettings>
            <smtp deliveryMethod="network">
                <network host="smtp.developernews.com"
    port="25" defaultCredentials="true" />
            </smtp>
        </mailSettings>
    </system.net>
</configuration>
```

Section: cryptographySettings

Although the .NET Framework contains base implementations for a number of cryptographic algorithms, such as the hashing function, there are times when it is necessary to override these algorithms. When this is required, the `cryptographySettings` section of the configuration file can be included to remap existing algorithm names, or map new names, to another implementation class.

Section: system.diagnostics

Debugging is always the hardest part of writing an application. It is made even more difficult when the application is in production and the error cannot be replicated in the debugging environment. One technique that is particularly important for debugging this type of error is to use trace statements:

```
Trace.WriteLine("The application made it this far before crashing...")
```

Both trace and debug statements work very similarly to events and event handlers. For the preceding `WriteLine` statement to have any effect, an object must be listening for this `WriteLine`. This is typically done by a `TraceListener` class. The framework supports a number of default trace listeners that can be wired up to the application via the diagnostics section of the configuration file, as shown in the following section in which an `EventLog` trace listener has been attached to the application:

```
<configuration>
    <system.diagnostics>
        <trace autoflush="true" indentsize="0">
            <listeners>
                <add name="MyEventListener"

type="System.Diagnostics.EventLogTraceListener, system,
version=1.0.3300.0, Culture=neutral, PublicKeyToken=b77a5c561934e089"
```

```
        initializeData="DeveloperApplicationEventLog"/>
                </listeners>
            </trace>
        </system.diagnostics>
    </configuration>
```

The `initializeData` attribute specifies a text string to be passed into the constructor for the trace listener. In the case of the event-log listener, this text corresponds to the name of the event log into which trace statements will be inserted.

Other elements can also be added to the diagnostics section of the configuration file — for example, to determine the level of trace logging to perform, which will determine how verbose the trace messages are; or to control whether the debug assertion dialog is displayed for an application or not.

Section: system.web

The `system.web` section of the configuration file is used to control how web applications behave. This is the section that can have quite a deep hierarchy, as configuration settings can be specified on a machine, web server, web site, web application, or even sub-folder basis. Because this section controls the security requirements for a web application, it is often used to restrict access to certain areas of the web application.

Section: webserver

Although web service applications use several configuration settings, such as `authentication` and `impersonation` sections, the `system.web` section of the configuration file contains some settings that are particular to the way that web services operate. For example, the following code snippet enables the use of `SOAP` and `Documentation` protocols, but removes the `POST` and `GET` protocols for the application:

```
<configuration>
    <system.web>
        <webServices>
            <protocols>
                <add name="HttpSoap"/>
                <remove name="HttpPost"/>
                <remove name="HttpGet"/>
                <add name="Documentation"/>
            </protocols>
        </webServices>
    </system.web>
</configuration>
```

By default, only `SOAP` and `Documentation` are enabled for web services. Quite often, for debugging purposes, it is convenient to allow the `POST` protocol so that the web service can be tested via a web browser. You should do this on an application basis by including the appropriate section in the configuration file within the application folder.

Section: compiler

The `compiler` section of the configuration file is used to list the compilers installed on a computer. The following snippet shows how the VB.NET compiler is referenced in the machine.config file. Within an application, this information can be accessed via the `CodeDomProvider` framework class.

```
<configuration>
    <system.codedom>
        <compilers>
            <compiler language="vb;vbs;visualbasic;vbscript" extension=".vb"
type="Microsoft.VisualBasic.VBCodeProvider, System, Version=2.0.0.0,
Culture=neutral, PublicKeyToken=b77a5c561934e089" />
        </compilers>
    </system.codedom>
</configuration>
```

Configuration Attributes

All configuration elements can specify a `configSource`, which is simply a redirection to a separate file. This can be useful if a configuration file becomes unwieldy in length. The following code snippet illustrates how a section of a configuration file can be extracted and subsequently referenced by means of this attribute:

```
<!-- Original Configuration File -->
<configuration>
    ...
    <WindowsApplication1.My.MySettings>
        <setting name="Button1_Text" serializeAs="String">
            <value>Press Me!</value>
        </setting>
    </WindowsApplication1.My.MySettings>
</configuration>

<!-- Reduced Configuration File using configSource -->
<configuration>
    ...
    <WindowsApplication1.My.MySettings configSource="MySettings.Config" />
</configuration>

<!-- Code from MySettings.Config -->
<WindowsApplication1.My.MySettings>
    <setting name="Button1_Text" serializeAs="String">
        <value>Press Me!</value>
    </setting>
</WindowsApplication1.My.MySettings>
```

Note a couple of limitations to using a `configSource`:

❑ There is no merging of configuration sections between the referenced file and the original configuration file. If you include the section in both files, a configuration error will be generated when you attempt to run the application.

- ❏ This attribute cannot be applied to configuration section groups. This can be a significant limitation, as the purpose of a section group is to group items that relate similar configuration sections. A logical separation could see all items in a particular section group in a separate configuration file.

- ❏ If the attribute is used within a web.config file, changing the referenced configuration file will not restart the ASP.NET application. In order for the configuration information to be reread, you need to either manually restart the ASP.NET application or modify the web.config file itself.

Each element within the configuration file inherits a number of attributes that can be set to control whether that element can be overridden or not. To prevent an element, or even an entire section, from being overridden, you can lock it. Five different locking attributes (outlined in the following table) can be used to specify any number of configuration attributes and elements that are to be locked.

Being able to lock configuration items is particularly relevant when you're dealing with web applications, which might contain a deep hierarchy of configuration inheritance. Windows applications inherit only from the machine.config file, so it is unlikely that you will need to lock items.

Table 38-1. Locking Attributes

Configuration Element	Description
LockItem	Locks the element to which this attribute is applied, including all other attributes provided on that element and all child elements
LockAttributes	Locks the comma-delimited list of attributes provided
LockAllAttributesExcept	Locks all attributes except those provided in the comma-delimited list
LockElements	Locks the comma-delimited list of child elements provided
LockAllElementsExcept	Locks all child elements except those provided in the comma-delimited list

Application Settings

Applications frequently have settings that do not fit into the default configuration schema. There are four mechanisms for storing this information.

Using appSettings

The first technique is to use the predefined appSettings section of the configuration file. This section can be used to store simple name-value pairs of application settings, which might be useful for storing the name of the server, as in the following example:

```
<configuration>
    <appSettings>
        <add key="PrimaryServer" value="http://www.softteq.com"/>
    </appSettings>
</configuration>
```

This value can easily be accessed within code by means of the `AppSettings` property of the new `ConfigurationManager` class (which requires a reference to the System.Configuration assembly):

```
Dim server As String = ConfigurationManager.AppSettings("PrimaryServer")
```

One of the weaknesses of this approach is that the name of the setting is specified as a string, rather than as a strongly typed property. It also assumes that the value will be a string, which is often not the case.

Project Settings

Using the Settings tab of the project properties designer, you can define application settings of a variety of types. Figure 38-1 illustrates how the `PrimaryServer` setting would appear in this designer.

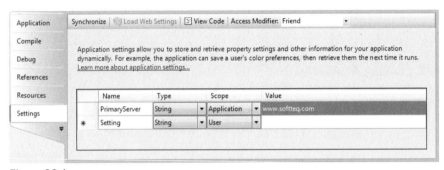

Figure 38-1

Adding application settings via this designer does not use the `appSettings` section as you might expect. Instead, it defines a new section in the configuration, as discussed earlier in the section on the `configSection` element and shown in the following snippet:

```
<configuration>
    ...
    <ConfigurationApplication.My.Settings>
        <setting name="PrimaryServer" serializeAs="String">
            <value>www.softteq.com</value>
        </setting>
    </ConfigurationApplication.My.Settings>
</configuration>
```

To access this setting in code, you can make use of the generated strongly typed access properties.

C#

```
string primaryServer = Properties.Settings.Default.PrimaryServer;
```

VB.NET

```
Dim primaryServer as String = My.Settings.PrimaryServer
```

Dynamic Properties

The third mechanism for storing application-specific information is the use of dynamic properties. These are typically used to dynamically set designer properties. For example, you could set the text on a Button1 using the following configuration block:

```
<configuration>
    ...
    <applicationSettings>
        <ConfigurationApplication.My.MySettings>
            <setting name="Button1_Text" serializeAs="String">
                <value>Press Me Now!</value>
            </setting>
        </ConfigurationApplication.My.MySettings>
    </applicationSettings>
</configuration>
```

You will note that the preceding code uses the same syntax as application settings defined using the project properties designer. In fact, they are one and the same, the only difference being that in the `InitializeComponent` method of the form there is a line of code that sets the button text:

```
Me.Button1.Text= Global.ConfigurationApplication.My.MySettings.Default.Button1_Text
```

When this application is deployed, the text displayed on Button1 is dynamically loaded from the configuration file. In the following steps, for example, we set the size of a control, Button1, to be dynamically loaded from the configuration file:

1. Select Button1 on the designer surface and press F4 to display the Properties window. Locate the Data category or the ApplicationSettings item in the alphabetic list, as shown in Figure 38-2.

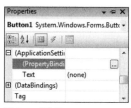

Figure 38-2

2. Press the ellipsis button (…) next to the `PropertyBinding` row. This will open a dialog that lists the available properties for Button1, along with any application settings that have been assigned, as shown in Figure 38-3.

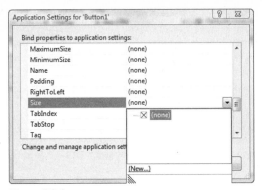

Figure 38-3

3. Select the drop-down next to the `Size` property and select New. This will open a dialog in which you can specify a default value, a name for the application setting, and the scope of the setting.

4. Specify a name for the application setting — for example, Button1_Size, and set the scope to Application. You can modify the default value or simply accept the value that has been extracted from the current properties of Button1, as shown in Figure 38-4.

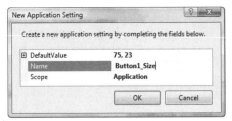

Figure 38-4

5. Click "OK" on both dialogs. If you open the app.config file that will be available from the Solution Explorer window, you will see a section that defines the Button1_Size setting.

Custom Configuration Sections

Developers often want to include more structured information in the configuration file than can be stored in the `appSettings` section. To solve this problem and eliminate any need for additional configuration files, you can create a custom configuration section. The new configuration section must be defined at the top of the configuration file via the `configSection` element, complete with a reference to a class that should be used to process that portion of the configuration file.

In the past this process was fairly complex, as the class needed to implement the IConfigurationSectionHandler interface. This exposed a simple method, `Create`, which was called the first time that section was referenced in code. There was little support from the framework to process the section, and a class implementing this interface often resorted to parsing the XML block to determine settings.

Visual Studio 2008 provides much better support for creating custom configuration sections via the `ConfigurationSection` and `ConfigurationElement` classes. These provide the bases for creating classes that map to the structure of the data being stored in the configuration files. Instead of mapping a class that processes the configuration section, we can now create a much simpler class that maps to the section. When the section is referenced in code, an instance of this class is returned with the appropriate data elements set. All the XML processing that would have been necessary in the past is now handled by the .NET Framework.

Although this mapping makes the process of writing a custom configuration section much easier, you may sometimes want more control over how the section is read. Two options can be used to give you this control.

❏   The first option is to go back to using a configuration section handler and manually process the XML file. This can be useful if the original XML representation is required. However, it still requires that the XML file be processed.

❏   The second strategy is to create an appropriate mapping class as an in-between measure. Instead of referencing this class directly, another class can be generated that exposes the configuration information in the right way.

If you need to use either of these options, it might be worth taking a step back and determining whether the configuration section structure is actually in a format suited to the data being stored.

Of course, the best way to illustrate this potential unsuitability is with an example. Our application requires a list of registered entities with which to work. One type of entity is a company, and we need to be provided with both the company name and the date on which it was registered. The XML snippet that we would like to have in the configuration file might look like the following:

```
<RegisteredEntities>
    <Companies>
        <add CompanyName="Random Inc" RegisteredDate="31/1/2005" />
        <add CompanyName="Developer Experience Inc" RegisteredDate="1/8/2004" />
    </Companies>
</RegisteredEntities>
```

Once generated, the corresponding classes that would map to the preceding snippet might look like the following (again, this requires a reference to the System.Configuration assembly):

```
Public Class RegisteredEntities
    Inherits ConfigurationSection

    <ConfigurationProperty("Companies")> _
    Public ReadOnly Property Companies() As Companies
        Get
            Return CType(MyBase.Item("Companies"),Companies)
        End Get
    End Property
End Class

<ConfigurationCollectionAttribute(GetType(Company))> _
Public Class Companies
```

(continued)

(continued)

```
        Inherits ConfigurationElementCollection

        Protected Overrides Function CreateNewElement() As ConfigurationElement
            Return New Company
        End Function

        Protected Overrides Function GetElementKey _
                            (ByVal element As ConfigurationElement) As Object
            Return CType(element, Company).CompanyName
        End Function

        Public Sub Add(ByVal element As Company)
            Me.BaseAdd(element)
        End Sub

    End Class

    Public Class Company
        Inherits ConfigurationElement

        <ConfigurationProperty("CompanyName",DefaultValue:="Random Inc",
    IsKey:=true, IsRequired:=true)> _
        Public Property CompanyName() As String
            Get
                Return CType(MyBase.Item("CompanyName"),String)
            End Get
            Set
                MyBase.Item("CompanyName") = value
            End Set
        End Property

        < ConfigurationProperty("RegisteredDate",DefaultValue:="31/1/2005",
    IsKey:=false, IsRequired:=false)> _
        Public Property RegisteredDate() As String
            Get
                Return CType(MyBase.Item("RegisteredDate"),String)
            End Get
            Set
                MyBase.Item("RegisteredDate") = value
            End Set
        End Property
    End Class
```

The code contains three classes that are required in order to correctly map the functionality of this section. The registered entities section corresponds to the `RegisteredEntities` class, which contains a single property that returns a company collection. A collection is required here because we want to be able to support the addition of multiple companies. This functionality could be extended to clear and/or remove companies, which might be useful if we had a web application for which we needed to control which companies were available to different portions of the application. Lastly, there is the `Company` class that maps to the individual company information being added.

To access this section from within the code, we can simply call the appropriate section using the `configurationManager` framework class:

```
Dim registered as RegisteredEntities= _
    ctype(configurationmanager.GetSection("RegisteredEntities"),RegisteredEntities)
```

Automation Using SCDL

You just saw how custom configuration sections can be written and mapped to classes. Although this is a huge improvement over writing section handlers, it is still a fairly laborious process that is prone to error. Furthermore, debugging the configuration sections is nearly impossible because it's difficult to track what's going wrong.

As part of another project to support ASP.NET developers, a development manager for the ASP.NET team at Microsoft recognized that the process of creating these mapping classes was mundane and could easily be automated. To this end, he created a small application entitled SCDL (`http://blogs.msdn .com/dmitryr/archive/2005/12/07/501365.aspx`) that could take a snippet of configuration data, such as the `RegisteredEntities` section discussed previously, and output both the mapping classes and a schema file that represented the section supplied. Once generated, this code can be included in the application. Furthermore, if the snippet of configuration data is to be included as a non-compiled file within the solution, it is possible to automate the generation of the mapping classes via a prebuild `batch` command. If changes need to be made to the structure of the section, they can be made in the snippet. That way, the next time the solution is built the mapping classes will be updated automatically.

IntelliSense

Even after you get the custom configuration sections correctly mapped, there is still no support provided by Visual Studio 2008 for adding the custom section to the configuration file. Unlike the rest of the configuration file, which has support for IntelliSense and will report validation issues, your custom section will not be able to be validated.

In order to get IntelliSense and validation for your custom configuration section, you need to indicate the structure of the configuration section to Visual Studio 2008. You can do this by placing an appropriate schema (as generated by the SCDL tool) in the XML Schemas folder, which is usually located at C:\Program Files\Microsoft Visual Studio 9.0\Xml\Schemas\. Unfortunately, this is where it gets a little bit more complex, as it is not enough to place the file in that folder; you also need to tell it that the schema should be included in the catalog used for parsing configuration files. To register your schema, follow these steps:

1. Generate your schema file from your configuration snippet:

```
Scdl.exe snippet.scdl snippet.vb snippet.xsd
```

2. Copy the schema file (in this case, snippet.xsd) to the schema folder.

3. Create a new text file called Config.xsd and include the following lines. Note that if your schema is called something different, you should update these lines appropriately. You may also add

additional lines to include more than one schema. Do not remove the `DotNetConfig.xsd` line because that will remove validation for the standard configuration sections.

```xml
<?xml version="1.0" encoding="utf-8" ?>
<xs:schema xmlns:xs="http://www.w3.org/2001/XMLSchema">
    <xs:include schemaLocation="DotNetConfig.xsd"/>
    <xs:include schemaLocation="snippet.xsd"/>
</xs:schema>
```

4. Open `Catalog.xml` in a text editor and replace `DotNetConfig.xsd` with `Config.xsd`. This effectively remaps the validation, and IntelliSense, for configuration files to use `Config.xsd` instead of `DotNetConfig.xsd`. However, because this file sources both `DotNetConfig.xsd` and your schema information, you will get validation for both your configuration section and the standard configuration sections.

Referenced Projects with Settings

As applications grow, it is necessary to break up the logic into assemblies that are referenced by the main application. In the past, if these referenced assemblies wanted to use an application setting, there were a number of gotchas that made it problematic. With Visual Studio 2008, it is now possible to share application settings among assemblies using the project properties designer. Figure 38-5 shows the Settings tab of the project properties designer for a reference assembly. In this case the Access Modifier drop-down has been set to Public to allow access to these settings from the main application.

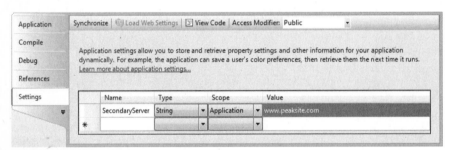

Figure 38-5

To access this property from the main application, you can again use the generated strongly typed access properties:

```
ReferencedAssembly.My.Settings.Default.SecondaryServer
```

A word of caution about using the project properties designer and referenced application settings: If you examine the code-behind file for the settings designer, you will note that for each of the settings you have defined there is a strongly typed access property, as previously discussed. What is important is the `DefaultSettingValueAttribute` that is applied. This is significant because it determines the value that will be returned by this property if the configuration file does not have any value specified.

In the following snippet, the default value of `www.peaksite.com` will be returned if there is no `SecondaryServer` element defined in the configuration file:

```
Namespace My
    Partial Friend NotInheritable Class MySettings
        Inherits Global.System.Configuration.ApplicationSettingsBase
        ...
<Global.System.Configuration.ApplicationScopedSettingAttribute(), _
Global.System.Diagnostics.DebuggerNonUserCodeAttribute(), _
Global.System.Configuration.DefaultSettingValueAttribute("www.peaksite.com")> _
        Public ReadOnly Property SecondaryServer() As String
            Get
                Return CType(Me("SecondaryServer "),String)
            End Get
        End Property
    End Class
End Namespace
```

Now, you might ask why this is important when you're dealing with referenced application settings. It is because although the project properties designer enables you to specify that you want to allow access to settings from another assembly, it doesn't enable you to indicate that an application does, in fact, reference settings from another assembly. The upshot is that when it compiles the application it takes only the app.config file in the application project folder, rather than combining the elements from the app.config files in the referenced assembly folder.

Unfortunately, because of the default value attribute you are unlikely to notice this until the application is deployed and you realize that some of the settings are missing from the app.config file. Because of this, you should make sure you manually combine these files. In our case the result would be this:

```
<configuration>
    ...
    <applicationSettings>
        <ConfigurationApplication.My.Settings>
            <setting name="PrimaryServer" serializeAs="String">
             <value>www.softteq.com</value>
            </setting>
        </ConfigurationApplication.My.Settings>
        <ReferencedAssembly.My.Settings>
            <setting name="SecondaryServer" serializeAs="String">
             <value>www.peaksite.com</value>
            </setting>
        </ReferencedAssembly.My.Settings>
    </applicationSettings>
</configuration>
```

Summary

In this chapter you have learned how configuration files can be used not only to control how your application runs, but also to store settings that may need to be adjusted at runtime. You should now be able to store simple name-value information, as well as more structured information, within the configuration file.

39

Connection Strings

A large proportion of applications need to persist data, and the obvious candidate for enterprise software is a relational database. The .NET Framework provides support for working with SQL Server, SQL Server Compact Edition, Oracle, ODBC, and OLE DB databases. To connect to any of these databases, you need to specify a connection string that determines the location, the database, authentication information, and other connection parameters. This chapter explains how to create and store connection strings. In addition, you learn about encrypting and working with connection strings in code.

Connection String Wizard

Connection strings are similar to XML in that, although they can be read, it is neither an enjoyable experience nor recommended to work with them directly. Because connection strings are strings, it is easy to introduce errors, misspell words, or even omit a parameter. Unlike XML, which can easily be validated against a schema, connection strings are harder to validate. The connection string wizard built into Visual Studio 2008 enables you to specify database connections without having to manually edit the connection string itself.

You can invoke the connection string wizard in a number of ways, as you will experience when you start working with any of the data controls in either the Windows Form or Web Form designers. For the purposes of illustrating the wizard, follow these steps to add a new data source to an existing Windows Forms application. You'll connect to the sample AdventureWorks database, which you will need to download from the Codeplex web site (www.codeplex.com and search for AdventureWorks).

1. From the Data menu within Visual Studio 2008, select Add New Data Source, which opens the Data Source Configuration Wizard.

2. Selecting Database enables you to determine the database connection to use. If a connection already exists, you can select it from the drop-down and the associated connection string will appear in the lower portion of the window, as shown in Figure 39-1.

Figure 39-1

The connection string will connect to the AdventureWorks database on the default database server on machine *drnick* with schema *dbo*. Later in this chapter you'll look at the properties of a SQL Server connection string in more detail.

3. To create a new connection, click the New Connection button to open the Add Connection dialog in which you can specify the properties of the connection string. Figure 39-2 shows the dialog as it would appear for a SQL Server database connection. This dialog is specific to the database source being configured.

Figure 39-2

Notice in Figure 39-2 that only the basic connection properties (such as server name, database name, and authentication information) are presented.

4. Click the Advanced button to open the Advanced Properties window, shown in Figure 39-3, where you can configure all properties for a SQL Server connection. At the bottom of this window is the connection string being constructed. The default values are omitted from the connection string. Once a value is set, it appears in the connection string and in bold in the Properties window. The list of available properties is again based on the data source being used.

Figure 39-3

5. Click OK to return to the Add Connection window, where you can change the type of data source by clicking the Change button. This opens the Change Data Source dialog, shown in Figure 39-4.

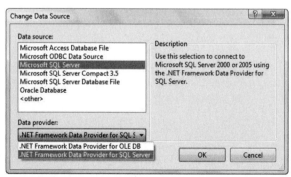

Figure 39-4

The list on the left contains all the data sources currently registered in the machine.config file. For a given data source, such as Microsoft SQL Server, there may be multiple data providers — in this case, the SQL Server and OLE DB providers.

Selecting an alternative data source-data provider combination will result in a different Add Connection dialog, displaying parameters that are relevant to that database connection. In most cases it is necessary to open the Advanced properties window to configure the connection itself.

6. After specifying the data source and connection settings using the Add Connection dialog, return to the Data Source Configuration Wizard. If you are creating a new connection, you will be given the option to save the connection string in the application configuration file, as shown in Figure 39-5. Unless you can guarantee that the location of the database, the authentication mode, or any other connection property will not change at a later stage, it is a good idea to store the connection string in the configuration file. Saving the connection string to the configuration file has the added benefit that the same configuration string can be reused throughout the application.

Figure 39-5

If you don't save the connection string to the configuration file, it is explicitly assigned to the connection object you are creating, which makes reuse difficult. Alternatively, saving the connection string in the configuration file means that other connection objects can access the same string. If the database connection changes at a later stage, you can easily update it in a single location.

7. The Data Source Configuration Wizard will continue to step you through selecting which database objects you want to be added to your data source. This is covered in more detail in Chapter 21 on working with DataSets.

When you save a connection string to an application configuration file, it is added to the `connectionStrings` configuration section, as illustrated in the following snippet from an app.config file (the same section can exist in a web.config file for a web application):

```
<?xml version="1.0" encoding="utf-8" ?>
<configuration>
    <appSettings />
    <connectionStrings>
        <add
        name="Connection_Strings.Properties.Settings.AdventureWorksConnectionString"
        connectionString="Data Source=drnick;Initial
Catalog=AdventureWorks;Integrated Security=True"
        providerName="System.Data.SqlClient" />
    </connectionStrings>
</configuration>
```

The `connectionStrings` section of a configuration file uses the standard element collection pattern, which allows multiple connection strings to be specified and then referenced in code. For example, the preceding connection string can be accessed in code as follows (this assumes your project has a reference to the System.Configuration assembly):

```
Private Sub OpenConnectionClick(ByVal sender As System.Object, _
                                ByVal e As System.EventArgs) _
                                          Handles BtnOpenConnection.Click
    Dim sqlCon As New SqlClient.SqlConnection
    sqlCon.ConnectionString = ConfigurationManager.ConnectionStrings _
                        ("AdventureWorksConnectionString").ConnectionString
    sqlCon.Open()
End Sub
```

A nice artifact of working with the connection string wizard is that it also adds strongly typed support for accessing the connection string from within your code. This means that you can access the connection string using the following strongly typed methods, rather than call them using a string constant:

C#

```
Properties.Settings.Default.AdventureWorksConnectionString;
```

VB.NET

```
My.Settings.AdventureWorksConnectionString
```

The other advantage of saving the connection string in the configuration file is that when you are editing the project settings, the connection strings are listed alongside other settings for the project as shown in Figure 39-6. Not only can you modify the connection string directly; you also have a shortcut to the connection string wizard, via the ellipsis button to the right of the connection string value, which enables you to adjust the connection properties without fear of corrupting the connection string.

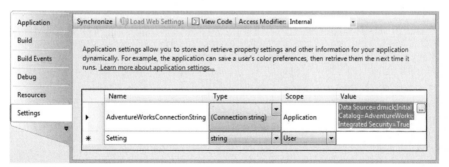

Figure 39-6

You will notice in Figure 39-6 that the name of the connection string excludes the rather lengthy prefix, Connection_Strings.Properties.Settings, which is in the application configuration file. This prefix is used to determine which connection strings should be included in both the project properties designer and for providing strongly typed support.

Given the inherent danger of getting data source properties wrong when manually editing the connection strings in the configuration file versus the benefits of using either the add data source wizard or the project properties designer, it is highly recommended that you avoid the manual approach wherever possible.

SQL Server Format

Probably the most familiar data provider is the SQL Server database provider, so Table 39-1 details some of the common connection properties you may need to specify to connect to your database server.

Table 39-1: Some Common Connection Properties

Connection Property	Description
Asynchronous Processing	Determines whether the connection will support asynchronous database calls. Most applications try to deliver a responsive user interface, so it is important for it not to freeze when retrieving data. In the past this could only be achieved by doing the data processing in a separate thread from the user interface. The data access methods, such as ExecuteNonQuery, now support calls using the Begin and End asynchronous pattern. For example, BeginExecuteNonQuery will return immediately so the user interface does not block while the data access is performed.
AttachDBFilename	Introduced in SQL Server 2005, this property means you can work with databases that aren't permanently attached to a SQL Server instance. This property is a path reference to the primary database file that contains the database. Specifying AttachDBFilename effectively attaches and detaches the database when required.
Connect Timeout	Determines the maximum length of time that the Open method will block when attempting to connect to the database. This should not be confused with the Timeout property on the SQLCommand class, which determines the timeout for a given command to execute.
Data Source	The host name or IP address of the instance of SQL Server that the connection will be accessing. In cases where multiple instances exist on a given machine, or where SQL Server has been assigned an instance name other than the default instance, this needs to be specified as part of the Data Source field, for example, 192.168.205.223\InstanceName.
Initial Catalog	Specifies the name of the database to connect to.

Connection Property	Description
Integrated Security	If Integrated Security is used, the Windows credentials of the current user will be used to connect to the database server. To provide user ID and password, this property must be set to false. Also be aware that when working with ASP.NET using Windows authentication without impersonation, if Integrated Security is enabled, the authenticated web user's credentials will be used to access the database server.
MultipleActiveResultSets	Allows multiple result sets to be returned across a given connection. For example, a single database command mightcontain two SELECT statements. If the MultipleActiveResultSets property is enabled, the results of both SELECT statements will be returned and can be used to populate a DataSet. This property is compatible only with SQL Server 2005 and above.
Password	Used for the SQL Server user account used to access the database server.
User ID	Specifies the SQL Server account used to access the database server. Mixed-mode authentication for the SQL Server must be enabled, and the Integrated Security property must be set to false.

Each connection string property must be specified as it appears in the preceding table, but they can be in any order in the connection string. A semicolon is used to separate each property. An example connection string might be as follows:

```
Data Source=drnick;Initial Catalog=AdventureWorks;Integrated Security=True;
   MultipleActiveResultSets=True
```

In-Code Construction

Although the connection string wizard in Visual Studio 2008 provides a convenient tool for writing connection strings, it is often necessary to build one dynamically — a feat easily done with the SqlConnectionStringBuilder class. In fact, there are also string builder classes for Oracle, ODBC, and OLE DB, and they all derive from the generic DBConnectionStringBuilder class, which exposes the ConnectionString property.

This example demonstrates creating a connection builder object, based on an existing connection string, changing the authentication mode to use the user ID and password provided by the user before assigning the new connection string to the connection object. In addition, the example demonstrates the use of the `MultipleActiveResultSets` property to retrieve multiple tables from the database using a single command object:

```
Private Sub LoadDataClick(ByVal sender As System.Object, _
                          ByVal e As System.EventArgs) Handles Button1.Click
    'Update the connection string based on user settings
    Dim sqlbuilder As New SqlClient.SqlConnectionStringBuilder _
                              (My.Settings.AdventureWorksConnectionString)
    If Not Me.TxtUserId.Text = "" Then
        sqlbuilder.IntegratedSecurity = False
        sqlbuilder.UserID = Me.TxtUserId.Text
        sqlbuilder.Password = Me.TxtPassword.Text
    End If
    sqlbuilder.MultipleActiveResultSets = True

    'Create the connection based on the updated connection string
    Dim sqlCon As New SqlClient.SqlConnection
    sqlCon.ConnectionString = sqlbuilder.ConnectionString

    'Set the command and create the dataset to load the data into
    Dim sqlcmd As New SqlClient.SqlCommand("SELECT * FROM Person.Contact;" & _
                                "SELECT * FROM Person.ContactType", _
                                sqlCon)

    Dim ds As New DataSet
    Dim rds As New SqlClient.SqlDataAdapter(sqlcmd)

    'Open connection, retrieve data, and close connection
    sqlCon.Open()
    rds.Fill(ds)
    sqlCon.Close()
End Sub
```

The important thing to note about this code sample is that the `MultipleActiveResultSets` property is enabled, which means that multiple SELECT statements can be specified in the SqlCommand object. The `SqlCommand` object is then used by the `SqlDataAdapter` object to fill the DataSet. The DataSet object will contain two data tables, each populated by one of the SELECT statements.

Encrypting Connection Strings

Although best practices state that you should use Windows authentication and integrated security wherever possible, this is not always the case; sometimes you have to resort to specifying a user ID and password in a connection string. It is recommended that this information not be hard-coded into your application, because it can easily be extracted from the assembly. As such, this information needs to be either specified by the users each time they use the system, or added to the connection string in the configuration file. The upshot of this is that you need a mechanism for encrypting configuration sections.

This walkthrough shows you how to encrypt a section of a configuration file for a web application, StagingWebsite, which has a web.config file as follows:

```xml
<?xml version="1.0"?>
<configuration>
    <connectionStrings>
        <add name="AdventureWorksConnectionString" connectionString="Data Source=
.\sqlexpress;Initial Catalog=AdventureWorks;Integrated Security=True"
            providerName="System.Data.SqlClient" />
    </connectionStrings>
    <!--
        ...
    -->
</configuration>
```

Using the command prompt, execute the following commands in sequence, replacing UserName with the name of the account that the web application will run as (for example, the AspNet account):

1. `cd\WINDOWS\Microsoft.NET\Framework\v2.0.50739`

2. `aspnet_regiis -pa "NetFrameworkConfigurationKey" "UserName"`

3. `aspnet_regiis -pe "connectionStrings" -app "/StagingWebsite"`

Executing these commands modifies the web.config file as follows (if you get an error saying that the RSA key container was not found, you may need to execute 'aspnet_regiis -pc "NetFrameworkConfigurationKey" -exp' to create the key container):

```xml
<?xml version="1.0"?>
<configuration>
 <connectionStrings configProtectionProvider="RsaProtectedConfigurationProvider">
  <EncryptedData Type="http://www.w3.org/2001/04/xmlenc#Element"
  xmlns="http://www.w3.org/2001/04/xmlenc#">
   <EncryptionMethod Algorithm="http://www.w3.org/2001/04/xmlenc#tripledes-cbc" />
   <KeyInfo xmlns="http://www.w3.org/2000/09/xmldsig#">
    <EncryptedKey xmlns="http://www.w3.org/2001/04/xmlenc#">
     <EncryptionMethod Algorithm="http://www.w3.org/2001/04/xmlenc#rsa-1_5" />
     <KeyInfo xmlns="http://www.w3.org/2000/09/xmldsig#">
      <KeyName>Rsa Key</KeyName>
     </KeyInfo>
     <CipherData>
         <CipherValue>Y4Be/ND8fXTK13r0CASBK0oaOSvbyijYCVUudf1AuQl
pU2HRsTyEpR2sVpxrOukiBhvcGyWlv4EM0AB9p3Ms8FgIA3Ou6mGORhxfO9eIUGD+M5tJSe6wn/
9op8mFV4W7YQZ4WIqLaAAu7MKVI6KKK/ANIKpV8l2NdMBT3uPOPi8=</CipherValue>
     </CipherData>
    </EncryptedKey>
   </KeyInfo>
   <CipherData>
       <CipherValue>BeKnN/kQIMw9rFbck6IwX9NZA6WyOCSQlziWzCLA8Ff/JdA0W/dWIidnjae1
vgpS8ghouYn7BQocjvc0uGsGgXlPfvsLq18//1ArZDgiHVLAXjW6b+eKbE5vaf5ss6psJdCRRB0ab5xao
NAPHH/Db9UKMycWVqP0badN+qCQzYyU2cQFvK1S7Rum8VwgZ85Qt+FGExYpG06YqVR9tfWwqZmYwtW8iz
```

(continued)

(continued)

```
    r7fijvspm/oRK4Yd+DGBRKuXxD6EN4kFgJUil7ktzOJAwWly4bVpmwzwJT9N6yig54lobhOahZDP05gtk
    Lor/HwD9IKmRvO1jv</
        CipherValue>
        </CipherData>
      </EncryptedData>
    </connectionStrings>
        <!--

              . . .

        -->
    </configuration>
```

As you can see from this example, the connection string is no longer readable in the configuration file. The commands you executed did two things. Ignoring the first command (because it simply changes the directory so you can access the `asp_regiis` executable), the second command permits access to the key container NetFrameworkConfigurationKey for the user Nick. This key container is the default container for the RSAProtectedConfigurationProvider, which is specified in the machine.config file. In order for your application to be able to decrypt data from the configuration file, the user that the application is running as must be able to access the key container. To determine the identity of this user, execute the following command:

```
System.Security.Principal.WindowsIdentity.GetCurrent().Name
```

The third command encrypts the `connectionStrings` section of the configuration file for the web application StagingWebsite. Other sections of the configuration file can also be encrypted using the same command. If at some later stage you need to decrypt the configuration section, execute the same command, but with –pd instead of –pe. For example:

```
aspnet_regiis -pd "connectionStrings" -app "/StagingWebsite"
```

Summary

This chapter showed you how to use Visual Studio 2008 to take charge of your application and configure it to connect to a database using a connection string. With the built-in support of the data classes in the .NET Framework, connection strings can be dynamically created and modified so you never have to handcraft a connection string again.

40

Resource Files

Developers often overlook the humble XML resource file, as it is often hidden by Visual Studio 2008 so as not to clutter the solution. Because its most common use is as a backing file for forms or web pages, you can write large applications without interacting directly with resource files. However, resource files are an important tool that developers need to be able to use in order to write applications that can be easily maintained and translated into other languages. The first part of this chapter explains why resource files are important and describes the features that enable developers to work with them. The remainder of the chapter explains how resource files are used to localize an application for different languages and cultures.

What Are Resources?

A resource is any data required by an application, whether it is a string, an icon, an image, or even an audio clip. Resources are non-executable and support the running of the application through the provision of data such as location, size, and other physical properties of controls. While most resources are strings, images, audio clips, or icons, there is no reason why a resource could not be a more complex object that supports serialization.

Three types of resource files can be compiled into an application: text, resx (XML resource file), and resources (binary resource file) file formats. Whole files can also be embedded as application resources where needed. Most developers who use Visual Studio 2008 will use resx files and embedded file resources.

Text File Resources

Text files are the most basic sort of resource because they are limited to providing string values. In applications for which a large number of string literals need to be managed, using a simple text file can be the easiest way to do it because that way they are not cluttered among the other resources of the application.

The format of strings defined in a text resource file is a name-value pair, where the name is used to reference the resource in code, as shown in the following example:

```
Error_Unable_To_Connect = Unable to connect to specified server
```

Because each name-value pair is delimited by a new line, this character cannot be added to the string. However, C-style escape characters can be used to insert new lines (\n) or tabs (\t) into the text.

You can add comments to the resource file by prefixing a line with a semicolon, as shown here:

```
;Error message to be displayed when a connection could not be made to the server
   Error_Unable_To_Connect = Unable to connect to specified server
```

Text resource files should be saved with the file extension of .txt or .restext. The latter is useful when you want to distinguish text resource files from regular text files.

Although text resource files are easy to edit and update, it is harder to integrate them into your application. As text files, they cannot be directly compiled into an application; they must instead be converted into either resx or resources files. Do this using the Resource Generator utility, resgen.exe, located in the \bin folder of the Windows SDK (located at C:\Program Files\Microsoft SDKs\Windows\v6.0A\bin):

```
resgen StringResources.txt StringResources.resources
```

Include the output file — in this case, StringResources.resources — in your application to give yourself access to those resources.

A prebuild event can be used to convert text resource files into a resources file that can be compiled into the main application build. This will ensure that the resources files contained in the application are always up to date. To do this, include the text resource file in the application and set the build action property to None. Navigate to the Project Settings window and on the Compile tab select Build Events. In the prebuild events, enter the Resgen command required to compile your text resource file:

```
"C:\Program Files\Microsoft Visual Studio 8\SDK\v2.0\Bin\resgen.exe"
   "$(ProjectDir)StringResources.txt" "$(ProjectDir) StringResources.resources"
```

Building the application will generate the resources file that needs to be included within your application with the build action property set to Embedded Resource. Figure 40-1 illustrates how both the text file and the resources file are included within an application with appropriate build action properties.

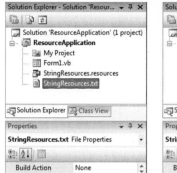

Figure 40-1

Resx Resource Files

A much more user-friendly format for resources is the XML resource file, commonly referred to as a resx file. This is a simple XML data file that contains name-value pairs of XML nodes. The advantage of this format is that the value is not restricted to just a string; it can be of any type that is serializable or that can be represented as a string.

The following XML snippet shows a resource named HelloWorld, with associated value and comment. As you can see from the code, no information is available about the type of data contained within the resource, as it is a string resource:

```
<data name="HelloWorld">
  <value>Say Hello</value>
  <comment>This is how we say hello</comment>
</data>
```

The next snippet illustrates how a more complex data type can be stored in a resource file as a string representation. It also shows how an assembly alias can be used to reference an external assembly that contains type information. When this resource is accessed, the type information will be used to convert the string value to an object of this type:

```
<assembly alias="System.Drawing" name="System.Drawing, Version=2.0.0.0,
Culture=neutral, PublicKeyToken=b03f5f7f11d50a3a" />
  <data name="Button1.Location" type="System.Drawing.Point, System.Drawing">
    <value>71, 43</value>
  </data>
```

Although resx files can be included in an application without your having to use the Resource File Generator (Resgen), they are still converted prior to being compiled into the application. During the build process, resources files are generated for each resx file in the application. These are subsequently linked into the application.

Binary Resources

The third resource format is the binary resource file, indicated by the `.resources` file extension. Behind the scenes, Visual Studio 2008 converts all resx files into `.resources` files as an intermediate step during compilation (you can see these files in the \obj\debug folder for your project), and as you saw earlier in this chapter, you must manually convert text resources into `.resources` files using Resgen. You can also integrate other binary resources into your project by simply including the `.resources` file and setting the build action to `Embedded Resource`.

Adding Resources

Visual Studio 2008 now supports a rich user interface for adding and modifying resource files. In the past it was possible to view the contents of a resource file within the IDE. However, unless the resource was a string, or had a string representation, it was not possible to modify the value within the resource file. The resource editor provides support for strings, images, icons, audio files, and more.

Double-clicking the My Project (VB.NET) or Properties (C#) node for a project in the Solution Explorer will open the project properties editor, from which you can select the Resources tab to open the default, or project, resource file. For C# projects you will then need to click the presented link to create the resource file (VB.NET projects already have a default resource file). When the default resource file opens you will see that in the top left-hand corner of the resource editor is a drop-down list that navigates among resources of different types, as shown in Figure 40-2. Double-clicking any resx file within the Solution Explorer will also bring up this resource editor.

Figure 40-2

The editor displays the resource in an appropriate format, according to its type. For example, strings are presented in an editable textbox, whereas images are presented as thumbnails that can be opened and edited. Adding new resources is as simple as selecting the Add Resource drop-down, choosing the appropriate resource type, and then adding the necessary information. Once you have added a resource it will appear in the resource editor, as shown in Figure 40-3.

Figure 40-3

Figure 40-3 shows an additional column that gives you the option to specify a comment alongside your resource. Unfortunately, the resource editor is the only place in Visual Studio 2008 where this comment is displayed. Figure 40-4 (C#) shows the previously created resource being accessed in code: you can see that the comment presented is not the one from Figure 40-3.

Figure 40-4

The comment presented in Figure 40-4 is the XML comment that appears in the automatically generated designer file for the resx file, whereas the comment in Figure 40-3 is contained in the resx file itself.

Embedding Files as Resources

It is often necessary to embed an entire file in an application. You can do this by including the file in the application and modifying the build action. Depending on the file type, when the item is included in the application, the build action (click the file and open the Properties window) is normally set to either `Compile` or `None`. If this is changed to `Embedded Resource`, the entire file will be added to the application as an embedded resource.

Alternatively, you can use the resource editor shown in Figure 40-2 to add a file resource. When images, icons, and other files are added to an existing resource file by means of the resource editor, they are added as a resxfileref item. The file will appear in the resources directory, but the build action will be `None`. When the application is built, these files are compiled into the resources file prior to being linked into the application. In the past the data from these files was pulled out and added to the resx file as a binary block. This meant that, once added, the data couldn't be easily modified. With the new file reference item, the data remains in an associated file and can easily be updated.

Naming Resources

Resources are named for the resource file to which they belong and the root namespace. For example, if you have a resource file called Sample.resources in a project called MyProject, the full resource name will be MyProject.Sample.

This is particularly important to remember when you make a file an embedded resource by changing the build action. You can access any file by prefixing the filename with the project name. Unlike with resource files, the name of the file retains the extension. For example, if you have a file called ASimpleDataDocument .doc in a project called MyProject, then it will need to be referenced as MyProject.ASimpleDataDocument.doc.

Any directory structure will be ignored for the purpose of naming embedded resources.

681

Accessing Resources

The method that you use to access resources depends on how they are embedded in the application. You have already seen that there are two ways to embed resources: the first is to add a file to the project and set the build action to `Embedded Resource`; the second is via the resource editor. In order to access resources added by a change to the build action, you need to use the `GetManifestResourceNames` and `GetManifestResourceStream` methods. The following code (VB.NET) retrieves the names of all the resources in the assembly by querying the manifest. It then creates a stream for accessing the relevant resource file. As we discussed in the previous section, the name of the embedded resource file returned by the `GetManifestResourceNames` method and accepted by the `GetManifestResourceStream` method is in the form *Root namespace.Filename.File_extension* (for example, MyProject. ASimpleDataDocument.doc).

```
Dim names = Reflection.Assembly.GetExecutingAssembly.GetManifestResourceNames
Dim resources = From n In names _
                Select Assembly.GetExecutingAssembly.GetManifestResourceStream(n)
For Each r In resources
    Using strm As New IO.StreamReader(r)
        MsgBox(strm.ReadToEnd)
    End Using
Next
```

Resources added via the resource editor can be accessed in code by means of a resource manager, which you can easily create from the name of the resource file to which they belong and a reference to the assembly from which the resource should be extracted:

```
Dim res As New ResourceManager ("MyProject.MyResources", _
                                Assembly.GetExecutingAssembly)
```

Once created, resources can be extracted by means of either the `GetObject` or `GetString` function:

```
res.GetObject("StringResource")
```

For more complex resources, such as files, you may also want to use the `GetStream` function. All three functions take the name of the resource as the only parameter.

Designer Files

The Resource Generator utility, Resgen, has a number of improvements that enable you to build strongly typed wrapper classes for your resource files. When you add a resx file to your application, Visual Studio 2008 will automatically create a designer file that wraps the process of creating a resource manager and accessing the resources by name. The accessor properties are all strongly typed and are generated by the designer to reduce the chance of invalid type conversions and references. For example, if you have a string resource, StringResource, contained in a resource file, MyResources, you can use the following code to access the string:

VB.NET

```
My.Resources.MyResources.MyStringResource
```

C#

```
MyResources.StringResource
```

You will notice that the designer-generated code is different for VB.NET and C#. This is because C# uses the generic ResXFileCodeGenerator custom tool to integrate the resource file into the My namespace, whereas VB.NET uses the VbMyResourcesResXFileCodeGenerator custom tool.

Unfortunately, Visual Studio 2008 does not automatically generate the designer file for text resource files, because text resource files cannot be explicitly added to the application. The process of generating a resource file from the text file can be extended to include the generation of the designer file.

A new argument has been added to Resgen that facilitates the generation of this designer file:

```
resgen sample.txt sample.resources /str:vb
```

Both of the output files need to be added to the application so that the resources are accessible. In order to ensure that the resources can be correctly accessed, you must ensure that the naming used within the designer file matches the naming of the compiled resources. You can provide additional parameters to control the namespace, class name, and output filename:

```
resgen sample.txt defaultnamespace.sample.resources /str:vb,defaultnamespace,sample,
    sample.vb
```

In this case, the fully qualified output class would be `defaultnamespace.sample`, and the use of this file would allow access to resources without an exception being raised. Once the correct command has been determined you can update your prebuild event to include the generation of the designer file. This way, every time the file is modified and saved and the application is compiled, the designer file will be recreated.

Resourcing Your Application

Writing an application often requires data such as images, icons, or sounds (collectively known as *resources*) to enhance the appearance of the application. Furthermore, best coding practices suggest that the use of constant strings throughout your application be avoided. In either case we can put together a custom solution that stores these resources in files that need to be shipped with the application.

An alternative is to include them in a resource file that can be compiled into your application. This way you not only have the resources in a format that you can work with, but they are also automatically available within your application.

In Visual Studio 2008, forms are initially represented by two files: the generated designer file (for example, Form1.Designer.vb) and the code-beside file (for example, Form1.vb). When a control, such as a button, is first added to the form, a resource file (for example, Form1.resx) is automatically created for the form. By default, this resource file contains very little data, as most properties are hard-coded into the designer file. This file becomes very important when localization is turned on for the form. When this is done, via the properties grid shown in Figure 40-5, the designer properties for the controls on the form are persisted to the resource file.

Figure 40-5

The following code snippet shows the designer-generated method `InitializeComponent`, which creates and sets properties on Button1. This is how the code would appear with the `Localizable` property on the form set to `False`:

```
Private Sub InitializeComponent()
    Me.Button1 = New Button
    '
    'Button1
    '
    Me.Button1.Location = New Point(71, 43)
    Me.Button1.Size = New Size(185, 166)
    Me.Button1.Text = "Button1"
    Me.Button1.TabIndex = 0
    Me.Button1.Name = "Button1"
    Me.Button1.UseVisualStyleBackColor = True
    '
    'Form1
    '
    Me.Controls.Add(Me.Button1)
End Sub
```

Once the `Localizable` property of the form has been set to `True`, the form uses the new `ComponentResourceManager` class to load and apply properties found in the associated resource file. (This framework class is covered in more detail later in this chapter.)

```
Private Sub InitializeComponent()
    Dim resources As New ComponentResourceManager(GetType(Form1))
    Me.Button1 = New Button
    '
    'Button1
    '
    resources.ApplyResources(Me.Button1, "Button1")
```

```
    Me.Button1.Name = "Button1"
    Me.Button1.UseVisualStyleBackColor = True
    '
    'Form1
    '
    Me.Controls.Add(Me.Button1)
End Sub
```

Although the resource files generated by the forms designer can be manually edited, this is not encouraged because changes may be overwritten the next time the file is regenerated by the designer.

When resource files are used properly, they can provide a number of benefits because they are a convenient place to store strings, icons, images, and other data that might be referenced by an application. The use of resource files, both for tracking form properties and for application data, is a must for any application that needs to be translated for a foreign culture. (We use the term "culture" here because more than language can differ among countries and ethnic groups.) Resource files enable developers to provide alternative data for different cultures. When the application is run, the .NET Framework uses the current culture information to determine which data to load, based upon the resource fallback process. (We'll discuss the fallback process in the section "Loading Culture Resource Files" later in this chapter.) Common examples of information that might need to be varied among cultures are prompts, titles, error messages, and button images.

Control Images

There are a number of Windows Forms controls that have images as properties. For example, the PictureBox control has Image, ErrorImage, and InitialImage properties. If you click the ellipsis in the value column of the Properties window for any of these properties, you will see the dialog shown in Figure 40-6, which enables you to select an image for the specified property.

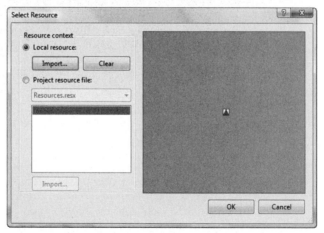

Figure 40-6

Before selecting an image, you have to decide whether you want to store it in the resource file associated with the current form (that is, a Local resource) or in a project-level resource file. The former option will store the image in a Base64-encoded block within the actual resource file, whereas the latter will add the image to the project and add an appropriate reference to the selected resource file. Clearly the latter is normally preferable, as it means that you can change the image without having to import it again.

Satellite Resources

One of the big advantages of placing data in a resource file is the resulting capability to translate the data for foreign cultures. Instead of all the languages being included in a single resource file, each culture's data is stored in a resource file that has a suffix defined by that culture.

Cultures

Cultures are defined by a combination of two lowercase letters, which represent the language, and two uppercase letters, which represent the country or region of the culture. These two pairs of letters are separated by a hyphen. For example, U.S. English and Australian English are represented as en-US and en-AU respectively. The corresponding resource files for these cultures would be MyResource.en-US.resx and MyResource.en-AU.resx. A full list of culture identifiers can be found at http://msdn2.microsoft .com/en-us/library/system.globalization.cultureinfo.aspx. If you are curious, you can look over all the available cultures, which are returned by CultureInfo.GetCultures(CultureTypes .AllCultures). There are about 220 of them, and they can be classified as follows:

❑   **Invariant culture:** No language or country identifier (for example, Form1.resx). Data is not dependent upon culture. For example, this might be the company logo, which will not vary and is not dependent upon culture information.

❑   **Neutral culture:** Language identifier (for example, Form1.en.resx). Data is dependent upon language alone — for example, a simple warning message that merely needs to be translated.

❑   **Specific culture:** Language and country identifier (for example, Form1.en-US.resx). Data is dependent upon both language and country/region — for example, form layout, color, and prompts should all be translated and adjusted for specific regions.

Creating Culture Resources

If you are creating additional resource files for a form, then it is important to ensure that the Localizable property is set to True. There are three ways to create culture-specific resource files:

❑   If you know the identifier of the culture for which you want to generate a resource file, you can simply save the resx file to *culture_identifier*.resx. For example, if you were converting the resource file Form1.resx to Australian English, you would save it as Form1.en-AU.resx. You will notice that when you do this, Visual Studio removes the original resx file from the solution and adds the new culture-specific resx file. In order to get both files to show up nested under the Form1 node, you actually need to exclude the new resx file, refresh the solution view (by closing and reopening the solution), and then put both files back into the project.

❑ Visual Studio supports a much better way to create culture-specific resource files for forms. From the Properties window for the form you can select `Language`. The name of this property is slightly misleading because it adjusts not only the language, but also the country/region of the form in designer mode. This property is initially set to `(Default)` and should always be returned to this setting after you have finished generating or modifying resource files for specific cultures. To generate the resource file for Australian English, select `English (Australia)` from the `Language` drop-down and make the appropriate changes to the form. Once you are comfortable with the new layout, save it and reset the `Language` property to `(Default)`.

❑ The last way to generate culture-dependent resource files is to use WinRes.exe. Although it's not added to the Start menu, it is available under the Windows SDK folder (located at C:\Program Files\Microsoft SDKs\Windows\v6.0A\bin) and is a graphical utility for generating resource files for forms. This utility can load an existing resource file, allow properties of all controls on the form to be modified, and then save the changes to a particular culture resource file. Before opening a form's resource file using this utility, make sure that the `Localizable` property is set to `True`; otherwise the file will not load properly.

Loading Culture Resource Files

At this point you might be wondering how resource files interact, and whether culture-specific resource files have to be created and compiled at the same time as the main application. The answer to both of these questions lies in the resource *fallback process*, which is the mechanism by which the `ResourceManager` class loads resources.

The fallback process has three levels, based upon the current user interface culture (UI culture) of the executing thread. This can be accessed in code via the `CultureInfo.CurrentUICulture` property. Be aware that this is different from `CultureInfo.CurrentCulture`, which is the current culture used in string comparisons, date formats, and so on. Unlike the current culture, which is based upon the regional settings of the computer (which you can adjust using Control Panel ⇨ Regional Settings), the default UI culture is dependent upon the Windows user interface language pack that is currently selected. Unless you have a Windows Multilingual User Interface Pack installed, you will not be able to modify the default UI culture for your applications.

Although you can't change the default user interface culture, you can adjust this property in code. A word of caution here, however: Without the interface pack installed, some cultures may not display correctly.

```
Thread.CurrentThread.CurrentUICulture = New CultureInfo("en-US")
```

Using the current user interface culture, the fallback process tries to locate resources based on a culture match. For example, if the UI culture is en-US, the process would start off by looking for specific culture resources that match both language (English) and country (U.S.). When no resource can be located, the process falls back to neutral culture resources that match just the language (English). If the fallback process still can't locate a resource, the process falls back to *invariant culture*, indicating there is no match for language or country.

Satellite Culture Resources

So far we have mentioned only how a resource can be converted into a new culture and added to an application. While this method gives you control over which cultures are deployed with your application, it would be better if you didn't have to rebuild your entire application whenever a culture resource needed to be modified, or when you decided to add support for a new culture.

When Visual Studio 2008 compiles culture resources, it splits the resource files into a hub-and-spoke arrangement, using satellite assemblies to contain culture resources. At the hub is the main assembly that would contain the invariant resources. Satellite assemblies are then created for each culture for which a resource has been created. The naming of the satellite assembly is of the form "MyApp.resources.dll" and it is located in a subdirectory named according to the culture under the main output path. Although there is an implicit relationship between specific cultures and neutral cultures (for example, between en-US and en), satellite assemblies for both types should reside in a subdirectory under the main output path.

Another alternative is for the main assembly and/or satellite assemblies to be installed into the Global Assembly Cache (GAC). In this case, each assembly must be strongly named so that it is unique within the cache.

Clearly, the resource fallback process needs to accommodate assemblies both in the GAC and in subdirectories. Hence, for each culture level (specific, neutral, and invariant) the GAC is checked first, followed by the culture subdirectory. Finally, if no resource is found, an exception is raised.

Note that culture resource files do not have to contain all the resources defined in the default resource file. The resource fallback process will load the resource from the default resource file if it is not located in a more specific resource file, so it makes sense to save in the specified culture only those resources that are different.

Accessing Specifics

Numerous shortcuts have been built into the .NET Framework to support the most common tasks related to accessing resources. These shortcuts include single-line image loading, cross-assembly referencing, and the use of the ComponentResourceManager class.

Bitmap and Icon Loading

Images and icons are two of the most common data types held in resource files. Therefore, both the Bitmap and Icon classes in the framework support a constructor that can create an instance directly from a resource without the need for a resource manager. For example, if you have an image, MyImage. bmp, that you included in your project by setting the build action to Embedded Resource, you can access the image directly using the following code:

```
Dim img As New Bitmap(GetType(ThisClass), "MyImage.bmp")
```

Here the class, ThisClass, can be any class in the root namespace of the project that contains the embedded resource.

Cross-Assembly Referencing

One of the features added to the resource editor in Visual Studio 2008 is the ability to control the accessibility level for resource files. In the past, if you wanted to make resources defined in one assembly accessible from another you had to do a lot of hard work and write custom code. Now, with the Access Modifier option in the resource editor, as shown in Figure 40-7, you can choose between keeping a resource internal to the assembly it is defined in (Friend) or making it publicly accessible (Public).

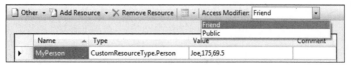

Figure 40-7

If you set the Access Modifier to Public, you can then access this resource from another assembly by prefixing the resource name with the assembly name. For example, in the following code the MyPerson resource is located in the CustomResourceType assembly.

```
Dim p As Person = CustomResourceType.My.Resources.MyPerson
```

ComponentResourceManager

In the first example in this chapter, after localization was turned on, a ComponentResourceManager object was used to retrieve resources associated with the form. The ComponentResourceManager extends the base ResourceManager by providing additional functionality for retrieving and applying component properties. Here are the original four lines required to set the properties defined for Button1:

```
Me.Button1.Location = New Point(71, 43)
Me.Button1.Size = New Size(185, 166)
Me.Button1.Text = "Button1"
Me.Button1.TabIndex = 0
```

Using the ComponentResourceManager, they can be condensed into just one line:

```
resources.ApplyResources(Me.Button1, "Button1")
```

In previous versions of Visual Studio, the code generated when localization was turned on was much more verbose. For each property, a separate call was made to the ResourcesManager to retrieve it by name, as shown in this code snippet:

```
Me.Button1.Location = CType(resources.GetObject("Button1.Location"), Point)
Me.Button1.Size = CType(resources.GetObject("Button1.Size"), Size)
Me.Button1.TabIndex = CType(resources.GetObject("Button1.TabIndex"), Integer)
Me.Button1.Text = resources.GetString("Button1.Text")
```

It is still possible to write this code because the GetObject method is still available on the ComponentResourceManager. The issue with writing this code is that each property that is going to be localized needs to be known at compile time. Because of this, every property on every control was added to the resource file. This added excess properties (even when they were no different from the default values) to the resource file. It also added huge overhead during the loading up of a form, as each property was set via a resource property.

The `ApplyResources` method in the `ComponentResourceManager` class works in reverse. When you specify a control name, which must be unique on a form, all resources that start with that prefix are extracted. The full resource name is then used to determine the property to set on the control. For example, a resource with the name Button1.Location would be extracted for the control called Button1, and the value used to set the `Location` property on that control.

This process eliminates the need to have all properties specified in a resource file. It also creates the need for culture resource files to specify additional properties that might not have been defined in the default resource file.

You might be wondering whether there are any additional penalties in using the `ComponentResourceManager`. In order to set a property on a control using the name of the property, the `ComponentResourceManager` uses *reflection* to find the appropriate property. Once it has been retrieved, it can be invoked. Each search that is done in order to set the property is relatively expensive. However, given the reduced number of properties to be set, the tradeoff is definitely worthwhile, as the application can easily be localized without recompilation of the main application.

Coding Resource Files

In addition to the rich visual tools that Visual Studio 2008 now provides for editing resource files, it is possible to use code to create resource files. The .NET Framework provides support for reading and writing resource files using two interfaces: IResourceReader and IResourceWriter. Once the resource files have been created, they need to be added to the application or manually linked so that they can be referenced within the application.

- ❏ **IResource Reader:** The reader interface ensures that resource readers have the following methods:

  - ❏ **GetEnumerator:** The `GetEnumerator` method retrieves an `IDictionaryEnumerator` object that permits the developer to iterate over each of the resources in the resource file.

  - ❏ **Close:** The `Close` method is used to close the resource reader and release any associated resources.

- ❏ **IResource Writer:** The writer interface ensures that resource writers have the following methods:

  - ❏ **AddResource:** There are three overloads to the `AddResource` method that support adding resources to the resource file. Both of the framework implementations of this interface have either an additional overload of this method or an alternative method for adding resources. The overloads that are part of this interface support adding resources in a name-value pair. Each method has the resource name as the first parameter and a value, such as a string, byte array, or object, as the second parameter. The final implementation that takes an object as a parameter may need to be serializable or converted to a string via a typeconverter.

❑ **Close:** The `Close` method writes resources out to the stream before closing it.

❑ **Generate:** Unlike the `Close` method, the `Generate` method simply writes the resources out to the stream without closing it. Once this method is called, any other method will cause an exception to be raised.

ResourceReader and ResourceWriter

ResourceReader and ResourceWriter are an implementation of the IResource interfaces to support reading and writing directly to resources files. Although reading and writing to this format is the most direct approach, as it reduces the need to use Resgen to generate the resources file, it does limit the quality of information that can be retrieved in reading from the file. Each resource is treated as a series of bytes where the type is unknown.

ResxResourceReader and ResxResourceWriter

ResxResourceReader and ResxResourceWriter are more versatile implementations of the IResource interfaces. In addition to supporting the IResource interface, ResxResourceWriter supports an additional overload of the `AddResource` method, whereby a ResxDataNode can be added. A ResxDataNode is very similar to a dictionary entry, as it has a key (in this case, the `Name` property) and a value (which you must set when the node is created). However, the difference is that this node can support additional properties such as a comment and, as an alternative to a value, a file reference (for example, one that indicates where an image needs to be added to a resource file).

As mentioned previously, it is possible to add a file reference to a resx file so that the file is still editable yet has the benefit of being compiled into the resource file by resgen.exe. The supporting class in the framework is `ResxFileRef`. This can be instantiated and added as a resource via the ResxResourceWriter. This inserts an XML node similar to the following snippet:

```
<data name="Figure_11_2" type="ResXFileRef, System.Windows.Forms">

    <value>..\Resources\CompanyLogo.tif;System.Drawing.Bitmap, System.Drawing,
Version=2.0.0.0, Culture=neutral, PublicKeyToken=b03f5f7f11d50a3a</value>
    </data>
```

Resource Files: A Word of Caution

Resource files are the best means of storing static application data. Although they are linked in to the application as part of the compilation process, their contents can easily be extracted and made human-readable. Because of this, however, resource files are not suitable for storing secure data such as passwords and credit card information.

Custom Resources

Although Visual Studio provides good support for international application development using resource files, there are times when it is not possible to get the level of control required using the default behavior. This section delves a little deeper into how you can serialize custom objects to the resource file and how you can generate designer files, which give you strongly typed accessor methods for resource files you have created.

Visual Studio 2008 enables you to store strings, images, icons, audio files, and other files within a resource file. You can do all this using the rich user interface provided. To store a more complex data type within a resource file you need to serialize it into a string representation that can be included within the resource file.

The first step in adding any data type to a resource file is to make that data type serializable. You can do this easily by marking the class with the `Serializable` attribute. Once it is marked as serializable, you can add the object to a resource file using an implementation of the IResourceWriter interface — for example, ResXResourceWriter:

```
<Serializable()> _
Public Class Person
    Public Name As String
    Public Height As Integer
    Public Weight As Double
End Class
Dim p As New Person
p.Name = "Bob"
p.Height = 167
p.Weight = 69.5

Dim rWriter As New ResXResourceWriter("foo.resx")
rWriter.AddResource("DefaultPerson", p)
rWriter.Close()
```

Serializing an object this way has a couple of drawbacks, however:

❑   You need to use code to write out this resource file before the build process so that the resource file can be included in the application. Clearly this is an administrative nightmare, as it is an additional stage in the build process.

❑   Furthermore, the serialized representation of the class is a binary blob and is not human-readable. The assumption here is that what is written in the generating code is correct. Unfortunately, this is seldom the case, and it would be easier if the content could be human-readable within Visual Studio 2008.

A workaround for both of these issues is to define a TypeConverter for the class and use that to represent the class as a string. This way, the resource can be edited within the Visual Studio resource editor.

TypeConverters provide a mechanism through which the framework can determine whether it is possible to represent a class (in this case a `Person` class) as a different type (in this case as a string). The first step is to create a TypeConverter using the ExpandableObjectConverter, as follows:

```vb
Imports System.ComponentModel
Imports System.ComponentModel.Design.Serialization
Imports System.Globalization

Public Class PersonConverter
    Inherits ExpandableObjectConverter

    Public Overrides Function CanConvertFrom(ByVal context As _
                                            ITypeDescriptorContext, _
                                            ByVal t As Type) As Boolean
        If t Is GetType(String) Then Return True
        Return MyBase.CanConvertFrom(context, t)
    End Function
    Public Overrides Function ConvertFrom( _
                                ByVal context As ITypeDescriptorContext, _
                                ByVal info As CultureInfo, _
                                ByVal value As Object) As Object
        If (TypeOf (value) Is String) Then
            Try
                If value Is Nothing Then Return New Person()
                Dim vals = CStr(value).Split(","c)
                If vals.Length <> 3 Then Return New Person()
                Return New Person With {.Name = vals(0), _
                            .Height = Integer.Parse(vals(1)), _
                            .Weight = Double.Parse(vals(2))}
            Catch
                Throw New ArgumentException("Can not convert '" & _
                                            value.ToString & _
                                            "' to type Person")
            End Try
        End If
        Return MyBase.ConvertFrom(context, info, value)
    End Function

    Public Overrides Function ConvertTo(ByVal context As ITypeDescriptorContext, _
                                ByVal culture As CultureInfo, _
                                ByVal value As Object, _
                                ByVal destType As Type) As Object
        If (destType Is GetType(String) And TypeOf (value) Is Person) Then
            Dim c = TryCast(value, Person)
            Return c.Name & "," & c.Height.ToString & "," & c.Weight.ToString
        End If
        Return MyBase.ConvertTo(context, culture, value, destType)
    End Function
End Class
```

The class being represented also needs to be attributed with the `TypeConverter` attribute:

```
<System.ComponentModel.TypeConverter(GetType(PersonConverter))> _
<Serializable()> _
Public Class Person
    • Public Name As String
      Public Height As Integer
      Public Weight As Double
End Class
```

Now you can add this item to a resource file using the string representation of the class. For example, an entry in the resx file might look like this:

```
<assembly alias=" WindowsApplication1" name="WindowsApplication1, Version=1.0.0.0,
    Culture=neutral, PublicKeyToken=null" />
<data name="Manager" type=" WindowsApplication1.Person, WindowsApplication1">
    <value>Joe, 175, 69.5</value>
</data>
```

Creating custom resource types is a difficult process, as Visual Studio 2008 doesn't refresh your TypeConverter after it has been loaded the first time. You can either strongly name the assembly in which the TypeConverter is located and increment the version number each time you change it, or you will have to restart Visual Studio in order for the changes to take effect.

Summary

This chapter demonstrated how important XML resource files are in building an application that can both access static data and be readily localized into foreign languages and cultures. The rich user interface provided by Visual Studio 2008 enables you to easily add resources such as images, icons, strings, audio files, and other files to an application.

The built-in support for localizing forms and generating satellite assemblies empowers developers to write applications that can target a global market. You have also seen that the user interface provided within Visual Studio 2008 is extensible, meaning that you can modify it to interact with your own custom resource types.

Part IX
Debugging

Using the Debugging Windows

Debugging applications is one of the more challenging tasks developers have to tackle, but correct use of the Visual Studio 2008 debugging windows will help you analyze the state of the application and determine the cause of any bugs. This chapter examines the numerous windows available in Visual Studio 2008 to support you in building and debugging applications.

Code Window

The most important window for debugging purposes is the code window. With the capability to set breakpoints and step through code, this window is the starting point for almost all debugging activities. Figure 41-1 shows a simple snippet of code with both a breakpoint and the current execution point visible.

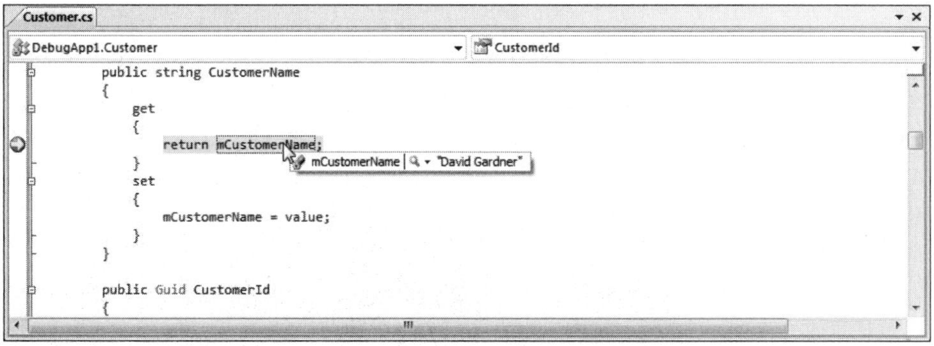

Figure 41-1

Breakpoints

The first stage in debugging an application is usually to identify the area that is causing the error by setting a breakpoint and gradually stepping through the code. Setting breakpoints and working with the current execution point is covered in more detail in the next chapter. Although you can't see the color in Figure 41-1, breakpoints are marked in the code window with a red dot in the margin of the page and red highlighting of the code itself.

When a breakpoint is encountered, the current execution point is marked with a yellow arrow in the margin and the actual code is also highlighted in yellow. As discussed in the next chapter, this marker can be dragged forward and backward to control the order of execution. However, this should be done sparingly because it modifies the behavior of the application.

Datatips

After hitting a breakpoint, the application is paused, or is in *Break* mode. In this mode, you can retrieve information about current variables simply by hovering your mouse over the variable name. Figure 41-1 shows that the value of the mCustomerName variable is currently "David Gardner". This debugging tooltip is commonly referred to as a *datatip*, and can be used to view not only the values of simple types, such as strings and integers, but also to drill down and inspect more complex object types, such as those made up of multiple nested classes.

> Datatips are used to both query, and edit, the value of a variable.

In Chapter 43 you learn how the layout of this datatip can be customized using type proxies and type visualizers.

Breakpoint Window

When debugging a complex issue, it is possible to set numerous breakpoints to isolate the problem. Unfortunately, this has two side effects. One, the execution of the application is hampered, because you have to continually press F5 to resume execution. More significantly, the execution of the application is slowed considerably by the presence of breakpoints; the more complex the breakpoint conditions, the slower the application will run. Because these breakpoints can be scattered through multiple source files, it becomes difficult to locate and remove breakpoints that are no longer required.

The breakpoint window, accessible via Debug ⇨ Windows ⇨ Breakpoints, is a useful summary of all the breakpoints currently set within the application. Using this window, breakpoints can easily be navigated to, disabled, and removed.

Figure 41-2 shows two currently active breakpoints in the Customer.cs file. The first is a regular breakpoint with no conditions. The second has a condition whereby the application will break only if the mAccountBalance variable has a value less than 1000. This condition is also in bold, because the application is currently in Break mode at that breakpoint.

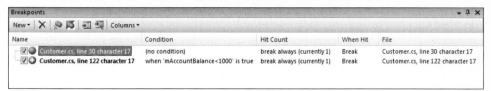

Figure 41-2

The Breakpoints window, like most other debugging windows, is made up of two regions: the Toolbar and the breakpoint list. From left to right, the breakpoint Toolbar icons are as follows: create, delete, delete all, and disable all breakpoints, go to source, go to disassembler, and finally column selection.

Each item in the breakpoint list is represented by a checkbox that indicates whether the breakpoint is enabled, an icon and breakpoint descriptor, and any number of columns that show properties of the breakpoint. The columns can be adjusted using the Columns drop-down from the Toolbar. You can set additional breakpoint properties by right-clicking the appropriate breakpoint.

Output Window

One of the first debugging windows you will encounter when you run your application for the first time is the Output window. By default, the Output window appears every time you build your application, and shows the build progress. Figure 41-3 shows the successful build of a sample solution. The final line of the Output window indicates a summary of the build, which in this case indicates three successfully built projects. In the output there is also a summary of the warnings and errors encountered during the build. In this case there were no errors, but there were three warnings. Although the Output window can be useful if for some reason the build fails unexpectedly, most of the time the errors and warnings are reported in the Error List.

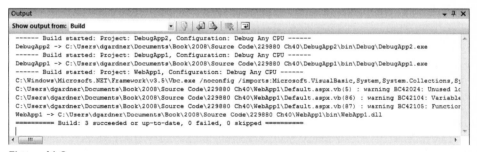

Figure 41-3

The Output window has a secondary role as the standard output while the application is running. The drop-down on the left of the toolbar can be used to toggle between output sources. Figure 41-3 shows the output of the build, but as you perform other activities in Visual Studio, additional entries will be created in the drop-down list. For example, when you run your application in debug mode, Visual Studio will create an entry called Debug, which will display any messages that either the runtime or your code has emitted using `Debug.Write` or `Debug.WriteLine`. Likewise, a Refactor entry will be created to show the results of any recent refactoring operation that was performed.

The output from external tools such as `.bat` *and* `.com` *files is normally displayed in the Command window. The output from these tools can also be displayed in the Output window by setting the Use Output Window option in the Tools ⇨ External Tools dialog box.*

The other icons on the Toolbar, in order from left to right, enable you to navigate to the source of a build message, go to the previous message, go to the next message, clear the window contents, and toggle word wrapping for the Output window.

Immediate Window

Quite often when you are writing code or debugging your application, you will want to evaluate a simple expression either to test a bit of functionality or to remind yourself of how something works. This is where the Immediate window comes in handy. This window enables you to run expressions as you type them. Figure 41-4 shows a number of statements — from basic assignment and print operations through to more advanced object creation and manipulation.

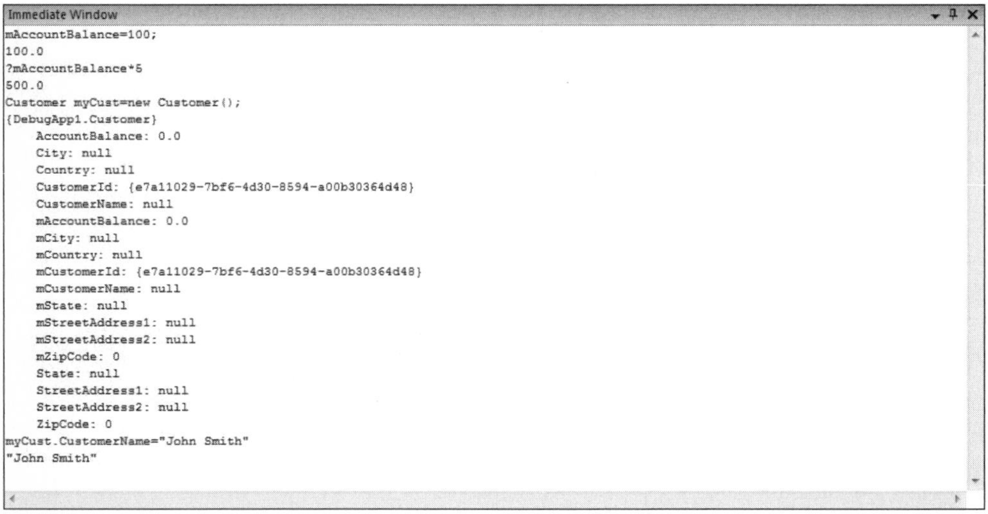

```
Immediate Window                                                          ▾ ╄ ✕
mAccountBalance=100;
100.0
?mAccountBalance*5
500.0
Customer myCust=new Customer();
{DebugApp1.Customer}
    AccountBalance: 0.0
    City: null
    Country: null
    CustomerId: {e7a11029-7bf6-4d30-8594-a00b30364d48}
    CustomerName: null
    mAccountBalance: 0.0
    mCity: null
    mCountry: null
    mCustomerId: {e7a11029-7bf6-4d30-8594-a00b30364d48}
    mCustomerName: null
    mState: null
    mStreetAddress1: null
    mStreetAddress2: null
    mZipCode: 0
    State: null
    StreetAddress1: null
    StreetAddress2: null
    ZipCode: 0
myCust.CustomerName="John Smith"
"John Smith"
```

Figure 41-4

Figure 41-4 shows a new `Customer` object being created in a C# project within the Immediate window. Within a Visual Basic project you can't do explicit variable declaration (for example, `Dim x as Integer`). Instead it is done implicitly using the assignment operator.

One of the more useful features of the Immediate window is that it can be used while you are writing code. When you create new objects in the Immediate window at design time, it will create an instance of that object using the Object Test Bench. If you invoke a method or property that contains an active breakpoint, Visual Studio will change to debug mode and break at the breakpoint. This is particularly useful if you are working on a particular method that you want to test without running the entire application.

The Immediate window supports a limited form of IntelliSense, and you can use the arrow keys to track back through the history of previous commands executed.

IntelliSense is only supported in the Immediate window when running in debug mode, not during design-time debugging.

The Immediate window also allows you to execute Visual Studio commands. To submit a command you must enter a greater than symbol (>) at the start of the line. There is an extremely large set of commands available; in fact almost any action that can be performed within Visual Studio is accessible as a command. Fortunately, IntelliSense makes navigating this list of available commands a little more manageable.

There is also a set of almost 100 predefined aliases for commands. One of the more well-known aliases is "?", which is a shortcut for the Debug.Print command that prints out the value of a variable. You can see the full list of predefined aliases by entering >alias, as shown in Figure 41-5.

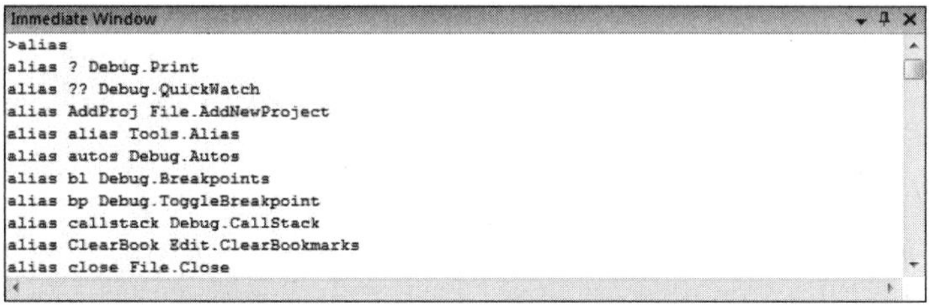

Figure 41-5

Watch Windows

Earlier in this chapter you saw how datatips can be used in the code window to examine the content of a variable by hovering the mouse over a variable name. When the structure of the object is more complex it becomes difficult to navigate the values using just the datatip. Visual Studio 2008 has a series of watch windows that can be used to display variables, providing an easy-to-use interface for drilling down into the structure.

QuickWatch

The QuickWatch window is a modal dialog that can be launched by right-clicking on the code window. Whatever you have selected in the code window is inserted into the Expression field of the dialog, as shown in Figure 41-6 where a Customer object is visible. Previous expressions you have evaluated appear in the drop-down associated with the Expression field.

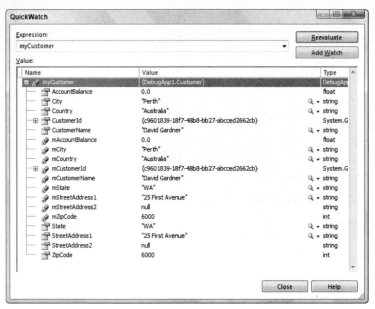

Figure 41-6

The layout of the Value tree in the QuickWatch window is similar to the datatip, without the annoyance of its disappearing. Each row shows the variable name, the current value, and the type of object. The value of the variable can be adjusted by typing in the Value column.

Use the Add Watch button to add the current expression to one of the watch windows. These are variables to be continuously watched.

Watch Windows 1–4

Unlike the QuickWatch window, which is modal and shows a variable value at a particular execution point, the watch windows can be used to monitor a variable value as you step through your code. Although there are four watch windows, a single window is sufficient in most cases. Having four separate windows means that you can have different sets of variables in the different windows, which might be useful if you are working through a more complex issue that involves multiple classes.

Figure 41-7 shows an `Order` and `Customer` class in a watch window. Similar to both the QuickWatch window and the datatips discussed previously, the user interface can be used to drill down into more complex data types.

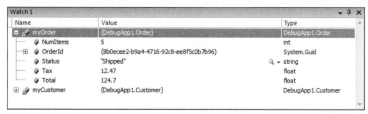

Figure 41-7

Additional variables to be watched can be added either by typing into the Name column on an empty line or by right-clicking the variable in the code window and selecting Add Watch from the context menu.

Autos and Locals

The Autos and Locals windows are two special watch windows in which the variables are automatically added by the debugger. The Autos window contains variables that are used in the current, preceding, and future lines of code. Similarly, the Locals window shows all variables used in the current method. Other than being automatically generated, these windows behave the same as the watch windows.

Call Stack

As applications grow in complexity, it is quite common for the execution path to become difficult to follow. The use of deep inheritance trees and interfaces can often obscure the execution path. This is where the call stack is useful. Each path of execution must have a finite number of entries on the stack (unless a cyclic pattern emerges, in which case a stack overflow is inevitable). The stack can be viewed using the Call Stack window, shown in Figure 41-8.

Figure 41-8

Using the Call Stack window, it is easy to navigate up the execution path to determine from where the current executing method is being called. This can be done by clicking any of the rows in the call stack, known as a *stack frame*. Other options available from the call stack, using the right-click context menu, enable viewing the disassembler for a particular stack frame, setting breakpoints, and varying what information is displayed.

Threads

Most applications make use of multiple threads at some point. In particular for Windows applications, in order for the user interface to always appear responsive, it is important to run time-consuming tasks on a thread separate from the main application. Of course, concurrent execution of threads makes debugging more difficult, especially when the threads are accessing the same classes and methods.

Figure 41-9 shows the Threads window, which lists all the active threads for a particular application. Notice that in addition to the threads created in the code, additional background threads have been created by the debugger. For simplicity, the threads used by this application, including the main user interface thread, have been given names so they can easily be distinguished.

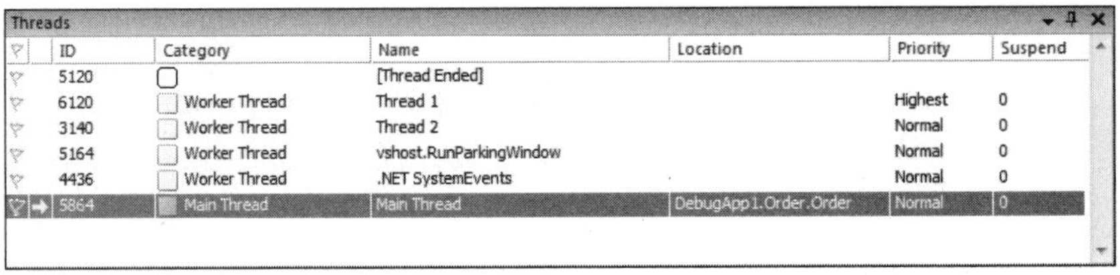

Figure 41-9

The Threads window shows a yellow arrow next to the thread that is currently being viewed in the code window. To navigate to another thread, simply double-click that thread to bring the current location of that thread into view in the code window and update the call stack to reflect the new thread.

In Break mode, all threads of an application are paused. However, when you are stepping through your code with the debugger, the next statement to be executed may or may not be on the same thread you are interested in. If you are only interested in the execution path of a single thread, and the execution of other threads can be suspended, right-click the thread in the Threads window and select Freeze from the context menu. To resume the suspended thread, select Thaw from the same menu.

Debugging multi-threaded applications is explained further in Chapter 45.

Modules

The Modules window (see Figure 41-10) shows a list of assemblies that are referenced by the running application. Those assemblies that make up the application will also have debugging symbols loaded, which means that they can be debugged without dropping into the disassembler. This window also provides useful assembly version information and indicates whether the assembly is optimized.

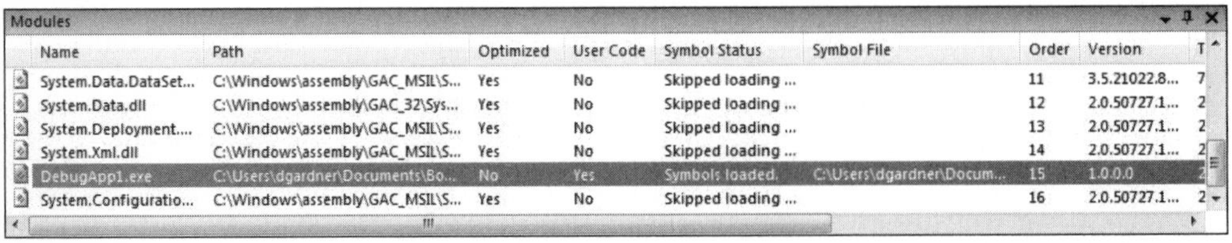

Figure 41-10

In Figure 41-10, the symbols have been loaded for the DebugApp1.exe application. All the other assemblies have been skipped, because they contain no user code and are optimized. If an appropriate symbol file is available, it is possible to load it for an assembly via the Load Symbols option from the right-click context menu.

Processes

Building multi-tier applications can be quite complex, and it is often necessary to have all the tiers running. To do this, Visual Studio 2008 can start multiple projects at the same stage, enabling true end-to-end debugging. Alternatively, you can attach to other processes to debug running applications. Each time Visual Studio attaches to a process, that process is added to the list of attached processes. Figure 41-11 shows a solution containing two Windows applications and a web application.

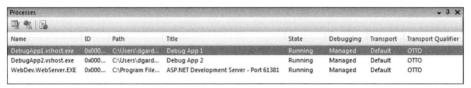

Name	ID	Path	Title	State	Debugging	Transport	Transport Qualifier
DebugApp1.vshost.exe	0x000...	C:\Users\dgard...	Debug App 1	Running	Managed	Default	OTTO
DebugApp2.vshost.exe	0x000...	C:\Users\dgard...	Debug App 2	Running	Managed	Default	OTTO
WebDev.WebServer.EXE	0x000...	C:\Program File...	ASP.NET Development Server - Port 61381	Running	Managed	Default	OTTO

Figure 41-11

The Toolbar at the top of the Processes window enables you to detach or terminate a process that is currently attached, or attach to another process.

Memory Windows

The next three windows are typically used for low-level debugging when all other alternatives have been exhausted. Stepping into memory locations, using a disassembler, or looking at registry values requires a lot of background knowledge and patience to analyze and make use of the information that is presented. There are only very rare cases while developing managed code when you would be required to perform debugging at such a low level.

Memory Windows 1–4

The four memory windows can be used to view the raw contents of memory at a particular address. Where the Watch, Autos, and Locals windows provide a way of looking at the content of variables, which are stored at specific locations in memory, the Memory window shows you the big picture of what is stored in memory.

Each of the four Memory windows can examine different memory addresses to simplify debugging your application. Figure 41-12 shows an example of the information that can be seen using this window. The scrollbar on the right of the window can be used to navigate forward or backward through the memory addresses to view information contained in neighboring addresses.

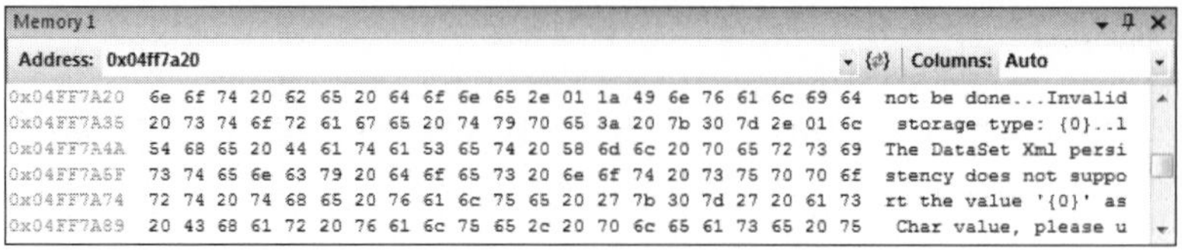

Figure 41-12

Disassembly

Interesting debates arise periodically over the relative performance of two different code blocks. Occasionally this discussion devolves to talking about which MSIL instructions are used, and why one code block is faster because it generates one fewer instruction. Clearly, if you are calling that code block millions of times, disassembly might give your application a significant benefit. However, more often than not, a bit of high-level refactoring saves much more time and involves much less arguing. Figure 41-13 shows the Disassembly window for a LinkLabel click — the runtime is about to construct a new Customer object. You can see MSIL instructions that make up this action.

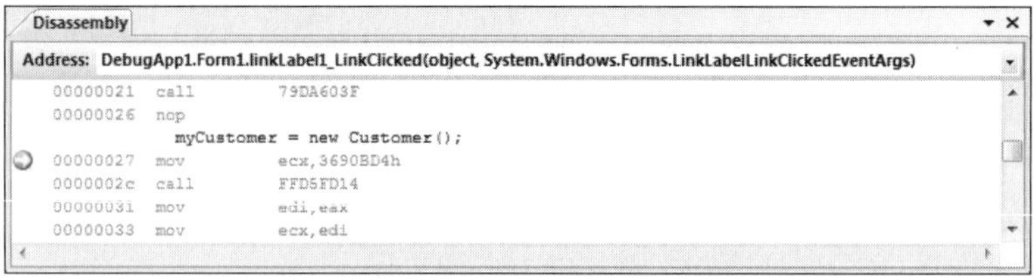

Figure 41-13

You can see from Figure 41-13 that a breakpoint has been set on the call to the constructor and that the execution point is at this breakpoint. While still in this window you can step through the lines of MSIL and review what instructions are being executed.

Registers

Using the Disassembly window to step through MSIL instructions can become very difficult to follow as different information is loaded, moved, and compared using a series of registers. The Registers window, shown in Figure 41-14, enables the contents of the various registers to be monitored. Changes in a register value are highlighted in red, making it easy to see what happens as each line is stepped through in the Disassembly window.

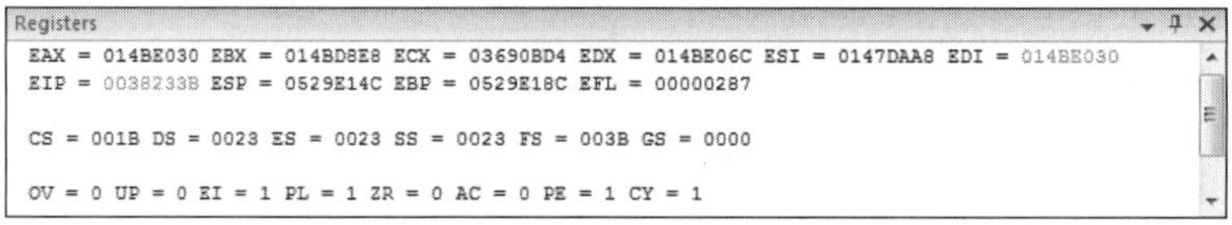

Figure 41-14

Exceptions

Visual Studio 2008 has a sophisticated exception handler that provides you with a lot of useful information. Figure 41-15 shows the exception assistant dialog that appears when an exception is raised. In addition to providing more information, it also displays a series of actions. The Actions list varies depending on the type of exception being thrown. In this case, the two options are to view details of the exception or copy it to the clipboard.

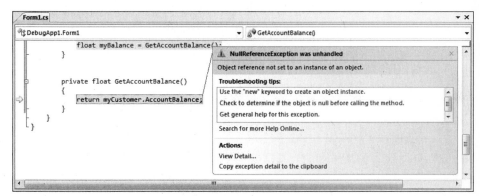

Figure 41-15

If you select the View Detail action item from the exception, you are presented with a modal dialog that provides a breakdown of the exception that was raised. Figure 41-16 shows the attributes of the exception, including the StackTrace, which can be viewed in full by clicking the down arrow to the right of the screen.

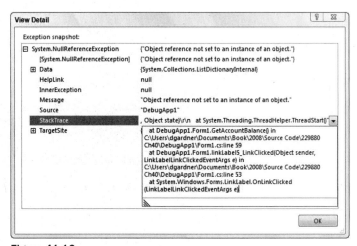

Figure 41-16

Of course, there are times when exceptions are used to control the execution path in an application. For example, some user input may not adhere to a particular formatting constraint, and instead of using a regular expression to determine whether it matches, a parse operation has been attempted on the string. When this fails, it raises an exception, which can easily be trapped without stopping the entire application.

By default, all exceptions are trapped by the debugger, because they are assumed to be exceptions to the norm that shouldn't have happened. In special cases, such as invalid user input, it may be important to ignore specific types of exceptions. This can be done via the Exceptions window, accessible from the Debug menu.

Figure 41-17 shows the Exceptions window, shown by selecting Debug ⇨ Exceptions, which lists all the exception types that exist in the .NET Framework. For each exception there are two debugging options. The debugger can be set to break when an exception is thrown regardless of whether it is handled. If the Just My Code option has been enabled, checking the "User-unhandled" box causes the debugger to break for any exception that is not handled within a user code region. More information on Just My Code is provided in Chapter 43, which examines debugging attributes.

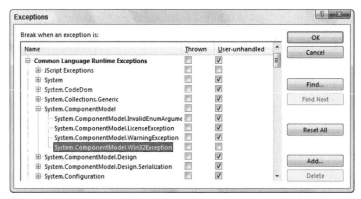

Figure 41-17

Unfortunately, the Exceptions window doesn't pick up any custom exception types that you may have created, but you can add them manually using the Add button in the lower-right corner of the window. You need to ensure that you provide the full class name, including the namespace; otherwise, the debugger will not break on handled exceptions. Clearly, unhandled exceptions will still cause the application to crash.

Customizing the Exception Assistant

As with a lot of the configurable parts within Visual Studio 2008, the information displayed by the Exception Assistant is stored in an XML file (C:\Program Files\Microsoft Visual Studio 9.0\ Common7\IDE\ExceptionAssistantContent\1033\DefaultContent.xml). This file can be modified either to alter the assistant information for existing exception types or to add your own custom exception types. If you have your own exception types, it is better practice to create your own XML document. Simply placing it in the same directory as the DefaultContent.xml is sufficient to register it with Visual

Studio for the next time your application is debugged. An example XML file is provided in the following code listing:

```xml
<?xml version="1.0" encoding="utf-8" ?>
<AssistantContent Version="1.0" xmlns="urn:schemas-
   microsoft-com:xml-msdata:exception-assistant-content">
   <ContentInfo>
       <ContentName>Additional Content</ContentName>
       <ContentID>urn:exception-content-microsoft-
   com:visual-studio-7-default-content</ContentID>
       <ContentFileVersion>1.0</ContentFileVersion>
       <ContentAuthor>David Gardner</ContentAuthor>
       <ContentComment>Additional Exception Assistant
   Content for Visual Studio 9.0.</ContentComment>
   </ContentInfo>
   <Exception>
       <Type>DebugApp1.myException</Type>
       <Tip HelpID="http://www.professionalvisualstudio.com/MyExceptionHelp.htm">
           <Description>Silly error, you should know better...</Description>
       </Tip>
   </Exception>
</AssistantContent>
```

This example registers help information for the exception type `myException`. The `HelpID` attribute is used to provide a hyperlink for more information about the exception. When this exception is raised, the debugger displays the window (see Figure 41-18).

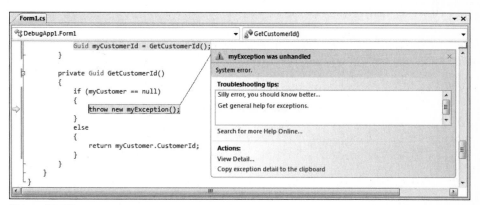

Figure 41-18

Unwinding an Exception

In Figure 41-19 there is an additional item in the Actions list of an exception helper window, which is to enable editing. This is effectively the capability to unwind the execution of the application to just before the exception was raised. In other words, you can effectively debug your application without having to restart your debugging session.

Figure 41-19

The "Enable editing" option will only appear if you have configured Visual Studio to break when an exception is thrown, as discussed earlier in this chapter. As with many of the debugging features, both the Exception Assistant and the capability to unwind exceptions can also be disabled via the Debugging tab of the Options window.

> *An alternative way to unwind the exception is to select the Unwind to This Frame item from the right-click context menu off the Call Stack window after an exception has been raised. This can be useful to check what the state of the application was just before the exception was thrown. You can only unwind an exception if it is handled (that is, contained within a* `try...catch` *block). You should also ensure that the debugger is set to break when the exception is thrown. You can do this via the Debug ⇨ Exceptions window.*

Summary

This chapter has described each of the debugging windows in detail so you can optimize your debugging experience. Although the number of windows can seem somewhat overwhelming at first, they each perform an isolated task or provide access to a specific piece of information about the running application. As such, you will easily learn to navigate between them, returning to those that provide the most relevant information for you.

The following chapter provides more detail about how you can customize the debugging information. This includes changing the information displayed in the datatip and visualizing more complex variable information.

Debugging with Breakpoints

Long gone are the days where debugging an application involved adding superfluous output statements to track down where an application was failing. Visual Studio 2008 provides a rich debugging experience that includes breakpoints and the Edit and Continue feature. This chapter covers how you can use these features to debug your application.

Breakpoints

A *breakpoint* is used to pause, or break, an application at a particular point of execution. An application that has been paused is said to be in Break mode, causing a number of the Visual Studio 2008 windows to become active. For example, the watch window can be used to view variable values. Figure 42-1 shows a breakpoint that has been added to the constructor of the Customer class. The application will break on this line if the Customer class constructor is called.

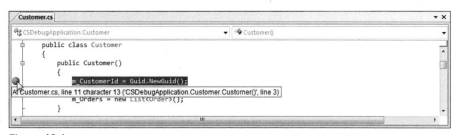

Figure 42-1

Setting a Breakpoint

Breakpoints can be set either through the Debug menu, using the Breakpoint item from the right-click context menu, or by using the keyboard shortcut, F9. The Visual Studio 2008 code editor also provides a shortcut for setting a breakpoint using a single mouse click.

An application can only be paused on a line of executing code. This means that a breakpoint set on either a comment or a variable declaration will be repositioned to the next line of executable code when the application is run.

Simple Breakpoints

A breakpoint can be set on a line of code by placing the cursor on that line and enabling a breakpoint using any of the following:

❑   Selecting Toggle Breakpoint from the Debug menu

❑   Selecting Insert Breakpoint from the Breakpoint item on the right-click context menu

❑   Pressing F9

❑   Clicking once in the margin of the code window with the mouse. Figure 42-1 shows the location of the mouse immediately after a breakpoint has been set using the mouse.

Selecting Location from the Breakpoint item on the right-click context menu for the line of code with the breakpoint set displays the File Breakpoint dialog, shown in Figure 42-2. Here you can see that the breakpoint is set at line 11 of the Customer.cs file. There is also a character number, which provides for the case in which multiple statements appear on a single line.

Figure 42-2

Function Breakpoints

Another type of breakpoint that can be set is a *function breakpoint*. The usual way to set a breakpoint on a function is to select the function signature and either press F9 or use the mouse to create a breakpoint. This will create a file breakpoint as you did previously. In the case of multiple overloads, this would require you to locate all the overloads and add the appropriate breakpoints. Setting a function breakpoint enables you to set a breakpoint on one or more functions by specifying the function name.

To set a function breakpoint, select Break at Function from the New Breakpoint item on the Debug menu. This loads the New Breakpoint dialog shown in Figure 42-3, in which you can specify the name of the function on which to break. There is a toggle to enable IntelliSense-checking for the function name. The recommendation is to leave this checked, because it becomes almost impossible to set a valid breakpoint without this support.

Figure 42-3

Unfortunately, the IntelliSense option doesn't give you true IntelliSense as you type, unlike other debugging windows. However, if you select the name of the function in the code window before creating the breakpoint, the name of the function is automatically inserted into the dialog.

When setting a function breakpoint, you can specify either the exact overload you wish to set the breakpoint on or just the function name. In Figure 42-3, the overload with a single Guid parameter has been selected. Notice that unlike a full method signature, which requires a parameter name, to select a particular function overload you should provide only the parameter type. If you omit the parameter information, and there are multiple overloads, you will be prompted to select the overloads on which to place the breakpoint, as illustrated in Figure 42-4.

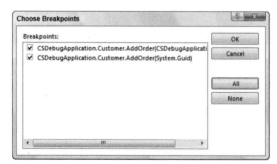

Figure 42-4

Address Breakpoints

Another way to set a breakpoint is via the Call Stack window. When the application is in Break mode, the call stack shows the current list of function calls. After selecting any line in the call stack, a breakpoint can be set in the same way as a file breakpoint, as described earlier (toggle Breakpoint from the Debug menu, use the F9 keyboard shortcut, or use Insert Breakpoint from the context menu). Figure 42-5 shows a short call stack with a new breakpoint set on a control event on Form1.

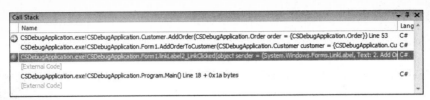

Figure 42-5

The call stack is generated using function addresses. As such, the breakpoint that is set is an address breakpoint. This type of breakpoint is only useful within a single debugging session, because function addresses are likely to change when an application is modified and rebuilt.

Adding Break Conditions

Though breakpoints are useful for pausing an application at a given point to review variables and watch application flow, if you are looking for a particular scenario it may be necessary to break only when certain conditions are valid. Breakpoints can be tailored to search for particular conditions, to break after a number of iterations, or even be filtered based on process or machine name.

Condition

A breakpoint condition can be specified by selecting Condition from the Breakpoint item on the right-click context menu for the breakpoint. This brings up the Breakpoint Condition dialog shown in Figure 42-6, which accepts a Boolean expression that determines whether the breakpoint will be hit. If the expression evaluates to `false`, the application continues past the breakpoint without breaking.

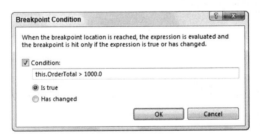

Figure 42-6

In the case of Figure 42-6, which is for a breakpoint set within the `Order` class, the condition specifies that the order total must be greater than 1000. As with most debugging windows, the Condition field provides rich IntelliSense support to aid in the writing of valid conditions. If an invalid condition is specified, the debugger throws an appropriate error message and the application will break the first time the breakpoint is reached.

When a condition, or a Hit Count as shown in the next section, is placed on a breakpoint, the breakpoint changes appearance. The solid red dot is replaced with a red dot with a white cross. When you move your mouse across this dot, the tooltip provides useful information about the breakpoint condition, as illustrated in Figure 42-7.

Figure 42-7

Sometimes it is more relevant to know when this condition changes status, rather than when it is true. The Has Changed option will break the application when the status of the condition changes. If this option is selected, then the application will not break the first time the breakpoint is hit, because there is no previous status to compare against.

Using multiple breakpoints with complex conditions can significantly slow down the execution of your application, so it is recommended that you remove breakpoints that are no longer relevant in order to speed up the running of your application.

Hit Count

Though it's perhaps not as useful as breakpoint conditions, it is also possible to break after a particular number of iterations through a breakpoint. To do this, select Hit Count from the Breakpoint item on the right-click context menu. Figure 42-8 shows the Breakpoint Hit Count dialog, which can be used to specify when the breakpoint should be hit.

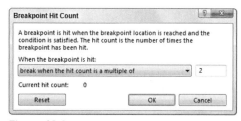

Figure 42-8

Every time the application is run, the hit counter is reset to zero, and it can be manually reset using the Reset button. The hit counter is also unique to each breakpoint. The hit count condition is one of four options:

- ❑ **Always:** Disregard the hit counter.
- ❑ **Is equal to:** Break if the hit counter is equal to the value specified.
- ❑ **Multiple of:** Break if the hit counter is a multiple of the value specified (as shown in Figure 42-8).
- ❑ **Is greater than or equal to:** Break if the hit counter is greater than or equal to the value specified.

Figure 42-9 shows the Breakpoints window, which provides additional information about the status of each of the breakpoints. In this case, the breakpoint is set to break every second time. The current hit counter is 4.

Figure 42-9

Filter

A single solution may contain multiple applications that need to be run at the same time. This is a common scenario when building a multi-tier application. When the application is run, the debugger can attach to all these processes, enabling them to be debugged. By default, when a breakpoint is reached all the processes will break. This behavior can be controlled from the Debugging (General) node in the Options window, accessible from the Options item on the Tools menu. Unchecking the "Break all processes when one process breaks" checkbox enables processes to be debugged individually.

If a breakpoint is set in a class library that is used by more than one process, each process will break when it reaches that breakpoint. Because you might be interested in debugging only one of these processes, you can place a filter on the breakpoint that limits it to the process you are interested in. If you are debugging applications on multiple machines, then it is also possible to specify a machine name filter.

In fact, filtering can be useful for a multi-threaded application for which you want to limit the breakpoints to a particular thread. However, in this case, when the breakpoint is hit (such as when the current thread being executed meets the filter criteria), all threads are paused regardless of whether they meet the filter criteria. Figure 42-10 shows the Breakpoint Filter dialog and the possible filter conditions.

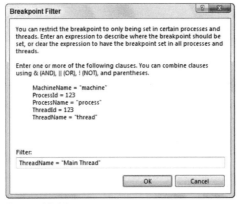

Figure 42-10

Working with Breakpoints

It's often necessary to adjust a breakpoint, because it might be in the wrong location or no longer relevant. In most cases it is easiest to remove the breakpoint, but in some cases — for example, when you have a complex breakpoint condition — it might be necessary to adjust the existing breakpoint.

Deleting

To remove a breakpoint that is no longer required, select it, either in the code editor or in the Breakpoints window, and remove it using the Toggle Breakpoint item from the Debug menu. Alternatively, the Delete Breakpoint item from the right-click context menu or the Delete Breakpoint icon from the Breakpoints window toolbar will remove the breakpoint.

Disabling

Instead of deleting a breakpoint, simply disabling the breakpoint can be useful when you have a breakpoint condition set or you are tracking a hit count. To disable a breakpoint, select it either in the code editor or in the Breakpoints window, and disable it using the Disable Breakpoint item from the right-click context menu. Alternatively, you can uncheck the checkbox against the breakpoint in the Breakpoints window. Figure 42-11 shows how a disabled breakpoint would appear in the code window.

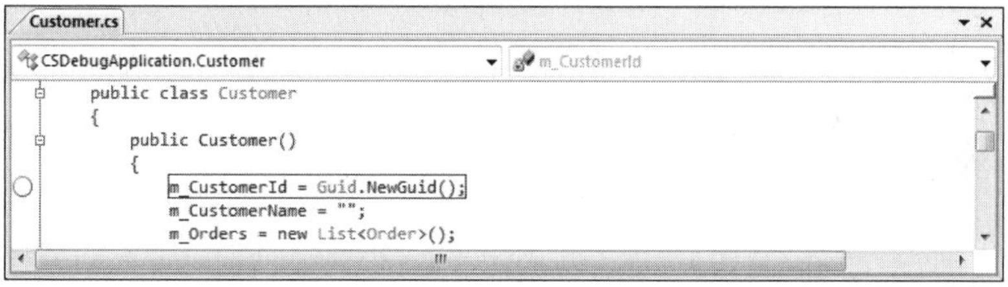

Figure 42-11

Changing Location

The location of a breakpoint can be modified by selecting Location from the Breakpoint item on the right-click context menu. Depending on what type of breakpoint has been set, the dialog shows the location of the breakpoint as either a line and character position in a file or function, or as an address within an assembly. If the location is either a file or function position, the breakpoint can be adjusted so it is in the correct location. Address breakpoints are harder to relocate, because you need to ensure that the new address is a valid location for a breakpoint.

Tracepoints

A *tracepoint* differs from a breakpoint in that it triggers an additional action when it is hit. In fact, for purposes such as applying filters, conditions, and hit counts, a tracepoint can be thought of as a breakpoint.

Tracepoints can be compared to using either Debug or Trace statements in your code, but they can be dynamically set as the application is being debugged and do not affect your code.

Creating a Tracepoint

Tracepoints can be created from either an existing breakpoint or the Breakpoint right-click context menu. To create a tracepoint from an existing breakpoint, select When Hit from the Breakpoint right-click context menu. The resulting dialog, shown in Figure 42-12, gives you the option of printing a message to the console window or running a macro. Alternatively, to create a tracepoint at a new location, select Insert Tracepoint from the Breakpoint item on the right-click context menu. This again loads the dialog shown in Figure 42-12 so you can customize the tracepoint action.

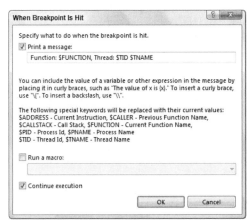

Figure 42-12

Once you set a tracepoint, the code window changes the appearance of that line of code to indicate that a tracepoint has been set. This is shown in Figure 42-13, where the tracepoint appears with a diamond in the margin. (The diamond is red, although this can't be seen in the figure.)

Figure 42-13

Tracepoint Actions

Two types of actions can be performed when a tracepoint is hit: either print a message to the console window or run a macro. In the dialog shown in Figure 42-12, you can indicate which action should be run when the tracepoint is hit. If both actions are unchecked, the tracepoint will fall back to being a breakpoint.

By default, once a tracepoint action has been indicated, the Continue Execution checkbox will be checked so the application will not break at this point. Unchecking this option causes the application to break at the tracepoint as if it were a breakpoint. The action defined will be performed prior to the application breaking. The appearance of this tracepoint will be the same as that of a breakpoint, because the visual cue indicates that the debugger will not stop at the tracepoint, rather than indicating that there are actions associated with the tracepoint.

Output Messages

As the dialog in Figure 42-12 suggests, a number of keywords can be used in conjunction with your trace message. However, a couple of keywords are not listed by the dialog: $FILEPOS, which gives the location of the current file, and $TICKS, which can be used as a relative time indicator.

Macros

Tracepoints can execute any Visual Studio macro, which includes macros you may have created. Because macros can be used to modify source code, be careful which macros you execute within a tracepoint. Modifying code while debugging an application may result in the source code being out of sync with the running application. Visual Studio macros are discussed in Chapter 53.

Execution Point

After reaching a breakpoint, it is often useful to be able to step through code and review both variable values and program execution. Visual Studio 2008 not only enables you to step through your code, it also permits you to adjust the execution point to backtrack or even repeat operations. The line of code that is about to be executed is highlighted and an arrow is displayed to the left, as shown in Figure 42-14.

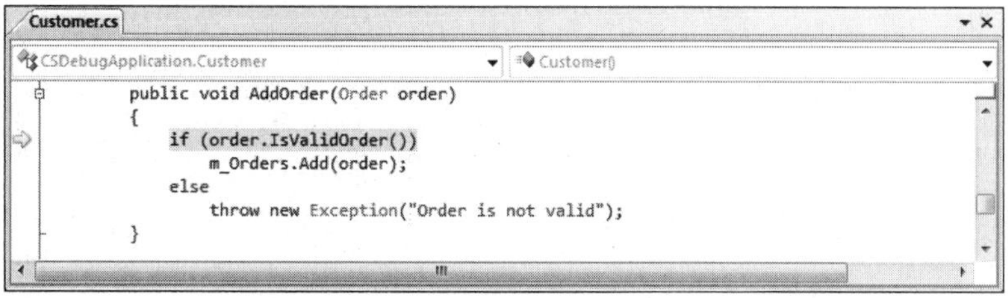

Figure 42-14

Stepping Through Code

The first step in manipulating the execution point is simply to step through code in the expected order of execution. Three size increments can be used to step the debugger forward. It is important to remember that when stepping through code it is actually being run, so variable values may change as you progress through the application.

Stepping Over (F10)

Stepping Over is fully executing the line that currently has focus and progressing to the next line in the current code block. If the end of the code block has been reached, stepping returns to the calling code block.

Stepping In (F11)

Stepping In behaves the same as Stepping Over when the line is a simple operator, such as a numeric operation or a cast. When the line is more complex, Stepping In steps through all user code. For example, in the following code snippet, pressing F10 through the TestMethod only steps through the lines of code within TestMethod. Pressing F11 steps through TestMethod until the MethodA call is made, and then the debugger steps through MethodA before returning to TestMethod:

```
public void TestMethod()
{
    int x = 5 + 5;
    MethodA();
}

private void MethodA()
{
    Console.WriteLine("Method A being executed");
}
```

Stepping Out (Shift+F11)

If you step into a long method by accident, it is quite often convenient to be able to step back out of that method without having to either step over every line in that method or set a breakpoint at the end of the method. Stepping Out moves the cursor out of the current method to where it was being called. Considering the previous snippet, if you entered MethodA, pressing Shift+F11 would immediately return the cursor to the end of TestMethod.

Moving the Execution Point

As you become familiar with stepping in and out of functions, you will find that you are occasionally overzealous and accidentally step over the method call you are interested in. In this case, what you really want to do is go back and review the last action. Though you can't actually unwind the code and change the application back to its previous state, you can move the execution point so the method is re-evaluated.

To move the current execution point, select and drag the yellow arrow next to the current line of execution (refer to Figure 42-14) forward or backward in the current method. Use this functionality with care, because it can result in unintended behavior and variable values.

Edit and Continue

One of the most useful features of Visual Studio 2008 debugging is Edit and Continue. Both C# and Visual Basic have support for Edit and Continue, enabling you to make changes to your application on the fly. Whenever your application is paused, you can make changes to your code and then resume execution. The new or modified code is dynamically added to your application, with the changes taking immediate effect.

Rude Edits

At this point, you are likely wondering whether there are any limitations on the changes that you can make. The answer is yes, and there are quite a few types of *rude edits*, which refer to any code change that requires the application to be stopped and rebuilt. A full list of rude edits is available from the Visual Studio 2008 help resource under the Edit and Continue topic, but they include the following:

❑   Making changes to the current, or active, statement

❑   Changes to the list of global symbols — such as new types or methods — or changing the signatures of methods, events, or properties

❑   Changes to attributes

Stop Applying Changes

When changes are made to the source code while the application is paused, Visual Studio has to integrate, or apply, the changes into the running application. Depending on the type or complexity of the changes made, this could take some time. If you wish to cancel this action, you can select Stop Applying Code Changes from the Debug menu.

Summary

Most developers who use Visual Studio 2008 will use breakpoints to track down issues with their applications. In this chapter, you learned how to optimize the use of breakpoints to reduce the amount of time spent locating the issue.

The following chapter examines the various debugging attributes that are available and explains how to create debugging proxy types and visualizers. This allows you to customize the debugging experience and reduce the time spent wading through unnecessary lines of code.

Creating Debug Proxies and Visualizers

Other than writing code, debugging is likely the most time-consuming activity when writing an application. If you consider all the time you spend stepping through code, looking at the watch window to see the value of a variable, or even just running the application looking for any exceptions being raised, you will realize that this is one of the most time-consuming parts of writing software.

Previous chapters have focused on how you can use the various debugging windows to retrieve information about the current status of your application, and how you can set breakpoints and tracepoints to generate debugging information. This chapter goes beyond what is provided out of the box, and looks at how you can customize the debugging experience to reduce the time spent wading through unnecessary lines of code.

Using debugging proxy types and visualizers, you can represent complex variables and data types in a useful way within the debugger. This allows you to filter out unnecessary information and zero in on the most relevant properties of an object, thereby making it easier to determine when your application is not functioning correctly and to trace the source of the issue.

Attributes

This section begins by outlining a number of debugging attributes that can be applied to code to affect the way the debugger steps through it. Some of the debugging attributes can also be used to customize the appearance of your types when you hover over them in Break mode.

The debugging attribute classes are contained within the System.Diagnostics namespace. Rather than specify the full namespace for each attribute, the source code examples in this chapter assume that it has been added as an import.

DebuggerBrowsable

The first attribute you can apply to fields and properties that belong to a C# class is the `DebuggerBrowsable` attribute. Although this attribute can be applied to both C# and Visual Basic code, it is only interpreted by the C# debugger. This attribute takes a single parameter that determines how the member is displayed in the variable tree. In the following code snippet, the field `Orders` is set to `Collapsed`:

```
public class Customer
{
    [DebuggerBrowsable(DebuggerBrowsableState.Collapsed)]
    public List<Order> Orders;

}
```

Figure 43-1 (left) shows the same snippet of code with `DebuggerBrowsable` initially set to `Collapsed` (or not specified). Figure 43-1 (center) shows the same snippet with `DebuggerBrowsable` set to the `RootHidden` value, where the actual `Orders` item does not appear, just the contents of the collection. Finally, in Figure 43-1 (right) the `Never` value is used for `DebuggerBrowsable`, in which case the `Orders` member does not appear at all.

Figure 43-1

DebuggerDisplay

When you hover your mouse over a variable while you are in Break mode, the first thing you will see in the tooltip is the type of object you are hovering over. In Figure 43-1, a mouse was initially hovering over the `Customer` class, followed by the `Order` class. This information is not particularly useful, because most of the time you have a fairly good idea about the type of object you are dealing with. It would be better for this single line to contain more useful information about the object. This is the case for well-known types such as strings and integers where the actual value is displayed.

The `DebuggerDisplay` attribute can be used to change the single line representation of the object from the default full class name. This attribute takes a single parameter, which is a `String`. The format of this String can accept member injections using the String.Format breakout syntax. For example, the attributes applied to the `Customer` and `Order` classes might be as follows:

```
[DebuggerDisplay("Customer {CustomerName} has {Orders.Count} orders")]
public class Customer

[DebuggerDisplay("Order made on {DateOrdered} which is worth ${Total}")]
public class Order
```

This would give you the debugger output shown in Figure 43-2, which indicates that customer John Smith has one order, which, as you can see from the description, was made on March 6 and is worth $50.

```
Customer c = new Customer();
c.CustomerName = "John Smith";
Order o = new Order();
o.Total = 50.00M;
c.AddOrder(o);
```

	c	Customer "John Smith" has 0x00000001 orders	
⊞	✔ CustomerId	{ecf627ed-9c35-4a66-955a-7b12e761acea}	
	✔ CustomerName	🔍 ▾ "John Smith"	
⊞	✔ [0x00000000]	Order made on {6/03/2008 12:12:08 AM} with is worth $50	
⊞	✔ Raw View		

Figure 43-2

Looking back at the syntax for the `DebuggerDisplay` attribute, you can see that the output string consists of both static text and field and property information from the object. For example, the `CustomerName` property for the `Customer` object is referenced using the `{CustomerName}` syntax within the static text.

DebuggerHidden

The `DebuggerHidden` attribute can be added to code that you don't want to step through when debugging. Code marked with this attribute is stepped over and does not support breakpoints. If this code makes a call to another method, the debugger steps into that method. Taking the following code snippet, a breakpoint can be set in both `ClickHandler` and `NotSoHiddenMethod`:

```csharp
private void ClickHandler(object sender, EventArgs e)
{
    HiddenMethod();
}

[DebuggerHidden()]
public void HiddenMethod()
{
    Console.WriteLine("Can't set a breakpoint here");
    NotSoHiddenMethod();
}

public void NotSoHiddenMethod()
{
    Console.WriteLine("Can set a breakpoint here!");
}
```

If you step through this code, the debugger goes from the call to `HiddenMethod` in the `ClickHandler` method straight to the `NotSoHiddenMethod`. The call stack at this point is shown in Figure 43-3, and you can see that `HiddenMethod` does not appear in the stack.

Figure 43-3

DebuggerStepThrough

Like the `DebuggerHidden` attribute, when the `DebuggerStepThrough` attribute is applied to a piece of code, that code is stepped over when debugging regardless of whether this code calls other methods.

Similar to the `DebuggerHidden` attribute, breakpoints cannot be set within a block of code marked with the `DebuggerStepThrough` attribute. However, if a breakpoint is set within a section of code that is called by that code, the attributed code will be marked as *external code* in the call stack. This is illustrated in Figure 43-4, which shows the code that was listed in the previous section. However in this case `DebuggerStepThrough` has been set on `HiddenMethod` instead of `DebuggerHidden`.

Figure 43-4

`DebuggerStepThrough` *is very useful when working with code that calls a lot of properties; for example, if you are calling a method that passes in a large number of properties as parameters. If you add the* `DebuggerStepThrough` *attribute to all the properties, you won't step into all of the properties when debugging the method call.*

Visual Studio 2008 supports the Just My Code option, configurable from the Debugging node in the Options dialog (select Tools ➪ Options). Unchecking this option makes all code contained within your application appear in the call stack, as shown in Figure 43-5. This includes designer and other generated code that you might not want to debug. Once this option is unchecked, breakpoints can also be set in blocks of code marked with this attribute.

Figure 43-5

DebuggerNonUserCode

The `DebuggerNonUserCode` attribute combines the `DebuggerHidden` and `DebuggerStepThrough` attributes. When the Just My Code option is selected, breakpoints cannot be set in blocks of code marked with this attribute, and the code will appear as external code in the call stack. However, stepping through code will step into any code called by that block of code in the same way it does for the `DebuggerHidden` attribute.

DebuggerStepperBoundary

DebuggerStepperBoundary is the least useful of all of the Debugger attributes, because it only comes into effect under specific conditions. It was added to avoid a misleading debugging experience that can occur when a context switch is made on a thread within the boundaries of the DebuggerNonUserCode attribute. It is entirely possible in this scenario that the next user-supplied code module stepped into may not actually relate to the code that was in the process of being debugged. To avoid this undesirable situation, the DebuggerStepperBoundary, when encountered under this scenario, will escape from stepping through code to running code.

Type Proxies

So far, you have seen how you can modify the tooltip to show information that is more relevant to debugging your application. However, the attributes discussed so far have been limited in how they control what information is presented in the expanded tree. The DebuggerBrowsable attribute enables you to hide particular members, but there is no way to add more fields. This is where the DebuggerTypeProxy attribute can be used to provide you with complete control over the layout of the tooltip.

The other scenario where a type proxy is useful is where a property of a class changes values within the class. For example, the following snippet from the Customer class tracks the number of times the OrderCount property has been accessed. Whenever the tooltip is accessed, the CountAccessed property is incremented by one:

```
public class Customer
{
    private int m_CountAccessed;
    public int OrderCount
    {
        get
        {
            m_CountAccessed++;
            return this.Orders.Count;
        }
    }

    public int CountAccessed
    {
        get
        {
            return this.m_CountAccessed;
        }
    }
}
```

Figure 43-6 illustrates the tooltip you want to be shown for the Customer class. Instead of showing the full list of orders to navigate through, it provides a summary about the number of orders, the maximum and minimum order quantities, and a list of the items on order.

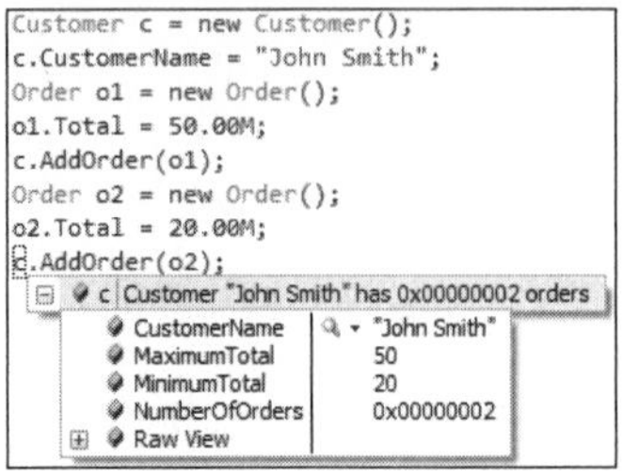

```
Customer c = new Customer();
c.CustomerName = "John Smith";
Order o1 = new Order();
o1.Total = 50.00M;
c.AddOrder(o1);
Order o2 = new Order();
o2.Total = 20.00M;
c.AddOrder(o2);
```

c	Customer "John Smith" has 0x00000002 orders	
	CustomerName	"John Smith"
	MaximumTotal	50
	MinimumTotal	20
	NumberOfOrders	0x00000002
	Raw View	

Figure 43-6

The first line in the tooltip is the same as what you created using the DebuggerDisplay attribute. To generate the rest of the tooltip, you need to create an additional class that will act as a substitute when it comes to presenting this information. You then need to attribute the Customer class with the DebuggerTypeProxy attribute so the debugger knows to use that class instead of the Customer class when displaying the tooltip. The following code snippet shows the CustomerProxy class that has been nested within the Customer class:

```
[DebuggerDisplay("Customer {CustomerName} has {Orders.Count} orders")]
[DebuggerTypeProxy(typeof(Customer.CustomerProxy))]
public class Customer
{
    private int m_CountAccessed;
    public int OrderCount
    {
        get
        {
            m_CountAccessed++;
            return this.Orders.Count;
        }
    }

    public int CountAccessed
    {
        get
        {
            return this.m_CountAccessed;
        }
    }

    public class CustomerProxy
    {
        public string CustomerName;
        public int NumberOfOrders;
        public decimal MaximumTotal = decimal.MinValue;
        public decimal MinimumTotal = decimal.MaxValue;

        public CustomerProxy(Customer c)
```

```
        {
            this.CustomerName = c.m_CustomerName;
            this.NumberOfOrders = c.m_Orders.Count;
            foreach (Order o in c.m_Orders)
            {
                this.MaximumTotal = Math.Max(o.Total, this.MaximumTotal);
                this.MinimumTotal = Math.Min(o.Total, this.MinimumTotal);
            }
        }
    }
}
```

There are very few reasons why you should create public nested classes, but a type proxy is a good example because it needs to be public so it can be specified in the `DebuggerTypeProxy` attribute, and it should be nested so it can access private members from the `Customer` class without using the public accessors.

Raw View

On occasion, you might want to ignore the proxy type. For example, this might be true if you are consuming a third-party component that has a proxy type defined for it that disguises the underlying data structure. If something is going wrong with the way the component is behaving, you might need to review the internal contents of the component to trace the source of the issue.

In Figure 43-6 you may have noticed at the bottom of the tooltip a node titled Raw View. Expanding this node will display the debugger tooltip as it is normally shown without any proxy types or debugger display values.

In addition, you can turn off all type proxies in Visual Studio through the Tools ⇨ Options menu. Under the Debugging node check the box that says "Show raw structure of objects in variables windows." Doing this will prevent all type proxies and debugger displays from being shown.

Visualizers

The last part of this chapter looks at a concept in Visual Studio 2008 that can be used to help debug more complex data structures. Two of the most common data types programmers work with are *Strings* and *DataTables*. Strings are often much larger than the area that can be displayed within a tooltip, and the structure of the `DataTable` object is not suitable for displaying in a tooltip, even using a type proxy. In both of these cases, a visualizer has been created that enables the data to be viewed in a sensible format.

Once a visualizer has been created for a particular type, a magnifying glass icon appears in the first line of the debugger tooltip. Clicking this icon displays the visualizer. Figure 43-7 shows the Text Visualizer dialog that appears.

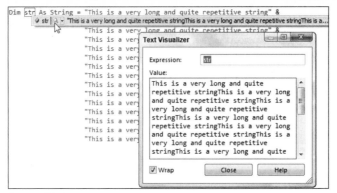

Figure 43-7

Before you can start writing a visualizer, you need to add a reference to the `Microsoft.VisualStudio` `.DebuggerVisualizers` namespace. To do this, right-click the project in the Solution Explorer and select Add Reference from the context menu. You should also add this namespace as an import to any classes for which you plan to create debugger visualizers.

A visualizer is typically made up of two parts: the class that acts as a host for the visualizer and is referenced by the `DebuggerVisualizer` attribute applied to the class being visualized, and the form that is then used to display, or visualize, the class. Figure 43-8 shows a simple form, CustomerForm, which can be used to represent the customer information. This is just an ordinary Windows Form with a couple of TextBox controls, a DataGridView control, and a Button. The only unique aspect to this form is that it has been marked as Serializable, and its constructor has been changed to accept a `Customer` object, from which the customer information is extracted and displayed, as shown in the following listing:

```
[Serializable()]
public partial class CustomerForm : Form
{
    public CustomerForm(Customer c)
    {
        InitializeComponent();

        this.txtCustomerId.Text = c.CustomerId.ToString();
        this.txtCustomerName.Text = c.CustomerName;
        this.dgOrders.DataSource = c.Orders;
    }

    private void btnOk_Click(object sender, EventArgs e)
    {
        this.DialogResult = DialogResult.OK;
        this.Close();
    }
}
```

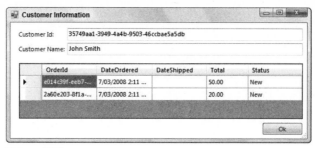

Figure 43-8

The next stage is to wire this form up to be used as the visualizer for the Customer class. This is done by creating the nested CustomerVisualizer class, which inherits from the DialogDebuggerVisualizer abstract class, as shown in the following code:

```
[Serializable()]
[DebuggerDisplay("Customer {CustomerName} has {Orders.Count} orders")]
[DebuggerTypeProxy(GetType(Customer.CustomerProxy))]
[DebuggerVisualizer(GetType(Customer.CustomerVisualizer))]
public class Customer
{
    ...

    public class CustomerVisualizer : DialogDebuggerVisualizer
    {
        protected override void Show(
                        IDialogVisualizerService windowService,
                        IVisualizerObjectProvider objectProvider)
        {
            Customer c = (Customer)objectProvider.GetObject();
            CustomerForm cf = new CustomerForm(c);
            windowService.ShowDialog(cf);
        }
    }
}
```

Unlike the type proxy, which interacts with the actual Customer object being debugged, visualizers need to be able to serialize the class being debugged so the class can be moved from the process being debugged to the process that is doing the debugging (and will subsequently be shown the visualizer). As such, both the Customer and Order classes need to be marked with the Serializable attribute.

The Show method of the CustomerVisualizer class does three things. To display the Customer object being debugged, first you need to get a reference to this object. You do this via the GetObject method on the ObjectProvider object. Because the communication between the two processes is done via a stream, this method does the heavy lifting associated with deserializing the object so you can work with it.

Next you need to pass the Customer object to a new instance of the CustomerForm. Finally, use the ShowDialog method on the WindowService object to display the form. It is important that you display the form using this object because it will ensure that the form is displayed on the appropriate UI thread.

Lastly, note that the `CustomerVisualizer` class is referenced in the `DebuggerVisualizer` attribute, ensuring that the debugger uses this class to load the visualizer for `Customer` objects.

As a side note, if you write components and want to ship visualizers separately from the components themselves, visualizers can be installed by placing the appropriate assembly into either the `C:\Program Files\Microsoft Visual Studio 9.0\Common7\Packages\Debugger\Visualizers` directory, or the `Documents\Visual Studio 2008\Visualizers` directory.

Advanced Techniques

Thus far, this chapter has covered how to display and visualize objects you are debugging. In earlier chapters you learned how to modify field and property values on the object being debugged via the datatip. The missing link is being able to edit more complex data objects. The final section in this chapter looks at how to extend your visualizer so you can save changes to the `Customer` object.

Saving Changes to Your Object

When you created the `CustomerVisualizer`, you had to retrieve the `Customer` object from the communication stream using the `GetObject` method. This essentially gave you a clone of the `Customer` object being debugged to use with the visualizer. To save any changes you make in the `CustomerVisualizer`, you need to send the new `Customer` object back to the process being debugged. You can do this using the `ReplaceObject` method on the ObjectProvider, which gives you a `CustomerVisualizer`.

Before you can call the `ReplaceObject` method you will need to make some changes to pass the modified `Customer` object back to the visualizer. This has been done by saving the `Customer` object to an internal variable when it is initially passed into the class, and exposing this variable via a read-only property. This is shown in the following listing:

```
[Serializable()]
public partial class CustomerForm : Form
{
    public CustomerForm(Customer c)
    {
        InitializeComponent();

        this.txtCustomerId.Text = c.CustomerId.ToString();
        this.txtCustomerName.Text = c.CustomerName;
        this.dgOrders.DataSource = c.Orders;

        m_ModifiedCustomer = c;
    }

    private Customer m_ModifiedCustomer;
    public Customer ModifiedCustomer
    {
        get
        {
            m_ModifiedCustomer.CustomerId = new Guid(txtCustomerId.Text);
            m_ModifiedCustomer.CustomerName = txtCustomerName.Text;
```

```
                    m_ModifiedCustomer.Orders = (List<Order>)dgOrders.DataSource;
                    return m_ModifiedCustomer;
            }
        }

        private void btnOk_Click(object sender, EventArgs e)
        {
            this.DialogResult = DialogResult.OK;
            this.Close();
        }
    }
```

You can now easily access the modified `Customer` object and save the changes back by calling the `ReplaceObject` method as shown here:

```
[Serializable()]
[DebuggerDisplay("Customer {CustomerName} has {Orders.Count} orders")]
[DebuggerTypeProxy(GetType(Customer.CustomerProxy))]
[DebuggerVisualizer(GetType(Customer.CustomerVisualizer))]
public class Customer
{
    ...

    public class CustomerVisualizer : DialogDebuggerVisualizer
    {
        protected override void Show(
                        IDialogVisualizerService windowService,
                        IVisualizerObjectProvider objectProvider)
        {
            Customer c = (Customer)objectProvider.GetObject();
            CustomerForm cf = new CustomerForm(c);
            if (windowService.ShowDialog(cf) ==
                                System.Windows.Forms.DialogResult.OK)
                    objectProvider.ReplaceObject(cf.ModifiedCustomer);
        }
    }
}
```

An alternate method would be to use `DataBinding` *for all of the Customer fields on the form with a* `BindingSource` *object. This* `BindingSource` *object could be exposed with a public modifier, thereby making it accessible from the visualizer class. All that is needed then is to set the* `Customer` *object as the data source of this* `BindingSource` *object by the* `visualizer` *class, and it will automatically synchronize changes back to the original* `Customer` *object.*

Summary

Debugging applications is one of the most time-consuming and frustrating activities in the development cycle. In this chapter you learned how you can take charge of Visual Studio 2008 by customizing the debugging experience.

Using debugging proxy types and visualizers, you can control how information is presented to you while you are debugging your application. This means that you can easily determine when your application is not functioning correctly and be able to trace the source of the issue.

Debugging Web Applications

With Visual Studio 2008, debugging solutions for the Web is just as straightforward as doing the same for Windows-based applications. You can use many of the same debugging windows already discussed in previous chapters, as well as deal with errors through the Exception Assistant. However, there are some differences and additional features specific to web applications that you can use to target your debugging practices more closely to the web paradigm.

In addition to the standard debugging techniques, ASP.NET also provides you with a comprehensive tracing capability, and even the capability to perform health monitoring on your system to ensure it is running in the manner you expect, as well as exposing problematic scenarios when it doesn't.

If you are using Windows Vista with UAC you will want to launch Visual Studio with administrator rights, or you are likely to find the debugger will not attach correctly to the local web server. Right-click the Visual Studio 2008 shortcut and select Run as Administrator. To always launch as administrator, right-click the shortcut and select Properties, and then select the Compatibility tab and check the "Run this program as an administrator" checkbox.

Debugging Server-Side ASP.NET Code

Before you can perform any level of debugging in a web application, you first need to ensure that ASP.NET debugging is enabled in your Web Application or Web Site Project. For Web Application Projects, enable debugging options by right-clicking the project entry in the Solution Explorer and selecting Properties. Select the Web tab option page and ensure that the ASP.NET debugger option is checked, as illustrated in Figure 44-1.

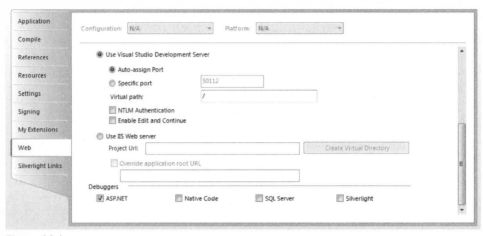

Figure 44-1

If you want to be able to include unmanaged code, stored procedures, or Silverlight in your debugging of the web applications, you can activate the Native Code, SQL Server, and Silverlight debuggers here. Native code and SQL Server debugging are explained in the next chapter and Silverlight debugging is discussed later in this chapter.

> *Enabling debugging in other Web Application Projects, such as ASP.NET Web Service or ASP.NET MVC applications, is exactly the same as for standard ASP.NET web applications. In fact, from a debugging perspective, there are really no differences between any of these project types.*

Because Web Site Projects do not have a project file, you must use a slightly different procedure to enable debugging. Enable debugging in Web Site Projects by right-clicking the project entry in the Solution Explorer and selecting Property Pages from the context menu. When the Property Pages dialog is displayed, navigate to the Start Options page, and ensure that the ASP.NET debugger option is checked, as shown in Figure 44-2.

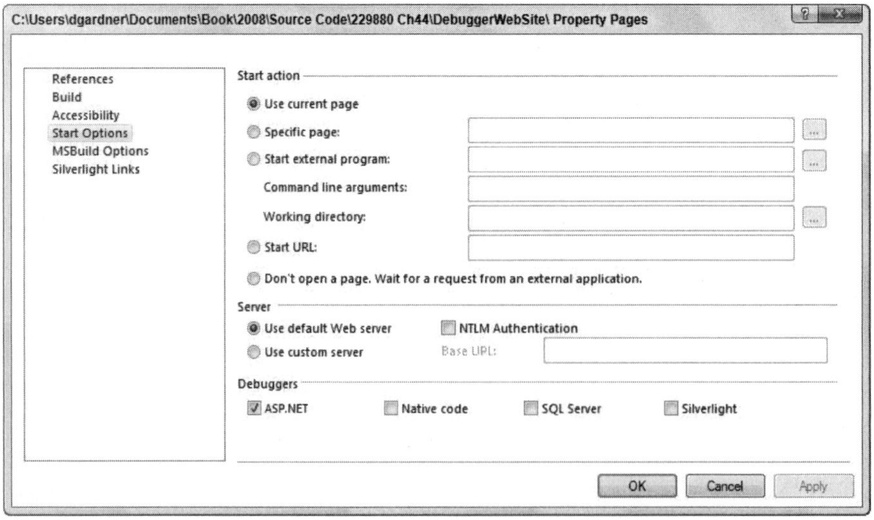

Figure 44-2

As with Web Application Projects, you can also customize how a Web Site Project is to be started, including not opening any specific page, but running the server so it listens for a request from another application.

An alternative method of implementing web debugging for any Web Site or Web Application Project is to use the web.config file. Locate the compilation node within system.web and set the debug attribute to true. The following listing shows a minimal web.config file with the debug option enabled, ready for hooking the debugger to the application:

```
<configuration>
    <appSettings/>
    <connectionStrings/>
    <system.web>
        <compilation debug="true" strict="false" explicit="true" />
    </system.web>
</configuration>
```

Note that even when you activate the ASP.NET debugger in the Start Options, without setting the debug attribute to true you will be unable to debug the application. However, Visual Studio will detect this discrepancy and present you with a dialog informing you that in order to debug you will need to change web.config. It also provides an option for Visual Studio to automatically change this attribute for you.

You should never deploy an ASP.NET application into production with the debug="true" *option set within the web.config file. Doing so will cause your application to run slower, use more memory, and prevent some things from being cached.*

Web Application Exceptions

By default, when your web application encounters an exception, the web application will display the ASP.NET server error page, as shown in Figure 44-3. Colloquially called the *Yellow Screen of Death*, this page displays the exception details including the stack trace.

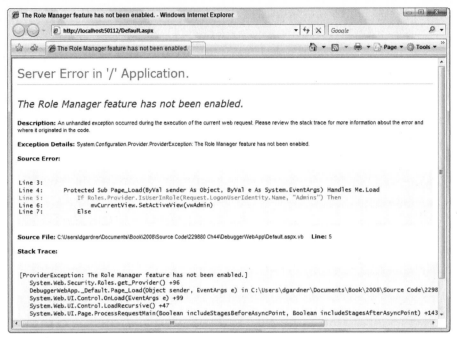

Figure 44-3

The server error page is generated under both debug and normal execution. Whereas it is useful to have this information during development, it is not something that you should be displaying to your end users. Fortunately, there is an easy way to configure redirections for exceptions, including standard HTTP errors, by editing the `customErrors` section in the web.config file.

Modifying the previous web.config file to include these redirection options for 403 (access denied) and 404 (page not found) can result in a configuration similar to the following:

```
<configuration>
    <appSettings/>
    <connectionStrings/>
    <system.web>
        <compilation debug="true" strict="false" explicit="true" />
        <customErrors mode="RemoteOnly" defaultRedirect="GenericErrorPage.htm">
            <error statusCode="403" redirect="AccessDenied.html" />
            <error statusCode="404" redirect="PageNotFound.html" />
        </customErrors>
    </system.web>
</configuration>
```

The `mode` attribute of the customErrors section defines three options for displaying a custom error page instead of the default server error page. These are:

❑   **On:** The custom error page will always be displayed.

❑   **Off:** The server error page will always be displayed.

❑ **RemoteOnly:** The server error page will be displayed if the browser request is coming from the local computer; otherwise the custom error page will be displayed.

The server error page is useful in production scenarios where you cannot run the application in debug mode. However, when debugging, it is much more useful to break execution as soon as an exception occurs. This can be done by enabling the "Break when an exception is" thrown option for the Common Language Runtime. Figure 44-4 shows how this option is set in the Exceptions dialog under the Debug ⇨ Exceptions menu item.

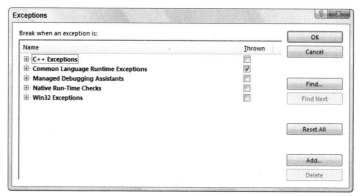

Figure 44-4

Once you have enabled this option, when an exception occurs, Visual Studio will drop back into the IDE and position the workspace so the statement at issue is visible. Just like Windows-based applications, Visual Studio can aid you when errors occur by displaying the Exception Assistant. As shown in Figure 44-5, web errors are fully detailed and include information about which part of the statement is in error.

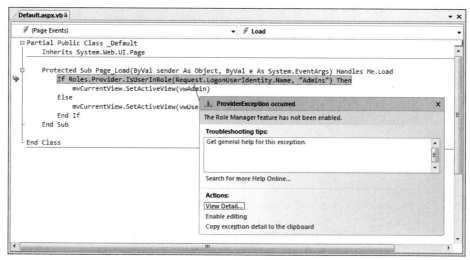

Figure 44-5

You can gather additional information on the error by clicking the View Detail link, which provides you with a comprehensive exception object visualizer that you can navigate to determine the content of the error at hand.

Edit and Continue

Edit and Continue, which enables you to modify code when the application is paused in a debug session, is disabled by default in ASP.NET web applications. This useful feature can be enabled by right-clicking the project entry in the Solution Explorer and selecting Properties. Under the Web tab option page check the Enable Edit and Continue option. This is only supported for the built-in Visual Studio development web server.

Web Site Projects do not support Edit and Continue, however; because they naturally support a very iterative style of development, it is not such a useful feature for those projects. Edit and Continue is explained in more detail in Chapter 42.

Error Handling

Though debugging your applications is indeed easy with the tools Visual Studio 2008 provides, it is always best to try to avoid error situations proactively. You can do this in web applications with structured Try-Catch exception handling, but you will also want to make your solutions more solid by including code to handle any errors that fall outside any Catch conditions.

> Notice we are using the term error handling and not exception handling here. This is because it is broader than trapping program exceptions and also covers HTML errors, such as Page Not Found and Authentication Required.

You can catch errors on two levels: On an individual page you can intercept unexpected errors and produce a custom-built error, or you can catch errors on an application-wide level through the implementation of a routine to handle errors in the global.asax file.

Page-Level Errors

To handle an error on an individual page, you need to implement an event-handler routine that intercepts the `MyBase.Error` event. When this event is raised, you can then perform whatever actions you need to take place when unexpected errors occur. A typical routine might look like this:

```
Private Sub Page_Error(ByVal sender As Object, ByVal e As System.EventArgs) _
    Handles MyBase.Error
    Response.Write("An unexpected error has occurred.")
    Server.ClearError()
End Sub
```

As discussed previously, you can also set custom redirections for standard HTTP error codes in the web.config file, so you should use this method only for errors that are not already handled and are specific to the individual page.

Application-Level Errors

At the web-application level, you can also trap a series of errors through the global.asax file. By default, Visual Studio 2008 web projects do not include this file, so you'll first need to add it to the project through the Add New Item dialog. Select the Global Application Class item, leave the name as global. asax, and click Add to add the file to your project.

When this class is added to the project, the template includes stubs for the commonly encountered application events, including the error event. To handle any errors that are not catered to elsewhere in the project, add your processing code to this `Application_Error` routine, like so:

```
Sub Application_Error(ByVal sender As Object, ByVal e As EventArgs)
    Server.Transfer("UnexpectedError.aspx")
End Sub
```

This sample routine simply transfers the user to an errors page that determines what to do by interrogating the `Server.GetLastError` property.

Debugging Client-Side JavaScript

One of the most anticipated new features of Visual Studio 2008 is the improved support for debugging client-side JavaScript code. Combined with the new IntelliSense support, this will significantly ease the difficulty of developing JavaScript code.

JavaScript debugging works only if you are using Internet Explorer as your web browser during the debug session.

Setting Breakpoints in JavaScript Code

Setting breakpoints for JavaScript code is no different from setting any other breakpoint. Within the editor window any breakpoints in JavaScript code are displayed with a diamond in the center, as shown in Figure 44-6.

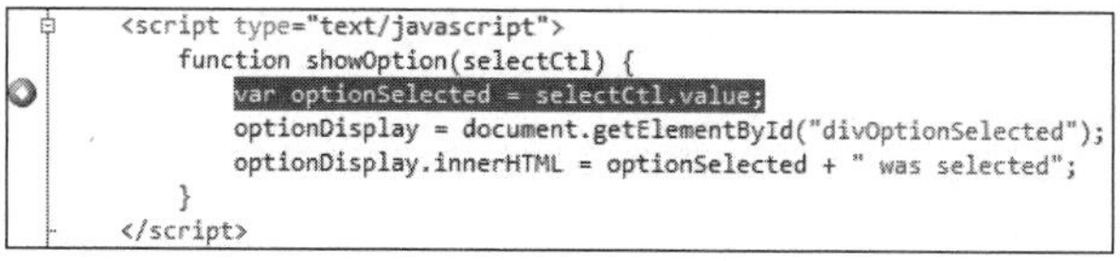

Figure 44-6

JavaScript breakpoints have the same functionality as standard breakpoints. This includes setting conditions, hit counts, or even running a macro as part of a tracepoint.

When the debugger hits a breakpoint it will pause execution and display the HTML code that has been rendered on the client, as shown in Figure 44-7. This provides a true debugging experience because it includes all client-side elements such as the ViewState and server controls rendered in HTML.

Visual Studio 2008 has also improved the watch visualizers for client-side elements. Figure 44-7 demonstrates this with a tooltip that shows the properties and methods of the document object.

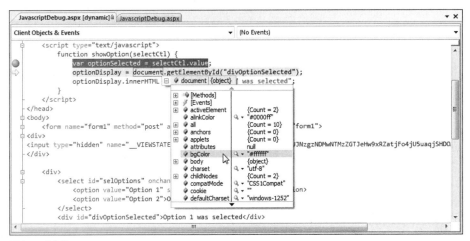

Figure 44-7

It is also possible to set both client-side JavaScript breakpoints and Visual Basic or C# server-side breakpoints at the same time on the same page. This will allow you to step through both the client-side and the server-side code in a single debug session.

Debugging Dynamically Generated JavaScript

There are several scenarios where ASP.NET sends down to the client JavaScript that has been dynamically generated on the server. For example, ASP.NET AJAX controls such as the Update Panel will send down to the client references to JavaScript files that are actually stored as resources in the ScriptManager control.

When you are running a web application in debug mode, the Visual Studio Solution Explorer will show a list of all the script references that the page you are debugging has loaded, as shown in Figure 44-8. Double-clicking any of the links under the Script Documents node will display the JavaScript code and allow you to set breakpoints within those scripts.

Figure 44-8

Debugging ASP.NET AJAX JavaScript

ASP.NET AJAX provides both Debug and Release versions of its client JavaScript libraries. The release version is optimized for performance and minimizes the size of the JavaScript that must be downloaded to the client. The Debug version is more verbose and provides additional debugging features at runtime, such as type and argument checking.

If debugging is enabled in the web.config file, ASP.NET AJAX will use a debug version of the client libraries. You can also enable the debug version on a per-page basis by setting `ScriptMode="Debug"` on the ScriptManager control.

ASP.NET AJAX also includes the `Sys.Debug` class, which can be used to add debug statements to your client JavaScript. This class can be used to display the properties of objects at runtime, generate trace messages, or use assertions.

Debugging Silverlight

The Microsoft Silverlight Tools for Visual Studio 2008 install a native debugger into Visual Studio that makes it easy to debug Silverlight 2 applications. When you create a new Silverlight 2 application, Visual Studio will prompt you either to generate an HTML test page to host the Silverlight application, or to utilize an existing or new web project, as shown in Figure 44-9.

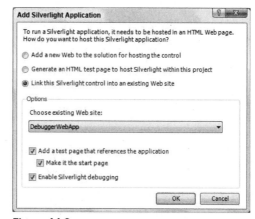

Figure 44-9

In Figure 44-9, we've chosen to create a test page that hosts the Silverlight application in the Web Application Project that is part of the existing solution, and to enable Silverlight debugging in this web application. If you select either of the other two options, you will not need to perform any additional steps to enable Silverlight debugging.

You can always enable or display support for Silverlight debugging in an existing Web Application Project under the Web option page of the project properties.

Once the Silverlight debugger is enabled, you will be able to set breakpoints in the code-behind class files of the XML pages. When the breakpoint is encountered during debug, the session will pause and display the current line of code, as shown in Figure 44-10. You will be able to step through the code, view the call stack, and interrogate the properties of objects, just as you would with any web or Windows Forms application.

The only major limitation with Silverlight 2 debugging is that Edit and Continue is not supported.

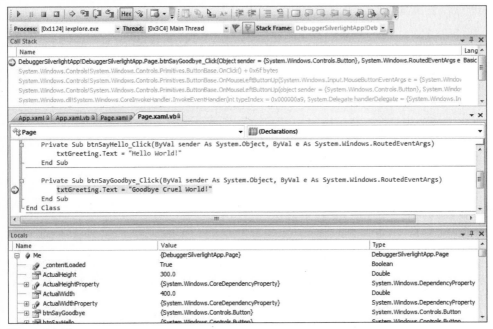

Figure 44-10

Tracing

In addition to actively debugging your web applications when things go wrong, you can also implement ASP.NET tracing functionality to look at the information produced in an individual page request. Using tracing enables you to add debug statements to your code that are only viewable when viewing locally; when the web application is deployed to the remote server, users do not see the trace information.

Trace information can include variables and simple objects to help you determine the state of the specific request and how it was executed. Note that ASP.NET tracing is different from using the `Trace` class in normal Windows applications in that its output is produced on the actual ASP.NET web page or in a stand-alone trace viewer, rather than the output windows that `Trace` commands use.

Page-Level Tracing

To implement page-level tracing, you simply need to include a `trace` attribute in the `@Page` directive at the top of the page you wish to trace. A simple Visual Basic page with tracing activated might look like the following:

```
<%@ Page Language="vb" Trace="true" AutoEventWireup="false"
    CodeBehind="ShowTrace.aspx.vb" Inherits="DebuggerWebApp.ShowTrace" %>

<!DOCTYPE html PUBLIC "-//W3C//DTD XHTML 1.0
  Transitional//EN" "http://www.w3.org/  TR/xhtml1/DTD/xhtml1-transitional.dtd">

<html xmlns="http://www.w3.org/1999/xhtml" >
```

```
<head id="Head1" runat="server">
    <title>Trace Example Page</title>
</head>
<body>
    <form id="form1" runat="server">
    <div>Hello!</div>
    </form>
</body>
</html>
```

In addition, you can specify how the tracing messages associated with the page request should appear by using the TraceMode attribute. Set this to SortByTime to output the tracing messages in the order that they were produced, or SortByCategory to categorize them into different message types. Figure 44-11 shows the trace output for the sample page defined in the previous listing when sorted by category.

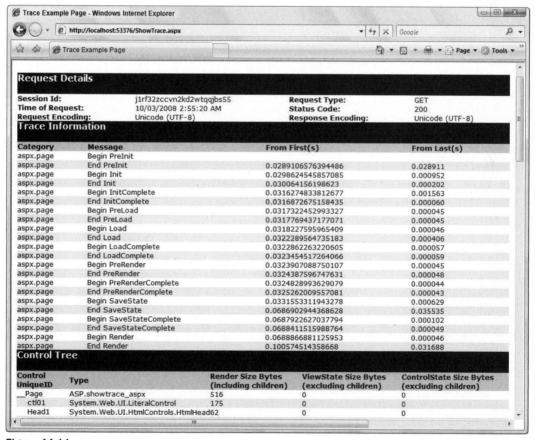

Figure 44-11

Application-Level Tracing

Application-level tracing can be enabled through the web.config file. Within the system.web node you need to include a trace node that contains the attribute `enabled` with a value of `true`. When using application-level tracing, you can control how the tracing is produced through the `pageOutput` attribute. When set to `true`, you receive the tracing information at the bottom of every page (similar to how it appears in Figure 44-11), whereas a value of `false` ensures that the tracing information never appears on the page, and is instead only accessible through the Trace Viewer (covered later in this chapter). You can also restrict the amount of information to trace with the `requestLimit` attribute. Including a trace node for the web.config file you saw earlier in this chapter results in a configuration like the following:

```
<configuration>
    <appSettings/>
    <connectionStrings/>
    <system.web>
        <compilation debug="true" strict="false" explicit="true" />
        <customErrors mode="RemoteOnly" defaultRedirect="GenericErrorPage.htm">
            <error statusCode="403" redirect="AccessDenied.html" />
            <error statusCode="404" redirect="PageNotFound.html" />
        </customErrors>
        <trace enabled="true" pageOutput="false" traceMode="SortByCategory"/>
    </system.web>
</configuration>
```

Trace Output

Tracing output is voluminous. The simple Hello page defined earlier produces almost three full printed pages of information, including the following categories of data:

❑ **Request Details:** The specific details of the current session, time of the request, what type of request it was, and the HTTP code that is returned to the browser

❑ **Trace Information:** A full listing of each event as it begins and then ends, including the amount of time taken to process each event

❑ **Control Tree:** A listing of all controls defined on the page, including the page object itself as well as HTML elements. Each object also has a size listed, so you can determine whether there are any abnormal object sizes affecting your application's performance.

❑ **Session State and Application State:** These two lists show the keys and their values for the individual session and the application overall.

❑ **Request Cookies Collection and Response Cookies Collection:** A list of any known ASP.NET request and response cookies on the system that your application may be able to access

❑ **Headers Collection:** A list of the HTTP headers included in the page

❑ **Response Headers Collection:** The HTTP headers associated with the response, indicating what type of object is being returned

❑ **Form Collection:** A list of any forms defined in the page

❑ **Querystring Collection:** A list of any query strings used in the page request

❑ **Server Variables:** A list of all server variables known to the ASP.NET server and application you're currently executing

As you can see, when tracing is implemented for a web page or application, you gain access to an enormous amount of information that you can then use to determine how your application is performing. You can see whether there are problems in the various collections in the way of missing or extraneous data, as well as analyze the Trace Information list to determine whether there are any abnormally long processing times for any specific events.

Trace Viewer

The Trace Viewer is a custom handler included in your web application when you have application tracing activated. When tracing is being reported at the application level, you can navigate to this page and view all page tracing output as it occurs. To view the Trace Viewer, browse to the trace.axd page in the root directory of your web site.

The Trace Viewer provides a summary table of all requests made in the application, along with the time the request was made and the HTTP status code returned in the response. It also provides a link to detailed information for each request (which is the same information that you can see on a page trace discussed earlier), as shown in Figure 44-12.

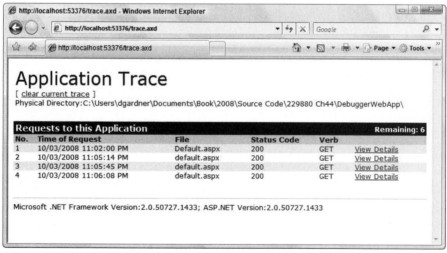

Figure 44-12

Custom Trace Output

You can supplement the default trace information with your own custom-built trace messages, using the `Trace.Warn` and `Trace.Write` methods. Both have the same set of syntactical overloads, and the only real difference is that messages outputted using the `Warn` method are displayed in red text.

The simplest form for these commands is to include a message string like so:

```
Trace.Warn("Encountered a potential issue")
```

However, you can categorize your warnings and messages by using the second and third forms of the methods, including a category and optionally an error object as well:

```
Trace.Warn("MyApp Error Category", "Encountered a potential issue", myAppException)
```

Health Monitoring

ASP.NET includes a built-in framework for generating and capturing events for the purposes of monitoring a web application. This feature, called Health Monitoring, allows you to become more proactive in managing your production web applications, enabling you to be notified as soon as a problem occurs.

The Health Monitoring feature does much more than just alerting you that an exception has occurred. You can also instrument your code and generate alerts for custom events (for example, if a user fails to log on or attempts to access a restricted area.)

Health Monitoring is enabled through the web.config file. Within the system.web node you need to include a healthMonitoring node that contains the attribute `enabled` with a value of `true`. This node will also contain the details of which provider to use and rules for handling different events. Extending the web.config file from earlier, we have created an SMTP provider and a rule that e-mails the details of any unhandled exceptions to the webmaster. The web.config file has also been modified to include a reference to an SMTP server, so that the provider can send the e-mail notifications.

```
<configuration>
    <appSettings/>
    <connectionStrings/>
    <system.web>
        <compilation debug="true" strict="false" explicit="true" />
        <customErrors mode="RemoteOnly" defaultRedirect="GenericErrorPage.htm">
            <error statusCode="403" redirect="AccessDenied.html" />
            <error statusCode="404" redirect="PageNotFound.html" />
        </customErrors>
        <trace enabled="true" pageOutput="false" traceMode="SortByCategory"/>
        <healthMonitoring enabled="true">
            <providers>
                <add name="SMTPProvider"
                    type="System.Web.Management.SimpleMailWebEventProvider"
                    from="server@yourdomain.com"
                    to="webmaster@yourdomain.com"
                    subjectPrefix="Exception on WebApp:"
                    bufferMode="Critical Notification"/>
            </providers>
            <rules>
                <clear />
```

```
                    <add name="All Errors Default"
                          eventName="All Errors"
                          provider="SMTPProvider" />
              </rules>
          </healthMonitoring>
      </system.web>

      <system.net>
          <mailSettings>
              <smtp><network host="mail.yourdomain.com"/></smtp>
          </mailSettings>
      </system.net>
  </configuration>
```

Once this is in place, any time an exception is generated and not handled, an e-mail is sent to the specified address. This e-mail message contains a large amount of useful troubleshooting information, including the exception details and stack trace. Figure 44-13 shows an example message.

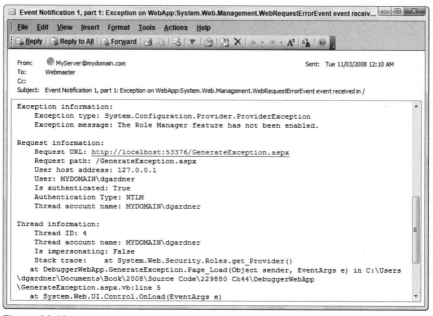

Figure 44-13

In addition to the SMTP provider, there is also an Event Log, WMI, and SQL Server provider. Quite complex rules can be enabled to direct the notifications to one or more of these providers. If none of these meets your needs, you can even write your own custom provider.

Summary

With the combination of Visual Studio 2008 and ASP.NET 2.0 server-side capabilities, you have a wide array of tools to help you look after your web solutions. These features enhance the already impressive feature set available with normal Windows application debugging, with web-specific features such as JavaScript and Silverlight debugging, page- and application-level error handling, and the capability to trace code, which you can use to monitor the way pages are being executed in your web applications without interrupting your end users.

In addition, the ASP.NET Health Monitoring framework allows you to proactively manage your production web applications by notifying you as soon as a problem occurs.

45

Advanced Debugging Techniques

As you've seen throughout the last several chapters, Visual Studio 2008 comes with a great variety of ways to debug and run through your applications, including catching errors and displaying them to you for action before the code executes too far; a number of techniques for effectively debugging web applications; and other features such as breakpoints and visualizing errors.

However, there is still more functionality to be found in Visual Studio that you can use to customize your experience with debugging projects, databases, unmanaged code, and even the .NET Framework itself. In this chapter you'll find advanced techniques for debugging your projects regardless of language or technology.

Start Actions

Visual Studio provides several ways to launch applications at the start of a debugging session. For most projects the default start option will be sufficient, which in the case of a Windows executable will launch the program directly. In the case of a web application, Visual Studio will open the default web browser and load the current page, or navigate to the root path of the web application if there is no active page.

There are some scenarios where you may want a different action to occur during a debugging session. For example, you may need to always open a specific web page when the web application is started. In these scenarios you can change the start options on the Debug or Web project property page. Figure 45-1 shows the start actions for a Windows Forms project.

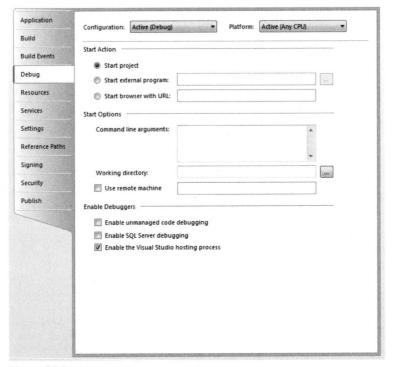

Figure 45-1

In addition to starting the project directly, you can also choose to start an external program that presumably will subsequently call your project into the execution process. Alternatively, you can choose to launch the default web browser on your system with a specific URL, again with the assumption that the URL will ultimately invoke your project.

Often, applications are built with the capability to exhibit different behavior depending on command-line arguments. If your project is of this variety and you need to test the different configurations, the "Command line arguments" textbox can be used to specify which set of arguments is to be included in the execution of the project. You should enter the command-line arguments in exactly the same way you expect the end user to when that user is invoking your application once it has been deployed.

You can override the default directory from which the application should be executed by setting the "Working directory" option. This equates to the same setting when you edit a Windows shortcut. In addition, you can also specify a different machine to control the debugging process of the application by activating the "Use remote machine" option. Note that you will need to explicitly specify the remote computer path, because it does not have an associated browse option.

The final section of the Debug page pertains to the different kinds of debugging that will be performed during the execution of your application. By default, the only debugging process active is the debugging of managed code inside the Visual Studio environment, but you can optionally include native unmanaged code or SQL Server stored procedures. These debuggers are discussed later in the chapter.

The configuration and platform settings are available only when you have the Show Advanced Build Configurations setting activated. This is in the Projects and Solutions ⇨ General options page and is on by default for all environment configurations except for Visual Basic programmers.

The start actions for ASP.NET web applications are found on the Web property page for the project, as shown in Figure 45-2. The default is to launch the web site with whichever page is currently open in the text editor. This can be changed to always use a specific page or URL. The other option is to start an external program or wait for a request from an external application. This is particularly useful when debugging a web service that is invoked by another application.

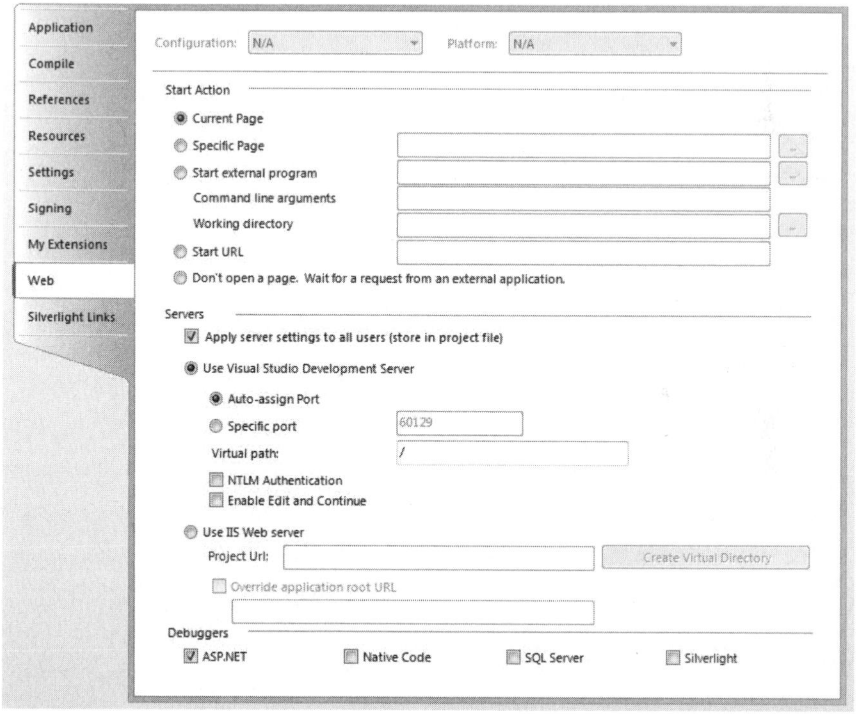

Figure 45-2

ASP.NET Web Application Projects can also choose from one of two web servers. The built-in Visual Studio Development Server is the most convenient, because it does not require installation or configuration. The Visual Studio Development Server also supports Edit and Continue.

Debugging with Code

Three classes ship with the .NET Framework under the System.Diagnostics namespace that can be used to build debugging support directly into your code — the `Debug`, `Debugger`, and `Trace` classes. When used properly, these classes provide a very powerful way for you to interact with the debugger.

The functionality provided by all three of these classes is exposed through static/shared methods and properties, which makes it easy to add them to your code.

The Debugger Class

The Debugger class provides programmatic access to certain debugger functions within Visual Studio. For example, the following code snippet will check whether the application is running under a debugger and, if not, launch one and attach to the process:

```
if (!Debugger.IsAttached)
{
    Debugger.Launch();
}
```

When this code is executed while the application is running normally outside Visual Studio, the program execution will pause, and you will be presented with a dialog box similar to the one shown in Figure 45-3. Selecting "New instance of Visual Studio 2008" will load the application in Visual Studio and continue executing the application in debug mode.

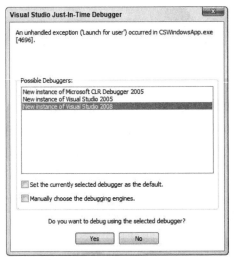

Figure 45-3

The Debug and Trace Classes

The Debug and Trace classes are used to output debugging information and trace the execution path of your application. Most of the properties and methods are common across the two classes, which may seem redundant. However, there is a key difference in the way these methods are implemented and the results presented to you.

The Debug class should be used if you only need to output information while running in debug mode. The Trace class can be used if you want output in both the Debug and Release versions. While you are debugging an application during development, both your tracing and debugging output go to the Output window in Visual Studio. However, in Release mode, any Debug statements will be suppressed by the compiler and not invoked during execution. This will ensure that you can include a large amount of debug code in your application without increasing the size or decreasing the performance of your release code.

> *The ability to use Trace and Debug statements in different build configurations is specified through compiler directives. Within Visual Studio you can enable or disable these directives from the project properties pages. These settings are located on the Build property page for C# projects, and under the Advanced Compiler Options button on the Compile property page for Visual Basic projects.*

The methods that are available to output debug messages in the Debug and Trace classes are listed in Table 45-1.

Table 45-1: Methods for Outputting Debug Messages

Method	Outputs
Write	The text or string representation and an optional category
WriteIf	The text and an optional category, if the condition specified as an argument evaluates to true
WriteLine	The text followed by a carriage return and an optional category
WriteLineIf	The text followed by a carriage return and an optional category, if the condition specified as an argument evaluates to true

You can also offset the output by increasing or decreasing the indenting through the Indent and Unindent methods.

You can also use the Assert method on the Debug and Trace classes to create an assertion, which tests a condition that was specified as an argument. If the condition evaluates to true, no action occurs. If the condition evaluates to false, the assertion fails. If you are running in debug mode, your program will pause execution, and a dialog box will be displayed, as shown in Figure 45-4.

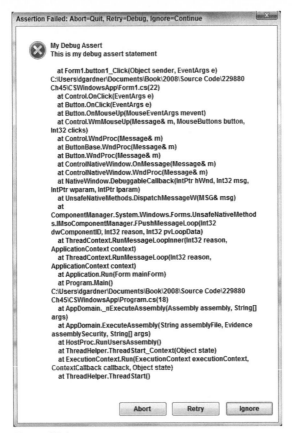

Figure 45-4

Selecting Abort will terminate the application execution. Retry will break at the statement and Ignore will continue execution.

While running in debug mode all output from the Debug and Trace classes is displayed in the Output window. However, with a Release build all trace output is collected by a listener. A listener is simply an object that receives trace output and writes it to an output device. An output device could be a text file, Windows event log, or some other custom logging repository.

Finally, Trace Switches are available, which allow you to enable, disable, and filter tracing output. Trace Switches can be declaratively enabled within the app.config file for an application.

Debugging Running Applications

Sometimes you'll need to debug an application that is running outside Visual Studio. There are many reasons why you would want to do this, such as if a defect appears only when an application is executed in production. Fortunately, Visual Studio provides a simple method for attaching and debugging a Windows executable or web application that is actively running.

Attaching to a Windows Process

Attaching to a running Windows process is a fairly straightforward task in Visual Studio. Ideally, you will have the original source code open in Visual Studio, in which case you will be able to debug the process as if you had launched it in debug mode from Visual Studio.

If you are debugging an executable without access to the source code, the available debugging features are limited. If the executable was built without debug information or symbols, available features are further limited and it is unlikely that you will gain much useful information by debugging it in this way.

From the Debug menu, use the Attach to Process command. This displays the Attach to Process dialog window (see Figure 45-5) from which you can browse all active processes. Locate the application that you wish to debug from the Available Processes list and click the Attach button.

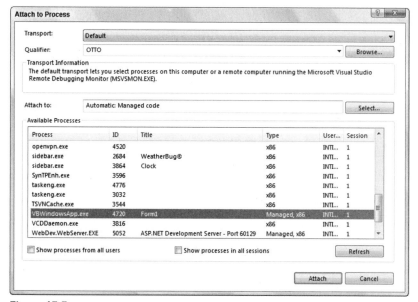

Figure 45-5

Because attaching to an application requires these manual steps, it is not well suited if you are trying to debug a problem that occurs during startup. Also, if you are debugging an application that does not require any user input and finishes quickly, you may not have time to attach to it. In both these scenarios it would be better to either launch the application in debug mode from within Visual Studio, or create a custom build with a `Debug.Break()` statement in the startup code of the application.

Once you've finished debugging an attached process, you should always cleanly detach from the process by selecting Debug ⇨ Detach All. You can also choose to end the application, by selecting Debug ⇨ Terminate All.

Attaching to a Web Application

Attaching to an ASP.NET web application is almost as easy as attaching to a Windows application. However, before you attach to a web application, you must ensure that it has debugging enabled by

757

editing the web.config file for the application. Locate the Compilation node within system.web and set the `debug` attribute to `true`. The following listing shows a minimal web.config file with the Debug option set, ready for attaching the debugger to the application:

```
<configuration>
    <appSettings/>
    <connectionStrings/>
    <system.web>
        <compilation debug="true" />
    </system.web>
</configuration>
```

ASP.NET automatically detects any changes to web.config settings and applies them immediately. Therefore, you don't need to restart the computer or the IIS service for this change to take effect. As discussed in Chapter 44, this change can have an adverse affect on performance, so you should not leave it enabled in production.

Once you have enabled debugging you can attach to the web application. The process you'll need to attach to is the ASP.NET worker process, which will either be the native process within IIS (called w3wp.exe for IIS 6.0 or higher, or aspnet_wp.exe on older versions of IIS) or the built-in Visual Studio 2008 development server WebDev.WebServer.exe.

Because the IIS process normally runs under the ASPNET or NETWORK SERVICE account, you will need to be running Visual Studio with Administrator rights to attach the debugger to it.

To begin debugging, select Attach to Process from the Debug menu in Visual Studio 2008. Select the "Show processes in all sessions" checkbox if you are attaching to ASP.NET under IIS. Locate the ASP.NET worker process from the Available Processes list and click the Attach button. As shown in Figure 45-6, you may be prompted to restart Visual Studio with elevated rights.

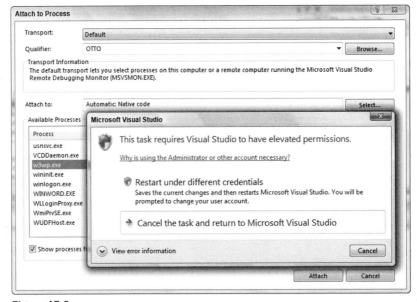

Figure 45-6

Remote Debugging

Remote debugging allows you to attach to an application that is executing on another machine. This can be useful for those cases where a bug is manifesting itself only on a non-programmer's computer, or if you need to debug a Windows Service or ASP.NET web application that is running on a production server.

Debugging a remote application is no different from debugging a local application. Once you have attached to the remote application you can set breakpoints, watch variables, and step through code. However, before you can attach to a remote process you must ensure that the Remote Debugging Monitor is running on the machine to be debugged.

The Remote Debugging Monitor, msvsmon.exe, is a small executable that is shipped with Visual Studio 2008. By default you will find the 32-bit version installed in the directory `C:\Program Files\ Microsoft Visual Studio 9.0\Common7\IDE\Remote Debugger\x86`.

> *The x64 version of msvsmon.exe is not installed by default with Visual Studio 2008 unless you are running a 64-bit version of Windows. The IA-64 version of msvsmon.exe is available only with Visual Studio Team System.*

You can simply copy this folder over to the remote machine and run it locally, or create a share and run it from a UNC path. You can also choose to install the Remote Debugging Monitor on the remote machine by running the setup MSI file that is on the Visual Studio installation DVD media under the `vs/Remote Debugger` directory.

When you launch msvsmon.exe on a remote computer for the first time, it will attempt to configure the Windows Firewall to open the network ports necessary to enable remote debugging. In some environments, such as on a Windows Server 2003, this will prompt you to make the necessary changes as shown in Figure 45-7. On the Developers machine, Visual Studio will make the necessary changes to the Windows Firewall to enable it to connect to a remote machine.

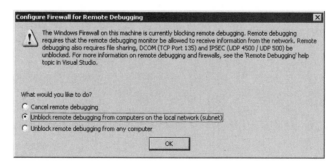

Figure 45-7

Once you have started the Remote Debugging Monitor it will simply listen on the network for incoming debugging requests. By default, remote requests must be authenticated, and only users who are Administrators have the necessary permissions to attach and debug applications. These security settings can be changed from the Tools ⇨ Options menu, as shown in Figure 45-8.

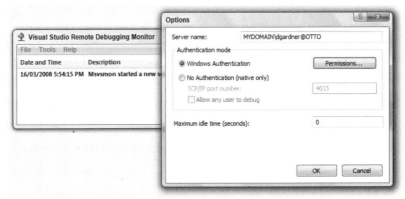

Figure 45-8

If you enable the "No Authentication" mode, your machine will be vulnerable to any user on the network. A remote user could launch applications on your computer, access data, or perform untold mischievous or destructive actions by using a debugger. You have been warned!

Once you have the Remote Debugging Monitor running on the remote machine, you can attach to an application on that machine through the Debug ⇨ Attach to Process menu. Enter the computer name or IP address of the remote machine in the field marked Qualifier. Visual Studio will connect to the Remote Debugging Monitor, authenticate you, and finally display the list of processes running on the remote machine. Simply select a process to attach and you will be able to debug as if you had attached to a local process.

.NET Framework Reference Source

One of the more interesting trends that has emerged from Microsoft in recent years is an increased openness and even willingness to embrace open source. The ASP.NET MVC framework, covered in Chapter 37, is a good example of this, because the source code for this has been released as a buildable Visual Studio project solution.

However, arguably more significant than this has been the release of the source code for a large number of base class libraries in the .NET Framework. Available under the read-only Microsoft Reference License, it allows you to step into and debug the .NET Framework code as part of a debugging session. Though we could always infer the programmer's intent by using Reflector, there is no comparison to browsing the actual source code, *including the inline documentation*. The really good news is that this documentation is quite comprehensive.

The first step to enabling access to the source code is to configure a couple of Debugger settings. Open the Tools ⇨ Options menu item and select the Debugging tab. If you are using the Visual Basic Profile, you'll need to select the Show All Settings option to see all these options. Ensure that the Enable Just My Code option is unchecked, and the "Enable source server support" option is checked, as shown in Figure 45-9.

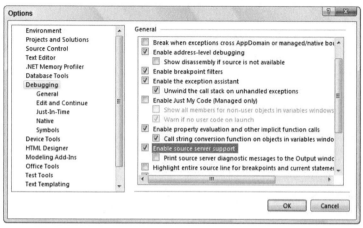

Figure 45-9

Secondly, navigate to the Symbols tab in the Options dialog and add a new symbol file location. Specify `http://referencesource.microsoft.com/symbols` as the new location. Next, enter a local directory to store the cached symbol files. It is important that you have read/write access to this directory without requiring elevated permissions. Finally, ensure that the "Search the above locations only when symbols are loaded manually" option is enabled. When you have finished, your screen should look similar to Figure 45-10.

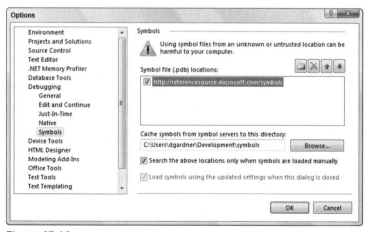

Figure 45-10

You will now be able to download and browse the .NET Framework base class libraries during a debugging session. Set a breakpoint in your application code and run in debug mode. When the breakpoint is hit, open the Call Stack window (Debug ⇨ Windows ⇨ Call Stack) to display the execution path. You can load the source code for a framework assembly by right-clicking the reference in the Call Stack window and selecting Load Symbols, as shown in Figure 45-11.

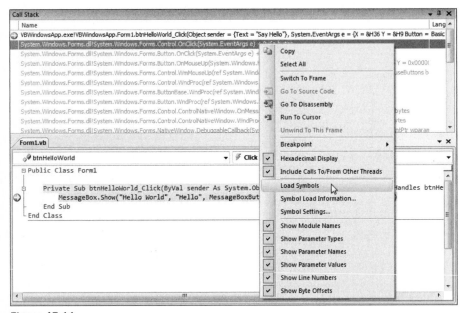

Figure 45-11

The Microsoft symbol server will be queried to determine which source code files are available. Once completed, the code that is available for debugging will no longer be grayed out, and you will be able to double-click the entry in the Call Stack to download the source code from the Microsoft symbol server and cache it on your local computer. If this is the first time you have downloaded the code, you will be prompted to accept the Microsoft Reference Library license.

Depending on the size of the assembly and your available bandwidth, the symbols could take a minute or so to download, during which time Visual Studio will be unresponsive. Once completed, you will be able to double-click the entry in the Call Stack, or step into the source code during your debug session, as shown in Figure 45-12.

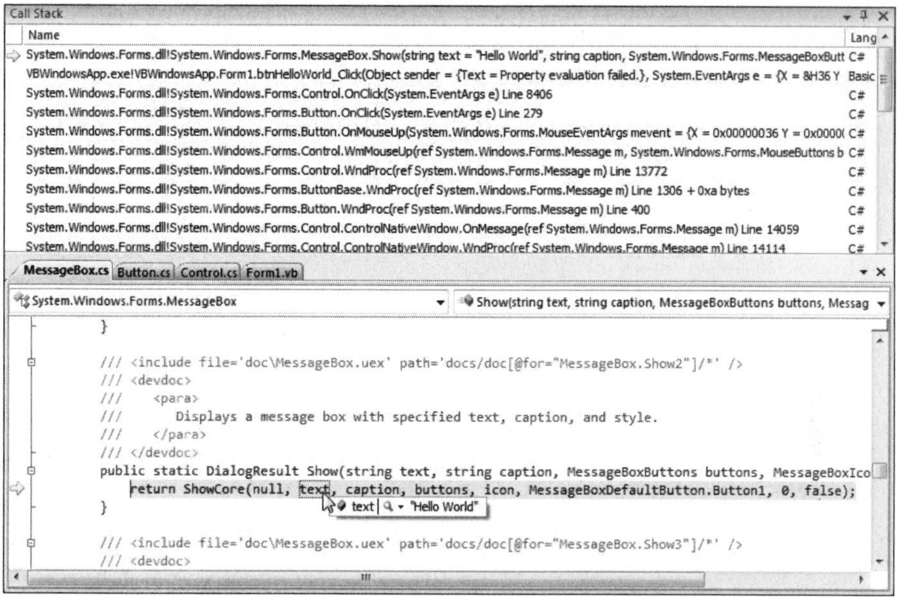

Figure 45-12

Multi-Threaded Debugging

Multi-threaded applications have traditionally been notoriously difficult to debug properly. Seemingly fundamental tasks, such as keeping track of which thread you are currently inspecting and what other threads are currently executing, are some of the reasons why this task is so hard. Fortunately, Visual Studio 2008 has improved the support available for debugging multi-threaded applications.

In Chapter 41 we discussed the Threads debug window, which lists all the active threads for a particular application. New functionality accessed through this window includes the ability to set a friendly name for a thread. You can also set flags on individual threads, which means that you don't have to spend as much time trying to keep track of thread IDs.

To further improve debugging, you can now identify each thread within the source code editor window. This is enabled from the Threads window, by right-clicking any entry and selecting Show Threads in Source. The result of this is shown in Figure 45-13, where a new thread marker icon (consisting of a red and blue wavy line) is displayed in the gutter. The thread marker indicates that a thread, or several threads, is stopped at this location. When you hover over the thread marker a tooltip will be displayed that identifies which threads are stopped here. The thread names listed are the friendly names that have been entered in the Threads window.

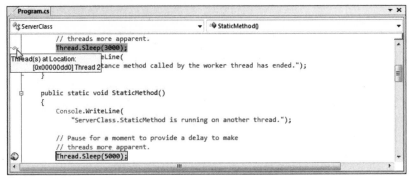

Figure 45-13

Within the Debug Location Toolbar, you can navigate between threads. When you select a different thread from the Thread drop-down list, the Call Stack will be updated with the selected thread's execution path, and the execution point moved to the current location in the source code. In Figure 45-14 we have also filtered the list of threads to show only those we have flagged. This is done using the button with the double-flag icon, next to the Threads drop-down.

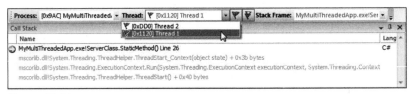

Figure 45-14

Although these features do not make it totally simple to debug multi-threaded applications, they do solve one of the more significant issues, which is keeping track of individual threads and where they are up to in your application.

Debugging SQL Server Stored Procedures

Another incredibly useful feature of the debugging model found in Visual Studio 2008 is the capability to debug stored procedures in SQL Server databases. You'll need to first check the "Enable SQL Server debugging" setting in the Debug property page of your project, as shown in Figure 45-15. Once activated, whenever your code encounters a stored procedure, you can debug the procedure code inline with your own code.

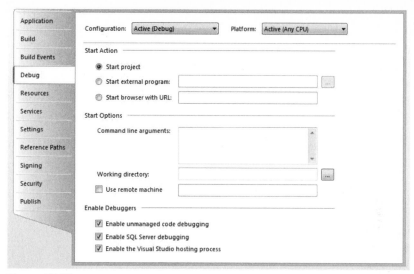

Figure 45-15

You can even include breakpoints within a stored procedure so you can trace through the SQL Server code without halting the application code execution.

Your Windows account must be a member of the sysadmin group on SQL Server in order to debug stored procedures.

Mixed-Mode Debugging

The final thing to discuss before we close out the section on debugging is mixed-mode debugging. A mixed-mode application is any application that combines managed code (Visual Basic, C#, Managed C++, and so on) with native code (typically C++). Debugging a mixed-mode application is generally no different from debugging a pure managed-code application; however, you must first configure the application to support native code debugging. Figure 45-15, in the previous section, shows the unmanaged code debugger enabled along with the SQL Server debugger.

There are a couple of limitations with mixed-mode debugging that you should be aware of. First, it is only available on Windows 2000 or higher operating systems. Also, when debugging a mixed-mode application, you may find that some operations such as stepping through code run very slowly. This can be improved by unchecking the option to "Enable and other implicit function calls" in the Debugger option page.

> *Because native call stacks and managed call stacks are different, the debugger cannot always provide a single complete call stack for mixed code. Though fairly rare, it is possible that there will be some discrepancies in the call stack. You can find more information on this in the MSDN library.*

Summary

This chapter completes the discussion on debugging your projects and applications, offering details about advanced debugging techniques. Visual Studio 2008 is capable of meeting a wide spectrum of debugging scenarios, such as multi-threaded applications, stored procedures, unmanaged code, and even the .NET Framework itself. These techniques provide you with a set of very effective debugging options for tracking down the issues in your projects regardless of language or technology.

Part X

Build and Deployment

46

Upgrading with Visual Studio 2008

Each time a new version of Visual Studio is released there is always a delay before developers start to use it. This is primarily due to the need to upgrade existing applications to a new version of the .NET Framework at the same time. For example, the migration from Visual Studio 2003 to Visual Studio 2005 required upgrading applications to version 2.0 of the .NET Framework. With the introduction of multi-targeting in Visual Studio 2008, you can now upgrade to the latest IDE independently of moving to the .NET Framework version. This is particularly important if you still need to target older versions of Windows for which there is no support for the newer .NET Framework versions.

In this chapter you see how easy it is to migrate existing .NET applications into Visual Studio 2008. This is done it two parts: upgrading to Visual Studio 2008 and then upgrading the .NET Framework version.

Upgrading from Visual Studio 2005

To begin with, let's start with a solution that contains a good mix of application types. Figure 46-1 shows a Visual Studio 2005 solution that contains Web Site, Class Library, Device Application, Web Service Application, and Windows Forms Application projects. The Web Site and Web Service applications both reference the Class Library, and the Windows Forms Application references the Web Service Application.

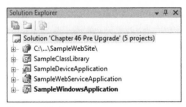

Figure 46-1

Upgrading this solution is as simple as opening it in Visual Studio 2008. This will automatically invoke the Visual Studio Conversion Wizard as shown in Figure 46-2. The wizard is relatively straightforward, with the only option being whether or not a backup is made of the solution before upgrading. This is highly recommended if your solution is not in a source control repository so that you have a backup. However, if you use a source control you can ignore this, because you can simply revert to the checked-in version if something goes wrong during the upgrade process.

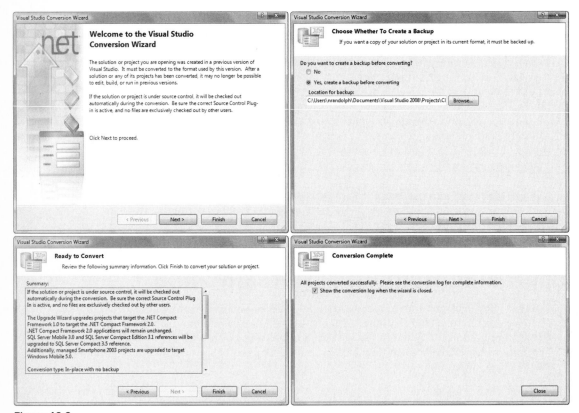

Figure 46-2

The Summary screen indicates that your solution will be checked out of source control so that changes can be made. It also indicates that in some cases there may be some framework and reference changes made as part of the upgrade. What you can't see in this screenshot is the list of projects that will be upgraded as part of the process.

Even if there are no errors raised during the upgrade process, it is still recommended that you look through the conversion log after the wizard closes. This log (UpgradeLog.XML, found in the solution folder) looks similar to Figure 46-3 and will typically list the solution and project files as the only things that have been upgraded. If you are upgrading a pre-Visual Studio 2005 solution, you may find that there are some conversion issues, because there are some known breakages between the framework versions. Despite being able to target multiple versions of the .NET Framework, Visual Studio 2008 is limited to version 2.0 and above. So, if you have a solution that uses a version prior to this, the conversion wizard will attempt to upgrade it.

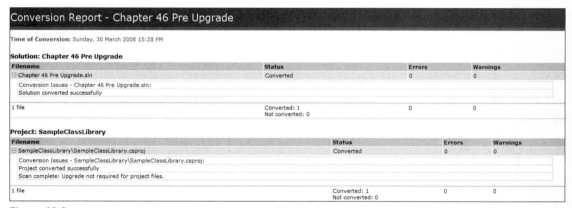

Figure 46-3

Upgrading this solution to Visual Studio 2008 will not change the version of the .NET Framework that the application targets. So, the question is what has been changed and what are the implications. The answer is that there are minimal changes to both the solution and project files. In the solution file the changes may be as subtle as the header. For example, the following:

```
Microsoft Visual Studio Solution File, Format Version 9.00
# Visual Studio 2005
```

becomes:

```
Microsoft Visual Studio Solution File, Format Version 10.00
# Visual Studio 2008
```

The changes to the project file include some additional elements and attributes. For example, the following:

```
<Project DefaultTargets="Build"
        xmlns="http://schemas.microsoft.com/developer/msbuild/2003">
    <PropertyGroup>
        <Configuration Condition=" '$(Configuration)' == '' ">Debug</Configuration>
        <Platform Condition=" '$(Platform)' == '' ">AnyCPU</Platform>
        <ProductVersion>8.0.50727</ProductVersion>
        <SchemaVersion>2.0</SchemaVersion>
        <ProjectGuid>{E9D90EE1-60A0-4740-8E3E-8F9E98202D50}</ProjectGuid>
        <OutputType>WinExe</OutputType>
        <StartupObject>SampleWindowsApplication.My.MyApplication</StartupObject>
        <RootNamespace>SampleWindowsApplication</RootNamespace>
        <AssemblyName>SampleWindowsApplication</AssemblyName>
        <MyType>WindowsForms</MyType>
    </PropertyGroup>
    ...
```

becomes:

```
<Project DefaultTargets="Build"
        xmlns="http://schemas.microsoft.com/developer/msbuild/2003"
        ToolsVersion="3.5">
    <PropertyGroup>
        <Configuration Condition=" '$(Configuration)' == '' ">Debug</Configuration>
        <Platform Condition=" '$(Platform)' == '' ">AnyCPU</Platform>
        <ProductVersion>9.0.21022</ProductVersion>
        <SchemaVersion>2.0</SchemaVersion>
        <ProjectGuid>{E9D90EE1-60A0-4740-8E3E-8F9E98202D50}</ProjectGuid>
        <OutputType>WinExe</OutputType>
        <StartupObject>SampleWindowsApplication.My.MyApplication</StartupObject>
        <RootNamespace>SampleWindowsApplication</RootNamespace>
        <AssemblyName>SampleWindowsApplication</AssemblyName>
        <MyType>WindowsForms</MyType>
        <OldToolsVersion>2.0</OldToolsVersion>
        <TargetFrameworkVersion>v3.5</TargetFrameworkVersion>
        <PublishUrl>publish\</PublishUrl>
        <Install>true</Install>
        <InstallFrom>Disk</InstallFrom>
        <UpdateEnabled>false</UpdateEnabled>
        <UpdateMode>Foreground</UpdateMode>
        <UpdateInterval>7</UpdateInterval>
        <UpdateIntervalUnits>Days</UpdateIntervalUnits>
        <UpdatePeriodically>false</UpdatePeriodically>
        <UpdateRequired>false</UpdateRequired>
        <MapFileExtensions>true</MapFileExtensions>
        <ApplicationRevision>0</ApplicationRevision>
        <ApplicationVersion>1.0.0.%2a</ApplicationVersion>
        <IsWebBootstrapper>false</IsWebBootstrapper>
        <UseApplicationTrust>false</UseApplicationTrust>
        <BootstrapperEnabled>true</BootstrapperEnabled>
    </PropertyGroup>
```

If you have developers working with a mix of Visual Studio 2005 and Visual Studio 2008, you can have them all work off a common set of project files by having two solution files, one for each version of Visual Studio. Even after upgrading the project to Visual Studio 2008, they can still be opened in both versions of the IDE. Unfortunately, the same is not true of MSBuild — once you upgrade your projects you must also upgrade your build process to use MSBuild version 3.5.

Upgrading to .NET Framework v3.5

Once you have migrated your application across to Visual Studio 2008 and tidied up your build environment, you should consider the upgrade path to .NET Framework v3.5. Unlike the upgrade to version 2.0 of the .NET Framework, where there were a number of breaking changes, the upgrade to v3.5 should be relatively painless. Though there are still some changes you may need to make, for the most part your existing application should be easily upgradable. The main reason for this is that the underlying CLR has not changed, only the libraries that sit above it.

In most cases upgrading your application is just a matter of changing the Target Framework project property. Figure 46-4 shows the project properties dialog for a web site. On the Build tab there is a drop-down that lists the different target frameworks that are available for you to select. For other application types, this property may be found in the Advanced Compile Options dialog for VB.NET projects (from the Compile tab of the project properties designer) and the Application tab of the project properties designer for C# projects. However, they all essentially allow you to change the version of the .NET Framework that the project is compiled against.

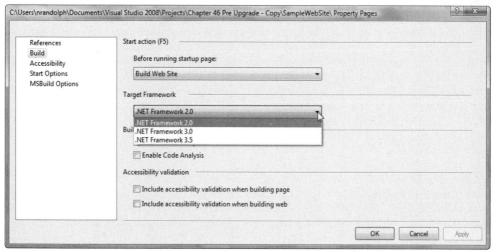

Figure 46-4

One exception to this is device applications. If you go to either the Advanced Compile Options dialog (VB.NET) or the Application tab (C#) of a device application, you will note that the Target Framework drop-down is disabled, preventing you from upgrading that project. To upgrade to version 3.5 of the .NET Compact Framework, you have to right-click the project in Solution Explorer and select Upgrade

Project from the shortcut menu (this is also available in the Project menu when the device project has focus in the Solution Explorer). Figure 46-5 shows the prompt you will see when you select to upgrade a device project. This is slightly different from the upgrade prompt you see when changing the target framework for other projects — this simply informs you that the project will be unloaded and reloaded so as to upgrade assembly references. The big difference is that the upgrade for a device project is not reversible, and you can't elect to target an earlier .NET Compact Framework version at a later stage.

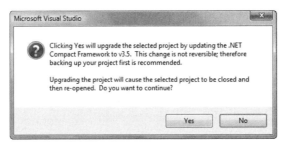

Figure 46-5

You can, in fact, reverse this upgrade by unloading the relevant project and editing the project to change the Target Framework version.

Upgrading from Visual Basic 6

Since the introduction of .NET many years ago, one of the ongoing challenges faced by organizations is how to upgrade their existing Visual Basic 6 applications. Initially, Microsoft's guidance was to use the fairly primitive upgrade tool within Visual Studio to automatically upgrade the application. It was recommended that you run the application through the upgrade tool, look at the results, and make changes to the initial application to address areas that did not upgrade smoothly.

More recently, the thinking has evolved slightly, and with the introduction of a compatibility pack it is possible to integrate .NET components into existing Visual Basic 6 applications and vice versa. In a similar approach to upgrading ASP to ASP.NET, you can now progressively migrate parts of your application over time.

With this in mind, there is still a Visual Basic 6 to .NET converter that is accessible from the File ⇨ Convert menu. Figure 46-6 shows the Convert dialog from which you can select one of the available converters. Visual Studio 2008 ships with a Visual Basic 2008 Upgrade Wizard, which as you can see is for upgrading Visual Basic 6 applications. Over time there are likely to be other converters made available to support the migration from other development platforms to .NET.

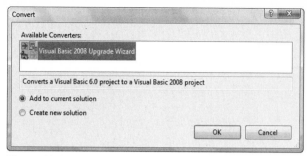

Figure 46-6

Stepping through this upgrade wizard will allow you to migrate your application, or parts of your application, to .NET. This is not a guaranteed process, and you need to thoroughly test the output to ensure that you haven't lost or broken any functionality in the upgrade process.

Summary

In this chapter you have seen how you can upgrade existing .NET applications to Visual Studio 2008 and version 3.5 of the .NET Framework. Using the latest toolset and framework version clearly has some advantages in performance, functionality, and usability. However, don't overlook the limitations that using the latest .NET Framework might impose. If your target market still uses old operating systems, such as Windows 2000, you may want to stay on version 2.0 of the .NET Framework, because this is supported on these platforms. Visual Studio 2008 allows you to have the best of both worlds, only upgrading as and when you want to.

Build Customization

Though you can build most of your projects using the default compilation options set up by Visual Studio 2008, occasionally you'll need to modify some aspect of the build process to achieve what you want. This chapter looks at the various build options available to you in both Visual Basic and C#, outlining what the different settings do so you can customize them to suit your own requirements.

In addition, you learn how Visual Studio 2008 uses the MSBuild engine to perform its compilations and how you can get under the hood of the configuration files that control the compilation of your projects.

General Build Options

Before you even get started on a project, you can modify some settings in the Options pages for Visual Studio 2008. These options apply to every project and solution that you open in the IDE, and as such can be used to customize your general experience when it comes to compiling your projects.

The first port of call for professional Visual Basic developers should be the General page of the Projects and Solutions group. By default, the Visual Basic setup of the IDE hides some of the build options from view, so the only way to show them is to activate the Show Advanced Build Configurations option.

When this is active, the IDE displays the Build Configuration options in the My Project pages, and the Build ➪ Configuration Manager menu command is also accessible. Other language environments don't need to do this, because these options are activated on startup (although you could certainly turn them off if you didn't want them cluttering your menus and pages).

The other option on this page relating to building your projects is whether or not to automatically show the Error List if compilation errors are encountered during the build process. By default, all language configurations have this option turned on.

The Build and Run options page (shown in Figure 47-1) in the Projects and Solutions group has many more options available to you to customize the way your builds take place.

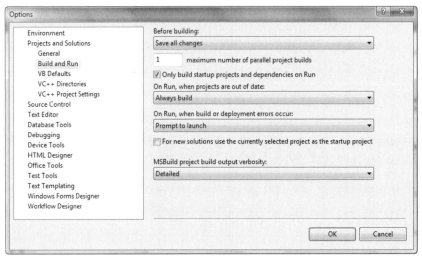

Figure 47-1

It's unclear from this page, but some of these options affect only C++ projects, so it's worth running through each option, what it does, and what languages it affects:

- ❑ **Before building:** This tells Visual Studio how to handle changes that have been made to any part of your project before the build process. You have four options:

  - ❑ **Save all changes** automatically saves any changes without prompting you. This is perhaps the best option, because you don't have to remember to save your work. This is the default setting.

  - ❑ **Save changes to open documents only** also automatically saves changes, but only to open documents. This excludes some changes to solution and project files.

  - ❑ **Prompt to save all changes** gives you the chance to save any changes before the build commences. When the build process is started, it displays a dialog prompting you to save the changes or not. If you decline to save the changes, the build still continues but uses the last saved version of the file. This option can be good to use when you want to know when you've made changes (perhaps inadvertently) to the source code.

  - ❑ **Don't save any changes**, as it suggests, doesn't save changes to any files, open in the editor or otherwise.

- ❑ **Maximum number of parallel project builds:** This controls how many simultaneous build processes can be active at any one time (assuming the solution being compiled has multiple projects). This option affects only how C++ solutions are built and has no effect on Visual Basic or C# projects.

❑ **Only build startup projects and dependencies on Run:** This option only builds the part of the solution directly connected to the startup projects. This means that any projects that are not dependencies for the startup projects are excluded from the default build process. This option is active by default, so if you've got a solution that has multiple projects called by the startup projects through late-bound calls or other similar means, they will not be built automatically. You can either deactivate this option or manually build those projects separately.

❑ **On Run, when projects are out of date:** This option is used for C++ projects only and gives you three options for out-of-date projects (projects that have changed since the last build). The default is "Prompt to build," which forces the build process to occur whenever you run the application. The "Never build" option always uses the previous build of out-of-date projects, while the "Prompt to build" gives you an option to build for each out-of-date project. Note that this only applies to the Run command, and if you force a build through the Build menu, projects are rebuilt according to the other settings in the build configuration and on this Options page.

❑ **On Run, when build or deployment errors occur:** This controls the action to take when errors occur during the build process. Despite official documentation to the contrary, this option does indeed affect the behavior of builds in Visual Basic and C#. Your options here are the default "Prompt to launch," which displays a dialog prompting you for which action to take; "Do not launch," which does not start the solution and returns to design time; and "Launch old version," which ignores compilation errors and runs the last successful build of the project.

The option to launch an old version enables you to ignore errors in subordinate projects and still run your application; but because it doesn't warn you that errors occurred, you run the risk of getting confused about what version of the project is active.

Note that when you use the "Prompt to Launch" option, if you subsequently check the "Do not show this dialog again" option in the prompt dialog, this setting will be updated to either "Do not launch" or "Launch old version," depending on whether you to choose to continue or not.

It is recommended that you set this property to "Do not launch" because this can improve the efficiency with which you write and debug code — one less window to dismiss!

❑ **For new solutions use the currently selected project as the startup project:** This option is useful when you're building a solution with multiple projects. When the solution is being built, the Visual Studio build process assumes that the currently selected project is the startup project and determines all dependencies and the starting point for execution from there.

❑ **MSBuild project build output verbosity:** Visual Studio 2008 uses the new MSBuild engine for its compilation. MSBuild produces its own set of compilation output, reporting on the state of each project as it's built. You have the option to control how much of this output is reported to you:

   ❑ By default, the MSBuild verbosity is set to Minimal, which produces only a very small amount of information about each project, but you can turn it off completely by setting this option to Quiet, or expand on the information you get by choosing one of the more detailed verbosity settings.

   ❑ MSBuild output is sent to the Output window, which is accessible via View ➪ Other Windows ➪ Output (under some environmental setups this will be View ➪ Output). If you can't see your build output, make sure you have set the "Show output from" option to Build (see Figure 47-2).

In order to select the output type, you need to have the Output window pinned so that the Toolbar is visible.

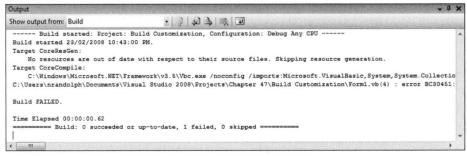

Figure 47-2

It's also worth taking a look at the other Options pages in the Projects and Solutions category, because they control the default Visual Basic compilation options (Option Explicit, Option Strict, and Option Compare), and other C++-specific options relating to build. Of note for C++ developers is the capability to specify PATH variables for the different component types of their projects, such as executables and include files, for different platform builds; and whether or not to log the build output.

Manual Dependencies

Visual Studio 2008 is able to detect inter-project dependencies between projects that reference each other. This is then used to determine the order in which projects are built. Unfortunately there are some circumstances where Visual Studio can't determine these dependencies, such as when you have custom steps in the build process. Luckily you can manually define project dependencies to indicate how projects are related to each other. You can access the dialog shown in Figure 47-3 by selecting either the Project ⇨ Project Dependencies or Project ⇨ Build Order menu commands.

Note that these menu commands are only available when you have a solution with multiple projects in the IDE.

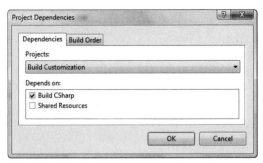

Figure 47-3

You first select the project that is dependent on others from the drop-down, and then check the projects it depends on in the bottom list. Any dependencies that are automatically detected by Visual Studio 2008 will already be marked in this list. The Build Order tab can be used to confirm the order in which the projects will be built.

Visual Basic Compile Page

Visual Basic projects have an additional set of options that control how the build process will occur. To access the compile options for a specific project, open My Project by double-clicking its entry in the Solution Explorer. When the project Options page is shown, navigate to the Compile page from the list on the left side (see Figure 47-4).

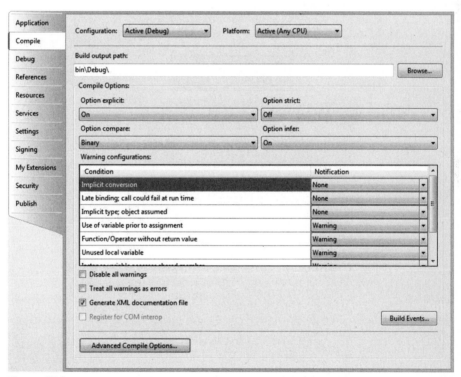

Figure 47-4

The "Build output path" option controls where the executable version (application or DLL) of your project is stored. For Visual Basic, the default setting is the `bin\Release\` directory, but you can change this by browsing to the desired location.

It is recommended that you enable the "Treat all warnings as errors" option because this will, in most cases, encourage you to write better, less error-prone code.

You should be aware of two additional sets of hidden options. The Build Events button in the lower-right corner is available to Visual Basic developers who want to run actions or scripts before or after the build has been performed. They are discussed in a moment.

Advanced Compiler Settings

Clicking the Advanced Compile Options button displays the Advanced Compiler Settings dialog (see Figure 47-5) in which you can fine-tune the build process for the selected project, with settings divided into two broad groups: Optimizations and Compilation Constants.

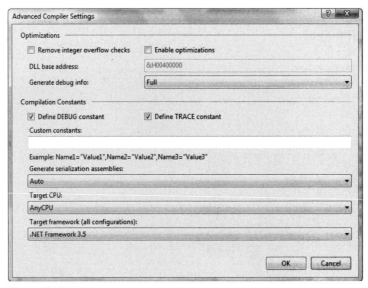

Figure 47-5

Optimizations

The settings in the Optimizations group control how the compilation is performed to make the built output or the build process itself faster or to minimize the output size. Normally, you can leave these options alone, but if you do require tweaks to your compilation, here's a summary of what each option does:

❑ **Remove integer overflow checks:** By default, your code is checked for any instance of a possible integer overflow, which can be a potential cause for memory leaks. Deactivating this option removes those checks, resulting in a faster-running executable at the expense of safety.

❑ **Enable optimizations:** Optimizing the build may result in faster execution with the penalty being that it takes marginally longer to build.

❑ **DLL base address:** This option enables you to specify the base address of the DLL in hexadecimal format. This option is disabled when the project type will not produce a DLL.

❑ **Generate debug info:** This controls when debug information will be generated into your application output. By default, this option is set to Full (for Debug configurations), which will enable you to attach the debugger to a running application. You can also turn debugging information off completely or set the option to pdb-only (the default for Release configurations) to generate only the PDB debugging information. The latter will mean that you can still debug the application when it is started from within Visual Studio 2008, but you will only be able to see the disassembler if you try to attach to a running application.

Compilation Constants

Compilation constants can be used to control what information is included in the build output and even what code is compiled. The Compilation Constants options control the following:

❑ **Define DEBUG constant and Define TRACE constant:** Enable debug and trace information to be included in the compiled application based on the DEBUG and TRACE flags, respectively.

❑ **Custom constants:** If your application build process requires custom constants, you can specify them here in the form ConstantName="Value". If you have multiple constants, they should be delimited by commas.

The last three options don't really fall under compilation constants, but they do allow you to further customize the way the project builds.

❑ **Generate serialization assemblies:** By default this option is set to Auto, which enables the build process to determine whether serialization assemblies are needed or not, but you can change it to On or Off if you want to hard-code the behavior.

❑ **Target CPU:** Depending on what CPU types are known to your system, this option enables you to optimize the build output to a specific platform. The default option of AnyCPU provides output that can be run on any CPU that supports the .NET Framework.

❑ **Target framework:** This is the only option in this dialog that applies to all configurations and is used to determine what version of the base class libraries the project is compiled against.

Build Events

You can perform additional actions before or after the build process by adding them to an events list. Click the Build Events button on the My Project Compile page to display the Build Events dialog. Figure 47-6 shows a post-build event that executes the project output after every successful build.

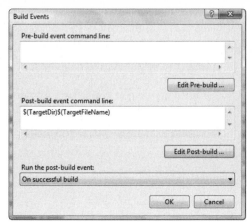

Figure 47-6

Each action you want to perform should be on a separate line, and can be added directly into either the "Pre-build event command line" text area or the "Post-build event command line" text area, or you can use the Edit Pre-build and Edit Post-build buttons to access the known predefined aliases that you can use in the actions.

Shown in Figure 47-7, the Event Command Line dialog includes a list of macros you can use in the creation of your actions. The current value is displayed for each macro so you know what text will be included if you use it.

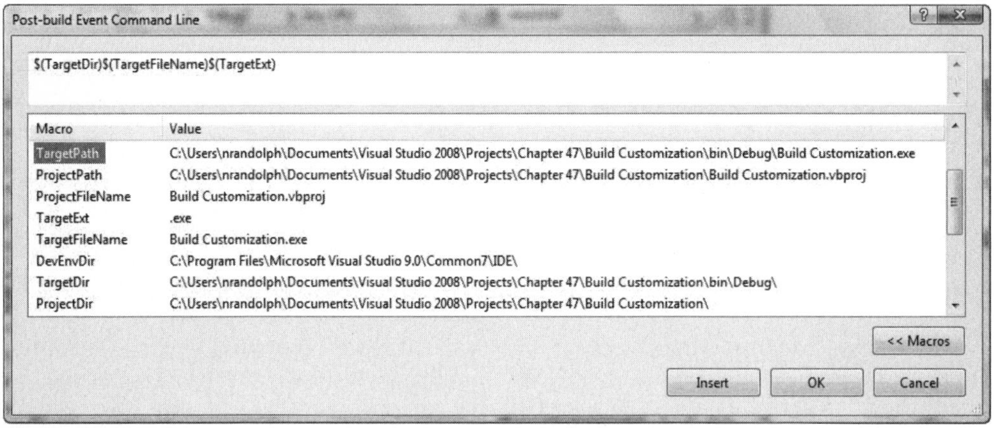

Figure 47-7

In this sample, the developer has created a command line of $(TargetDir)$(TargetFileName) $(TargetExt), assuming that it would execute the built application when finished. However, analyzing the values of each of the macros, it's easy to see that the extension will be included twice, which can be amended quickly by either simply removing the $(TargetExt) macro or replacing the $(TargetFileName) macro with $(TargetPath).

C# Build Pages

C# provides its own set of build options. In general, the options are the same as those available to a Visual Basic project, but in a different location because C# programmers are more likely to tweak the output than are Visual Basic developers, who are typically more interested in rapid development than in fine-tuning performance.

Instead of a single Compile page in the project property pages, C# has a Build page and a Build Events page. The Build Events page acts in exactly the same way as the Build Events dialog in Visual Basic, so refer to the previous discussion for information on that page.

As you can see in Figure 47-8, many of the options on the Build page have direct correlations to settings found in the Compile page or in the Advanced Compiler Settings area of Visual Basic. Some settings, such as the "Define DEBUG constant" and the "Define TRACE constant," are identical to their Visual Basic counterparts.

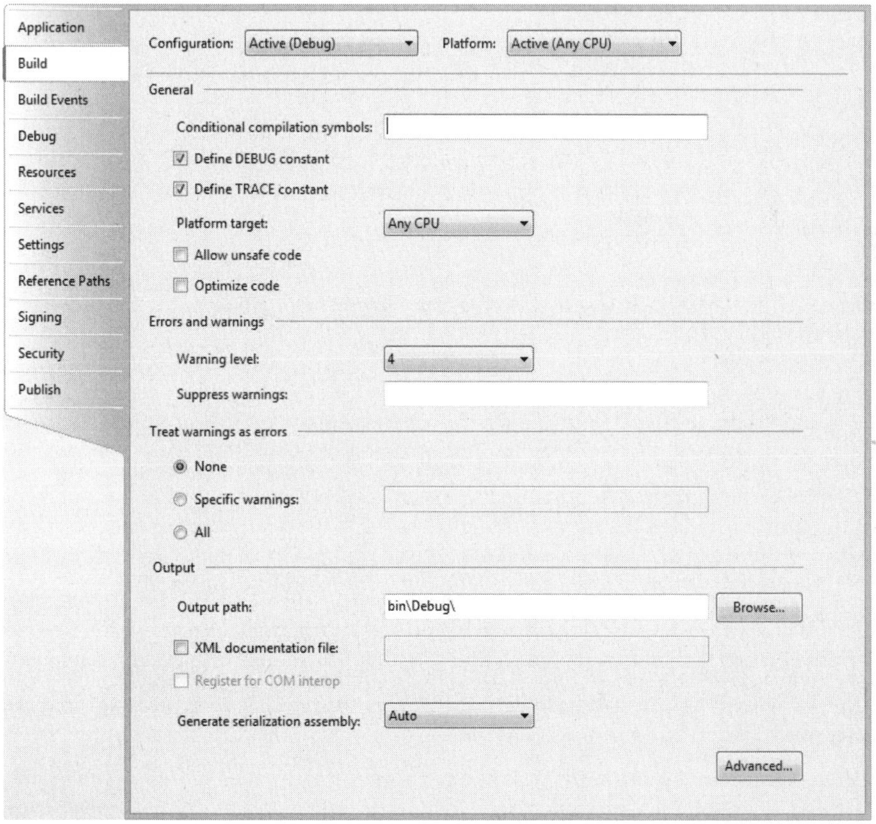

Figure 47-8

However, some are renamed to fit in with a C-based vocabulary; for example, "Optimize code" is equivalent to "Enable optimizations." As with the Visual Basic compile settings, you can determine how warnings are treated, and you can specify a warning level.

Clicking the Advanced button on the Build page invokes the Advanced Build Settings dialog, shown in Figure 47-9, which includes settings that are not accessible to Visual Basic developers. These settings give you tight control over how the build will be performed, including information on the internal errors that occur during the compilation process and what debug information is to be generated.

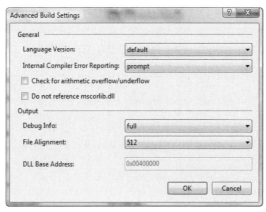

Figure 47-9

These settings are mostly self-explanatory, so the following list is a quick summary of what effect each one has on the build:

❑ **Language Version:** Specifies which version of the C# language to use. The default is to use the current version. In Visual Studio 2008, the other options are ISO-1 and ISO-2, which restricts the language features to those defined in the corresponding ISO standard.

❑ **Internal Compiler Error Reporting:** If errors occur during the compilation (not compilation errors, but errors with the compilation process itself), you can have information sent to Microsoft so it can add it to its revision of the compiler code. The default setting is prompt, which asks you whether you want to send the information to Microsoft.

Other values include none, which won't send the information; send, to automatically send the error information; and queue, which adds the details to a queue to be sent later.

❑ **Check for arithmetic overflow/underflow:** Checks for overflow errors that can cause unsafe execution. Underflow errors occur when the precision of the number is too fine for the system.

❑ **Do not reference mscorlib.dll:** By default, the mscorlib.dll, which defines the System namespace, is automatically referenced in your project, but you can check this option to build your own System namespace and associated objects.

❑ **Debug Info:** Identical to the Visual Basic Generate debug info setting.

❑ **File Alignment:** Used to set the section boundaries in the output file, and enables you to control the internal layout of the compiled output. The values are measured in bytes.

❑ **DLL Base Address:** Identical to the Visual Basic setting of the same name.

Using these settings for your projects enables you to closely control how the build process will perform. However, you have another option with Visual Studio 2008, which is to edit the build scripts directly. This is made possible because Visual Studio 2008 uses MSBuild for its compilations.

MSBuild

MSBuild is the new compilation engine Microsoft released with Visual Studio 2005. It uses XML-based configuration files to identify the layout of a build project, including all of the settings discussed earlier in this chapter, as well as what files should be included in the actual compilation.

In fact, since Visual Studio 2005, Visual Studio uses MSBuild configuration files as its project definition files, in place of the old project file formats used by previous versions of Visual Studio. This enables the MSBuild engine to be used automatically when compiling your applications within the IDE because the same settings file is used for both your project definition in the IDE and the build process.

How Visual Studio Uses MSBuild

As already mentioned, the contents of Visual Studio 2008 project files are based on the MSBuild XML Schema and can be edited directly in Visual Studio so you can customize how the project is loaded and compiled.

However, to edit the project file, you need to effectively remove the project's active status from the Solution Explorer. Right-click the project you want to edit in the Solution Explorer and choose the Unload Project command from the bottom of the context menu that is displayed.

The project will be collapsed in the Solution Explorer and marked as unavailable. In addition, any open files that belong to the project will be closed while it is unloaded from the solution. Right-click the project entry again and an additional menu command will be available to edit the project file (see Figure 47-10).

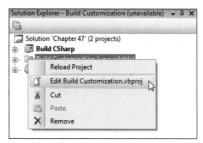

Figure 47-10

The XML-based project file will be correspondingly opened in the XML editor of Visual Studio 2008, enabling you to collapse and expand nodes. The following listing is a sample MSBuild project file for an empty Visual Basic project:

```xml
<?xml version="1.0" encoding="utf-8"?>
<Project ToolsVersion="3.5" DefaultTargets="Build" xmlns="http://schemas.microsoft
.com/developer/msbuild/2003">
  <PropertyGroup>
    <Configuration Condition=" '$(Configuration)' == '' ">Debug</Configuration>
    <Platform Condition=" '$(Platform)' == '' ">AnyCPU</Platform>
    <ProductVersion>9.0.21022</ProductVersion>
    <SchemaVersion>2.0</SchemaVersion>
    <ProjectGuid>{DE305706-4F2E-44CE-A6CA-6DD4D03B0091}</ProjectGuid>
    <OutputType>WinExe</OutputType>
    <StartupObject>Build_Customization.My.MyApplication</StartupObject>
    <RootNamespace>Build_Customization</RootNamespace>
    <AssemblyName>Build Customization</AssemblyName>
    <FileAlignment>512</FileAlignment>
    <MyType>WindowsForms</MyType>
    <TargetFrameworkVersion>v3.5</TargetFrameworkVersion>
    <OptionExplicit>On</OptionExplicit>
    <OptionCompare>Binary</OptionCompare>
    <OptionStrict>Off</OptionStrict>
    <OptionInfer>On</OptionInfer>
  </PropertyGroup>
  <PropertyGroup Condition=" '$(Configuration)|$(Platform)' == 'Debug|AnyCPU' ">
    <DebugSymbols>true</DebugSymbols>
    <DebugType>full</DebugType>
    <DefineDebug>true</DefineDebug>
    <DefineTrace>true</DefineTrace>
    <OutputPath>bin\Debug\</OutputPath>
    <DocumentationFile>Build Customization.xml</DocumentationFile>
    <NoWarn>42016,41999,42017,42018,42019,42032,42036,42020,42021,42022</NoWarn>
  </PropertyGroup>
  <PropertyGroup Condition=" '$(Configuration)|$(Platform)' == 'Release|AnyCPU' ">
    <DebugType>pdbonly</DebugType>
    <DefineDebug>false</DefineDebug>
    <DefineTrace>true</DefineTrace>
    <Optimize>true</Optimize>
    <OutputPath>bin\Release\</OutputPath>
    <DocumentationFile>Build Customization.xml</DocumentationFile>
    <NoWarn>42016,41999,42017,42018,42019,42032,42036,42020,42021,42022</NoWarn>
  </PropertyGroup>
  <ItemGroup>
    <Reference Include="System" />
    <Reference Include="System.Data" />
    <Reference Include="System.Deployment" />
    <Reference Include="System.Drawing" />
    <Reference Include="System.Windows.Forms" />
    <Reference Include="System.Xml" />
    <Reference Include="System.Core">
      <RequiredTargetFramework>3.5</RequiredTargetFramework>
    </Reference>
    <Reference Include="System.Xml.Linq">
```

```
            <RequiredTargetFramework>3.5</RequiredTargetFramework>
          </Reference>
          <Reference Include="System.Data.DataSetExtensions">
            <RequiredTargetFramework>3.5</RequiredTargetFramework>
          </Reference>
      </ItemGroup>
      <ItemGroup>
        <Import Include="Microsoft.VisualBasic" />
        <Import Include="System" />
        <Import Include="System.Collections" />
        <Import Include="System.Collections.Generic" />
        <Import Include="System.Data" />
        <Import Include="System.Drawing" />
        <Import Include="System.Diagnostics" />
        <Import Include="System.Windows.Forms" />
      </ItemGroup>
      <Import Project="$(MSBuildToolsPath)\Microsoft.VisualBasic.targets" />
      <!-- To modify your build process, add your task inside one of the targets below
and uncomment it.
          Other similar extension points exist, see Microsoft.Common.targets.
      <Target Name="BeforeBuild">
      </Target>
      <Target Name="AfterBuild">
      </Target>
      -->
    </Project>
```

The XML contains the information about the build. In fact, most of these nodes directly relate to settings you saw earlier in the Compile and Build pages, but also include any Framework namespaces that are required. The first PropertyGroup element contains project properties that apply to all build configurations. This is followed by two conditional elements that define properties for each of the two build configurations, Debug and Release. The remaining elements are for project references and project-wide namespace imports.

When the project includes additional files, such as forms and user controls, each one is defined in the project file with its own set of nodes. For example, the following listing shows the additional XML that is included in a standard WindowsApplication project, identifying the Form, its designer code file, and the additional application files required for a Windows-based application:

```
    <ItemGroup>
      <Compile Include="Form1.vb">
        <SubType>Form</SubType>
      </Compile>
      <Compile Include="Form1.Designer.vb">
        <DependentUpon>Form1.vb</DependentUpon>
        <SubType>Form</SubType>
      </Compile>
      <Compile Include="My Project\AssemblyInfo.vb" />
      <Compile Include="My Project\Application.Designer.vb">
        <AutoGen>True</AutoGen>
        <DependentUpon>Application.myapp</DependentUpon>
      </Compile>
```

(continued)

(continued)

```
        <Compile Include="My Project\Resources.Designer.vb">
          <AutoGen>True</AutoGen>
          <DesignTime>True</DesignTime>
          <DependentUpon>Resources.resx</DependentUpon>
        </Compile>
        <Compile Include="My Project\Settings.Designer.vb">
          <AutoGen>True</AutoGen>
          <DependentUpon>Settings.settings</DependentUpon>
          <DesignTimeSharedInput>True</DesignTimeSharedInput>
        </Compile>
      </ItemGroup>
      <ItemGroup>
        <EmbeddedResource Include="Form1.resx">
          <DependentUpon>Form1.vb</DependentUpon>
          <SubType>Designer</SubType>
        </EmbeddedResource>
        <EmbeddedResource Include="My Project\Resources.resx">
          <Generator>VbMyResourcesResXFileCodeGenerator</Generator>
          <LastGenOutput>Resources.Designer.vb</LastGenOutput>
          <CustomToolNamespace>My.Resources</CustomToolNamespace>
          <SubType>Designer</SubType>
        </EmbeddedResource>
      </ItemGroup>
      <ItemGroup>
        <None Include="My Project\Application.myapp">
          <Generator>MyApplicationCodeGenerator</Generator>
          <LastGenOutput>Application.Designer.vb</LastGenOutput>
        </None>
        <None Include="My Project\Settings.settings">
          <Generator>SettingsSingleFileGenerator</Generator>
          <CustomToolNamespace>My</CustomToolNamespace>
          <LastGenOutput>Settings.Designer.vb</LastGenOutput>
        </None>
      </ItemGroup>
```

You can also include additional tasks in the build process in the included Target nodes for BeforeBuild and AfterBuild events. However, these actions will not appear in the Visual Studio 2008 build events dialog discussed earlier. The alternative is to use a PropertyGroup node that includes PreBuildEvent and PostBuildEvent entries. For instance, if you wanted to execute the application after it was successfully built, you could include the following XML block immediately before the closing `</Project>` tag:

```
<PropertyGroup>
  <PostBuildEvent>$(TargetDir)$(TargetFileName)</PostBuildEvent>
</PropertyGroup>
```

Once you've finished editing the project file's XML, you need to re-enable it in the solution by right-clicking the project's entry in the Solution Explorer and selecting the Reload Project command. If you still have the project file open, Visual Studio will close it automatically.

MSBuild Schema

An extended discussion on the MSBuild engine is beyond the scope of this book. However, it's useful to understand the different components that make up the MSBuild project file so you can look at and update your own projects.

Four major elements form the basis of the project file: *items*, *properties*, *targets*, and *tasks*. Brought together, you can use these four node types to create a configuration file that describes a project in full, as shown in the previous sample Visual Basic project file.

Items

Items are those elements that define inputs to the build system and project. They are defined as children of an ItemGroup node, and the most common item is the Compile node used to identify to MSBuild that the specified file is to be included in the compilation. The following snippet from a project file shows an Item element defined for the Form1.Designer.vb file of a WindowsApplication project:

```
<ItemGroup>
  <Compile Include="Form1.Designer.vb">
    <DependentUpon>Form1.vb</DependentUpon>
    <SubType>Form</SubType>
  </Compile>
</ItemGroup>
```

Properties

PropertyGroup nodes are used to contain any properties defined to the project. Properties are typically key/value pairings. They can only contain a single value and are used to store the project settings you can access in the Build and Compile pages in the IDE.

PropertyGroup nodes can be optionally included by specifying a Condition attribute, as shown in the following sample listing:

```
<PropertyGroup Condition=" '$(Configuration)|$(Platform)' == 'Release|AnyCPU' ">
    <DebugType>pdbonly</DebugType>
    <DefineDebug>false</DefineDebug>
    <DefineTrace>true</DefineTrace>
    <Optimize>true</Optimize>
    <OutputPath>bin\Release\</OutputPath>
</PropertyGroup>
```

This XML defines a PropertyGroup that will only be included in the build if the project is being built as a Release for the AnyCPU platform. Each of the five property nodes within the PropertyGroup uses the name of the property as the name of the node.

Targets

Target elements enable you to arrange tasks (discussed in the next section) into a sequence. Each Target element should have a Name attribute to identify it, and it can be called directly, thus enabling you to provide multiple entry points into the build process. The following snippet defines a Target with a name of BeforeBuild:

```
<Target Name="BeforeBuild">
</Target>
```

Tasks

Tasks define actions that MSBuild will execute under certain conditions. You can define your own tasks or take advantage of the many built-in tasks such as Copy. Shown in the following snippet, Copy can copy one or more files from one location to another:

```
<Target Name="CopyFiles">
    <Copy
        SourceFiles="@(MySourceFiles)"
        DestinationFolder="\\PDSERVER01\SourceBackup\"
    />
</Target>
```

Assembly Versioning via MSBuild Task

One aspect of most automated build systems is planning application versioning. In this section you see how you can customize the build process for your project so that it can accept an external version number. This version number will be used to update the AssemblyInfo file, which will subsequently affect the assembly version. Let's start by looking at the AssemblyInfo.vb file, which typically contains assembly version information such as the following:

```
<Assembly: AssemblyVersion("1.0.0.0")>
```

What our build customization needs to do is replace the default version number with a number supplied as part of the build process. To do this we have elected to use a third-party MSBuild library entitled Microsoft.Sdc.Task, which is a project on CodePlex (http://www.codeplex.com). This includes a Replace task that can be used to match on a regular expression. Before we can use this task we need to include the source assembly in our MSBuild file (that is, the project file — Build Customization.vbproj):

```
<Project ToolsVersion="3.5" DefaultTargets="Build" xmlns="http://schemas.microsoft
.com/developer/msbuild/2003">
    <UsingTask TaskName="Microsoft.Sdc.Tasks.File.Replace"
    AssemblyFile="c:\MyDownloads\MSBuild SDC Tasks\Microsoft.Sdc.Tasks.dll" />
    <PropertyGroup>
    . . .
```

Because we want to update the AssemblyInfo file before the build, we need to include the BeforeBuild target, as follows:

```
<Import Project="$(MSBuildToolsPath)\Microsoft.VisualBasic.targets" />
<Target Name="BeforeBuild">
<!-- Change the core version files using current build label -->
```

```
    <Replace Path="$(ProjectDir)\My Project\AssemblyInfo.vb"
    NewValue="Version(&quot;$(buildversion)&quot;)"
    RegularExpression="Version\(&quot;[0-9]+\.[0-9]+\.[0-9]+\.[0-9]+&quot;\)"
    IgnoreCase="False" Force="True" />
    </Target>
</Project>
```

You will notice here that we are using a couple of properties, namely $(ProjectDir) and $(buildversion). Whereas the ProjectDir is a predefined property, buildversion is not, so we need to define this property so that our project will build even if this property is not supplied as an MSBuild argument:

```
<PropertyGroup>
    <buildversion>0.0.0.0</buildversion>
    <Configuration Condition=" '$(Configuration)' == '' ">Debug</Configuration>
```

This is all we have to do in order to accept a version number as part of the build process through the property buildversion. When building this project in Visual Studio 2008, this property will not be specified, so it will use the default value of 0.0.0.0. In your automated build process you can specify the version number as an argument to the MSBuild call. For example:

```
MSBuild "Build Customization.vbproj" /t:Rebuild /p:Configuration=Debug;
/p:buildversion=1.2.3.4
```

If you get an error such as "The element <BuildingProject> beneath element <PropertyGroup> is unrecognized," it may be that your command is calling the wrong version of MSBuild. You may need to use the fully qualified MSBuild.exe command which is located at C:\Windows\Microsoft .NET\Framework\v3.5.

Summary

The default build behavior can be customized with an enormous range of options in Visual Studio 2008, particularly for Visual Basic and C# projects because they're based on the MSBuild engine. Within the project file you can include additional actions to perform both before and after the build has taken place, as well as include additional files in the compilation.

Assembly Versioning and Signing

When you create your .NET projects, they compile down to an assembly. By default, this assembly is open and doesn't have any security on it to ensure that your users are consuming the correct version of the binary file. However, signing your assembly can rectify that issue by strongly naming the compiled application or component, which can then uniquely identify it to other applications and even system administrators who can apply a security policy against it.

In this chapter, you learn how to use Visual Studio 2008 to set the assembly version number and how you can use a digital signature to sign your assembly so that it can't be tampered with. This will also result in a strongly named assembly, which can be added to the Global Assembly Cache.

Assembly Naming

Every .NET assembly, whether it is an executable or a class library, contains a manifest that contains information about the assembly's identity. Primarily, this includes the name and version number of the assembly but can also include a culture and public key if it is a strong-named assembly. This information can be easily viewed by opening an assembly in Lutz Roeder's .NET Reflector, as shown in Figure 48-1.

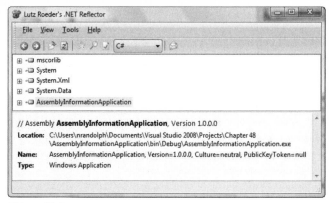

Figure 48-1

In Figure 48-1 the assembly AssemblyInformationApplication.exe does not have a public key. Other assemblies, like System.Data, have a full name such as:

```
System.Data, Version=2.0.0.0, Culture=neutral, PublicKeytoken=b77a5c561934e089
```

Specifying the name of your assembly in Visual Studio 2008 is done via the project properties editor, as shown in Figure 48-2. You can see in this figure the Assembly name field on the main Application tab and the Assembly Version field in the inset, which is accessible via the Assembly Information button.

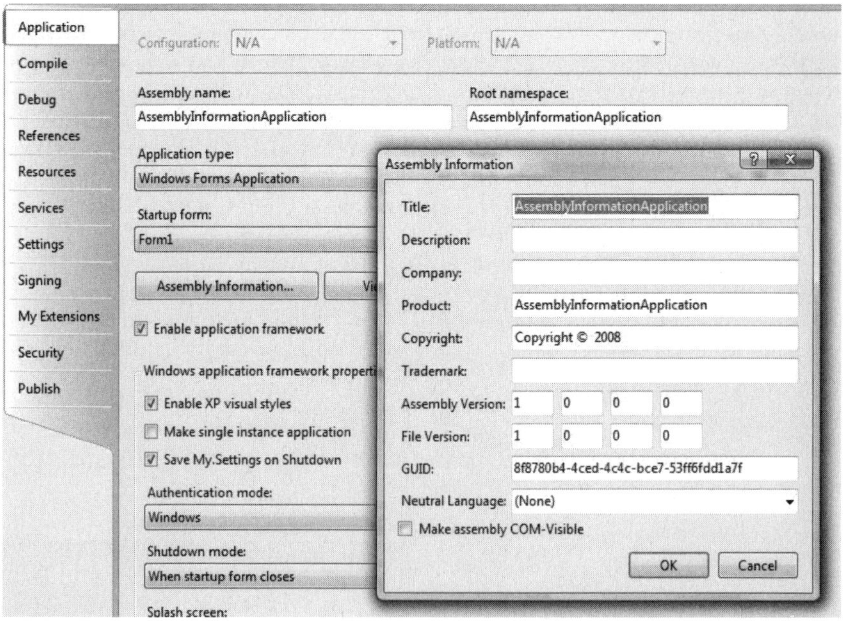

Figure 48-2

The assembly properties that are presented in the inset dialog in Figure 48-2 all appear in the AssemblyInfo file that is, by default, a hidden file in the project — select the Show All Files button to reveal the AssemblyInfo file. The following snippet illustrates the `AssemblyVersion` and `AssemblyFileVersion` assembly attributes that are used to define the version and file version of the assembly:

```
' Version information for an assembly consists of the following four values:
'
' Major Version
' Minor Version
' Build Number
' Revision
'
' You can specify all the values or you can default the Build and Revision Numbers
' by using the '*' as shown below:
' <Assembly: AssemblyVersion("1.0.*")>
<Assembly: AssemblyVersion("1.0.0.0")>
<Assembly: AssemblyFileVersion("1.0.0.0")>
```

In case you were wondering what the difference is between the version and file version of an assembly, it comes down to usage. The assembly version information is used by the .NET Framework when resolving assembly and type information. On the other hand, the file version is what is displayed within Windows Explorer when you look at the file properties.

> *There is much debate over whether the assembly version and file version numbers should be in sync, but essentially it is up to you. Some developers prefer keeping them in sync because it means that they can determine the assembly version via Windows Explorer. Alternatively, other organizations use the file version to represent changes to an assembly (for example, a hotfix or service pack), while the assembly version is used for new versions of the application.*

As the comments explain, there are four components to assembly version numbers — Major, Minor, Build, and Revision. Again, how you increment these is completely up to you. In fact, you could even elect for Visual Studio 2008 to increment them for you by specifying a * for the build and/or revision numbers. One fairly common strategy is to use the Major or Minor number to represent the actual version of the product being worked on. Incrementing just the Minor number would perhaps represent minor fixes and minimal new functionality (similar to a service pack), whereas the Major number would represent new core functionality.

This leaves the Build and Revision numbers that can be used to perhaps tie into the build process. For example, the Build number might represent the week number into development for a particular release, whereas the revision number might represent the most recent revision number in the source repository. This last value then becomes very important because it can be used, in isolation, to access the exact source code from the repository that was used to build a particular version.

Version Consistency

The default project configuration doesn't lend itself easily to having a consistent version number across all projects within a solution. However, with the ability to include linked files in a project, you can coerce Visual Studio 2008 into giving you version consistency. This is particularly important if you have an automated build system that automatically increments the version number. Instead of having to update any number of AssemblyInfo files, it can simply modify a single file and have all projects be updated.

You need to start by creating an additional AssemblyInfo file, say GlobalAssemblyInfo.vb, in the solution folder. To do this, right-click the solution node and select Add New Item. The new item will be added to a Solution Items folder in your solution. Into this file you need to move the `AssemblyVersion` and `AssemblyFileVersion` attributes from the AssemblyInfo file in your projects (you will also need to import the System.Reflection namespace unless you fully qualify the attribute names).

Once you have done this, you then need to add this file to each of your projects. You do this via the Add Existing Item right-click menu item for the projects in the Solution Explorer tool window. When you have located the right AssemblyInfo file, make sure you select the Add As Link item from the Add drop-down, as shown in Figure 48-3.

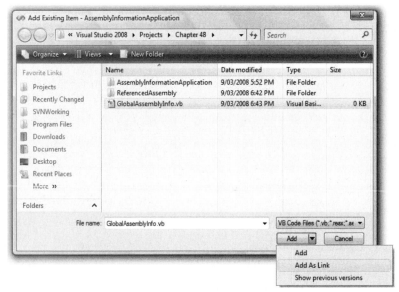

Figure 48-3

This one AssemblyInfo file can be used by any number of projects, the one limitation being that it is specific to VB.NET. If you have a solution that uses a mix of VB.NET and C# projects, you will need to have a central AssemblyInfo file for each language — this is still better than having to maintain the version information in a separate file for each project. Note that you can include other assembly attributes in these central files, such as the `AssemblyCopyright`, `AssemblyCompany`, and `AssemblyTrademark` if appropriate.

Strong-Named Assemblies

A strong name consists of the parts that uniquely identify an assembly's identity. This includes the plain-text name and a version number. Added to these elements are a public key and a digital signature. These are generated with a corresponding private key. Because of this private/public key system being coupled with a digital signature, strong names can be relied on to be completely unique. Further, by signing your assembly you are preventing someone maliciously tampering with your code. .NET assemblies are relatively easy to reverse-engineer, modify, and compile as a modified assembly. The hash that is created as part of the signing process will change as the assembly is modified — in effect providing a security mechanism against unauthorized modifications.

Using a strong name can also ensure that the version of your assembly is the one that has been shipped. No modification can be made to it without affecting its signature and thus breaking its compatibility with the generated strong name.

As mentioned previously, using strong names also gives administrators the ability to explicitly set security policy against your solutions by referring to their unique names. This can give a corporation confidence that once deployed, the software will run as expected because it cannot be tampered with without affecting the signing of the strong name.

> *Once you start using strong-named assemblies in your solution, you will have to use strong-named files right down to the chain of references, because allowing an unsigned assembly as part of the chain would break the very security that strong-naming your assembly was intended to implement.*

The Global Assembly Cache

Every computer that has the .NET Framework installed has a system-wide cache, called the Global Assembly Cache (GAC), which can be used to store assemblies that are to be shared by multiple applications. Assemblies that are added to the GAC are accessible from any .NET application on the same system. This itself can be a huge savings for organizations where you have common functionality that you want to share between applications.

In this cache (usually stored in a folder within the Windows directory) you'll find the common language runtime components as well as other globally registered binary files that you, and anyone else, can consume. If an assembly is only going to be used by a single application, then it should be deployed in that application's folder.

> *It is important to note here that adding assemblies to the GAC is not recommended unless you really need to share assemblies between applications, and they are too large to redistribute alongside each application.*

If you do decide to share the assembly between applications, you will need to know how to store it in the GAC. Your assembly must also be strong-named. You don't have a choice in the matter, because the cache interrogates all files to ensure that their integrity is valid; hence, it needs the strong-name versioning to compare against.

Signing an Assembly

Previously, signing an assembly in Visual Studio required the generation of a strong-name key (.snk) file via an external utility and then editing the assembly attributes of your application's configuration file. Thankfully, Visual Studio has built-in support for signing all managed code projects using the Signing tab in the project properties editor, as you can see from Figure 48-4.

The Signing tab enables you to sign the assembly in the lower half of the page. You first should select the "Sign the assembly" checkbox to indicate that you will be generating a strong name. You will then need to select the strong name key file to use when signing the assembly.

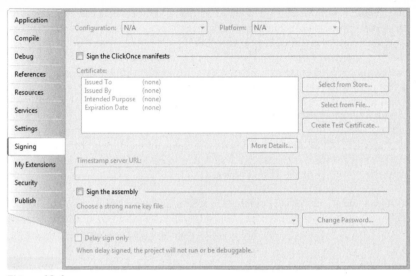

Figure 48-4

Existing key files in either the older `.snk`-paired key file format or the new `.pfx` format can be used. From the drop-down list, select the Browse option to locate the file in your file system and click OK in the dialog to save the key file to the Signing page settings.

Alternatively, you can create a new strong-named key by selecting the New option from the drop-down list. When you choose New, you will be able to create a new `.pfx`-formatted strong-named file. Figure 48-5 shows the Create Strong Name Key dialog. You can simply choose a filename to use for the key or you can additionally protect the key file with a password. If you do decide to add a password, you will be prompted to enter the password if you build your application on any other computer the first time. Thereafter, Visual Studio will remember the password.

Figure 48-5

Either way, once you've created and selected the key file, it will be added to your project in the Solution Explorer, enabling you to easily include it for deployment projects.

One of the main reasons you might want to sign your assemblies is to ensure that they cannot be modified. For this reason, most organizations place a high level of security around the strong name key file that is used to sign their assemblies. As such it is likely that you won't have access to the private key to successfully sign the assembly. When you're in this situation, you may still need to dictate that the application will be digitally signed. However, instead of providing the full strong name key file, which contains the public and private key information, you provide only a file containing the public key information and select the "Delay sign only" checkbox. Later, perhaps as part of your build process, you would need to sign the assemblies using the full key:

```
sn -R AssemblyInformationApplication MyOrganisationsStrongkey.snk
```

If you select to delay the signing of your assemblies you won't be able to debug or even run the application, because it will fail the assembly verification process that is part of the pre-execution checks that the .NET Framework does on assemblies. Actually, this is a little inaccurate because it is possible to register your assembly (or, in fact, any assembly signed with the same public key) so that the verification step will be skipped:

```
sn -Vr AssemblyInformationApplication.exe
```

You should only register assemblies to skip verification on development machines. Further, you can unregister an assembly (or all assemblies signed with the same public key) using the sn *command with the* –Vu *parameter.*

Summary

Strong-naming your application and thus safeguarding it from improper use is now straightforward to implement, and can be done completely from within the Visual Studio 2008 IDE. The Signing page gives you the ability to both create and set the key file without having to edit the application's assembly attributes directly.

ClickOnce and MSI Deployment

One area of software development that is often overlooked is how to deploy the application. Building an installer is a simple process and can transform your application from an amateur utility to a professional tool. This chapter looks at how you can build a Windows installer for any type of .NET application.

Visual Studio 2008 also includes support for a ClickOnce deployment, which can be used to build applications that can be dynamically updated. This is particularly important for rich client applications that periodically need updating, because it solves the problem of how to roll out those updates.

Installers

The traditional way to deploy applications is to use an installer, which can typically be used to install and, in most cases, uninstall an application. Visual Studio 2008 comes with a rich user interface for building an installer for any type of .NET application. That said, there are a number of tricks to building installers for services and mobile applications. Building installers for mobile applications is covered in the next chapters.

Building an Installer

To build an installer with Visual Studio 2008 you need to add an additional project to the application that you want to deploy. Figure 49-1 shows the available setup and deployment project types. The Setup Project should be used for Windows Forms or service applications, and the Web Setup Project should be used for ASP.NET web sites or web services. If you want to build an installer that will be integrated into a larger installer, you may want to build a merge module.

Alternatively, a CAB Project can be used to create an alternative package that can be deployed via a web browser. The Setup Wizard steps you through the process of creating the correct project for the type of application you're deploying.

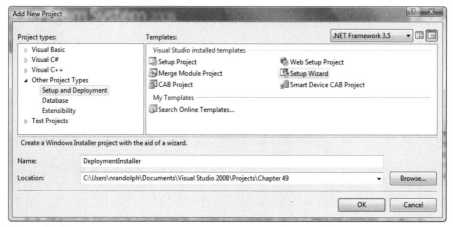

Figure 49-1

In this case we are going to use the Setup Wizard to create an installer for a simple Visual Basic Windows Forms Application, Simple Application. After acknowledging the Setup Wizard splash screen, the first decision is specifying whether you want to create an installer or a redistributable package. For an installer, you need to choose between either a Windows application or a web application installer. The basic difference is that the Windows application installer places the application in the appropriate folder within Program Files, whereas the web application installer creates a virtual directory under the root folder for the specified web site. In the case of a redistributable package, the choice is between a merge module, which can be integrated into a larger installer, or a CAB file.

Regardless of the type of deployment project you are creating, the next step in the Setup Wizard is the most important because it determines the set of files to be deployed. Figure 49-2 shows the third screen in the Setup Wizard, which prompts you to select which files or project outputs will be included in the deployment project. In this case, the primary output for our Sample Application has been selected, because you want to include the main executable and any assemblies on which this executable depends. The Content Files item has also been selected, which will include any files with the build action set to Content. In the remaining step in the Setup Wizard, you can choose to add files that were not part of any existing project. For example this might include release notes, licensing information, getting started samples, or documentation and README files.

Occasionally you may choose to deploy debug symbols with your application, because this can aid you in diagnosing a failing application in production. However, it is not generally deemed good practice to do this, because you should incorporate sufficient logging or other diagnostic instrumentation for this purpose.

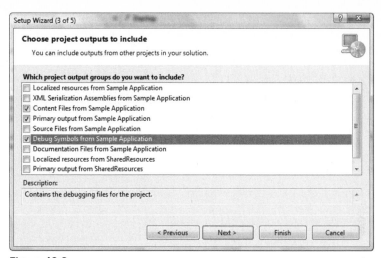

Figure 49-2

Once the deployment project has been created, it is added to the Solution Explorer, as shown in Figure 49-3. Although you didn't explicitly add any files or output from the SharedResources class library to the deployment project, it has been added as a calculated dependency. If the dependencies are guaranteed to exist on the target computer, they can be manually excluded from the deployment project by selecting the Exclude item from the right-click context menu. For example, if this were an add-in for another application that already has a copy of the SharedResources assembly, you could exclude that from the dependency list. The resulting installer would be smaller, and thus easier to deploy.

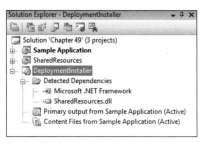

Figure 49-3

If the dependencies between your projects vary, it may be necessary to force a recalculation of these dependencies. You can do this by selecting Refresh Dependencies from the right-click shortcut menu on the Detected Dependencies node.

When a deployment project (DeploymentInstaller) is selected, a number of new icons appear across the top of the Solution Explorer window, as can be seen in Figure 49-3. Unlike other project types, where the project properties appear in the main editor area, clicking the first icon (Properties) opens the Property Pages dialog, as shown in Figure 49-4. This can be used to customize how the deployment module is built. This dialog can also be accessed via the Properties item on the right-click context menu for the deployment project in the Solution Explorer.

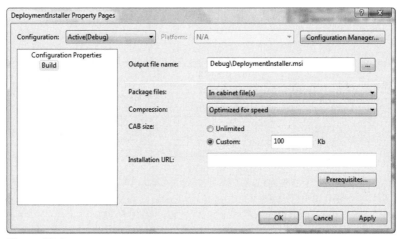

Figure 49-4

By default, the `Package files` property is set to "In setup file," so all executables and associated dependencies are placed into the `.msi` file that is created. The deployment project also creates a Setup.exe file that checks for minimum requirements, such as the presence of the .NET Framework, prior to calling the `.msi` file to install the application. Although the compression can be adjusted to optimize for file size, including everything into a single distributable might be an issue for large projects. An alternative, as shown in Figure 49-4, is to package the application into a series of CAB files. In this scenario, the size of the CAB file is limited to 100Kb, which will aid deployment over a slow network. Another scenario where this would be useful is if you were planning to deploy your application via CD, and your application exceeded the capacity of a single CD.

The final property on this page is the Installation URL. If you are planning to deploy your application via a web site, you can elect to package everything into a single file, in which case you do not need to specify the Installation URL because you can simply add a reference to the Setup.exe file to the appropriate web site and a user can install the application simply by clicking on the link. Alternatively, you can package your application into smaller units that can be incrementally downloaded. To do this you must specify the Installation URL from which they will be installed.

As just discussed, the default deployment project creates a Setup.exe file. The Prerequisites button opens a dialog like the one shown in Figure 49-5, where you can configure the behavior of this file. You can indicate that a setup file should not be created, in which case the application can be installed by double-clicking the .msi file. This, of course, removes the initial check to ensure that the .NET Framework has been installed.

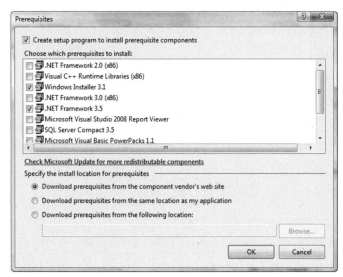

Figure 49-5

In addition to the .NET Framework, you can also specify that other components, such as SQL Server Compact 3.5, need to be installed. These checks will be carried out, and the user prompted to install any missing components before the main installer file is invoked. Depending on how you want to deploy your application, having all the prerequisites in the same location as your application may be useful and will eliminate time spent looking for the appropriate download.

Returning to the Solution Explorer and our DeploymentInstaller project (and just to confuse matters), there is an additional Properties window for deployment projects that can be opened by selecting the appropriate project and pressing F4. This opens the standard Properties window, shown in Figure 49-6, which can be used to tailor the deployment details for the application it is installing.

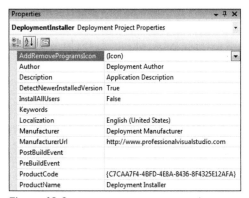

Figure 49-6

The properties for the deployment project shown on this screen configure the appearance, icons, and behavior of the installation wizard. It is highly recommended that you adjust these properties so your application is easily identifiable in the Add/Remove Programs dialog, and so that the installation looks professional rather than half-finished. As you can see from Figure 49-7, some of these properties are used to tailor the installer dialog.

Figure 49-7

Once the application has been installed, some of these properties also appear in the Programs and Features dialog (Add/Remove Programs under Windows XP) accessible via the Control Panel, as shown in Figure 49-8. Here you can see the AddRemoveProgramsIcon, the ProductName, and the Manufacturer properties. More properties can be displayed by right-clicking the header bar and selecting More.

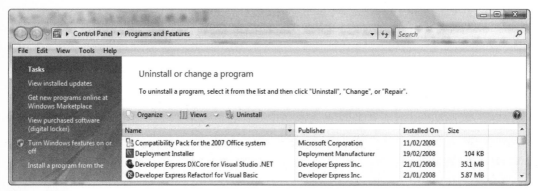

Figure 49-8

In order to test your installer, you can select the Install *(and subsequently* Uninstall*) item from the shortcut menu that is displayed when you right-click the setup Project in the Solution Explorer. If this option is disabled, you may need to build the setup Project first.*

Customizing the Installer

The remaining icons at the top of the Solution Explorer are used to customize what is included in the deployment package. In addition to the shortcut icons, these views of the deployment project can be accessed via the `View` item on the right-click context menu. Start with the File System view, which indicates where files will be installed on the target machine. By default, the primary output for a Windows application is added to the Application Folder, as shown in Figure 49-9. Selecting this node and looking at the Properties window shows that this folder has a default location of `[ProgramFilesFolder][Manufacturer]\[ProductName]`. This location is made up of three predefined installation variables: `ProgramFilesFolder`, `Manufacturer`, and `ProductName`, which will be evaluated and combined during installation. As you can see in Figure 49-7, the installation wizard allows users to change this location when they install the application.

Earlier you saw that the Sample Application had a dependency on the SharedResources assembly. Here this assembly has been removed from the Application Folder and placed instead in the Global Assembly Cache Folder. When this application is installed, the main executable will be installed in the relevant directory under Program Files, but the SharedResources assembly will be installed in the Global Assembly Cache so it is available to any .NET application. To achieve this, you first need to create the new folder in the File System view by selecting the Global Assembly Cache Folder from the Add Special Folder item on the right-click context menu. You can install files to a number of other special folders as part of the installer. The next step is to move the SharedResources assembly to the Global Assembly Cache by selecting the assembly in the right pane of the File System view and changing the `Folder` property from Application Folder to Global Assembly Cache Folder. Alternatively you can drag the item from the Application Folder to the Global Assembly Cache Folder.

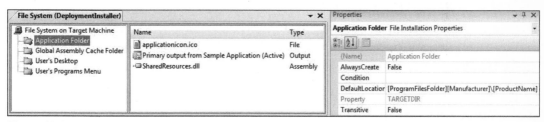

Figure 49-9

In addition to installing files on the target machine, you can also add keys to the registry. Some developers argue for and other developers argue against the use of the registry. Although it can provide a convenient store for per-user configuration information, the new application settings with user scope are an alternative that makes them easier to manage. The Registry view, as shown in Figure 49-10, can be used to add registry keys and values. To add a new key, right-click the appropriate node in the Registry tree and select Add Key from the context menu. To add a new value, select the appropriate key in the Registry tree and select the type of value from the `New` item on the right-click context menu off the right pane shown in Figure 49-10. The Name and Value can then be set using the Properties window.

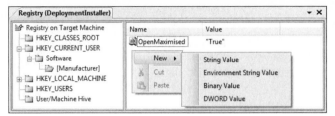

Figure 49-10

Figure 49-11 shows the File Types view of the deployment project. This view is used to add file extensions that should be installed. For example, in this case you are installing the extension .nic. You can specify an icon for this type of file as well as specify the executable that should be called for this file type. In most cases this will be the primary output for your application. To add a new file type, right-click the root node of the File Types tree and select Add File Types from the context menu. This creates a node for the new file type and for the default action (in bold) for that file type. For the .nic extension, the default action is Open, and it can be executed by double-clicking a file of the appropriate file type. The Open action also appears, again in bold, in the right-click context menu for a file with the .nic extension. Other actions can be added for this file type by selecting Add Action from the right-click context menu for the file type. An alternative action can be made the default by selecting Set as Default from that action's context menu. You can change the order in which the actions appear in the context menu by moving the action up or down in the tree.

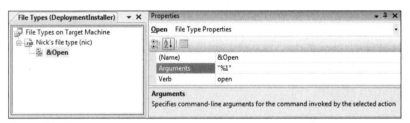

Figure 49-11

.NET applications can be autonomous so that their list of dependencies may only contain the .NET Framework. However, web applications require IIS, and more complex applications may require SQL Server to be installed. You can check for these dependencies by using a *launch condition* via the view shown in Figure 49-12. By default, the .NET Framework is added to this launch condition. Previously you saw that Setup.exe also did a check for the .NET Framework and would install it if it was not found. Launch conditions are embedded in the .msi file and, unlike conditions in the Setup.exe file, are validated even if the .msi file is installed directly. The only limitation is that the launch conditions only provide a warning message and a URL reference for more information.

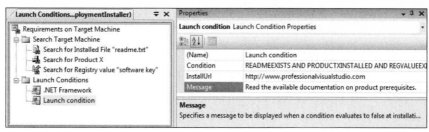

Figure 49-12

The tree in the left pane of Figure 49-12 is actually split into two sections. The top half of the tree is used to specify searches to be performed on the target machine. Searches can be carried out for files, for installed components or applications, and for registry values. Properties for a file search include the search folder, version and modification dates, and file size. To search for an installed component, you need to know the Component ID, which is embedded in the .msi file used to install the product. This information can be retrieved using a product such as MSI Spy, which is included in the Windows Installer SDK that can be downloaded from the Microsoft web site (www.microsoft.com/downloads/). A registry search requires properties indicating the key, name, and value to search for. In each of these cases the search needs to be assigned a Property identifier. If the search is successful, the installer property with that identifier is True.

The Property identifiers assigned to searches on the target machine can be used by a launch condition in the lower half of the tree. As you can see in Figure 49-12, there are conditions that check for the .NET Framework, as well as a custom launch condition. The Condition property is set to a logical AND operation across the three search results. If any of the searches fails, the associated property identifier is replaced with False, making the whole logical expression false. This will prevent the application from installing, and a warning message will be displayed.

Note that some other views have a Condition property for some of the tree nodes. For example, in the File System view, each file or output has a Condition property that can be specified. If this condition fails, the file is not installed on the target machine. In each of these cases the syntax of the Condition property must be valid for the MsiEvaluateCondition function that is called as part of the installation process. This function accepts standard comparison operators, such as equals (=), not equals (<>), less than (>), and greater than (<), as well as Boolean operators NOT, AND, OR, and XOR. There are also some predefined Windows installer properties that can be included in the condition property. The following is a subset of the full list, which you can find in the documentation for the Windows Installer SDK:

- ❑ ComputerName: Target computer name

- ❑ VersionNT: Version of Windows on the target computer

- ❑ ServicePackLevel: The service pack that has been installed

- ❑ LogonUser: The username of the current user

- ❑ AdminUser: Whether the current user has administrative privileges

- ❑ COMPANYNAME: The company name, as specified in the installation wizard

- ❑ USERNAME: The username, as specified in the installation wizard

One of the main reasons for creating an installer is to make the process of deploying an application much smoother. To do this you need to create a simple user interface into which an end user can specify values. This might be the installation directory or other parameters that are required to configure the application. Clearly, the fewer steps in the installer the easier the application will be to install. However, it can be better to prompt for information during the installation than for the user to later sit wondering why the application is not working. The User Interface view, shown in Figure 49-13, enables you to customize the screens that the user sees as part of the installation process.

Figure 49-13

Two user interfaces are defined in this view: the standard installation and an Administrative install (not visible). Both processes follow the same structure: Start, where you typically collect information from the user before installing the product; Progress, used for providing a visual cue as to the installation's progress; and End, at which point the user is presented with a summary of the installation. The Administrative install is typically used when a network setup is required, and can be invoked by calling `msiexec` with the `/a` flag.

You can customize either of the installation processes by adding and/or removing dialogs from the user interface tree. To add a new dialog, right-click any of the three stages in the installation process and select Add Dialog from the context menu. This displays a list of the predefined dialogs from which you can choose. Each of the dialogs has a different layout; some are used for accepting user input and others are used to display information to the user. Input controls are allocated a property identifier so that the value entered during the installation process can be used later in the process. For example, a checkbox might be used to indicate whether the tools for a product should be installed. A condition could be placed on an output in the File System view so the tools are installed only if the checkbox is enabled.

Adding Custom Actions

It is often necessary to perform some actions either before or after the application is installed. To do this, you can create a custom action to be executed as part of the install or uninstall process. Adding a custom action entails creating the code to be executed and linking the appropriate installer event so that the code is executed. Custom actions use an event model similar to what Windows components use to link the code that you write to the appropriate installer event. To add a custom action to an installer event, you need to create a class that inherits from the `Installer` base class. This base class exposes a number of events for which you can write event handlers. Because writing custom installer actions is quite a common task, the Add New Item dialog includes an Installer Class template item under the General node. The new class (added to the SharedResources project) opens using the component designer, as shown in Figure 49-14.

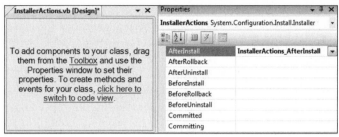

Figure 49-14

From the Events tab of the Properties window, select the installer event for which you want to add an event handler. If no event handler exists, a new event handler will be created and opened in the code window. The following code is automatically generated when an event handler is created. A simple message box is inserted to notify the user that the AfterInstall event handler has completed:

```vb
Imports System.ComponentModel
Imports System.Configuration.Install

Public Class InstallerActions

    Public Sub New()
        MyBase.New()

        InitializeComponent()
    End Sub

    Private Sub InstallerActions_AfterInstall(ByVal sender As Object, _
                                    ByVal e As InstallEventArgs) _
                                              Handles Me.AfterInstall
        MessageBox.Show("Installation process completed!")
    End Sub
End Class
```

As with forms and other components, the rest of this class is stored in a designer class file where you can see that the partial InstallerActions class inherits from the Installer class and is attributed with the RunInstaller attribute. This combination ensures that this class is given the opportunity to handle events raised by the installer.

The InstallerActions class you have just created was added to the SharedResources assembly. For the events to be wired up to the InstallerActions class, the installer needs to know that there is a class that contains custom actions. To make this association, add the SharedResources assembly to the Custom Actions view for the deployment project by right-clicking any of the nodes shown in Figure 49-15 and selecting Add Custom Action from the context menu. In this case, you want to wire up the SharedResources. In Figure 49-15, this association has been made only for the Install action. If you want to wire up the `Custom Action` class for all of the actions, you need to add the custom action to the root Custom Actions node.

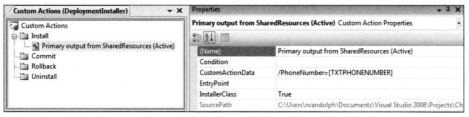

Figure 49-15

To complete this discussion, understand that it is important to be able to pass information collected from the user during the Start phase of the installation process to the custom action. Unfortunately, because the custom action is invoked after the installer has finished, you have to use a special channel to pass installer properties to the custom action event handler. In the Custom Actions view (refer to Figure 49-15), select Properties Window from the right-click context menu for the Primary output node. The `CustomActionData` property is used to define name/value pairs that will be sent through to the custom installer. For example, you might have `/PhoneNumber= "+1 425 001 0001"`, in which case you can access this value in the event handler as follows:

```
Private Sub CustomActions_AfterInstall(ByVal sender As Object, _
                                    ByVal e As InstallEventArgs) _
                                                    Handles Me.AfterInstall
    MessageBox.Show("Number: " & Me.Context.Parameters("PhoneNumber").ToString)
End Sub
```

Of course, hard-coded values are not a good idea and it would be better if this were a user-specified value. To use a property defined in the installer user interface, replace the specified string with the property identifier in square brackets. For example, `/PhoneNumber=[TXTPHONENUMBER]` would include the text in the TXTPHONENUMBER text box.

Service Installer

You can create an installer for a Windows Service the same way you would create an installer for a Windows application. However, a Windows Service installer not only needs to install the files into the appropriate location, it also needs to register the service so it appears in the services list. You can do this using the `ServiceInstaller` and `ServiceProcessInstaller` components from the System. ServiceProcess namespace (you'll probably need to add these to the Toolbox, because they are not visible by default). An instance of each of these components needs to be dragged onto the designer surface of a custom installer, as shown in Figure 49-16.

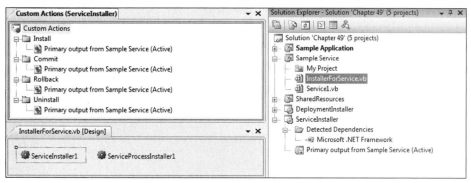

Figure 49-16

The `ServiceInstaller` class is used to specify the display name (the name of the service as it will appear in the Windows services list), the service name (the name of the service class that will be executed when the service is run), and the startup type (whether it is manually started or automatically started when Windows starts up). For each service you want to install you need to create a separate instance of the `ServiceInstaller` class, specifying a different display and service name. Only a single instance of the `ServiceProcessInstaller` class is required, which is used to specify the account information that the service(s) will run as. In the following example, the `InstallerforService` constructor specifies that the class `Service1` should be installed as a service, and that it should automatically start using the `NetworkService` account:

```
Imports System.ComponentModel
Imports System.Configuration.Install

Public Class InstallerForService

    Private Const cServiceDisplayName As String = "My Generic Service"
    Private Const cStartAfterInstall As String = "STARTAFTERINSTALL"
    Private Const cNETProcessName As String = "Net"
    Private Const cNETStart As String = "Start ""{0}"""
    Private Const cNETWaitTimeout As Integer = 5000
    Private Const cNETWaitError As String = "WARNING: Process took longer than
expected to start, it may need to be restarted manually"

    Public Sub New()
        MyBase.New()

        'This call is required by the Component Designer.
        InitializeComponent()

        'Add initialization code after the call to InitializeComponent
        Me.ServiceInstaller1.DisplayName = cServiceDisplayName
        Me.ServiceInstaller1.ServiceName = GetType(Service1).ToString
        Me.ServiceInstaller1.StartType = ServiceProcess.ServiceStartMode.Automatic
```

(continued)

(continued)

```
            Me.ServiceProcessInstaller1.Account = _
                                    ServiceProcess.ServiceAccount.NetworkService
        End Sub

        Private Sub InstallerForService_AfterInstall(ByVal sender As Object, _
                                          ByVal e As InstallEventArgs) _
                                          Handles Me.AfterInstall
            'Retrieve the user input (unchecked box can return empty string,
            'whereas a checked box will return "1")
            Dim startString As String = Me.Context.Parameters(cStartAfterInstall)
            If startString = "" Then Return
            Dim shouldStart As Boolean = CBool(startString)
            If Not shouldStart Then Return

            'Service should be started, so create a process and wait for completion
            Dim proc As Process = Process.Start(CreateNetStartProcessInfo)
            If Not proc.WaitForExit(cNETWaitTimeout) Then MsgBox(cNETWaitError)

        End Sub

        Private Function CreateNetStartProcessInfo() As ProcessStartInfo
            Dim x As New ProcessStartInfo(cNETProcessName, _
                                    String.Format(cNETStart, cServiceDisplayName))
            x.WindowStyle = ProcessWindowStyle.Hidden
            Return x
        End Function
    End Class
```

Also included in this listing is an event handler for the AfterInstall event that is used to start the service on completion of the installation process. By default, even when the startup is set to automatic, the service will not be started by the installer. However, when uninstalling the service, the installer does attempt to stop the service.

The user interface for this deployment project includes a Checkboxes (A) dialog using the User Interface view for the project. Refer to Figure 49-13 for a view of the default user interface. Right-click the Start node and select Add Dialog from the context menu. Highlight the dialog titled Checkboxes (A) from the Add Dialog window and click OK. This will insert the new dialog at the end of the installation process. The order of the dialogs can be adjusted using the Move Up/Down items from the right-click context menu on the nodes in the User Interface window.

Selecting Properties Window from the right-click context menu on the new dialog will bring up the Properties window. Set the property identifier for Checkbox1 to STARTAFTERINSTALL and then set the Visible property for the remaining checkboxes to false. As discussed earlier in the chapter, you also needed to add /STARTAFTERINSTALL=[STARTAFTERINSTALL] to the CustomActionData property for the assembly in the Custom Actions view of the deployment project. With this user input you can decide whether to start the service when the installer completes.

ClickOnce

Using a Windows installer is a sensible approach for any application development. However, deploying an installer to thousands of machines, and then potentially having to update them, is a daunting task. Although management products help reduce the burden associated with application deployment, web applications often replace rich Windows applications because they can be dynamically updated, affecting all users of the system. *ClickOnce*, introduced in version 2.0 of the .NET Framework, enables you to build self-updating Windows applications. This section shows you how to use Visual Studio 2008 to build applications that can be deployed and updated using ClickOnce.

Click to Deploy

To demonstrate the functionality of ClickOnce deployment, this section uses the same application we used to build the Windows Installer, Simple Application, which simply displays an empty form. To deploy this application using ClickOnce, open the Publish tab of the project properties designer. Publishing the application deploys the current version of the application to the location defined in the Publishing Folder Location path (in the case of Figure 49-17, `http://localhost/DeploymentSample/`) along with a deployment manifest that details the application components and security. Although the publish location appears as a drop-down list, it is only populated with previous locations to which you have published the application, so initially it will be empty. Clicking the ellipsis button displays the Open Web Site dialog, which assists you in specifying the publishing location.

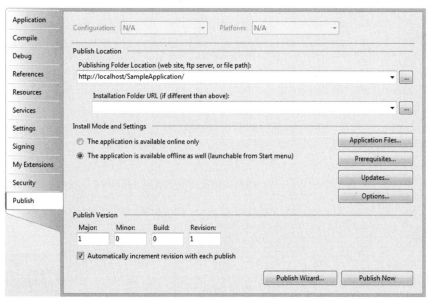

Figure 49-17

In the Publish Options dialog (click the Options button) enter the name of a Deployment web page (for example `publish.htm`) and ensure the "Automatically generate deployment web page after every publish" option is checked. Back in the project properties editor, click once on the Publish Now button shown in lower-right corner of Figure 49-17. After this process has completed, the installation URL is launched, as shown in Figure 49-18.

This process may fail if you don't have appropriate permissions. To work around this you may need to run Visual Studio 2008 as Administrator.

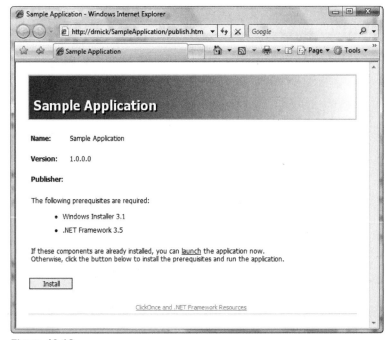

Figure 49-18

Clicking the Install button at this location displays a dialog prompting you to run or save Setup.exe. This is a bootstrap that enables your application to install correctly and means that ClickOnce can now be used to deploy Office add-ins as well as Windows applications. Selecting Run will show the Launching Application dialog, shown in Figure 49-19, while the components of your application are being retrieved from the server.

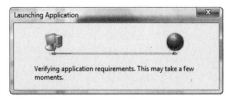

Figure 49-19

After information about the Sample Application has been downloaded, a security warning is launched, as shown in Figure 49-20. In this case, the security warning is raised because although the deployment manifest has been signed, it has been signed with a certificate that is not known on the machine on which it is being installed.

Figure 49-20

Three options are available when it comes to signing the deployment manifest. By default, Visual Studio 2008 creates a test certificate to sign the manifest, which has the format `application name_ TemporaryKey.pfx` and is automatically added to the solution (this happens when the application is first published using the Publish Now button). Though this certificate can be used during development, it is not recommended for deployment. The other alternatives are to purchase a third-party certificate, from a company such as VeriSign, or to use the certificate server within Windows Server to create an internal certificate.

The advantage of getting a certificate from a well-known certificate authority is that it can automatically be verified by any machine. Using either the test certificate or an internal certificate requires installation of that certificate in the appropriate certificate store. Figure 49-21 shows the Signing tab of the project properties window, where you can see that the ClickOnce manifest is being signed with a certificate that has been generated on the local computer. An existing certificate can be used by selecting it from the store or from a file. Alternatively, another test certificate can be created.

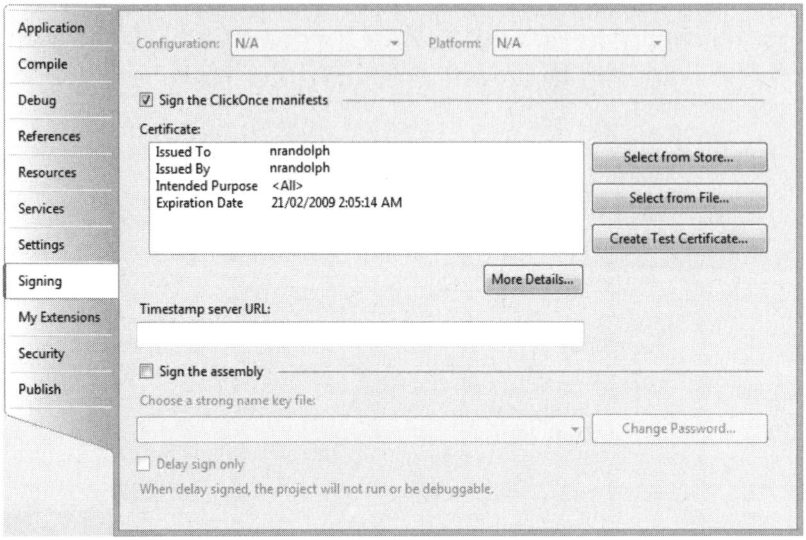

Figure 49-21

If you want your application to install with a known publisher, you need to add the test certificate into the root certificate store on the machine on which you're installing the product. Because this also happens to be the deployment machine, you can do this by clicking More Details. This opens a dialog that outlines the certificate details, including the fact that it can't be authenticated. (If you are using the certificate created by default by Visual Studio 2008, you will need to use the Select from File button to re-select the generated certificate, and then use the More Details button. There seems to be an issue here in that the details window does not show the Install Certificate button without this additional step.) Clicking Install Certificate enables you to specify that the certificate should be installed into the Trusted Root Certification Authorities store. This is not the default certificate store, so you need to browse for it. Because this is a test certificate, you can ignore the warning that is given, but remember that you should not use this certificate in production. Now when you publish your application and try to install it, you will see that the dialog has changed, looking similar to the one shown in Figure 49-22.

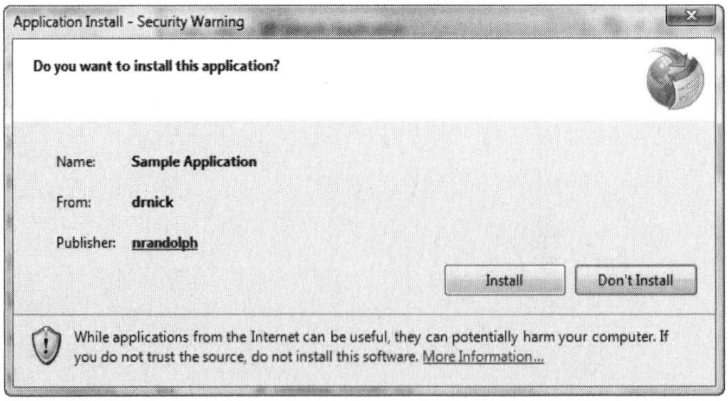

Figure 49-22

Although you have a known publisher, you are still being warned that additional security permissions need to be granted to this application in order for it to execute. Clicking the rather minimalist More Information hyperlink opens a more informative dialog, shown in Figure 49-23. As with the security coding within Windows XP SP2 and Windows Vista, there are three icons: green for positive security, red for potential security weaknesses, and yellow for informative or best practice guidance.

Figure 49-23

ClickOnce deployment manifests are rated on four security dimensions. You've just seen how you can specify a well-known publisher, critical for safe installation of an application. By default, ClickOnce publishes applications as full trust applications, giving them maximum control over the local computer. This is unusual, because in most other cases Microsoft has adopted a security-first approach. To run with full trust, the application requires additional security permissions, which might be exploited. The Sample Application will be available online and offline; and though this isn't a major security risk, it does modify the local file system. Lastly, the location from which the application is being installed is almost as important as the publisher in determining how dangerous the application might be. In this case, the application was published within the local network so it is unlikely to be a security threat.

Because this application doesn't really do anything, you can decrease the trust level that the application requires. As shown in Figure 49-24, this application is made a partial trust application based on the Local Intranet zone. This changes the Machine Access icon to green, leaving only the Installation icon yellow. Unfortunately, the only way you can get this to be green would be to not install the application, which means that it would not be available offline.

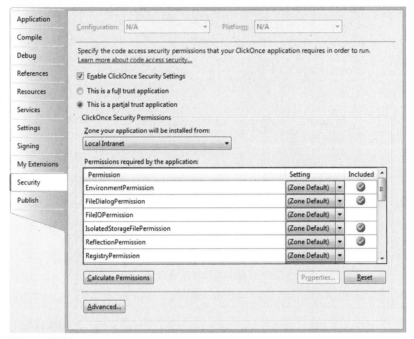

Figure 49-24

Ideally, you would like to be able to bypass the Application Install dialog and have the application automatically be granted appropriate permissions. You can do this by adding the certificate to the Trusted Publishers store. Even for well-known certificate authorities, in order for the application to install automatically, the certificate needs to be added to this store. With this completed, you will only see the progress dialog as the application is downloaded, rather than the security prompt in Figure 49-22.

Once installed the application can be launched either by returning to the installation URL (Figure 49-18) or by selecting the shortcut from the newly created Start Menu folder with the same name as the application.

Click to Update

At some point in the future you might make a change to your application — for example, you might add a button to the simple form you created previously. ClickOnce supports a powerful update process that enables you to publish the new version of your application in the same way you did previously, and existing versions can be upgraded the next time they are online. The default behavior of ClickOnce applications is that they do not check for updates at all. However, if you select the Updates button on the Publish tab of the project properties designer (Figure 49-17), you will see the Application Updates dialog, shown in Figure 49-25. Here you can select when the application will check for updates — we have opted for the application to check before startup.

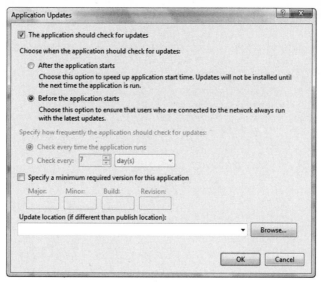

Figure 49-25

With this change, now when you publish a new version of your application, any existing users will be prompted to update their application to the most recent version, as shown in Figure 49-26.

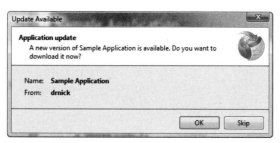

Figure 49-26

One of the most powerful features of ClickOnce deployment is that it tracks a previous version of the application that was installed. This means that at any stage, not only can it do a clean uninstall, it can also roll back to the earlier version. The application can be rolled back or uninstalled from the Programs and Features list from the Control Panel.

Note that for users to receive an update they do need to be able to contact the original deployment URL when the application performs the check for a new version (in this case when the application starts). You can also force all users to upgrade to a particular version (that is, they won't get prompted) by specifying the minimum required version in the Application Updates dialog (Figure 49-25).

Summary

This chapter walked you through the details of building installers for various types of applications. Building a good-quality installer can make a significant difference in how professional your application appears. ClickOnce also offers an important alternative for those who want to deploy their application to a large audience, and with the changes introduced with version 3.5 of the .NET Framework, it can now be used for a much wider range of applications.

Web and Mobile Application Deployment

In the previous chapter you saw how to deploy your Windows application via either an installer or using ClickOnce. But how do you go about deploying other types of applications? This chapter walks you through deploying both web and mobile applications.

One of the most important aspects of building your application is to think about how you will package it so that it can be deployed. While a large proportion of web applications are only for internal release, where a simple copy script might be sufficient, if you do want to make your web application available for others to purchase and use, then you really need to focus on making the deployment process as simple as possible.

This is equally true with mobile applications. With the ever-decreasing cost of data plans, more mobile applications are being deployed straight to the device. However, for those users who still synchronize their devices with their main computers, it is worth building an installer for Windows that can automatically deploy your application to their devices the next time they synchronize.

Web Application Deployment

There are a variety of ways to deploy web applications that range from building an installer capable of creating the necessary virtual directory to using FTP to copy the web site to a remote server. In this section you see a number of the options you can use from within Visual Studio 2008.

Publish Web Site

One of the simplest ways to deploy a web site from Visual Studio 2008 is to publish it via the Publish item on the Build menu. Exactly what options are displayed when you go to publish your web site will depend on whether you are using the ASP.NET Web Application or the ASP.NET Web Site project template. Figure 50-1 displays the two different dialogs that are presented: on the left are the options for publishing a web site and on the right are the options for publishing a web application. As you can see, some of the options that are presented for the web site are not relevant to a web application, or they are contained in the project settings that can be accessed via the Web tab of the project properties editor.

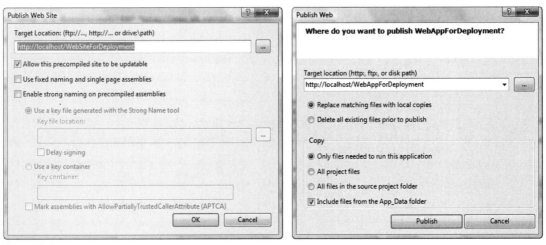

Figure 50-1

Irrespective of whether you are publishing a web site or a web application, you need to define the target location, which can be a local instance of IIS, an FTP site, elsewhere on the file system, or a remote instance of IIS. Clicking the ellipses button next to the Target Location textbox in Figure 50-1 brings up a dialog to specify the details of where you want to publish to, as shown in Figure 50-2.

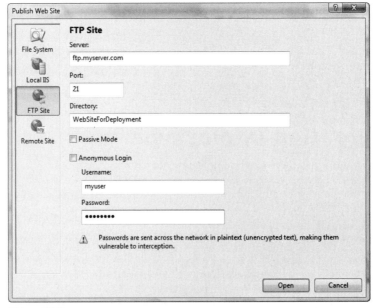

Figure 50-2

Here we are publishing to a private FTP account, and if this is the first time we are publishing this site we may have to define this folder as an IIS application in order for the web site to function.

Copy Web Project

Once a web site has been published, it is important that you have some way of updating it. One option is to go through the process of publishing your web site. However, this will publish the entire web site, even if only a single file needs to be updated. An alternative is to use the Copy Web Site tool, shown in Figure 50-3, to synchronize files between your development project and the web site. This tool can be accessed from the right-click context menu in the Solution Explorer, or via the web site menu.

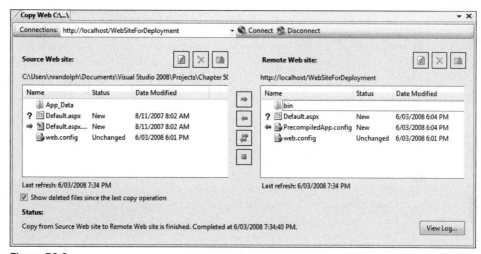

Figure 50-3

In order to view the existing files on the remote web site, you need to either select a recent connection from the drop-down list or click the Connect button. This will open a dialog similar to Figure 50-2 where you can specify how to connect to the remote web site. Once you have connected you can see which files are out of sync. You can then use the right and left arrows to move files between your local project and the remote web site.

Note that this tool is only available for ASP.NET Web Site Projects.

Web Deployment Projects

Despite having two different ways to build ASP.NET web applications there are still some constraints when it comes to customizing the deployment process for web applications. Due to a significant amount of feedback requesting features such as the ability to specify different configuration settings depending on the build type, Microsoft has released the Visual Studio 2008 Web Deployment Projects (available as a download from www.microsoft.com). These project types complement both Web Site and Web Application projects so that you can package your application ready for deployment. Unlike other project templates that appear in the New Project dialog, Web Deployment Projects need to be created via the right-click context menu in the Solution Explorer, as illustrated in Figure 50-4.

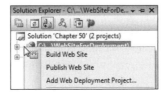

Figure 50-4

Because there is a one-to-one association between a Web Site/Application Project and a Web Deployment Project, you need to ensure you have the correct project selected before you select Add Web Deployment Project from the shortcut menu. This will then prompt you for a name and location before going ahead and creating the project in your solution.

It is recommended that you use a Solution Folder to group together each web site/application with the associated Web Deployment Project, particularly if you have a large solution with many projects. This becomes even more relevant when you then build an installer for your web application — by grouping the three projects together they become much easier to manage.

To begin configuring the Web Deployment Project right-click the project in the Solution Explorer tool window and select Property Pages. This will open a modal dialog that allows you to define the usual project properties such as output folder, whether debugging information is generated, the assembly version and signing information, as well as some web application specifics. Some of the properties specific to web applications include how the assemblies are built and defining configuration file section replacements.

In most cases you will only want to select the creation of a single output assembly. However, for large web applications where it may be necessary to update portions of the site independently, it may be preferable to create separate assemblies for each folder. This is configurable via the Output Assemblies page in the Property Pages dialog.

In Figure 50-5 you can see the Deployment page of the Property Pages dialog, which is where you can define configuration file section replacements. As you can see from the tooltip, this is displayed when you click the examples link, the idea being that you provide a separate file that contains the relevant configuration information. You will notice that these properties are defined for a specific build configuration. This means that you can have one set of settings that you use during debugging and another set that is used when you do a release build. For more information on using separate files for different configuration sections, see Chapter 38.

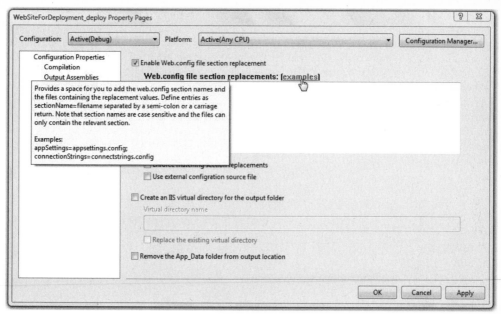

Figure 50-5

A Web Deployment Project is essentially just an MSBuild file that you can open by selecting Open Project File from the right-click shortcut menu off the project in the Solution Explorer tool window. Not only will this open the project file using the XML editor, but you will see that there is also IntelliSense support for making changes. In Figure 50-6, you can see the IntelliSense provided when adding a Copy task to the AfterBuild event of the Web Deployment Project.

```
<Import Project="$(MSBuildExtensionsPath)\Microsoft\WebDeployment\v9.0\Microsoft.WebDeployment.targets" />
<!-- To modify your build process, add your task inside one of the targets below and uncomment it.
     Other similar extension points exist, see Microsoft.WebDeployment.targets.
-->
<Target Name="AfterBuild">
  <Copy
</Tar
Proj
```

Condition
ContinueOnError
DestinationFiles
DestinationFolder
SkipUnchangedFiles

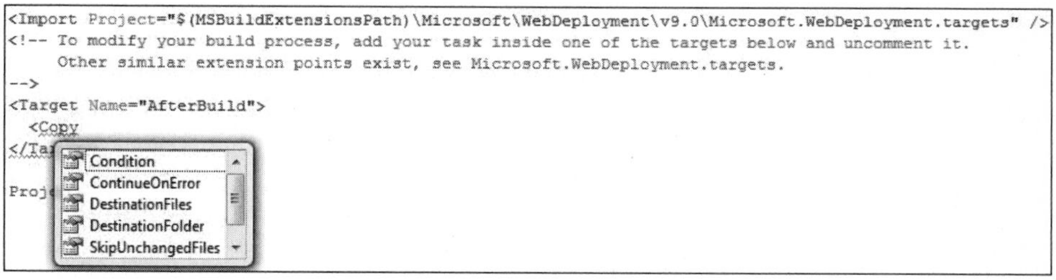

Figure 50-6

Figure 50-6 also shows the Import element, which includes the relevant targets so that MSBuild knows how to build the Web Deployment Project types. As the comment implies, there is more information in the targets file on how you can further customize the build process.

Web Project Installers

Whether you use a Web Deployment Project or not, if you are redistributing your web application you will want to create a Windows Installer that is capable of installing the web application and configuring IIS. To do this you will need to create a Web Setup Project from the Other Project Types ⇨ Setup and Deployment node in the New Project dialog. This is essentially a normal setup project that has been configured with the relevant output folder (see the File System view) and user interface (see the User Interface view) for deploying web applications. Once you have created the setup project, you will need to add the appropriate project outputs. The left image of Figure 50-7 shows the Add Project Output Group dialog for adding a web site to the setup project. Because a web site contains only content files, this is the only option available.

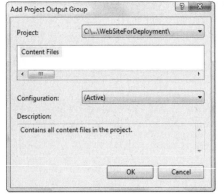 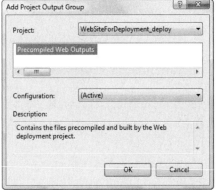

Figure 50-7

Alternatively, when you are using a Web Deployment Project you will want to select the Precompiled Web Outputs of that project to add to the setup project, as shown in the right image of Figure 50-7. Lastly, if you are adding a web application to the setup project, you will need to remember to include both the Primary output and Content Files to ensure the application will function correctly.

One of the unique features of the Web Setup Project is the screen that is added to the user interface to enable the user to define the web site, virtual directory, and application pool that will be used by the web application being installed. Figure 50-8 illustrates this dialog as part of the installation process.

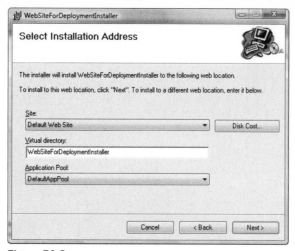

Figure 50-8

In previous versions of Visual Studio, the web site installation wizard would only prompt the user to specify the name of the virtual directory into which the application was to be installed, and this directory would then be created in the default web site. If multiple web sites were hosted on the same server (often the case with products such as SharePoint installed), then this could result in the application being installed on the wrong web site. Being able to specify the web site during installation reduces any post-installation administration that would have been required in the past.

Mobile Application Deployment

Deployment of device applications has been a much-debated topic, and numerous white papers have been written about how to package an application for installation. In the past, packaging an application required considerable fiddling within Visual Studio to generate an installer for a mobile application. Although Visual Studio 2008 provides good support for building CAB files, several steps are still required to deliver an easy-to-install application. This section looks at how you can use CAB files to install your application, and describes how a desktop MSI installer can really make your application look professional.

CAB Files

The easiest way to deploy your application is via a CAB file, which is essentially a compressed file that contains all the assemblies and resources that your application requires in order to run. It can also contain registry settings that may need to be applied during installation. To install an application, the CAB file needs to be downloaded to the device before being executed. Executing the CAB file decompresses the contents, installs the application, and performs any installation activities. The final stage is to remove the CAB file from the device. If you use a storage card to deploy a CAB file to multiple devices, it is a good idea to make the card read-only so the CAB file does not get removed.

Visual Studio 2008 contains a project type called a Smart Device CAB Project, which is listed under Setup and Deployment projects in the Add New Project window, shown in Figure 50-9.

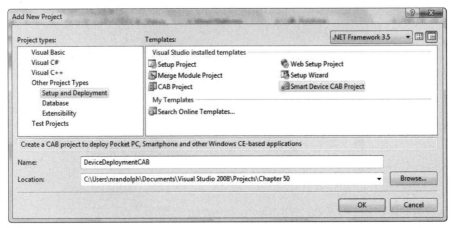

Figure 50-9

Selecting this project type adds a CAB project to your solution. Unlike an installer for the desktop, which has a number of views, the Smart Device CAB Project has only two views, of the file system and the registry settings. This is shown in Figure 50-10, where the primary output for the project DeviceDeploymentExample has been added to the CAB project; this is achieved by right-clicking the CAB project and selecting Add ⇨ Project Output from the context menu.

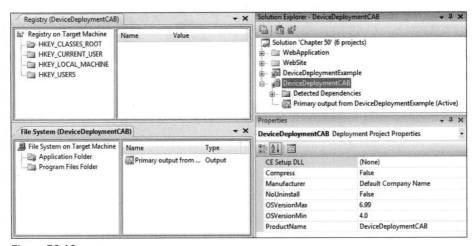

Figure 50-10

The File System view can be used to add files and shortcuts on the device itself. Right-clicking the Target Machine node in the File System view enables you to select Add Special Folder. This includes directories such as Programs, Start menu, and Startup. Right-clicking one of the folders prompts you to add sub-folders, project output, or files. These will be installed on the target machine when the CAB file is installed.

> It is good practice to include a shortcut to your application in the Programs Folder because this will make your application much more readily accessible. Instead of users having to locate your application using File Explorer, they can instead go to Start ⇨ Programs, and your application will be listed alongside the other applications installed on the device.

In the Properties window are several properties that can be configured for the CAB file itself. It is, of course, good practice to ensure that the Manufacturer and ProductName reflect the application being deployed.

MSI Installer

The CAB project enables developers to create a CAB file that can be installed on a mobile device. The difficulty lies in getting the CAB file onto the device in the first place. Although as a developer you can easily copy the file to the device via ActiveSync, or even download the CAB file from a web site, unless your application is designed for fellow developers or IT professionals, it is necessary to have an easier mechanism by which the application can be installed.

This can be done using a desktop installer with a custom action to install the CAB using the ActiveSync CEAppMgr application (which can be run from C:\Windows\WindowsMobile\CEAppMgr.exe under Windows Vista or C:\Program Files\Microsoft ActiveSync\CEAppMgr.exe under Windows XP). The installer works as follows:

1. The end user double-clicks the MSI installer (for example, MyApplication.msi).

2. The MSI installer copies files to the installation directory.

3. The MSI installer launches a custom installer action.

4. The custom installer action copies the installed files to an application directory used by CEAppMgr.

5. The custom installer action launches CEAppMgr to install CAB files on the device.

6. The Uninstaller: The custom installer action cleans up installed files in the application directory used by CEAppMgr.

The first step in creating this installer is to add a setup project, which is done the same way as you would create an installer for a desktop application. Select Add ⇨ New Project from the right-click context menu in Solution Explorer and then select Setup Project from the Setup and Deployment node. The desktop installer needs to do two things: copy the CAB file onto the desktop and initiate the custom installer action, which will install the CAB file on the device. To add the CAB file to the installer, right-click the Setup Project node in the Solution Explorer window and select Add ⇨ Project Output. In the Add Project Output Group dialog, you then select Build Outputs from the CAB project to add to your setup project. This automatically adds the Build Outputs to the application folder, and because you will be copying the CAB file into the appropriate location with the custom installer action, it doesn't matter where the files are initially placed.

The next step is to add custom installer actions to copy the installed files to the CEAppMgr application folder and then to run the CEAppMgr, which installs the CAB file on the device. To create the custom installer actions, perform the following steps:

1. Create a Class Library project within the existing solution.

2. Remove the default Class1 that is in the solution.

3. Add a new item based on the Installer Class item template.

4. Add event handlers for the BeforeInstall and BeforeUninstall.

5. Add an INI file to the Class Library project (for example, DeviceDeploymentExample.ini) and set the Build Action property to Content. You can do this by adding a new item based on the Text file item template — just change the filename to end in .ini.

6. Add class library primary output and content files to the desktop setup project. You can do this by selecting Add ⇨ Project Outputs, from the right-click context menu from the Setup Project node in Solution Explorer, then specifying the Primary output and Content Files from the class library.

7. Wire up custom installer actions to the Setup Project. Select View ⇨ Custom Actions from the right-click context menu from the Setup Project node in Solution Explorer. Right-click the Custom Actions node and select Add Custom Action. Select the Primary output from the class library from within the application folder. This attaches the necessary event handlers to the Windows installer to ensure that the custom installer actions are executed as part of the installation process.

These steps set up the template for the file structure and the custom installer actions. What remains is to fill in the contents for the INI file, which is used by CEAppMgr to install the correct CAB files, and to fill in the event handlers for the custom installer actions. The INI file needs to define the CAB files that are to be installed on the device for a particular application. The CEAppManager section is required, because it indicates that this is a configuration file for the CEAppMgr application and lists the components to be installed. The component section describes the application and provides a comma-delimited list of CAB files, without spaces, that are to be installed for this application:

```
[CEAppManager]
Version = 1.0
Component = DeviceAps

[DeviceAps]
Description = Device Deployment Example
CabFiles = DeviceDeploymentCAB.cab
```

The BeforeInstall event handler needs to copy the application files from where they are installed by the desktop installer to an application folder that sits within the ActiveSync folder. It then needs to run the CEAppMgr process, passing it the INI file just created. The BeforeUninstall event handler has to clean up the application folder under ActiveSync to ensure that the application is entirely removed. The following code provides a template with which you can include your own installer activities:

```vbnet
Imports System.ComponentModel
Imports System.Configuration.Install
Imports System.IO
Imports Microsoft.Win32

Public Class DeviceDeploymentInstallerActions

    Public Sub New()
        MyBase.New()
        'This call is required by the Component Designer.
        InitializeComponent()
    End Sub

    Private Shared Function CEAppMgrApplicationDirectory() As String
        Dim activeSyncKey As RegistryKey = _
            Registry.LocalMachine.OpenSubKey(My.Resources.ActiveSync_Registry_Key)
        Dim activeSyncPath As String =  _
        CStr(activeSyncKey.GetValue(My.Resources.CEAppMgr_Install_Dir_Registry_Key))
        Dim installPath As String = activeSyncPath + _
                                                My.Resources.Application_Directory
        activeSyncKey.Close()
        Return installPath
    End Function

    Private Shared Function CEAppMgrExecutable() As String
        Dim appMgrKey As RegistryKey = _
                    Registry.LocalMachine.OpenSubKey(My.Resources.CEApp_Mgr_Path)
        Dim appMgrPath As String = CStr(appMgrKey.GetValue(Nothing))
        appMgrKey.Close()
        Return appMgrPath
    End Function

    Private Sub ActionBeforeInstall(ByVal sender As Object, _
                            ByVal e As InstallEventArgs) _
                                                Handles Me.BeforeInstall
        'Copy installation files to the CEAppMgr application directory
        Dim installPath As String = CEAppMgrApplicationDirectory()
        Dim tmpPath As String = (New FileInfo(Me.Context.Parameters.Item _
                (My.Resources.Installation_Context_Assembly_Key))).DirectoryName
        My.Computer.FileSystem.CopyDirectory(tmpPath, installPath, True)

        'Run CEAppMgr to install the application on the device
        System.Diagnostics.Process.Start(CEAppMgrExecutable, _
                            """" + Path.Combine(installPath, _
                            My.Resources.Application_Cab_INI_File) + " "" ")
    End Sub

    Public Sub ActionBeforeUninstall(ByVal sender As Object, _
                            ByVal e As InstallEventArgs) _
                                                Handles Me.BeforeUninstall
        'Remove the installation files we manually copied
        My.Computer.FileSystem.DeleteDirectory(CEAppMgrApplicationDirectory, _
                            FileIO.DeleteDirectoryOption.DeleteAllContents)
    End Sub
End Class
```

This code makes use of a number of resources that are embedded in the Custom Installer Action class library. These constants are provided as shown in Figure 50-11, which illustrates the String resource editor tab of the project properties window.

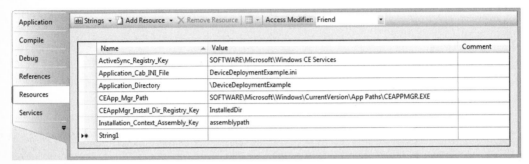

Figure 50-11

The installer is now ready to be built and deployed to your clients. You can be sure that not only will the application be easy to install, it can also be successfully uninstalled without leaving any traces on the desktop computer. Clearly, in order for the application to be installed on the device, the device needs to be connected to the desktop computer through the Windows Mobile Device Center (ActiveSync on pre-Windows Vista versions of Windows). However, CEAppMgr can be run at a later stage to install the application on any device attached to the computer.

> By default, the CAB project will not be included in the build configuration, which means when you go to build this solution you will find that the desktop setup installer will fail to build because it can't find the CAB output. You can either manually build the CAB project or add it to the build configuration using the Configuration Manager.

Summary

In this chapter you have seen how to use a number of the features of Visual Studio 2008 to package your web applications ready for deployment. Using a Web Deployment Project you can effectively customize your application so that it can be deployed with a minimal set of files. This helps ensure that the application is not modified in production.

You have also seen how to package a mobile application using both the built-in CAB setup project and a customized desktop installer. Depending on how you plan to deliver your mobile application, it may be appropriate to use either or both of these techniques. For example, if you want users to be able to browse to your web site and download and install the application directly from their devices, you will need to ensure that you have a link to the CAB file. Alternatively, those browsing the site using their desktops, or those without a data connection directly from their devices, may wish to download the desktop installer.

Part XI
Automation

The Automation Model

Visual Studio 2008 is an integrated development environment (IDE) that lets you build several types of desktop, web, and embedded device applications and components. Despite being one of the premiere IDEs, there is something obvious that you will notice during your use of the IDE — the repeating of some tasks.

The development process itself contains many repetitive tasks and common pieces of code. In all development technologies and IDEs, we seek solutions to save time, spare developers from doing these repetitive tasks, and let them use tools to automatically insert codes and automate their development.

Visual Studio 2008, one of the most common and well-known IDEs, isn't an exception, and there are many features to provide this automation. Many aspects of the Visual Studio extensibility options are created to automate such repetitive tasks, including add-ins, macros, code snippets, and templates. In this part of the book you are introduced to the Visual Studio 2008 automation model and two extensibility options associated with it: add-ins and macros.

You'll learn that the automation model is a set of tools and APIs included in Visual Studio from the earlier versions, which let you access common functions in the IDE from your code rather than working directly with the IDE. This allows you to write code that automates processes.

Though the automation model is a set of APIs collected and inserted in a single architecture, they cover various aspects of the Visual Studio 2008 environment. Some of the Visual Studio Extensibility (VSX) options apply this model to provide different extensibility and automation features for Visual Studio out of the box. Add-ins and macros are two famous and common instances of these extensibility options. Both these options apply the automation model, but they have different goals and applications that are covered in the next two chapters.

In this chapter you walk through the principles of the automation model and its code representation, Development Tools Extensibility (DTE), which is one of the most common APIs in Visual Studio 2008. Before continuing to the main body of the chapter, let's discuss the automation model in more detail.

Introduction to the Automation Model

The automation model is a set of smaller models included in the Visual Studio architecture to provide access to different pieces of the Visual Studio functionality via code. It lets you automate all the tasks that you can accomplish in the IDE via .NET code and consists of some smaller models, including:

❏ **Environment model:** This model is at the core of the automation model and collaborates with all other models in order to provide some common functionality for developers to use.

❏ **Project model:** This model is responsible for providing some features to work with solutions, projects, and project items in the automation model.

❏ **Editor model:** This model is responsible for documents in editors in general. It provides some tools to manipulate the text in the editor for different documents.

❏ **Code model:** This model is responsible for manipulating different pieces and types of code.

❏ **Forms model:** This model lets you manipulate Windows Forms elements, user controls, and some other user interface elements via your code.

❏ **Debugger model:** This model lets you get access to some information and methods of the Visual Studio debugger in order to work with debugging features on the fly.

❏ **Build model:** The last model is the build model, which lets you manipulate the build process automatically and from within your code.

Figure 51-1 shows a schematic view of these models and their associations in the automation model. As you can see, the common environment model is in the core and other models are placed around it and have collaborations with this model in order to make things possible.

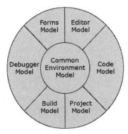

Figure 51-1

The features provided by the automation model are almost consistent between different .NET programming languages. However, a few features are supported by Visual C++ only. In general, Visual C++ is the main language behind the automation of Visual Studio, because the IDE is built on top of the traditional Visual C++ and COM programming.

The Automation Model and Visual Studio Extensibility

The automation model is strongly correlated with Visual Studio Extensibility and the options it provides. These options apply the automation model in order to work.

Of the various extensibility options provided by Visual Studio, three are more common, relevant, and use the automation model more than others. These three extensibility options have different goals and applications and are designed specifically for a particular level of extensibility.

Add-ins, macros, and VSPackages are the three extensibility options that apply the automation model in order to provide different tools for the developer to automate tasks in Visual Studio and extend this environment.

You can group these three options in some ways from the ease-of-development point of view and the depth of integration they provide for you. Figure 51-2 shows this in a schematic view.

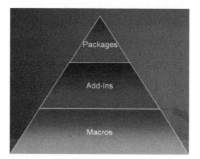

Figure 51-2

As you can see, VSPackages are at the top, add-ins are in the middle, and macros are in the lowest level. From the top down your development process is easier; going up the pyramid, the level and depth of integration with Visual Studio increases.

It's crucial to mention here an important point about VSPackages. VSPackages have been with Visual Studio for a long while and are known as the deepest way to extend it. With VSPackages you have access to the same underlying API of Visual Studio that internal teams at Microsoft have access to and use to add new functionality to Visual Studio.

However, in Visual Studio 2008, Microsoft had a revolution in Visual Studio Extensibility and after merging a few teams that were working around Visual Studio Extensibility (VSX), it also released Visual Studio Shell as a new feature included in the Visual Studio SDK.

Visual Studio Shell comes in two modes: integrated mode and isolated mode. Integrated mode is a new name for VSPackages, so don't worry if you haven't heard about it; isolated mode is a nice way to create your own IDEs based on the Visual Studio IDE elements but without requiring installation of the Visual Studio core API. This was a big limitation for everyone who wanted to use Visual Studio IDE elements in an IDE. Now, after installing a free stand-alone package, you're able to build your own IDEs with Visual Studio elements.

This book doesn't get into the topic of VSPackages because it's a broad one and isn't relevant here, but the next couple of chapters introduce you to add-ins and macros.

The last point to mention about the automation model is the availability of this model in the Visual Studio Macros IDE. In Chapter 53 you will learn that there's an IDE named Macros IDE, which is similar to the main Visual Studio IDE for macro development. The automation model is also available in this IDE to automate tasks. It gets more interesting when you learn that macros themselves use the automation model!

Development Tools Extensibility (DTE)

The automation model is somewhat abstract and related to the architecture of Visual Studio, but its core representation is known as Development Tools Extensibility, which is a set of APIs that implement the automation model. Development Tools Extensibility is abbreviated as DTE, and you'll commonly encounter this term in some of the Visual Studio 2008 extensibility classes.

DTE is the object in the automation model and is actually an interface that implements another interface, which is _DTE.

Here it's necessary to note that Visual Studio is an old IDE and was originally built on top of the COM programming model. Over the years Microsoft replaced its COM programming model with the .NET development model, but because the Visual Studio core was left unchanged, Visual Studio is still a COM-based IDE. In COM programming you deal with interfaces and components that implement these interfaces. So in Visual Studio Extensibility and DTE you see lots of interfaces and their associated components that implement each interface. Sometimes developers worry about this, especially those who aren't very familiar with COM programming. In general, the COM nature of Visual Studio has made some parts more complicated than if Visual Studio were designed in .NET.

During these years, though, Microsoft has tried to implement new features in a way that's compatible with .NET development, keeping the underlying COM layers hidden from your eyes. This is something that you experience when working with code snippets, for example. In fact, code snippets operate on top of a COM programming model, but you don't feel this because there is a separation between what you see and what goes on behind the scenes.

Development Tools Extensibility (DTE) contains a wide range of APIs related to different models included in the main automation model. These APIs are grouped in different interfaces and classes, and you'll notice the difference after coding against them for a while.

As you learned earlier in the chapter, DTE consists of several COM interfaces and their associated implementations. So you can expect to see lots of pair classes: an interface and its implementation. The root object, the _DTE interface, and its implementation, DTE, are no exception. Figure 51-3 shows that the DTE class (which is an interface itself) is implementing the _DTE interface.

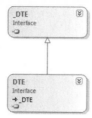

Figure 51-3

The other point is about number indexes at the end of object names. When working with DTE you may notice that some objects have such number indexes. The question is where these indexes are coming from.

You should know that an interface is a programming concept that doesn't support extensibility easily. In other words, you can't update an interface and extend it when writing new versions of your code. Actually, interfaces should be kept constant; any change in their structure breaks the structure of any class that implements the original interface.

In Visual Studio things are written based on the interfaces in COM programming, but over time new requirements and changes have forced developers at Microsoft to add new features to these interfaces. By their nature, it wasn't possible to modify existing interfaces, so what was the solution?

Microsoft developers decided to use new versions of an interface by deriving from the previous version and adding new requirements to it. After adding new features, they also updated each name with a number index to represent the new version; the larger number is the newer version.

You may encounter such interfaces in DTE. For example, you can check out the Debugger, Debugger2, and Debugger3 interfaces. The Debugger interface was a part of Visual Studio 2003 and was the original interface. Debugger2 is an updated version of Debugger for Visual Studio 2005, and Debugger3 is an updated version of Debugger and Debugger2 for Visual Studio 2008. You can see the hierarchy structure of these three interfaces in Figure 51-4.

Figure 51-4

The root DTE interface also has a new version called DTE2, and usually you need to use this class rather than its old version.

A Quick Overview of DTE

Now that you have a background about the automation model and its code representation, Development Tools Extensibility (DTE), let's look at some general information about the DTE and its main parts. In general, DTE covers some main aspects of Visual Studio including solutions and projects, documents and windows, code files, commands, debuggers, and events.

Some other things in the IDE can be accessed by the DTE, but the items just mentioned are the ones you usually care about. As you can see, there's an association between the main aspects of the DTE and the main models in the automation model; in fact each of these parts represents one of these models.

Even though we can't talk about all these parts in this book, this section gives a quick overview of some basic parts, including solutions, commands, and events.

To explain the concepts in the next few subheadings, I'll use some code snippets that are actually macros. You'll get familiar with macros in Chapter 53. For now, just focus on the source code and general idea behind examples.

Solutions and Projects

As a part of DTE you can work with solutions, projects, and project items in your code and get access to their properties and methods easily. Not only can you find information like the names of items and their counts, but you can also use methods to dynamically perform the same actions you do manually in the IDE, such as adding new projects to a solution or removing a project item from a project.

For example, the following is a macro that lists all the project names in the current solution. To execute this code simply place it into a macro module via the Macros IDE (Tools ⇨ Macros ⇨ Macros IDE):

```
Sub SolutionSample()
    If (DTE.Solution.Projects.Count > 0) Then
        Dim output As String = "Available Projects:" & vbCrLf

        For Each project As Project In DTE.Solution.Projects
            output = output & project.Name & vbCrLf
        Next

        System.Windows.Forms.MessageBox.Show(output, "Projects")
    End If
End Sub
```

This piece of code first checks the number of projects in the solution. If there are any projects, it then steps into the main logic where it creates a string output and iterates through all the available projects in order to add their names to the output. At the end, it shows the output in a MessageBox.

Running this macro for a sample solution (shown in Figure 51-5), you will see the output displayed in Figure 51-6. Note that the Solution Items folder is also considered as a separate project.

Figure 51-5

Figure 51-6

Documents and Windows

You can also work with text documents and open windows in the IDE. Visual Studio 2008 lets you have access to the list of all documents and windows and provides a set of methods to perform different tasks. The following is a macro that, using the properties of the DTE object, shows the name of the current open document in a MessageBox, then performs an Undo operation on the content of this document:

```
Sub DocumentSample()
    If (Not String.IsNullOrEmpty(DTE.ActiveDocument.Name)) Then
        System.Windows.Forms.MessageBox.Show(DTE.ActiveDocument.Name, "Window Name")
    End If

    DTE.ActiveDocument.Undo()
End Sub
```

Now suppose that you have opened a document in the IDE like the one you see in Figure 51-7, and that you temporarily add some text to the document (notice the "k" character in the code).

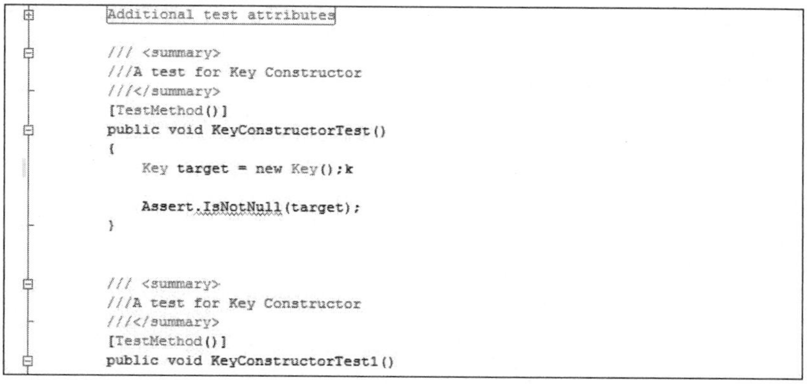

Figure 51-7

Now run the macro. First you will see the MessageBox shown in Figure 51-8.

Figure 51-8

After this you will notice the Undo operation in the document (Figure 51-9).

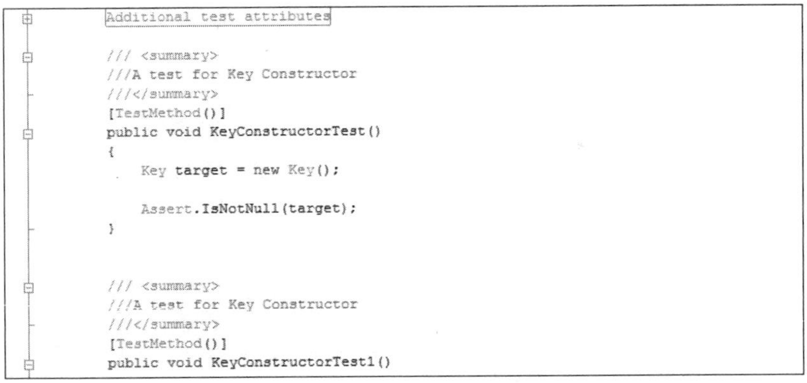

```
Additional test attributes

/// <summary>
///A test for Key Constructor
///</summary>
[TestMethod()]
public void KeyConstructorTest()
{
    Key target = new Key();

    Assert.IsNotNull(target);
}


/// <summary>
///A test for Key Constructor
///</summary>
[TestMethod()]
public void KeyConstructorTest1()
```

Figure 51-9

Commands

The fundamentals of the Visual Studio ecosystem are built on top of commands. In fact, every time you do something in the IDE you're probably running a specific command for a task. Many of the operations and tasks in the IDE are associated with a single command of their own. You can create your own commands for specific purposes and add them to the list of commands in Visual Studio, then run them via your code in order to perform a task.

Commands come into play especially when you're working with add-ins or VSPackages, and there are a few key classes that you need to be aware of. But for now we'll just look at a very basic example of commands in Visual Studio, where I display the number of available commands in the IDE in a MessageBox. Code for this sample macro is as follows:

```
Sub CommandSample()
    System.Windows.Forms.MessageBox.Show(String.Format("There are {0} commands
available in the IDE.", _

                                        DTE.Commands.Count),

"Commands Count")
End Sub
```

The output shows that 3,818 commands are available in my IDE (Figure 51-10).

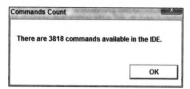

Figure 51-10

Debugger

Debugging is also important enough to have its own part in the DTE. Sometimes you may need to automate the debugging process for your projects or extend the debugger somehow. In such cases, this part of the DTE will come in handy.

The following code provides a macro that shows in a MessageBox the total number of breakpoints inserted in the code:

```
Sub DebuggerSample()
    System.Windows.Forms.MessageBox.Show(String.Format("There are {0} breakpoints
inserted in your code.", _
                                                    DTE.Debugger.Breakpoints
.Count), "Breakpoints Count")
End Sub
```

If you insert three breakpoints in your code and run the macro, you will get the output shown in Figure 51-11.

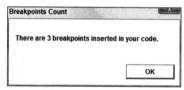

Figure 51-11

Limitations of the Automation Model

Although the automation model tries to cover everything in the Visual Studio IDE, and is very powerful in this way, there still may be some areas that remain uncovered.

You use the automation model and DTE in order to write programming code to automate something or to extend the Visual Studio IDE. But there are some limitations if you try to get access to the underlying layers of the Visual Studio ecosystem.

The automation model is suitable for common tasks and normal integration scenarios as well as many automation processes, but it's not suitable for deeper integrations and adding some major features to the Visual Studio environment.

The solution is to use underlying APIs via VSPackages to extend Visual Studio. The topic of Visual Studio Shell and VSPackages is broad and can't be covered here. Even though the automation model has been the most common way to extend and automate the IDE, it's not the only way, and there is something more powerful behind the scenes — Visual Studio Shell API and VSPackage as the deepest extensibility options in Visual Studio.

Summary

In this chapter you were introduced to the automation model, which is the basic concept of extensibility in Visual Studio.

After getting a quick overview of the automation model, its structure, its goals, and its architecture, you learned about its code representation in the Visual Studio API and Development Tools Extensibility (DTE), as well as some key points about the DTE. After that, you saw a quick overview of the main topics in DTE to get you familiar with its structure, and finally some limitations there may be with the automation model.

In the next couple of chapters you see more examples of DTE applications in add-ins and macros, two common ways for automating your tasks in the Visual Studio IDE.

52

Add-Ins

Among the most popular and well-known extensibility options in Visual Studio 2008, and one of the two main automation options, are add-ins.

Add-ins are a built-in part of the Visual Studio IDE, so you can start developing add-ins by installing one of the commercial editions of Visual Studio. Some of the other extensibility options require the installation of the Visual Studio SDK to work.

Moreover, add-ins have been with Visual Studio for a long time and along with macros are one of the most common extensibility and automation options in this IDE.

One of our goals in this part of the book is to get you started with these two automation options (add-ins and macros). In this chapter you will find a good introduction to add-ins teaching you how to develop them, deploy them, and start using them.

The topic of add-ins is much broader than a single chapter can cover, so if you want to step into real development of add-ins, you may need to refer to more resources to learn more about the topic. As you read in Chapter 51, the key point in your success with add-in and macro development is learning about the automation model and how to use the Development Tools Extensibility API to write good add-ins or macros.

Some of the major topics covered in this chapter include:

- ❑ An introduction to add-ins
- ❑ A step-by-step guide to using the Add-in Wizard in Visual Studio
- ❑ The anatomy of an add-in
- ❑ The structure of .AddIn files
- ❑ How to start developing an add-in
- ❑ How to debug your add-ins
- ❑ How to deploy your add-ins

These are the main topics directly related to getting started in add-in development. But the most important thing that can help you with add-in development is having an understanding of the automation model and the smaller models included in it.

Introduction

Add-ins are actually COM components that run as a part of the Visual Studio IDE and let users use their functionality to extend Visual Studio features or automate something in the IDE. Add-ins integrate with the Visual Studio IDE and can't run separately from the IDE.

Previously you had to register the COM component for add-ins to work, but with the introduction of a new mechanism for add-ins Microsoft has tried to hide their COM nature. This simplifies the process of add-in development and deployment, making it more like regular .NET development.

You'll read more about the technical details of add-ins and their development, but for now it's worthwhile to know that add-ins can be developed by multiple .NET languages including Visual C#, Visual Basic, and Visual C++ (CLR and ATL). However, the development language for an add-in doesn't matter because the anatomy and structure is the same for all the languages.

One thing you need to understand is the application of add-ins and how they differ from macros and other extensibility options. This is because the variety of extensibility options and their similarities to other options may make it confusing for a developer to choose the most appropriate option for his development.

Add-ins are an integrated component of Visual Studio 2008 and have access to the automation model API via Development Tools Extensibility (DTE), so their functionality is restricted to what the DTE provides. As a result of this we can conclude that for the underlying functionality of Visual Studio, add-ins aren't a good choice and some other options, like VSPackages, should come into the play.

By the way, add-ins are generally a great and common way to extend Visual Studio because the DTE addresses the common requirements that users may have.

On the other hand, you may have some difficulty choosing between add-ins and macros. So, what are the differences, and what are the pros and cons of each one? Even though you will see a more detailed discussion of macros in Chapter 53, at this point it's worthwhile covering the differences between add-ins and macros.

Add-ins are COM components that can be deployed on all machines that have Visual Studio installed, but macros are just uncompiled code packages that are harder to deploy. Moreover, macros can't be integrated with the IDE and can only automate something for you, whereas add-ins can be integrated with the IDE and can also bring extensibility features to the IDE. In general, macros are a quick and easy way to automate some tasks in the IDE, and add-ins are a more professional way to automate complex scenarios and extend the IDE.

As you work with both macros and add-ins, develop some instances of each, and see some examples, you will build a good understanding of their differences. This will help you identify where you can best use either extensibility option.

Add-In Wizard

The first step in creating an add-in project, as you might expect, is using the New Project dialog to get started. In this dialog you need to open the Extensibility node located in Other Project Types in order to see Visual Studio templates related to its extensibility (Figure 52-1). Here you will see the Visual Studio Add-in template, which is a built-in template for Visual Studio. You may or may not see some templates that are shown in Figure 52-1, such as the Visual Studio Shell Isolated template. Both the Visual Studio Add-in and Shared Add-in templates are built-in parts of the Visual Studio installation.

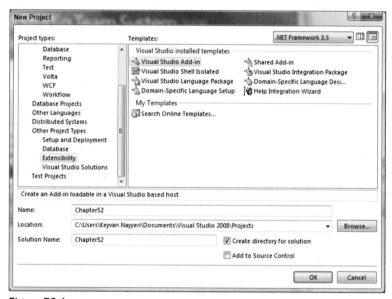

Figure 52-1

After choosing a name for the project, a wizard dialog appears called the Add-in Wizard. This wizard helps you to get started with your add-in through an initial code that is generated for you. This wizard consists of six pages and a welcome page.

Here you can see a walkthrough of this wizard and read a description about each step. As a general note, you need to know that this wizard has buttons to the next and previous steps and to cancel the wizard. At any step you can go back and forth between steps.

There is a welcome page at the start, which gives a short description of the wizard (Figure 52-2).

Figure 52-2

In the first step of the Add-in Wizard (Figure 52-3) you need to choose a development language for your add-in. There are four options for you — Visual C#, Visual Basic, Visual C++ / CLR, and Visual C++ / ATL. Visual Studio generates appropriate code for the language that you choose here.

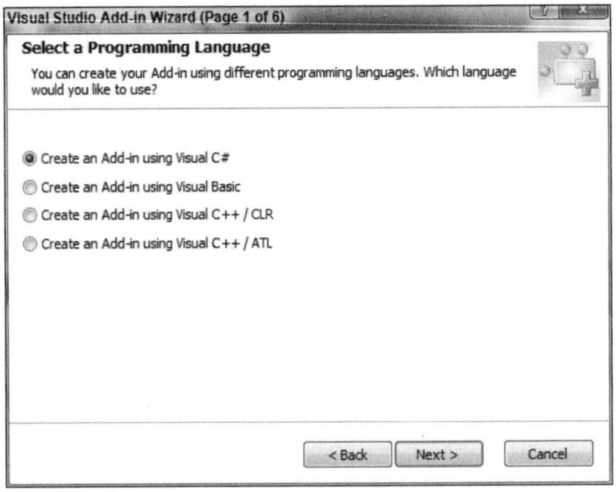

Figure 52-3

In the second step you choose an application host for your add-in. Two application hosts are available for your add-ins: the Visual Studio IDE and the Visual Studio Macros IDE (Figure 52-4). You can check or uncheck each host to select or deselect it. Your add-in is available to the application host(s) that you choose here.

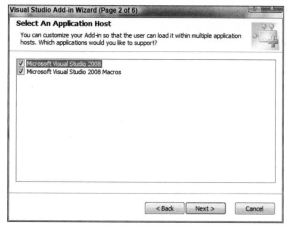

Figure 52-4

Page 3 is where you enter a name and description for your add-in (Figure 52-5). This information is what end users see in the Add-in Manager dialog in Visual Studio for your add-in.

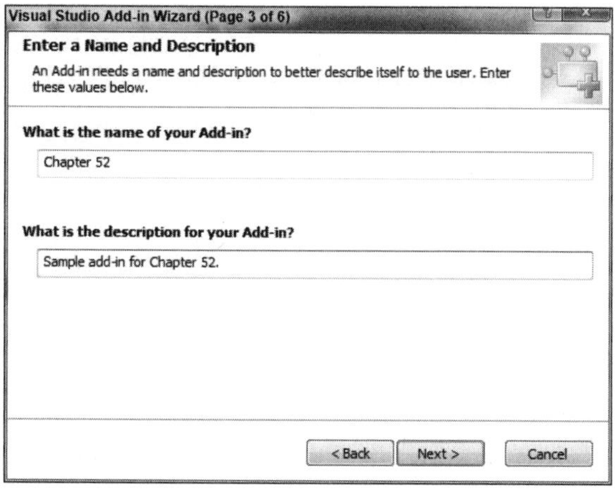

Figure 52-5

In the next step you see a page where you can choose some options for your add-in. There are three options that you can check to include in your add-in (Figure 52-6). The first option specifies that your add-in can have a user interface element as an item in the Tools menu. If you check this item, then the item appears in that menu. The second option indicates that you would like to load your add-in when the Visual Studio IDE or Visual Studio Macros IDE starts, and the third option indicates that your add-in doesn't show any modal user interfaces, and thus can be used with command-line builds.

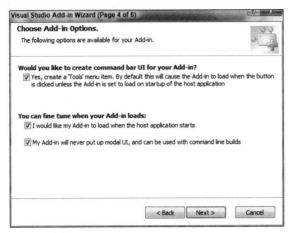

Figure 52-6

On Page 5 you can enable an About box for your add-in and enter a text description for it (Figure 52-7). The description appears in the About box for the Visual Studio IDE as a separate product.

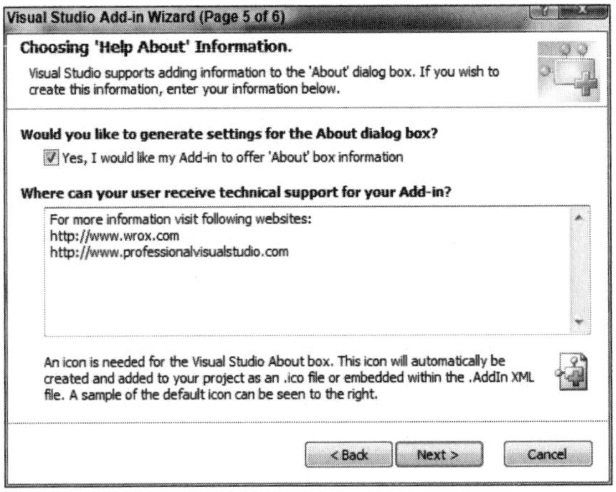

Figure 52-7

In the last page you just see a summary of what you have chosen in your wizard (Figure 52-8). At this stage, you can go back and change your options or click the Finish button to generate the solution and initial code for your add-in.

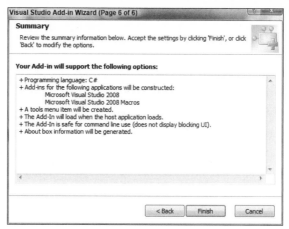

Figure 52-8

After clicking the Finish button, Visual Studio generates a solution with some files that you can use as a good starting point for your development. In the next sections you'll read more details about the anatomy of an add-in and the structure of these generated files.

The Anatomy of an Add-In

The Add-in Wizard generates a solution with a single project in it. This project contains a Connect.cs file, which is the main implementation file for the add-in, as well as two files with the .AddIn extension and a resource file for command bar resources.

The main parts of the add-in are the Connect.cs file and an .AddIn file. In earlier versions of Visual Studio you had to register the COM component by hand for an add-in on the machine, so deployment was harder than what you see in Visual Studio 2005 and 2008, but with the introduction of .AddIn files this process has been made simpler. .AddIn files are XML files that act as configuration files for add-ins. You'll read more about them in the next section, but for now let's focus on the add-in anatomy and the Connect.cs file.

First, look at the generated code for the Connect class:

```
using System;
using Extensibility;
using EnvDTE;
using EnvDTE80;
using Microsoft.VisualStudio.CommandBars;
using System.Resources;
using System.Reflection;
using System.Globalization;

namespace Chapter52
{
    public class Connect : IDTExtensibility2, IDTCommandTarget
    {
        public Connect()
        {
        }

        public void OnConnection(object application, ext_ConnectMode connectMode,
            object addInInst, ref Array custom)
        {
            _applicationObject = (DTE2)application;
            _addInInstance = (AddIn)addInInst;
            if (connectMode == ext_ConnectMode.ext_cm_UISetup)
            {
                object[] contextGUIDS = new object[] { };
                Commands2 commands = (Commands2)_applicationObject.Commands;
                string toolsMenuName;

                try
                {
                    //If you would like to move the command to a different menu,
change the word "Tools" to the
                    //  English version of the menu. This code will take the
culture, append on the name of the menu
                    //  then add the command to that menu. You can find a list of
all the top-level menus in the file
                    //  CommandBar.resx.
                    string resourceName;
                    ResourceManager resourceManager = new
ResourceManager("Chapter52.CommandBar",
                        Assembly.GetExecutingAssembly());
                    CultureInfo cultureInfo = new CultureInfo(_applicationObject
.LocaleID);

                    if (cultureInfo.TwoLetterISOLanguageName == "zh")
                    {
                        System.Globalization.CultureInfo parentCultureInfo =
cultureInfo.Parent;
                        resourceName = String.Concat(parentCultureInfo.Name, "Tools");
                    }
                    else
                    {
                        resourceName = String.Concat(cultureInfo
```

```
                .TwoLetterISOLanguageName, "Tools");
                        }
                        toolsMenuName = resourceManager.GetString(resourceName);
                }
                catch
                {
                        //We tried to find a localized version of the word Tools,
but one was not found.
                        //  Default to the en-US word, which may work
for the current culture.
                        toolsMenuName = "Tools";
                }

                //Place the command on the tools menu.
                //Find the MenuBar command bar, which is the top-level command
bar holding all the main menu items:
                Microsoft.VisualStudio.CommandBars.CommandBar menuBarCommandBar =
                        ((Microsoft.VisualStudio.CommandBars.CommandBars)_
applicationObject.CommandBars)["MenuBar"];

                //Find the Tools command bar on the MenuBar command bar:
                CommandBarControl toolsControl = menuBarCommandBar.
Controls[toolsMenuName];
                CommandBarPopup toolsPopup = (CommandBarPopup)toolsControl;

                //This try/catch block can be duplicated if you wish to add
multiple commands to be handled by your Add-in,
                //  just make sure you also update the QueryStatus/Exec method to
include the new command names.
                try
                {
                    //Add a command to the Commands collection:
                    Command command = commands.AddNamedCommand2(_addInInstance,
"Chapter52",
                        "Chapter52", "Executes the command for Chapter52", true, 59,
                        ref contextGUIDS, (int)vsCommandStatus.
vsCommandStatusSupported +
                        (int)vsCommandStatus.vsCommandStatusEnabled,
                        (int)vsCommandStyle.vsCommandStylePictAndText,
                        vsCommandControlType.vsCommandControlTypeButton);

                    //Add a control for the command to the tools menu:
                    if ((command != null) && (toolsPopup != null))
                    {
                        command.AddControl(toolsPopup.CommandBar, 1);
                    }
                }
                catch (System.ArgumentException)
                {
                    //If we are here, then the exception is probably because
a command with that name
                    //  already exists. If so there is no need to recreate
the command and we can
                    //  safely ignore the exception.
```

(continued)

(continued)

```csharp
                }
            }
        }

        public void OnDisconnection(ext_DisconnectMode disconnectMode,
ref Array custom)
        {
        }

        public void OnAddInsUpdate(ref Array custom)
        {
        }

        public void OnStartupComplete(ref Array custom)
        {
        }

        public void OnBeginShutdown(ref Array custom)
        {
        }

        public void QueryStatus(string commandName, vsCommandStatusTextWanted
neededText,
            ref vsCommandStatus status, ref object commandText)
        {
            if (neededText == vsCommandStatusTextWanted.
vsCommandStatusTextWantedNone)
            {
                if (commandName == "Chapter52.Connect.Chapter52")
                {
                    status = (vsCommandStatus)vsCommandStatus.
vsCommandStatusSupported |
                        vsCommandStatus.vsCommandStatusEnabled;
                    return;
                }
            }
        }

        public void Exec(string commandName, vsCommandExecOption executeOption,
            ref object varIn, ref object varOut, ref bool handled)
        {
            handled = false;
            if (executeOption == vsCommandExecOption.vsCommandExecOptionDoDefault)
            {
                if (commandName == "Chapter52.Connect.Chapter52")
                {
                    handled = true;
                    return;
                }
            }
        }
        private DTE2 _applicationObject;
        private AddIn _addInInstance;
    }
}
```

At first glance you notice that this class is implementing two interfaces: IDTExtensibility2 and IDTCommandTarget. IDTExtensibility2 is the interface that all add-ins must implement, but IDTCommandTarget is an interface that is implemented to display the Tools menu item. Based on your choices in Page 4 of the Add-in Wizard, your add-in code may be simpler than this and may not implement the IDTCommandTarget interface.

So, you can see that an add-in is a COM component that implements an IDTExtensibility2 interface. Figure 52-9 shows the structure of the Connect class in its simplest form (when it's not implementing IDTCommandTarget).

Figure 52-9

IDTExtensibility2 has five methods to implement that are actually five events in the add-in lifecycle. The structure of this interface is shown in Figure 52-10.

Figure 52-10

Here is a short description of the methods of IDTExtensibility2:

❑ OnAddInsUpdate: Occurs whenever an add-in is loaded or unloaded into or from Visual Studio

❑ OnBeginShutdown: Occurs whenever the Visual Studio IDE is shutting down so add-ins unload automatically

❑ OnConnection: Occurs whenever an add-in is loaded into the Visual Studio environment

❑ OnDisconnection: Occurs whenever an add-in is disconnected from Visual Studio

❑ OnStartupComplete: Occurs whenever an add-in is loaded when Visual Studio starts

Besides implementing interfaces, the `Connect` class also has two fields: one is `_applicationObject` of `DTE2` type and the other is `_addInInstance` of `AddIn` type. The `_applicationObject` gives you the access to the current instance of Development Tools Extensibility to be able to do lots of things, and `_addInInstance` gives some information and tools for the current instance of the add-in.

The `IDTCommandTarget` interface provides two methods that let you manage the process of displaying the Tools menu item, but this is just one of several results of its original goal, which is enabling you to execute commands in the IDE.

This interface has two methods:

❑ `QueryStatus`: Visual Studio calls this method to check whether there is any command associated and available for the add-in to execute. If there isn't, then the second method, `Exec`, can't be called.

❑ `Exec`: This method is called whenever the command associated with the add-in is called by the IDE or a user. In other words, if the add-in command runs somehow, then the `Exec` method is called to handle the command.

The last note before going to the next section is that you commonly implement your add-in logic in the `OnConnected` method of the add-in class, but there are still some cases where you need to use other methods to get access to specific events.

The Structure of .AddIn Files

Besides the add-in assembly, which is like its heart and contains all its implementation, there is also an XML file that acts as its configuration file with an `.AddIn` extension. This `.AddIn` file was first introduced in Visual Studio 2005 to simplify the process of add-in deployment. Prior to this version, you had to register the add-in COM component to deploy it, and this had its own difficulties. But now, thanks to `.AddIn` files, deployment is much easier.

An `.AddIn` file is an XML file with a specific schema that is defined by the `http://schemas .microsoft.com/AutomationExtensibility` namespace. When you create an XML file and set its XML namespace to this, Visual Studio automatically gives you IntelliSense to work with `.AddIn` files and edit them easily.

Like any other XML file, `.AddIn` files have their own special structure and format. Discussing all elements and attributes of this file is beyond the scope of this book, but you can find a detailed discussion about this file in Chapter 6 of *Professional Visual Studio Extensibility* (ISBN: 9780470230848).

Here in a nutshell is an introduction to the structure.

An `.AddIn` file has an `<Extensibility />` root element, which contains two possible child elements including `<HostApplication />` and `<Addin />`.

`<HostApplication />` defines a host application for an add-in and `<Addin />` configures the add-in with some information about it to set it up. Visual Studio looks into these elements to find the necessary information and load an add-in.

Let's finish the discussion about .AddIn files by pointing to a technique that can help you update Visual Studio 2005 add-ins to Visual Studio 2008. Generally, there haven't been any major changes in add-in development between Visual Studio 2005 and 2008, so many of the add-ins for Visual Studio 2005 should work with Visual Studio 2008. But they will need a modification in their .AddIn files for them to be loaded by Visual Studio 2008.

`<HostApplication />` has a child `<Version />` element that must be set to the version number of the compatible host application. For a Visual Studio add-in there are two possible host applications, including Visual Studio IDE and Visual Studio Macros IDE that both use the same version numbers. For Visual Studio 2005 the `<Version />` element was set to 8.0 (the internal version number of Visual Studio 2005) and for Visual Studio 2008 it must be set to 9.0. So if you have an existing Visual Studio 2005 add-in and are sure its code can work with Visual Studio 2008, then you can simply update it by modifying these version numbers to 9.0.

Develop an Add-In

A common step in building an add-in is developing it. Many common steps of the add-in creation process are automated by the Add-in Wizard, Visual Studio templates, and other tools, but you still need to write your own programming code to get what you desire from an add-in.

This development process depends on your requirements and your programming language and programming knowledge, but overall the development process is similar for all programming languages and add-ins.

As in other development projects, you can use classes, modules, methods, and other programming concepts to write an add-in, but the important point is the right usage of add-in methods to make them work. There are five methods (related to five events) in the add-in lifecycle that you need to apply in order to start and activate your add-in. There are also two methods for command handling and showing user interface elements.

To get started with the development process for an add-in, you can look at the following quick example covering the main aspects of add-in development. In this example you learn how to develop an add-in that lets you copy a piece of selected text in an editor to a clipboard.

After creating the add-in project and checking the checkboxes to include Tools menu items, you have an initial generated code to get started with. To write such an add-in you need to handle the command associated with the add-in in the `Exec` method in order to copy the selected text to the clipboard.

The following code is an updated version of the generated code you saw earlier to add this functionality. Notice the highlighted code:

```csharp
using System;
using Extensibility;
using EnvDTE;
using EnvDTE80;
using Microsoft.VisualStudio.CommandBars;
using System.Resources;
using System.Reflection;
using System.Globalization;
using System.Windows.Forms;

namespace Chapter52
{
    public class Connect : IDTExtensibility2, IDTCommandTarget
    {
        public Connect()
        {
        }

        public void OnConnection(object application, ext_ConnectMode connectMode,
            object addInInst, ref Array custom)
        {    // This method hasn't been modified.    }

        public void OnDisconnection(ext_DisconnectMode disconnectMode,
ref Array custom) {          }

        public void OnAddInsUpdate(ref Array custom){          }

        public void OnStartupComplete(ref Array custom){          }

        public void OnBeginShutdown(ref Array custom){          }

        public void QueryStatus(string commandName, vsCommandStatusTextWanted
neededText,
            ref vsCommandStatus status, ref object commandText)
        {    // This method hasn't been modified.    }

        public void Exec(string commandName, vsCommandExecOption executeOption,
            ref object varIn, ref object varOut, ref bool handled)
        {
            handled = false;
            if (executeOption == vsCommandExecOption.vsCommandExecOptionDoDefault)
            {
                if (commandName == "Chapter52.Connect.Chapter52")
                {
                    CopyToClipboard();

                    handled = true;
                    return;
                }
            }
        }
    }
```

```
        private void CopyToClipboard()
        {
            TextSelection selection = this._applicationObject.ActiveDocument.
Selection as TextSelection;

            Clipboard.SetText(selection.Text);
        }


        private DTE2 _applicationObject;
        private AddIn _addInInstance;
    }
}
```

Note that there is a new method call added to the Exec method in order to copy the selected text to the clipboard. In the CopyToClipboard method you see a very simple code that uses the TextSelection class in the code model (which is a smaller model in the automation model) to get access to the selected text in the editor. There isn't enough space here to discuss this object and other objects in the automation model, but the code should be self-explanatory.

Now you can open a document in the Visual Studio editor (whether it be a text file, code file, or any other material) and select a text like what you see in Figure 52-11.

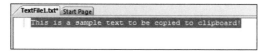

Figure 52-11

If you run the add-in, your selected text should be copied to the clipboard and you can paste it somewhere to see the result. Figure 52-12 shows the selected text that is pasted from the clipboard to Notepad.

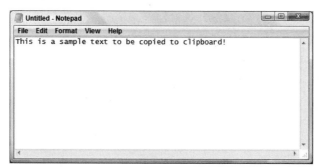

Figure 52-12

Debugging

Debugging an add-in may look harder than normal .NET applications because you're developing add-ins with Visual Studio and need to debug them in Visual Studio. So how to work around this?

In Visual Studio there is an option for debugging your projects that involves starting an external program in order to run the project. This option is in the Start Action section in the Debug tab of project properties (Figure 52-13).

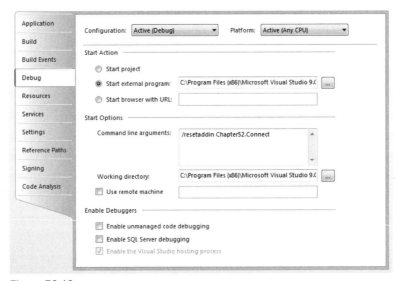

Figure 52-13

By default, an add-in project is set up to use the Visual Studio IDE to run the output of the project and debug it. So when you choose to debug an add-in project (whether by choosing appropriate menu items or by pressing F5 on the keyboard), the Visual Studio IDE shows up with the add-in enabled for you to test it.

As with any other .NET code, you can insert breakpoints in your code and run the add-in to debug your code, then use some options like visualizers or the watch window to monitor the values of variables, objects, and methods to see what's wrong with your code.

Deployment

Deployment of a Visual Studio add-in was harder before Visual Studio 2005, but thanks to the simplification of the deployment process in this version and the introduction of .AddIn files, deployment has been made much simpler.

To deploy an add-in you need to copy two files for the add-in to specified paths. One file is the assembly DLL file for an add-in and the second file is its .AddIn file. When you deploy both of these files in a specified path and load the Visual Studio IDE, the add-in is actually deployed and you can start using it.

To deploy an add-in for the current user of a machine, you need to deploy these files to the Add-ins folder in the Visual Studio folder installation path, in the personal documents folder. The personal documents folder is My Documents in Windows 2000, XP, and 2003, and Documents in Windows Vista.

You can automate this deployment by using a setup project that copies these two files to the specified folder on the end user's machine, or you can use the Visual Studio Content Installer, which is simpler and automatically deploys add-in files to specified paths. The Visual Studio Content Installer is a great option to deploy some common extensions for Visual Studio just by adding them to a single package and adding an XML configuration file for the installer.

After deploying your add-ins, they should appear in the Add-in Manager dialog available in the Tools menu in the Visual Studio IDE (Figure 52-14).

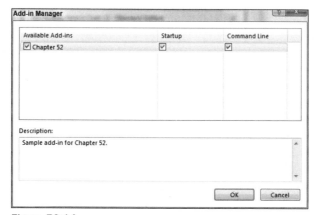

Figure 52-14

This dialog lets you enable or disable add-ins in the IDE. You can do this just by checking or unchecking the checkbox before the name of the add-in. You can also enable or disable the ability of the add-in to load with the IDE startup or run from the command line.

Shared Add-Ins

Besides Visual Studio add-ins you have another type of add-in called the shared add-in. Shared add-ins let you build add-ins for Microsoft Office products in a way similar to building an add-in for the Visual Studio IDE.

You can create shared add-in projects by choosing the Shared Add-in project template in the New Project dialog in Visual Studio and passing the same wizard that you saw for Visual Studio add-ins. In general, there aren't many differences between Visual Studio add-ins and shared add-ins. One of the differences is in the name and the numbers of host applications for a shared add-in. The generated code and development process for shared add-ins is similar to Visual Studio add-ins, but to develop a shared add-in you need to use Microsoft Office APIs rather than the automation model and the DTE.

However, because this book targets Visual Studio, we won't go any further into the topic of shared add-ins. You should be able to get started with them just by having this background in Visual Studio add-ins.

Summary

After talking about the automation model in Chapter 51, in this chapter you were introduced to Visual Studio add-ins and learned how to build, debug, and deploy them in general.

After getting an introduction to the add-ins and their applications, you saw a step-by-step guide on how to use the Add-in Wizard in Visual Studio to generate a starting code for yourself. After that you learned about the anatomy of an add-in and the generated code for your add-ins, as well as the structure of an .AddIn file as an XML file that acts like a configuration file for your add-ins.

After this basic information you saw a simple example to teach you about the development process for an add-in. Finally, you read some notes about the debugging and deployment of add-ins and finished the chapter by being introduced to shared add-ins.

53

Macros

The last chapter of this part of the book is dedicated to macros. Like add-ins, macros are a very common extensibility option in Visual Studio and a built-in one. Macros are the best way to automate a task in the Visual Studio IDE.

Repetitive tasks are a common part of our daily lives, and programming is no exception. The growing number of these tasks yields many tools and applications to automate them. Many code-generation tools and applications for automating parts of programming have been introduced in recent years.

Visual Studio is an old development IDE that is being used by many developers around the world and can be used for various purposes and different application types. One of the main positive points about Microsoft products is their usability for end users, so Microsoft was one of the first companies that introduced tools for automating repetitive tasks in its products. One of the main automation options in such Microsoft products as Visual Studio, Microsoft Office, Microsoft Word, Microsoft Excel, and some other IDEs and tools was the macro.

The nice point about macros is that they can be generated by the macro recorder and can also be developed with programming tools, so someone without any knowledge of programming can also create a macro.

The topic of this chapter is macros in Visual Studio. You'll read some helpful information about macros, including the following:

- ❑ The anatomy of a macro
- ❑ Macro Explorer windows in the Visual Studio IDE
- ❑ Visual Studio Macros IDE
- ❑ How to record a macro

❑ How to develop a macro

❑ How to run a macro

❑ How to deploy a macro

Let's get started with an introduction to macros by discussing the anatomy of a macro.

The Anatomy of a Macro

A Visual Studio macro (it's actually called VSMacro but is commonly known just as a macro among developers) is a stand-alone package of uncompiled code that can be run by the Visual Studio IDE to automate a task.

In fact, a macro is a piece of code and nothing else. Visual Studio has a specific extension for macro packages. A file with the .vsmacros extension is a macro package and is a known extension to Visual Studio.

A .vsmacros file can contain several components. One of these components is code modules. A code module can contain one or more macros, so you can include as many macros as you like in a .vsmacros file.

A macro itself is a public method in a module that takes no parameter and returns nothing and applies the Development Tools Extensibility (DTE) API to automate something in the IDE.

The nature of macros (which are code packages) makes their deployment a little difficult. You need to move and import the package in order to deploy a macro. This is covered later in the chapter.

You saw that a macro is a subroutine without parameters but can apply any object-oriented programming concept like class or enumeration types to get its job done. You can include other classes and modules to divide your code into smaller pieces and make your job easier.

When working with macros you don't have to deal with the same concepts like solutions and projects as you have to in the Visual Studio IDE. Instead, you have to deal with a Visual Studio macros system that works as a single root solution for all macros. This system includes your macro projects that are actually separate .vsmacros files. Each project consists of one or more modules, classes, and other programming material.

Moreover, you don't need to build and compile a macro project because a macro is a piece of code that Visual Studio runs on demand.

There is only one development language that you can use to write macro code and that is Visual Basic. Previously you had to use Visual Basic for Applications (VBA) to write a macro code for Visual Studio or Microsoft Office, but after the birth of .NET you can simply use Visual Basic to do this.

Macro Explorer

The first element of the Visual Studio IDE that comes in handy when working with macros and assists you in dealing with them is the Macro Explorer window (Figure 53-1), which is a built-in Visual Studio window like many other windows including the Solution Explorer, Toolbox, and Properties windows.

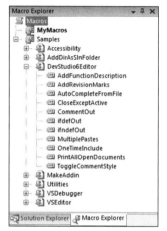

Figure 53-1

Macro Explorer is an equivalent to the Macro dialog for Solution Explorer and lets you navigate between macro projects, macro modules, and macros in order to apply some common tasks to them.

Note that Macro Explorer doesn't let you do as many things as you can do in the Macros IDE (which is described in the next section), but it's a quick and easy way for common tasks. For example, you can load and unload a macro project or run a macro via this window and open a module or edit a module or macro in the Macros IDE.

Generally, even though Macro Explorer is very handy and helpful, the Macros IDE is the main place for macro development.

Macros IDE

The Visual Studio Macros IDE is an IDE very similar to the Visual Studio IDE but independent from it. The Macros IDE has the same look and feel as the Visual Studio IDE, as you can see in Figure 53-2.

Figure 53-2

The Visual Studio Macros IDE is independent from the Visual Studio IDE. It has a similar look and feel but can't run as a stand-alone program and can only be loaded via Visual Studio.

The Macros IDE has some user interface elements that are similar to what you have in the Visual Studio IDE. Working with this IDE is similar to working with the main Visual Studio IDE, and you don't need to worry about it. There are some windows like Toolbox, Properties, Task List, and Error List that do the same things as those windows in the main IDE.

You can create macro projects to develop a macro in this IDE or open existing macros to edit them in the editor.

There is a Project Explorer window that works like Solution Explorer in the main Visual Studio IDE and provides more functionality than Macro Explorer in the Visual Studio IDE.

How to Record a Macro

When it comes to macros, one of the very cool features of Microsoft products is the capability of recording a macro with a macro recorder without having any knowledge of programming. The macro recorder records whatever you do in an IDE and then generates all the necessary programming code for you to use it.

Visual Studio has a built-in macro recorder as well. Even though we can be almost sure that users of Visual Studio IDE are technical developers, this recorder is still helpful for two reasons:

❑   It can help a developer build a macro in less time rather than spending his or her time on writing programming code.

❑   With the macro recorder you can generate an initial code for your macro, then start developing your macro based on this existing code. This is a common technique among developers to save the time and energy it would take to write all the code.

Using the macro recorder is easy. You need to open the Visual Studio IDE, then navigate to Tools ⇨ Macros ⇨ Record TemporaryMacro or simply press Ctrl+Shift+R to start recording a macro. Then do whatever you like in the IDE such as opening items, windows, or menus, and many other common tasks.

When you open the macro recorder a window appears in the IDE to let you work with the macro recorder and pause, stop, cancel, or continue recording the macro (Figure 53-3).

Figure 53-3

After recording your macro, you can stop the recording process and then open the generated TemporaryMacro in the Macros IDE to see the code. You can also rename this macro to a more relevant name for your needs. This macro is recorded in a module named RecordingModule in the MyMacros project by default, but you can move it to other projects or rename the module.

For example, the following code shows a macro that simply opens a Task List window for view:

```
Option Strict Off
Option Explicit Off
Imports System
Imports EnvDTE
Imports EnvDTE80
Imports EnvDTE90
Imports System.Diagnostics

Public Module RecordingModule
    Sub TemporaryMacro()
        DTE.ExecuteCommand("View.TaskList")
    End Sub
End Module
```

You can see how the macro recorder converts your actions to Visual Basic programming code. This is very handy and helpful in saving you time while building macros.

Even though the macro recorder is an excellent tool, don't forget that it can't accomplish all professional tasks. A professional macro may need hand-written code to make full use of the Development Tools Extensibility (DTE).

How to Develop a Macro

Developing a macro with programming code is an easy task. You just write your code and debug it and don't need to worry about compilation and other stuff. You may notice that macro development is easier in comparison with other development scenarios like developing an add-in or a Windows application.

However, macro development applies your knowledge in object-oriented programming by using concepts like classes, modules, and methods to build a macro.

You can even use user interface elements like Windows Forms in your macros. This isn't a common scenario, but it can be done easily. As with a normal project, you add a reference to Windows Forms assemblies in your macro project, then add Windows Forms to your project and load them in your code. However, here we won't get into details about this here.

The best way to understand the development process is by seeing an example. Here you see an example that is a built-in part of Visual Studio. The accessibility module located in the Samples macro project that comes with the default Visual Studio installation is a module that contains a few macros to improve the accessibility of the Visual Studio IDE by changing the size of fonts and their colors. The code for this module is shown here:

```
Imports EnvDTE
Imports System
Imports EnvDTE80
Imports System.Diagnostics
Imports Microsoft.Win32

Public Module Accessibility

    Private Const fontSizeIncrement As Integer = 2
    Private Const minimumSupportedEditorSize As Integer = 3
    Private whiteColor As UInt32 = Convert.ToUInt32(&HFFFFFF) ' FFFFFF is hex value
of the RGB color white.
    Private blackColor As UInt32 = Convert.ToUInt32(0)        ' 0 is the value of
the RGB color white.

    ' Changes the font size to match the font size of the operating system.
    Public Sub UpdateTextEditorFontSizeToMatchDisplayProperties()
        Dim textEditorFontsAndColors As Properties
        Dim font As System.Drawing.Font
        Dim pointSize As Integer
        Dim fontSize As [Property]

        ' Get font size from menu font to use as an approximation.
```

```
        font = System.Windows.Forms.SystemInformation.MenuFont
        pointSize = font.GetHeight() - 3 ' Subtract 3 for adjustment.

        ' Update the text edit font size.
        textEditorFontsAndColors = DTE.Properties("FontsAndColors", "TextEditor")
        fontSize = textEditorFontsAndColors.Item("FontSize")
        fontSize.Value = pointSize
    End Sub


    ' Increases the font size used within the editor.
    Public Sub IncreaseTextEditorFontSize() ' Useful to bind to a keystroke, like
Ctrl+Alt+Shift+DownArrow.
        Dim textEditorFontsAndColors As Properties

        textEditorFontsAndColors = DTE.Properties("FontsAndColors", "TextEditor")
        textEditorFontsAndColors.Item("FontSize").Value += fontSizeIncrement
    End Sub


    ' Decreases the font size used within the editor.
    Public Sub DecreaseTextEditorFontSize() ' Useful to bind to a keystroke, like
Ctrl+Alt+Shift+UpArrow.
        Dim textEditorFontsAndColors As Properties
        Dim fontSize As [Property]

        textEditorFontsAndColors = DTE.Properties("FontsAndColors", "TextEditor")
        fontSize = textEditorFontsAndColors.Item("FontSize")
        If fontSize.Value >= minimumSupportedEditorSize Then
            fontSize.Value -= fontSizeIncrement
        End If
    End Sub


    ' Turns all colors used within the editor to black and white, or
    '    restores the colors used before the colors were turned black and white.
    Public Sub ToggleTextEditorGrayScale()
        Dim applicationRegistryRootKey As RegistryKey
        Dim accessibilityKey As RegistryKey
        Dim textEditorFontsAndColors As Properties
        Dim fontsAndColors As FontsAndColorsItems
        Dim editorInGrayScale As Boolean

        ' Determine whether the user has toggled grayscale by looking up info in
registry.
        applicationRegistryRootKey = Registry.CurrentUser.OpenSubKey
(DTE.RegistryRoot, True)
        accessibilityKey = applicationRegistryRootKey.OpenSubKey
("Accessibility", True)

        ' Create key if it does not exist.
        If accessibilityKey Is Nothing Then
            applicationRegistryRootKey.CreateSubKey("Accessibility")
```

(continued)

(continued)

```
                accessibilityKey = applicationRegistryRootKey.OpenSubKey
("Accessibility", True)
                accessibilityKey.SetValue("TextEditorInGrayScale", 0)
        End If

        ' Get current editor grayscale state.
      ' editorInGrayScale = CType(accessibilityKey.GetValue
("TextEditorInGrayScale"), Boolean)

        ' Get the Fonts and Colors object.
        textEditorFontsAndColors = DTE.Properties("FontsAndColors", "TextEditor")
        fontsAndColors = textEditorFontsAndColors.Item("FontsAndColorsItems")
.Object

        ' Determine whether grayscale settings or previous settings should be
applied.
        If editorInGrayScale Then
            ' Revert to previous colors found from the registry.
            For Each displayItem As ColorableItems In fontsAndColors
                displayItem.Background = UInt32.Parse(accessibilityKey.GetValue
(displayItem.Name + "_BG"))
                displayItem.Foreground = UInt32.Parse(accessibilityKey.GetValue
(displayItem.Name + "_FG"))
            Next

            ' Toggle flag in registry to indicate text editor is not in gray scale
state.
            accessibilityKey.SetValue("TextEditorInGrayScale", 0)
        Else
            ' Write current colors into registry and apply grayscale.
            For Each displayItem As ColorableItems In fontsAndColors
                accessibilityKey.SetValue(displayItem.Name + "_BG", displayItem
.Background.ToString)
                accessibilityKey.SetValue(displayItem.Name + "_FG", displayItem
.Foreground.ToString)
                displayItem.Background = whiteColor
                displayItem.Foreground = blackColor
            Next

            ' Toggle flag in registry to indicate text editor is in gray scale
state.
            accessibilityKey.SetValue("TextEditorInGrayScale", 1)
        End If
    End Sub

    ' Makes tool windows appear in the MDI document space.
    Public Sub MaximizeToolWindowsInEnvironment()
        For Each window As Window In DTE.Windows
            ' Check that this is a tool window and not a document window.
```

```
        If (window.Document Is Nothing) Then
            ' Turn off auto-hiding.
            Try
                If window.AutoHides = True Then
                    window.AutoHides = False
                End If
            Catch exception As Exception
            End Try

            ' Set to undockable (which means show the document as maximized).
            Try
                window.Linkable = False
            Catch
            End Try
        End If
    Next
End Sub

End Module
```

Let's take a quick look at this module to get some information about macro development.

First, you see a few definitions for private constants and fields in the code. Then there are five public subroutines without any parameters, which are actually five macros that accomplish different tasks. Code comments make the code more readable and easier to understand, but as a case study let's determine the code for the UpdateTextEditorFontSizeToMatchDisplayProperties macro.

This macro changes the font size for the Visual Studio IDE to match the font size of the system.

It defines four variables for its work. First it gets the system font size by calling the `System.Windows .Forms.SystemInformation.MenuFont`. Then it reduces the height of the font size. The next step is to get the font and color properties of the Visual Studio text editor by calling the `Properties` method of the `DTE` object and passing the string names of the property and object names.

This `Properties` object contains a list of some properties for its own. Its `FontSize` property can be updated to change the font size for the editor at the last stage.

The second macro is IncreaseTextEditorFontSize, which increases the text editor font size by a constant value to make it more readable. This macro is simpler and uses the same approach to get access to the `FontsAndColors` property of the text editor. It then increases the `FontSize` property by the `fontSizeIncrement` constant value.

The last example is the MaximizeToolWindowsInEnvironment macro. This macro maximizes all tool windows in the IDE in the MDI space.

This macro first iterates through all the Windows instances in Visual Studio that are accessible via the `DTE.Windows` property. In each iteration, it checks for the `Document` property of the window to see if it's null, because if this property is null then the window is a tool window, not a document window.

Inside the if case it checks for the `AutoHides` property of the window and sets it to false, then sets the `Linkable` property to false. This latter property maximizes the window.

Before finishing the discussion about macro development it's worthwhile to point out that macro debugging is similar to debugging any other type of .NET application. You simply start your macro project in debug mode by pressing F5 or choosing appropriate menu items in the Macros IDE. You can use the same debugging tools like breakpoints and visualizers in your macro projects as well.

Running a Macro

There are some options to run a macro, but before listing them suppose that you have a very simple macro that updates the text-in-progress bar like what you see in the following code:

```
Imports System
Imports EnvDTE
Imports EnvDTE80
Imports EnvDTE90
Imports System.Diagnostics

Public Module Chapter53
    Sub SetStatusText()
        DTE.StatusBar.Text = "Wrox Professional Visual Studio 2008"
    End Sub
End Module
```

Here are the options to run a macro:

❑   Double-click the name of the macro in Macro Explorer.

❑   Press F5 or Ctrl+F5 in the Macros IDE when the cursor is inside the macro code.

❑   Associate a command in the IDE with a macro to run it via a comment.

❑   Run the macro via programming code when appropriate.

Usually you work with the first two options in your daily job, but the third and fourth options are also helpful for very common macros.

For example, if you double-click the name of the SetStatusText macro in Macro Explorer to update the status text, you will get an output like that shown in Figure 53-4.

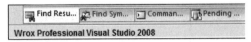

Figure 53-4

When you run a macro, a tape icon then appears in the bottom-right corner of the IDE and in the task bar. To examine this icon, which normally hides quickly, you can run a macro like the following code to keep the icon for a few seconds:

```
Imports System
Imports EnvDTE
Imports EnvDTE80
Imports EnvDTE90
Imports System.Diagnostics

Public Module Chapter53
    Sub ShowTapeIcon()
        System.Threading.Thread.Sleep(10000)
    End Sub
End Module
```

When you run this macro, the tape icon appears for a longer time in the task bar (Figure 53-5).

Figure 53-5

If you right-click this icon, you can stop running macros.

Deployment

As stated in the first sections of the chapter, the structure of a macro is different from normal applications and it's a stand-alone code package that can't be compiled into binary form.

A macro package with a .vsmacros extension must be deployed to the end user's machine in order to let the user use the macros included in the package. These files must be deployed to a specified path on the destination machine.

Macros must be deployed to the VSMacros80 folder located in the Projects folder of your Visual Studio 2008 folder in personal documents. The personal documents name is Documents in Windows Vista and My Documents in Windows XP or 2003. The path for your projects can be changed in Visual Studio via the Options dialog.

You can automate the deployment process with a Windows installer setup or Visual Studio Content Installer setup files to avoid deploying the macro packages manually.

Summary

In the third and last chapter of this part of the book you read about macros as the easiest and fastest way to automate some tasks in the Visual Studio IDE.

You explored briefly all the major topics concerning macros and got started with them. First you read about the anatomy of macros and their structure, then learned about Macro Explorer and the Macros IDE as two common and important Visual Studio elements and tools that aid you with macros.

After this basic information, you read about recording macros with the Visual Studio macro recorder and developing macros with programming code.

Obviously you need to know how to run a macro and deploy it to other machines, so the final sections of this chapter were dedicated to these topics.

Visual Studio automation and extensibility is a wider topic than what you saw in this part of the book, but it covered all the major topics that you need to get started. Visual Studio Extensibility is a major category of its own in the .NET community, and you may be interested in following this topic in more detail.

Part XII

Visual Studio Team System

VSTS: Architect Edition

The Architect Edition aids in designing applications and datacenters, as well as planning for the deployment of these applications. This is not another UML tool. It goes far beyond what simple diagrams could give us. Thanks to the tight integration with the platform and IDE, the artifacts used for the diagrams will translate nicely to other concepts already used. The diagrams go from simple documents to definitions that can actually be validated to see ahead from day one.

This chapter covers the different diagrams used to model Distributed Systems. To start, you look at the Application Designer and see how you can model the communication paths. Then you see how the Logical Datacenter Designer (LDD) allows you to define a view of your servers and the way you connect them through the different communication boundaries. Also, you see how an LDD can constrain servers to host only certain kinds of applications or allow for only certain communications. Finally, you see how the Deployment and System Designer will map applications and systems to servers and allow you to evaluate how the deployment meets the constraints and settings of both the applications and servers.

All designers include general tools to add comments and connections and to zoom in and out. You can add diagrams by right-clicking the solution and selecting Add New Distributed System Diagram from the Add menu. There you have three options: Application Diagram (AD), Logical Datacenter Diagram (LDD), and System Diagram (SD). There's a fourth type, the Deployment Diagram (DD), but this is created from the AD or SD.

Case Study

During this chapter you will be architecting a solution for a hypothetical customer. He has three plants around the world. The corporate office located in Torreon, Mexico, has the main datacenter and will be exposing existing services from a corporate directory and SAP. It also has a manufacturing system that you can use through a proprietary API. You will build a new Corporate Portal and a WPF planning application that will consume different services and will be run from all the offices.

To start the project, your Solution Architect will have to work with the customer's infrastructure architect to plan for deployment and be sure you can get access to all the services you need.

Keep in mind that the proposed solution is meant to show the different features of the Distributed System Diagrams and not act as guidance or show good architectural patterns.

Application Designer

The Application Diagrams will be used to configure and connect applications to each other. To create one, you can select File ⇨ New Project, and in the Distributed System Diagram choose Application Diagram. This will create a new solution with the Application Diagram. If you are starting with an existing solution, you can right-click it and choose Add ⇨ New Distributed System Diagram. This will look for projects you have in your solution and add them to the Application Diagram if those projects are compatible with the application types available.

From the Toolbox you have three categories. The first one, General Designer, is available for all the diagrams and includes the connection tool and comments. The Applications category includes application prototypes that will map to projects in your solution. You have eight types of applications. The Endpoints represent connection points between applications, and these are specific for the different prototypes — for example, you can use only a Web Content and .NET Web Service Endpoint in applications mapping to web sites or web applications.

> *You can extend the Application Designer to include custom application prototypes. Please see "Extending Distributed System Designers" on MSDN.*

For this case study you will start with a new solution and a new Application Diagram. Figure 54-1 shows the final result. We added a generic application to represent the Manufacturing system. The SAP Services and Corporate Directory are modeled as external web services, and when you add them you need to specify their WSDLs to define their endpoints. This is needed because the Application Designer will use it to create proxies for applications connecting to them. There's more behind these three pieces, but for this solution we only care about their interfaces — that's why we don't model the databases or other services used by this application.

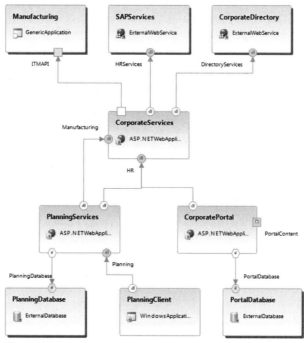

Figure 54-1

In the center we have a CorporateServices application modeled as an ASP.NET Web Application. It has consumer endpoints for the three applications we mentioned and has two provider endpoints that are consumed by the PlanningServices and the CorporatePortal. The PlanningServices application will connect to this database and provide services for the PlanningClient.

We can compare ADs to UML Component diagrams. You can think of endpoints as interfaces and applications as components, but the difference is that the AD will map directly to implementation concepts. You have the option to implement a specific application or all the applications defined in the diagram; when you do this, Visual Studio will create projects in the solution based on the selected template, proxies for its web service consumer endpoints, and web services for the web service provider endpoints. It will add a connection string to the configuration file for each database consumer endpoint. Other settings, specified in the Settings and Constraints Editor (described later), are also included in the config files. There are some prototypes that can't be implemented; for example, the external web services and the generic application we used are only references for the rest of our application.

Before implementing the projects you can change their names by selecting them and then making changes in the properties tool window. By default it will have the same name as the application. All applications are set to use Visual Basic, but you can change this from this window. You can also select a template to implement the prototype. For example, by default Visual Studio will use a WinForms project to implement your Windows application, but we chose to use a custom template and selected WPF. You can change other things like the namespace and framework version. Figure 54-2 shows the Solution Explorer with the applications implemented. As you can see, our PlanningClient was implemented using a WPF project, and a proxy for the planning endpoint was created.

Figure 54-2

For your web services provider endpoints you can define operations, similar to the way you add methods to a class in the Class Designer as you saw in Chapter 18. From the Properties window you can add attributes specific to web methods, like SOAP Action, Cache Duration, and Enable Session.

Logical Datacenter Designer

This designer is used to define the servers, zones, and ports. You create a Logical Datacenter Diagram (LDD for short) in a way similar to what you did for the Application Diagram in the last section. In the Toolbox you have Logical Servers, which include Generic Servers, Databases, IIS, Windows Clients, and Zones, that will allow you to define communication boundaries. Figure 54-3 shows the LDD created by our customer's Infrastructure Architect; later we will use it as a base for our Deployment Diagram.

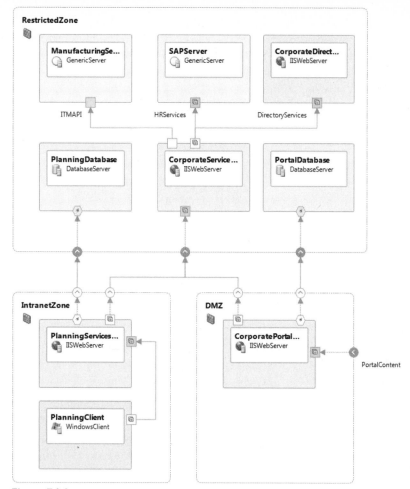

Figure 54-3

LDDs are similar to UML Deployment Diagrams except that the former is used to model logical environments and the latter is used for modeling physical environments. In LDDs you can capture additional details of the servers and endpoints using the Settings and Constraints Editor (explained later). This will help you validate that your applications can effectively be deployed to the logical servers.

You can right-click an IIS web server and select Import Settings. A wizard will guide you to get the entire current configuration from a particular machine — for example, application pools, authentication mode, and web sites.

Deployment Designer

The Deployment Diagram is used to specify which applications each logical server will host. To create one of these, you need to first have an Application and a Logical Datacenter Diagram. To add it, right-click the design surface of the Application Diagram and select Define Deployment. You will need to select an LDD to validate against. This will create a new diagram based on the LDD but with additional space on each server to add applications. In this case you won't work from the Toolbox; you need to open the system view from the menu View ⇨ Other Windows ⇨ System View. In it you will have all the applications in your Application Diagram and can simply bind them to a server. Figure 54-4 shows the DD for our Application Diagram and LDD.

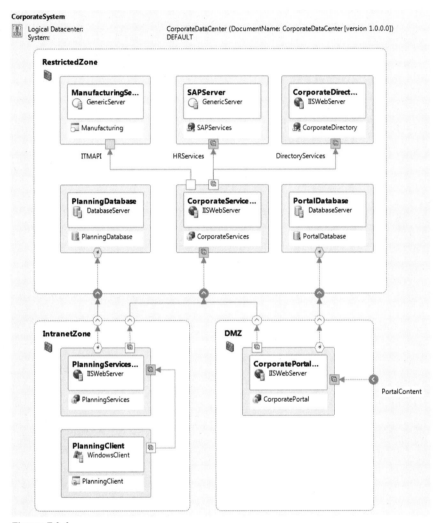

Figure 54-4

Settings and Constraints Editor

To simplify the explanation of the Application and Logical Datacenter diagrams we intentionally left out one of their most important features, Settings and Constraints. This is better understood from the context of the Deployment Diagram. When you have your applications inside your servers, as shown in

Figure 54-5, you can choose to validate the diagram (after right-clicking the design surface). This will ensure that all the settings in the Application Design match constraints in the Logical Datacenter Design, and that settings in the LDD match constraints in the AD.

To specify settings and constraints from View ⇨ Other Windows ⇨ Settings and Constraints, you can open the editor. Then, by selecting an application, endpoint, server, or zone, you can specify its settings and constraints. In the chapter's example for the WPF application, you need to specify that it needs to have Windows Vista, .NET 3.5, and Office 2007.

For the purposes of this hypothetical case, let's assume that these settings weren't specified in the LDD by the infrastructure architect, so that when you hit Validate you would clearly see that there were going to be problems and that you would need to talk these over with the (imagined) architect. If this were actually happening, he might tell you that .NET 3.5 isn't a problem, and he can install it in the clients; all his machines have Office 2003, but he can upgrade them to Office 2007, and he doesn't really need Vista — XP with SP2 is enough for the application.

This scenario could be extended, but the point of the story is to resolve such questions at the beginning of the project.

System Designer

The last step in having everything set up to start coding is to plan the deployment for the remaining offices. You have a system ready to be deployed at the corporate headquarters of your hypothetical company. But your planning application will be run from all the plants. The IT department from one of those plants might create an LDD for you to validate your application as shown in Figure 54-5.

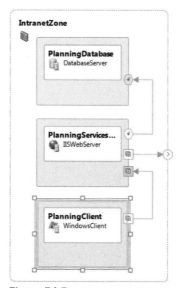

Figure 54-5

From your Application Diagram you'll create a new system, selecting the applications you'll need to separate as a new deployment unit. In this case choose PlanningServices, PlanningDatabase, and PlanningClient, and then click Design Application System from the context menu. You will have to add two Web Service Consumer Endpoints to the system boundary and connect them to the existing HR and Manufacturing endpoints. Figure 54-6 shows the end result for the planning system.

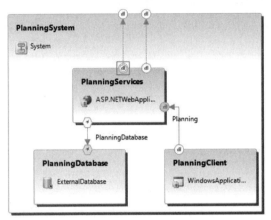

Figure 54-6

This system will be deployed to each plant, so you need to create new Deployment Diagrams. To do this, right-click the designer surface and select Define Deployment. For this example choose the LDD for a hypothetical plant in Sydney. Figure 54-7 shows the final Deployment Diagram for this plant. You can choose to validate to be sure your new system is compatible with the definitions in this LDD.

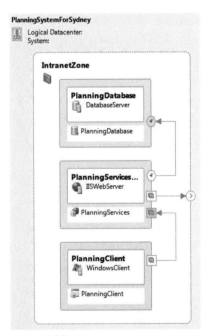

Figure 54-7

The System Designer will be based on your Application Diagram and will define systems that can be evaluated for deployment. A system is a deployment unit that includes other systems or applications. For each system you can override the application's configuration.

To create a System Diagram you can right-click your Application Diagram and select Design Application System or add a new Distributed System Diagram directly from the solution. With the first option you will start with all the applications already connected; with the second you will start from scratch designing your system. From both options you can remove endpoints and applications and override settings.

You can work in a bottom-up approach as we did in this case, starting from the Application Diagram and then creating the Planning System, or you could have started by defining the systems and subsystems and then their applications.

Summary

In this chapter you saw, through a hypothetical case study, what the flow would be between the different diagrams. You started by defining the services and applications needed for your solution. You implemented these to create Visual Studio projects, proxies, and configurations like connection strings. Then you revised the Logical Datacenter Diagrams, which will let you specify how logical servers will work and communicate. After that, you created a Deployment Diagram and analyzed how settings and constraints will impact the validation of these diagrams, ensuring that the application's requirements are met by the infrastructure, and that infrastructure constraints are compatible with the application's configuration. Finally, you saw how the System Designer would let you approach your solution in smaller, deployable pieces.

VSTS: Developer Edition

Many people would ask themselves, isn't Visual Studio 2008 a product for developers? Why do we need a Developer Edition of a developer tool? It's like saying there was a Halo 3 Gamer Edition. Well, as you can imagine, probably the gamer edition would have features for hardcore gamers. VSTS Developer Edition has advanced features mainly for quality improvement, like code metrics, static analysis, profiling tools, and code coverage. It's not that you can't develop quality software with other editions or that using these tools will make sure your software performs well. Obviously, there's more to it than using a few tools, but these can be of great help and will reduce the time invested in other tasks like code review and debugging.

Code Metrics

Code metrics will serve as a reference to know how maintainable your code is. This feature is new in Visual Studio 2008; in this version it comes with five metrics. All of them have to be looked at with care, and you have to set your own context at the time you evaluate your projects. Figure 55-1 shows the Code Metrics window for a sample project. You open this window from the Analyze ⇨ Windows ⇨ Code Metric Results menu. To calculate the metrics you should hit the button on the top-left corner. The Code Metrics window shows a hierarchy of the projects, namespaces, types, and members.

Directly from the list you can filter any of the metrics to show methods that fall within a specified range, export to Excel, configure columns to remove metrics, or create a work item. Export to Excel is particularly useful to generate reports using pivot tables or to work with a flat view of the information using filters and sorts. For example, if you want to look for methods with more than 15 lines of code, filtering directly in the Code Metrics window will get you a lot of namespaces and types, but you will have to expand each to see whether there are any methods, whereas in Excel you can easily filter out namespaces and types and only look at methods.

> *Work items are activities assigned to someone working on a team project. Team projects and work items are explained in more detail in Chapter 58.*

When you see each metric's detail, keep in mind that lower numbers are better for all the metrics except the Maintainability Index.

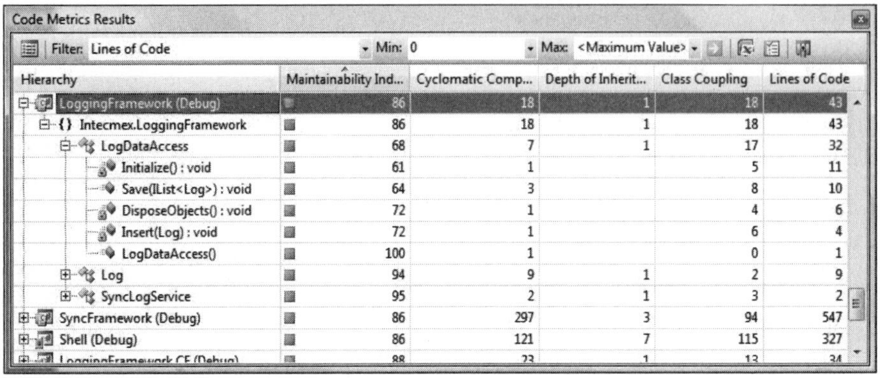

Code Metrics Results

Filter: Lines of Code · Min: 0 · Max: <Maximum Value>

Hierarchy	Maintainability Ind...	Cyclomatic Comp...	Depth of Inherit...	Class Coupling	Lines of Code
LoggingFramework (Debug)	86	18	1	18	43
Intecmex.LoggingFramework	86	18	1	18	43
LogDataAccess	68	7	1	17	32
Initialize() : void	61	1		5	11
Save(IList<Log>) : void	64	3		8	10
DisposeObjects() : void	72	1		4	6
Insert(Log) : void	72	1		6	4
LogDataAccess()	100	1		0	1
Log	94	9	1	2	9
SyncLogService	95	2	1	3	2
SyncFramework (Debug)	86	297	3	94	547
Shell (Debug)	86	121	7	115	327
LoggingFramework CF (Debug)	88	23	1	13	34

Figure 55-1

Lines of Code

The name is self-explanatory; however, it's worth mentioning that the purpose of this metric should be only to get a clue of the complexity of the code, and must *not* be used to measure progress. Clearly, a method with five lines of code that calls other methods will be simpler than if you inline all 25 lines of code in that method.

```
public class OrdersGenerator
{
public void GenerateOrder(Order order)
{
IsUnderCreditLimit(order);
IsCustomerBlocked(order.Customer);
AreProductsInStock(order);
IsCustomerBlocked(order);
SaveOrder(order);
}
// remaining methods are omitted.
}
```

If you compare a class with six methods as shown in the preceding code with a class having the same functionality, but with all the code inlined in one method, the latter will have 25 lines. Assuming the remaining methods have five lines each, the former will be 30 lines long although it is simpler. You have to be careful about how to consider this metric; a longer class might be better than a short one.

As you saw in Chapter 17, Extract Method refactoring can help you simplify the code.

Depth of Inheritance

This metric counts the base classes; some recommendations are to have a value lower than six. But this, like other metrics, has to be looked at with special care. It's hard to give a recommended value and it's relative to which classes you are inheriting from. If you inherit from LinkLabel, you will have a depth of 4, but your base classes are less likely to change than if you inherit from ProviderXComponent and have a depth of 1. It's more probable that ProviderX will change his component and break yours, while Microsoft will take more care not to break code. But you'll probably never update ProviderX's library. The point is that this metric is relative to what base classes you have.

Class Coupling

This counts the dependencies an item has on other types except for primitives and built-in types like Int32, object, and string. The more dependencies you have, the harder it's supposed to be to maintain, because it would be more probable that changes on other types will cause a break in your code. Similarly to depth of inheritance, the importance you give is relative to the dependencies you have. A class referencing System libraries is less likely to have a break than classes referencing other types on active development. You can see a value for this metric at each level of the hierarchy (project, namespace, type, and member).

Cyclomatic Complexity

The different branches a code may have, caused by such statements as if, do/while, for, and switch will cause your code to increase its cyclomatic complexity.

Maintainability Index

This index is calculated using a formula that considers cyclomatic complexity, lines of code, and the Halstead volume, which is a metric that considers the total and distinct number of operators and operands. It will give you a range between 0 and 100, the higher being the better.

Excluded Code

Code marked with the `CompilerGenerated` and `GeneratedCode` attributes won't be considered in the metrics. Datasets and WebServiceProxies are examples of code marked with the `GeneratedCode` attribute, but other generated code like WindowsForms isn't marked and will be considered in the metric's results.

Managed Code Analysis Tool

This is a tool based on FxCop, a Microsoft internal tool, released to the public a few years ago and finally integrated into the IDE. It will allow you to perform static code analysis using a set of rules. You can activate it from the project's property window as shown in Figure 55-2.

To use it you can right-click a project and select Run Code Analysis, or if you selected Enable Code Analysis on Build in the project's property window, you can simply compile it. The rules will be evaluated and if there is any violation (and believe me, there will be sooner or later) you will have a set of warnings in the Error List window. By default each violation will appear as a warning, but you can change this behavior by selecting Treat Warning as Error.

If you right-click a warning and select Show Error Help, you will have a description of the rule, the cause, steps on how to fix violations, and suggestions on when to suppress warnings.

You have more than 200 rules conveniently organized in 11 categories, and you can add custom rules if needed. Depending on your project, you might want to exclude some categories or some particular rules. For example, if you don't need globalization and don't have plans in the future to support it, you might exclude that category. Another option is to suppress a particular warning by right-clicking it in the Errors window.

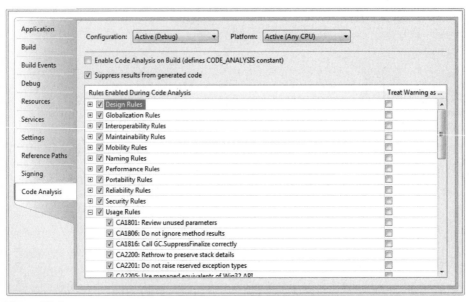

Figure 55-2

I recommend starting with all the rules activated and excluding them or suppressing warnings as needed (or even better, fixing violations). This is an excellent way of learning best practices. After a couple of iterations, new code written will be less prone to violate a rule.

> *The rules in the maintainability category complement the code metrics you saw in the last section.*

C/C++ Code Analysis Tool

This tool is similar to the Managed Code Analysis Tool, but works for unmanaged code. To activate it simply go to your C++ project's properties window, look for the Code Analysis node inside the Configuration Properties, and select Yes for the Enable Code Analysis for C/C++ on Build. Every time you compile your project, the tool will intercept the process and attempt to analyze each execution path.

It will help you detect crashes that are otherwise hard to find with other techniques like debugging that are very time consuming. It's able to detect memory leaks, uninitialized variables, pointer management problems, and buffer over/under runs.

Profiling Tools

Profiling tools will allow you to detect and correct performance and memory issues in your projects. The Profiler has two ways of getting its information. Sampling will periodically interrupt the application to capture its current state, and instrumentation will insert additional lines of codes to the selected assemblies. Instrumentation is more accurate but has more overhead than sampling.

The easiest way to start is by launching the Performance wizard from the Analyze menu. You need to select a project, executable, DLL, or web site to profile. Next you select the profiling type (sampling or instrumentation); you can start with sampling and change it later if you need to get more accurate results on a particular area. With that information, the Profiler wizard creates a performance session and opens the Performance Explorer window. You could also create a blank session from the Performance Explorer or from a test in the Test Results window.

In the Performance Explorer (Figure 55-3) you can change between instrumentation and sampling. Using the combo box, you could start the wizard again or manually create a new performance session. You could add targets to the performance session. Although you can instrument or sample a DLL, you need a point of entry for your application to run when you start the session, so be sure to include an executable, web site, or test as target.

Figure 55-3

Configuring Profiler Sessions

To configure your session, simply right-click and select Properties. In the General section you can change between sampling and instrumentation (Figure 55-4), and choose if you want to activate .NET memory profiling collection, the output for the reports, and the report names.

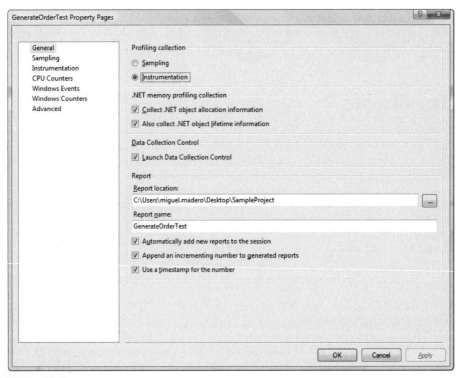

Figure 55-4

In the Sampling section you can select when to take samples; by default this is set to 10,000,000 clock cycles. Depending on what you want to track, you can change the sample event to page faults, system calls, or a particular performance counter.

The Instrumentation section is used to specify pre- and post-instrument events, for example to sign an assembly with a strong name. These settings are set on a per-target basis. The last section in the property page, Advanced, is also used when instrumentation is selected, and there you can specify additional command arguments. To see a list of available options, search for VSInstr on MSDN. VSInstr is the tool used to instrument binaries.

The remaining sections are used to specify the collection of different counters or events. CPU Counters will let you capture additional low-level information and will be displayed as extra columns in the different report views. These are only available for instrumentation. The Windows Counters are system performance counters and you will be able to see the results in the Marks report view. The Windows

Events section will let you specify event trace providers. To see the information on Windows events you would need to manually get a text report using the following command:

```
Vsperfreport c:\<path>ReportName.vsp /calltrace /output:c:\<path>
```

Reports

Once you are all set, you can start the application, test, or web site from the Performance Explorer. It will run as usual, but will be collecting data. Once your application terminates, a report will be generated. Table 55-1 shows a description of some of the report views.

Table 55-1: Some Report Views

Summary	Shows function information. Sampling it will show functions causing the most work and functions with the most individual work. With instrumentation it will show the most called functions with the most individual work and functions taking the longest. From here you can navigate to the Functions view. If "Collect .NET object allocation information" is selected as shown in Figure 55-4, it will show functions allocating the most memory and types with the most memory allocated and most instances.
Call Tree	Contains a hierarchy of the functions called. The Call Tree has a feature called Hot Spot that will point you to child functions taking most of the time.
Modules	Information about the module sampled or instrumented.
Caller/Callee	Will let you see which functions a particular function called and which functions called it.
Functions	Will present a list of all the functions sampled or instrumented. Double-clicking each function will let you navigate to the caller/callee window.
Allocations	You can see the number of instances and bytes allocated of a particular type.
Object Lifetime	Will show you how objects got cleaned on each generation.

Additional reports can be generated using the command tool VSPerfReport. For more information, you can consult the MSDN documentation.

Allocation and Object Lifetime are only available if you select "Collect .NET object allocation information" and "Also collect .NET object lifetime information," respectively, in the session's property page. Some of the report views are different depending on the configuration. To see a description of a particular column, simply hover over its title. I suggest you go through the documentation on MSDN to get a thorough description on each report.

In all the views you can use the filter from the Toolbar to get to specific information. You can add or remove columns by right-clicking a header and sort using a particular column. Reports can be exported to either XML or CSV.

Stand-Alone Profiler

This is a command-line tool useful when you need to profile an application without having to install Visual Studio on the machine — for example, in a production environment. To install this tool you need to execute vs_profiler.exe from the VSTS installation media located in the Standalone Profiler folder. It will install the tools in the directory `%ProgramFiles%\Microsoft Visual Studio 9.0\Team Tools\Performance Tools`. I suggest adding this path to the system path.

The following commands profile an application using sampling with the default settings. The first line enables the trace. Then you specify it to use sample and the output for the report. In this case the report will be saved in the ApplicationToProfile directory on a file named Report.vsp. Then you launch the application, interact with it as usual, and when you are done you finally shut down the Profiler. You can then open and inspect the generated report in Visual Studio.

```
C:\ApplicationToProfile>vsperfclrenv /traceon
Enabling VSPerf Trace Profiling of managed applications (excluding allocation
profiling).
. . .
C:\ApplicationToProfile>vsperfcmd -start:sample -output:Report
Microsoft (R) VSPerf Command Version 9.0.21022 x86
. . .
C:\ApplicationToProfile>vsperfcmd -launch:Application.exe
Microsoft (R) VSPerf Command Version 9.0.21022 x86
. . .
Successfully launched process ID:2896 Application.exe
C:\ApplicationToProfile>vsperfcmd -shutdown
Microsoft (R) VSPerf Command Version 9.0.21022 x86
. . .
Shutting down the Profile Monitor
```

Application Verifier

This tool allows the dynamic testing of unmanaged applications. It lets you troubleshoot handles, locks, and heaps. To configure it, go to the project properties window at the end of the Configuration Properties node and find the Application Verifier section as shown in Figure 55-5.

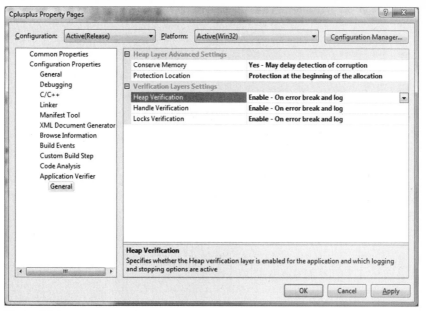

Figure 55-5

In this section you can specify if you want to conserve memory. If No is selected, a guard page will be inserted at the beginning or end of the allocation as selected in the Protection Location setting. These will detect buffer underruns and overruns.

The next three options specify how you want to handle the heap, handles, and locks. You have the options to disable the verification layer, break and log, log and continue, or simply break.

To start your program using Application Verifier, from the Debug menu select Start with Application Verifier. It will instrument your code and once it is run will verify different areas such as memory allocation and exceptions.

Code Coverage

This is a very useful tool. It will instrument the code to help you see which lines of code are really being executed. First, you need to have a Test Project on your solution. As an example you will use "Your First Test Case" described in Chapter 20. Assuming you already created the SubscriptionTest class and CurrentStatusTest is passing, you will now activate Code Coverage.

To open the TestRun properties window, you can double-click the LocalTestRun.testrunconfig file in Solution Explorer or go to the menu Test ⇨ Edit Test Run Configurations and select your active configuration. Figure 55-6 shows the Code Coverage options.

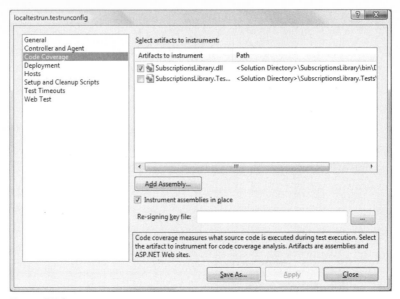

Figure 55-6

You need to select the assemblies to instrument. In case you are signing your assemblies, similar to the procedure when you are profiling using instrumentation, you need to resign them.

Now simply run your test and from the Test Results window right-click it and select Code Coverage. Figure 55-7 shows the Code Coverage window indicating the not-covered and covered blocks for each assembly, namespace, type, and member. Double-clicking a member will open the code file with the executed lines highlighted in blue (light shading in the figure) and untouched lines in red (darker shading in the figure) as shown in Figure 55-8.

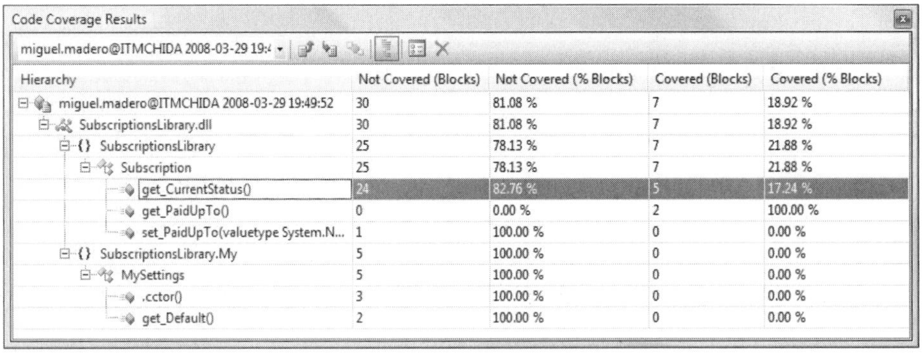

Figure 55-7

```
Public ReadOnly Property CurrentStatus() As Status
    Get
        If Not Me.PaidUpTo.HasValue Then Return Status.Temporary
        If Me.PaidUpTo.Value > Now Then
            Return Status.Financial
        Else
            If Me.PaidUpTo >= Now.AddMonths(-3) Then
                Return Status.Unfinancial
            Else
                Return Status.Suspended
            End If
        End If
    End Get
End Property
```

Figure 55-8

As you can see, the `get_CurrentStatus()` has 82.76 percent in not-covered blocks. The first option is evaluated and returned, so the remaining branches are never being touched. This is an indication that you will need additional test cases. This was covered in the "Data" section in Chapter 20 where you specify a DataSource with the additional input.

When you have code that is never touched, this can lead you to think three things:

❑　It is code that really isn't used and is only getting in your way, decreasing your project's maintainability. Solution: simply delete it.

❑　That code isn't being tested. Solution: create a new test.

❑　The code is so simple that there's probably no need to test it. Think twice about this, even for simple properties or methods. The code is likely to be referenced elsewhere in your application, in which case any errors in the code may cause issues elsewhere in your application. This is a good reason to write a new test case. Right-clicking the member and selecting Find All References can help you see if this is unused code, but it won't find references from data-bound properties or projects not in the solution.

It's not necessary to take this practice to an extreme and look for 100 percent Code Coverage. In many projects it's not worth it, especially if you have legacy code or you didn't start using unit testing. What you need to keep in mind is not to let your code coverage go down. Iteration after iteration, or better yet (if you are using continuous integration as you will see in Chapter 58), check-in after check-in, your percentage should increase, or at least remain constant. Most important, rather than looking at the numbers at a test suite level, it's useful to look at them at the code level to see if you're missing critical test cases.

Summary

In this chapter you saw a couple of advanced features that are part of the Developer Edition in Visual Studio Team System. All of these target quality improvement. Code Metrics and the Analysis Tool will analyze your code or binaries statically, collecting metrics and evaluating rules. The metrics will be useful to see how maintainable your code is. For the analysis you have rules for different categories that will help you ensure that your code will perform well before it runs. On the other hand, the Profiling Tools, Application Verifier, and Code Coverage will evaluate your code at runtime. The Profiler will let you detect and correct performance and memory issues, and the App Verifier that targets unmanaged code will allow you to troubleshoot handles, locks, and heaps. Finally you saw Code Coverage, which will point you to code that isn't being tested.

VSTS: Tester Edition

In previous chapters you saw different testing features of Visual Studio 2008, such as Unit Tests and the Test List Editor in Chapter 20 and Code Coverage in the previous chapter. You also saw other quality tools targeting developers. In this chapter you look at additional features, mainly focused for testers, although some of these features are also available for other Visual Studio editions. Web, Load, Manual, and Generic tests are available only on this edition. The rest of the topics can be used in Visual Studio Professional and the other Team System editions.

Web Tests

These tests will simulate web requests and allow you to inspect the responses and evaluate different conditions to determine if the test passes. To create a new Web Test, right-click your Test Project from the Add submenu and select Web Test. This will open Internet Explorer with the Web Test Recorder enabled as shown in Figure 56-1. Point to your site as if you were a normal user and interact with your application. Once done, simply click Stop. This will open the Web Test's designer shown in Figure 56-2. There you can customize your test, adding validation and extraction rules, context parameters, comments, data sources, and calls to other Web Tests, or inserting transactions.

You will often need to run the same set of tests against different web servers; to do this you configure this as a context parameter. From the Web Test Designer you can right-click the main node and select Parameterize Web Servers. Visual Studio will inspect the URLs in each request and determine the context parameters it will need to create.

You can link your requests using the output from one of them as input for the next; to do this you add extraction rules to a specific request. You can extract from fields, attributes, http headers, hidden fields, and text, or even use regular expressions. The result of an extraction will set a context parameter, which can then be used, for example, as a form or query string parameter in further requests. You could add a product and then search for it using the ID in another request.

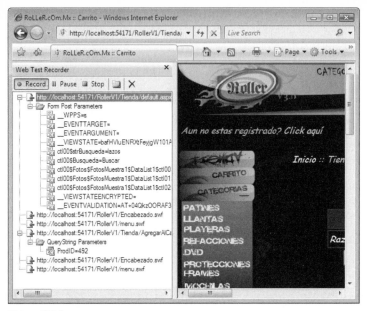

Figure 56-1

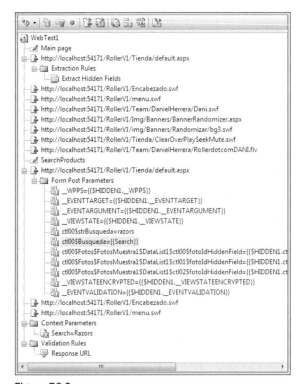

Figure 56-2

You can add extraction rules and form and query string parameters from the context menu of a request. By selecting a form or query string parameter from the properties window you can set its value to a Context Parameter or bind it to a data source.

No test framework would be complete without validations. When you record a test, a Response URL Validation Rule is added asserting that the response URL is the same as the recorded response URL. This is not enough for most scenarios. From the context menu at a Web Test or request level you can add validation rules. You can check that a form field or attribute has a certain value or that a particular tag is included, find some text, or ascertain that the request doesn't take more than a specified length of time.

Double-clicking the testrunconfig file in Solution Explorer will allow you to further customize how Web Tests are run. There you can choose the number of iterations, the browser and network type, and if the test engine should simulate think times. You can have many Test Run Configurations and from the Test menu select the active one.

Web Tests as well as any other type of tests will be displayed in the Test List Editor window as you saw in Chapter 20. From there you can run your Web Test and group it inside a particular test list. You can also run it directly from the Web Test Designer. Once a test is run you can see its details by double-clicking it in the Test Results window. To open this window, select Test Results from the Test ⇨ Windows menu. There you can see each request's status, total time, and bytes. When you select a request you will see the used request and received response, values of the context parameters, validations and extraction rules, and a web-browser-like view displaying the web page. An example is shown in Figure 56-3.

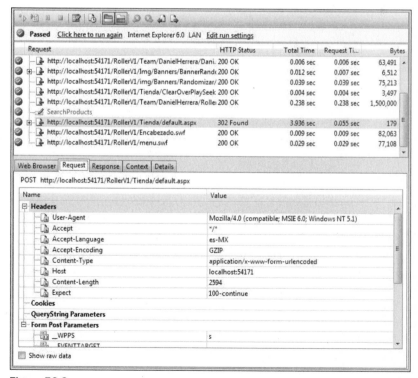

Figure 56-3

If you need additional flexibility, you can code the Web Tests using .NET and the Web Testing Framework. The best way to learn how to use the framework and start coding your test is by generating code for a recorded Web Test. You have this option in the Web Test context menu.

Although Team System provides some ASP.NET-specific features, you can use Web Tests for sites built using other technologies.

Load Tests

While web and load testing are meant to test functional requirements, Load Tests will run a set of tests repeatedly so you can see how your application will perform. To create a Load Test, right-click your test project and select Load Test from the Add sub-menu. This will present you with a wizard that will guide you through the necessary steps. First, you'll need to create a scenario; here you will define if you want to use think times. When you recorded the Web Tests, the time you took between each request was also recorded and can be used as the think time. It can be edited for each Web Test request in the properties window.

As part of the scenario you will define the load pattern; for example, a constant load of 100 users or a load incrementing by 10 every 10 seconds until you get to 200 users. The next steps, Test, Browser, and Network Mix, define how tests will be run by virtual users according to Test Mix, specifying which browsers are used and simulating which kind of networks. In the Test Mix step you can add Generic, Ordered, and Web Tests.

Finally, in the Counter Sets step, you add the computers that you want to monitor and the performance counters you are interested in. For example, you can monitor your Database Server and IIS. In the last step, Run Settings, you can specify the test duration or test iterations, how often samples will be taken for performance counters, a test description, how many identical errors will be recorded, and the validation level. We defined a validation level for each Validation Rule in our Web Tests. Since evaluation of these rules can be expensive, in Load Tests only rules with a level equal to or below the specified validation level will be evaluated.

When you hit Finish you will be presented with the Load Test Designer as shown in Figure 56-4. There you can add additional scenarios, counter sets, or new run settings.

When you run the tests you will see the Load Test Monitor; by default it will show the Graphs view. In the left-side pane you have a treeview of the Counter. You can select items there to add them to the graphics. From the toolbar you can change to Summary or Tables view, export to Excel or CSV, and add analysis notes. In the Graphs view at the bottom you will have a legends pane as shown in Figure 56-5. There you can select/deselect the counters that you want to include in the graphs. While the test is running, the monitor will be updated on each sample interval. In the Tables view you can see the Requests, Errors, Pages, SQL Trace, Tests, Thresholds, and Transactions.

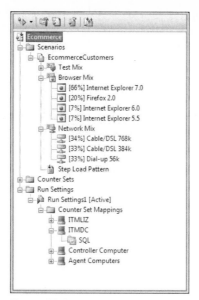

Figure 56-4

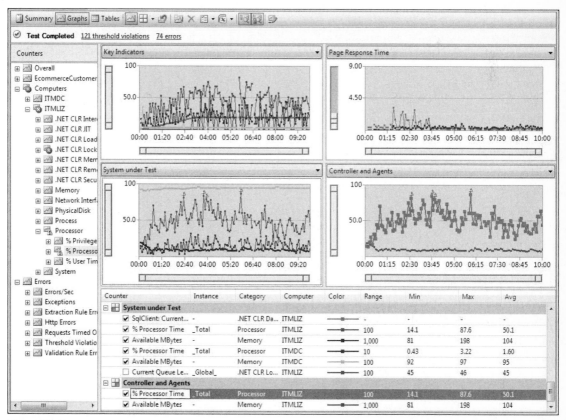

Figure 56-5

Thresholds are particularly important. These are values for each performance counter that will allow you to spot problems. In the graphs you can see points where violations occurred marked with a warning or error icon.

Test Load Agent

For large-scale applications, one computer might not be enough to simulate the desired load. Visual Studio Team System 2008 Test Load Agent can distribute the work across different machines. It can simulate approximately 1,000 users per processor. This product requires a separate installation and requires one controller and at least one agent. To configure the environment select Administer Test Controller from the Test menu. There you can select a Controller and add Agents. Then from the Test Run Configuration window in the Controller and Agent node you can select to run the tests remotely and select the configured controller.

Manual Tests

Sometimes there's no way to automate a test, as you saw in Chapter 20 and previously in this chapter, as a Web Test. When this happens you need detailed instructions to manually reproduce a test case. Anyway, you still need to log and report the results of such tests in an easy and integrated way as explained at the end of this chapter.

These tests are simple. Team System will provide you with a template to fill in the instructions. Once you have them you can say your test is designed. Now when you run your test you will be presented with the instructions, and from there you can simply run the application, write a comment, and state that the test passed or failed.

Keep in mind it's better to try to automate all tests and only leave Manual Tests for cases where automating is impossible or too expensive.

Generic Tests

Not every kind of test is covered in Team System. This is why Microsoft included the concept of Generic Tests so that you can easily use custom tests, but still be able to use the rest of the features like Test Results, Test List, Assign Work Items, and Publish Test Results.

To configure a Generic Test you need to specify an existing program and optionally specify its command-line arguments, additional files to deploy, and environment variables. The external application can communicate the test result back to Team System in two ways. One is with the Error Level, where a value of 0 indicates success and anything else is considered a failure. The other is to return an XML file that conforms to the SummaryResult.xsd schema located in Visual Studio's installation path. In MSDN you can find information about this schema and how to report detailed errors using XML.

Ordered Tests

Ordered Tests are used when you need to group tests and run them as a whole or if tests have dependencies on each other and need to be run in a particular order. It's a good practice to create atomic Unit Tests to be able to run them in isolation with repeatable results. I don't recommend using Ordered

Tests just to deal with dependencies between Unit Tests. A good reason for creating Ordered Tests could be to create a performance session for more than one test.

In the Ordered Test Editor you will have a list of the available tests that you can add to the Ordered Test — the same test can be added more than once. You can also choose to continue after a failure. When the test is run, it will execute each of the selected tests in the specified order.

Test Management

The easiest way to manage your tests is through the Test List Editor explained in Chapter 20. There you can add the tests to lists, select the tests or lists to run, sort, group, filter, and enable or disable them. To display the Test List Editor select it from the Test ⇨ Windows menu.

Another option is to use the Test View window, which is simpler compared to the Test List Editor. From there you can also run tests and filter tests, but can't group them in test lists.

When you run a set of tests you will be presented with the Test Results window. In case it doesn't appear automatically you can open it from the Test ⇨ Windows menu. There you can sort the tests and results and see error messages. You can select what tests to rerun; by default failing, inconclusive, and not-executed tests will be checked, and passed tests will be unchecked. Because the list of results can be big, you can use sorting, filtering, and grouping or even change the view to display a left pane with the Test Lists and use the same organization defined in the Test List Editor.

From the Test Results window you can export the Test Result to save a .trx file containing all the details and a folder with the test output. You can simply send the files to someone else who can import them from the Test Results window, selecting the .trx file. This person can see the same results the tester saw and even rerun the tests to reproduce the error on his or her machine. The latter is possible since the binaries are included with every test output.

Instead of passing Test Result files from one computer to another, it would be better to publish them to Team Foundation Server. This option is available in the Test Results window's toolbar. You will be prompted to select a team project. The team project must have a build configured, as you will see in Chapter 58 in the section "Team Foundation Build." The benefit of publishing, besides making the data available to other people, is that the data can also be used for reports.

Summary

In this chapter you saw the different types of tests included in Visual Studio 2008. You started with Web Tests, which will allow you to reproduce a set of requests, and then you continued with Load Tests, which help to simulate several users executing your tests simultaneously to stress your application. Then you saw how Manual Tests covered scenarios where test automation is impossible or too expensive, how Generic Tests can be used to wrap existing tests that are using other mechanisms, and how Ordered Tests can help you run a set of tests sequentially. Finally, you looked at options to manage your tests like grouping them in lists and publishing the results to Team Foundation Server.

VSTS: Database Edition

This chapter talks about the newest edition in the VSTS suite. It was introduced late in 2006 and was welcomed for database developers and application developers, and has been slowly adopted for DBAs too. It targets two main areas: SQL-CLR development and tools to help teams working with databases. The first will aid in developing and deploying .NET code that will be hosted inside SQL Server. The second will allow us to version schema changes, isolating developers and allowing them to compare changes, auto-generate data, and share their modifications easily with other developers or DBAs.

SQL-CLR Database Project

In the New Project dialog inside either Visual Basic or C# is a Database node that contains the "SQL Server Project." It's used to create managed classes to use inside a SQL Server. When you create a new project of this type, you will be prompted for a connection and to enable CLR debugging. Use CLR debugging only on development database servers and isolated from other developers as explained later in the "Best Practices" section.

> *There's another way to get to the SQL Server Projects, and this is located in Database Projects/ Microsoft SQL Server/SQL-CLR. There you will select the flavor according to your language. You will see the projects inside the Database Projects node in the Offline Database Schema section.*

You can add to this project some types like Aggregates, User-Defined Functions, Stored Procedures, Triggers, User-Defined Types, and Classes. You can think of this as a normal VB/C# project; you can add classes, references, and even web references. You can create unit tests for your methods as explained in Chapter 20, refactor your code, and build, in the same way you would for other library projects. However, the debugging history is a bit different, since your code is running in an SQL Server context. First you will need to allow VS to remote debug the code. This is needed only the first time you debug your project. However, the point of entry for your code will be through a script that will use any of your managed objects. As you may have noticed when you created the project, there's already a file named Test.sql, which is used to use and test your types.

The test scripts can grow quickly, and long script files are not easy to maintain. You can add new test scripts and right-click to set them as Default Debug Script. This is similar to the way you would set an ASP.NET page as the start page. You can set a breakpoint on the script or the classes you are testing and hit F5 (or from the menu Debug ⇨ Start Debugging). This will build the project, drop the assembly from SQL Server in case it was previously deployed by Visual Studio, and then register the assembly again with SQL Server using the Create Assembly procedure. Finally, it will attach to the SqlServr.exe process to allow you to debug scripts and managed code. You can also create Database Unit Tests that use your SQL-CLR objects as explained in the section on unit testing.

Offline Database Schema

There's another type of Database Project and it's inside the Microsoft SQL Server node as shown in Figure 57-1. As you can see, you have four options, but it's basically the same project type; the difference between them is the use of a wizard and the SQL Server version being targeted. Some options are available only from the creation of the project using the wizard, so I suggest you start using that. These projects will let you have an offline representation of your DB schema, so that you can version it along with your code. It will create a file for each schema object and deploy the changes to a database.

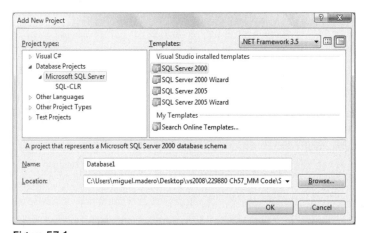

Figure 57-1

If you run the wizard for SQL Server 2005, the first option will let you choose whether to organize the files by schema or object type (tables, views, stored procedures, and so on). This is important because you can't change this option once the project is created, although you will find yourself working on the Schema View most of the time instead of doing it directly on the files — from that window you can select or deselect the filter by Schema View. However, if you select "No" to organizing by schema inside the types, you can still distinguish the schema because of the prefix added to each filename. On the other hand, if you select to organize by schema, inside of each you will have folders for each type. Figure 57-2 shows at the left the Schema View filtered by schema. You could change this option to organize all the objects by type. The Solution Explorer (at the right) shows two different projects where files are physically organized differently.

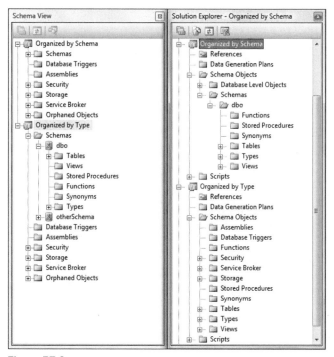

Figure 57-2

The database options are the next step of the wizard; if you don't know your defaults now, don't be afraid to choose something and change it once you get this information from either your DBA or your production DB. You can select to import this configuration directly from a DB. If you can connect to your production DB it's a good idea to import them at this moment. To do this, simply go to the next step in the wizard and mark the needed checkboxes as shown in Figure 57-3.

The last step is to configure the build and deployment options. You will need more deployment configurations, so here you will only select your development database. Keep in mind this doesn't have to be the same as in the previous step — here you are configuring your development database and in the previous step, if available, you would import existing objects and configuration from a production DB. You will see the three configurations needed in more detail later, so for now you can go with the default options. The final step will take awhile, especially if you have many objects to import.

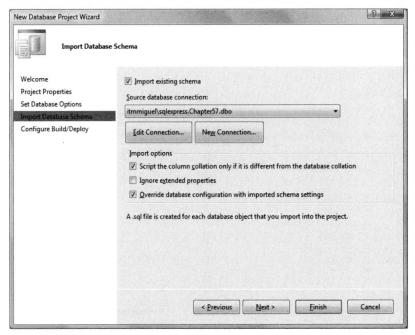

Figure 57-3

Once the wizard finishes, you can add, edit, or delete schema objects right from the Solution Explorer or the Schema View (View ⇨ Schema View) — these will be represented as files. When you build the project, a .sql file containing all the DML necessary to re-create your schema will be generated and evaluated. The script can then be deployed to SQL Server. You could also choose to deploy on every build, so your DB will always get your last changes.

When working with Source Control this type of project becomes really useful. The scenario would be that each developer works on his own server instance. One of them has made changes to the schema and his .NET code and deployed them to his instance. He then tests the .NET application and it works fine with the new database changes. Then he checks in all of his changes to the server and another developer retrieves the changes. When the second developer deploys his database instance it is also updated with the latest changes, and he will be running the new code changes along with the new schema changes applied to his SQL Server instance.

Data Generation

As well as versioning the schema, you might want a way to generate data for testing purposes. To do this, you need to add a Data Generation Plan. If you right-click the Offline Schema project under the Add menu, you will find the option for Data Generation Plan. By default all the tables on the schema will be selected, but you can override these settings. In the top section of Figure 57-4 only the Products table is checked. The Categories and Suppliers tables are automatically added (darkened checkboxes) because of the Foreign Key between Products and Suppliers and Products and Categories.

Keep in mind these generation plans are only for development and testing purposes. Don't run them on production servers.

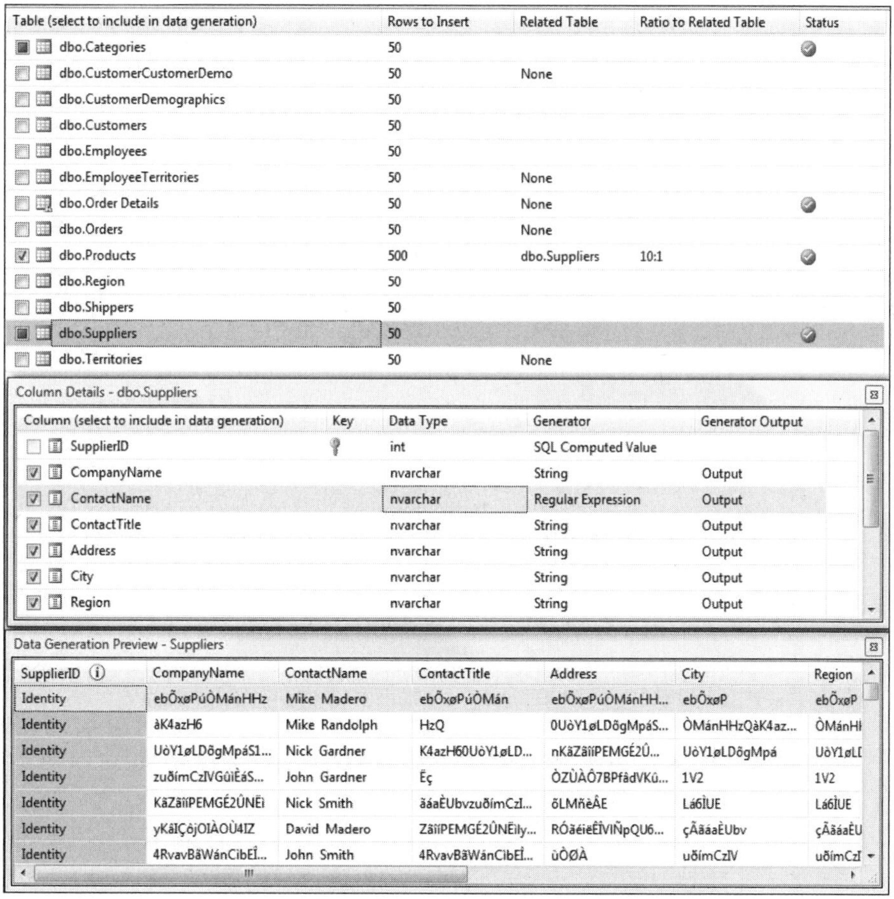

Figure 57-4

From the Data ⇨ Data Generator menu you can open the Column Details and Preview Data Generation windows.

In the plan, you can select the ratio between Related Columns; for example, in Figure 57-4 we are specifying to have 10 products for each supplier (10:1).

In the Column Details window, all columns are selected except for the SupplierID, which is an identity column. You can deselect columns as long as they have either a Default value or allow nulls. In the properties window you can specify the percentage of nulls to be generated.

For each column you can also specify the type of generator to use. By default a generator will be selected depending on the data type, or in case a column is a foreign key, the values will come from the related table's primary keys. You can use other generators. In the example in Figure 57-4, for the ContactName on the Suppliers table we used a regular expression to mix first names and last names. Another option would be to use a Data Bound Generator. In that case, you would need to specify a connection string and a select query to get the values to insert. You could also create a Custom Generator and implement your own logic simply by implementing a base class and registering your assembly as a Customer Generator. For more information see "Creating Custom Generators" on MSDN.

To run the Data Generation Plan simply select Generate Data from the Data ⇨ Data Generator menu. Remember to run this plan only on a development or testing database.

Database Unit Testing

You already looked at unit testing in Chapter 20; this section expands the topic to databases. This kind of test is useful to verify the functionality and design of your schema objects and can work hand-in-hand with your Data Generation Plans and Schema Database Projects. To create a new Database Unit Test, from the Tests menu select New Test and choose the template for Database Unit Test, then create a new project if needed. For the first DB Unit Test in the project you will be prompted for a database to run the tests against. You can change this later from the Database Test Configuration option under the Test menu. It's highly recommended to have a dedicated database for test purposes for each developer. You can also select to deploy the project before running the tests. This will guarantee you are always running the tests against the latest version of the schema. Finally, you can select to use a Data Generation Plan to re-create the data for the unit tests.

To create and edit the tests you have a designer (Figure 57-5). From there you can select the different test methods or create new ones and add new test conditions. The conditions available are Empty ResultSet, Execution Time, Inconclusive, Not Empty ResultSet, Row Count, and Scalar Value. When selected, you can configure them from the properties windows — for example, to set the value for the row count. You can also create your own test conditions. The Power Tools (explained at the end of the chapter) include two additional test conditions, CheckSum and ExpectedSchema.

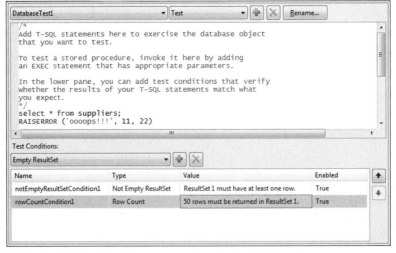

Figure 57-5

There are other two ways to verify your tests. One is by raising errors from your T-SQL code. The `RAISERROR` function will take an error message (this will be displayed on the Test Results window in case of failure), error severity, and error state. If error severity is above 10 it will cause the unit test to fail.

The other way is from your C# or VB.NET script. If you right-click your test and select View Code, you will see it's structured as a regular unit test as explained in Chapter 20 and simply has methods that call SQL scripts. When you execute a script you will get back in your .NET code an ExecutionResult array; each ExecutionResult object will contain a `DataSet`, number of rows affected, and the `Execution Time`. Using those properties you can make your assertions. The `Execute` method of the TestService also takes SqlParameters that could be passed to your script and can be returned to your C# code for further verification.

Database Refactoring

We talked about refactoring in Chapter 17. For databases you have only one refactoring task, Rename. If you install the Power Tools described at the end of this chapter, you will have additional refactoring tasks like Move Schema and Extend to Type DataSets, but we won't cover these here.

You can rename tables, columns, stored procedures, constraints, and indexes as well as other database objects. You can also rename the references to other servers or databases if a cross-database reference is used in the scripts.

To rename an object from the Schema View, right-click it and select Rename from the Refactor sub-menu. When renaming an object you will see a preview of the changes as shown in Figure 57-6. In the upper pane you will see the old version and in the lower pane the new one for all the dependencies.

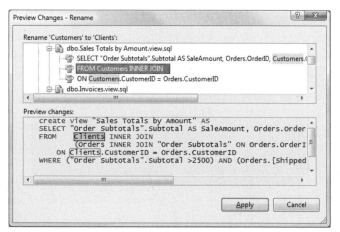

Figure 57-6

Renaming is easily done on an offline schema version, but for tables and columns it can be hard to deploy to the database. Because the old object will be dropped and re-created, this can result in data loss. If you have a Data Generation Plan, you can regenerate the data after the changes are deployed, but if you need to preserve your data you should either modify the deployment script or apply the refactoring manually. See "Protecting Data during a Renaming Operation" on MSDN for more information.

Schema Compare

This tool will allow you to compare schemas between databases or Database Projects. To use it, select New Comparison from the Data ⇨ Schema Compare menu. You will have to select a project or database as Source and a project or database as Target. When you do that you will be presented with a window similar to the one shown in Figure 57-7. The lower pane will show both versions of the selected object with the changes highlighted. It's handy to use the filters from the Toolbar; by default all objects will be shown. I recommend selecting Non Skip Objects to see only the differences.

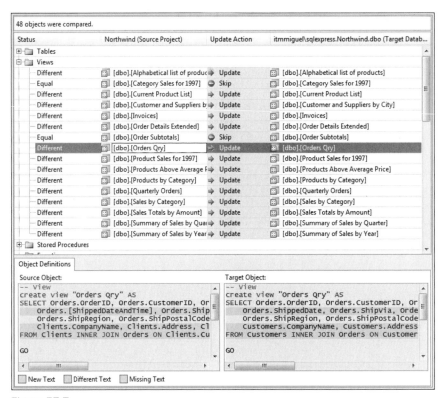

Figure 57-7

For each DB object you can see the action that will be applied Then from the Toolbar you can either select Write Updates to apply all the changes or Export to Editor to get the SQL statements used for the update in case you need to do manual changes or hand it out to your DBA.

To customize the options for Schema Comparisons, go to Tools ⇨ Options and to the Schema Compare node under Database Tools. By default, "Block Schema updates if data loss might occur" is selected; this is recommended but can cause some updates to fail. You can uncheck this option, but be sure you're running on a test database and that you can regenerate the data. Such other options as Ignore White Space can be useful to reduce unnecessary changes.

Remember that if you are using a Database Project the deploy option will write the changes from your Database Project to the database selected in the build option in the project's properties. This tool can be useful to see the changes or do manual tweaking.

Data Compare

This tool is useful to copy data from one database to another. Go to Data ⇨ Data Compare ⇨ New Data Comparison to start the wizard. You will need to select the Source and Target database and the records to compare. Depending on what you want to do, you can choose between the different Compare options, "Different Records" for updates, "Only in Source" for inserts, "Only in Target" for deletes, and identical records just as a reference. Finally, you can select which tables and columns to compare.

You will be presented with all the objects selected in the last step of the wizard, but only the objects with differences will be selected. I recommend filtering the view to show only the Selected Records. From there you can check/uncheck the changes you want to apply either at a table or row level.

Figure 57-8 shows the comparison results between two versions of the Northwind table. The upper pane shows the tables and the lower pane the records for the selected table. The Different Records tab in the lower pane will show side by side each Source and Target column, so you can see where the differences are.

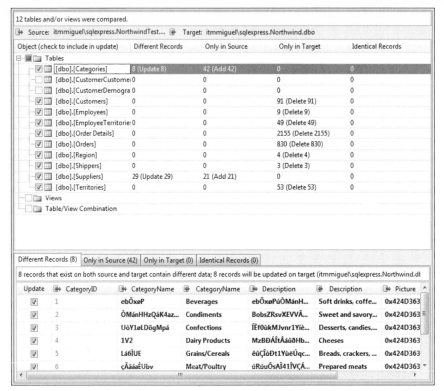

Figure 57-8

From the Toolbar you can select either Write Updates or Export to Editor to manually apply the changes.

T-SQL Editor

This editor allows you to work with T-SQL code directly in Visual Studio. To open it, you can double-click a `.sql` file in Solution Explorer or from the Schema View of a Database Project. Another option is to start with a blank editor — to do this go to Data ➪ T-SQL Editor and select New Query Connection. Now you can start to write your T-SQL, with nice coloring and having most of Visual Studio's shortcuts and features like bookmarks and search and replace. From the Toolbar or the T-SQL Editor menu, you can validate syntax, execute your code, include client statistics, disconnect to work offline, and reconnect once you need to run a query. When you run the queries, the results can be displayed on a grid or text format or be exported to a file. You can also change this behavior from the menu or Toolbar.

Power Tools

From MSDN you can freely download the "Visual Studio Team System 2008 Database Edition — Power Tools." Some of the nice features it will add to your Database Edition are a Data Generator Wizard, the Dependency Tool, T-SQL Static Code Analysis, MSBuild tasks, additional refactoring options like Move Schema and Extend to Typed DataSets, and two test conditions for database unit tests — CheckSumCondition and ExpectedSchemaTestCondition.

Best Practices

The following is a list of best practices we compiled through our work with Database Professional and which have worked for us on small and medium-sized projects:

❑ Each developer works with his own local SQL database instance, one for development and another for testing. This is necessary to isolate uncommitted and untested changes and avoid affecting other developers working on the database at the same time. It is strictly necessary for managed-code debugging purposes, because starting a debugging session will cause all managed threads to stop. From the project properties for Database Projects you can specify the database to target for each Solution Configuration, but SQL-CLR projects can only target one database.

❑ Each developer works with two databases, one for development and one for unit testing because different data will be used for each.

❑ Use (local) or 127.0.0.1 for the hostname instead of, say, mikesComputer or 192.168.2.6, which would work only on one machine.

❑ If you are using database instances, be sure all your developers have an instance with the same name.

❑ All developers should have the same SQL Server version. Although SQL Server Express can be used for design-time validation and testing purposes, some features, like text Indexing, are not supported.

❑ Clear the "Block incremental deployment if data loss might occur" checkbox in the project properties window for the Solution Configuration used for Test Databases. Because you will have a Data Generation Plan, data will be easy to re-create after changes have been made to the schema.

❑ When deploying to a production database, build the Database Project and then modify the build script to manually deploy it to the server. You can lean on the Schema Comparison tool to have a more granular view of the changes made.

Summary

This chapter covered some of the most important features in Database Edition. You saw how easy it is to develop code for SQL-CLR and how the Offline Schema Projects will help you work on a team, versioning and merging your changes. Advanced features like refactoring and unit testing will change the way you develop databases, and tools like Schema Compare, Data Compare, Data Generation, and the T-SQL Editor will support the process as well.

58

Team Foundation Server

Software development is a hard job, from the project manager to the tester and even for the customers. Since you've made it all the way to Chapter 58, you're certainly involved in this area. So I don't need to give you statistics on how badly some development projects can go. That's why many shops have implemented quality models like CMMI, methodologies such as RUP, or Agile Practices, Scrum, or Continuous Integration. We need a tool to support all the pieces necessary to do our work better.

The basic thing, even for the smallest one-person projects, is to have a source-control repository. For bigger ones we would need more sophisticated features such as labeling, shelving, branching, and merging. We need to assign, prioritize, and track activities, and to be sure (at the end of the day or better yet after every change is checked in to our repository) that everything builds and all tests are passing. To make this process smoother and improve team communication, we need a way to report to our project managers or peer developers.

Team Foundation Server allows us to do all this. In this chapter you will see how version control works, how it integrates with work item tracking, and how after each change is made it can trigger a team build. You will also see how project managers can see reports to get a better understanding of the project status and how they can work using Excel and Project to assign work items. The team can interact using the project's portal in SharePoint and different stakeholders can get the information they need through the report server or configure it to get their reports directly by e-mail.

Process Templates

To begin working with TFS you need to create a team project. When you do it, you need to select the process template. Select the one that better suits your organization's process or methodology. Out of the box, Team System comes with two templates, both based on the Microsoft Solution Framework. One flavor is for Agile Development and the other for CMMI Process Improvement.

Both options are great as starting points, but if your company has a defined process, it can be incorporated into TFS or can use a third-party process template. As you can see in Figure 58-1, we have different templates installed. For the rest of this chapter we will use MSF for Agile Software Development and refer to the CMMI version when necessary.

Figure 58-1

A process template will create the environment for the team project. This usually consists of defining work item types (as you will see in the section titled "Work Item Tracking"), creating default groups and permissions, preparing a version-control repository, and configuring reports and a custom SharePoint portal with document structure and process guidance. A different process could omit some of these or add custom tasks.

When the wizard finishes it opens the Guidance Page, which details the process used, defines the responsibilities of the roles involved, explains the different types of work items, and provides step-by-step guidance about specific tasks like "How to create a Vision Statement." Figure 58-2 shows the Project Guidance and the Team Explorer windows.

You will navigate to the different features of TFS through Team Explorer. It has Work Item Queries, a convenient way to access the documents stored in the Team Portal, links to Reports, a list of the Team Builds, and the Source Control node.

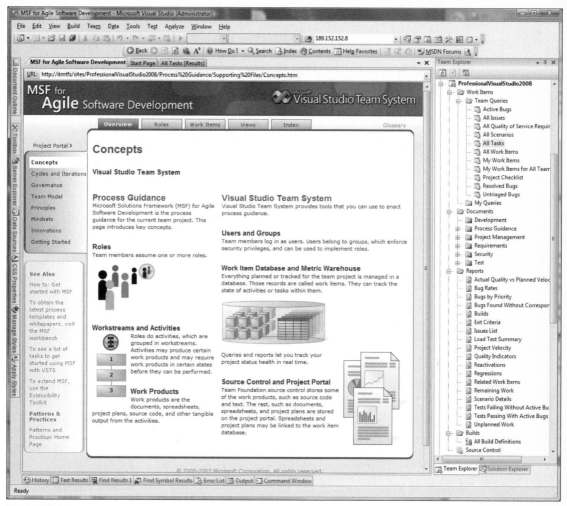

Figure 58-2

Work Item Tracking

Team Foundation allows you to manage activities using work items. As you will see in the following sections, you can search for work items using work item queries and you manage them using Visual Studio, Excel, Project, or Team System Web Access. There are different types of work items like bugs, tasks, and risks, and later in the chapter you will see how to create custom types.

Initial Work Items

The template defined some pending tasks. These are represented as work items and by default will be assigned to the person who created the team project. You will be completing this list throughout the chapter, but for now you can close the Set Permissions, Migration of Source Code, and Migration of Work Items, and assign the ones in the Requirements, Test, and Project Management disciplines to the appropriate persons.

You can select each work item and edit its details. You will usually change the state (active, resolved, closed), rank, remaining work, or the "assign to" fields. In Figure 58-3 you can see a list of the work items edited in Visual Studio.

The initial work item list may vary depending on the process template.

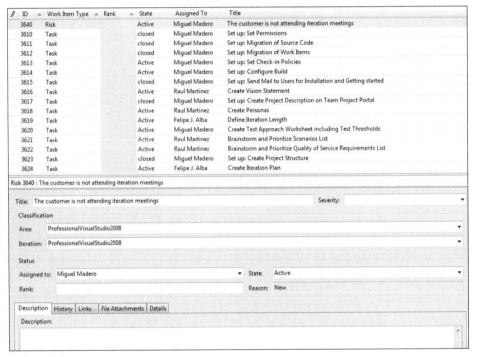

Figure 58-3

Work Item Queries

The work items shown in Figure 58-3 are all tasks in the selected team project. You could look for different work items using the work item queries from Team Explorer. The template process includes eleven team queries (Figure 58-2) like Active Bugs, All Work Items, or My Work Items. Most of the time those queries will be enough, but you have the option to create new ones. If you're a project administrator you can add new team queries to make them available to everyone with access to this project. And if you can modify the process template, you can add new team queries, so projects created with the edited templates will include them. Changes in the templates don't apply to team projects already created. If you don't have these permissions or you want to create a personal query, you can do that, too.

When you notice you are creating the same queries over and over from one project to another, you should add those to your process templates. Over time, there will be less need to create custom queries.

To create a new query right-click the My Queries node and select Add Query (Figure 58-4).

Now you can visually design your query. In this case you only care about the work items of the selected project, assigned to the current user and under Iteration 1. You specify this using the @me and @Project variables. You can also specify which columns you want visible in the grid and sorting options (Figure 58-5). You can then run the new query to see a sub-list of the work items.

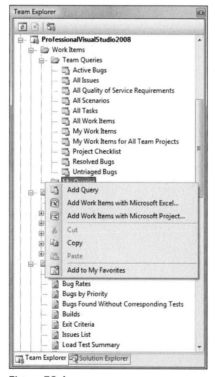

Figure 58-4

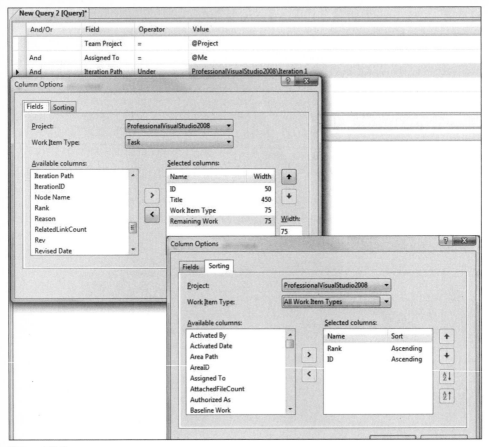

Figure 58-5

Work Item Types

In MSF for Agile Development you have five types of work items: bugs, risks, scenarios, quality-of-service requirements, and tasks. Each work item has different fields depending on its type. For example, a bug will have a triage state and test information field, whereas a risk is a simpler work item. Contrasting it with the MSF for CMMI template, you have a change-request work item, which doesn't exist in the Agile version. CMMI also has a risk work item, but this case is not so simple; it now requires a mitigation and contingency plan and has other fields such as severity, priority, probability, and estimate. All these fields are customizable either at a template or team-project level.

Adding Work Items

The basic way of adding work items is via the Team ⇨ Add to Work Item menu option (Figure 58-6) and selecting the work item type you want to add. Another convenient way to add work items is through the Test Results window, which was explained in Chapter 56.

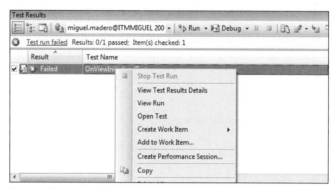

Figure 58-6

When you do it this way you will usually create a bug and also create a link between it and the selected test. You can navigate from the bug to the test or see the test and its related work items (Figure 58-7). If the test fails again, you can see the work items associated with it and track it back to their related change sets, as you will see later in the "Version Control" section. Team System also associates the test result with the work item and optionally uploads the assemblies being tested; that way the developer assigned to correct the bug can easily reproduce it.

Figure 58-7

Excel and Project Integration

Looking at, adding, or editing work items can get a bit complicated and won't scale well when you have hundreds of tasks. This can be problematic especially for project managers who are not used to working inside Visual Studio. They usually prefer to work from Excel or Project. This integration is really easy using the provided add-ins.

Excel

From the ribbon simply click New List and choose a Team Project and Work Item Query. This will retrieve all the information from a web service and display it in Excel. Once it's there you can sort, filter, edit, and publish changes back to the server, refresh the changes made by others, add links or attachments, and choose columns to be displayed.

Another way of doing this is from Team Explorer. From a work item query's context menu, select Open in Microsoft Excel. This will create a new Excel worksheet with the information. Figure 58-8 shows both options and Figure 58-9 shows the results in Excel.

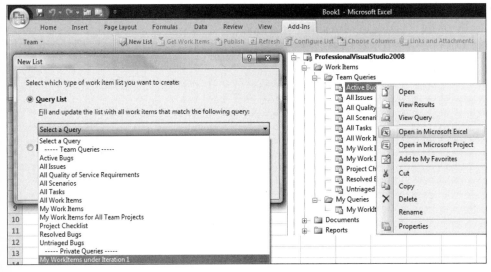

Figure 58-8

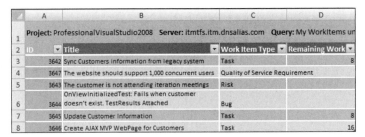

Figure 58-9

Project

There is also an add-in for Project. Similarly to Excel, you can connect to a server, choose a team project, and select a work item query, but instead of using the entire list, you have to choose each of the work items you want to import to your project, as shown in Figure 58-10.

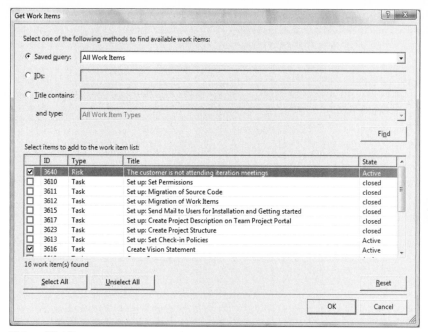

Figure 58-10

Once your work items are imported you can edit each of their fields directly in Project. This is possible thanks to the Column Mappings between TFS fields and MS Project Columns. For example, Resource Names in Project will map to the Assigned to field in TFS. Fields that exist only in Team System will be mapped to Text Fields in Project; for example, Work Item Type is mapped to Text 24. This is preconfigured in the process template.

You can add new work items, nest them in iterations or areas, assign them to people, choose a work item type, balance workloads between resources, see project reports, and refresh the progress from the server after each developer changes the work remaining or work item state.

There are important differences that make the integration a bit tricky:

❑ This TFS 2008 doesn't have a notion of hierarchical work items; this will be improved for the next version. Work items can be related, but it isn't a parent/child relationship; some process templates overcome this by relating different work item types; for example, a Product Backlog Item in Scrum associated to a Sprint Backlog Item would be a parent/child relationship and you can represent that in Project as well. The problem with this approach is that you can't have the N-level relationships commonly used for work breakdown structures (WBS). You could have that in Project but the relationship won't be persisted in TFS.

❑ Iterations and areas are represented as fields, while in Project you tend to nest activities under iterations or areas. This is a similar problem and is more a restriction of the MSF process templates than of TFS.

❑   In Project you can have many resources for the same activity, but TFS only accepts one entry. One approach could be to add a custom field to the work item type, but then the mapping won't work because you would need to have one column in Project mapped to two fields in TFS. The workaround is to add the activity once for each resource.

❑   There's no concept of predecessor and successor in TFS, a concept commonly used in pert charts for project managers. Again, you could use this concept in Project, but it won't be persisted in TFS. Or you could modify your work item types to include this field and add the mappings for Project.

❑   There's no Project server/TFS integration out of the box. There are a couple of third-party tools that do this for you. The next version of Team System will include it, as well as project management improvement across multiple projects for load balancing of resources.

Version Control

You can open Source Control Explorer from your Team Explorer window or View ⇨ Other Windows ⇨ Source Control Explorer to get to the window shown in Figure 58-11. You will need to define mappings between paths on the server and local folders to configure your workspace. You could define a different local folder for each path, but a good practice would be to have only one mapping; this helps keep all the solutions and projects relative to each other even between different team projects. To define this mapping, open the workspace combobox and select Workspace.

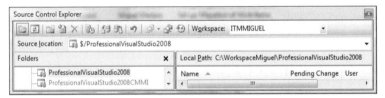

Figure 58-11

Now you can get the latest version of the source code and start working with it, add files, check out files (mark as edit) or check in (upload/persist) changes, view change history, and compare folders.

Working from Solution Explorer

When you create a new project you have the option to add it to Source Control. Team System will automatically bind it and add it according to the mapping previously defined. That's why you need to set the location to a folder inside your workspace (the local path you mapped to), as seen in Figure 58-12.

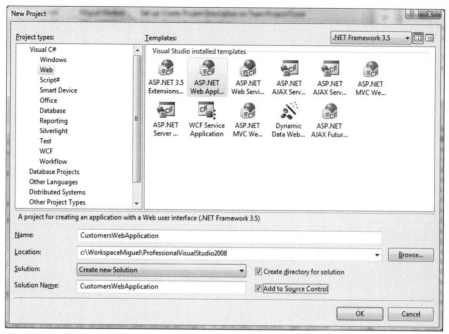

Figure 58-12

The Solution Explorer you are used to working with in Visual Studio will be the main place to interact with your Source Control System. Every time you add a new file to the solution, it will be added to Source Control; when you open a file and VS detects you're editing it, it will be automatically checked out for you. Once you are done working you can simply right-click the solution and choose Check In to persist your changes in the server.

Check Out

Files under Source Control are by default read-only; in TFS terms you would say the file is checked in. To start editing a file you need to check it out. This is done for you automatically when you modify it from VS. When the file is a text file (that is, a C#, VB, or XML file), the IDE will do a shared check-out; if it's a binary file (that is, a Word document, SQL Server Compact Edition Database, or another resource) an "exclusive check-out" will be made.

Shared check-outs will allow two or more developers to modify a file at the same time, whereas an exclusive check-out will prevent a second developer from checking it out. You can choose to do an exclusive check-out on a text file if you need to prevent anyone from modifying it. This is not a recommended practice, and I encourage you to only use it when you really need it. Martin Fowler has written an excellent article about Code Ownership (`http://martinfowler.com/bliki/CodeOwnership.html`).

Word, Excel, and other document types can be stored in a SharePoint document list. But you certainly want to version libraries in TFS, and I strongly recommend having strict policies about dealing with them.

Check In

To preserve your changes in the server, you will need to check in the edited files. You can select which files to include in this change set, add comments to it, associate it with work items, and add check-in notes (Figure 58-13).

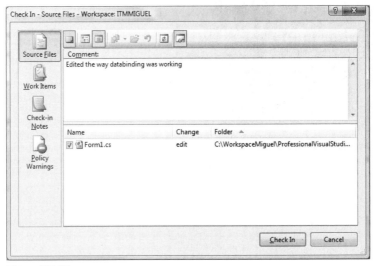

Figure 58-13

Depending on the policies defined for the team project, you might need to associate your check-in with a work item, run code analysis, have it pass tests, or at least successfully build the solution. To modify a team project's policies, open the Source Control Settings window (Team ⇨ Team Project Settings ⇨ Source Control) and go to the Check-in Policy tab. Once the policies are defined, you will get Policy Warnings (Figure 58-14); these can be overridden.

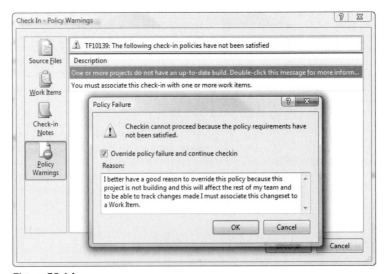

Figure 58-14

History

Every change you made is persisted in the server and you can get to any specific version of a file; a great way to do it is through the History window. Simply right-click a file in Source Control or Solution Explorer and select View History. From there you can see how a file has evolved over time (Figure 58-15). When you right-click any version, you can compare it to your version, open it, and view details of the change set (including the comments and related work items).

Chang...	Change	User	Date	Comment
4691	edit	miguel.mad...	3/10/2008 4:27:00 PM	Se libero versión 3.0.0.8 de GE Se arreglo el Data Access
4661	edit	miguel.mad...	2/28/2008 1:18:50 AM	Se cambio en todos lados donde se usaba un reader y command para...
4617	rename	miguel.mad...	2/15/2008 10:26:38 AM	Se movieron los blocks a otro lado
3249	rename	miguel.mad...	8/15/2007 10:54:04 PM	Se agregarton referencias a EntLib, CAB, Resco, Intecmex Se moviero...
2793	add	miguel.mad...	6/2/2007 12:54:00 PM	Se agrego la ventana de SaldoPendiente Se arreglaron y probaron pas...

History - C:\WorkspaceMiguel\JTM MCSF\JtmBlocks\DataAccessFramework\DataAccessFramework.CF\DataAccess.cs

Figure 58-15

Annotate

You can see when and who edited each line of code (Figure 58-16). From each of the changes made, you can get to each particular change set to see details, get that particular version, compare it to its previous version, locate the file in the History window, or annotate from that version.

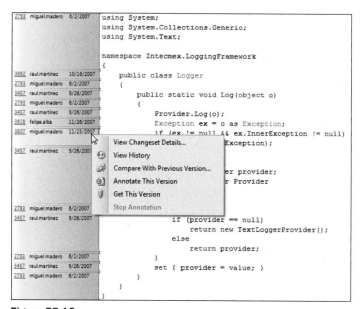

Figure 58-16

Resolve Conflicts

Shared check-outs can lead to conflicts, and these can easily be resolved with the help of Visual Studio. From the Resolve Conflicts window (Figure 58-17) you can compare versions and look at all the changes to that file. To resolve it, you can use Auto Merge and let Visual Studio merge the changes for you, undo your local changes, discard server changes, or merge changes manually in the merge tool (Figure 58-18).

When the changes were made in different parts of the file (for example, two different methods), VS can automatically resolve changes, but if changes were made in the same line you have to either choose a version or manually merge both files using the Merge Changes Tool.

> *Visual Studio will compare text to determine if changes overlap, but this will not guarantee the resulting file will even compile or behave as expected. This option is really useful, but has to be used with caution. Over time, you will have more confidence in choosing which files to automerge to save time and which are worth a quick look just to be sure.*

In the Merge Changes Tool (Figure 58-18), you will have a view of "their" version (that is, the server version), your version, and a merged version. You can navigate easily between changes and conflicts. In the case of conflicts, you can manually edit the offending lines or select a version to keep. When all conflicts are resolved, you can accept the changes, keep the new file as your current version, and proceed to check-in.

> *After resolving conflicts, I recommend running the automated tests again to ensure there are no breaking changes. As you will see in the "Team Build" section, this test can be run automatically in the server after each check-in.*

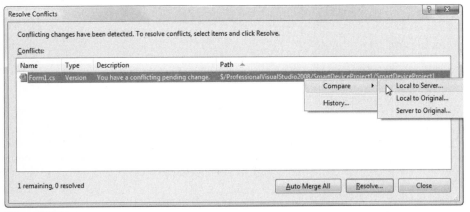

Figure 58-17

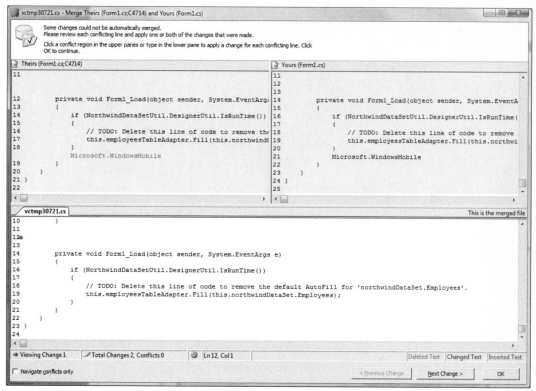

Figure 58-18

Working Offline

Team Foundation Server uses HTTP and web services and can work perfectly through the Internet and allow for collaboration of distributed teams, but in case you don't have an available connection VS will allow you to work offline when you try to open a bound project.

All files under Source Control are read-only. When you save a file you will be warned and should simply choose Overwrite. When the connection with TFS can be reestablished, you can select to go online from Solution Explorer or by right-clicking the solution. VS will look for files in the solution without the read-only attribute; if those are not in Source Control it will add them, and if they exist it will check them out.

> *Files modified outside the solution won't be detected and you would have to manually check them out. To make this easier you can compare your local copy to the latest version by right-clicking a folder in Source Control Explorer.*

Label

Labeling a specific version allows you to refer to it easily. To create a label you simply right-click a folder in Source Control Explorer that you want to mark, add additional files if necessary, and write a Name and optionally a Comment (Figure 58-19). Similarly, you can get to a specific version using the label. The perfect use for this is to release a version.

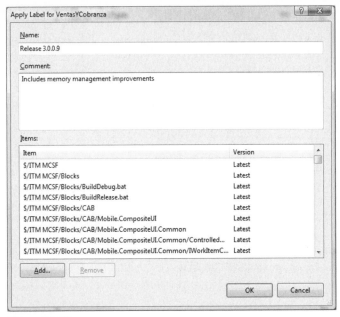

Figure 58-19

To get a labeled version right-click a file or folder in Source Control Explorer and select Get Specific Version from the context menu. On the Type combobox in the Get window (Figure 58-20) select Label. You can search for labels by name, team project, and owner. Once you find the label, to be sure you are getting the exact labeled version, you will probably choose to overwrite writable files.

> *I recommend undoing, shelving, or checking-in pending changes before getting a specific version, to separate the latest changes in your workspace from the labeled version.*

If you want to get the version in a different location, you can create a branch. You will see this later in the chapter.

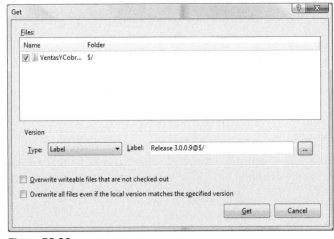

Figure 58-20

Shelve

When you check in a file, that change is automatically made available to others. Sometimes you need to persist your changes without affecting everyone — a scenario that can happen when you need to work from another computer and want to upload your changes and send them somewhere else, or when you are in the middle of something and are assigned a new task.

Shelving persists your changes in the server. You can associate a shelve set to WorkItems and add comments and check-in notes, much as you would when checking in. You can optionally evaluate check-in policies before shelving and choose to undo local changes after the shelve is done. The latter is useful when you need to work on some other work item without the shelved changes interfering with what you are doing. Shelving changes is also useful if you are moving to another machine and don't want to have to make the same change in both places. To get to the changes you can unshelve and your files will be checked out again.

Branch

Branch will allow you to create a parallel version of your code. This is useful for different purposes. Here are a couple of examples:

❑   Hot fixes or bugs for stable versions while working on new ones. When you release 1.0 you label all your source code and start working on 2.0. Then a critical bug is found. (I know, this never happens — this is just to an example.) Version 2.0 is months away from being ready. You will branch from version 1.0 (you can get to this version using the label). Then you can fix the bug in the new branch and release version 1.1. Later you can merge the change made and integrate it with the main branch.

❑   Creating a branch from the latest version to do a big refactoring or a change you are not sure will work and thus don't want to affect the main branch. If it works you can merge it with the main branch and if it doesn't you can simply delete it.

You have to choose wisely what branching strategy is better for your organization, type of product, and process, or when you could substitute by simply labeling a version or shelving a change. Abuse of branching can exponentially complicate source-code management. Codeplex hosts branching guidance that provides additional scenarios (`http://www.codeplex.com/BranchingGuidance/`).

Team Foundation Build

Team Foundation Build is a tool, part of TFS, and its responsibility is to get the latest version from Source Control to a local workspace, build the projects as configured, run tests, do other MSBuild tasks, and finally report the results and leave the output in a shared folder. We will refer to a computer with TFB installed as a build agent.

> *MSBuild is the build platform for Microsoft and Visual Studio. It can be run from the command line and extended using Custom Tasks, which includes tasks such as copy, makedir, and C# compiler (csc).*

To create a new build definition right-click the Builds folder in Team Explorer and select New Build Definition (Figure 58-21). In the General tab you need to write the build name and optionally a description. Configuring the workspace will be used in complex scenarios where you have dependencies between team projects, so the defaults in that tab might be enough.

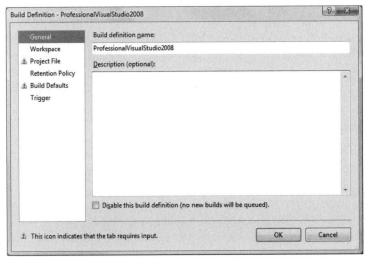

Figure 58-21

You can select an existing MSBuild project in the Project File tab or create a new one (Figure 58-22). To create one, select which solutions to build, in which configuration (that is, debug, release, custom ones), and finally decide which test to run and if code analysis will be performed.

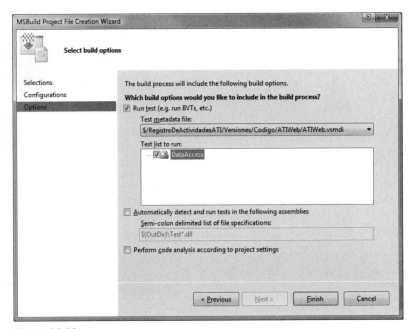

Figure 58-22

In the build defaults you can choose a build agent and a shared folder to drop the output into. These will be used for triggered builds, but for manual builds this can be overridden. The retention policy will let you choose how the builds left in the shared folder will be deleted. I would recommend the Keep All option now with adjustments as necessary.

By default the build has to be manually queued, but in the Trigger tab you can modify this behavior. You have four options, as shown in Figure 58-23. I would recommend choosing "Build each check-in"; this will generate more builds and has many advantages. If a build breaks or a test fails, you will know exactly which build caused it and the error will be easier to detect. Depending on how big your project is, how long it takes to build and run the tests, and how often the team checks in, this option may cause some overhead. The third option, "Accumulate check-ins until the prior build finishes," will definitely help alleviate the workload, but it's better to wait until you find you need it.

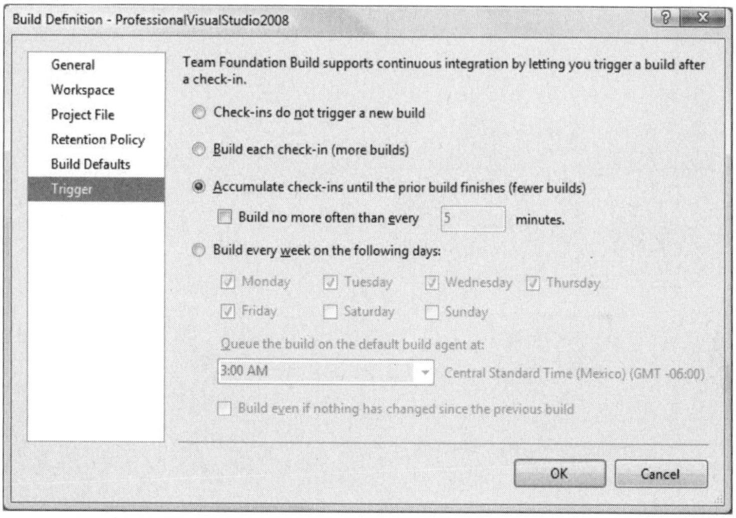

Figure 58-23

Reporting and Business Intelligence

TFS uses Report Server, which is part of Microsoft SQL Server 2005, to provide useful information for project managers, customers, and developers. Reports can be accessed directly from Team Explorer, the reports site (http://mytfs/reports/), SharePoint, or Team System Web Access, or they can be configured as a subscription from the Reports site to be left in a Windows fileshare or sent through e-mail.

The great benefit these have is that developers can focus on their work instead of manually filling out reports. All the information is collected during their daily work, checking out and checking in code, fixing bugs, and relating what they are doing to work items. This way project managers and stakeholders can get to the information they need from the reports TFS provides.

Each process template provides its own set of reports. The CMMI version provides three additional reports and templates like Scrum for Team System from Conchango, and has reports appropriate for the Scrum methodology like Delta Report and Burndown Charts. Again, we will focus on MSF for Agile Development here.

Some of the reports included are Actual Quality vs. Planned Velocity, Bug Rates, Bugs by Priority, Bugs Found Without Corresponding Tests, Quality Indicators, Remaining Work, Regressions, and Test Failing With and Without Active Bugs. Figure 58-24 shows how the work has been resolved over a couple of years and how much work is left. In the report you can filter by dates, work item type, iteration, and area. You can export to XML, CSV, TIFF, PDF, Web, and Excel.

You don't need two years of information to get useful reports. Depending on the nature of the data displayed, you might not see anything at the beginning. For example, the Test Failing reports will need to have at least one test in your MSBuild project, or to have data for the Regressions report you need Passing tests that are now failing. Similarly, the Scenarios Details report will need you to register at least a Scenario Work Item. After a couple of iterations of working with TFS you will have a lot of useful metrics for free.

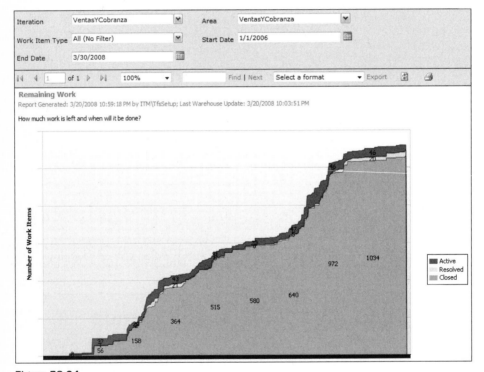

Figure 58-24

Team Portal

Team Foundation uses SharePoint to create a portal for each team project. It has all the benefits of SharePoint, but is customized for each process template. The home in each team portal will include the most important reports, latest announcements, and useful links.

Documents

Depending on the process template, certain documents will be included as templates. For example, MSF for Agile Software Development includes Word documents for creating personas and scenarios. These documents are also available from the Team Explorer's document folder.

Process Guidance

Inside SharePoint are documents that define the process (Figure 58-25). This guidance is available to all developers on the team.

SharePoint Lists

You can have picture libraries, discussion boards, surveys, announcements, links, events, contacts, and custom lists. This will help improve team collaboration.

Team System Web Access

This is a separate, free tool from Microsoft that integrates with TFS and allows you to do pretty much everything you can do from VS, but in a web interface. You can create and modify work items as well as work item queries, see the reports and documents, and initiate and monitor builds. The only area with limited functionality is Source Control. You can see history and change-set details, but you can't check out/check in documents due to the web client nature.

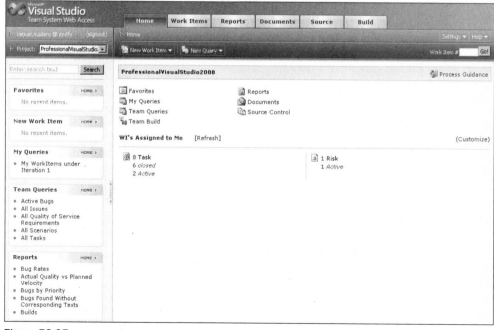

Figure 58-25

TFS Automation and Process Customization

Throughout the chapter you have seen how the process templates define most of the behavior of TFS; for example, they define work item types, process guidance, and reports. To close the chapter we will briefly introduce how you could customize a process template or edit work item types.

To edit either work item types or process templates, you could modify the XML that defines them, but it's easier to use the Process Editor, which is part of the Team Foundation Server Power Tools, downloadable from the Microsoft site.

Work Item Types

From the Tools ⇨ Process Editor ⇨ Work Item Types menu, you can open a work item type directly from an existing team project and start to edit it. Working this way will cause all your changes to be immediately propagated to all users. Another approach is to export the work item type to a file and then open it for editing and finally import it back to a team project. All these options are located in the same sub-menu.

> *I recommend having a team project dedicated to testing changes before importing or editing work item types in active team projects.*

Once you are editing a work item type, either directly from a team project or from a file, you will have three tabs to work with — Fields, Layout, and Workflow (Figure 58-26).

The first tab has a list of fields with their data types and a reference name. The ref name is used to uniquely identify fields from different work item types. For example, a title for a bug and a title for a task have the same System.Title Ref Name; other fields might have the same names but refer to different things.

The second tab allows you to modify the layout. You don't have a visual designer here, but you can work in a tree designer to nest groups, columns, and controls. Each control will be mapped to a field name using the ref name.

On the third tab you can modify the workflow, and from the Toolbox you can add states and transition links. The bug shown in Figure 58-26 shows how it can transition between active and resolved. If you double-click the transition, you can define reasons, actions, and fields. The last is used to set default values to fields after a transition; for example, when the bug transitions from active to resolved, it is assigned to the person who created the bug, the Resolved By field is set to the current user, and the Resolved Date is set to the server's current date.

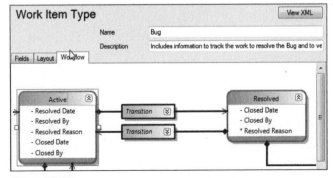

Figure 58-26

In the next section you will see how you can include work item types on a process template.

Customizing the Process Template

To serve as an example for process template customization, you will modify MSF for Agile Development. To create a local copy you need to open the Process Template Manager from the Team ⇨ Team Foundation Server Settings menu and select Download. Now you can open it in the Process Template Editor from the Tool ⇨ Process Editor ⇨ Process Template ⇨ Open Process Template menu and select the processtemplate .XML file just downloaded.

In the Process Template Editor window (Figure 58-27) you have a treeview to configure the different areas of a team project. In the Work Item Tracking node you can modify the Initial Work Item List, create default work item queries, and import work item types. In Areas & Iteration you can configure default values for these lists and specify the field and column mappings for Microsoft Project Integration. You can specify permissions and settings under Source Control. In the Portal node you can add documents that will be added to Document Libraries for SharePoint, and finally in the Reports node you can add Report Definition files.

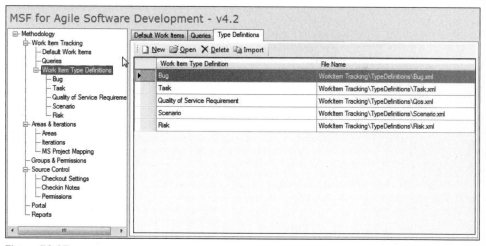

Figure 58-27

Although this tool can tremendously simplify the required work, you will need to edit the XML files for several tasks. For example, there's no way to specify a SharePoint template for the portal.

Summary

In this chapter you saw how Team Foundation Server can help you get the work done by integrating the different roles involved. The project managers will be filing and monitoring work items in either Excel or Project, while architects, developers, and testers will be working with the Visual Studio Projects using the version control features, easily relating changes to their assigned work items. Optionally, after each change a team build will be triggered. TFS will be monitoring everything and generating metrics for reports that can be viewed through the different interfaces like Visual Studio, Team Portal, and Team System Web Access. At the end of the chapter you saw how the whole process can be customized by modifying the process templates and work item types to better suit each organization's needs.

Index

Index

Programmer to Programmer

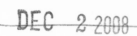

DEC 2 2008

WITHDRAWN

Tak brary
whe u go.

Now you can acces
online, wherever you
screen capture, ar
subscription to the
and where you nee
subscribe today!

ELKHART PUBLIC LIBRARY
Elkhart, Indiana

books on

NET   • .NET
C++   • Open Source
base   • PHP/MySQL
eral   • SQL Server
             • Visual Basic
             • Web
osoft Office • XML

DEMCO

wrox™

w.wrox.con